TRANSIENT AND PERMANENT

*The Transcendentalist Movement
and Its Contexts*

MASSACHUSETTS HISTORICAL SOCIETY
STUDIES IN AMERICAN HISTORY AND CULTURE

TRANSIENT
AND PERMANENT

The Transcendentalist Movement and Its Contexts

EDITED BY

Charles Capper *and*
Conrad Edick Wright

PUBLISHED BY THE

Massachusetts Historical Society
Boston, 1999

DISTRIBUTED BY

Northeastern University Press

MASSACHUSETTS HISTORICAL SOCIETY
Studies in American History and Culture, No. 5

*Editing of this book was made possible in part by the proceeds
of an endowment fund created with the assistance of a Challenge Grant
from the National Endowment for the Humanities, a federal agency
that supports research, education, and public programming
in the humanities.*

Designed by Steve Dyer

Library of Congress Cataloging-in-Publication Data
Transient and Permanent: the transcendentalist movement and its
contexts / edited by Charles Capper and Conrad Edick Wright.
    p.   cm. — (Studies in American history and culture; no. 5)
Includes bibliographical references and index.
ISBN 0-934909-76-8
1. American literature—19th century—History and criticism Congresses.
2. Transcendentalism (New England) Congresses. 3. Literature and society—
New England—History—19th century Congresses. 4. American literature—
New England—History and criticism Congresses. 5. New England—
Intellectual life—19th century Congresses. 6. Transcendentalism in
literature Congresses. 7. Transcendentalism in art Congresses.
I. Capper, Charles. II. Wright, Conrad Edick. III. Series: Studies
in American history and culture (Boston, Mass.); no. 5.
PS217.T7T75   1999
810.9'384—dc21
99-35220
CIP

Contents

Transcendentalism and the Critics

Preface

Conrad Edick Wright

H AVE THE TRANSCENDENTALISTS, THE NEW ENGLAND RELI-
gious reformers and intellectuals who challenged both spiritual
and secular orthodoxies between the 1830s and the 1850s, ever received
more attention from first-rate scholars than they do today? Has the quality
of the most insightful research on Transcendentalism ever been better than
it is now? The premise underlying this collection of essays is that the best
recent writing on the Transcendentalists illuminates them more clearly
than ever before, perhaps more lucidly than scholarship has ever illuminated any other major American intellectual circle. In view of the quality
and diversity of current writing on the movement, this seems an appropriate time to take stock of what we know about Transcendentalism and the
Transcendentalists.

The Transcendentalists are hardly a new subject for historians, literary
critics, or scholars from a host of other disciplines. As Charles Capper
recognizes in "'A Little Beyond': The Problem of the Transcendentalist
Movement in American History," the first essay in this collection, their
earliest chroniclers came from their own ranks. Octavius Brooks Frothingham, the author of *Transcendentalism in New England: A History*
(1876), was a junior member of their circle, and Caroline Healey Dall, the
author of *Transcendentalism in New England: A Lecture* (1897), also
occupied a place on its margins. Since Frothingham and Dall's day,
the movement has attracted the attention of scholars in most of the
humanities disciplines—history, literature, philosophy, religious studies,
art history, music history.

Notwithstanding many generations of serious interest in the history of
the movement, Transcendentalism has been and remains today a difficult
term to define. Persuaded of the importance of private judgment, the individuals who identified themselves with Transcendentalism did not sub-
scribe to a single, rigid theological, philosophical, and social orthodoxy.
They differed in enough ways to make most generalizations about them

and their beliefs suspect. It is possible, however, to point to a few characteristics and doctrines that most Transcendentalists shared:

- *Religious background.* The spiritual roots of Transcendentalism were in reformed Protestantism. At several removes, the Transcendentalists were heirs to the faith of John Calvin as interpreted by his Puritan followers both in England and New England. More immediately, with very few exceptions the Transcendentalists grew in the spiritual soil of American Unitarianism, the movement of Liberal Christians, centered in Boston in the early nineteenth century, who tested inherited Calvinist doctrines against reason—common sense—and found many of these beliefs wanting.
- *Belief in the immanence of the divine.* Religious faith for the Transcendentalists was personal and immediate. In attaining fundamental religious experience there were no intermediaries—neither scriptures nor prophets—between the divine and the believer. God existed in the heart and soul of every man and woman. Knowledge of the divine, therefore, was best achieved through introspection, which in turn yielded religious truths that tested doctrines, reason, and sense experience.
- *Intellectual influences.* Transcendentalism was an American expression of European Romanticism complemented by the ideas of important Asian thinkers. When he chronicled the history and achievements of the movement, Frothingham devoted the first five chapters of *Transcendentalism in New England* to German, French, and English authors whose works influenced its adherents, writers such as Friedrich Schleiermacher, Victor Cousin, and Samuel Taylor Coleridge. For the Transcendentalists, life was a spiritual and intellectual quest, a summons to self-cultivation, and the ideas of subtle thinkers, no matter what their origins, promised insights into the mysteries of life, society, and the universe.
- *Social critique.* At a time of substantial social change and challenges—industrialization, immigration, slavery, gender relations—most Transcendentalists were critical of important aspects of their society. They believed that all too often common customs and practices constrained the individual. Although their critiques and proposed solutions took many different shapes, most pursued reforms intended to liberate individual human potential.

The essays in this collection attempt to capture New England's Transcendentalists in all their complexity. Because personal interests and outlooks rather than shared orthodoxies guided the activities of individual members of the movement, no-one was equally involved in every issue that modern scholars are likely to identify with it. In recognition of this circumstance, the volume is organized according to a series of themes, each of which engages individual Transcendentalists in varying degrees. The collection has seven sections: Transcendentalism and the Historians, Transcendentalism and the New England Religious Tradition, Transcendentalism and the Cosmopolitan Discourse, Transcendentalism and Society, Transcendentalism and American Reform, Transcendentalism's Cultural Legacy, and Transcendentalism and the Critics.

Transcendentalism's enduring interest for many scholars is the subject of the collection's opening and closing sections, each comprising a single essay. In their contributions, Capper (on historians) and Lawrence Buell (on literary critics) both concede that the Transcendentalists sit less securely at the center of the field of vision of scholarship on American culture than they did in the past, when for many historians and critics the New England experience seemed to epitomize that of the nation as a whole. Notwithstanding increased competition from other historical and literary subjects for the attention of researchers, the number of capable scholars writing on the movement remains substantial, the sophistication of much current research on it impressive. Capper and Buell both acknowledge important work on Transcendentalism by past generations of writers and point out fruitful directions for further research.

Transcendentalism's place within New England's religious tradition is the subject of essays by David M. Robinson and Dean Grodzins. Robinson reveals "certain shared assumptions" among leading Transcendentalists on such theological issues as the relationship of reason to faith and prospects for the millennium, each of which helps to establish the movement's Unitarian bloodlines. In his piece, Grodzins creates a portrait of Boston's Twenty-Eighth Congregational Society, which was organized in 1845 by admirers of Theodore Parker as a place for the minister to promote his theological and social doctrines. Grodzins's study demonstrates Parker's continuity with longstanding New England teachings and ways as well as some radical changes.

Potentially provincial in view of its deep roots in the New England religious tradition, Transcendentalism became the most cosmopolitan movement of its time thanks to the interest of its leading figures in the ideas of European and Asian writers. The four essays brought together under the rubric "Transcendentalism and the Cosmopolitan Discourse" reveal how German, French, English, and Indian writings influenced Ralph Waldo Emerson, Henry David Thoreau, and other prominent Transcendentalists.

The early writings of Friedrich Schleiermacher confirmed for his avid American followers that "religion is basically an inward matter," as Robert D. Richardson, Jr., explains in his contribution to this collection. In her essay in this book, Barbara Packer shows that Emerson found confirmation of a different sort in the writings of three French-speaking intellectuals—Pierre Laplace, a mathematician and scientist; Charles Fourier, a philosopher and visionary; and Adolph Quetelet, an astronomer and statistician. Laplace, Fourier, and Quetelet affirmed for Emerson an optimistic message, nature's essential regularity and predictability. By comparing Thoreau's *Walden* with English (and New York) nature writing of the eighteenth and nineteenth centuries Nina Baym shows how the American was able to adapt a transplanted literary form into a defense of the New England countryside. And by studying Thoreau's understanding of Hindu writings after 1840, Alan D. Hodder reveals how the presuppositions of a noted American reader shaped the sense he made of the literature of a foreign culture.

At the same time that the Transcendentalists were engaging the ideas of European and Asian writers, domestic conditions in the United States influenced both what they thought about important issues and what their contemporaries thought about them. The four essays gathered together in the section "Transcendentalism and Society" show different ways in which members of the circle interacted with the world around them. In "Transcendentalism and the Spirit of Capitalism," John Patrick Diggins inquires into the relationship between social forces and the movement's metaphysical truths, "flesh and spirit," at a time of fundamental economic change. Robert A. Gross places the Transcendentalists in the town that is synonymous with them in "The Celestial Village: Transcendentalism and Tourism in Concord." A languid, pastoral image of the town has long obscured a much more energetic reality in Concord according to Gross. As astute observers of and commentators on the United States in the 1830s, '40s, and '50s, the Transcendentalists absorbed many of the trends of the day; in his essay in this collection, "'A Chaos-Deep Soil': Emerson, Thoreau, and Popular Culture," David S. Reynolds shows how popular language and rhetoric shaped the way that the movement's two most important literary figures expressed themselves. In "Transcendentalism in Print: Production, Dissemination, and Common Reception," Mary Saracino Zboray and Ronald J. Zboray analyze how the Transcendentalists' writings passed from their desks to their readers' libraries and how their audience responded to them.

Men and women who probed their social circumstances, who understood the power of the challenges facing their society, were ripe for reform and advocacy. At a time when causes and philosophies from abolitionism to feminism, from communalism to individualism, were proposing radically different ways to make the United States a better place, Transcendentalists pursued a variety of avenues to improvement. Ralph Waldo Emerson's commitment to reshaping American beliefs about slavery is the subject of Albert J. von Frank's challenge to the common notion that the Sage of Concord was too other-worldly to become a serious and steadfast opponent of the practice. The "Woman Question," the puzzle over woman's proper place in society, that activists began to address in the 1840s, did not result in a uniform Transcendentalist answer, as Phyllis Cole points out in her contribution to this volume. Margaret Fuller and Emerson, each socially progressive, came to significantly different conclusions about how women should lead their lives. In an essay on communalism's appeal for many Transcendentalists, Carl J. Guarneri explains how Fourierism and nationalism combined to transform their utopian visions. And Philip F. Gura's essay in this collection demonstrates how in the hands of William B. Greene, a minister in the central Massachusetts town of West Brookfield, Transcendentalist beliefs and sensibilities might undergird a program of radical individualism.

It often seems convenient to close the book on Transcendentalism sometime before the start of the Civil War, but four essays in this collection comment on its continuing ability to influence American thought and culture. Richard F. Teichgraeber III shows in his contribution that Emerson, best remembered today for his writing in the 1830s and early 1840s, remained a visible and influential force in American letters into the 1870s and a revered figure at the time of his death in 1882. The movement was still sufficiently immediate in 1897 to Caroline Healey Dall, the subject of Helen R. Deese's contribution, that it deserved a substantial reappraisal "from the margins" when she wrote a major lecture on it. Nancy Stula's essay on Christopher Pearse Cranch contends that the energetic, turbulent, and underappreciated landscapes of this artist, the only Transcendentalist to take up painting as a career, constituted the movement's most direct contribution to the visual arts during the second half of the nineteenth century. And Michael Broyles and Denise Von Glahn analyze the central influence of Transcendentalism on Charles Ives's *Concord* Sonata, composed between 1900 and 1915, revealing the enormous complexities of translating philosophy into music.

No collection of essays can hope to provide as full a portrait of a subject as a monograph can, not even a volume as large as this one. Transcendentalism's place in education and its transplantation from New England to the West are examples of the subjects that are missing from this book for want of space. Nevertheless, this compilation will serve its purpose if it stimulates discussion about a movement that has never ceased to engage inquiring minds and testifies to the vigor of current scholarship on the Transcendentalists.

ACKNOWLEDGMENTS

Most of the essays in this volume were presented in preliminary form at a conference at the Massachusetts Historical Society in May 1997. In organizing the program and then preparing this collection the editors accumulated dozens of obligations. It is a happy duty to acknowledge the many individuals and institutions who made our project possible. We are grateful to the following for generous financial support: Charles Francis Adams, John W. Adams, Mr. and Mrs. James B. Ames, Oliver F. Ames, Leo L. Beranek, The Boston Foundation, Stimson Bullitt, Levin H. Campbell, Melville Chapin, Louise I. Doyle, Mrs. John H. Fitzpatrick, Mr. and Mrs. Oscar Handlin, The Lowell Institute, Ruth B. Oliver, Stanley C. Paterson, Kathryn L. C. Preyer, Mr. and Mrs. William L. Saltonstall, L. Dennis and Susan R. Shapiro, Louis L. Tucker, and the Unitarian Universalist Historical Society. Conference participants, in addition to most of the essayists in this volume, who contributed to that stimulating event included: Daniel Aaron, Andrew Delbanco, Julie Ellison, Lilian Handlin, James Hoopes, Daniel Walker Howe, William R. Hutchison, James T. Kloppenberg, Mary Kelley, Stephen A. Marini, Leo Marx, Joel Myerson, Lewis C. Perry, Stephen Prothero, Nancy L. Rosenblum, Alan Trachtenberg, and C. Conrad Wright. The conference that has resulted in this collection was a complicated program to organize, and it never would have taken place without the considerable efforts of the staff of the Massachusetts Historical Society, particularly Louis L. Tucker, Peter Drummey, Len Travers, Ondine E. Le Blanc, Anne E. Bentley, Christopher A. Carberry, Sharon DeLeskey, Judy Greene, James Harrison III, Joice Himawan, Elizabeth J. Krimmel, Daniel McCormack, Alyson Reichgott, and Jennifer Smith. The editors owe extra words of thanks to Adam Tuchinsky, who provided Charles Capper with valuable research assistance, and to Ondine E. Le Blanc, the Society's assistant editor of publications, who has lived with this collection for longer than she believed possible. Without her editorial skill, organizational ability, and persistence this collection would not have been published. Manuscript from the collections of Houghton Library, Harvard University, are used by permission; those from the Boston Public Library are used by the courtesy of the Trustees of the Boston Public Library.

Charles Capper's contribution to this collection, "'A Little Beyond': The Problem of the Transcendentalist Movement in Amercan History," previously appeared in the *Journal of American History* 85(2) (September 1998): 502-539. It appears in this collection by permission of the *Journal.*

Charles Capper
Conrad Edick Wright

Transcendentalism
and the Historians

"A Little Beyond"

The Problem of the Transcendentalist Movement in American History

Charles Capper

Something strange has happened in American historiography. Transcendentalism, once a mainstay of surveys of American thought, has virtually vanished from the historical radar screen. This is somewhat ironic, since during the past decade prominent public intellectuals as disparate as Stanley Cavell, Richard Poirier, Irving Howe, Cornel West, Christopher Lasch, and George Kateb have made leading Transcendentalists such as Ralph Waldo Emerson and Henry David Thoreau the natal sources of their various post-1960s critical "genealogies." Nor have the Transcendentalists exactly starved for lack of scholarly attention. Joel Myerson's review of research on the movement for the Modern Language Association, published a little over a decade ago, lists nearly four thousand publications, while hefty biographies of both well-known and lesser-known Transcendentalists continue to pour from major presses. But neither critical acclaim nor academic productivity constitutes the history of a movement. That requires some sense of its contours, phases, and significance as a past, multiform, collective entity, interacting with other such entities in various "times." When one raises *these* questions about Transcendentalism, the recent literature, mostly written by scholars in American literature, shrinks down considerably. As a historical movement, Transcendentalism would seem to have entered into a long eclipse.[1]

Long, of course, is a relative notion. In fact, this eclipse has been a fairly recent one, roughly since the 1970s. Also, the reasons for Transcendentalism's long life in American historical writing have hardly been trivial or ephemeral ones. For one, over the past three-quarters of a century the subject has often found secure, if changing, professional and methodological footholds in the major disciplines of both history and literature. For another, historical Transcendentalism has been long buoyed up by that protean trio of cultural configurations that Alexis de Tocqueville, writing in the decade of the movement's rise in the 1830s (and completely ignorant of its existence), first virtually identified with "America" itself: liberal religion, individualist democracy, and national identity. Finally, these Transcendentalism concepts have been neither pristine nor static. On the contrary, they have been shaped, reshaped, and in some cases subverted by some of the nation's most important historians and critics, who have enlisted the Transcendentalists variously as allies or foils in their own successive Victorian, modernist, progressivist, "Americanist," liberal religious, and left ideological projects, and so have written Transcendentalism into the major designs of American history.[2]

The prospective issue then becomes neither the isolated present moment nor past Transcendentalism scholarship as such, but two retrospective historiographic questions. How have these successive Tocquevillean and post-Tocquevillean *conceptualizations* of Transcendentalism maintained or undermined the movement's presence in American history? What are the prospects for Transcendentalism scholarship now that these discursive plots have lost something of their force in the last couple of decades? Armed with answers to these questions, and a little critical imagination, we then ought to be able at least to get (in the Transcendentalists' fellow traveler Almira Barlow's catchy definition of their movement) "*a little beyond*" its current historiographic eclipse.[3]

When did the Transcendentalist movement become history? One could begin with the Transcendentalists themselves. Puritan and Revolutionary idealism, the birth of an American culture, the tradition of religious revivalism, the contemporary surge of antinomian reform movements, the rise of European Romantic literature and philosophy, the discovery of Asian literature, the spread of American democracy, the repression of the spiritual in rationalistic liberal Protestantism, the "modern" longing for an organic culture—these and other historical contexts for situating their movement, the Transcendentalists themselves articulated long before historians came along to do it for them. But these historicizations were sporadic and eclectic—as one might expect from adherents, in Emerson's words, not of the party of "Memory," but of the party of "Hope." A better temporal vantage point from which first to observe historical Transcendentalism would be during the time of its afterlife following the Civil War. By then, after a decade of steady diffusion of Transcendentalist ideas and writings, the movement's most aggressively radical leaders—such as Thoreau, Margaret Fuller, and Theodore Parker—had died, its avant-garde cultural edge had begun to dull, and its collective reform energies had been largely absorbed by antislavery impulses within the Union. Not surprisingly, it was around these years that several Transcendentalists wrote the first retrospectives of their movement.[4]

The most justly famous of these was Emerson's "Historic Notes of Life and Letters in New England." He wrote most of its sections in 1867 and delivered a patched-together version of them thirteen years later, by which time he had become afflicted with aphasia. In the opening section, he establishes the period's central motif of self-conscious individualism.

> The key to the period appeared to be that the mind had become aware of itself. . . . This perception is a sword such as was never drawn before. It divides and detaches bone and marrow, soul and body, yea, almost the man from himself. It is the age of severance, of dissociation, of freedom, of analysis, of detachment.

Emerson's self-consciousness fuse set, he then lets it explode into a historical bricolage of antebellum "severances": from tender child worship and burly free trade to hypertender come-outers and "genial" mesmerism. But at this point something remarkable happens: after recalling that this age of separation brought forth "young men . . . born with knives in their brain," he wanders into a surprisingly warm parlor-room reminiscence of his once "corpse-cold" intellectual Boston Unitarian fathers and a tenderly patronizing portrait of the leading Transcendentalists and their socialist compatriots. Then, suddenly, their circle disappears. "There was no concert," he assures us, but "only here and there two or three men or women who read and wrote, each alone, with unusual vivacity." Finally, he concludes, not with a hopeful prophecy of "seething brains" and "admirable radicals," as he had twenty-five years earlier in his lecture "The Transcendentalist," but with a very different kind of prophecy. After contentedly observing that the socialist Brook Farmers' "prophecies" were now being realized by giant corporations and cheap rooming houses, he closes with the pleasing thought "that our American mind is not now eccentric or rude in its strength . . . but normal, and with broad foundation of culture, and so inspires the hope of steady strength advancing on itself, and a day without night." So, in the end, the old Transcendentalist trickster takes his crew and together they go marching gently into post–Civil War Victorian America.[5]

Emerson's failure to connect his self-consciousness soil and its flourishing antebellum wildflowers with the more manicured landscape of the postbellum years was not only, or perhaps not even mainly, a function of his worsening aphasia and the haphazard circumstances of his essay's production. Like all other Transcendentalists linked to the past through memory, he was caught between two opposite and equally problematic pressures. One was the temptation of a soft triumphalism. These were the years, after all, when old abolitionists, who had once chafed at the circle's political aloofness, were now crediting it with constructing their crusade's philosophy; when liberal Christian Transcendentalists such as James Freeman Clarke were applauding their Unitarian denomination's progressive shedding of its old dualistic rationalist-supernaturalist dogmas; when Clarke and Samuel Johnson were producing their pioneering studies of comparative religion; and when even more theologically radical second-generation Transcendentalists were joining with ex-Unitarians, free thinkers, and assorted "spiritualists" to help found the period's two most important intellectual reform organizations, the Free Religious Association and the American Social Science Association. On the other hand, there was the temptation of despair, since below this surface Transcendental assimilation one could hear some highly discordant rumblings. Not idealist philosophy, individualism, "amateur" social science, and an intuitively understood fire of faith, but science, institution building, academic professionalism, and an anxious moralism were fast becoming the lingua franca of Victorian liberal intellectuals. No longer America's avant-garde, the now dead Transcendental greats seemed to many Unitarian establishment young bloods absurd, if not incomprehensible. The *North American Review*'s editor, the up-and-coming Harvard historian Henry Adams, characteristically explained to its readers in 1876, in calculated deadpan, what the Transcendentalists had been up to:

> Transcendentalists . . . renounced allegiance to the Constitution, continuing the practice of law; went through a process when they bought a piece of land which they called "releasing it from human ownership"; sought conspicuous solitudes; looked out of windows and said, "I am raining"; clad themselves in strange garments; courted oppression; and were, in short, unutterably funny.[6]

It is not, then, terribly surprising, given this contradictory situation, that Emerson seized on a plot of ironic "descendentalism" as a way out. New England Transcendentalism was not exactly dead, but it was rapidly ceasing to be (in the term of that post-Transcendentalist William James) a "living option." To survive, it had to become something more than ironic or incongruous memory. It had to become history.[7]

That could not be professional history, of course. Institutionally focused and culturally provincial, the newborn profession was decidedly unwelcome turf for Transcendentalism historians. Inevitably, then, the first historians of Transcendentalism—Octavius Brooks Frothingham, Thomas

Wentworth Higginson, and Caroline Healey Dall—wrote their narratives in an older tradition of "amateur" or "literary" history. As former Transcendentalists, they also wrote "insider" history. Yet this was not, except for Dall's, highly apologetic history. Even the insistent Dall in her polemical 1897 lecture on the movement quite originally traced Transcendentalism back to Anne Hutchinson and onward to the later women's rights movement. And the more intellectually surefooted Frothingham and Higginson, although hardly disinterested, strove at least to keep their more substantial accounts of the movement both comprehensive and dispassionate, while preserving an immediacy (as good insider histories often do) that professional historians can usually only envy.[8]

As the son of a prominent anti-Transcendentalist Unitarian minister and the first president of the non-Christian and vaguely scientistic Free Religious Association, Frothingham was the consummate religious liberal insider-outsider, and so in many ways was his 1876 *Transcendentalism in New England: A History*. Covering all the movement's European Romantic philosophical and literary antecedents, major phases, and leading figures—as well as maintaining an intellectually capacious and lucid yet also ideologically engaged and personally knowledgeable perspective—his *History* remains the only book on the subject ever written truly deserving of that subtitle. Furthermore, despite his genteel slighting of the Transcendentalists' radical literary figures, such as Thoreau (whom he only once barely mentions), the book's perspective on the movement's (to him) more eccentric figures, such as Bronson Alcott and Fuller, often manages to be both sober *and* empathetic.[9]

Yet therein lies the book's central problem: Frothingham cannot seem to get over Transcendentalism, and especially its ethical élan, but he does not know what to do with it historically. The result is that his history is strangely fractured. This characteristic is most glaringly apparent in his failure to connect the long first third of his book, on European Romantic thinkers, to its subsequent chronicle of New England Transcendentalism: after he begins the latter, he virtually never refers back to the former. Indeed, he tells us, in an astonishing concession that opens the second part, "it may be said that there never was such a thing as Transcendentalism outside of New England," because only in New England did it address popular and practical concerns. But why that was or how it made a difference in the way the Transcendentalists addressed the philosophical questions he chronicled in the European chapters of his book is not at all clear. So, in the end, Frothingham's Transcendentalists float far away, not only from the new spirit of his scientific, "sensuous," and "external" Victorian world, but from America altogether. "Their philosophy may be unsound," he concludes his book, "but it produced noble characters and human lives. The philosophy that takes its place may rest on more scientific foundations; it will not more completely justify its existence or honor its day." If Emerson's ethical prophecies about Transcendentalism were ironically triumphal, Frothingham's were uncertainly elegiac.[10]

By contrast, Frothingham's Free Religious Association colleague, "minor prophet," and fellow Transcendentalism memorializer Higginson, who wrote on the movement in the following two decades, had all the qualities of a *counter*-elegy-maker: humor, vigor, and a recollected fondness for his youthful militant abolitionist activism. Almost inevitably, the two also had very different takes on the Transcendentalist movement. Whereas the sober Frothingham had taken up his cousin Henry Adams's European-minded cosmopolite preoccupation with modern "science" and had been unable to find a clear historical space within it for his Romantic Transcendentalists, the left-mugwump and popular "man of letters" Higginson took up instead the other preoccupation of Victorian New England intellectuals—America's uplifting cultural nation building—and confidently construed the Transcendentalists as its bumptious forerunners. First, he said, explicitly countering Frothingham, the Transcendentalist movement's primary object was not a European-inspired philosophy, but a new American literature. Second, its form was not, as Frothingham implied, a compact intellectual coterie, but a loose association of highly individualistic figures who interacted with a broader social and cultural movement. Finally, that movement was principally created, not by the ideas of a few European writers, nor by a theological crisis within Unitarian liberal Protestantism, but by something called "the newness." As he portrayed it, this was a sudden awakening in the early 1840s of religiously liberal, middle-class New England young people, who earnestly experimented with new semi-bohemian, egalitarian, and "self-reliant" lifestyles and vocational identities. Poetically summing up his argument in his 1884 biography of Margaret Fuller, Higginson wrote:

> What is called the Transcendental movement amounted to essentially this: that about the year 1836 a number of young people in America made the discovery that, in whatever quarter of the globe they happened to be, it was possible for them to take a look at the stars for themselves.[11]

Higginson's generational and nationalist cultural Transcendentalist plot would turn out to be seminal. It was adopted wholesale in George Willis Cooke's elaborate 1902 history of the *Dial*, and one can find remnants of it down through post–World War II American Studies and new social history

Transcendentalism scholarship. Of course, Higginson's plot, too, had its blind spots. Not all the Transcendentalists were youths (even if they liked to affect the stance), not all of the movement's incongruities were (as he liked to portray them) quaintly humorous, and not all the stars they were looking at mirrored dreams that were likely to be consummated, as *his* were, in heroic war service and then a successful literary career. Higginson knew all this. He knew that some Transcendentalists struggled painfully to puzzle out a Romantic metaphysic, seriously dreamed utopian social dreams, loved and hated, acted irrationally, took dangerous risks, and plunged into mystical ecstasies. He also knew, from having to deal with his brother-in-law Ellery Channing, that Transcendentalism also produced many lazy, selfish, irresponsible, and, as he once confessed, "morally wasted" young men. But none of this seemed the point, which, for Higginson, was almost always an invigorating or uplifting one—both of which he showed effectively in his pioneering biography of Fuller, even as he deliberately suppressed her darker and wilder utopian sides. Ultimately, Higginson's historical plot for the Transcendentalist movement (which he lays out most clearly in his characteristically titled essay "The Sunny Side of the Transcendental Period") ran something like this: It began in fervid aspiration, got purged of its self-absorption by the "perpetual tonic" of the antislavery struggle, and finally flowered in an American literature that united Oliver Wendell Holmes and James Russell Lowell, Emerson and (after his purging) Thoreau, and Nathaniel Hawthorne (at least in his genial character), all the while dispensing with all the "gloom" that for some unknown reason beclouded European literature at this time. And so, with wit, charm, remembered courage, literary ingenuity, and a great deal of social perspicacity, Higginson cheerfully tucked Transcendentalism into the warm womb of the American "genteel tradition."[12]

By the time Higginson died in 1911, virtually all the movement's Victorian era "minor prophets" had also passed from the scene. Meanwhile, as the historical profession continued to eschew noninstitutional history, and as most English departments did the same with American literature, except for a few flimsy works in the venerable philological subfield of European source studies, Transcendentalism scholarship likewise continued to languish. One potential bright spot was the emergence, in revolt against the sort of Victorian scientistic and genteel evasions that had burdened Frothingham's and Higginson's histories, of a new generation of buoyantly irreverent, "modern"-minded critics centering around liberal and radical magazines such as the *New Republic* and *Seven Arts*. But unfortunately for

Transcendentalism, a number of these "Young American" critics, who despised the Victorian notion (as they saw it) of elevating the ethereal "ideal" above society's sordid realities, accepted Higginson, Harvard's Barrett Wendell, and other "genteel" critics' view that the Transcendentalists had helped with this elevating. So these young turks applied the cultural lash to them also. Indeed, Van Wyck Brooks, their most prominent figure, saw the Transcendentalists, with their eccentric behavior, fuzzy-minded "high ideals," and, in the case of Emerson, individualist "catchpenny realities," as almost the worst of the ethereal lot. "Since the day of Emerson's address on 'The American Scholar,'" Brooks wrote disgustedly in his influential *America's Coming-of-Age*,

> the whole of American literature has had the semblance of one vast, all-embracing baccalaureate sermon, addressed to the private virtues of young men. It has been one shining deluge of righteousness, purity, practical mysticism, and at the end of ninety years the highest ambition of Young America is to be—do I exaggerate?—the owner of a shoe-factory.

As for the socialist Transcendentalists at Brook Farm, "They were like high-minded weathercocks on a windless day."[13]

There was much unintended irony in this indictment. In fact, the overwhelming majority of American Victorian genteel critics had always *disdained* the "transcendental crew," as their New York poet Bayard Taylor called the circle, precisely because they had thought the Transcendentalists "introverted" and unpolished and therefore thoroughly *un*genteel. Moreover, by denouncing the Transcendentalists as (unlike Brooks's hero, Walt Whitman) failed cultural nationalists, Brooks perpetuated the very fundamentalist national category that had permeated Victorian readings of their movement. Finally, by treating the Transcendentalists' Tocquevillean individualism as nothing more than a category of moral uplift, Brooks missed what was culturally radical about much Transcendentalist thought—namely, that its Romantic individualism was self-reflexive and therefore implicitly challenged the very "highbrow"/"lowbrow" cultural split that he diagnosed as America's fatal disease.[14]

The first to recover this premodernist Transcendentalist viewpoint was not only no nationalist, radical or otherwise, but he was also the most penetrating non-American critic of the United States intellectual scene since Tocqueville: Spanish-born, Boston-"adopted," Harvard philosophy professor George Santayana. In his now classic essay "The Genteel Tradition in American Philosophy," which he delivered at the University of California at Berkeley in 1911 and published in 1913, two years before Brooks's book, after famously encapsulating the two-Americas problem ("The American Will inhabits the sky-scraper; the American Intellect inhabits the colonial mansion"), he then traced back the conundrum's intellectual origins to Calvinism and Transcendentalism. With Calvinism, to the materialist Catholic fatalist Santayana, the malady was clear: its "agonised" idealization of human sin and misery as manifestations of God's perfect omnipotence, however ironically self-abasing and exalting, was grossly evasive of natural instincts and therefore part and parcel of the genteel tradition. In the case of Transcendentalism, however, Santayana displayed profound ambivalence. Although he hated the sentimental projections of the self onto nature, in which he thought most Transcendentalists extravagantly indulged, at its core their philosophy was luminously modern:

> Transcendentalism is systematic subjectivism. It studies the perspectives of knowledge as they radiate from the self; it is a plan of those avenues of interference by which our ideas of things must be reached, if they are to afford any systematic or distant vistas. In other words, transcendentalism is the critical logic of science. Knowledge, it says, has a station, as in a watchtower; it is always seated here and now, in the self of the moment. The past and the future, things inferred and things conceived, lie around it, painted as upon a panorama. They cannot be lighted up save by some centrifugal ray of attention and present interest, by some active operation of the mind.

"As a method I regard it as correct," he concluded, "and, when once suggested, unforgettable. I regard it as the chief contribution made in modern times to speculation."[15]

With this brilliant categorization, Santayana accomplished three new and immensely important things for the historiography of American Transcendentalism. To begin with, he put on view a new method for thinking about the movement that went beyond both Frothingham's dry philosophical exposition and Higginson's earnest cultural appreciation: a mix of the "history-of-ideas" approach then being introduced by his colleague Arthur O. Lovejoy and the cultural criticism genre pioneered by the new pre–World War I generation of literary intellectuals. Second, he shifted the entire discussion from the moralistic nationalist paradigms that had dominated American Transcendentalism scholarship from Higginson through Brooks, back to an appreciation of Emerson's original paradigm of a hyperindividualist Transcendental ethos. Third, in giving that ethos a radically self-reflexive epistemological twist by defining it as an experiential "transcendental method," he brought Transcendentalism for the first

time in American intellectual history into the ongoing stream of modern
philosophy, including the radical empiricism of William James and the
modernist *overthrow* of the genteel tradition.[16]

This new link of individualist Transcendentalism to modern intellectual
culture soon became American modernist gospel. James himself had given
it his imprimatur in his "Address at the Emerson Centenary in Concord,"
but it was literary intellectuals of the 1920s who transformed it into an
evangelical doctrine. And the range was astonishing. James's progressive
pragmatist colleague John Dewey hailed Emerson as the only American
thinker "fit to have his name uttered in the same breath with that of Plato."
The conservative New Humanist critic Paul Elmer More declared Emerson the natal star of American literature. Indeed, the canonization of
Emerson was practically the *only* thing that both the New Humanists and
their often bitter liberal enemies agreed on.[17]

The most Romantically modernist claim for Emersonian Transcendentalism, though, came from an unexpected source: Brooks's younger Young
American colleague, the future critic of modern technology, Lewis Mumford. Brooks had called for a "usable past," yet Brooks's own historical
jeremiad had almost nothing usable in it. By contrast, Mumford's 1926
book, *The Golden Day*, had a great deal. For in it he defined for the first
time what we roughly think of today as "the American Renaissance"—not,
that is, the late nineteenth-century constellation of Emerson, Hawthorne,
Longfellow, and Lowell, but that of Emerson, Thoreau, Whitman, Hawthorne, Melville, and Poe. Even more important for Transcendentalism
historiography, Mumford defined a distinctly modernist, or forward moving *and* self-conscious, rationale for creating this canon—namely, that this
"Renaissance" was a plainly *post*-pioneer phenomenon; that the *collective*
dialectical play of its writers' imaginations allowed for a *variously* light
and dark interplay between mind and nature; and, finally, that because of
this *dialectical* "idealism," these authors were able symbolically to reconstitute American identity, and thereby make it available for our modern
"use." Just as Santayana had found a place for Transcendentalism at history's modernist philosophical table, so now Mumford found a spot at its
literary one.[18]

From the point of view of Transcendentalism history, however, there
was one serious flaw in all this early modernist appropriation, whether
cosmopolitan-individualist (as Santayana's) or individualist-nationalist (as
Mumford's): it settled on Emerson (or, in More's and Mumford's cases,
Emerson and Thoreau) as the sole Transcendentalists at the modernist
table. Indeed, Santayana had explicitly argued that, whereas Emerson
was at heart an experimental and "contemplative" stoic Platonist (rather

like himself!), all the rest of his Transcendentalist pals were just the oppo-site. *They* embraced, not the transcendental "method of discovery for the mind," but, following those "colossal egotists" the German post-Kantians, its self-flattering conversion into a "sham system" of "evolution in nature and history." (He did concede they sometimes somehow managed to seduce even Emerson into talking as though he, too, actually believed in his "metaphysical fables.") A historian of Transcendentalism, then, has to ask: What happened to all of Frothingham's and Higginson's "prophets," and where did *they* fit into the modernist "golden day"? "Much . . . of the power now attributed to Emerson [was] really the unconscious result of the total movement," Higginson had written, and he then had gone on to instance the various Transcendentalists whom Emerson had "boldly robbed." Ironically, in returning to the Victorian habit of canonizing Emer-son virtually alone, both the sophisticated cosmopolitan Santayana and the cultural radical Mumford proved, in this respect at least, more evasive (and therefore more "genteel") than the cheerfully provincial Higginson. For-tunately for the historical survival of Emerson's exploited fellow-laborers, Transcendentalism moved the next year from a shiny modern historical house to a sturdier "progressive" one.[19]

It is difficult to exaggerate the historiographic achievement of Vernon Louis Parrington's *Main Currents in American Thought.* The first intellec-tual history of the United States by a professional historian, it had little or no connection to the scholarship being done in either English or history departments. Furthermore, while Parrington's vision of American history as an enduring struggle between the forces of "progress" and democracy versus those of regression and elitism clearly aligned him with the progres-sivist historiography of Charles Beard, unlike Beard and his colleagues, who were largely economic determinists, Parrington was a Jeffersonian romantic. In Parrington's volumes, individuals drove history, and, if they seemed free-spirited and on the right side of the populist/elitist divide, he treated their ideas, if not their art, as semi-autonomous creations.[20]

Parrington's softly romantic progressivism accomplished two things for Transcendentalism historiography apart from just continuing the post-Vic-torian push beyond monolithically nationalist framings: it provided the most congenial methodological approach yet for treating the free-spirited Transcendentalists as a collective historical movement, and it gave them a democratic progressivist plot. He worked out with great ingenuity the details of both that method and plot in his extensive portrayal of the Tran-scendentalist movement in the second volume of his *Main Currents in*

American Thought. To begin with, following Frederick Jackson Turner, he divides his book into three regional "minds" (South, Middle East, and New England), which has the effect of relegating to New England virtually the entire intellectual component of his progressive "current." (And currents are always flowing together and forward in Parrington, unless they get stopped by retarding "reefs" and "sand bars.") He then inserts Poe, Melville, and Hawthorne as half-"transcendentalist" but also unfortunately "abnormal," "pessimistic," or "aloof" isolatoes in their respective regions. They are not barriers, but they are definitely not flowing with the current! (The "genteel" and anti-democratic New England literary Brahmins, of course, are *ineffective* barriers.) But Parrington does not stop at giving the Transcendentalists the progressive New England stream; he gives them virtually the whole river. He gives the game away with the subtitle to his volume: "The Romantic Revolution in America." This title has always puzzled scholars, and Parrington is certainly pretty watery about it. Basically, he seems to mean four things: eighteenth-century French Rousseauean "utopianism," Enlightenment humanitarian liberalism, the "romantic" hopefulness of antebellum individualist change, and an assertive psychocultural rebelliousness. The key, however, is this: although other currents contribute to all this flowing "romantic" current (such as Jeffersonianism, Unitarianism, Jacksonianism, and perfectionism), none is as clear as Transcendentalism. Thus, whereas the western populist Parrington does not flinch, as did most of his progressive colleagues, in acknowledging the exploitative and "acquisitive" cast of his subsumed (respectively) southern and western "minds" or (as he also calls them) "imperialisms," the Transcendentalists he portrays as virtually the self-conscious incarnation of American idealism.[21]

Finally, beyond practically deifying Transcendentalism in the larger narrative of American history, Parrington breaks new ground in *theorizing* the Transcendentalist movement. To start with, he was the first modern scholar to link together his leading Transcendentalists—Emerson, Thoreau, Parker, and Fuller—by seeing them, again for the first time, not as philosophical or literary figures, but as radical social and political critics. Too often in Parrington this approach to literature as politics by other means yields meager results, but in the case of the Transcendentalists, this is not so, and the reason is simple: although they were certainly other things, they *were* social critics. Moreover, Parrington's deep sympathy for them as "romantic" rebels leads him to original insights, for example, his elucidation of Thoreau's pre-William Morris organicist critiques of capitalism. It also encourages some surprising ones, such as his nuanced explication of Emerson's anti-politics politics and Thoreau's anti-populist pop-

ulism. Finally, there are his two metanarratives for the genesis and significance of their movement. One is his psychocultural interpretation of
Transcendentalism as a sort of historical Mighty Mouse, propelled by
New England's long-repressed idealism, flying through the narrow channel of European Romanticism, and suddenly landing as a stranger in a
strange new land of kaleidoscopic movements and romantic dreams. The
other schema is his more sober political one of the Transcendentalists as
heroic and self-conscious, if ultimately thwarted, carriers of "romantic"
versions of American liberalism.

Of course, like so much else in Parrington, his treatment of these "romantic" designs had its own naïvely romantic sides—beginning with (to
name the most glaring) his "masculine" distaste for Transcendental "mysticism," his deafness to anything smacking of an aesthetic sensibility, and his
1920s Freudianism, which caused him to portray the Transcendentalists
anachronistically as Rousseauean "rebels" victimized by repressive "Puritanism." In the end, though, Parrington's "Romantic Revolution" paradigm
served historical Transcendentalism well: it offered the first schema since
Higginson's for situating the Transcendentalists politically; it corresponded
to major "currents" within their movement; and it was presented with
enough passion, rhetorical power, and melodrama (all pure Parrington
traits) to ensure its survival in historical discourse for many years.[22]

Compared with Parrington's onrushing flood, Transcendentalism scholarship in the "progressivist" 1930s was something of a backwater, and
perhaps inevitably so. Certainly the hardships of the depression and the
public's yearning for federal government intervention were not the sorts of
things that easily nurtured favorable feelings toward mystical-minded individualist rebels, whether genteel *or* "romantic." Nor was the attraction
of many intellectuals to certain kinds of "Marxism" helpful. Early 1930s
Communist party critics' formulaic dismissal of Transcendentalism (as in
Granville Hicks's *The Great Tradition*) as an escapist and reactionary bourgeois individualism hardly encouraged major breakthroughs in the field. It
is true that with the Communist party's turn away from "proletarian" ultra-
leftism to an all-embracing (except for critics of Joseph Stalin) Popular
Front at the end of the decade, some left-wing critics touted the "bourgeois democratic" and anti-big business rhetoric of the Transcendentalists.
But even the most critically savvy of these, Bernard Smith, in his *Forces in
American Criticism*, denounced the circle's "mysticism" and individualism—or, in other words, the very things that distinguished the Transcendentalists from their generic role of fighters "on the side of humanity." Finally, by far the most intellectually sophisticated Marxists, the anti-Stalinist
circle around the *Partisan Review*, were too preoccupied with incorporat-

ing into the American radical discourse the boldly fractured tradition of European literary modernism to pay much attention to a group whose idealism seemed to many of them so evasive of "experience."[23]

On the 1930s popular and academic fronts, things were slightly more transcendentally "progressive." The founding of *American Literature* in 1929 had signaled the emergence of a reasonably secure group of Americanists, including some who took Transcendentalism under their wings. Yet the best of these works, such as Frederic Ives Carpenter's and Arthur Christy's studies of "Oriental" influences in American Transcendentalism, were still roughly in the mold of the old philological source studies and thus largely sidestepped the crucial question of how their chronicled "influences" shaped, or were shaped by, the Transcendentalist movement. Slightly better on this last score were the period's biographical studies, such as Odell Shepard's chronicle of Bronson Alcott, Henry Seidel Canby's study of Thoreau, and Madeleine Stern's life of Margaret Fuller. Written in variously breezy and sentimental styles, and directed at the mushrooming market for uplifting, American-centered, "middlebrow" biographies, they provided, if nothing else, the first detailed scholarly studies of leading Transcendentalists.[24]

The central figure, though, in this little Transcendentalism renaissance was, in one of the most astonishing reversals in American literary history, none other than the Young American's Jeremiah, Van Wyck Brooks. After plunging into a frightening depressive breakdown while trying to put together a life of his nemesis Emerson, Brooks reemerged to write *The Flowering of New England*. In his 1936 book he now portrayed, as the apotheosis of America's "usable past," the very antebellum New England literary tradition that he had once excoriated as the hated mother of America's "genteel tradition." Gaining overnight best-seller status and a Pulitzer Prize, his volume also earned him a worthy place in Transcendentalism history. By including the largest cast of Transcendentalists that had yet figured in a historical narrative, mixing them in with their Brahmin opponents, and surrounding them all with a mass of well-researched social and literary bric-a-brac, he conjured up what seemed to his eventually hundreds of thousands of readers a compellingly intimate atmosphere of New England Transcendentalism's literary life—in a word, a sort of genteel, provincial counterpart to the Communist party's Popular Front (which Brooks ardently supported). He also had a major influence on the period's Transcendentalism biographers, most of whom mimicked his semifictionalized style, as well as copied his central conceit of literature as social encounters. But, like the Victorian interiors Brooks's chapters resemble, more was not exactly better. By converting texts, psychologies, even his subjects' words into his own cozy prose of interior monologues, he carefully kept complex ideas and hard feelings from defiling his precious social ambiance. Here, too (with the partial exception of Canby's sentimentally Freudian *Henry David Thoreau*), the Transcendentalists' biographers did the same, only adding to the mix a dash more of concern for the personal "idealism" of their quaintly provincial heroes. Historiographically speaking, Transcendentalism, as Parrington might have said, had hit another reef—or perhaps was even flowing back the other way.[25]

That last possibility was partly forestalled with the emergence around World War II of a *nationalist* progressivism in Transcendentalism scholarship. The Columbia historian of philosophy Herbert W. Schneider characterized the Transcendentalists in his erratically perceptive *A History of American Philosophy*, the first such history in over a generation, as sometimes going to extremes in their love of nature and natural spontaneity, but more often staying the course as "genial" critics and "constructive" idealists, "vigorous, good-natured" even in their social rebelliousness—in a word, level-headed, moderate "liberals." In an even more expansive mood, Ralph W. Gabriel portrayed them, in *The Course of Democratic Thought*, as exponents of an ethical "individualism" hostile alike to a mindless "collectivism" and to the "materialism of American business and politics," a sort of Transcendentalist version of the modern, world-enlightening American "democratic faith" that was the theme of Gabriel's book. The apotheosis of this progressivist liberal view of the Transcendentalists was Daniel Aaron's 1951 *Men of Good Hope*. Roughly in line with the view of the best Transcendentalism book to have come out of the progressivist 1930s—Henry Steele Commager's *Theodore Parker: Yankee Crusader*—Aaron presented a spirited picture of Emerson and Parker as moderate but principled reformers, whose social idealism, despite occasional false steps (Aaron alluded to but then dismissed Parker's racism), led on to a central nineteenth-century moral-minded reform tradition that lasted until it was done in by the bogus Progressivism of Theodore Roosevelt.[26]

Yet Aaron's generously liberal take on Transcendentalism, as he conceded in his preface, was already out of step with the predominant post–World War II liberal and scholarly trends, which were politically "tough-minded" and, if liberal, increasingly hostile to anything that smacked of effete individualistic idealism. Characteristic of that turn was the pro-New Deal historian Arthur Schlesinger, Jr., who had written a sympathetic biography of the Jacksonian and sometime Transcendentalist Orestes Brownson. In his Pulitzer Prize-winning 1945 *The Age of Jackson*, dispensing with Parrington's Transcendentalist-led "romantic revolution," Schlesinger made the litmus test rudely political: did the Transcendentalists support Jackson's urban-led, anti-big business Democratic party or were they aloof fence-sitters, timid escapists, and precious naysayers? When he banged down the historical gavel for the latter verdict, they were (except for Brownson) summarily expelled from the "age of Jackson."[27]

Fortunately for Transcendentalism, a new generation of sophisticated American history and literature scholars had by this time emerged, ready to mount a critical rescue operation. One set were historians associated with the rising school of post–World War II "consensus history." Actually the term is misleading, since most of them, including their leading figure, Richard Hofstadter, were often critical of the American capitalist consensus, although, in the wake of totalitarianism abroad and McCarthyism at home, they were also highly skeptical of sweeping neopopulist claims on behalf of the virtues of "the people." Moreover, suspicion does not necessarily mean dismissal. In the arsenal of post–World War II American historiography, Transcendentalism became, in an abrupt return to the grand theme of the grandfather of unillusioned liberalism, Tocqueville, the proof-text of consensus America's idealist individualism.

The key text was Stanley Elkins's enormously influential 1959 book, *Slavery: A Problem in American Institutional and Intellectual Life*. The subtitle revealed his thesis. Slavery, Elkins argued, had been a wrenching political problem because of the relative absence of the sort of mediating institutions, such as a state church and a strong central government, that had peacefully abolished slavery in Britain. Without such institutions, reform devolved upon rootless intellectuals who framed the issue in abstract moral terms, making any resolution short of civil war impossible. Although Elkins, in good consensus fashion, held as equally responsible for this calamity southern ideological pundits and, naturally, the abolitionists, it was on the Transcendentalists that he placed the largest responsibility:

> By the 1830s the closest thing to an intellectual community in the United States consisted of men with no concrete commitment to system at all. They were men who had no close commitment to any of society's institutions. They were truly men without responsibility.

Ignoring the obvious differences between the morally absolutist and denunciatory abolitionists and the ethically introspective and ostentatiously "self-reliant" Transcendentalists, Elkins portrayed them both as symbiotically connected central players in bringing about, through their injection of a dangerously radical antinomian spirit into northern culture, the one terrible collapse of the American consensus.[28]

Of course, the classic Tocquevillean theme of American individualism can be played out, as it was by Tocqueville himself, in several ways, not all of them quite so darkly insidious as in Elkins. This is where the new literary scholars, who had found both Parrington's and Schlesinger's reduction of ideas to either onward-flowing currents or mere political referents highly problematic, came into the picture. The key rescuer this time was F. O. Matthiessen, his vehicle was his 1941 *American Renaissance*, and his approach was nearly the exact opposite of Parrington's—to return to Mumford's canon of Romantic writers (minus the darkly cosmopolitan Poe) and to focus, not on their professed politics, but on their artistic theories and practices, and particularly their use of language, as they facilitated the emergence of an American literature in an extended Western modernist discourse. In a word, Matthiessen returned to the early modernism of Mumford, gave it a darker Augustinian and European flavor, and offered up as the result a cosmopolitan modernist version of the new post–World War II Tocquevillean Americanist plot.[29]

The notion of Matthiessen as a Transcendentalism rescuer may seem wildly implausible. As a Popular Front socialist, neo-orthodox Christian, and a high modernist critic, he was a highly complex figure hardly cut out for simple gestures. Moreover, his notion of "democracy," by which he claimed in his book to connect and judge all his Romantic writers, *is* indeed (as it was in his life) extremely fuzzy. Sometimes he seems to mean by it their espousal of anticapitalist opinions, sometimes their dialectical play of language, and sometimes (with Hawthorne and Melville) their tragic view of life. Finally, Matthiessen's view of New England Transcendentalism was a rather unfriendly one. His hiving off of Emerson and Thoreau from their New England colleagues, his modernist distaste for the antinomian reform culture that they attached themselves to, his naturalistic antipathy to Emerson's spiritualistic brand of symbolism, his Popular Front dismissal of Thoreau's political libertarianism, and, finally, his categorization of both Emerson and Thoreau as the moral and artistic inferiors of both Whitman, the superior democrat, and their two dark Romantic anti-soul-mates, Hawthorne and Melville—none of this conjures up the image of a warm incubator of modern Transcendentalism scholarship.[30]

But major scholarly roads are rarely smooth and straight. Just as Elkins "saved" historical Transcendentalism by making it politically important through its assimilation of antebellum "individualism," so Matthiessen's book saved it by making it culturally important through its imperfect assimilation of American "democracy." For one thing, he made the Transcendentalists accessible to a generation of intellectuals, of varying political persuasions, for whom Parrington's "liberal" notions of inevitable progress ensuing from dualistic struggles between the forces of the "people" and agents of privilege and superstition ceased to correspond not just to the Cold War but to the realities of the entire post–World War II modern world. For another, despite his severe strictures of them, by casting Emerson as the fountainhead of his book's entire American philosophical-artistic tradition and Thoreau as its greatest Transcendentalist artist, Matthiessen created for them a powerful intellectual genealogy. Furthermore, by placing Emerson and Thoreau in conversation with three of the most intellectually influential writers in American history, and all five within a thick narrative of philosophical and literary discourse from the Renaissance through the modernist era, Matthiessen hardly dealt with them, as is often charged, as isolated, ahistorical artifacts. Last, although he avoided engaging with Emerson and Thoreau's immediate discursive context (he cryptically called the two books on this larger discourse that he conceded that he had *not* written *The Age of Swedenborg* and *The Age of Fourier*), he uncovered in Emerson's and Thoreau's ideas resonant languages that simply could not be decoded without paying some attention to the Transcendental duo's benighted colleagues and compatriots.[31]

Over the next couple of decades, two groups of literary scholars did just that. One set, led most importantly by Charles Feidelson, honed in even more rigorously than had Matthiessen on the epistemology and aesthetics of the Transcendentalists and their ideas of symbolic representation. Meanwhile, more important for historians, a second group, self-identified with the burgeoning American Studies field, such as R. W. B. Lewis, John William Ward, and Leo Marx, refashioned Matthiessen's symbolistic approach to his Romantic texts into a tool for extracting from a variety of cultural artifacts answers to broad post–World War II Tocquevillean questions concerning American identity, which directly bore on Transcendentalism. First, they often drew heavily on Transcendentalist texts and themes, such as nature and individualism. Also, they generally constructed their works, not as accounts of conflicts *à la* Parrington and Schlesinger, but more as (in Lewis's term) "conversations." If this Tocquevillean downplaying of contention sometimes led them to fuse a little too easily their discussants, at its best their discursive method had a crucial benefit for the Transcendentalists: it brought them into relation with a large number of antebellum writers, both popular and elite, whose questions resonated with theirs, but whose answers often did not. Finally, their American Studies mode reflected, along with a shared method, a related shared political sensibility, which allowed them to see something in Transcendentalism that progressive liberals such as Parrington had been closed to. This was not its religious vision, or its antinomian style, which they largely missed. This was, rather, in Marx's term for his and his colleagues' method, its dialectical liberal imagination: the Transcendentalists' capacity to engage with American culture as a way, not of escaping it, nor even necessarily reforming it, but interrogating it, symbolizing it, and so opening it up to possibilities of democratic renewal.[32]

What these critics did *not* do, however, was to make the Transcendentalists' *party* a central one. Except for Lewis, who included Parker, they did not drift very far from Matthiessen's Emerson and Thoreau duo. Nor, except sporadically, did they concern themselves with tracing out Transcendental philosophical ideas, or connecting them, as Matthiessen had done, with non-American influences. Nor, finally, did they place Transcendentalism in the murky temporal stream that historians (to borrow from Thoreau) like to go a-fishing in. They had other symbolic fish to fry. Yet, all of these things had to be done if Transcendentalism was to be conceptualized for post-World War II scholarship as a significant historical movement.

These tasks were taken up by their older American Studies colleague Perry Miller. Actually, the often applied "American Studies" label is misleading here. Miller was an intellectual historian with a strong comparatist flair, although not (as is often claimed) in the Lovejoyan sense of a historian who narrates largely decontextualized philosophical ideas, but quite the opposite. Miller was America's first dramatically *discursive* American intellectual historian. In particular, he constructed narratives of past intellectually self-conscious figures who struggled to impose meaning on their cultures by dint of struggle with others, as well as with their own darker selves, in particular historical situations, often with unintended results. These results did not flow, either forward *or* (despite the common claim that he was a declensionist) backward. Ultimately Miller was an ironist—sometimes Promethean, sometimes (though he denied it) H. L. Mencken-like, but basically existential. His central ironic conflicts revolved around two main themes: American intellectuals wrestling with their European cultural inheritance in conflict with America's provincial openness, and, closely related, their coming to terms with modernity, by which he meant a world without verifiable transcendent meaning, but which nonetheless required our engagement.[33]

Miller's philosophical outlook bore directly on the plot that he created for the Transcendentalist movement. Curiously, in some ways, that plot almost mimicked Parrington's. Not, of course, methodologically: Miller's method of making ideas problematic so that they might propel his narrative discur-

sively while he penetrated their surface calm to their esoteric patterns beneath was poles apart from Parrington's literal-minded and often one-di-
mensionally political way of looking at texts and ideas. Still, on the surface,
Miller's Transcendentalism plot was not too different from Parrington's: the
movement's sudden bursting on the scene in the guise of a "romantic" cultural revolt. But there the similarity ends. For Miller, it was not "idealism"
that had been repressed, but modernity, and its bursting was made at once
radical and innocent because American intellectuals, as he wrote in his
essay "New England Transcendentalism: Native or Imported?" had never
had, as Alfred North Whitehead once said, "an eighteenth century." That is,
they had never experienced the extremes of skepticism, revolution, and dis-
illusionment that European intellectuals had all passed through in the
second half of the century. The Transcendentalists' "innocent" rebellion
was made especially poignant, Miller argued in this essay and elsewhere, by
the fact that they had to channel it through one small, archaically rationalist
intellectual community that was, nonetheless, the most "liberal" one in
America. Finally, Miller noted, there was poignancy in the further fact that
their often prescient Romantic critiques of utilitarian modern capitalism
were swallowed up in the Civil War and postwar American economic
expansion and seemed, therefore, to lead to nothing. When one considers
that the only historical appraisal of the Transcendentalists' world since
Parrington's was Van Wyck Brooks's provincially self-congratulatory *Flowering of New England*, one can see how truly extraordinary Miller's achievement was.[34]

Of course, Miller's Transcendentalism plot, too, is a kind of metahistory,
unless or until it can produce an empirically grounded historical narrative.
Unfortunately, Miller died before completing more than a small part of his
projected multivolume "life of the mind" from the Revolution to the Civil
War, in which he had planned to include a full portrait of the Transcendentalist movement in the context of American Romanticism. He did publish in the 1950s and early 1960s several pioneering studies of individual
Transcendentalists. But his most important work on Transcendentalism
was the one he finished in 1950, near the beginning of his research—
his comprehensive, and still unsurpassed, anthology of the movement's
writings, *The Transcendentalists*. Actually, anthology gives a misleading
impression. Its organization, selection, and interwoven commentaries provide a virtual skeleton history. It is hardly a flawless skeleton, however. The
hyperbolic and condescending tone of some of his headnotes can be dis-
tracting, if not downright off-putting. One problem, perhaps, was their
hit-and-run format, which may have encouraged the Mencken sort of
swaggering that in his fuller and denser narratives he usually managed to

check or sublimate. Also, he does not seem to have yet found the right voice for dealing with intellectuals whose styles, while certainly inviting irony, required a more delicate version of it than he had been in the habit of using for his blunter Puritans. Whether he would have found such a voice is impossible to say. But whether he would or would not have, as they are, these commentaries display a verve, erudition, and profundity that had never been manifested before in Transcendentalism scholarship.[35]

Ultimately, what made Miller's anthology an enduring classic was its central and truly original idea that Transcendentalism, at its heart, was a "religious demonstration." The historiographic importance of this new paradigm was immense. By highlighting the Transcendentalists' religious sensibility, he brought back to life what had, indeed, been the animating center of Transcendentalism, yet one that had been nearly effaced by the overwhelmingly secular and literary preoccupations of its twentieth-century scholarly chroniclers. The Tocquevillean issues of individualism and democratic national identity in Transcendentalism remained important, but always as they were constructed by the religious language used by its movement's adherents. Also, this religious paradigm gave him an entrée as well into its specific historical characteristics. First, by devoting substantial sections to the Transcendentalists' debates with their conservative Unitarian opponents, he placed Transcendentalism's genesis in a specific historical site, as well as showed dramatically how it actually functioned in its early phase *as* a movement. Second, his broad religious focus also allowed him not only to recover dozens of important figures who had virtually disappeared in modern scholarship but also to reveal something of the sheer numbers of people involved in the movement. Third, by cleverly using the term "demonstration," which can mean both an outward verbal expression and a public display in favor of a cause, he captured precisely the double-sided individual-literary and collective-political shape of historical Transcendentalism. Indeed, by including sizable sections on both the Transcendentalists' literary writings *and* their radical social and political critiques, and highlighting the latter because he believed "this element in the story has been most lost sight of today," he did two remarkable things. One was to bring forward female cultural critics such as Fuller and Elizabeth Peabody, whom scholars had never before written about as serious intellectual figures, and radical intellectuals such as Orestes Brownson, who had never even figured in histories of the movement. But even more important historiographically, his religio-political reconfiguration represented simultaneously a rebuke to Matthiessen's restricted casting and Christian anti-Romanticism and a return to Parrington, though now, in the spirit of Frothingham, on a broadly religious and international, rather than

narrowly secular and national, basis. In sum, Miller's anthology was nothing less than the first effort to construct a broadly conceived, historiographically sophisticated, and narratively exciting picture of Transcendentalism as a historical movement. It was not a history, but it was a great
second.[36]

Miller died in 1963, the year of President John F. Kennedy's assassination.
Leaping over Miller's 1920s heart and post-1930s mind, historical Transcendentalism, like much scholarship of the era, lurched to the left.
Moreover, it was a prototypical 1960s lurch—which is to say, rather like
Transcendentalism's own antebellum time, it lurched in several different
directions at once. Returning to a new civil rights-conscious version of the
"old" progressivist line of the 1930s, Aileen Kraditor, in her *Means and
Ends in American Abolitionism*, while spiritedly defending the radical
abolitionist Garrisonians from the aspersions Elkins had cast on them as
social irresponsibles, happily threw the impossibly individualistic Transcendentalists to the same political dogs to which Schlesinger had fed
them. Meanwhile, literary scholars exploited heightened 1960s social sen-
sitivities to weigh in against the Transcendentalists. Characteristic was the
Columbia University American literature scholar Quentin Anderson. In
his wide-ranging *The Imperial Self*, Anderson, echoing Kraditor's distaste
for "irresponsible" intellectuals but applying it to cultural matters, charged
Emerson and his followers with fleeing from society into the "empire of
the self" and so "decreasing our ability to imagine society as the primary
scene of human accomplishment." These by now well-worn neo-Elkins
assaults, of course, left two rather large question marks. First, assuming
that the Transcendentalists had at least *thought* they were trying to bring
about a new society, what positively *was* their social ideal? Second, if the
Transcendentalists had disdained both institutions and movements, how
explain their historical influence?[37]

By the end of the 1960s, younger scholars were starting to give three sets
of comparatively friendly answers to these questions. One answer was to
say the Transcendentalists were exponents of individualistic and holistic *alternatives* to capitalist cultural modes and therefore contributors to a powerful, if unacknowledged, countercultural tradition down to our own day.
This answer came in Marxist, libertarian, and environmentalist renderings,
but the most capacious version was advanced by the New Left historian-
activist Staughton Lynd in his 1968 *Intellectual Origins of American Radicalism*. Returning to a kind of Parringtonian view of the Transcendentalists
as Rousseauean pre-Marxian Romantics, Lynd placed Transcendentalism

as expressed by its most metapolitical figure, Thoreau, within a broad tradition of Anglo-American radicalism incorporating strands of the ethical religiosity of eighteenth-century Protestant Dissenters, the agrarianism of early-nineteenth-century artisan republicanism, and the moral fundamentalism of antebellum abolitionism. In Thoreau's hands, Lynd argued, the Transcendentalist reworking of this tradition produced a political ideology that counterposed personal integrity to utilitarian compromise, creative associationism to static social contracts, and "joyful labor" and human growth to economic exploitation and commodity fetishism.[38]

A second set of answers to dismissals of the "irresponsible" Transcendentalists was given by other left-liberal scholars, who sought to rescue them, not by claiming them for a radical countercultural tradition, but, almost the opposite, by embedding them in the main currents of nineteenth-century culture. Leo Marx, for example, in what was arguably the most important American Studies text of the 1960s, *The Machine in the Garden*, argued that Transcendentalists such as Emerson and Thoreau expressed neither industrialism nor agrarianism, but a "middle landscape" vision, which differed from that embraced by many conventional antebellum pundits only in its deep sensitivity to the moral and metaphorical tensions required by a humane psychic movement back and forth between the poles of the "pastoral" and the "civilized." But it was an intellectual historian, George M. Fredrickson, who went the furthest in appropriating the Transcendentalists to this liberal neo-consensus framework. Fredrickson explicitly *accepted* Elkins's view that the essence of the Transcendentalist ethos was individualistic and anti-institutional but then added a crucial historicist twist. Noting that a "perfectionist" or "Romantic" ethos was an essential, if not defining, ingredient in northern antebellum culture as a whole, Fredrickson argued in his widely read, 1965 *The Inner Civil War: Northern Intellectuals and the Crisis of the Union* that that same sensibility in the Transcendentalists was therefore both adaptive and contributory to American reform and national identity. Virtually echoing the decomposing and atomizing social trends in the family, church, and state that Emerson had listed in his "Historic Notes" as dissolving traditional sources of authority and social control—but labeling them the "natural conditions of a capitalist society in the state of rapid economic and geographical expansion"—Fredrickson concluded that not just Emersonian Transcendentalism but antebellum revivalism and reform generally "can be seen as a response to these conditions. If man was not to be governed, he must be taught to govern himself. God's grace or his own awakened conscience would have to take the place of external authority."[39]

In essence, then, Fredrickson's historicization of Emersonian Transcen-

dentalism returned Transcendentalism scholarship to the founder of the
liberal theory of American democracy, Tocqueville, but now in an altered
reformist form and applied to the Transcendentalists: antebellum democracy equaled individualism, individualism was paradoxically atavistic and
adaptive, and that paradoxical individualism was fully expressed in the
thinking of the Transcendentalists. Yet this neo-liberal Tocquevillean rescue was a cautious one. For one thing, it put a large period at the end of the
Transcendentalist impulse. In Fredrickson's rendering, with the Civil War
and the rise of corporate America, Transcendentalist ideas, now irrelevant
to the needs of an increasingly bureaucratized society, disappeared from
the American reform discourse. Two other aspects of Transcendentalism
also largely dropped out of Fredrickson's left Tocquevillean picture: the
movement's specific theology and its collective character. Without these,
Transcendentalism's historiographic box, having been expanded to the size
of America, suddenly shrank down to the size of that afforded it before Parrington and Miller.[40]

Working to expand that box was a group of 1970s scholars who gave yet
a third set of answers to the questions of what the Transcendentalists were
for and what sustained them historically. These answers grew directly out
of Miller's claim that the Transcendentalist movement was America's first
premodern "religious demonstration," but without the temporal prefix and
with "liberal" added. The first attempt to assimilate Transcendentalism to
mainstream liberal Protestantism had been made nine years after Miller's
anthology, in William Hutchison's *The Transcendentalist Ministers*, soberly
subtitled, as though a simultaneous rejoinder to Matthiessen's formalist
and Miller's and Elkins's antinomian portrayals, *Church Reform in the New
England Renaissance*. Specifically, Hutchison's study struck at a serious
weakness in Miller's chain of argument: his stark counterposition of the
Transcendentalists and their Unitarian opponents. Here Miller's Parringtonian taste for melodrama, especially when it came to head-heart dualisms, had betrayed him. Hutchison persuasively demonstrated that
Miller had exaggerated both the differences *between* the two camps and
the unities *within* each. But Hutchison did more than revise Miller. He
also portrayed the church reform efforts of his Transcendentalist ministers
as part of a seminal renewal movement within liberal Christianity, whose
effects were felt well into the later nineteenth century.[41]

The 1970s and early 1980s scholars who picked up Hutchison's liberal
church tradition plot reworked it in two somewhat opposite ways. On one
hand, they expanded it into the broader realms of literature and society. On
the other hand, reflecting both the growing knowledge of minor movement figures afforded by Joel Myerson's publication of Transcendentalist

documents in his *Studies in the American Renaissance* and the post-1960s scholarly preoccupation with "local knowledge" and marginalized groups, scholars increasingly concentrated on Transcendentalism in historiographic miniature. In literary studies, the most imaginative work of this period was Lawrence Buell's *Literary Transcendentalism: Style and Vision in the American Renaissance* (1973). Ignoring the European Romantic, Americanist-minded, and partly New Critical preoccupations of Matthiessen and his generation of post–World War II critics, Buell showed not only that Transcendentalist literary ideas—such as the sacredness of secular literature and the concept of the poet-preacher—evolved out of Boston-area Unitarianism, but that those hybrid notions also nurtured the very nonfictive discursive genres and sublimely "common" rhetorical strategies that produced the Transcendentalists' contribution to American literature.[42]

Meanwhile, energized by the new social history of the 1970s, which emphasized the study of communities, with special attention to issues of economic development, class formation, and collective behavior in "private" associations, two historians fashioned new resonant miniatures of Transcendentalism as a local social phenomenon. In *Transcendentalism as a Social Movement, 1830–1850*, Anne Rose revealed the Boston Unitarian social and denominational roots of Transcendentalism's religious quarrels, communitarian projects, and private transgressive social experiments. At the same time, Robert Gross, in three contemporaneous articles, returned the subject of Transcendentalism to its traditional American Studies duo of Emerson and Thoreau but this time rooted their cultural critiques of capitalism and urbanism, not in the metaphorical "middle landscape" of Leo Marx, but in the literal, if conflict-ridden, place of suburban Concord.[43]

This post-Miller Boston turn brought Transcendentalism scholarship home, in several senses. First, of course, it broadened considerably an awareness of Unitarianism's contribution to Transcendentalism. Second, it captured the peculiar liberal religious *and* literary ethos of Transcendentalism that most literature scholars had always occluded or, in the case of Matthiessen, treated with some contempt. Most important, it sympathetically assimilated the movement to a tradition that both Miller's Puritan-focused Romantic view and its various progressivist and liberal secular alternatives had also elided: American religious liberalism, or the ongoing attempt since the early nineteenth century to bring Protestant religion within modernist modes of thinking without sacrificing its sacred center. Finally, in the hands of Rose and Gross, this Boston regional focus suggested how Transcendentalism in the margins might reveal the local but implicitly wider worlds of work, community, and economy.

Still, this hybrid Boston Unitarian synthesis had a few worldly elisions of its own. One was theological. In fact, once the Unitarian-Transcendentalist controversy died down, most of the leading Transcendentalists developed religious ideas that were not only post-Unitarian but radically post-Christian as well. Another was Transcendentalist reform, which encompassed much more than behavioral changes within the extended Boston Unitarian community. But the largest gap in the Unitarian synthesis was contextual. Assuming that religious liberalism and cultural reform were at the center of Transcendentalism, the question remained: how did that center radiate outward to the broader national culture either in the movement's heyday or since? To imagine how these problems might be addressed today, we need to move from this last turn in Transcendentalism scholarship to a few backward and forward glances.

Looking backward, it is clear that certain past methodological approaches will continue to be essential to any Transcendentalism project. In particular, as the leading Transcendentalists were self-conscious intellectuals whose languages borrowed from a wide range of discourses, discursive intellectual history will necessarily be one of them. Likewise, others, given the importance of literary practice to the Transcendentalists, will necessarily blend the empirical and contextualist methods of history and the linguistic and intrapsychic ones of literary studies. Nor, finally, should the sheer variety of past approaches to Transcendentalism stop scholars from getting a fix on what exactly was the *movement* in the movement. A movement can be defined in many ways: intellectual coterie, social current, religious demonstration, cultural trend, philosophical genealogy, literary tradition, and others, depending on the purposes of one's narrative. The key is to develop within each narrative a conceptualization of "movement" that actually *moves*. This means doing at least three things: maintaining some sense, whether microscopic or macroscopic, of the movement's temporality; distinguishing the *Transcendentalism* component of one's narrative from others within it; and keeping the avenues open to other such distinguishable Transcendentalist elements in different narrative contexts.[44]

When one looks forward, it is also clear that the three Tocquevillean paradigms of much classic Transcendentalism scholarship—liberal religion, individualist democracy, and national identity—will clearly need to be both revitalized and revised in light of all the corroding acids applied to them by postliberal and postmodernist discourses since the 1960s. Certainly Transcendentalist religion needs to remain central, yet its mongrel character needs much more attention than it has received from either Millerite or post-Millerite scholars. Catherine Albanese's *Corresponding Motion: Transcendental Religion and the New America* is one of the few studies that tries to get at this problem by linking Transcendentalism to broad worldwide religious currents as well as to rapid social change and correspondent rhetorics of "speed" and "ecstasy" in antebellum America. Yet her suggestive social-science phenomenological approach still leaves critical dimensions unaddressed. One is the specific intellectual conduits of Transcendentalist religious comparatism. For example, how did it fit within early comparative religious and mythographical studies, to which the Transcendentalists were the first important American contributors? What were the links connecting syncretic Transcendentalism to contemporary Catholic, Anglican, non-Christian, and quasi-scientistic religions, to which many Transcendentalists later converted? Then, too, there is the further liminal fact that the more theologically radical Transcendentalists were thought by many, both at the time and since, to have founded a new religion. Yet the character, parameters, and sources of that religion have never been very clear, especially in relation to the explosion of antebellum antichurch "come-outer" sects, which vitally influenced Transcendentalist ideas of church, state, and society.[45]

Finally, there is comparative Romanticism, or what M. H. Abrams has aptly called the religion of "natural supernaturalism." After three-quarters of a century of modern Romantic scholarship, during which time Transcendentalism has repeatedly been glibly characterized as "American Romanticism," what was specifically "American" or "Romantic" about it remains almost as hazy as ever. And it is likely to remain so until Transcendentalism scholars begin formulating questions that would make any set of Romantic comparisons historically meaningful. One of these is the diversity of Romanticisms within nineteenth-century American culture generally. Literary scholars have written volumes about the connections and disconnections between the Transcendentalist "children of light" and the "dark Romanticism" of Hawthorne and Melville, but virtually nothing has been done to explore the same overlapping polarities between Transcendentalism and the various liberal, confessional, and sentimental Romantic cultures that began to emerge in the late 1840s in both Protestant and popular discourses. Another question is that of Romantic politics. It has long been recognized that the Transcendentalists were politically neither on the right nor (for the most part) on the classical, European-style left. Recently the political theorists Nancy Rosenblum and George Kateb have tried to define a "liberal" Romanticism in which classical liberal commitments to negative freedom are modified by positive concerns with the self's "inner ocean" and a noncontractualist community, a discourse that might fruitfully be used to expose the fault lines of Transcendentalism's contributions to both American liberalism and Western Romanticism. Yet a third comparative question is that of Romantic "modernity." The issue was sketchily raised by Miller: not simply the Transcendentalists' foreign "sources" but what these borrowings signified—the depth and character of their participation in the West's great problematic leap into cultural modernity. Certainly, if modernity means, as postmodernist philosophers tell us, a self-reflexive engagement in a world seemingly without fixed "foundations," the leading Transcendentalists, although idealists to the core, pushed closer to that leap than did any other intellectual circle before the twentieth century.[46]

Besides Romanticism, another nineteenth-century ersatz religion that deserves a place at a new historical Transcendentalist table is culture. Nineteenth-century notions of culture, as Raymond Williams long ago pointed out, vacillated among concepts of life, thinking, and symbolic construction, and the Transcendentalists sought to express and relate all three. In the first category was the surprisingly still underdeveloped subject of generational culture, encompassing issues ranging from family life to vocational identity. Not only were the Transcendentalists born into a period of radical domestic change, but they were the first intellectual group in American history to make liberation from the "sepulchres of the fathers" (in Emerson's phrase) the exhilarating (and covertly anxious) center of their social world view. Likewise resonating with Transcendentalism was the nineteenth-century culture of the "private." Indeed, it is hard to imagine a better venue for exploring such private cultures as friendship, family life, work, and the alternately bright and dark (in Tocqueville's phrase) "solitude of . . . heart" than with the Transcendentalists, whose very collective identity and communitarian experiments were paradoxically closely bound up with the lonely and the inward. On the more formal cultural side, besides engaging in an astonishing array of artistic and educational practices themselves, the Transcendentalists, through their Romantic concepts of "genius," "talent," "nature," and spirituality, directly engaged with all the major contested cultural questions of the nineteenth century: the interplay among "high," "low," and "middlebrow" cultures; the status of the artist and intellectual in a consumer-capitalist market; the powers of "sentiment" versus those of the intellect; and the boundaries between the "cultural" and the "political." As America's first self-consciously highbrow, avant-garde searchers for the "common," the Transcendentalists' cultural genealogy can even be extended right through the "culture wars" of the late twentieth century.[47]

The second traditional category of Transcendentalism scholarship that is ripe for radical revision is what Tocqueville called "democracy," but which most scholars since the 1950s have preferred to call more neutrally the ideology of "reform." Remarkably enough, it has only been during the last few years that Carl Guarneri and Richard Francis, extending outward from the work of Anne Rose, into, respectively, Fourierism and Transcendentalist social science, have given us modern scholarly accounts of Transcendentalist socialism. Meanwhile, only now, thanks to such works as John d'Entremont's biography of Moncure Conway, Len Gougeon's monograph on Emerson's abolitionism, and Alfred von Frank's study of the 1854 Anthony Burns rendition case, are we beginning to get a picture of Transcendentalist abolitionism alternative to that of Elkins. Even environmentalism—which Donald Fleming has called the Transcendentalists' "main institutional legacy"—has only in recent years been given much systematic attention. Likewise, liberal feminism—the movement's other modern reform legacy—is just now, with the proliferation of works on Margaret Fuller and her circle, beginning to enter historical narratives. Also remaining to be understood are perhaps the two most distinguishing questions of all of Transcendentalist reform. One is how the Transcendentalists' conception of individual freedom intersected with the three main conceptual modes of antebellum reform: moral law, individual rights, and human sympathy. The other question, cutting even closer to the Transcendental bone, is how the Transcendentalists understood their literary and performative styles—and, closely related to that, their acute self-consciousness about their special cultural responsibilities as intellectuals—in shaping their social and political commitments. Finally, there is the recent decades' "race-class-gender" paradigm. No intellectual group in antebellum America so thoroughly addressed these constructions as did the Transcendentalists. But to get at how they did this, it will be necessary to heed Transcendentalism as a conceptual and linguistic *constitutive* category. That means asking such questions as not just how gender, race, class, and the market shaped *Transcendentalism* but how *Transcendentalism* shaped *them*. Only then can Transcendentalism scholarship become contributive to, rather than merely derivative of, those ubiquitous discourses.[48]

This question of reform ideology is closely related to the third Tocquevillean paradigm: the national question. Indeed, this issue has reverberated more consistently than any other in the literature on Transcendentalism since its first emergence after the Civil War down through the post-World War II era of American Studies. Most recently, the national question has been raised in a new ideological form by scholars associated with what is sometimes labeled the "New American Studies." Its claim to newness rests on three grounds: its change of focus from single "myths" to shifting "rhetorics," its heightened sensitivity to oppressed minorities, and, following closely on the last, its reformulation of the old Tocquevillean "American exceptionalist" question to read: why has America had such a seemingly undifferentiated ideological culture *despite* the obvious facts of race, class, and gender divisions?[49]

The scholar who has most persistently applied this project to Transcendentalist themes and figures has been Sacvan Bercovitch. Specifically, his characteristic plot has highlighted the Transcendentalists' reworking of the Puritan jeremiad rhetoric of tribal self-flagellation in the service of American self-aggrandizement into a rhetoric by which the interrogated self expands outward to nature, which in turn becomes a trope for a hegemonic, forward-looking, capitalist "American self." From the point of view of American Studies approaches to Transcendentalism, Bercovitch's project has had two beneficial effects. For one thing, in focusing on religious language, it has resonated more directly with Transcendentalist constructs than did the more secular 1950s Tocquevillean mythic models. Also, in keeping the ideologically unfashionable paradigms of New England Puritanism and national identity as his nodal points for Transcendentalism, Bercovitch has shown amazing resourcefulness and staying power. But as a way of historicizing Transcendentalism, his ideological project raises several difficulties. First, the quasi-evangelical rhetoric that he uses to Americanize the Transcendentalists insufficiently accounts for their more important Romantic locutions, especially in the writings of post-Christian Transcendentalists such as Emerson, Fuller, and Thoreau. Nor does Bercovitch's even larger trope of the "American self" do full justice to the Transcendentalists' Romantic cultural stances, to their group identity concerns, or to the rapidly changing political developments with which they engaged over the two decades leading up to the Civil War—nor, for that matter, to the still underexplored question of *non*-New England sites of Transcendentalist culture.[50]

Of course, the historical question of Transcendentalism's relation to American national capitalist ideology is no easier a puzzle to solve now than it was when the Marx-conscious Louis Hartz first formulated that latter consensus paradigm in his *The Liberal Tradition in America* over forty years ago. Since World War II we have gone through a long trajectory of scholarly solutions to this conundrum: from the responsible 1940s and 1950s, when the Transcendentalists appeared narcissistic, escapist, or innocent; through the 1960s, when they seemed healthily adaptive or countercultural; through the post–Vietnam War 1970s and 1980s, when they seemed entrepreneurially canny, ideologically submissive, or imperialistically elitist; until the period since the late 1980s, when they have increasingly appeared in American scholarship as "organic intellectuals," "connected critics," modern "professionals," artisan-minded "populists," "democratic individuality" liberals, and even postmodernist "corporate superliberals." Such a dizzying historiographic catalogue of interpretations might seem to confirm the intractability of the nationalist ideology problem, but in fact it reveals two positive historical lessons. The first is, by becoming luminous screens on which successive generations have projected some of their deepest ideological fears and desires, the Transcendentalists have shown they matter. The second is, when it comes to a complex historical subject, more *is* often better, if it keeps us from getting stuck with only one set of conceptual glasses before we have had a chance to discover our own.[51]

For a glimpse of what that one lens set might be, one might consider the most recent formulation of the "national question" that can usefully be brought to bear on Transcendentalism. This might be called the "transnational" paradigm. On one hand, after a generation of postmodernist and "postcolonial" critiques of the idea of the nation—or at least the idea of the *American* or *Western* nation—a swarm of new furies has arisen. These range from the rise of genocidal tribalism in Eastern Europe and Africa to the globalization of market-driven economic inequalities and the multiculturalist destabilizing of yesterday's multiculturalist racial categories. The cumulative result of these developments has forced back into the public discourse the question of the nation as a potentially "progressive" entity. On the other hand, simultaneously, talk about a new "cosmopolitanism" is now being heard among public intellectuals, raising for the first time in over a generation profoundly difficult questions about identity, community, and individual freedom. It is always risky to try to link historical experiences with present-day interests, but sometimes it is just the thing to help break out of dead protective shells. Certainly no intellectual circle in early America other than the Transcendentalists thought so self-consciously of itself—and in its criticism and actions tried to act on that perception—as at once individualist, nationalist, and cosmopolitan, and that during a period in American history when an anxiously hopeful kind of national self-consciousness was at its height. As our considerably more purely anxious civic present and future seem increasingly to hang on getting this trinity right, it seems not too utopian to suppose that, not a further vanishing, but a shock of recognition in Transcendentalism studies is in order.[52]

A version of this article has been published in the Journal of American History *85(1998):502-539.*

I wish to thank the following readers of earlier versions of this essay for their helpful criticisms and suggestions: Catherine Albanese, Ruth Bloch, Lawrence Buell, Carole Capper, Mary Cayton, Elizabeth Clark, Andrew Delbanco, Robert Ferguson, Carl Guarneri, Philip Gura, David Hall, David Hollinger, Daniel Howe, John Kasson, Henry May, Joel Myerson, David Nord, Barbara Packer, Lewis Perry, Daniel Rodgers, and Conrad Edick Wright.

NOTES

1. Stanley Cavell, *This New Yet Unapproachable America: Lectures after Emerson after Wittgenstein* (Albuquerque, 1989); Richard Poirier, *The Renewal of Literature: Emersonian Reflections* (New Haven, 1987); Irving Howe, *The American Newness: Culture and Politics in the Age of Emerson* (Cambridge, Mass., 1992); Cornel West, *The American Evasion of Philosophy: A Genealogy of Pragmatism* (Madison, 1989), 9–68; Christopher Lasch, *The True and Only Heaven: Progress and Its Critics* (New York, 1991), 168–295; George Kateb, *The Inner Ocean: Individualism and Democratic Culture* (Ithaca, 1992); Joel Myerson, ed., *The Transcendentalists: A Review of Research and Criticism* (New York, 1984); Charles Capper, *Margaret Fuller: An American Romantic Life*, vol. 1: *The Private Years* (New York, 1992); Robert D. Richardson, Jr., *Emerson: The Mind on Fire* (Berkeley, 1995); Dean David Grodzins, "Theodore Parker and Transcendentalism" (Ph.D. diss., Harvard University, 1995); Phyllis Cole, *Mary Moody Emerson and the Origins of Transcendentalism: A Family History* (New York, 1997); Bruce A. Ronda, *Elizabeth Palmer Peabody: A Reference on Her Own Terms* (Cambridge, Mass., 1999); Wesley T. Mott, ed., *Biographical Dictionary of Transcendentalism* (Westport, Conn., 1996); Wesley T. Mott, ed., *Encyclopedia of Transcendentalism* (Westport, Conn., 1996). Only five years ago there appeared the first major overview of the movement in over a generation, Barbara L. Packer's "The Transcendentalists," in *The Cambridge History of American Literature*, ed. Sacvan Bercovitch (Cambridge, 1994–), 2:329–604. Although necessarily limited by its publication date, the best bibliographical survey is Lawrence Buell, "The Transcendentalist Movement," in *The Transcendentalists: A Review of Research and Criticism*, ed. Joel Myerson (New York, 1984), 1–36.

2. Alexis de Tocqueville, *Democracy in America*, ed. Phillips Bradley (1835, 1840; New York, 1945).

3. Ralph Waldo Emerson, Oct. 6, 1836, in *The Journals and Miscellaneous Notebooks of Ralph Waldo Emerson*, ed. William H. Gilman et al. (Cambridge, Mass., 1960–1982), 5:218.

4. Ralph Waldo Emerson, "The Conservative," in *The Collected Works of Ralph Waldo Emerson*, ed. Alfred R. Ferguson et al. (Cambridge, Mass., 1971–), 1:184. For samples of contemporary attempts by Transcendentalists to historicize their movement, see Margaret Fuller, "Modern British Poets," *American Monthly Magazine* 8(Oct. 1836):320–322; Orestes A. Brownson, *New Views of Christianity, Society, and the Church* (Boston, 1836); Ralph Waldo Emerson, "Lectures on the Times," in *Col-*

lected Works, 1:161–216; and Margaret Fuller to William Henry Channing, 1840, *The Letters of Margaret Fuller*, ed. Robert N. Hudspeth (Ithaca, 1983–1994), 2:108–109. Ambitious historical appraisals of Transcendentalism by sympathetic contemporaries may be found in William Dexter Wilson, "The Unitarian Movement in New England," *Dial* 1(Apr. 1841):409–443; J. A. Saxton, "Prophecy—Transcendentalism—Progress," *Dial* 2(July 1841):83–121; and James Murdock, "American Transcendentalism," in his *Sketches of Modern Philosophy* (Hartford, Conn., 1842), 167–188. For three important Transcendentalist retrospectives published in the 1850s, see *Memoirs of Margaret Fuller Ossoli*, ed. R. W. Emerson, J. F. Clarke, and W. H. Channing (Boston, 1852), 1:322–323, 2:12–39, 72–80; Orestes A. Brownson, *The Convert; or, Leaves from My Experience* (New York, 1857); and Theodore Parker, *Theodore Parker's Experience as a Minister, with Some Account of His Early Life* (Boston, 1859).

5. Ralph Waldo Emerson, "Historic Notes of Life and Letters in New England," in *The Complete Works of Ralph Waldo Emerson*, ed. Edward Waldo Emerson (Boston, 1903–1904), 10:326, 329, 337, 342, 369–370; Ralph Waldo Emerson, "The Transcendentalist," in *Collected Works*, 1:207–208.

6. Henry Adams, review of *Transcendentalism in New England* by Octavius Brooks Frothingham, *North American Review* 123(Oct. 1876):470–471.

7. William James, *The Will to Believe and Other Essays in Popular Philosophy* (1897; Cambridge, Mass., 1974), 14.

8. Caroline Healey Dall, *Transcendentalism in New England: A Lecture* (Boston, 1897). The best succinct discussion of professional history in this period remains John Higham, *History: Professional Scholarship in America* (1965; Baltimore, 1983), 6–25, 92–103, 158–170. Transcendentalism apologetics in these years generally fell into one of two camps: quasi-official Unitarian histories that portrayed the movement as a renewal current within Unitarianism, and unreconstructed defenses of Transcendentalism as a still sound and relevant philosophy. For Unitarian histories, see Joseph Henry Allen, *Our Liberal Movement in Theology* (Boston, 1882), 196–244; *Unitarianism: Its Origins and History* (Boston, 1890), 196–244; John White Chadwick, *Old and New Unitarian Belief* (Boston, 1894), 1–34, 217–246; and George Willis Cooke, *Unitarianism in America* (Boston, 1902), 155–186. For Transcendentalist defenses, see Cyrus A. Bartol, *Radical Problems* (Boston, 1872); Samuel Johnson, "Transcendentalism," *Radical Review* 1(Nov. 1877):447–478; and George Ripley (completed by George P. Bradford), "Philosophic Thought in Boston," in *The Memorial History of Boston*, ed. Justin Winsor (Boston, 1881), 4:295–330.

9. Octavius Brooks Frothingham, *Transcendentalism in New England: A History* (New York, 1876). For contrasting appraisals of Frothingham's thought, see Sydney E. Ahlstrom, "Introduction," in Octavius Brooks Frothingham, *Transcendentalism in New England* (Philadelphia, 1959), ix–xxiv; and Stow Persons, *Free Religion: An American Faith* (New Haven, 1947), 28–31, 55–74.

10. Frothingham, *Transcendentalism in New England*, 105, 383.

11. Thomas Wentworth Higginson, *Margaret Fuller Ossoli* (Boston, 1884), 133. For other works of Higginson's that also discuss Transcendentalism, see his *Cheerful Yesterdays* (Boston, 1898), *Old Cambridge* (New York, 1899), and *Part of a Man's Life* (Boston, 1905).

12. George Willis Cooke, *An Historical and Biographical Introduction to Accompany the* Dial (Cleveland, 1902), 2:1–39; Thomas Wentworth Higginson, "The Sunny Side of the Transcendental Period," in Higginson, *Part of a Man's Life*, 14, 16, 25.

13. Barrett Wendell, *A Literary History of America* (New York, 1900), 233–446; Van Wyck Brooks, *America's Coming-of-Age* (New York, 1915), 7, 70, 84–85, 89. The meager state of academic American literary scholarship in these years is amply documented in Howard Mumford Jones, *The Theory of American Literature* (1948; Ithaca, 1965), 118–159. See also Kermit Vanderbilt, *American Literature and the Academy: The Roots, Growth, and Maturity of a Profession* (Philadelphia, 1986), 3–28, 123–240. Of the various Transcendentalism source studies published in the 1900s, the most complete is Henry Clarke Goddard, *Studies in New England Transcendentalism* (New York, 1908). For Brooks and his circle of cultural critics, see James Hoopes, *Van Wyck Brooks: In Search of American Culture* (Amherst, Mass., 1977); and Casey Nelson Blake, *Beloved Community: The Cultural Criticism of Randolph Bourne, Van Wyck Brooks, Waldo Frank, and Lewis Mumford* (Chapel Hill, 1990). The unsurpassed work on the early-twentieth-century intellectual revolt against the "genteel tradition" remains Henry F. May, *The End of American Innocence: A Study of the First Years of Our Own Time, 1912–1917* (1959; New York, 1994). An unusually positive pre–World War I radical appraisal of Emerson and especially Thoreau as social rebels may be found in the socialist critic John Macy's *The Spirit of American Literature* (New York, 1913), esp. v–viii, 3–17, 45–76, 171–188. But Macy makes no attempt, unlike the later Vernon Louis Parrington, whose assessment Macy anticipates, to put his figures in any significant historical context.

14. Bayard Taylor, "My Mission," in his *The Poet's Journal* (Boston, 1863). Although there were important differences between the Boston and New York "genteel critics," their attitudes toward the Transcendentalists were not among them. For a good study, see John Tomsich, *A Genteel Endeavor: American Culture and Politics in the Gilded Age* (Stanford, 1971).

15. George Santayana, "The Genteel Tradition in American Philosophy," in his *Winds of Doctrine* (London, 1913), 188, 190, 193–194.

16. Santayana, "Genteel Tradition," 195. A good account of Lovejoy's early scholarship in the history of ideas can be found in Daniel J. Wilson, *Arthur O. Lovejoy and the Quest for Intelligibility* (Chapel Hill, 1980), 33–35, 139–156. For later histories of philosophy that have followed Santayana's lead in linking Transcendentalist philosophy to pragmatism and thereby to modernism, see Woodbridge Riley, *American Thought: From Puritanism to Pragmatism and Beyond* (New York, 1915), 328–331; Herbert W. Schneider, "American Transcendentalism's Escape from Phenomenology," in *Transcendentalism and Its Legacy*, ed. Myron Simon and Thornton H. Parsons (Ann Arbor, 1967), 215–228; William A. Clebsch, *American Religious Thought: A History* (Chicago, 1973), 69–187; and Morton White, *Science and Sentiment in America: Philosophical Thought from Jonathan Edwards to John Dewey* (New York, 1972), 71–119. I do not mean to imply here that there was nothing innocent about early American modernism. Yet for many American literary intellectuals, the darker and more self-reflexive strains of "high modernism" that had long marked European modernism, and would later define much of its post–World War II variant, were already beginning to appear in the 1920s, and Lewis Mumford's later canonization of both the Transcendentalists and "dark Romantics" such as Hawthorne and Melville

is a case in point: see Lewis Mumford, *The Golden Day* (New York, 1926). On the variety of modernisms, see Hugh Kenner, *A Homemade World: The American Modernist Writers* (New York, 1975); Daniel Joseph Singal, ed., *Modernist Culture in America* (Belmont, Calif., 1991); and Peter Nicholls, *Modernisms: A Literary Guide* (Berkeley, 1995).

17. William James, "Address at the Emerson Centenary in Concord," in his *Memories and Studies* (New York, 1911), 17–34; John Dewey, "Ralph Waldo Emerson," in his *Characters and Events* (New York, 1929), 1:76; Paul Elmer More, "Emerson," in his *Shelburne Essays* (Boston, 1904–1921), 11:69–94. For the modernist recovery of America's literary "usable past" in the 1910s and 1920s, see Jones, *Theory of American Literature*, 118–159; and Richard Ruland, *The Rediscovery of American Literature: Premises of Critical Taste, 1900–1940* (Cambridge, Mass., 1967), 1–165. Although more crotchety than previous volumes, the last volume of René Wellek's monumental history of critical thought is constantly illuminating on the period's critical scene. See René Wellek, *History of Modern Criticism, 1750–1950*, vol. 4: *American Criticism, 1900–1950* (New Haven, 1986).

18. Mumford, *Golden Day*.

19. Santayana, "Genteel Tradition," 194, 195, 199; Higginson, *Old Cambridge*, 62–63. For a balanced consideration of Santayana's strengths and weaknesses as an intellectual historian of Transcendentalism, see Joe Lee Davis, "Santayana as a Critic of Transcendentalism," in *Transcendentalism and Its Legacy*, 150–184. See also James's fascinating discussion of the similarities and differences between Emerson and Santayana (all to Emerson's advantage), in William James to Dickinson S. Miller, Nov. 10, 1905, quoted in Ralph Barton Perry, *The Thought and Character of William James* (Boston, 1935), 1:399.

20. Vernon Louis Parrington, *Main Currents in American Thought: An Interpretation of American Literature from the Beginnings to 1920* (New York, 1927–1930). For varying appraisals of Parrington and his *Main Currents*, see Robert Allen Skotheim, *American Intellectual Histories and Historians* (Princeton, 1966), 124–148; Richard Hofstadter, *The Progressive Historians: Turner, Beard, Parrington* (New York, 1968), 349–434; and H. Lark Hall, *V. L. Parrington: Through the Avenue of Art* (Kent, Ohio, 1994).

21. Parrington, *Main Currents in American Thought*, 2:58, 61, 258, 379, 445, 473.

22. Parrington, *Main Currents in American Thought*, 2:384, 434.

23. Granville Hicks, *The Great Tradition: An Interpretation of American Literature since the Civil War* (New York, 1933); Bernard Smith, *Forces in American Criticism: A Study in the History of American Literary Thought* (New York, 1939), 120; Philip Rahv, "Paleface and Redskin" (1939), and "The Cult of Experience in American Writing" (1940), in his *Literature and the Sixth Sense* (Boston, 1970), 1–6, 21–37. For popular, early 1930s, left-wing "Freudian" dismissals of the Transcendentalists as "Puritan" palefaces, see Ludwig Lewisohn, *Expression in America* (New York, 1932), 105–152; and V. F. Calverton, *The Liberation of American Literature* (New York, 1932), 244–298. The connection between the Great Depression and antipathy to Transcendentalism comes through clearly in James Truslow Adams's widely admired savaging of Emerson; see James Truslow Adams, "Emerson Re-Read," *Atlantic Monthly* 146(Oct. 1930):484–492. For somewhat comparable 1930s critiques by two conservative critics, see Henry Bamford

Parkes, "Emerson," *Hound and Horn* 5(July-Sept. 1932):581–601; and Yvor Winters, *Maule's Curse: Seven Studies in the History of American Obscurantism* (Norfolk, Conn., 1938), 125–136. Still valuable for the 1930s critical scene is Alfred Kazin, *On Native Grounds: An Interpretation of Modern American Prose Literature* (New York, 1942), 400–452. Post-1960s "left"-conscious appraisals may be found in Grant Webster, *The Republic of Letters: A History of Postwar American Literary Opinion* (Baltimore, 1979); and Vincent B. Leitch, *American Literary Criticism from the 30s to the 80s* (New York, 1988), 1–114. Despite the abundance of (often partisan) recent appraisals of the *Partisan Review* circle, a thorough historical assessment of its cultural criticism is still needed. The best overall study is Terry A. Cooney, *The Rise of the New York Intellectuals: Partisan Review and Its Circle* (Madison, 1986).

24. Frederic Ives Carpenter, *Emerson and Asia* (Cambridge, Mass., 1930); Arthur Christy, *The Orient in American Transcendentalism: A Study of Emerson, Thoreau, and Alcott* (New York, 1932); Odell Shephard, *Pedlar's Progress: The Life of Bronson Alcott* (Boston, 1937); Henry Seidel Canby, *Henry David Thoreau* (Boston, 1939); Madeleine B. Stern, *The Life of Margaret Fuller* (New York, 1942). See also Mason Wade, *Margaret Fuller: Whetstone of Genius* (New York, 1940). For the turn toward sentimental and nationalist-minded narrative styles in biography writing in the late 1930s and early 1940s, see John A. Garraty, *The Nature of Biography* (New York, 1957), 138–151. For the period's "middlebrow" literary culture, see Joan Shelley Rubin, *The Making of Middlebrow Culture* (Chapel Hill, 1992).

25. Van Wyck Brooks, *The Flowering of New England, 1815–1865* (New York, 1936).

26. Herbert W. Schneider, *A History of American Philosophy* (New York, 1946), 281, 286, 289; Ralph Henry Gabriel, *The Course of Democratic Thought: An Intellectual History since 1815* (New York, 1940), 42, 46, 50, 51; Daniel Aaron, *Men of Good Hope* (New York, 1951); Henry Steele Commager, *Theodore Parker: Yankee Crusader* (New York, 1936). For a somewhat tougher-minded but still liberal democratic appreciation of the Transcendentalists by a student of Gabriel's, see Stow Persons, *American Minds: A History of Ideas* (New York, 1958), 201–213. Merle Curti, the major American intellectual historian of the post–World War II era, wrote a kind of Parringtonian progressivist history, but his method of narrating a mass of small artifacts organized into broad thought "patterns" driven by social institutions and practices did not leave much room for self-consciously intellectual groups such as the Transcendentalists; in his *Growth of American Thought* (New York, 1943), Transcendentalists are given a total of 3 out of over 900 pages.

27. Arthur M. Schlesinger, Jr., *Orestes A. Brownson: A Pilgrim's Progress* (Boston, 1939); Arthur M. Schlesinger, Jr., *The Age of Jackson* (Boston, 1945), 361–390.

28. Stanley M. Elkins, *Slavery: A Problem in American Institutional and Intellectual Life* (1959; Chicago, 1976), 141. Elkins's theories about the effects of slavery on the personality of the slave drew the most critical assaults, followed by his negative appraisal of the abolitionists. When the Transcendentalists were discussed at all, they were usually folded into the latter topic. For critiques of Elkins and his various rejoinders, see ibid., 140–266; and Ann J. Lane, ed., *The Debate over Slavery: Stanley Elkins and His Critics* (Urbana, Ill., 1971).

29. F. O. Matthiessen, *American Renaissance: Art and Expression in the Age of Emerson and Whitman* (New York, 1941). For an influential critique of Parrington's one-

dimensional way of handling ideas in his narrative, see Lionel Trilling, "Reality in America," in his *The Liberal Imagination: Essays on Literature and Society* (New York, 1950), 3–21. For a comparable view by a younger intellectual historian, who would later become a critic of consensus history, see John Higham, "The Rise of American Intellectual History," *American Historical Review* 56(1951):453–471.

30. The literature on Matthiessen is large and often contentious. For sympathetic appraisals, see Paul M. Sweezy and Leo Huberman, eds., *F. O. Matthiessen: A Collective Portrait* (New York, 1950); Giles Gunn, *F. O. Matthiessen: The Critical Achievement* (Seattle, 1975); and Frederick C. Stern, *F. O. Matthiessen: Christian Socialist* (Chapel Hill, 1981). For two left multiculturalist critiques, see Jonathan Arac, "F. O. Matthiessen: Authorizing an American Renaissance," in *The American Renaissance Reconsidered*, ed. Walter Benn Michaels and Donald E. Pease (Baltimore, 1985), 90–155; and William E. Cain, *F. O. Matthiessen and the Politics of Criticism* (Madison, 1988).

31. In Matthiessen's two comments on Parrington in his text, he dissents from his criticism but respectfully appropriates his history. Matthiessen, *American Renaissance*, 472n, 638.

32. Charles Feidelson, Jr., *Symbolism and American Literature* (Chicago, 1953), esp. 119–161. For other important post-Matthiessen works on Transcendentalist literary epistemology, see Sherman Paul, *Emerson's Angle of Vision: Man and Nature in American Experience* (Cambridge, Mass., 1952); and Tony Tanner, *The Reign of Wonder: Naivety and Reality in American Literature* (Cambridge, 1965), 1–93. R. W. B. Lewis, *The American Adam: Innocence, Tragedy, and Tradition in the Nineteenth Century* (Chicago, 1955); John William Ward, *Andrew Jackson: Symbol for an Age* (New York, 1955); Leo Marx, *The Machine in the Garden: Technology and the Pastoral Ideal in America* (New York, 1964); Leo Marx, *The Pilot and the Passenger: Essays on Literature, Technology, and Culture in the United States* (New York, 1988), xi. Marx borrowed the "dialectical" imagination formulation from Trilling's anti-Parringtonian essay "Reality in America." Recent helpful appraisals of the early American Studies discipline may be found in Russell J. Reising, *The Unusable Past: Theory and the Study of American Literature* (New York, 1986); and Evan Carton and Gerald Graff, "Criticism Since 1940," in *Cambridge History of American Literature*, 8:305–323. For a cogent discussion of the discursive character of many American Studies texts, see David A. Hollinger, *In the American Province: Studies in the History and Historiography of Ideas* (Bloomington, 1985), 130–151, 210–213.

33. Arthur O. Lovejoy's approach to the history of ideas is succinctly presented in Arthur O. Lovejoy, "The History of Ideas" (1938), in his *Essays in the History of Ideas* (Baltimore, 1948), 1–13. For an example of the view, frequently stated by 1970s social and cultural historians, that both Perry Miller and Lovejoy followed the same method, which "raised the level of intellectual history by stripping it of any concern for social context," see Robert Darnton, "Intellectual and Cultural History," in *The Past Before Us: Contemporary Historical Writing in the United States*, ed. Michael Kammen (Ithaca, 1980), 327, 329. A roughly similar argument may be found in Skotheim, *American Intellectual Histories and Historians*, 186–212. For (in my opinion) convincing counterviews, see Hollinger, *In the American Province*, 152–166, 213–215; and Francis T. Butts, "The Myth of Perry Miller," *American His-*

torical Review 87(1982):665–694. Several interesting assessments by Miller's colleagues of his methods and mind-set appear in "Perry Miller and the American Mind: A Memorial Issue," *The Harvard Review* 2(1964).

34. Perry Miller, "New England's Transcendentalism: Native or Imported?" in *Literary Views: Critical and Historical Essays*, ed. Carroll Camden (Chicago, 1964), 115–129.

35. Perry Miller, ed., *The Transcendentalists: An Anthology* (Cambridge, Mass., 1950). Completed portions of Miller's multivolume project were posthumously published in Perry Miller, *The Life of the Mind in America: From the Revolution to the Civil War* (New York, 1965).

36. One additional contribution to Transcendentalist historiography that Miller probably deserves to be partly credited with was the second major spate of biographies of "minor" Transcendentalists. See Arthur S. Bolster, Jr., *James Freeman Clarke: Disciple to Advancing Truth* (Boston, 1954); Charles Crowe, *George Ripley: Transcendentalist and Utopian Socialist* (Athens, Ga., 1967); and Edwin Gittleman, *Jones Very: The Effective Years* (New York, 1967). For an early study that anticipated Miller's denominational conflict focus, see C. H. Faust, "The Background of the Unitarian Opposition to Transcendentalism," *Modern Philology* 35(Feb. 1938):297–324. Other works of Miller's dealing largely with the Transcendentalists include his *Errand into the Wilderness* (Cambridge, Mass., 1956), 184–216; *The American Transcendentalists: Their Prose and Poetry* (Garden City, N.Y., 1957); *Consciousness in Concord: The Text of Thoreau's Hitherto "Lost Journal" (1840–41), together with Notes and a Commentary* (Boston, 1958); *Margaret Fuller, American Romantic: A Selection from Her Writings and Correspondence* (Garden City, N.Y., 1963); and several essays in Miller's posthumously published collection *Nature's Nation* (Cambridge, Mass., 1967), esp. 121–240.

37. Aileen S. Kraditor, *Means and Ends in American Abolitionism: Garrison and His Critics on Strategy and Tactics* (New York, 1969), 11–38; Quentin Anderson, *The Imperial Self: An Essay in American Literary and Cultural History* (New York, 1971). For a comparably unfavorable contemporaneous account of Transcendentalist social thought by an intellectual historian influenced by Elkins, see R. Jackson Wilson, *In Quest of Community: Social Philosophy in the United States, 1860–1920* (New York, 1968), 1–31.

38. Staughton Lynd, *Intellectual Origins of American Radicalism* (New York, 1968), esp. 67–129. For two, respectively, Marxist and left libertarian countercultural interpretations of Transcendentalism, see David Herreshoff, *Origins of American Marxism: From the Transcendentalists to De Leon* (1967; New York, 1973); and Taylor Stoehr, *Nay-Saying in Concord: Emerson, Alcott, and Thoreau* (Hamden, Conn., 1979). For contemporaneous positive presentations of Transcendentalist environmental thought, see Roderick Nash, *Wilderness and the American Mind* (New Haven, 1964), 84–95; Edwin Fussell, *Frontier: American Literature and the American West* (Princeton, 1965), 175–231; Donald Fleming, "Roots of the New Conservation Movement," *Perspectives in American History* 6(1972):7–91; and Donald Worster, *Nature's Economy: The Roots of Ecology* (Garden City, N.Y., 1977), 59–111.

39. Marx, *Machine in the Garden*, 220–265; George M. Fredrickson, *The Inner Civil War: Northern Intellectuals and the Crisis of the Union* (New York, 1965), 9. An-

other important 1960s study that stressed the socially adaptive cast of Transcendentalist ideology was John L. Thomas, "Romantic Reform in America," *American Quarterly* 17(1965):656–681. See also the critique of Quentin Anderson in Maurice Gonnaud, "Emerson and the Imperial Self: A European Critique," in *Emerson: Prophecy, Metamorphosis, and Influence*, ed. David Levin (New York, 1975), 107–128.

40. For an important contemporaneous synthesis that placed the beginning of the post-individualist turn in nineteenth-century American culture *before* the Civil War, see John Higham, *From Boundlessness to Consolidation: The Transformation of American Culture, 1848–1860* (Ann Arbor, 1969).

41. William R. Hutchison, *The Transcendentalist Ministers: Church Reform in the New England Renaissance* (New Haven, 1959). A related line of argument was developed a few years later by Unitarianism historians Daniel Walker Howe and Conrad Wright, who treated that denomination with greater respect than had Miller but also stressed its differences from Transcendentalism. See Daniel Walker Howe, *The Unitarian Conscience: Harvard Moral Philosophy, 1805–1861* (Cambridge, Mass., 1970); and Conrad Wright, *The Liberal Christians* (Boston, 1970).

42. Joel Myerson, ed., *Studies in the American Renaissance* (Boston, 1977–1982; Charlottesville, 1983–1996); Lawrence Buell, *Literary Transcendentalism: Style and Vision in the American Renaissance* (Ithaca, 1973). Two scholars who extended Buell's Unitarianism-inspired literary-religious synthesis into other cultural aspects of Transcendentalist writing were Philip F. Gura and David Robinson. See Philip F. Gura, *The Wisdom of Words: Language, Theology, and Literature in the New England Renaissance* (Middletown, 1981); and David Robinson *Apostle of Culture: Emerson as Preacher and Lecturer* (Philadelphia, 1982).

43. Anne C. Rose, *Transcendentalism as a Social Movement* (New Haven, 1981); Robert A. Gross, "'The Most Estimable Place in All the World': A Debate on Progress in Nineteenth-Century Concord," in *Studies in the American Renaissance 1978*, ed. Joel Myerson (Boston, 1978), 1–15; Robert A. Gross, "Culture and Cultivation: Agriculture and Society in Thoreau's Concord," *Journal of American History* 69(1982):42–61; and Robert A. Gross, "Transcendentalism and Urbanism: Concord, Boston, and the Wider World," *Journal of American Studies* 18(1984):361–381.

44. For instructive approaches to this problem of linking "text" and "context" in a historical narrative, see Dominick LaCapra, *Rethinking Intellectual History: Texts, Contexts, Language* (Ithaca, 1983); and Martin Jay, "The Textual Approach to Intellectual History," in Martin Jay, *Force Fields: Between Intellectual History and Cultural Critique* (New York 1993), 158–166, 220–222.

45. Catherine L. Albanese, *Corresponding Motion: Transcendental Religion and the New America* (Philadelphia, 1977). For works on aspects of Transcendentalist non-Christian religious connections since Christy's *Orient in American Transcendentalism*, see Robert D. Richardson, Jr., *Myth and Literature in the American Renaissance* (Bloomington, 1978); Carl T. Jackson, *The Oriental Religions and American Thought: Nineteenth-Century Explorations* (Westport, Conn., 1981); and Arthur Versluis, *American Transcendentalism and Asian Religions* (New York, 1993). Catholic-Transcendentalist links are illuminated in Jenny Franchot, *Roads to Rome: The Antebellum Protestant Encounter with Catholicism* (Berkeley, 1994), 302–366;

and Patrick Allitt, *Catholic Converts: British and American Intellectuals Turn to Rome* (Ithaca, 1997), 61–85. The subject of Transcendentalist science is virtually *terra incognita*, but new works are beginning to fill in some empty spaces. For an overview, see Frederick C. Dahlstrand, "Science, Religion, and the Transcendentalist Response to a Changing America," in *Studies in the American Renaissance 1988*, ed. Joel Myerson (Charlottesville, 1988), 1–25. More specialized recent studies are Laura Dassow Walls, *Seeing New Worlds: Henry David Thoreau and Nineteenth-Century Natural Science* (Madison, 1995); and Lee Rust Brown, *The Emerson Museum: Practical Romanticism and the Pursuit of the Whole* (Cambridge, Mass., 1997). The literature on antebellum come-outerism is ample, but very little of it addresses the movement's connections with Transcendentalism. An exception is the cogent discussion of Transcendentalism and come-outer nonresistance in Lewis Perry, *Radical Abolitionism: Anarchy and the Government of God in Antislavery Thought* (Ithaca, 1973), 81–88, 252–257. For a sweeping appropriation of Emersonian Transcendentalism for a post-Christian religious tradition, see Harold Bloom, *The American Religion: The Emergence of the Post-Christian Nation* (New York, 1992). Explorations of the links between Transcendentalism and post–Civil War social science likewise remain largely uncharted territory, but for scattered probings, see Persons, *Free Religion*; Thomas L. Haskell, *The Emergence of Professional Social Science: The American Social Science Association and the Nineteenth-Century Crisis of Authority* (Urbana, 1977), 48–62; and William Leach, *True Love and Perfect Union: The Feminist Reform of Sex and Society* (New York, 1980).

46. M. H. Abrams, *Natural Supernaturalism: Tradition and Revolution in Romantic Literature* (New York, 1971); Nancy L. Rosenblum, *Another Liberalism: Romanticism and the Reconstruction of Liberal Thought* (Cambridge, Mass., 1987); Kateb, *Inner Ocean*; Miller, "New England's Transcendentalism." The only full-length examination of European Romantic and American Transcendentalist philosophical and literary concepts is Leon Chai, *The Romantic Foundations of the American Renaissance* (Ithaca, 1987). For earlier attempts to present a comparative theory of Transcendentalist-European Romantic connections, see René Wellek's two essays on the Transcendentalists and German philosophy, reprinted in his *Confrontations: Studies in the Intellectual and Literary Relations between Germany, England, and the United States during the Nineteenth Century* (Princeton, 1965), 153–212; R. A. Yoder, "The Equilibrist Perspective: Toward a Theory of American Romanticism," *Studies in Romanticism* 12(1973):705–740; and Duane E. Smith, "Romanticism in America: The Transcendentalists," *Review of Politics* 35(1973):302–325. The comparative strains of American Romantic religion await their historian, but for works that touch on aspects relating to Transcendentalism, see Richard A. Grusin, *Transcendentalist Hermeneutics: Institutional Authority and the Higher Criticism of the Bible* (Durham, N. C., 1991); Walter H. Conser, Jr., *God and the Natural World: Religion and Science in Antebellum America* (Columbia, S. C., 1993); and Peter Carafiol, *Transcendent Reason: James Marsh and the Forms of Romantic Thought* (Tallahassee, Fla., 1982). For the transmutation of Transcendentalist and Romantic religious currents after the Civil War, see William R. Hutchison, *The Modernist Impulse in American Protestantism* (1976; Durham, 1992); and Anne C. Rose, *Victorian America and the Civil War* (Cambridge, 1992). Especially suggestive for European Romantic comparisons with American Transcendentalist conceptions of the

"modern self" are Charles Taylor, *Sources of the Self: The Making of the Modern Identity* (Cambridge, Mass., 1989); Gerald N. Izenberg, *Impossible Individuality: Romanticism, Revolution, and the Origins of Modern Selfhood, 1787–1802* (Princeton, 1992); and Peter Gay, *The Bourgeois Experience: Victoria to Freud*, vol. 4: *The Naked Heart* (New York, 1995). For a valuable recent discussion of the theme in early American intellectual history, see Daniel Walker Howe, *Making the American Self: Jonathan Edwards to Abraham Lincoln* (Cambridge, Mass., 1997).

47. Raymond Williams, *Culture and Society: 1780–1950* (1956; New York, 1983). Transcendentalist social psychology remains woefully underdone, but see three older studies: Albert Gilman and Roger Brown, "Personality and Style in Concord," in *Transcendentalism and Its Legacy*, 87–122; Charles Strickland, "A Transcendentalist Father: The Child-Rearing Practices of Bronson Alcott," *Perspectives in American History* 3(1969):5–73; and Elizabeth R. McKinsey, *The Western Experiment: New England Transcendentalists in the Ohio Valley* (Cambridge, Mass., 1973). For a valuable recent discussion of the vocational question in Emerson's career and era, see Mary Cayton, *Emerson's Emergence: Self and Society in the Transformation of New England, 1800–1845* (Chapel Hill, 1989), 83–160. For a pioneering coverage of several of the circle's important cultural forms, see Buell, *Literary Transcendentalism*, 75–139. A suggestive discussion of Transcendentalist ideas about work and writing may be found in Nicholas K. Bromell, *By the Sweat of the Brow: Literature and Labor in Antebellum America* (Chicago, 1993), 15–39, 80–95, 213–239. A recent print study collection incorporates Transcendentalist authors: Kenneth M. Price and Susan Belasco Smith, eds., *Periodical Literature in Nineteenth-Century America* (Charlottesville, 1995). For recent or recently revised discussions of Transcendentalist arts theory, see Neil Harris, *The Artist in American Society: The Formative Years, 1790–1860* (1966; Chicago, 1982); Barbara Novak, *Nature and Culture: American Landscape and Painting, 1825–1875* (1980; New York, 1995); Bryan Jay Wolf, *Romantic Re-Vision: Culture and Consciousness in Nineteenth-Century American Painting and Literature* (Chicago, 1982); and Michael Broyles, *"Music of the Highest Class": Elitism and Populism in Antebellum Boston* (New Haven, 1992). A general study of Transcendentalist cultural theory remains to be written, but three important works connect Transcendentalists to ideas of popular culture, democracy, and modernity, respectively; see David S. Reynolds, *Beneath the American Renaissance*; Kenneth Cmiel, *Democratic Eloquence: The Fight over Popular Speech in Nineteenth-Century America* (Berkeley, 1990); and Lewis Perry, *Boats against the Current: American Culture between Revolution and Modernity, 1820–1860* (New York, 1993). The Transcendentalist cultural topic that has attracted the most attention recently has been the literary market. For various appraisals, see Michael T. Gilmore, *American Romanticism and the Marketplace* (Chicago, 1985), 1–51; Leonard N. Neufeldt, *The Economist: Henry Thoreau and Enterprise* (New York, 1989); Howard Horwitz, *By the Law of Nature: Form and Value in Nineteenth-Century America* (New York, 1991), 3–19, 57–84, 171–191; Stephen Fink, *Prophet in the Marketplace: Thoreau's Development as a Professional Writer* (Princeton, 1992); and Richard F. Teichgraeber III, *Sublime Thoughts/Penny Wisdom: Situating Emerson and Thoreau in the American Market* (Baltimore, 1995).

48. Carl J. Guarneri, *The Utopian Alternative: Fourierism in Nineteenth-Century America* (Ithaca, 1991); Richard Francis, *Transcendental Utopias: Individual*

and Community at Brook Farm, Fruitlands, and Walden (Ithaca, 1997); John d'Entremont, *Southern Emancipator: Moncure Conway: The American Years, 1832–1865* (Cambridge, Mass., 1987); Len Gougeon, *Virtue's Hero: Emerson, Antislavery, and Reform* (Athens, Ga., 1990); Alfred von Frank, *The Trials of Anthony Burns: Freedom and Slavery in Emerson's Boston* (Cambridge, Mass., 1998); Fleming, "Roots of the New Conservation Movement," 8. For a recent, penetrating consideration of Transcendentalist ecological writing, see Lawrence Buell, *The Environmental Imagination: Thoreau, Nature Writing, and the Formation of American Culture* (Cambridge, Mass., 1995). See also Catherine L. Albanese, "Having Nature All Ways: Liberal and Transcendental Perspectives on American Environmentalism," *Journal of Religion* 77(1997):20–43. Important issues relevant to Transcendentalist social ethics are raised in Elizabeth B. Clark, "'The Sacred Rights of the Weak': Pain, Sympathy, and the Culture of Individual Rights in Antebellum America," *Journal of American History* 82(1995):463–493. For recent discussions of Fuller's Transcendentalist feminism, see Capper, *Margaret Fuller*, esp. 252–306; Bell Gale Chevigny, *The Woman and the Myth: Margaret Fuller's Life and Writings* (1976; Boston, 1994); Christina Zwarg, *Feminist Conversations: Fuller, Emerson, and the Play of Reading* (Ithaca, 1995); and Annette Kolodny, "Inventing a Feminist Discourse: Rhetoric and Resistance in Margaret Fuller's *Woman in the Nineteenth Century*," *New Literary History* 25(1994):355–382. For post-1960s works that imaginatively use the gender category for elucidating Transcendentalist themes and figures, see Ann Douglas, *The Feminization of American Culture* (New York, 1977); David Leverenz, *Manhood and the American Renaissance* (Ithaca, 1989); Nina Baym, *Feminism and American Literary History* (New Brunswick, 1992), 136–150; and Julie Ellison, *Delicate Subjects: Romanticism, Gender, and the Ethics of Understanding* (Ithaca, 1990). Among the few discussions of Transcendentalism and class are Gross's articles cited above (note 42) and Bromell, *By the Sweat of the Brow*. The most notable exception to the dearth of discussions of Transcendentalism and "race" may be found in West, *American Evasion of Philosophy*, 9–41. See also Michael Fellman, "Theodore Parker and the Abolitionist Role in the 1850s," *Journal of American History* 61(1974):666–684.

49. For an outstanding collection of essays by leading "New Americanists," see Philip Fisher, ed., *The New American Studies: Essays from Representations* (Berkeley, 1991). A slightly earlier and more self-consciously "ideology"-centered collection of essays by both older and newer American Studies scholars is Sacvan Bercovitch and Myra Jehlen, eds., *Ideology and Classic American Literature* (Cambridge, 1986). For a feisty wholesale assault on the entire nation-centered project of "American Literary Scholarship," which uses as its number one exhibit Transcendentalism literary historiography, see Peter Carafiol, *The American Ideal: Literary History as a Worldly Activity* (New York, 1991).

50. Bercovitch's classic narrative of the national mythos is *The American Jeremiad* (Madison, 1978). For his take on Emersonian Transcendentalism, see his *Puritan Origins of the American Self* (New Haven, 1975), 136–186. In the last few years Bercovitch seems to have shifted a bit in allowing at least some subtle forms of cultural "dissensus." See Sacvan Bercovitch, *Office of* The Scarlet Letter (Baltimore, 1991); and Sacvan Bercovitch, *Rites of Assent: Transformations in the Symbolic Construction of America* (New York, 1993), 1–67, 307–376. We badly lack studies of

regional Transcendentalism, but see Henry A. Pochmann, *New England Transcendentalism and St. Louis Hegelianism* (Philadelphia, 1948); McKinsey, *Western Experiment*; Robert D. Habich, *Transcendentalism and the* Western Messenger: *A History of the Magazine and Its Contributors, 1835–1841* (Rutherford, N.J., 1985); and Mary Kupiec Cayton, "The Making of an American Prophet: Emerson, His Audiences, and the Rise of the Culture Industry in Nineteenth-Century America," *American Historical Review* 92(1987):597–620.

51. Louis Hartz, *The Liberal Tradition in America* (New York, 1955). In the era of Ronald Reagan, as in the 1930s, hostile views of the Transcendentalists have been by no means a monopoly of the Left. Compare the left multiculturalist portrayal of Transcendentalist ideology in Myra Jehlen, *American Incarnation: The Individual, the Nation, and the Continent* (Cambridge, Mass., 1986), 76–122, with the comparably hostile depictions in Kenneth S. Lynd, "Emerson the Man," *Commentary* 73(Mar. 1982):76–80; R. Jackson Wilson, *Figures of Speech: American Writers and the Literary Marketplace, from Benjamin Franklin to Emily Dickinson* (New York, 1989), 161–218; and Lewis P. Simpson, *Mind and the Civil War: A Meditation on Lost Causes* (Baton Rouge, 1989). The recent, more positive labels for Transcendentalists flagged in this paragraph may be found developed in Cayton, *Emerson's Emergence*, 3–32; Teichgraeber, *Sublime Thoughts/Penny Wisdom*; Grusin, *Transcendentalist Hermeneutics*; Lasch, *True and Only Heaven*, 168–295; Kateb, *Inner Ocean*; Horwitz, *By the Law of Nature*, 3–19, 57–84, 171–191; and Rosenblum, *Another Liberalism*, 103–124. But as proof that left censures of liberal Transcendentalism still remain alive and well, see the vigorously pursued "socialist" critique of Emerson's inegalitarian "submissive" liberalism in Christopher Newfield, *The Emerson Effect: Individualism and Submission in America* (Chicago, 1996).

52. Recent writings in political theory on individuality, the nation, and the cosmopolitan ideal abound, but for especially useful works for scholars of American Transcendentalism, see Nancy L. Rosenblum, ed., *Liberalism and the Moral Life* (Cambridge, Mass., 1989); Scott Lash and Jonathan Friedman, eds., *Modernity and Identity* (Cambridge, Mass., 1992); David A. Hollinger, *Postethnic America: Beyond Multiculturalism* (New York, 1995), 79–104, 131–163; and Kateb, *Inner Ocean*. Transcendentalist cosmopolitanism has not received the attention it deserves, but for manifestations of it, see Benjamin T. Spencer, *The Quest for Nationality: An American Literary Campaign* (Syracuse, 1957), 156–194; Buell, *Literary Transcendentalism*, 188–207; Alfred J. von Frank, *The Sacred Game: Provincialism and Frontier Consciousness in American Literature, 1630–1860* (Cambridge, 1985), 1–10, 97–158; and Larry J. Reynolds, *European Revolutions and the American Literary Renaissance* (New Haven, 1988). For a fine collection of international writings by the movement's chief cosmopolitan figure, see Margaret Fuller, *"These Sad But Glorious Days": Dispatches from Europe, 1846–1850*, ed. Larry J. Reynolds and Susan Belasco Smith (New Haven, 1991).

Transcendentalism
and the New England
Religious Tradition

"A Religious Demonstration"

The Theological Emergence of
New England Transcendentalism

David M. Robinson

W HEN PERRY MILLER CONTENDED IN 1950 THAT "THE TRAN-
scendental movement is most accurately to be defined as a religious demonstration,"[1] he revealed his disposition to read the movement's
works within the framework of American theological discourse and to
show its emergence from a legacy of New England religious history that
he had interpreted with unmatched authority in his studies of the Puritans. Miller's emphasis on the theological context of the Transcendentalist
movement is still of importance, even though it has not proved to be the
primary direction that its scholars have taken in the past half century.
Revisiting Miller's interpretation of Transcendentalism as a "religious
demonstration" can help us, however, in recovering a vital sense of context for the movement. Perhaps more importantly, it can reveal not only
some shared assumptions among the Transcendentalists but some significant divergences of opinion and emphasis among them. Such a re-
examination can lead us to clarify and qualify what we mean when we
speak of Transcendentalism as a unified whole and characterize it as a
"movement."

Miller published his comments on the religious character of the Transcendentalist movement in the introduction to *The Transcendentalists:
An Anthology*, a comprehensive gathering of primary source documents,
arranged with Miller's interspersed commentary into a narrative of the
movement.[2] Miller's volume, certainly the most influential and inclusive
gathering of documents on the movement, nevertheless carried a substantial omission, one that he explained in very practical terms:

> As a record of the facts, this volume must confess at once to a seri-
> ous incompletion: it omits, except for a few unavoidable citations,

> Emerson and Thoreau. The reason is frankly utilitarian; there is
> not enough space. Moreover, the works of these two men are eas-
> ily accessible, at least in anthologies.[3]

Without doubting Miller's judgment that their inclusion would have made
the anthology far too lengthy, it must also be said that their exclusion had
another effect, one that was much in accord with Miller's interpretive purpose. It eliminated the two most accomplished "literary" figures from the
movement, leaving a collection of decidedly theological authors and writings. In assembling an anthology of what most English professors would
have deemed the "minor" Transcendentalists, Miller also assembled a collection of predominantly religious writings by Transcendentalist authors,
revealing thereby just how deeply theological were Ralph Waldo Emerson's and Henry David Thoreau's contexts and foundations.

   Miller was disposed to see the movement in theological terms because
of his previous work on New England Puritanism, a monumental scholarly
enterprise that he could achieve in large part because he was able, and
willing, to read reams of quite remote theological texts. In commenting on
his undertaking in Puritan scholarship in the preface to *Errand into the
Wilderness*, Miller made it clear that it was not "a personal predilection"
toward Puritan theology, or even toward theology in general, that motivated him, but the desire to uncover and understand American origins.

> The beginning I sought was inevitably—being located in the sev-
> enteenth century—theological. This was not a fact of my choosing:
> had the origin been purely economic or imperial, I should have
> been no less committed to reporting. Since the first articulate
> body of expression upon which I could get a leverage happened to
> be a body of Protestant doctrine, I set myself to explore that doc-
> trine in its own terms.[4]

Miller's inevitable tendency was thus to link Emerson and Thoreau with
the strand of theological discourse that had carried forward through the
eighteenth century, eventually erupting into the Transcendentalist controversy.

   Miller's understanding of the theological roots of Transcendentalism had
a certain urgency because of the alternative reading of the movement that
had emerged at mid century from literary critics who were increasingly
committed to aesthetic judgments based on the principles of close textual
explication. The densely layered, highly metaphorical prose of both Emerson and Thoreau proved very amenable to this sort of interpretation, as
Miller's Harvard colleague F. O. Matthiessen had brilliantly demonstrated

a decade before in *American Renaissance: Art and Experience in the Age of Emerson and Whitman*.[5] Although Matthiessen was a critic with a deep awareness of the historical dimension of literary study, who based his volume on a designated historical moment of great cultural importance, his emphasis on symbolic constructs and aesthetic structures was of greatest appeal to the generation of scholars that followed him, as Miller surely understood. Miller's claim of Transcendentalism for the history of theology, then, was more than a Puritan historian's venture into the nineteenth century—it was a counterstatement about the aims and assumptions of literary interpretation, intended to bolster the place of history in literary studies.

In describing Transcendentalism as a "religious demonstration," Miller had a particular variety of religion in mind: the Puritan and Edwardsian tradition that, though admittedly a "dual heritage," had resurfaced in a somewhat truncated form in Emerson's *Nature* and the resulting insurgence of the "new views" of his Transcendentalist followers. Part of this religious sensibility, Miller had explained in "From Edwards to Emerson," was "a piety, a religious passion, the sense of an inward communication and of the divine symbolism of nature." This experiential religion represented a vital legacy, but one that was restrained by "a social code demanding obedience to external law, . . . aimed at propriety and decency, the virtues of middle-class respectability, self-control, thrift, and dignity, at a discipline of the emotions." In the course of New England theological history that latter strain had become dominant, settling into a passionless and conventionally minded liberalism against which the Transcendentalists rebelled. In the introduction to *The Transcendentalists* Miller argued that "Emerson and Parker were throwbacks to the messy emotionalism and the dangerous mysticism that 'liberal Christianity' had striven for a century to exorcise." Their insurgency was, as Miller saw it, the resurfacing of Edwardsian passion in the barren landscape of Boston Unitarianism.[6]

But it has been the historical rehabilitation of the Arminian and Unitarian traditions rather than a deeper investigation of the Edwardsian tradition that has, in recent years, accounted for the theological interpretation of Transcendentalism. Several decades of this work, which began soon after Miller published his anthology, have resulted in a consensus that the Transcendentalists can be understood as extenders of Unitarian premises rather than rebels against them. Any discussion of Transcendentalism in theological terms must now refer to Chauncy, Buckminster, Channing, and the younger Ware as more immediately determinative figures than the Mathers, Edwards, or Hopkins.[7] While Transcendentalism was clearly a movement with many sources, ranging from the texts of classical antiquity to German and English Romanticism, its roots in the evolving American liberal religious tradition seem now to be much clearer, as we have come to understand that tradition more completely.

This recovery of Unitarianism as an important contributing source of the religious energy of Transcendentalism has yielded several important insights. We now understand, thanks largely to the work of Daniel Walker Howe, that there was a prominent element of emotional pietism within Unitarianism; Emerson himself can be productively read as in part the product of this legacy of Unitarian pietism. Such a recognition complicates the tendency to see Transcendentalism as the rebellion of a passionate younger generation of Romantics rejecting the Enlightenment-based rationalism of their religious inheritance. We understand that Emerson was not alone among Unitarians in his concern, expressed in the "Divinity School Address," that the "great and perpetual office of the Preacher is not discharged,"[8] since Unitarians of a variety of theological positions were calling for a revitalization of preaching.[9] We understand that Andrews Norton spoke for some, but by no means all, Unitarians in his attacks on Transcendentalism, and that Unitarian reactions to Emerson ranged from warm admiration to puzzlement to worried concern. And we understand that Emerson's fundamental doctrine of self-culture, which described the moral life as a continuing effort to cultivate the growth of the soul, was an extension of a central line of Unitarian theological reflection most impressively articulated by Channing.[10]

Unitarianism was not the monolith that Emerson sometimes makes it seem. A diverse movement that achieved a broad anti-Calvinist consensus, it had much less unity in its theological doctrines or even its religious sensibility than conventional knowledge assumes. Divided by dispute and controversy almost from its beginning, Unitarianism finally settled, in the late nineteenth century, into one doctrinal position—we shall have no creed.[11] Our enhanced understanding of the complexity of early Unitarianism has thus complicated our interpretation of Transcendentalism by bringing forward intellectual continuities where we have earlier seen breaks. But it has made clearer the theological grounding of the Transcendentalism, confirming in a different way Miller's view of the religious nature of the movement.

This sense of the complexity and diversity of Unitarianism can be extended into analysis of Transcendentalism itself, for when we look at it as a "religious demonstration" the differing emphases and concerns of its participants, and their varied personalities and sensibilities, become clearer. While I still believe it is important to recognize the cultural significance of the Transcendentalist movement, I have also repeatedly come up against the problem of fixing it with any kind of clear definitional identity. If, after all, one muddies the lines of demarcation between Unitarianism and Transcendentalism, how is one to know who the Transcendentalist is? And if, further, one notes the divisions among the Transcendentalists, can there be said to have been such a movement? We enter uncertain ground when we focus on distinction rather than accord, but it is important to understand the Transcendentalists not only as like-minded insurgents, but also as intellectual experimenters who had not reached consensus on many important questions.

Three of the originating figures of the movement—Emerson, Orestes Brownson, and Theodore Parker—authored theologically-centered texts that illustrate both the common ground and the important divergences within Transcendentalism. Emerson's *Nature* and Brownson's *New Views of Christianity, Society, and the Church* appeared in 1836, constituting a determined intervention into antebellum religious discourse. Emerson followed in 1838 with his "Divinity School Address," an extension of his developing philosophy in an explicitly church-centered context. Parker's *A Discourse of Matters Pertaining to Religion* (1842) most closely approximates a Transcendentalist systematic theology, a book written under the pressure of the attack of his enormously controversial ordination sermon *A Discourse on the Transient and Permanent in Christianity* (1841). His book is a more systematic elaboration of the key conceptual structure of that sermon. These texts were written from within a theological framework of ideas, using religious discourse, in an attempt to reformulate the received religious opinion of their day. Theological intervention does not exhaust what these three thinkers attempted and achieved, especially in the case of Emerson, but it captures the fundamental thrust of their texts.

These works confirm that certain shared assumptions and a sense of new beginnings bound their authors together. In each of them we find an anti-supernatural approach to religion that downplayed both ecclesiastical and Biblical authority. This theological liberalism was combined with an optimistic expectancy about human development that expressed itself in an anticipation, grounded in nineteenth-century Protestant millennialist thinking, of a revolutionary era in human religious practice. This combination of millennialist progressive expectancy and essentially post-Christian theological premises fueled the Transcendentalists' remarkable intellectual upsurge in the mid 1830s.[12]

As scholars such as Ernest Lee Tuveson and James Moorhead have shown, there is a strong and influential tradition of millennialist theorizing in American Protestantism, which has focused on the American nation as the vehicle through which the Biblical prophecies of the final redemption of the world would be fulfilled. Rejecting the idea of a sudden divine intervention into human history that would reverse its course and instantly establish a kingdom of God on earth, an important line of thinkers, as Tuveson notes, instead "thought that the kingdoms of this world are destined to become those of Christ."[13] In this view, human progress, in both a spiritual and a secular sense, could be seen as the sign of the coming perfection of society prophesied in the book of Revelation.

The most prevalent interpretation of the final days within antebellum evangelical Protestantism was postmillennialism, which held, as Moorhead explains, that "the Second Coming would occur after the millennium," bringing an era of continuing human progress and enlightenment. Human history would thus develop through progressive improvement into the state of social harmony and perfection that would precede and make possible the Second Coming. Even though postmillennialist thinkers held this progressive view of history, they also mixed "symbols of the Apocalypse" with their vision of progress. In this sense, their outlook "was a compromise between a progressive, evolutionary view of history and the apocalyptic outlook of the book of Revelation." Moorhead's stress on the postmillennialist quality of antebellum Protestant thought is important, for it suggests how progressivist thinking about the course of human history could be reconciled with the religious view that the Second Coming of Christ would end human history. As Moorhead explains, postmillennialists assumed that the gradual perfection of human society through spiritual and social progress was a necessary precondition for the return of Christ and the establishment of a God's reign over the earth. In this sense, the signs of progress in the nineteenth century, which could be taken to be either material and technological advances, indications of religious revival, or indications of political or social reform, could be interpreted by postmillennialist thinkers as confirmations that the course of history was indeed leading to its perfected end.[14]

This theory of history appealed to the Transcendentalists since it fit well with their sense of human perfectibility and their commitment to political and social reform.[15] While they were much less inclined than most antebellum Protestants to accord definitive authority to the Bible without a wide latitude of interpretation, they were still influenced by the Christian view of history entailed in postmillennial thinking and inclined to a kind of utopian excitement and expectancy.

This strand of millennialist hope is an important but largely overlooked aspect of Emerson's *Nature*, in which we hear repeatedly the ardent voice of prophetic change. Emerson's millennialism is distinct, of course, in that it is not Christologically centered; it suggests the dawn of a new era without recourse to any of the mythological elements of Christianity. The Platonic and Neoplatonic traditions, bolstered by the revived idealism of the Romantic movement, are central to Emerson's vision in *Nature*. But even in the absence of the Christology of the millennialist outlook, his opening call for "an original relation to the universe" and "a religion by revelation to us" captures the mood of revitalization characteristic of millennialist thinking. Such expectancy leads directly to the demand for a new course of action: "Let us demand our own works and laws and worship" (*CW*, 1:7). The opening builds toward an even more intense set of prophetic declarations from the voice of the "Orphic poet" who enters the text in its final chapter, "Prospects": "Know then, that the world exists for you. For you is the phenomenon perfect. . . . Build, therefore, your own world. As fast as you conform your life to the pure idea in your mind, that will unfold its great proportions" (*CW*, 1:44-45). Emerson ends *Nature* with this prophetic, future-oriented mood, hoping to translate the expectation for a new revelation of religious truth into a call for work and change in the lives of his readers. Part of the secret of Emerson's appeal to a younger generation lay in his impassioned sense of the possibility of new beginnings. *Nature* and the "Divinity School Address" are texts of spiritual and ethical encouragement in which Emerson supplies the hope and courage to believe that the past is not absolutely determinative and that the course of Western religious history, largely derailed from its proper direction for the past two millennia, could be righted.

In his "Divinity School Address" Emerson expounds a religion founded on the "moral sentiment" with its "insight of the perfection of the laws of the soul" (*CW*, 1:77). "This sentiment," he writes, "lies at the foundation of society, and successively creates all forms of worship" (*CW*, 1:79). Christianity, the form of worship in which Emerson and his hearers "have had our birth and nurture," thus holds "great historical interest for us" (*CW*, 1:80-81), an interest all the more pressing because of "two errors in its administration, which daily appear more gross" (*CW*, 1:81) from the perspective of the moral sentiment. Those erroneous assumptions, a false reverence for the person of Jesus and the conviction that no further divine inspiration is available, constitute a kind of religious paralysis that distances the church from its religious source. Emerson brings the message that these errors can and must be corrected, thus restoring its intuitive and inspirational roots.

Brownson and Parker shared Emerson's belief in the need for an immediate renewal of religious energy, and each of them constructed a theological program based on the dual gesture of beginning anew and of returning to a lost source. Brownson's *New Views* assaulted the church in even stronger terms than Emerson would use two years later in the "Divinity School Address." Arguing that the church, like all institutions, is "mutable and transitory," he also posited an enduring "reproductive energy of religion" that, transcending institutions, was able to "survive all mutations of forms."[16] For Brownson, the church "must be spoken of as one which was, not as one which is." What exists today is no more than a corpse, "the body after the spirit has left it" (*NV*, 5). But even this metaphor of the corpse may overstate Brownson's sense of the relevance of the church, for he seemed to draw back from his suggestion that there once *was* life in the church, to argue that because Jesus was completely misunderstood by his own age, the church had never been "the real body of Christ" (*NV*, 7). The work of the present generation, given this failure in history, was to synthesize the exclusive "spiritualism" represented in Christian history by Catholicism with the exclusive "materialism" represented by Protestantism. Each by itself was incomplete, missing the full import of Jesus's message. The reconciliation of the spiritual and material, which is Brownson's motivating vision, would realize "the atonement" (*NV*, 32). Brownson regarded the atonement as the work or process of history, continuing in the present and moving toward complete human synthesis and reconciliation.

Parker shared in the utopian millennialism of Emerson and Brownson, and offered a similar grounding for his views by insisting that religion is "an original necessity of man's nature,"[17] pervasive throughout human history and culture. This religious necessity, analogous to Emerson's concept of the moral sentiment and Brownson's "conception, or sentiment, of the Holy" (*NV*, 3), is what he described as the "permanent" element of religion, one which underlay the transient and evanescent attempts to define or sharply conceptualize God and to establish institutions and creeds.

For Parker, the distance between the persisting religious desire in humanity and its mutable expression restricted even the authority of Christianity and its founder, Jesus. Parker argued that "Christianity can be no greater than the religious sentiment, though it may be less" (*D*, 240). In this sense Christianity was at best a vehicle for an enduring human aspiration, at worst a corruption of it. He located Christian authority not in the person or mission of Jesus, but exclusively in Christ's message of a pure or "absolute" religion. "If Christianity be true at all," he argued, "it would be just as true if Herod or Catilene had taught it" (*D*, 244). In rhetorical force this went a step beyond even Brownson in its rejection of the authority of the established church. Parker's conception of "absolute religion," a religion that cannot be defined or restricted by historical versions of theology or organized worship, served as a standard against which to judge the contemporary church. In Parker's view, absolute religion demanded a state of perpetual discontent with established religious forms and acts as a force continually working to undercut their authority.

This shared sense of a necessary and impending shift in the course of Christian history, signaled by a broadening universality and inclusivity in the conception of religion that was simultaneously a return to abandoned religious fundamentals, represents the core of the Transcendentalists' "religious demonstration." While consonant with the thought of many Protestant postmillennialists in its emphasis on a quickening of the course of historical developments that indicated the coming fulfillment of the prophecies of a perfected social order, it of course departed from them in its skepticism of ecclesiastical institutions and authority, and in its inclination to define this religious awakening in terms that were not necessarily restricted to Christianity. The Transcendentalists thus espoused a program of religious insurgency, but one grounded in the liberalizing of New England theology represented by the Arminian and Unitarian movements.

The Transcendentalists' critique of Unitarianism, at times critical to the point of hostility, has tended to obscure the extent to which their theological project extended Unitarian assumptions. While Emerson was silent on Unitarianism in *Nature*, his "Divinity School Address" contained a veiled but quite obvious critique of the movement's failure, especially in the performance of its preachers. Even so, he urged the ministerial graduates to stay the course and revivify religion from within their established denomination. Both Brownson and Parker claimed continuity with the recent Unitarian reformist efforts, invoking Unitarianism explicitly as both authority for their vision and audience for their calls to reform. Brownson, whose conversion to Unitarianism was influenced heavily by William Ellery Channing, referred in his *New Views* to Channing as a great exemplar of a new prophetic movement of synthesis or "eclecticism" in modern theology and termed Channing's "Likeness to God" "the most remarkable [sermon] since the Sermon on the Mount" (*NV*, 46). For Brownson, the appearance of a preacher like Channing was a clear indication that a new era of progressive religious reform had already begun. Brownson declared that "it is from the Unitarians that must come out the doctrine of universal reconciliation" (*NV*, 39), the final synthesis of Catholic "spiritualism" and Protestant "materialism" that together expresses the full religious potentialities of the human race.

Parker devoted a section of his *Discourses* to the Unitarian movement, and given the controversy within Unitarian circles over his *A Discourse of the Transient and Permanent in Christianity*, of which his volume was an expanded version, it is not surprising to find his attitude more cautious than Brownson's, who wrote his *New Views* still in the flush of his conversion to Unitarianism. Arguing that the principles of the early Unitarian movement (the 1815–1830 anti-Calvinist movement led by Channing) were close to the pure principles of the Reformation, Parker averred that Unitarianism "had great work to do and did it nobly. The spirit of reformers was in its leading men" (*D*, 468). But he warned that "the time has come for Unitarianism—representing the *movement party* in theological affairs,—to do something; develop the truth it has borne, latent and unconscious in its bosom" (*D*, 470). Parker feared that the progressive momentum of Unitarianism was beginning to harden into a new form of institutional conservatism. Unitarianism must *"affirm the great doctrines of absolute Religion,"* Parker's term for his version of Transcendentalist theology, or it must give up its identity of progressive leadership in theology, and *"cease to represent the progress of man in theology"* (*D*, 475-476). In moments like these, Transcendentalism seems not only like a "religious demonstration," but like a contest for leadership within a particular religious party. Its status as an intra-Unitarian affair becomes more apparent. To say this is not to try to limit or reduce the aims or sources of any of these three thinkers. They were all widely read and vitally open to a range of disparate influences, both theological and literary. But it does remind us that their ability to conceive their historical moment as one of significant change was built on a set of assumptions that they had inherited or adopted from a theological movement that had defined its purpose as interventionist and had broadened the limits of Christian of religion.

Emerson, Brownson, and Parker were thus bound together by their common expectation of a shift in the course of religious history, an outlook which they shared with many Protestant postmillennialist thinkers. They extended in sometimes radical ways the antisupernatural directions of New England liberal religion, thus creating a unique form of millennialism marked by liberal or, in the cases of Emerson and Parker, post-Christian tendencies. It is important to note, however, that within this broad framework of shared beliefs, there were significant divergences of perspective and modulations of emphasis among them. They differed both in their conceptions of the origins or basis of religion and in the various foci of their concern for religious reformation.

Emerson, Brownson, and Parker all addressed in some depth the question of the source of the religious impulse, using this point of origin as a principle of authority with which to criticize the state of theology and worship as they now found it. The most buoyantly utopian and optimistic of the three was Brownson, whose *New Views* located the basis of religion in the quality of "progressiveness" in humanity; he raised this quality of progressiveness to a prophetic principle, basing his sense of the possibility of constructive change on the idea that the desire for such change is an inherent aspect of human nature. Brownson described the current state of religious crisis as the result of the divergence between the static church and the ever-enlarging tendency of the human character: "We are creatures of growth; it is, therefore, impossible that all our institutions should not be mutable and transitory" (*NV*, 4). Expanding on this definition of humans as "creatures of growth," he specified the "capacity for progress" as "the chief glory of our nature." For Brownson, such progress, a form of perpetual self-education, was a permanent aspect of our experience, constituting our very principle of life: "The being which can make no further progress, which has finished its work, achieved its destiny, attained its end, must die" (*NV*, 52). There can be no finality of understanding or achievement, according to Brownson, for it is in our very constitution to resist the established or achieved nature of things as we find them, and to refuse the finality of any theory or body of knowledge.

As an expression of the vitality of our will, this "capacity for progress" also "makes us moral beings" (*NV*, 52). The series of choices that constitutes the work of the will is also the mode through which our characters achieve a crucial self-expression and self-possession, either in the execution of particular acts or the achievement of certain interior intellectual or emotional capacities. The personality, for Brownson, was never fully matured, never finally formed; it was instead in perpetual development, and he regarded the drive or energy fueling that development as the religious impulse.

Brownson's exposition of religion as the "progressive" quality of human nature was heavily determined by his reading of Channing, whose "Likeness to God" represented the spiritual life in terms of progressive moral and intellectual growth. By conceiving the religious life as a process of increasing God-likeness, in which the soul grew in a kind of organic development toward identity with divinity, Channing placed theological emphasis on both the inherent spiritual qualities of the self and on the idea of its culture, or progressive development. Both these ideas were central to the Transcendentalists. Brownson's *New Views* was a fervent and impassioned articulation of the conception of "self-culture" that was shaped by Channing and other Unitarians as the answer to the Calvinist doctrine of innate depravity. For Channing, the soul's capacity to become more and more akin to God was the counter-image of the Calvinist conception of the unbridgeable gulf between the human and the divine natures. Brownson seized on this conception of self-culture and transposed it into a prophetic sign of the possibility of a new religious and social age.

Emerson, also a pupil of Channing, extended a radical version of the doctrine of self-culture in his sermons and early lectures, and the idea permeated both *Nature* and the "Divinity School Address." Brownson's insistence that the capacity for growth is "the chief glory of our nature" accorded with the concluding chapter of *Nature*, "Prospects," in which Emerson urged an emboldened program of self-empowerment: "As fast as you can conform your life to the pure idea in your mind, that will unfold its great proportions. A correspondent revolution in things will attend the influx of the spirit" (*CW*, 1:45). But what is striking when one reads *Nature* alongside Brownson's contemporaneous *New Views* is Emerson's emphasis on the *experience* of this "influx of the spirit." While Brownson certainly offered his vision with fervency and emotional intensity, he provided very little description of the internal phenomenon of religious experience. Emerson's more experiential account of the inrush of God, something that stands as an unexpected link to the more evangelical wing of American Protestantism, is one of the aspects of his work that has had a sustained appeal to readers up to the present. Though he certainly avoided the language of revivalism in his work, he did offer an appeal to immediate experience that seems to arise from the same roots. Brownson, whose theological terminology was much closer to that of the evangelicals, did not rely on such direct descriptions of religious experience.

The differences between Emerson and Brownson are also evident in their depictions of the nature of the revolutionary change that they both feel is afoot. This is a very important distinction in their intellectual outlook. Brownson envisioned the coming atonement as a revolution in human social interaction which would "remodel all our institutions" and "create a new civilization" (*NV*, 47). But when Emerson spoke of a "revolution in things" that accompanied the "influx of spirit" he referred primarily to a radical shift in perception and consciousness which would allow the individual to see the world with transformed eyes. This of course might result in far-reaching social change—that is Emerson's strong implication—but the *internal* revolution of consciousness is for him primary. Brownson's energy was devoted first to a more conceptual explanation of the reconciliation of "spiritualism" with "materialism" that represented the full potential of human nature and human society. But he also envisioned the social consequences of that reconciliation in a coming era of the perfected human society. He described less the change that would happen to particular individuals than the perfected world in which these individuals would find themselves.

Brownson's work was in this sense more typically utopian, in that it displayed utopian projections of a perfected society and perfected individuals, while Emerson offered a detailed witness to the perceptual, psychological, and emotional dynamics of the soul's encounter with the divine. There has been a wealth of commentary on Emerson's representation of consciousness and perception in *Nature*, enough to have established him as a major contributor to the development of Romantic epistemology.[18] It is not my purpose to rehearse or extend that commentary here except to underline how integral a part perception and experience play in Emerson's description of the nature and work of religion, and how this seems to distinguish him from other key Transcendentalists. The Emerson who is often classified as abstract or ethereal seems, on close examination, to be quite clearly concerned with lived moments of experience. The contrast with Brownson can be illustrated effectively in a comparison of two brief but important and representative sentences. In looking forward to the coming period of atonement, Brownson described the result of humanity's recognition of its grounding in divinity. Human nature will be elevated, he argued: "It will be felt to be divine, and infinite will be found to be traced in living characters on all its faculties" (*NV*, 48). Emerson, by contrast, described an experience in the woods in which he was momentarily transfigured into a "transparent eyeball," both egoless and infinitely perceptive: "The currents of the Universal Being circulate through me; I am part or particle of God" (*CW*, 1:10).

Each statement advances essentially the same idea, asserting the unity of the human with the divine. But the tone and impact of each is markedly different, largely because Brownson depicted a coming state-of-affairs as an observer and Emerson described an achieved experience from within. Emerson assumed the role of expounder of an experientially centered conception of religion and Brownson as the bearer of a broader prophetic message about the course of history and the fate of the human race. Certainly Emerson's thinking did not lack a prophetic dimension, nor did Brownson's completely displace religious experience, but the difference in emphasis between them approached a difference in kind. Emerson's message appeals to an experience so wholly unique and private that it sets his reader apart as an individual; Brownson's appeals to a desire for large-scale transformation in which the individual participates as part of a much larger movement of history.

The contrast between a theology based on the experience of the holy and one espousing a prophetic sense of historical progress and social transformation is significant, but the picture is further complicated when we consider Parker's conception of the basis of religion. The grounding of re-

ligion in the principle of progressive growth or in the reception of transcendent experience was answered by something quite different in Parker.
While Emerson and Brownson offered different versions of the belief
in human power and capacity representative of the Unitarian and Transcendentalist intervention into nineteenth-century theological discourse,
Parker offered a quite different definition of the religious sentiment as "A
SENSE OF DEPENDENCE" (D, 18). Like Emerson and Brownson, Parker
argues that "there is in man a spiritual nature, which directly and legitimately leads to Religion" (D, 15), but he associated this spiritual nature not
with power but with a recognition of the lack of it.

For Parker, religion arises from our intuition that we are incomplete and
from our resulting desire for fulfillment or completion. The experiential
basis of Parker's religion is in this sense a negative one. Rather than describing religion as the influx of spirit, as Emerson did, he instead argued
that religion begins in the recognition of dependent or contingent nature.
As Leon Chai has demonstrated, Parker was heavily influenced by
Friedrich Schleiermacher in this conception of the origins of religion,
drawing from him both a desire to found the religious impulse on consciousness itself and a recognition that the structure of consciousness
inevitably implied a dependent relationship. As Chai explained, the "whole
existence [of perception] is one of pure receptivity, consequently one
dependent upon the existence of that which it perceives." Thus for Parker,
the mind's lack of self-existence implied its derivation from a power that
transcended it.[19]

One of the most powerful moments in Parker's *Discourse* is his expression of the human recognition of its incompleteness, a passage that becomes a profound meditation on human frailty, limitation, and mortality:

> We are not sufficient for ourselves; not self-originated; not self-
> sustained. A few years ago, and we were not; a few years hence,
> and our bodies shall not be. A mystery is gathered about our little
> life. We have but small control over things around us; are limited
> and hemmed in on all sides. Our schemes fail. Our plans miscarry.
> One after another, our lights go out. Our realities prove dreams.
> Our hopes waste away. (D, 16)

This is not the kind of rhetoric that we expect from a Transcendentalist. It
does not exalt human capacity for spiritual perception and growth and the
human access to the God within, as the works of Emerson, or even Channing, usually do. The Calvinists or evangelicals of Parker's day would have
found it far more congenial than most of what they might have found in
Emerson or Brownson, for despite Parker's firmly anti-Calvinist orienta

tion, his emphasis on incompletion and dependence as the basis of religion had some resonance with the Calvinist doctrine of innate depravity, or the evangelical's description of the individual's conviction of a sinful state. While Parker used the sense of dependence to construct a much larger theological program, the distinctiveness of Parker's theology among the Transcendentalists was its acknowledgment of the fragility of life. Emerson would not arrive at a public statement of anything like this sense of the contingency of human experience until his "Experience" of 1844, an essay generally acknowledged to represent a departure from his earlier articulation of Transcendentalism and as the initiation of a new and different phase of his thought.[20]

Parker's strategy in emphasizing this concept of human inadequacy was to build from it by analogy, reasoning that the sense of the dependence necessarily implies the existence of a force that would bring completion, which he named God. "We find in nature that every want is naturally supplied," he wrote. "That is, there is something external to each created being to answer all the external wants of that being" (*D*, 183). This law of the relation of supply to want also holds, he believed, in the realm of the soul. Thus the human "sense of dependence," he argued, is "a proof by implication of its object,—something on which dependence rests" (*D*, 20). Parker read the perception of dependence as a sign of the removed presence of God, reasoning that only such a presence could account for such a lack: "A belief in this relation between the feeling in us and its object independent of us, comes unavoidably from the laws of man's nature. There is nothing of which we can be more certain" (*D*, 20). The rising intensity of Parker's insistence on certainty here marked this assumption as a place of profound concern for him. Without the correspondence of need and possible fulfillment, of desire and its object, the possibility of an ordered and coherent universe is lost. Parker's adamant rejection of that possibility constituted his most fundamental statement of faith.

Even though Parker's account of human dependence as the origin of the religious sentiment had close affinities with the more traditional theologies of the Calvinist tradition, his rejection of contemporary Christianity was harsher and more absolute than Brownson's or Emerson's. He asserted the cultural relativity of religious concepts and practices, arguing that "the phenomena of Religion—like those of Science and Art—must vary from land to land, and age to age" (*D*, 50). Nothing, therefore, of Christian institutions, theology, or practices of worship can be regarded as necessary or inevitable. Parker spared no edge in aggressively challenging the regnant pieties regarding Jesus and his miracles. The scornful irony with which he regarded the argument for the credibility of the Biblical miracles, Andrews

Norton's final basis for Christian belief, typified his rejection of established religion. There is more evidence for the credibility of witchcraft in 1690s Salem, he wryly observed, than for the miracles reported in the New Testament.

Parker's assumption of human dependence as the origin of religious belief yielded, however, an advocacy of a strongly individualistic "Absolute Religion," which he defined as "INWARD AND OUTWARD OBEDIENCE to the law [God] has written on our nature" (D, 46). The operative term here is "our nature," especially if we contrast it with more conventional sources of spiritual authority such as the Bible or the Church. The church, Parker argued, only has those powers "delegated by the individuals who compose it" (D, 387), and as a voluntary organization it has an important but limited role in the cultivation of the spiritual life. "THE SOUL IS GREATER THAN THE CHURCH" (D, 482), he contended, devolving religious authority ultimately on the individual conscience.

As we have seen, the version of millennialist expectancy that these Transcendentalists held in common was based in part on somewhat different accounts of the basis of the religious sensibility, a difference that in Parker's case seems quite striking. But even their shared belief in an impending historical change in the course of the religious history of humanity yielded different visionary postulates of the nature of the redeemed world. These differences not only further our sense of the diversity of the Transcendentalist religious demonstration, but help us to understand the various manifestations of the reformist fervor and political insurgency that marked Transcendentalism as a movement.

This is most readily seen when we compare Brownson's work with that of Emerson and Parker, for in 1836 he was by far the most fervently millennialist of the three. In his New Views, Brownson presented a vision of history moving toward a moment in which all established human institutions and patterns of interaction would be swept away in an utterly renewed world. In presenting Brownson in this way I confirm the generally received opinion that for a period in his career he was the most politically radical of the Transcendentalists. In "The Laboring Classes" he offered a thorough analysis of American class divisions and mounted a searching critique of the ultimate futility of liberal reform methods. Brownson subjected even his mentor Channing to rigorous criticism, arguing that clerical calls for self-culture were likely to leave undisturbed the social and economic conditions that prevented both adequate self-development and the possibility of a harmonious and unified social system.[21] Brownson's phase of political radicalism partook of a quite ancient tradition of Christian social prophecy, one which we can recognize in the almost feverish reimagining of the world in his *New Views*.

In Chapter IX of that book, Brownson offered a vision of the Christian doctrine of the atonement which expressed, in its utopian sentiments, his conviction of the sweeping changes needed in human civilization. His "new doctrine of the atonement" reconciled "the warring systems" of materialism and spiritualism, establishing matter and spirit as "separate elements of the same grand harmonious whole." Such a reconciliation, he believed, would "remodel all our institutions" and "create a new civilization" (*NV*, 47), which, as Brownson described it, was part heaven-on-earth and part the envisioned triumph of nineteenth-century progressive politics.

Beginning with the principle of the sacredness of humanity, Brownson addressed one of the central political and moral questions of his era by predicting the end of slavery: "Slavery will cease. . . . When man learns the true value of man, the chains of the captive must be unloosed and the fetters of the slave fall off" (*NV*, 48). This was the beginning of a series of prophetic images through which Brownson sketched his expectations for a coming new age. "Wars will fail. . . . Education will destroy the empire of ignorance. . . . Civil freedom will become universal. . . . The church will be on the side of progress. . . . Industry will be holy. . . . The earth itself and the animals which inhabit it will be counted sacred. . . . Man's body will be deemed holy" (*NV*, 48-49). The sweep of Brownson's vision here marked the furthest extension of the utopian urge that reflected a discontent with existing social arrangements. Elements of this utopianism colored the sensibility of everyone associated with the Transcendentalist movement. This utopianism was put into practice in such experiments as Brook Farm and Bronson Alcott's Fruitlands, and it was even reflected in Thoreau's experiment at Walden Pond. Each of these projects reflected the movement's widely shared conviction that the era promised a significant reform of social structures.[22]

When read against Brownson, Emerson's visionary energy is remarkably interior in its orientation. Alan D. Hodder has shown very perceptively how in *Nature* Emerson transmuted the idea of the apocalypse into one of inward revelation, keyed to the full apprehension of *Luke* 17:21: "Behold, the kingdom of God is within you." Having gradually abandoned his earlier belief in the coming of a literal, external apocalypse, much to his aunt Mary Moody Emerson's dismay, Emerson eventually came to understand more fully that "the Kingdom is not a new world; it is just the same old world transfigured in vision." *Nature*, as Hodder argues, is not "a rhetoric of rep-

resentation but a rhetoric of provocation," designed to move the reader toward an altered perspective or vision of the world.[23]

Whereas Brownson prophecied a thoroughly remade social world,
Emerson prophecied a thoroughly remade perception of the world. This
is most readily apparent in one of the oddest of the several unusual passages in *Nature*, his declaration that our realization of the full extent of our
potential perceptual powers would result in a revolution that would protect us from all the disagreeable elements in the external world. Compare
to Brownson's vision of the new heaven on earth this declaration of Emerson's, the first part of which I quoted earlier:

> Build, therefore, your own world. As fast as you conform your life
> to the pure idea in your mind, that will unfold its great propor-
> tions. A correspondent revolution in things will attend the influx of
> the spirit. So fast will disagreeable appearances, swine, spiders,
> snakes, pests, mad-houses, prisons, enemies, vanish; they are tem-
> porary and shall be no more seen. The sordor and filths of nature,
> the sun shall dry up, and the wind exhale. (*CW*, 1:45)

The passage shows us the extent to which Emerson committed his text—
and the entire focus of his efforts as a preacher to the world-at-large—to
the proposition that individuals could recover a remarkable new perceptual power that would absolutely transform their relationship to the world.
Read in the most generous light possible, the above passage offers the
promise that those who assertively begin to remake their lives in terms of
their highest principles will find the world a surprisingly pliant medium.
The small annoyances of life, as well as the fearful obstacles to change and
progress, will be found to have less power over us than we feared; these
constraints will, in our new capacity to perceive the world more completely, vanish.

We might say that at the beginning of the Transcendentalist insurgency,
Emerson and Brownson aim their millennial energies in different directions; the trajectories of their respective careers confirm this fundamental
difference. Brownson was more concerned with social reform in the late
1830s and 1840s than was Emerson, whose evolution toward political
engagement, though real, was more cautious and gradual. Emerson continued to define himself vocationally as the "scholar," or at times the "poet,"
trusting that the work of language was a sufficient calling.[24]

The divergence of Emerson and Brownson over the program of Transcendentalist reform is further complicated when we examine Parker. Like
Brownson, Parker saw the promise of Transcendentalism in social and institutional terms, and can thus be aligned against Emerson if we are

tempted to divide the reformers from the poets as different wings of the movement. But Parker lacked the visionary sweep or apocalyptic intensity of either Brownson or Emerson. Parker was, by comparison, much more engaged in a program of ecclesiastical reform, one connected in general with the evolution of the Protestant church but focused on the development of New England Unitarianism.

Parker wrote his *Discourse* less in a state of exalted prophetic intensity, which is the tone of Brownson's *New Views* and key parts of Emerson's *Nature*, and more as an embattled, even victimized, proponent of liberalization within his church. While Brownson and Emerson had had their share of theological infighting, and would have more after their respective texts were published, Parker wrote his *Discourse* in the blaze of controversy that his sermon on *The Transient and Permanent* had struck. The book is, in conception, an enlargement of that sermon, made possible by the encouragement of George Ellis and others who rented the Masonic Temple in 1842 in order to provide Parker a venue for his expanded views. The five lectures Parker delivered there, published as the *Discourse*, were aimed, as Perry Miller has argued, quite strategically at exposing the limits of the current Unitarian synthesis.[25] Parker's "absolute religion" is the state of faith that Unitarianism has not yet achieved and, perhaps more disturbingly to Parker, is no longer earnestly pursuing.

The new lectures and their publication as a book only deepened the already serious rift between Parker and the more conservative Unitarians. Miller noted that soon after the publication of the *Discourse*, Nathaniel L. Frothingham attacked Parker's position in relation to Unitarianism as the "difference between no Christianity and Christianity." More broadly, as Dean Grodzins has shown in his new edition of Parker's account of his 1843 "Conference with the Boston Association," the radical theology of Parker's *The Transient and Permanent* contributed to a general air of ecclesiastical and political restlessness that alarmed the Unitarian old guard into an aggressively defensive posture.[26]

In the 1961 essay in which he sought simultaneously to recover Parker's "majestic nobility" and uncover his "neurotic compulsions," Miller argued that Parker's challenge to Unitarianism was a representative crisis in American liberalism, generated by the inevitably self-consuming nature of liberalism's intellectual progress, in which one's past belief, and those persons and institutions still holding it, became the fundamental target of destruction.[27] The more closely we read Parker's *Discourse*, with its sweeping characterization of the entire course of Western Christianity, the more clearly we understand it as an embattled text rooted in a local theological controversy. The section of the book mentioned earlier that is devoted exclusively to the contemporary position of Unitarianism is quite revealing, especially since Parker chooses to emphasize unlimited free inquiry as the foundation of the Unitarian movement. The Unitarian "old school," he argued, "assumes a position abhorred by primitive Unitarianism, which declared that FREE INQURY SHOULD NEVER STOP BUT WITH A CONVICTION OF TRUTH" (D, 472). Parker's strategy was to demonstrate that those who felt he had taken his critique of the authority of Jesus too far for Unitarianism were in fact abandoning the movement's cardinal principle. Parker and his Transcendentalist colleagues were, in this sense, the "true" Unitarians, carrying on the necessary work of perpetually expanding the boundaries of faith.

There are also more subtle signals of Parker's sense that his basic mission was a denominational or sectarian one, despite the contempt with which sectarianism was generally held among the Transcendentalists. He used as an epigraph to the volume's conclusion two quotations, one from Emerson and the other from Andrews Norton. The Norton quotation was drawn from one of his earlier anti-Calvinist tracts, in which he noted that the rapidity of change made it essential *not* to cling to a "form of false religion, because it is called religion" (D, 488). Norton, of course, meant Calvinism; Parker means Unitarianism. By quoting the battling younger Norton, himself then embroiled in a struggle to establish a new form of religious culture, Parker made a slyly ironic reference to his own position as an embattled Transcendentalist.[28] He extended that reference by quoting Emerson's indictment of "the loss of Worship" in contemporary society and by providing an answer to that loss: "In the Soul let the redemption be sought" (D, 488). Parker's *Discourse* was a declaration that Unitarianism must now take a new direction, one indicated by the work of the Transcendentalists.

It is important to note that while Brownson and Emerson were controversial figures in their day, no one disturbed the religious establishment, especially the liberal religious establishment, more than Parker. He was seen as a threat in ways that Emerson and Brownson were not, in large part because many Unitarian leaders understood that he was aiming less at a sweeping reformulation of society or a profound inner revolution of perspective than at a revision of the core beliefs and fundamental direction of the New England Congregational churches that had declared themselves Unitarian. The comparatively limited and highly focused nature of Parker's aims made him more dangerous because his demands were more concrete and more capable of being realized. Emerson and Brownson could be regarded with a certain amount of bemusement; Parker had to be taken seriously. Since he was at once the most Unitarian and the most radical of the Transcendentalists, his stature and impact are due to be reevaluated.

If the theological diversity among these leading Transcendentalists suggests that the movement was less than cohesive, and I believe it does, it also reinforces the idea that theological issues were at the center of their concerns. These differences do not, of course, negate the shared concerns that established an intellectual sympathy among them and brought them together in a range of shared projects. They still understood themselves to be engaged in a common struggle to establish the legitimacy of a set of "new views" of religion, which stressed the authority of intuition over tradition and aspired to a pure or absolute religion, rooted in Christianity but aiming at a more universal vision of cultivating the spiritual potential of every individual. But at this moment in the course of Transcendentalist historiography, it is important to understand more fully the distinctions among them, as well as to recognize their shared purposes. In order to make such distinctions, we will have to revisit their texts with some attention—more attention, I believe, than we are used to paying to some of the "minor" Transcendentalists.

That there has been a tradition of study of the "movement" of Transcendentalism among historians and critics, a tradition dating back to the Transcendentalists themselves, has meant that those associated with the movement have been accorded at least some mention in the historical record. Granted, Jones Very, Bronson Alcott, Christopher Pearse Cranch, and George Ripley are not household names; they do, however, have the historical security of association with Emerson, the *Dial*, and Brook Farm. They were part of the movement. But I sometimes think that we do not carry this analysis much further. In this sense, their identification as "Transcendentalists" becomes a screen which obscures the particularity of their lives or works from us. A renewed sense of the *variety* of the movement, of its fluid categories, divergent directions, and conflicting personalities, may bring us back to a deeper engagement with the intellectual work to which they were dedicated.

NOTES

1. Perry Miller, ed., *The Transcendentalists: An Anthology* (Cambridge, Mass., 1950), 8.
2. Miller's anthology has served as the primary history of the Transcendentalist movement for several decades. The recent publication of Barbara Packer's section on

"The Transcendentalists" in the second volume of the *The Cambridge History of American Literature* now provides an authoritative modern narrative history of the Transcendentalist movement. See Packer, "The Transcendentalists," *Cambridge History of American Literature*, ed. Sacvan Bercovitch (Cambridge, 1994–   ), 2:329–604.

3. Miller, *Transcendentalists*, 3.

4. Perry Miller, *Errand into the Wilderness* (Cambridge, Mass., 1956), ix.

5. F. O. Matthiessen, *American Renaissance: Art and Expression in the Age of Emerson and Whitman* (New York, 1941).

6. Miller, *Errand into the Wilderness*, 192; Miller, *Transcendentalists*, 11. For a more detailed discussion of Miller's attitude toward New England Unitarianism and its implications for his reading of Emerson and Transcendentalism, with particular reference to Miller's "From Edwards to Emerson," see my "The Road Not Taken: From Edwards, through Chauncy, to Emerson," *Arizona Quarterly* 48(1992):45–61.

7. The key works in the reconsideration of American Unitarian history are Conrad Wright, *The Beginnings of Unitarianism in America* (Boston, 1955); Conrad Wright, *The Liberal Christians* (Boston, 1970); Conrad Wright, *The Unitarian Controversy* (Boston, 1994); Daniel Walker Howe, *The Unitarian Conscience: Harvard Moral Philosophy, 1805–1861* (Cambridge, Mass., 1970); Lawrence Buell, *Literary Transcendentalism: Style and Vision in the American Renaissance* (Ithaca, 1973); Andrew Delbanco, *William Ellery Channing: An Essay on the Liberal Spirit in America* (Cambridge, Mass., 1981); David Robinson, *Apostle of Culture: Emerson as Preacher and Lecturer* (Philadelphia, 1982); David Robinson, *The Unitarians and the Universalists* (Westport, Conn., 1985); and Conrad Edick Wright, ed., *American Unitarianism, 1805–1865* (Boston, 1989).

8. Ralph Waldo Emerson, *The Collected Works of Ralph Waldo Emerson*, ed. Alfred R. Ferguson et al. (Cambridge, Mass., 1971–   ), 1:85. Hereafter cited in text as *CW*.

9. On Unitarian pietism, see Howe, *Unitarian Conscience*, 151–173. On Unitarian preaching in the nineteenth century, see Wright, *The Liberal Christians*, 41–61; Buell, *Literary Transcendentalism*, 21–54, 102–139; David Robinson, "Poetry, Personality, and the Divinity School *Address*," *Harvard Theological Review* 82(1989):185–199; and Wesley T. Mott, *"The Strains of Eloquence": Emerson and His Sermons* (University Park, Penn., 1989).

10. See Robinson, *Apostle of Culture*, for an account of the development of Emerson's concept of self-culture from its Unitarian roots.

11. For the history of Unitarian discourse on creeds and statements of doctrinal principles, see Robert Hemstreet, "Identity and Ideology: Creeds and Creedlessness in Unitarianism and Universalism," *Unitarian Universalist Advance Study Paper No. 3* (Walkerton, Ind., 1977).

12. The Transcendentalists occupy the opposite pole, theologically, from the American evangelicals and revivalists, and they are usually not considered fully enough, therefore, within a larger framework of American religious history. But the post-millennialist sensibility that we find in many of their works should remind us of the link that still existed between them and their American Protestant context.

13. Ernest Lee Tuveson, *Redeemer Nation: The Idea of America's Millennial Role* (Chicago, 1968), 232. Tuveson's survey of millennialist thinking focuses primarily

on more orthodox and evangelical Protestant figures, and does not include a discussion of the Transcendentalists. But as some of the originating texts of the movement show, the Transcendentalists were also under the sway of millennialist theories, and the hopes for social redemption that these brought.

14. James H. Moorhead, "Between Progress and Apocalypse: A Reassessment of Millennialism in American Religious Thought, 1800–1880," *Journal of American History* 71(1984):525, 541. The optimism that we associate with Transcendentalists such as Emerson and Thoreau, and also with Walt Whitman, who was strongly influenced by Emerson, can be linked to these broader theological assumptions about the progressive nature of history that were shaped in part by millennialism.

15. Anne C. Rose has noted the millennialist tendencies of Bronson Alcott and a similar outlook in the Brook Farm community in its engagement with Fourierism. See Rose, *Transcendentalism as a Social Movement, 1830–1850* (New Haven, 1981), 117–118 and 150–161.

16. Orestes Brownson, *New Views of Christianity, Society, and the Church*, vol. 4 of *The Works of Orestes A. Brownson*, ed. Henry F. Brownson (New York, 1966), 4. Cited hereafter in text as *NV*.

17. Theodore Parker, *A Discourse of Matters Pertaining to Religion* (1842; New York, 1972), 30. Cited hereafter in text as *D*.

18. Notable discussions of Emerson's theory of perception include Sherman Paul, *Emerson's Angle of Vision: Man and Nature in American Experience* (Cambridge, Mass., 1952); Barbara L. Packer, *Emerson's Fall: A New Interpretation of the Major Essays* (New York, 1982); and David Van Leer, *Emerson's Epistemology: The Argument of the Essays* (Cambridge, 1986).

19. Leon Chai, *The Romantic Foundations of the American Renaissance* (Ithaca, 1987), 181–182. See Chai's detailed discussion of Parker's encounter with Schleiermacher's work, 178–185. He also notes the somewhat less direct impact of Kant on Parker's attempt to found the basis of religion on the structure of consciousness.

20. It is important to remember, of course, that Emerson's Journals do not always convey, even in his early career, the kind of optimism that marks early public addresses and essays. In his Journals we find Emerson struggling with doubt, skepticism, and a lack of a sense of enlightenment or fulfilling religious experience.

21. On "The Laboring Classes," see Miller, *Transcendentalists*, 436–446; and Rose, *Transcendentalism as a Social Movement*, 91–92.

22. For two excellent analyses of this dimension of Transcendentalism, see Taylor Stoehr, *Nay-Saying in Concord: Emerson, Alcott, and Thoreau* (Hamden, Conn., 1979); and Richard Francis, *Transcendental Utopias: Individual and Community at Brook Farm, Fruitlands, and Walden* (Ithaca, 1997).

23. Alan D. Hodder, *Emerson's Rhetoric of Revelation: Nature, the Reader, and the Apocalypse Within* (University Park, Penn., 1989), 90, 101.

24. On Emerson's vocational struggle and his changing use of the concept of the "scholar" as a term of self-definition, see Merton M. Sealts, Jr., *Emerson on the Scholar* (Columbia, Mo., 1990). Emerson's later engagement in questions of politics and social ethics, especially the antislavery cause, is traced in Len Gougeon, *Virtue's Hero: Emerson, Antislavery, and Reform* (Athens, Ga., 1990). In *Emerson and the Conduct of Life* (New York, 1993) I recount Emerson's experience of a fading mysticism, and his deepening focus on questions of ethical purpose and social relations.

25. Miller, *Transcendentalists*, 315.

26. Miller, *Transcendentalists*, 315; Dean Grodzins, "Theodore Parker's 'Conference with the Boston Association,' January 23, 1843," *Proceedings of the Unitarian Universalist Historical Society* 23(1995):66–101. Grodzins connects Parker's journal account of this conflict to several interrelated conflicts at the time, including the purely theological dispute over the source of religious authority, and an altercation between the congregation of the Hollis Street Church and their minister, John Pierpont, over his preaching of social reform.

27. Perry Miller, *Nature's Nation* (Cambridge, Mass., 1967), 148–149.

28. On Norton's early work as an anti-Calvinist controversialist, see Lilian Handlin, "*Babylon est delenda*—the Young Andrews Norton," in *American Unitarianism*, 53–85.

Theodore Parker and the 28th Congregational Society

The Reform Church and the Spirituality of Reformers in Boston, 1845–1859

DEAN GRODZINS

Let us imagine you are in Boston some summer Sunday morning in the mid 1850s. You decide to go hear Theodore Parker, the famous Transcendentalist minister, preach to the 28th Congregational Society. Having never been, you arrange to accompany a friend who attends regularly.

As the two of you turn the corner from Tremont onto Winter Street, you are struck by the sheer size of the crowd gathered there. The sight of nearly three thousand people massing for a routine religious service is a novel one. The press of incoming worshipers is strong. Anyone walking this way right now would have difficulty not going to hear Mr. Parker, jokes your friend. Slipping into the human stream, you and your companion go down a narrow, dark alley to the entrance of the Boston Music Hall.

Inside, you pass through one of the many sets of diamond-windowed double doors that open into a large, airy, and elegantly decorated chamber, lit from large semicircular windows near the ceiling. You take seats together in one of the rows of small, connected, blue-upholstered, oval-backed chairs; they are filling up, as are the two narrow balconies that run along the walls to your right, to your left, and behind you. Before you is a low stage on the back of which stands a large bronze statue of Ludwig van Beethoven, reminding you what the room is used for the rest of the week. On the stage in front of the statue are ten rows of freestanding chairs, where, you suspect, Mr. Parker's special admirers sit. Immediately in front of them is the preacher's desk.

The desk is plain. On it sit a Bible and hymn book, a red velvet cushion ready for the sermon manuscript, and a vase of fresh cut lilies. Your friend explains that a few women bring a different kind of flower each week—

73

*usually whatever sort has just bloomed. Mr. Parker was the first minister in
Boston to have flowers on his pulpit, and only a few other clergy, such as Mr.
Clarke at the Church of the Disciples, follow the practice. Others think
flowers on the pulpit irreverent.*

*Mr. Parker has not yet arrived. While waiting for him, you look around.
This congregation, although generally prosperous looking, is less decorous
and more motley than ones with which you are familiar. You are not used to
seeing blacks and whites, laborers, merchants, and threadbare foreign
scholars sitting side by side. As a group they seem inappropriately noisy,
and you note that many of them are reading books and even newspapers.
Your friend assures you that Mr. Parker really does not approve of the reading, but he says nothing publicly because he fears to rob some poor laborer
with no spare time of a precious few minutes for self-education. While
preaching, he has rebuked members of his audience for only one thing: letting the double doors bang behind them when they leave before the service
is over.*

*A wave of silence starts from the front of the hall. Mr. Parker has come in,
although you cannot see him just yet because he has taken a seat behind his
desk. Once all is quiet, he stands and you get a clear view: small man, plain
featured, with a high forehead and large farmer's hands, dressed in a carefully tailored dark suit. He recites from memory the "lesson" (which includes not only Scripture, but a poem by Longfellow), then a hymn, in a
strong, clear, deep voice. Music follows, provided by an organist and a choir
of professional singers.*

*Mr. Parker now starts to pray, arms extended, head bowed. It is different
from any public prayer you have heard before—something like a soliloquy
in the open air—and wholly free of the theological language with which you
are used to hearing God addressed. After the "Amen," the minister puts on
his spectacles and announces the topic for the day. This sermon, he says,
continues a series he has been preaching since the previous September concerning God, Man, and the relationship between the two.*

*The discourse lasts exactly an hour, is unusually eloquent without being
distractingly so, and is delivered with hearty conviction. Although there is a
scriptural text quoted at the beginning, you quickly realize there is to be no
exposition of it; it is to be used only as a motto. In the part of the sermon
attacking the absurdities and limitations of the Ecclesiastical Idea of God,
the preacher's tone is severe. At one point, he refers to Satan as the fourth
and most powerful Person in the Orthodox Trinity. This remark prompts
a movement in the congregation—for a moment, they seem about to ap-
plaud—but to your relief they do not. While discussing the beauties of the
Philosophical Idea of God, the preacher mentions the Lilies of the Field and*

draws out one of flowers from the vase beside him for illustration. His per-
oration—about how our goal in life should not be pleasure, fame, or wealth,
but perfect wisdom, justice, love, and holiness—is stirring. You remember
your own failings and resolve to do better.

A few people head for the exits as the sermon is ending (the doors do bang
annoyingly), but you and your friend stay until the service is over. There is
another hymn, and Mr. Parker gives a benediction. Then you exit slowly,
with the crowds, through the dark alley, into the midday sunshine. . . .[1]

THE 28TH CONGREGATIONAL SOCIETY ORIGINATED IN 1845 AS a way of giving a Boston pulpit to Theodore Parker, then minister of the tiny Unitarian society in West Roxbury, who due to his controversial views had been shut out of other city churches. On January 22, a committee of the "Friends of Theodore Parker," meeting in the Marlboro Chapel, passed a resolution to give him a "chance to be heard in Boston." The Melodeon Theater was rented from the Handel and Haydn Society, and Parker preached his first sermon there on February 16, a cold, wet Sunday morning. Initial interest was high, but there was no guarantee it would last, so Parker kept his West Roxbury position. But week after week, the Melodeon seats were filled. In November, Parker's Boston supporters, counting the experiment a success, offered him a permanent call. He accepted. His installation as minister of the newly organized Society took place on January 4, 1846, and a month later he took official leave of his West Roxbury church.

Over the following years, Parker's fame and that of his Society grew. By 1852 the church had outgrown the Melodeon and so moved to the new Music Hall, which seated nearly twice as many people. By the mid 1850s, regular weekly services were drawing audiences of 2,500—or nearly 2 per-cent of all non-Catholics in Boston. Many more would attend whenever there was expectation that he would pronounce on some particularly excit-ing topic. What one woman exclaimed in 1856, when she learned that the antislavery senator from Massachusetts, Charles Sumner, had been beaten senseless in Washington by a southern congressman, was merely the ex-pression out loud of a thought that flashed across Boston whenever news of a crisis spread: "What a sermon Theodore Parker will preach about this next Sunday!"[2]

The halcyon days of the Society ended when Parker's health began to fail in 1857. He had to give up preaching in 1859, when he suffered a physical collapse brought about by tuberculosis, and he died the following year. His Society tried to replace him, but none of the successors they appointed lasted long, and attendence continued to decline. Services continued to be offered until 1889, when the Society formally dissolved itself, but as early as the 1870s it had become principally a charitable organization.[3]

Technically, there were no "members" of the 28th Congregational Society. Those who wanted to worship with Parker needed to make no profession nor endorse any document. They only had to show up from week to week. A membership roll was never kept. A Society Book did exist for people to sign—it had been opened in late 1845 to help meet the legal requirements for establishing a new church—but after the first few months it was maintained very carelessly; the names of some of the most active Parkerites do not appear in it. Yet a great many people participated in Society activities; in this looser sense, there were a large number of members. Over 1,200 different names appear in one or another of the Society records between 1845 and 1859.[4]

What drew all these people to Parker? A common observation among his contemporaries is that whatever his appeal was, it could not have been religious. He was accused of hosting a mere "Sunday *Lyceum*, where he harangued a promiscuous audience on all themes of thought, science, or politics."[5] Such complaints came even from among his admirers. The reformer and educator Dr. Samuel Gridley Howe is an example. Howe, who had Parker baptize his first child in 1844, supported the 28th Congregational Society for a number of years after its founding in 1846, contributing money and attending with his wife. He withdrew, however, when his children became old enough to attend public worship. As he explained to Parker in 1851, he and his wife did not find the devotions there "religious" enough.

The criticism struck Parker deeply—in his journal he called it "the most painful of my ministry"—and he wrote Howe a searching letter in which he analyzed at length his own religious life and that of his church. Although Parker professed to be surprised that anyone would attend on his preaching, he was glad that most came for some religious, moral, or intellectual purpose, and that no one came for reasons of fashion, as to be there was "dis-respectable": "The audience I speak to is composed mainly of persons from that class of men least under the influence of aesthetic considerations, or of mere social conventions, & most under the influence of moral & religious principles & sentiments."[6]

A great many agreed with this more positive assessment of the religiousness of Parker's ministry—including, as it turned out, Howe's wife, the poet and reformer Julia Ward Howe. She later revealed that she

thought Parker a great religious teacher and had withdrawn from his congregation only at her husband's insistence. She remained so displeased
with Mr. Howe on this point that she avoided the churches he preferred
(either the Unitarian/Anglican King's Chapel or the Swedenborg Chapel).
Instead, she sometimes went by herself to hear Parker; in 1854, she found
a spiritual home in the Church of the Disciples, ministered by Parker's
friend James Freeman Clarke.[7]

Others always kept their spiritual home with Parker. Among these loyal-
ists was the writer, reformer, and philanthropist Ednah Dow Littlehale
Cheney. Cheney joined Parker's Society at its founding in 1845, and she
remained faithful to it thereafter; her mother and two of her sisters were
also members. She served as a Sunday School teacher for the church; she
also organized the committee of women who ensured a bouquet of flowers
would be on Parker's preaching desk every Sunday. A number of women in
his "parish" she counted among her prized friends and associates, and she
devoted several pages of her memoirs to lauding them and their benevolent works.[8]

While Julia Howe, in her *Reminiscences*, recalls Parker principally as a
great preacher and moral crusader, Cheney's *Reminiscences* concentrate
on his pastoral role. He met her when she was still named Ednah Littlehale, at a time of great sorrow, after her dearest sister had died from a sudden illness. Littlehale invited him to call on the recommendation of a
friend, and his visit left her "changed in mind": "I felt that I could still live
for [my sister], and with her, and that her loving presence would go with
me through life."[9] Several years later, in 1850, when she herself fell seriously ill, Parker called on her almost every day, even though at the time he
was deeply involved in a major political crisis—the Craft fugitive slave
case.[10] In 1853, Parker was the minister who married her to the artist Seth
Cheney, himself a longtime Parker admirer.[11] When, sadly, Seth died a few
years later, Parker did not hesitate to interrupt his hectic schedule and go
down to Connecticut from Boston to conduct the funeral. No wonder
Ednah wrote in her memoirs that she would never be able to tell all that
Theodore Parker had been to her.[12]

The history of the 28th Congregational Society was bound up with that of
three Boston Unitarian churches: the Suffolk Street Chapel, the Church
of the Disciples, and the Hollis Street Church. In the winter of 1844–
1845, the first two of these churches experienced crises while at Hollis
Street a long period of bitter controversy drew to a close. These events
resulted in Parker's call to preach in Boston. They also shook many people

free of their traditional church allegiances so that they could join Parker's Society.[13]

The background for the crises at Suffolk Street and the Church of the Disciples was a theological controversy. It had opened in 1841, when Parker began publicly attacking the idea that Christianity was a miraculous revelation. In his sermon "On the Transient and Permanent in Christianity" (1841) and his book *A Discourse of Matters Pertaining to Religion* (1842), both regarded as Transcendentalist manifestoes, he argued that the foundation of Christianity was not the Bible, nor even Jesus, but a religious element within the human soul. Parker made a particular point of attacking the authority of the Bible, which he regarded as merely an historical document, very spiritually valuable in parts but shot through with myths and mistakes about morals and religion.

Most Unitarians, who believed in the miraculous authority of Scripture, thought Parker an infidel. They saw him, too, as an embarrassment to the denomination. For decades they had fought off the charge of their evangelical opponents that the Unitarian faith was but a "half-way house to infidelity." Now evangelicals were gleefully holding up Parker as proof they had been right all along.

Many Unitarians felt they had to do something about their renegade, especially because he was embarrassingly popular; from 1841 on, his lectures drew large audiences. The Unitarian range of reaction, however, was limited both by their congregational form of polity and by their liberal ideology. Due to the former, they could not expel Parker from the ministry. He owed his position only to his West Roxbury congregation, which could keep him as long as it wanted. Nor had the Unitarians, for ideological reasons, much inclination to develop formal procedures of excommunication or censure. From the birth of their denomination a generation earlier they had gloried in their lack of a creed and had boasted that they would extend fellowship to any moral, pious person who claimed to be a follower of Christ. That Parker was such a person—he was universally conceded to be upright and devout, and he never ceased to identify himself as a Christian—made his case all the more exasperating.

Unitarians never were able to make a unified denominational response to Parker, despite the clamor for one from their evangelical critics and even from some fellow liberals. Nonetheless, what actions Unitarians did take, although all piecemeal and ad hoc, had considerable cumulative effect. Unitarian ministers, each claiming to speak for no one but himself, made public statements in which they denounced Parker's theology.[14] The editors of the leading denominational publications—the *Register*, the *Miscellany*, and the *Examiner*—let it be understood that, although their periodicals all had published writings by Parker before the controversy began, his submissions were no longer welcome.[15] Harvard College, dominated by Unitarians, stopped inviting him to examine its students in ancient languages.[16] But the most important Unitarian sanction against Parker was the limitation placed on where he could preach. The restriction was accomplished by denying him pulpit exchanges.

Swapping churches for a Sunday was an old and popular custom among the clergy in and around Boston. It had arisen as a matter of convenience. Ministers liked it because it relieved them from having to write new sermons every week and because it gave the sermons they did write a wider audience; congregations also liked the practice because it allowed them to hear a greater variety of preaching.

Pulpit exchanging gained theological significance only in the early nineteenth century, during the controversy that split the old congregational Standing Order of Massachusetts into liberal/Unitarian and evangelical/Orthodox camps, when evangelical ministers refused to switch places with their liberal colleagues on the grounds that to do so would facilitate the spread of deadly theological errors. Unitarians resented this treatment so strongly that a tradition began among them of regarding pulpit exchanges as a fundamental right of Christian fellowship, one that should never be restricted on grounds of theology.

Even so, during the first year of the Parker controversy, 1841–1842, the large majority of Boston-area Unitarian ministers stopped offering him exchanges.[17] At first, very few made any attempt to reconcile what they were doing with their professed liberal principles. Some refused to admit—at least to Parker himself—that they were shutting him out. Instead, when possible exchanges came up they would beg off, claiming ill health or bad weather, while hoping Parker would take the hint and let the matter drop (something he learned very quickly to do). A few confessed to Parker that they could think of no religious reason to exclude him from their pulpits and that they felt guilty about doing so, but that an exchange would upset unduly some conservatives in their congregations, who were typically among the oldest, wealthiest, and most active members.

Rationales for denying Parker exchanges developed some years later. Two major ones were advanced. The first was that Unitarians in fact had a creed—not a formal, complicated or "irrational" one, like that of the Orthodox, but a creed nonetheless: belief in the miraculous authority of Jesus as the Savior and in the Bible as the guide to faith and practice. Parker, by rejecting these broad articles of faith, had stepped beyond the pale. The second rationale was that when Unitarians denied Parker pulpit exchanges, they did so in a manner fundamentally different from how the Orthodox denied Unitarians pulpit exchanges. The Orthodox had denounced the Unitarians as unworthy of Christian fellowship. Most Unitarians, by contrast, professed to believe that Parker was at least in some sense a Christian—if only a "Christian in life"—and therefore fully entitled to "Christian fellowship," which they claimed to give him gladly and freely. They merely were denying him *"ministerial* fellowship," which was not a right but a convenience.[18]

These rationales did not convince everyone. In fact, they were worked out because, in the winter of 1844–1845, two Unitarian ministers of Boston, John T. Sargent of Suffolk Street Chapel and James Freeman Clarke of the Church of the Disciples, began insisting that the principles of Unitarianism obligated them to exchange with Parker. Sargent and Clarke thus forced the issue of exchanges, for the first time, into serious public debate.

Sargent, pastor of a chapel for the poor sponsored by the Benevolent Fraternity of Churches, a Unitarian charitable organization, conducted an exchange with Parker in November 1844. A few days later, Sargent learned that his act had upset the board of the Fraternity and certain members of his congregation. He responded by resigning his position. When the Fraternity offered him his job back if he would agree not to exchange with Parker again, he flatly refused.

Sargent's case generated considerable public sympathy. The church he left was one he had built up from nothing. When he started his ministry, he had no congregation and no place of worship; by the time he resigned, he had gathered a congregation of 130 families, which worshiped in a chapel his own family's money had helped to build.[19] Then, too, he won sympathy because he insisted that he had acted strictly on the principle of a free pulpit, rather than out of any agreement with Parker's particular theological opinions. Sargent in fact appears to have been committed to the belief, which Parker rejected, that Jesus had a special, divinely ordained mission.

Sargent did not go quietly into retirement. In early December, he made a strong case for freedom of the pulpit, as he understood it, in "The Obstacles to the Truth," a sermon preached before the Hollis Street Church; when the discourse was published some weeks later at the request of several Hollis Street members, he added an appendix in which he printed his heated correspondence with the Executive Committee of the Benevolent Fraternity.[20] Meanwhile, the Fraternity had issued a quarterly report containing a letter by another of its ministers, Robert Waterston of the Pitts Street Chapel, attacking Parker as an infidel and justifying the policy of excluding him from Fraternity pulpits. Sargent felt obligated to reply and wrote a pamphlet, *The True Position of Rev. Theodore Parker*, vigorously defending Parker's religious character.[21] This opened a public controversy between Sargent and Waterston and others, which played out in a long series of pamphlets and in the newspapers.[22]

While these events were unfolding, on January 12, 1845, James Freeman Clarke of the Church of the Disciples, as a protest against what had happened to Sargent, announced that he would conduct an exchange with Parker on January 26. Like Sargent, Clarke professed to disagree strongly with Parker's understanding of the mission of Christ. Clarke's decision sparked an intense debate among the Disciples. Members of the congregation accused Clarke of overstepping his authority by inviting someone to preach whom they did not want, and one group—small, but among them some of the most active supporters of the Church—declared it would secede in protest.

The debate within the Disciples received considerable attention in the religious press, and a young lawyer in the congregation, the future Civil War governor of Massachusetts, John A. Andrew, first came to public notice when he made a speech at one of the church meetings declaring himself not a "come-outer" but a "stay-iner" and pleading with the seceders not to go. Some in his audience reportedly were moved to tears, but the "Come-Outers" remained implacable.[23] Clarke, meanwhile, stuck to his principles, and the Parker exchange took place as scheduled. The seceders responded by organizing a new church with Robert Waterston, Sargent's debating opponent, as their pastor.

At the height of the controversies over Sargent's resignation and Clarke's exchange, on January 22, the Friends of Theodore Parker passed their resolution declaring he had a "right to be heard." Some of those who voted for the resolution were concerned principally with freedom of the Unitarian pulpit, which, like Sargent and Clarke, they believed was under threat. Among the Friends who thought this way appears to have been the merchant Mark Healey, normally a member of the West Church and an interesting example because he is known to have been more conservative than Parker on many matters, notably the slavery issue: Parker was an abolitionist, while Healey was an anti-abolitionist Democrat. Yet Healey proved willing to serve on the standing committees both of the Friends of Theodore Parker and later of the 28th Congregational Society during its first year. In early 1847, however, he resigned from both the Standing Committee and from the Society itself. Pulpit freedom was a cause that could sustain his support for Parker for only so long.[24]

Most of the Friends of Theodore Parker appear to have shared a stronger motive for supporting him. They had been members of the Suffolk Street Chapel and were friends and admirers of John Sargent. Angry at the treatment of their minister, they turned to Parker as an obvious alternative. Sargent himself encouraged them to do so. His pamphlet on the *True Position of Theodore Parker* was perhaps the most ringing endorsement of the Transcendentalist to appear in print. When Parker preached his first sermon at the Melodeon Theater on the morning of February 16, 1845, Sargent substituted for him in West Roxbury and in the afternoon conducted a service at the Melodeon itself. This arrangement with Sargent lasted for the first few weeks of Parker's Boston experiment.

Several people who appear in the records of the 28th Congregational Society can be identified as former members of the Suffolk Street Chapel, prominent among them Dr. John Flint, who served on the Standing Committee of the Friends of Theodore Parker, and Martin Lincoln, for six years the director of the Suffolk Street Sunday School. Sargent, who frequently attended services at the 28th Congregational Society and sometimes preached there in later years, estimated that up to one hundred of his former parishioners now belonged to Parker's Society.[25]

When Sargent, shortly after resigning his position at Suffolk Street, preached the "Obstacles to Truth," his defense of the free pulpit, he did so at the Hollis Street Church. There he knew he would receive a sympathetic hearing. This was the only large, old Unitarian church in Boston where Parker had been admitted on exchange. That same evening, a committee of seven Hollis Street members requested he publish the sermon; of these, four soon would join the 28th Congregational Society—Francis Jackson, Samuel May, Stephen Child, and Adam Thaxter.[26]

That Jackson, May, and others at Hollis Street were supportive of Parker might seem surprising at first, because for many years they had sat happily under the preaching of John Pierpont, whose theology was thoroughly un-Transcendental. He firmly believed in the miraculous origin of Christianity, and he even held that Sabbath observance was "ordained by divine authority."[27] Pierpont was controversial nonetheless. For years, his congregation had been torn apart by a bitter and very public dispute over whether to retain him as pastor. His supporters included a majority of the worshipers; his opponents included most of the church Proprietors—that is, those who owned the pews in his meeting house and so had financial control over the church property.

The trigger of the revolt against Pierpont had been the temperance issue.[28] In 1838, Pierpont had been a leader in rallying public support for the first state law attempting significant restriction of alcohol sales,[29] and he had preached against the sinful traffic in ardent spirits. His activities mortified his Proprietors, many of whom had grown rich in the liquor trade. They charged him with having introduced "exciting topics" into his sermons and asked him to resign. He refused to do so, declaring that freedom of the pulpit was at stake. His enemies next tried to fire him, but they lacked the votes in the congregation. They began increasing their share of ownership in church property, both by purchasing more pews themselves and by persuading allies, some of whom had no association with the Hollis Street Church, to purchase pews. Once the Proprietors won majority control, they began withholding Pierpont's salary. Meanwhile, their list of complaints against him lengthened. Eventually they were accusing him of neglecting his duties, of being offensive and irreverent in the pulpit and in his communications with them, and even of having made dishonest business deals. Pierpont responded by charging them with underhanded tactics and low motives.

By 1840, both sides agreed that they were incapable of reaching a settlement and that an outside body was needed to adjudicate one. For that purpose, they invited ministers of Unitarian churches in and around Boston to convene an extraordinary ecclesiastical council. The proposed task was thankless, but the ministers agreed to come. The Hollis Street Council considered the complaints against Pierpont in the summer of 1841, just as the uproar began over Parker's theology.[30]

The Council was anxious to resolve the Hollis Street controversy, which had become a major embarrassment to the denomination. They also intended to reaffirm clerical authority. Yet many Councilors privately disapproved of Pierpont's course. They thought he was destroying his church for mere personal and political reasons. The "Result" or report of the Council reflected these mixed sentiments. It vindicated Pierpont only to a degree. Although the Council declared there was no evidence to sustain the charges against him of personal malfeasance or neglect of official duties, it did not commend him for preaching on temperance, and it criticized him for lacking a "Christian temper" in dealing with his opponents. To these, the Council issued only the mild admonition to take offense less easily. The "Result" concluded by urging the two sides to reconcile.[31]

This irenic recommendation pleased no one. Pierpont's opponents rejected it outright, and the dispute dragged on for years. Pierpont's supporters, meanwhile, were disgusted. In this group was Parker.

As Parker viewed the situation at Hollis Street, Pierpont was wholly in the right: a pastor crusading to put down actual sin in his own parish. Because the "Result" did not recognize this, Parker considered it a craven document. Even worse, he thought it "worthy of a college of Jesuits."[32] The members of the Council, he believed, were mostly hostile to reformers and dearly wanted to condemn Pierpont outright, as many of them had condemned Parker himself, but feared the public reaction, for popular opinion was on Pierpont's side. They therefore had done their best to undermine him without appearing to do so.[33] Parker was not the only minister to read the "Result" this way,[34] but he was the only one brave enough to make his opinion public. He condemned the work of the Council in a sensational article that appeared in the *Dial* in October 1842. It won him the enduring enmity of many Unitarian leaders but the lasting goodwill of Pierpont's friends.[35]

Another bond formed between the two ministers because Pierpont, despite disapproving of Transcendentalism, kept his pulpit open to Parker—one of the very few Boston ministers to do so. Parker, for his part, was one of the few ministers to keep his pulpit open to Pierpont, who also faced ostracism by his colleagues. Of the twelve ministers who signed the Council "Result," nine never thereafter gave Pierpont a pulpit exchange. As one of these nine later declared in Parker's hearing, the Brethren all "perfectly well understood" how they were to treat Pierpont after the Council.[36]

One of the three Council members who evidently had not understood this, and who had continued to exchange with Pierpont, was John Sargent.[37] He understandably saw a "singular . . . parallel" between the Pierpont and Parker cases. In one of his letters to the directors of the Benevolent Fraternity of Churches in November 1844, he used the Pierpont example to reject their argument that he should keep Parker out of his pulpit because the other Fraternity ministers kept him out of theirs. No one pretends, wrote Sargent, "that Mr. Pierpont is *theologically* a heretic," yet would not this "same rule which would exclude Mr. Parker from Suffolk Street Chapel . . . also close the door of that chapel against Mr. Pierpont?" In that case, concluded Sargent, the "prejudice of the several pastors in your churches must be the criterion or condition of my fellowship or exchange with others, . . . [and] I should prefer to vacate a pulpit so constrained."[38]

By the time this letter was published in early 1845, the Hollis Street controversy was at long last sputtering to a close. In May of that year, just as Parker started his engagement at the Melodeon, Pierpont resigned his pulpit when the Proprietors finally agreed to pay his long-withheld salary.[39] In October he left for Troy, New York, to start a new ministry there. Parker sent him a farewell letter, telling him that he left "in triumph," for without his "manly voice" none of the great moral causes of the day would be so far advanced.[40] A few months later, in "The True Idea of a Christian Church,"

Parker's sermon on being installed as minister of the 28th Congregational Society, he lamented Pierpont's fate:

> [H]as there not just been driven out of this city, and out of this state, a man conspicuous in all . . . [the movements of the times], after five and twenty years of noble toil; driven out because he was conspicuous in them! You know it is so, and you know how and by whom he is thus driven out![41]

Among those in Parker's audience who felt they knew very well "how and by whom" were Francis Jackson, Samuel May, and Daniel Child. Jackson and May, both senior members of Pierpont's church, had been two of his most vocal supporters at Hollis Street, and both had testified at length on his behalf before the Council. Child, a much younger man, had testified briefly for Pierpont at the Council, and he was one of the minority of Hollis Street Proprietors who consistently had backed their pastor.[42]

Jackson, a prosperous land agent, was very active in the antislavery movement. He served for several years as president of the Massachusetts Anti-Slavery Society and later as vice-president of the American Anti-Slavery Society, and he was such close friends with the radical abolitionist leader William Lloyd Garrison that Garrison named a son after him.[43] After Pierpont left Boston, Jackson became a stalwart of the 28th Congregational Society; in a fundraising subscription list from 1847, he appears as one of the top contributors ($100), and his name surfaces repeatedly in the Society records. He and Parker exchanged many letters on business, political, and religious matters, and in 1850 they worked together to organize the Boston Vigilance Committee, which sought to prevent the return of fugitive slaves by any means necessary; Jackson served as its treasurer, and Parker as chair of its Executive Committee.[44]

May, a well-to-do hardware merchant, usually referred to as "Deacon" May because that had been his position at Hollis Street for many years, belonged to a family of reformers. He was the uncle of the famous abolitionist Unitarian minister Samuel Joseph May and his sister Abigail May Alcott, who was herself the wife of the Transcendental educator Bronson Alcott and the mother of the writer Louisa May Alcott. The Deacon's own children included Samuel May, Jr., who also became an abolitionist of note, and Abby W. May, the antislavery and women's rights crusader. The Deacon, his wife Mary Goddard May, and all of his children show up prominently in the 28th Congregational Society records. On the 1847 fundraising list, the Deacon is down for $200, the largest contribution noted. Mary served on the Benevolent Committee and in April 1855, when the Society made a self-conscious gesture in favor of women's rights by becoming one of the first congregational churches—if not the first—to elect women to its Standing Committee (three of the seven seats were reserved for females), she was one of those chosen.[45]

Child, although comfortably well off, was comparatively less rich than either Jackson or Deacon May. At the time Parker's Society was founded, he was a clerk at the Boston Locomotive Works (later he rose to become its treasurer); in the 1847 fund drive, he donated only $40. Nonetheless, like the older men, he was sympathetic to reform. According to the daily diary that he diligently kept with his wife, Mary Guild Child,[46] he often read William Lloyd Garrison's abolitionist newspaper, the *Liberator*, aloud to his family, and he went with Mary to the annual antislavery fairs. Daniel became a significant member of the 28th Congregational Society, serving on its Standing Committee from 1847 to 1854. Mary also appears in the Society records, as do their children, his sister, his brother, his brother's wife, two of Mary's brothers, and her uncle; in 1850, he and Mary had Parker perform a christening ceremony for one of their sons.

Daniel and Mary's diary provides a detailed picture of how two Hollis Street parishioners made the transition to Parker. He first appears in the diary in May 1840, less than a year after their marriage, when they note that "Mr. Parker of Roxbury" called on them in Boston; the visit was probably purely personal—Mary came from Roxbury, and Parker almost certainly was acquainted with her. In September of that year, they record hearing him preach for the first time, on an exchange at their church.

They liked what they heard. From 1841 through early 1845, as the storm around Parker raged, they showed their continuing support for him by going to hear him preach in the pulpits where he was still admitted (including a few outside of Boston), attending his lectures, and reading what he published.

All this time they remained loyal to the embattled Pierpont, who almost invariably is referred to in their journal as "our pastor." Then one evening in February 1845, two days after Parker began regular preaching in Boston at the Melodeon, when Daniel was at Francis Jackson's house for a gathering of "Mr. Pierpont's friends," Pierpont himself dropped by and read to them a letter in which he announced his resignation. He would leave his post in May.

In March and April, Daniel and Mary apparently debated whether to stay at Hollis Street. Daniel records reading, often aloud to Mary, samples of the controversial literature, then growing daily, that surrounded Parker's exchanges with Sargent and Clarke. On Thursday, April 3, Fast Day, Daniel went for the first time to hear Parker preach at the Melodeon; the following Sunday found him back listening to Pierpont. By May 4, when "our pastor, Mr. Pierpont" officiated at services for the last time, the Childs had made up their mind. Starting the following Sunday, Daniel, Mary, and their family were in Parker's audience. Late that year, Daniel participated in some of the meetings that organized the 28th Congregational Society. After Parker formally was installed as its minister in January 1846, he began to be described in the Childs' diary as "our pastor."

The 28th Congregational Society, in which the Suffolk Street and Hollis Street refugees found a home, was supposed to be a new kind of church. Parker was very involved in the wide-ranging church reform movement of the day, which among the Unitarians had produced numerous experiments with new ecclesiastical institutions.[47] Parker pastored one of the two most well-known of these reformed churches; his Society was imitated in the 1850s by "Free Churches" established in Worcester, Lynn, West Newton, and Charlestown. The other famous reform society was the Church of the Disciples, founded in 1841 and pastored for nearly fifty years by James Freeman Clarke.[48] The two churches are worth comparing in order to see some of the distinctive features of the 28th Congregational Society model.

Although Parker's traumatic exchange in 1845 indicates that some of the Disciples were considerably more conservative than he was, in fact, because Parker and Clarke supported Transcendentalism and social reform, the two ministers appealed to many of the same people. As Elizabeth Palmer Peabody, an original Disciple, noted in 1841, some of those in her church actually preferred Parker to Clarke as a preacher, "& of those in the city who are thinking to join Clarke—very many want to see if Parker after all may not be invited in."[49] There were, too, at least a few people like Julia Ward Howe, who moved from one of the two churches to the other depending on whether they felt they best could benefit from, in Howe's words, Parker's "drastic discipline" or Clarke's "tender and reconciling ministry."[50]

As Howe here implies, the differences between Parker and Clarke were as marked as their similarities. The most obvious of these differences is that Clarke usually is numbered among the "Christian Transcendentalists," whereas Parker, although he was a Transcendentalist who identified himself as a Christian, is not. The grounds for this classification are not unreasonable. Clarke believed that Jesus was, in some unique, divine sense, a mediator between God and humankind, and that He had been specially inspired by God to preach a perfect revelation. Parker denied Jesus was in any sense a mediator or that he had been inspired in any special sense; Parker even argued later in his career that this "son of Joseph the carpenter" had made some significant theological errors (about the existence of Hell, for example). Parker did praise Jesus as the greatest religious genius of history and admire him as a martyr, but for Clarke, Jesus was "the Christ."[51] At the Church of the Disciples, therefore, members signed a statement that their "faith is in Jesus, as the Christ, the Son of God," and pledged to "cooperate together in the study and practice of Christianity." At the 28th Congregational Society, those who signed the Society Book were merely endorsing a statement that they "wished to join the society worshiping in the Melodeon [or Music Hall] under the instruction of Theodore Parker."

The willingness of the Disciples to identify with the Christian tradition made their church more palatable to the Boston Unitarians than Parker's Society ever could be. Even so, Clarke met with resentment when he started his work in 1841, partly because he associated with Transcendentalists and reformers, partly because the innovative worship practices of the Disciples implied criticism of how more conservative churches conducted their business, and partly because his Church was felt to have lured worshipers away from churches longer established (one Unitarian minister even referred to Clarke as "a thief and a robber").[52] The Disciples came to be regarded in some quarters as a "decidedly unfashionable" congregation.[53] Yet Parker's Society was seen as worse—outright "dis-respectable." Its presence on Clarke's "left" probably won him support as a "reasonable" and "moderate" alternative.

Although the Church of the Disciples and the 28th Congregational Society differed in outlook and social position, they were both characterized by significant practical reforms in their ecclesiastical arrangements.[54] One of the most significant involved how the two churches were financed. Money was raised entirely by subscription, a practice called the "voluntary principle."

This principle defied the tradition of funding a church by selling the meetinghouse pews, a practice almost all church reformers condemned. They argued that it shut the poor out and destroyed the spirit of free Christian worship by binding people to a church for pecuniary rather than religious reasons. The reformers complained of pew owners who did not attend the services, leaving their seats empty, and expressed pity for those who attended only because of their financial investment. The Hollis Street controversy added a new spectre, that of wealthy pew owners having undue influence on church affairs. The image of rich Proprietors, many of whom did not go to services at Hollis Street, ousting Pierpont over the objections of the majority of those who actually did attend was seared in the memory of Parkerites such as Francis Jackson, Samuel May, and Daniel Child. Meanwhile, James Freeman Clarke alluded pointedly to the problems raised by the Pierpont controversy in a sermon on "principles and methods" of the Disciples:

> [T]hese pew owners are not necessarily the friends of Christian and humane movements. One is a distiller or a retailer of ardent spirits, and he does not like to hear anything said strongly about Temperance. Another owns a plantation in Cuba, or has security on negroes in New Orleans, or his son has married a slaveholding lady in Georgia, and he does not wish to hear anything said against Slavery. Another is a Captain or Colonel in the militia, and does not approve of ultraism in the cause of Peace. Another is a good, easy man, who means to enjoy life, and does not like to hear too much said about Eternity, Judgment and Retribution. They consult together and find that they compose a majority of the pew holders; the church belongs to them; what right has the minister to use their church to say things which they disapprove? In a mercantile point of view perhaps they are right; the building doubtless is their property; but in a Christian point of view it is unfortunate that such considerations should ever control the pulpit.[55]

Of course there were no pews in the halls where Parker's Society always worshiped or where the Disciples worshiped for many years, and the rented seats could not be sold. But they could have been assigned and sublet. Both the Disciples and the Parkerites considered seat rental "a great improvement" over seat ownership; in 1846, Clarke declared that renting half the pews, and leaving the rest "entirely free," was "perhaps as good a method as can be devised, until Christians shall become liberal enough to give freely the whole amount necessary for erecting a church."[56] The Parkerites also for a time considered renting some seats. Yet, as the Standing Committee declared in its annual report for 1846, renting was a fundraising method of last resort. In the end they rejected it as too restrictive: "[We] have been very desirous that *all* should have an opportunity to come & hear what we believe to be the truth; and . . . think [voluntary subscription] is clearly the most effectual way to put down forever the misrepresentations with which the public ear is filled, as to the character of Mr. Parker's preaching."[57]

The Society even rejected assigned seating, which Clarke allowed as a way of ensuring that families could sit together and that regular worshipers could get to know one another.[58] In the Melodeon or the Music Hall,

although some of the more devoted attendees took to sitting regularly near
Parker's desk on the stage, no places ever were set aside or designated for
them. This feature of the Society proved very attractive to some people.
African Americans, including the historian William Nell, found the 28th
Congregational Society congenial in part because it was one of the few
racially unsegregated churches in the city; Nell became a loyal member
and starting in 1855 served as the sexton.[59] Then, too, many recent mi-
grants to Boston liked the open seating arrangement. The young Louisa
May Alcott, new to the city and learning to live on her own, attended
Parker's Society for a few years in the late 1850s. She later remarked that
she enjoyed "the freedom and good will there, for people sat where they
liked, and no one frowned over shut pew doors at me, a stranger."[60]

An obvious difference between the 28th Congregational Society and the
Church of the Disciples was that the former had no afternoon service on
Sunday. Since Puritan times, New Englanders had been accustomed to
spending nearly the whole of Sabbath in church, hearing two or even three
sermons in succession. Clarke did not depart from that tradition, but
Parker did. As he explained in a sermon:

> I am pained to see a man spend the whole of a Sunday going to
> church,—and forgetting himself in getting acquainted with the
> words of the preachers. I think most intelligent hearers, and most
> intelligent and Christian preachers, will confess that two sermons
> are better than three, and one is better than two. One need only
> look at the afternoon face of a congregation in the city, to be satis-
> fied of this.[61]

The time freed could, he believed, be used for nonecclesiastical pursuits
of a spiritual or moral nature, such as self-culture or perhaps social reform.[62]

The afternoon service was a hard habit to break, however, and Parker
did not at first propose to do away with it. When he started preaching in
Boston in February 1845, John Sargent offered second services to the congregation. How long they continued is not clear, but probably not more
than a few weeks because the demand for them appears not to have been
high. When Parker was invited to settle in Boston later in 1845, some of his
supporters apparently expected afternoon services would resume, but
Parker now discouraged the idea, and most of his followers agreed with
him. As the first Standing Committee report noted in April 1846, Parker's
suggestion that there be only one Sunday service "has been found to give
general satisfaction."[63]

Still, Parker never felt entirely comfortable having his Sunday afternoons to himself. He frequently used the time to drop by other Boston churches to hear what the other preachers were saying (he never comments on the cold stares he must have received while doing this). He also tried to fill the time with a number of worthwhile activities—at one time or another a biblical study class, a Sunday School, and a meeting for free conversation. All these endeavors eventually fell through, the primary cause of the failures being insufficient interest.

Parker's most enduring and successful Sunday afternoon activity was an informal one that did not strictly speaking involve his Society. In 1847, after he moved from West Roxbury to Boston, he began holding receptions at his townhouse several hours after services. Guests would talk on elevated themes and sometimes sing hymns. Regular attendants included non-Society members, such as the reformers Wendell Phillips and Caroline Healey Dall, but Society members also came routinely, among them the abolitionist William Lloyd Garrison,[64] the reformer Franklin Sanborn, and Julia Ward and Samuel Gridley Howe. Julia Howe, at one of these receptions in 1853, befriended Garrison, whom her husband regarded as a fanatic and always had told her not to like.[65] Louisa May Alcott attended these gatherings faithfully in 1856 and 1857—a self-described "large, bashful girl" who would sit in the corner listening to the conversation until Parker or his wife came over to say a kind word to her.[66] Alcott may have witnessed the best-remembered event to take place at one of these receptions, in January 1857, when Capt. John Brown, fresh from the Kansas War, debated the pacifist Garrison on whether violence was justified in trying to overthrow slavery.[67]

Parker's efforts to change the Church were shaped by his general distrust of institutional authority, one that he shared with other Transcendentalists and reformers. He was never, however, hostile to institutions as such. He recognized their usefulness, but he saw any institution as valuable only until humanity could devise something better.

An instructive comparison may be made between him and a more extreme anti-institutionalist, the abolitionist and sometime 28th Congregational Society member William Lloyd Garrison. Both Garrison and Parker thought the United States Constitution recognized slavery, but they drew quite different conclusions from this premise. For Garrison, constitutional political action and abolitionism were obviously incompatible; he therefore refused to vote or to propose constitutional legislative programs. For Parker, the Constitution was but the temporary, flawed expression of the "great national idea" of democracy. Insofar as it truly expressed that idea, it

was antislavery and should be honored and obeyed; insofar as it endorsed
slavery, it should be defied until it could be improved upon. Holding such
views, Parker felt free to endorse both constitutional political activity, such
as voting for antislavery politicians, and extra-constitutional action, such as
financing John Brown's effort to start a slave insurrection in Virginia.[68]

Parker's process-oriented view of institutions had a profound effect on
the 28th Congregational Society, giving it a permanently transient character. This quality was symbolized by the venues in which the congregation
worshiped. To hold services in a rented space for a few years is a common
occurance in the early history of many a church. For most, renting is a
temporary expedient until a permanent sanctuary can be found or built.
But Parker's church always used halls. These it held for years at a time as
mere tenants at will, without lease. On at least three occasions (1853,
1854, 1858) it came close to being evicted for reasons either political or
financial.[69]

The finances of the Society were as precarious as its hold on a worship
space. Having done away with seat rentals, Parkerites found no adequate
substitute, and the burden of supporting the Society ended up on the
shoulders of a small number of dedicated members. The annual financial
reports of the Standing Committee and of the Treasurer,[70] delivered aloud
to the congregation at its business meeting each April, are notable for their
exasperated tone. Repeatedly they complained of the "very unequal distribution of the weight of pecuniary responsibility." They pleaded that the
"Apostolic injunction 'Bear ye one another's burdens,' so often & forcibly
urged by our Pastor, be exemplified in practice." They issued stern reminders that "the Age of miracles has passed, & . . . along with it, (at least
as taught in our pulpit) that of *vicarious* discharge of personal duty." In
case anyone somehow missed the point of these reports, despite their
"great plainness of speech" and "more than ordinarily distinct" statements,
in 1854 notices were placed on the doors of the Music Hall reminding the
congregation that "the expenses are large, and the means of paying them
depend upon voluntary contributions." Society officers were stationed
nearby, ready to take donations.

All to no avail. The percentage of the audience who contributed money
to the Society remained consistently smaller than 10 percent, and often no
more than 5 (even less, in other words, than the proportion of a modern
audience that contributes to its public radio station). The Society repeatedly skirted the "rocks & shoals of bankruptcy" and for years at a time was
in debt. For most of the 1850s, even as attendance doubled, expenses
could only be met because Parker annually returned $400 of his $2,000
salary.

His Society was weak by intention. That it never got a "house of its own" was no accident; as one Society member noted, Parker and his friends "preferred the use of halls."[71] To start raising money for a building was proposed at a Standing Committee meeting in 1845, voted down, and never brought up again. The Standing Committee did not even mind that they held their halls as tenants at will, a condition they celebrated as "untrammelled by lease." That the Society was constantly short of money was a matter of greater concern, but not such concern that any effort was made to build an endowment.

The leaders of the 28th Congregational Society did not believe in building up a strong church. Parker himself was leery of such institutions, which he saw as potentially restrictive, over time, of individual spiritual freedom. Any organization for religious purposes, he believed, although founded with prayers, sacrifice, and blood, "soon shows it is not wide enough for *man*."[72] The spirit that would found a church was larger than any ecclesiastical institution, any creed or ritual, it possibly could create. Once created, these institutions, creeds, and rituals inevitably outlived their usefulness as humanity outgrew them. They then became stumbling blocks to spiritual progress. For Parker, the best church (like the best national constitution) was a disposable one, easily discarded when no longer helpful.

This outlook probably lay behind the failure of so many extra-pulpit activities at his Society. Sunday schools and societal meetings naturally would be difficult to sustain without church structures to support them.[73] An interesting comparison may be made here with the Church of the Disciples. Clarke, like Parker, worried about ecclesiastical oppression. His solution, however, was to organize not a weak church, but a democratic one, at which the management was "subject to the vote of the majority of the regular worshipers."[74] The strong organization of the Disciples provided a framework in which extra-pulpit activities flourished.

Parker's interest in church reform was limited by his conviction that full reform of the Church would require a complete reformation of society. He had not always held this position. In fact, he once had believed just the opposite—that reform of the Church would *result in* a complete reformation of society.

This last belief lay behind a series of sermons and speeches he delivered in 1840, before the controversy broke that made him famous.[75] In these pronouncements he attacked any claim that creeds or church institutions (e.g., the sacraments, the Sabbath, or the ministry) were sanctioned by either God or Jesus. Parker assumed that once the Church was recognized as a merely human creation its ability to oppress the soul would disappear. Its creeds and institutions could be rethought, refigured, or even abandoned to suit present spiritual needs. Such steps, he argued, were a necessary prelude to any substantial social reform. The church was the oldest and greatest oppressor of the human spirit, and once this boulder was removed, all other forms of oppression would have to give way.

Parker's early outlook was shared in some measure by a great many other social reformers in 1840, such as those who packed the famous religious reform conventions at Groton and at the Chardon Street Chapel in Boston that year. Parker's fellow Transcendentalists, meanwhile, thought the link between reform and the creation of a new church important enough to discuss it at four of the five meetings of the so-called Transcendental Club in 1840. Even Orestes Brownson, the Locofoco Transcendentalist whose views on many political and religious subjects were very different from those of Parker, demanded reform of the church in his controversial (and today, widely misinterpreted) articles on the "Laboring Classes." These usually are remembered for their proto-Marxist analysis of worker exploitation and for their recommendation that inherited private property be abolished. Yet Brownson devotes most of his pages to the abolition of the priesthood, which he argued was the first step towards liberating the workers and one that should be taken at once. Abolition of inherited private property, by contrast, he held to be a distant goal for which civilization was not yet prepared.[76]

In the years after 1840, Parker's thoughts about church reform began to change, and by the time the 28th Congregational Society was organized in 1845 they had undergone a revolution. Parker expressed his new view in a sermon preached early in 1846.

His topic was "Education." Like many other social reformers, before and since, Parker put great stock in education, which he here defined very broadly. Our schools and colleges, he said, were our least important educators. Instead, the education of a people principally came from four sources. Ranked in descending order of importance, these were, first, politics, which he said regulated the pendulum of the nation and determined the character of all its institutions; second, the "material action" of the country—that is, its trade and business activity; third, the press; and last and least, the churches. "I once looked to the [churches], for the highest ed[ucational]. work," he remarked.

> Some of you may have been as simple. But they are not organized for that; their servants not hired for that, not paid for it. . . . The Ch[urch] . . . cannot show the living genius for Rel[igion].—

wh[ich] |shall| [Christianize] . . . the P[ress], Trade & Politics. Itself it is secularized, barbarized by these 3 & partitioned by them.[77]

The reference here is to the partition of the old Polish Kingdom by Prussia, Austria, and Russia a half-century before—an act that Parker elsewhere ranked among the most monstrously unjust in modern political history.[78] Obviously, he was dismayed just as much by this "partition" of the Church. That the Church would regain its independence and "living genius" was his hope. He certainly expected the 28th Congregational Society to play an independent prophetic role and so help Christianize the city and the nation.[79] Yet he no longer believed that any of the reforms he had helped institute at his Society would change the world. The Church, he now realized, did not hold together the social order.

Two events had been decisive in this change of outlook. One was the Hollis Street controversy. Parker's conviction that John Pierpont had been driven from his pulpit by "rum and the Unitarian clergy"[80] provided him with an object lesson that the Church was not an independent force in society. The implications of this lesson grew on Parker in 1843–1844, when he spent a Sabbatical year touring Europe, his first trip outside the United States. He went abroad as a kind of religious tourist. At each stop, he visited churches, cathedrals, and sacred sites, listened to sermons, called on theologians, and examined the theological manuscripts in the local library. He made his longest stay in Rome, where he spent four months. Yet when he had recrossed the Atlantic and could reflect on his experiences, particularly on the factors that most sharply distinguished America from Europe, the religious differences, although important, seemed less significant than the political and economic ones.[81] Politics and economics, not the Church, seemed to order society. Within months of his return from Europe Parker declared that "the greatest of all human enterprises was the *formation of a state*," and God's purpose for America was a political one—to "organize the *Rights of Man*."[82]

Parker never discounted the role of the Church in social reform, but the nature of that role had changed. Its function became instead to alter the sentiments and ideas of the economic group he now saw as the real power brokers. He identified them in a published sermon from November 1846 on "Merchants."[83]

The "merchant class," Parker said, possessed the "most powerful and commanding" position in the country. They held the most prestigious social rank; they owned the "machinery of society"—its wealth and resources; they controlled American politics; they controlled, too, American churches.

Parker criticized merchants for their selfishness and conservatism, yet he also insisted that if their temptations were great, their power for doing good was greater still. He told them:

> You may develope [sic] the great national idea, the equality of all men. . . . It is for you to organize the rights of man. . . . If this be not done, the fault is yours. . . . If you do the national duty that devolves on you, then are you the saviours of your country, and shall bless not that alone, but all the thousand million sons of men. Toil then for that. If the church is in your hands, then make it preach the Christian truth. . . . Help build the American church. . . . The church of America, the church of freedom, of absolute religion, the church of mankind, where Truth, Goodness, Piety, form one trinity of beauty, strength, and grace—when shall it come? Soon as we will. It is yours to help it come.[84]

Merchants were principally responsible for the realization of the American Idea—and for reform of the Church.

Parker's turn away from the church as the focus of reform to the merchant class was part of his general emphasis on the importance to religion of the middle class.[85] In his day, middle-class people were coming to be aware of themselves as a distinct social group, defined by a way of life and a cultural style. He was one of their champions, and as such, was one of the thinkers who helped define what the middle class was for his time and place.[86]

True, Parker rarely used the term "middle class" as such and did not consistently use the word "class" in its usual modern sense of social stratum; sometimes it meant for him merely a classification or group. For example, in his sermon on the "merchant class," his definition of that "class" is functional: all who "live by buying and selling," regardless whether the trade is out of "a basket, a wheelbarrow, a cart, a stall, a booth, a shop, a warehouse, counting-room, or bank."[87] On the other hand, he generally did conceive of society as having three horizontal layers, each with a distinct character, and he saw the middle one as the most important for social progress.

In the bottom layer of society, said Parker, were the manual laborers, that is, those who acted on the world by means of "brute force" alone. Among this group, he believed, could be found the "perishing classes" (the abjectly poor) and most of the "dangerous classes" (that is, the criminals). People at this level in society generally were degraded because they had been unable to develop their spiritual natures. Yet Parker had no general concept of this group as a threat nor of a proletariat locked in combat with the bourgeoisie. Instead, he believed that the lower layer of society should be aided and elevated. He constantly praised the dignity of manual work and attacked the social prejudices against it, and he supported a wide variety of reforms he believed would alleviate poverty and degradation, from better public schools to temperance to a shorter work day.[88]

At the top of society, Parker believed, was a group that influenced the world by means of its capital. He sometimes called this the "controlling" class (because it controlled the state, the press, and church) or the "capitalists." This class Parker portrayed as neither terribly moral nor terribly religious. Its members thought religion vulgar and decidedly low, good for ordinary people but not for them. They used their vast influence to oppose any reform of church, state, or society. As such, they struck Parker as a far greater threat to social progress than the degraded but largely powerless lower class.[89]

Parker put his hopes for social progress in neither the laboring nor controlling classes, but in the middle group, which he believed constituted the large majority of society. Members of this group, he said in a sermon from 1846, were characterized by seriousness and earnestness of purpose, for they had made their own way in the world. They had "mingle[d] more with all sorts of men" than had members of the other two classes and so had learned to feel the common nature of humanity, to ignore the accidents of situation, and to appreciate the spiritual value of "man as man." Among these people, religious ideas had always found a home. The mission of this middle group was to help the class below them and to challenge the class above them.[90]

According to Parker, true religious ideas emerged in a fundamental way only from middle-class experience. Certainly, his religious ideas emerged from his middle-class experience, as did the picture of society that he expressed here.

Parker was a self-made man. One simple measure of his success is to compare his wealth with that of his father, a farmer and pumpmaker. John Parker was worth about $1,500 when he died in 1836, just as the son was starting his ministerial career. By contrast, at the height of that career Theodore was earning nearly $5,000 a year from his salary and lecture fees alone. When he died in 1860, he and his wife together were worth $50,000, placing them in the top 1 percent of Bay Staters.[91] Yet these numbers only hint at what was a more complicated story. For although Parker had succeeded in some respects, his youthful ambitions in fact had been thwarted. "O Blindness O the Future . . . ," he wrote in a typical lament in his journal on this theme. "Alas my life has been far other than I dreamed of, prayed for."[92]

Parker originally had aspired to join the "controlling class" of Boston—the group known in the later nineteenth century as the "Brahmins." Already in the antebellum period it was perhaps the most clearly defined and powerful elite in America.[93] This network of about forty mercantile, banking, and manufacturing families, closely intermarried, had risen to unprecedented wealth and power by establishing and controlling the first great textile mills. It was united not only by kinship networks, but by world view, being overwhelmingly Whig in politics and Unitarian in religion.[94] This patriciate had enormous influence over the politics of Massachusetts and dominated its leading cultural institutions—Harvard University, the Boston Athenaeum, the oldest and most prestigious churches, the major newspapers and journals.

Parker's ambition to join this elite was not unreasonable, for it was, in his youth, still fairly open. All a poor boy needed to do was work hard, find patrons, get an education, enter an acceptable profession, join the Whig Party and Unitarian Church, and most importantly, marry well.

Parker made all the right moves. He decided to become a Unitarian minister.[95] He voted Whig.[96] He pursued his education with a terrifying intensity—and largely on his own, because his family could not afford to send him to college. Despite this handicap, by the age of twenty-five he had studied at Harvard Divinity School (which he had entered with the help of a patron) and learned to read twenty languages (among them, Latin, Greek, Hebrew, French, German, Spanish, Italian, Swedish, Icelandic, and Aetheopic). He also "married up." His wife, Lydia, was a Cabot and as such a member of perhaps the most eminent family of the Boston bourgeois aristocracy (as the old saw goes, Boston is where the Lowells talk to the Cabots, and the Cabots talk only to God).[97]

In 1834, he wrote to Lydia with reference to another poor boy who had made good, the dean of the Divinity School, John Gorham Palfrey:

Nothing is too much for young *ambition* to hope, no eminence too lofty for *his* vision; no obstacle too difficult for his exertions and no excellence unattainable. Patience, Perseverance, Prayer have done *something* already, and when we consider that sincere desires are never neglected, and real endeavors never unassisted, we need not *despair* of making some *approaches* at least to the eminence Mr. Palfrey now occupies. Would not this be truly delightful?[98]

This "truly delightful" dream failed him. First, he and his wife's family did not get along; he came to regard them as so many insufferable philistines, and they in turn cut his wife out of a major inheritance.[99]

Through personal acquaintance he discovered that aristocrats of Boston were not his kind of people. Then, too, the Boston elite defined itself as conservative in theology and politics. Parker, largely through his association with New England Transcendentalism, came to define himself as a radical.[100] As a consequence, they shut him out of their clubs and homes as well as their churches.

The disdain Parker developed for them was considerable. Throughout his career, he would direct much of his social criticism and many of his most barbed comments against these "snobs" and their institutions, such as Harvard and its Divinity School, which he once had aspired to lead. He famously remarked that while the Egyptians took three months to embalm a dead man, the Divinity School took three years to embalm a live one.[101] Parker's disdain was mixed with anger towards the elite for trying to keep him down. It was the rage of a self-made man. "*Why* have I been opposed," he asked in an autobiographical note from 1846, ". . . not because [I] said what was not *true*, . . . not *honest*, not friendly to the *interests of Man.* . . . *With what intention* have I been opposed? To ruin me, to give me no chance."[102]

Ironically, the more he was denounced and renounced by the establishment, the more popular he seemed to become. As he often said, when he spoke to the people, they heard his words gladly. He had tapped into what turned out to be a widespread popular resentment among middle-class Unitarians against the pretensions of the Boston elite.[103] In particular, he drew a following from people like himself—those who were middle class or who had middle-class aspirations.

The social composition of Parkerism is indicated by the data presented in the appendix. Here are compared the socioeconomic profiles of a sample of all Boston male household heads (1850) and a sample of the most active members of the 28th Congregational Society, male and female (1845–1859).[104] The Parkerites are revealed to have been strikingly more middle class than the general Boston population. Nearly a third of the latter were unskilled or semi-skilled laborers, whereas only 1 percent of Parkerites were of such status; by contrast, more than a third of Parkerites had the status of clerks or professionals (lawyers, doctors, architects), whereas that was true of fewer than one in ten Bostonians overall. The largest block of Parker supporters, nearly 40 percent, were of merchant status ("Proprietors"), almost twice the proportion of their fellow citizens.

These results are not surprising. Much of the membership of the 28th Congregational Society was made up of dissident Unitarians, and Unitarianism was famously not a working-class religious movement. Yet there does appear to have been a significant social difference between the Parkerites and regular Unitarians; as Parker himself so often claimed, his following was drawn from a different "class of men." Which class is indicated by Jane and William Pease's examination of the Hollis Street controversy and especially by their comparison of the relative wealth, power, and social standing of Pierpont's supporters—many of them future paladins of Parkerism—and his opponents, who remained Unitarian communicants. The Peases found the former group to have been much less economically and politically powerful—less "elite"—than the latter. The core membership of Parker's Society, in sum, appears to have been disproportionately middle class when compared to the general Boston population, but less oriented towards the elite than the conservative Unitarian churches of Boston, where he was forbidden to preach.[105]

Parker's appeal to his middle-class followers ran deeper, however, than simply social resentment. Theirs was an age in which rising industrialization and consumerism were reorganizing everyday life. Parker showed them a way to be *in* this brave new world but not *of* it.

He always hailed economic development and the rising level of material comfort that consumerism brought about. He bought stocks in railroads, mills, and banks and came to live a typically Victorian bourgeois lifestyle, complete with a tailored suit, a bric-a-brac stuffed house, and a maid. Yet even when he insisted, as he frequently did insist, that a Christian should seek material comfort, he always held that this was but the first, preliminary step towards spiritual self-culture. The moment you lost sight of this was the moment you became too rich. The sure sign that you were too rich was that you ceased to value "man as man"—that you became, in other words, like the conservative elite of Boston whom Parker opposed. By contrast, if you pursued spiritual self-culture (that is, you worked constantly to improve yourself mentally, morally, affectionally, and religiously); if you worked to turn society into a place in which all people, especially the weakest and poorest, could pursue their own spiritual self-culture; and above all if you pursued both these goals in the face of public hostility and scorn, then you could be assured that you still valued "man as man." Or to use an older theological language that Parker avoided, you were assured of salvation.

How Parker's model of salvation worked in the lives of his followers can be seen in the religious histories of two of them, Caroline Healey and Henry Wilcox. Although Healey never became a regular member of the 28th Congregational Society, and Wilcox lived too far away to join, their life stories reveal tendencies common among Parkerites.

Healey was a young Unitarian woman from a wealthy Boston family that attended the West Church. She first encountered Parker when she heard him deliver a series of lectures on religion in 1841. In her journal she expressed enthusiasm for what she heard. More than once she declared that Parker's words had made her "stronger."[106] She was in awe of his bravery in speaking his mind and thought that if she "lived in the atmosphere of such a life as his" she "should be always right." His appeal to live a divine life made her painfully aware of what she saw as her own "false and degrading" position as a young woman in a well-to-do family. After the last lecture, she felt ashamed that she had "consented, but a few hours before to waste a day at least in preparing for a ball."[107]

Parker's theological ideas were "shocking" to her at first, but on reflection she decided she agreed with him. She was seized by the idea that if she declared her "new faith" it must separate her "forever" from her closest friends:

> I had seen Mr Parker making a great effort to speak what he believed to be the truth[,] the perspiration starting to his forehead— and his hands trembling as he said that he spoke "well knowing what it meant—" what would close the door of every pulpit in our land against him—rob him of his brother's heart—put his hand against every man's and every man's hand against him—I had loved him for his independence—and I wondered if I too—could do this—[108]

Thinking such thoughts, she prayed earnestly for "truth[,] faith and power."

Over the following weeks she often was restless and unable to sleep. She found herself defending Parker to her friends. She started a correspondence with him. Finally, after some months had passed, she made a public confession of faith. She announced to her Bible class that she was a "humanitarian" and a "disciple of Theodore Parker's." This declaration sparked, as might be expected, a warm discussion, in which Healey nearly burst into tears. "I struck my own death blow," she wrote in her journal that night, "God forgive me the suicide." She clearly expected (hoped?) that she would be made an outcast like Parker himself.

This did not in fact happen (perhaps because those around her thought she was a young woman going through a phase), yet her conversion experience was a turning point for the young Healey—her first major break from social and intellectual conventions. She would continue to break from these conventions her entire life. Later, as Caroline Healey Dall, she would become an important member of the women's rights movement and a pio-

neer social scientist. She always would list Parker as mentor and a great
religious influence on her.[109]

The second example of how the Parker model of salvation worked is that
of Henry A. Wilcox, a young man who hailed from what was then the frontier town of Mendon, Illinois. Unlike Dall, he never became famous, but
his case is interesting nonetheless. Wilcox opened a correspondence with
Parker in 1856, when the westerner was struggling to get ahead and find a
respectable career. One of the Bostonian's books had fallen into his hands
the year before. Promptly, he ordered more from back East. He described
their effect on him in a letter to their author: "I feel like one that has just
awoke from a horrid dream. I have found there is something to live for, and
that instead of my pocket I have a mind to cultivate."[110]

Wilcox, in other words, could now satisfy himself that he could be self-
made without being a man on the make. He improved his mind. Not only
did he start to standardize the spelling and punctuation in his letters, but
his prose, which in the early letters was plain, grew fancy. Wilcox began
composing self-consciously "literary" passages in which he waxed lyrical
about, for example, farming. Even more strikingly, he transformed his life
into a kind of *imitatio Parkeri*. He started theological arguments with local
evangelicals and identified himself with the antislavery movement by giving a lecture in which he argued that opposition to slavery was a religious
duty. He won a local reputation as an infidel, which made him a social outcast. He resolved to be a preacher who would work to tear down the
"dreadful theology" around him.

Wilcox's new faith was put to the ultimate test in September 1858, when
he grew gravely ill. He later described what happened in a letter to his
hero:

> Frequently while discussing religious subjects with others, they
> have said that my belief would do to *live* by, but it would not do to
> *die* by. The day of trial came. On the evening of the 26th of Sep-
> tember, I felt I could not live till morning. My stand being close to
> the bedside, while my friends were absent for a few minutes, I
> with great effort wrote these words on a piece of paper: "I die in
> the belief in which I live," dated and signed it, and placed it with
> my other papers. When my friends returned, I told them I thought
> I was going to die; and I settled up my worldly affairs. The physi-
> cian and my friends conversed with me, and tried to shake my
> belief, but in vain: . . . there was no doubt, no fear, but a peaceful
> happiness came over me. Gradually I lost all consciousness, my
> body lost its feeling, my pulse was gone. I lay in that state for sev-

eral hours, when, contrary to expectation, I rallied; for a week life hung in the balance. . . . Part of the time I was conscious, and conversed freely with those that came to see me; my bed was besieged daily by church members and ministers; daily I was urged to renounce my belief, but daily that belief grew stronger, and the contrast between natural and ecclesiastical religion grew wider and more distinct. At the end of a week, my youth and excellent constitution triumphed.[111]

By Wilcox's own lights, he had not only survived, he had achieved a kind of sanctification.

The stories of Wilcox and Dall show how powerfully the example of Parker's life—his rise to accomplishment, prosperity, and fame while becoming martyr for his convictions—resonated with his contemporaries. His supporters in the 28th Congregational Society could work to get ahead in the world, with their pastor's encouragement, yet could be redeemed, like him, by having "respectable" people persecute them for championing reform. Parkerism, in other words, to work religiously, required "respectable" enemy inquisitors.

The principal religious problem the 28th Congregational Society faced after Parker's death, one that they could not overcome, was that this inquisition faded away. The theology that Parker had been ostracized for proclaiming in the 1840s began to win wide acceptance in the 1860s and 1870s, after the rise of Darwinism made belief in traditional theological constructs impossible for many. A common observation of his old followers, rereading his works decades after his death, was that his ideas—about the inspiration of scripture, for example—which once appeared strange and shocking, now seemed familiar and unexceptionable. Also, major parts of his political program, abolitionism in particular, triumphed and so ceased to be controversial. Finally, the simple absence of the man made his Boston following less "dis-respectable." The personal animus so many in the city elite felt towards Parker—a rancor built up over many years of controversy and mutual recrimination—had been transferred to his supporters; but without his presence continually to irritate the old wounds, they began to heal, and the elite enmity towards Parkerites started to soften. With this softening, the spiritual key to Parkerism was lost, its mainspring could not be rewound, and the movement inevitably stopped.

APPENDIX. A socioeconomic profile of Boston household heads (1850)
compared with a profile of the most active members (MAM)
of the 28th Congregational Society (1845-1859)

Socioeconomic Status Group	Boston 1850	28th CS MAM
Unskilled and Semi-Skilled Labor	32.5%	1%
Skilled Labor	25.4%	14%
Clerical or Sales	3.9%	19%
Proprietors, Managers, and Officials	21.3%	39%
Semi-Professional or Professional	4.2%	15%
Miscellaneous and unknown	12.7%	12%
Total Sample Size:		182

SOURCES: The profile of Boston household heads is adapted from Peter Knights, *The Plain People of Boston, 1830–1860: A Study in Growth* (New York, 1971), Table V-2 (p. 87). The methods used in compiling the profile of the 28th Congregational Society are explained in the Note to the Appendix, below.

NOTE TO THE APPENDIX

I compiled the list of members of the 28th Congregational Society from the following sources:

- Signers of the 28th Congregational Society Book [1845-1858]. (In the Theodore Parker Church, West Roxbury.)
- Officers of the Society or of its predecessor, the Friends of Theodore Parker (members of the Standing Committee or Benevolent Committee, Treasurer, Secretary, Sexton) [1845-1858]. (Compiled from various archives of the 28th Congregational Church [Parker Memorial], Boston, Records, bMS 7, Andover-Harvard Theological Library, Harvard Divinity School, Cambridge, Mass.)
- Those for whom Parker conducted a baptism, marriage, or funeral [1845-1858]. (Gathered from his record of these, at the Theodore Parker Church, West Roxbury.)
- Donors who subscribed to give funds to the Society [1847]. (In the 28th Congregational Church [Parker Memorial], Boston, Records, bMS 7, Andover-Harvard Theological Library, Harvard Divinity School, Cambridge, Mass.)
- Donors who contributed to buying for Parker a watch and for Parker and his wife a silver fork set [1852]. (Listed in a letter tipped into Parker's Journal O, p. 339a [Nov. 20, 1852], Theodore Parker, Papers, bMS 101, Andover-Harvard Theological Library, Harvard Divinity School, Cambridge, Mass.)
- Donors who contributed to buying for the Parkers a piano [1853]. (Listed in a

letter tipped into Parker's Journal O, p.424a [Dec. 24, 1853], Theodore Parker, Papers, bMS 101, Andover-Harvard Theological Library, Harvard Divinity School, Cambridge, Mass.)
- Signers of a congregational epistle to the London Free Religious Association, pastored by Johannes Ronge [Nov. 14, 1854]. (Copy in the 28th Congregational Church [Parker Memorial], Boston, Records, bMS 7, Andover-Harvard Theological Library, Harvard Divinity School, Cambridge, Mass.)
- Signers of a congregational epistle to Theodore Parker [Jan. 11, 1859]. (At the Theodore Parker Church, West Roxbury.)
- Those not in other Society records who in letters, diaries, memoirs, etc., describe attending Parker's services regularly (Louisa May Alcott, for example).

The total number of names, cross-correlated, was 1,126. Included on this list were 488 women, 650 men, 41 children (under age 18), and 47 whose sex/age I could not determine.

My sample of the Most Active Members (MAM) of the 28th Congregational Society included the following persons:

- Those whose names appear in three or more of the various records described above.
- Those who signed both the Society Book (which only certain members chose to sign) and the 1859 congregational letter (which was reputed to include among its signatories the core membership of Parker's Society at that time).
- Those who were Society officers.
- Those whom I knew from other evidence were very active in the Society (e.g., Frank Sanborn).
- The immediate family members of the people in the first four groups who also appear in the church records (parents, spouses, siblings, and children). In many cases, when I could not identify the social status of a given most active member (e.g., a woman), I could identify the presumably similar status of an immediate family member (e.g., her father, husband, or son).

My final total sample was 102 men, 80 women, and 20 children (under 18 years of age). This number is not unduly small; most anecdotal evidence indicates that the core membership of Parker's Society numbered not more than about 300.

To identify the socioeconomic status of the 182 adult sample members, I first identified either their occupations or the occupation of a close family member (parent, spouse, sibling, child). I made the identifications using the following sources:

- The Boston City Directories for 1847 and 1858.
- The fundraising list from 1847, on which the occupations of donors are listed.
- Biographies and biographical articles.

- Parker's journal and letters and notes he made while recording marriages, baptisms, and funerals.

From these sources I was able to identify the occupations of 92 men and 3 women; I was also was able to identify the occupation of a close family member (parent, spouse, sibling, child) of an additional 4 men and 59 women, bringing the total with some status identification to 158.

I then classified my occupation data according to categories described by Knights, *Plain People of Boston*, 149-156. I lumped together some of his categories because I did not think all his distinctions were relevant for my inquiry—for example, between "Unskilled" and "Semi-Skilled" laborers, or between "Semi-Professionals" and "Professionals."

A more difficult decision was to combine Knights's category of "Proprietors," merchants who owned more than $1,000 of real and personal property, with his category of "Petty Proprietors," who owned less than $1,000 of real and personal property. Some may argue that I here am folding a non-middle-class group in with a middle-class one. I felt justified in making this combination, however, for two reasons. First, Parker himself would have classified both groups as "merchants," and he considered all non-Brahmin merchants above the level of street peddler "middle class." Second, various evidence indicates that few if any of the 35 merchants in my sample were in fact "Petty Proprietors." I have biographies or personal reminiscences of about 5 of them, who were all quite wealthy; for example, Alvan Adams was the founder of one of the most important express companies in nineteenth-century America, and Mark Healey was at one point known to be among the richest men in Boston. Of the remaining 30, the City Directories reveal that 2 owned factories, 7 others were importers, an enterprise requiring considerable capital, and almost all of them had enough capital to have a place of business distinct from their residence.

One complication I had making the classifications is that some sample members changed categories between 1847 and 1858—for example, moving from a Merchant to a Bank President. My solution to this problem was to classify all sample members by the earliest identified occupation.

I classified the occupations as follows:

- *Unskilled and Semi-Skilled Labor:* Fisherman; Truckman.
- *Skilled Labor:* Bookbinder; Engraver; Hatter; Housewright; Jeweller; Piano Maker; Piano Varnisher; Printer; Tailor; Watchmaker.
- *Clerical or Sales:* Assessor; Business Agent; Clerk; Land Agent; Police Clerk.
- *Proprietors, Managers, and Officials:* Bookseller; Builder; Captain; Carriage Manufacturer; Commission Merchant; Confectioner; Crockery; Custom House [Government Official]; Dry Goods; English Goods; Express [Propri-

etor]; Fancy Goods; Grocer; Hardware; Importer; Iron Dealer; Merchant; Merchant Tailor; Millener; Oil Factory; Oil Merchant; Proprietor Boston Bazaar; Provisions; Provisions Merchant; Publisher; Shoe Store; Surveyor of Lumber; West Indian Goods; Wood and Coal; Wool Merchant.

- *Semi-Professional and Professional*: Agent (American Anti-slavery Society); Ambrotypist; Apothecary; Architect; Counsellor; Doctor; Druggist; Editor; Lawyer; Minister; Optician; Physician; Portrait Painter; Schoolteacher.
- *Miscellaneous, Unknown*: Widow; Woman; Unknown (Man). Note: I only placed in this category those women whom I was unable to place in another category, according to the methods already described.

The MAM sample is biased in certain respects, but I believe these biases are not strong enough to compromise my conclusions. The MAM sample is dominated by men, and in this respect it resembles the overall list of adult members of the 28th Congregational Society from which it is drawn. Yet I am not convinced that the Society actually was predominantly male; anecdotal evidence indicates Parker's audiences were made up mostly of women—an observation that, if accurate, would be consistent with the predominant pattern of most American congregations. There may be biases in the sources from which the sample, and the overall list, were drawn: more Society Records survive that list men than list women. For example, the Benevolent Committees were exclusively female, and there is a record of only one of them (that of 1854); the Standing Committees were exclusively male until 1855, and there is a record for each one of them (1845-1858). Again, the 1847 fundraising list is overwhelmingly male (95 percent), because subscriptions were taken at places of business. Actually, for reasons that are not clear to me, all the Society Records listed at the beginning of this Note are mostly male, except for the gift subscriptions to Parker and his record of marriages, deaths, and baptisms.

The male bias of the MAM sample would have a significant effect on my findings only if a major percentage of the women excluded belonged to the "Unskilled and Semi-Skilled Labor" category. But this does not seem to be the case. Most of the women who appear in the Society Records seem to have been related closely to men in the Society Records (as wives, sisters, daughters) and therefore presumably shared in their families' middle-class socioeconomic status. This presumption may not be made in the case of widows, for obvious reasons, and therefore I classify these women separately.

I suspect, too, there is also some bias in the MAM sample in favor of wealthier members, who would be more likely to become congregational leaders. Probably the proportion of Unskilled and Semi-Skilled laborers was higher in Parker's total audience than the MAM sample indicates. On the other hand, I do not think the proportion was so high that that audience could not be described as predominently "middle class."

Notes

1. The details of the service here described have been gleaned from various sources: reminiscences, including those of Ednah Dow Littlehale Cheney in John Weiss, *Life and Correspondence of Theodore Parker* (Boston, 1864), 1: 414–421, and in her *Reminiscences* (Boston, 1902), Julia Ward Howe in her *Reminiscences, 1819–1899* (Boston, 1899), and Louisa May Alcott, who in *Work: A Novel of Experience* (Boston, 1875) features Parker (hereafter "TP") and his society, thinly disguised as the free church of the infidel preacher "Thomas Power"; eyewitness accounts, including a hostile one in the *New Englander* for Feb. 1858 and a favorable one from the *Liverpool Northern Times* (Feb. 1859), describing a service the previous summer (a clipping found in the Society Book, which is in the 28th Congregational Church [Parker Memorial], Boston, Records, bMS 7, Andover-Harvard Theological Library, Harvard Divinity School, Cambridge, Mass.); and the 28th Congregational Church (Parker Memorial), Boston, Records, bMS 7, Andover-Harvard Theological Library, Harvard Divinity School, Cambridge, Mass. (Cited hereafter as AHTL.) No actual sermon by TP is here described, but the themes, structure, and phrasing are characteristic of hundreds of his sermons that I have read. See also Dean Grodzins and Joel Myerson, "The Preaching Record of Theodore Parker," *Studies in the American Renaissance 1994*, ed. Joel Myerson (Charlottesville, 1994), 55–65. For an example of a minister who disliked flowers on the pulpit, see William C. Gannett, *Ezra Stiles Gannett: Unitarian Minister in Boston, 1824–1871* (Boston, 1875), 271; for James Freeman Clarke's use of flowers see Howe, *Reminiscences*, 249. The bronze statue of Beethoven now stands at the New England Conservatory of Music in Boston just inside the Huntington Avenue entrance to Jordan Hall.
2. Frank Preston Stearns, *The Life and Public Services of George Luther Stearns* (Philadelphia, 1907), 114–115.
3. TP's formally installed successors were David A. Wasson (1865–1866), James Vila Blake (1868–1871), J. L. Dudley (1877–1879), and James K. Appleby (1882–1886); others who "filled the desk" for a time but were never installed included S. R. Calthorp (1864–1865) and Samuel Longfellow (1867–1868). In 1872–1873, the Society built the Parker Memorial Building, which was dedicated principally to charitable purposes; the Society Records at AHTL indicate that management of the building became the focus of Society activity. When the building was turned over to the Benevolent Fraternity of Churches in 1889, the Society ceased to exist. See the *Boston Journal*, Sept. 22, 1873; *The Commonwealth*, Sept. 23, 1873; and the *Christian Register*, Feb. 14, 1889.
4. For a description of these, see the Note to the Appendix. Later references to Society Records (e.g., the Society Book, the 1847 fundraising list) come from this list, unless otherwise noted.
5. Cheney in Weiss, *Theodore Parker*, 1:415.
6. See TP's Journal O, 155–157 (Dec. 1851), Theodore Parker, Papers, bMS 101, AHTL; Howe to TP (Dec. 1851, tipped into Journal O, 157–158); TP to Howe, Dec. 6, 1851, °44M-314 (1576) Houghton Library, Harvard University. Journal O is catalogued in the AHTL collection as Journal vol. 3 of the Theodore Parker Papers.

7. Howe, *Reminiscences*, 244–247; see also 164–165, her account of listening to TP's famous sermon on the death of Daniel Webster (Oct. 31, 1852). The discourse was long, so she came home late and found her family impatiently waiting dinner for her. "Let no one find fault!" she exclaimed. "I have heard the greatest thing I shall ever hear!" No other member of her family had heard TP that day because her husband had withdrawn them all from his Society some time earlier. Julia obviously still attended. Howe, *Reminiscences*, 245, says her husband "cherished an old predilection for King's Chapel"; TP in Journal O, 155, notes S. G. Howe "goes to the Swedenborg Chapel." Theodore Parker, Papers, bMS 101, AHTL.

8. Cheney, *Reminiscences*, 104–109; see also Cheney's memoir of Abby May, in *Memoirs of Lucretia Crocker and Abby W. May* (Boston, 1893).

9. Cheney, *Reminiscences*, 102–104.

10. William and Ellen Craft, two fugitives from Georgia who attended the 28th Congregational Society and who were married by TP, were under threat of being returned to slavery under the Fugitive Slave Act of 1850. TP was a central figure in the Vigilance Committee, which prevented this from happening by use of methods both legal and extra-legal. The same week TP was calling daily on Cheney, he was harboring Ellen Craft in his own house, with a loaded revolver kept on his desk at all times. Weiss, *Theodore Parker*, 1:419–420, 2:95–102.

11. See Weiss, *Theodore Parker*, 1:294; Ednah Dow Littlehale Cheney, *Memoir of Seth W. Cheney, Artist* (Boston, 1881), 3, 110–114, 133.

12. Cheney, *Reminiscences*, 102.

13. There was a third controversy in the winter of 1844–1845, over whether TP should be allowed to preach the regular Thursday Lecture at the First Church. By tradition, the lecture was delivered in rotation by members of the Boston Association of Congregational Ministers, to which TP belonged. Other members of the Boston Association wished to exclude him from the Thursday Lecture and after much debate succeeded in doing so by voting to reconfigure it so that it was delivered by invitation of the minister of the First Church (who was at the time Dr. Nathaniel Frothingham, a staunch anti-Transcendentalist). Although these maneuverings received considerable attention at the time and led TP to write his *Letter to the Boston Association of Congregational Ministers* (Boston, 1845), I believe they had only an indirect bearing on the creation of the 28th Congregational Society. TP had already been invited to preach in Boston before the Association voted to exclude him from the Lecture. I therefore will not discuss this controversy here.

14. See, for example, the comments of Samuel K. Lothrop in *The South-Boston Unitarian Ordination* (Boston, 1841).

15. All three publications contained strong attacks on TP's views in 1841. Thereafter, he ceased making submissions to the *Register* and the *Miscellany*, evidently believing there was no point in doing so. He did submit an article on J. A. Dorner's *Christology* to the *Examiner* (see TP's Journal I, 124 [Nov. 18, 1841]), but the piece was rejected. He later had it published in the Transcendentalist journal, the *Dial* (Apr. 1842), and submitted no more material to the *Examiner* until secretly requested to do so many years later. Journal I is catalogued as Journal vol. 2 of the Theodore Parker Papers, bMS 101, of the AHTL collection.

16. See TP's Journal I, 197 (July 11, 1842), Theodore Parker, Papers, bMS 101, AHTL.

17. See also Dean Grodzins, "Theodore Parker's 'Conference with the Boston Association,' January 23, 1843," *Proceedings of the Unitarian Universalist Historical Society* 23(1995):68–70.

18. For examples of such arguments, see on creeds Nathaniel Frothingham, *Deism or Christianity? Four Discourses* (Boston, 1845), 23–35; on ministerial fellowship [Ezra Stiles Gannett,] "Mr. Parker and his Views," *Christian Examiner* 37(Mar. 1845), esp. 268–271.

19. See John T. Sargent, *Ministry at Suffolk Street Chapel; its Origin, Progress and Experience* (Boston, 1845), passim; also, TP's *Letter to the Boston Association*, 7.

20. John T. Sargent, *Obstacles to the Truth* (Boston, 1845), 17–20.

21. On the Fraternity's quarterly report and Waterston's letter, see the *Christian Register*, Jan. 18, 1845; see also [John T. Sargent,] *The True Position of Rev. Theodore Parker* (Boston, 1845).

22. Besides the pamphlets and articles already cited, see the following: [R. C. Waterston,] *Questions Addressed to Rev. T. Parker and his Friends* (Boston, 1845); [John T. Sargent,] *An Answer to "Questions Addressed to Rev. T. Parker and his Friends"* (Boston, 1845); [anon.,] *Remarks on an Article from the Christian Examiner, entitled "Mr. Parker and his Views"* (Boston, 1845); [James Freeman Clarke?,] *Answers to Questions Contained in Mr. Parker's Letter to the Boston Association of Congregational Ministers* (Boston, 1845); A. B. Muzzey, *A Plea for the Christian Spirit* (Boston, 1845); W. H. Furness, *The Exclusive Principle Considered: Two Discourses on Christian Union and Truth in the Gospels* (Philadelphia, 1845); William Ware, *Righteousness before Doctrine* (Boston, 1845). See also the *Christian Register* and *Christian World* for early 1845.

23. See Henry Greenleaf Pearson, *The Life of John A. Andrew, Governor of Massachusetts, 1861–1865* (Boston, 1904), 1:37–38; Howe, *Reminiscences*, 261–262.

24. He had also been influenced by his daughter Caroline, a Parker enthusiast, about whom more will be said later.

25. John T. Sargent, *The Crisis of Unitarianism in Boston* (Boston, 1859), 23. As passages in this pamphlet indicate, Sargent appears to have grown somewhat bitter towards the 28th Congregational Society, perhaps because the Suffolk Street Chapel, his creation, had faded away due to so many defections to TP's congregation; ironically, among the defectors were some who had criticized Sargent for exchanging with TP in 1844. Sargent seems to have resented, too, that his former parishioners, when he came to the 28th Congregational Society to preach, now preferred to hear TP. See for example his letter to the Society, July 13, 1858, Society Records, AHTL.

26. All four of these men are in the "Most Active Member" sample described in the Note to the Appendix. Jackson and May are discussed at greater length below.

27. Dean Grodzins, "Theodore Parker and Transcendentalism" (Ph.D. diss., Harvard University, 1993), 413.

28. Pierpont also made remarks against slavery that some in his congregation found offensive, but temperance appears to have been the principal cause of the dispute. The next few paragraphs appeared in slightly different form in Grodzins, "Theodore Parker's 'Conference with the Boston Association,'" 72–73.

29. The "Fifteen gallon law" made illegal all sales of liquor less than fifteen gallons. Intended to end the retail liquor business, it never was widely enforced.

30. See Samuel K. Lothrop, *Proceedings of an Ecclesiastical Council* (Boston, 1841). Most of the information I have been able to find on the Hollis Street controversy comes from this pamphlet, but see also Jane H. Pease and William H. Pease, "Whose Right Hand of Fellowship? Pew and Pulpit in Shaping Church Practice," in *American Unitarianism, 1805–1865*, ed. Conrad Edick Wright (Boston, 1989), 194–200. Note that there had been months of negotiations and hearings prior to opening of the Council in July 1841, but these had been to determine its jurisdiction.

31. Lothrop, *Proceedings of an Ecclesiatical Council*, 374–383.

32. Theodore Parker, "Hollis Street Council," *Dial* 3(1842):220.

33. In TP's Journal I, 107 (July 1841), Theodore Parker, Papers, bMS 101, AHTL, he records (in Greek characters) and comments on a remark of Dr. Francis Parkman, Moderator of the Council: "'The Council could not condemn Mr. P. for that would only produce a reaction in his favor, so strong was the public opinion of his merit.' Dr P. counted this a fine piece of diplomacy. Is it not Christian?"

34. According to TP, others who did so included George Ripley and Dr. Henry Ware, Jr.

35. Prominent among those who never forgave TP for his attack on the Council were the principal author of the "Result," Ezra Stiles Gannett (later Dr. Gannett), and Dr. Francis Parkman.

36. The speaker was Dr. Francis Parkman, in remarks to the Boston Association. See TP's Journal M, 200 (Nov. 10, 1845), Massachusetts Historical Society. Journal M is catalogued in the M.H.S. collection as vol. 2, Theodore Parker Papers.

37. The other two were Sargent's opponent on the TP issue, Robert Cassie Waterston, and Ezra Stiles Gannett. See Pierpont to TP, Mar. 22, 1845, Parker Papers, vol. 12, Massachusetts Historical Society, where he corrects TP's erroneous statement in the *Letter to the Boston Association* that the three were Gannett, Sargent, and James Freeman Clarke; Clarke did exchange with Pierpont but was not on the Council. Gannett appears to have taken the "Result" at face value, while most of the rest of the Council apparently did not. Sargent, meanwhile, although he signed the "Result," seems to have come around to TP's view of the document once he saw how the other members of the Council treated Pierpont.

38. Sargent to the Executive Committee of the Benevolent Fraternity of Churches, Nov. 29, 1844, in *Obstacles to the Truth*, 20. See also TP's *Letter to the Boston Association*: "I am told that Mr. Pierpont was quite as effectually excluded from the actual fellowship of your association, as even myself. . . . Yet I think he is guilty of no heresy,—*theological* and *speculative* heresy I mean, for in practical affairs it is well known that his course is the opposite of that pursued by most of his brethren in the city" (9–10).

39. Pease and Pease, "Whose Right Hand of Fellowship," 199. Pierpont's resignation did not wholly end the dispute; lawsuits related to the case continued to drag out in the courts for some time.

40. TP to Pierpont, Oct. 15, 1845, printed in Weiss, *Theodore Parker*, 1:256–257.

41. Theodore Parker, *Speeches, Addresses, and Occasional Sermons* (Boston, 1852), 1:35. Cited hereafter as *SAOS*. In TP's famous sermon on the "Perishing Classes," preached a few months later, he identified the how and the who: "[Pierpont], benevolent and indefatigable, where is he? He trod the worm of the still under his feet, but the worm of the pulpit stung him, and he too is gone; that champion of

temperance, that old man eloquent driven out of Boston. Why should I not tell an open secret?—driven out by rum and the Unitarian clergy of Boston." *SAOS,* 1:150–151.

42. Child was evidently a relative of the Stephen Child who, with Jackson and May, signed the above-mentioned request to publish John Sargent's *Obstacles to the Truth,* but the relationship is unclear.

43. Another namesake, his grandson Francis Jackson Meriam, would in 1859 join the secret "army" with which John Brown planned to liberate the slaves of Virginia.

44. See Austin Bearse, *Reminiscences of Fugitive Slave Law Days in Boston* (Boston, 1880), 6.

45. The other two were also stalwarts of the Benevolent Committee, Caroline Thayer and Sarah Hunt.

46. Diary of Daniel and Mary Child, Daniel F. Child Papers, Massachusetts Historical Society.

47. See Grodzins, "Theodore Parker and Transcendentalism," chap. 5, and William R. Hutchison, *The Transcendentalist Ministers: Church Reform in the New England Renaissance* (New Haven, 1959).

48. Except for a period from 1849 to 1854, when Clarke, principally for reasons of health, suspended his ministry. See Edward Everett Hale, ed., *James Freeman Clarke: Autobiography, Diary and Correspondence* (Boston, 1899), 187–188; Howe, *Reminiscences,* 245–246.

49. Peabody to John Sullivan Dwight, June 10, 1841, in *Letters of Elizabeth Palmer Peabody, American Renaissance Woman,* ed. Bruce A. Ronda (Middletown, Conn., 1984), 252–253. There had been some discussion at the time that TP would be invited in as the successor of George Ripley at the Purchase Street Church, Ripley having resigned the year before to start Brook Farm. In the end, the Purchase Street congregation thought TP too controversial and did not invite him.

50. Howe, *Reminiscences,* 247.

51. When TP was preparing for his installation as pastor of the 28th Congregational Society, he originally asked Clarke to take part in the service; Clarke tentatively agreed to do so, but only if he could express dissent at the service from some of TP's doctrines: "[T]here is probably no Unitarian minister in the city who agrees less with *a part* of your theology than I do. Some doctrines which you reject, especially the mediation of Christ, are very dear and important to my mind." Clarke to TP, Dec. 9, 1845, bMS AM 1569 (577), Houghton Library, Harvard University. In the end, Clarke did not take part in the installation. Almost 15 years later, in Clarke's otherwise warmly appreciative memorial sermon for TP, he nonetheless continued to insist that his late friend "was wanting in some of the perception and utterance of some of the truths of the gospel." See Clarke, *Memorial and Biographical Sketches* (Boston, 1878), 127.

52. Hale, *James Freeman Clarke,* 145.

53. Howe, *Reminiscences,* 246. Howe remarks that a friend of hers found the bonnets worn at the Church of the Disciples "of so singular a description, as constantly to distract her attention from the minister's sermon."

54. See also Hutchison, *Transcendentalist Ministers,* chap. 5.

55. Clarke, *A Sermon on the Principles and Methods of the Church of the Disciples* (Boston, 1846), 22–23.

56. Clarke, *Principles and Methods*, 23–24.
57. In Society Records, AHTL.
58. Clarke, *Principles and Methods*, 21–22.
59. The number of African Americans in TP's Society is hard to determine; so far, I have been able to identify only about 15 among the more the more than 1,200 people named in the Society records, including Nell, the abolitionist Lewis Hayden, and the fugitive slaves William and Ellen Craft. Anecdotal evidence indicates, however, that there were many more, especially after 1850, when the Boston Vigilance Committee named TP minister-at-large for all fugitive slaves in the city. That Nell preferred TP's Society to any of the local black churches (two Baptist and three Methodist) is no surprise. Nell firmly supported integrated over separate black institutions. He campaigned successfully for the abolition of the segregated black school in Boston—a cause TP also championed—and criticized the idea of segregated churches.
60. Alcott, *Work*, 202.
61. Theodore Parker, "Some Thoughts on the Most Christian Use of the Sunday," in *SAOS*, 1:369.
62. See "A sermon of Sunday" (MSS sermon #212, Nov. 15, 1840), Theodore Parker, Papers, bMS 101, AHTL. See also "Some thoughts on the most Christian use of Sunday," in *SAOS*, 1:337–391, and TP's speech and resolutions to the Sabbath Convention in the *Liberator*, Mar. 31 and May 12, 1848.
63. In 28th Congregational Church (Parker Memorial), Boston, Records, bMS 7, AHTL.
64. In 1860, Garrison declared that "he did not strictly consider himself a member of Mr. Parker's Society, though he had always attended his ministrations when in his power." *Liberator*, June 8, 1860. Garrison and wife, Helen Benson Garrison, apparently did go regularly to services at the 28th Congregation, and Helen gave money to buy TP a gold watch and silver fork set in 1852. The Garrisons also requested that TP help conduct the funerals of two of their sons and of William's aunt. These activities, taken together, qualify William and Helen as "Most Active Members" of the Society (see Note to the Appendix), despite William's disclaimer, which was prompted, I suspect, by his principled dislike of claiming fealty to any religious institution.
65. Howe, *Reminiscences*, 152–153: "The Parkers had then recently received the gift of a piano from members of their congregation. A friend began to play hymn tunes upon it, and those of us who could sing gathered in little groups to read from the few hymn-books which were within reach. Dr. Howe presently looked up and saw me singing from the same book with Mr. Garrison. He told me afterwards that few things in the course of his life had surprised him more."
66. Ednah Dow Littlehale Cheney, *Louisa May Alcott, Her Life, Letters and Journals* (Boston, 1890), 85, 90. See also Joel Myerson, Daniel Shealy, Madeleine B. Stern, eds., *The Journals of Louisa May Alcott* (Boston, 1989), 79–81.
67. Wendell Phillips Garrison and Francis Jackson Garrison, *William Lloyd Garrison, 1805–1879* (New York, 1885), 3:487–488. Although Alcott was attending the receptions in January 1857, she makes no mention of Brown in her journal; see *Journals of Louisa May Alcott*, 84.
68. To call TP simply uninterested in institutions, as Stanley Elkins has done, is a

mistake. See Elkins, *Slavery: A Problem in American Institutional and Intellectual Life*, 3d ed. (Chicago, 1976), 167–168. In general I agree with the many critics of Elkins's exaggerated and disparaging view of the abolitionists' "anti-institutionalism"; see especially Aileen Kraditor, *Means and Ends in American Abolitionism: Garrison and His Critics on Strategy and Tactics, 1834–1850* (New York, 1969). For a lengthier analysis of TP's view of the Constitution, its links to his religious outlook, and its effects on his political behavior and his position in the antislavery movement, see Dean Grodzins, "Why Theodore Parker Backed John Brown: The Political and Social Roots of Support for Abolitionist Violence," *John Brown: The Man, the Myth and the Legacy*, ed. Paul Finkleman and Peggy Russo (forthcoming).

69. In 1853 and 1858, the problem was meeting the rent or proposed rent. In 1854, TP's public denunciations of Edward G. Loring, Commissioner in the Anthony Burns fugitive slave case, prompted one of Loring's relations, a member of the board of the corporation that owned the Music Hall, to try to terminate the lease the Society then had. See TP's *The Trial of Theodore Parker* (Boston, 1855), 206.

70. In 28th Congregational Church (Parker Memorial), Boston, Records, bMS 7, AHTL.

71. From an unidentified and undated newspaper clipping pasted into the Society Book, 28th Congregational Church (Parker Memorial), Boston, Records, bMS 7, AHTL.

72. Theodore Parker, "Of the one thing needful in Religion and the Church thereof" (MSS sermon #360, Dec. 30, 1844), Theodore Parker, Papers, bMS 101, AHTL.

73. The only notable exception to the rapid demise of Parkerite extracurricular institutions was the Parker Fraternity, started in 1858, only months before the onset of TP's final illness, as a social and educational group for young men and women in the congregation. The Fraternity continued to sponsor lecture courses for the public until the Society went out of existence in 1889. In fact, as the years passed, the Society seems to have rested more and more on the financial and social resources of the Fraternity than the other way around. Fraternity records, including a scribal newspaper, are at AHTL.

74. Hale, *James Freeman Clarke*, 147. Clarke also insisted people refer to the "Church of the Disciples" and not "Mr. Clarke's church"; to designate a church by the name of its minister was conventional in Boston, but to Clarke the name sounded autocratic. See Hale, *James Freeman Clarke*, 146.

75. Grodzins, "Theodore Parker and Transcendentalism," 401–418. See, for example, TP's "The Christianity of Christ, of the Church, and of Society," originally printed in the *Dial* in 1840 and reprinted in *The Critical and Miscellaneous Writings of Theodore Parker* (Boston, 1843), 1–24. Here TP argued that the Christianity of Society was but an "imperfectly realized" version of the Christianity of the Church, which was itself a drastic departure from the (in TP's interpretation, Transcendentalist) Christianity of Christ. The evils of Society would begin to be reformed, TP implied, if the Church were reformed so as to present Society with a higher ideal to aspire to, that of the Christianity of Christ.

76. Orestes Brownson, "Laboring Classes," *Boston Quarterly Review* 3(1840): 358–395, 412–513.

77. "A Sermon of Education" (MSS sermon #412, Feb. 1, 1846), 15–16, Theodore

Parker, Papers, bMS 101, AHTL. "Christianize" reads "Xtianize" in original manuscript.

78. Theodore Parker, "The Mexican War," *Massachusetts Quarterly Review* 1(1847):47.

79. See his installation sermon, "The True Idea of a Christian Church," in *SAOS*, 1:17–45.

80. See TP, "Hollis Street Council," 201–221; and TP, "A Sermon of the Perishing Classes in Boston," in *SAOS*, 1:150–151, quoted in note 41.

81. He began this process of reflection in "A sermon of travels, or the lesson wh[ich] the old world has to offer the new" (MSS sermons #339–340, Sept. 8, 1844), Theodore Parker, Papers, bMS 101, AHTL.

82. Theodore Parker, "A Service to Pay for a Service Given: A Thanksgiving Sermon" (MSS sermon #353, Nov. 28, 1844), Theodore Parker, Papers, bMS 101, AHTL.

83. Theodore Parker, "A Sermon of Merchants," in *SAOS*, 1:163–200.

84. *SAOS*, 1:167, 174, 198–199.

85. Parts of the paragraphs that follow appear in the forthcoming "Why Theodore Parker Backed John Brown."

86. The literature on how the middle class formed is extensive. One book I have found especially useful, because of the subtlety and flexibility of its interpretation, is Stuart Blumin, *The Emergence of the Middle Class: Social Experience in the American City, 1760–1900* (Cambridge, 1989).

87. See TP, "A Sermon of Merchants," in *SAOS*, 1:164.

88. See his "Thoughts on Labor," *Critical and Miscellaneous Writings*, 109–135; "On the Education of the Laboring Class," *Critical and Miscellaneous Writings*, 192–219; "A Sermon of the Perishing Classes of Boston," in *SAOS*, 1:133–162; "A Sermon of the Dangerous Classes of Society," in *SAOS*, 1:201–238; and "A Sermon of Poverty," in *SAOS*, 1:239–260.

89. TP, "A Sermon of Merchants," in *SAOS*, 1:163–200; Theodore Parker, "The Obstacles Practically in the Way of Christianity" (MSS sermon #426, May 10, 1846), Theodore Parker, Papers, bMS 101, AHTL.

90. See TP, "The Obstacles Practically in the Way of Christianity," Theodore Parker, Papers, bMS 101, AHTL.

91. The figure for John Parker's wealth is the assessment made at his death, in the Middlesex County Probate Records. TP's own real and personal property at his death, according to the assessment in the Suffolk County Probate Records, was worth nearly $43,000 (almost half of which was in books). His wife's property in the 1860 federal census, taken a few months after TP's death, was estimated to be worth $30,000. She just had received $15,000 from the estate of her late husband, and their house after mortgage was estimated as worth $8,000 (most of the balance of TP's estate, consisting of his 13,000-volume library, he had bequeathed to the city). When TP died, therefore, her personal wealth, independent of his, was at least $7,000, and their combined worth must have been at least $50,000.

92. TP, Journal M, 50 (Mar. 22, 1845), Massachusetts Historical Society.

93. For three different portrayals of this elite, each valuable, see Ronald Story, *The Forging of an Aristocracy: Harvard and the Boston Upper Class, 1800–1870*

(Middletown, Conn., 1980); Robert Dalzell, *Enterprising Elite: The Boston Associates and the World They Made* (Cambridge, Mass., 1987); Betty G. Farrell, *Elite Families: Class and Power in Nineteenth-Century Boston* (Albany, 1993).

94. Pease and Pease, "Whose Right Hand of Fellowship?" 181–206. For a sympathetic view of their religious and political outlooks, see Daniel Walker Howe, *The Unitarian Conscience: Harvard Moral Philosophy, 1805–1861* (Middletown, Conn., 1988), and *The Political Culture of the American Whigs* (Chicago, 1979), 96–108, 210–237; also, Dalzell, *Enterprising Elite*, 164–190.

95. TP considered becoming an evangelical in 1831, but decided against it, perhaps because the Evangelicals were predominantly lower class, representing what he wanted to leave, while the Unitarians represented the class he wanted to join. See Grodzins, "Theodore Parker and Transcendentalism," 36.

96. TP apparently voted Whig in every election through 1844, with the exception of 1840, when the Whigs' Log Cabin and Hard Cider campaign so disgusted him that he elected not to vote at all. After 1844, TP voted for antislavery candidates and parties.

97. This famous phrase was coined by John Collins Bossidy (1860–1928) in a toast at a Holy Cross College alumni dinner in 1910.

98. TP to Lydia Cabot (later Lydia Parker), Feb. 20, 1834, in Franklin Sanborn's Notes for a Memoir of TP, bMS AM 1342.1, Houghton Library, Harvard University, 16–17.

99. Grodzins, "Theodore Parker and Transcendentalism," chap. 3. The inheritance was from Lucy Cabot, aunt of TP's wife, Lydia. Although Lucy lived in the Parker household for the last dozen years of her life, she, in a will drawn up by her brother-in-law, Judge Charles Jackson, left most of her money to the Jackson family; during the administration of the estate, none of the money promised Lydia went to her directly. TP, in his journal, later estimated that Judge Jackson had cheated Lydia out of thirty or forty thousand dollars. See Lydia's notes to TP's missing Journal N, Theodore Parker Papers, Library of Congress.

100. See Grodzins, "Theodore Parker and Transcendentalism," chaps. 3–5.

101. TP to Samuel Joseph May, Oct. 24, 1853, Autograph File, Houghton Library, Harvard University.

102. Note to "Farewell Sermon to West Roxbury" (MSS sermon #413, Feb. 6, 1846), Ms.E. 2.7, Theodore Parker Papers, Boston Public Library.

103. See Story, *Forging of an Aristocracy*, 135–159; Dalzell, *Enterprising Elite*, 198–224. John R. Mulkern, *The Know-Nothing Party in Massachusetts: The Rise and Fall of a People's Movement* (Boston, 1990), is useful for emphasizing the class dimensions of Massachusetts politics in the 1840s and 1850s; he errs, however, in denying the significance of slavery to the controversy and in insisting that the fulcrum of conflict was between the working class and the elite, rather than between the middle class and the elite. His analysis of the Know-Nothing movement has been partly superseded by Tyler Anbinder, *Nativism and Slavery: The Northern Know Nothings and the Politics of the 1850's* (New York, 1992).

104. When only the 102 males in the sample are considered, the results are nearly identical: 2% Unskilled etc; 17% Skilled; 20% Clerical; 40% Proprietor; 16% Professional; 5% Unknown.

105. Pease and Pease, "Whose Right Hand of Fellowship?" 196–197.

106. Journal of Caroline Healey Dall, Oct. 6 and Nov. 4, 1841, Massachusetts Historical Society.

107. Dall, Journal, Nov. 4, 1841.

108. Dall, Journal, Oct. 27, 1841.

109. Her enthusiasm for TP surely helped persuade her father, Mark Healey, to give him support in 1845–1847 (see above). Meanwhile, William Dall, her husband's uncle, would serve as treasurer of the 28th Congregational Society from 1847 until after TP's death. See also Helen R. Deese, "Tending the 'Sacred Fires': Theodore Parker and Caroline Healey Dall," *The Proceedings of the Unitarian Universalist Historical Society* 23(1995):22–38.

110. In Weiss, *Theodore Parker*, 1:440.

111. Weiss, *Theodore Parker*, 1:444.

Transcendentalism and the Cosmopolitan Discourse

Schleiermacher and the
Transcendentalists

ROBERT D. RICHARDSON, JR.

T RANSCENDENTALISM WAS—AND TO SOME EXTENT STILL IS—A
many-faceted movement in American thought, having a literary
side, a philosophical side, a religious side, and a social and political side.
Many of our best historians and commentators have been quick to recognize the religious origins of the movement, yet many people still think of
the religious aspect of Transcendentalism in negative terms, defining it
mainly as a protest against Unitarianism, much as we often see early Unitarianism as a protest against Calvinism and orthodox trinitarian Congregationalism. But great religious movements are seldom just negative, mere
reactions or protests against something. American Transcendentalism was
more than a rejection of "corpse-cold" Unitarianism; it was, and is, a positive religious movement. It has roots reaching back to Plato and the long
tradition of Liberal Platonism. It owes something to George Fox and the
Quakers; to Jacob Boehme and the mystics; to the seventeenth-century
Neoplatonic and Plotinian spirituality of the Cambridge Platonists; to the
Romantic religious thought of Samuel Taylor Coleridge, Thomas Carlyle,
and John Sterling; to the *sentiment religieux* of Benjamin Constant; to
the moral sense of the Scottish Common Sense Philosophers; to Jonathan
Edwards, Jonathan Mayhew, and William Ellery Channing. But the central
religious impulse of Transcendentalism most nearly resembles the early
religious position of Friedrich Schleiermacher, and many of the defining
moments and documents of Transcendentalism clearly exhibit his direct
influence.[1]

Ralph Waldo Emerson's "Divinity School Address" has strong parallels
with the Schleiermacher of the *Reden* and the *Monologen*. Andrews Norton's attack on Emerson's address takes him as one of its targets, and
George Ripley's defense of Emerson includes a detailed, monograph-
length defense of Schleiermacher as well. The German philosopher and

121

theologian was a major inspiration for Ripley, who once said, "I regard Schleiermacher as the greatest thinker who ever undertook to fathom the philosophy of religion." Theodore Parker's *Discourse of Matters Pertaining to Religion*—which O. B. Frothingham said "presents his philosophy of religion in a systematic form nowhere else attempted"—is based directly and explicitly on Schleiermacher. Frederic Henry Hedge's *Reason in Religion*, which Barbara Packer calls "the definitive statement of mainstream or moderate Transcendentalism," has as its epigraph the opening sentence of Schleiermacher's *Monologen*: "Keine vertrautere Gabe vermag der Mensch dem Menschen anzubieten als was er im Innersten des Gemuthes zu sich selbst geredet hat." (No more precious gift can a person make to others than what he says to himself in his innermost being.)[2]

Friedrich Schleiermacher (1768–1834) had four main claims to the attention of the American Transcendentalists, as he has, indeed, to modern attention: as interpretation theorist, as Plato scholar and translator, as theologian, and as primary religious witness.[3] He is currently best known as the founder of modern hermeneutics, the first to pay serious attention to the phenomenology of reading, the first to recognize the claims of the reader as well as the writer of any given text. He is perhaps least generally known for his work in Plato studies, though he is always acknowledged by Plato scholars themselves. Schleiermacher was the first modern editor and translator of Plato to make a determined effort to present the dialogues in the order in which they were written. His was also the first attempt to present Plato's texts for themselves alone, and not as neoplatonic or proto-Christian. Werner Jaeger calls Schleiermacher the "founder of modern Platonic scholarship."[4]

As a theologian, Schleiermacher has frequently been singled out, even by his bitterest opponents, as the greatest Protestant theologian since Calvin. One recent, admiring commentator says, "Schleiermacher has a secure place among the very few giants of Christian thought from whom theology will always have to take its bearings. He belongs, in other words, in the company of Augustine, Aquinas, Luther and Calvin." Sidney Ahlstrom observed that "for Christian thought, the comprehensive genius of the [Romantic] epoch and the 'father of modern theology' was Friedrich Schleiermacher." Karl Barth, who devoted much of his career to refuting Schleiermacher and undoing his influence, said of his great antagonist, "the first place in the history of the theology of the most recent times belongs and will always belong to Schleiermacher, and he has no rival." Hans Kung says Schleiermacher is "the paradigmatic theologian of modernity."[5]

Perhaps the least recognized, at least in English speaking countries, but arguably the most important of Schleiermacher's achievements is as a personal witness, a primary news-bringer, the single most important person to describe and announce modern liberal experiential religion. This is the Schleiermacher of the *Uber die Religion: Reden an die Gebildeten unter ihren Verachtern* (usually translated as *On Religion: Speeches to its Cultured Despisers*, and hereafter called *Reden*) and the *Monologen* (*Soliloquies*), the Schleiermacher who decisively revolutionized and re-oriented our understanding of religion, a hundred years before William James, by locating the authoritative source of Christianity in common human experience, and not in bibles, a historical church, or a historical Jesus. The modern focus on the validity or authority of personal religious experience starts with the rigorous post-Kantian work of Schleiermacher.

"There are two points of view," Schleiermacher wrote, "from which everything taking place in man or proceeding from him may be regarded. Considered from the center outwards, that is, according to its inner quality, it is an expression of human nature, based in one of its necessary modes of acting. . . . Regarded from the outside, according to the definite attitude and forms it assumes in particular cases, it is a product of time and history." Our bibles and churches, our rituals and dogmas are products of time and history. One cannot find in them the origin of genuine religious feeling; they are the external results or indicators of it. Therefore, Schleiermacher says, "if you have only given attention to these dogmas and opinions . . . you do not yet know religion itself, and what you despise is not it." Schleiermacher insists that we shift our gaze from the outer manifestations to the inner. "I ask, therefore, that you turn from everything usually reckoned religious, and fix your regard on the inward motions and dispositions." Schleiermacher is quite clear about the inner location, the inner nature, and the inner function of true religion. It is, he says in a much-quoted passage, a basic element of human nature: "I maintain that in all better souls piety springs necessarily by itself; that a province of its own in the mind belongs to it, in which it has unlimited sway, that it is worthy to animate most profoundly the noblest and best, and to be fully accepted and known by them." In this reformulation, religion becomes religious feeling. Schleiermacher specifies: "the contemplation of the pious is the immediate consciousness of the universal significance of all finite things, in and through the Infinite, and of all temporal things in and through the Eternal. Religion is to seek this and find it in all that lives and moves, in all growth and change, in all doing and suffering. . . . It is to have life and to know life in immediate feeling." Schleiermacher locates true religion not in doing or in knowing, but specifically in feeling. "Your feeling is piety," he wrote, "insofar as it is the result of the operation of God in you by means of the operation of the world upon you." Religion then, in Schleiermacher's view, can manifest itself only through the individual (though we will see later that communication of religious feeling to others is also a basic constitutive element of religion for Schleiermacher and for his American followers—for George Ripley in particular).[6]

Just as Emerson would say that his central and permanent belief was in the infinitude of the private man, so Schleiermacher before him said that "each individual, in his inner nature is a necessary complement of a complete intuition of humanity. . . . You are a compendium of humanity. In a certain sense your single nature embraces all human nature."[7]

With this revolutionary relocation of religion in the religious experience of the individual, Schleiermacher boldly redefines and relocates (his enemies would say he psychologizes) the basic elements of Christianity. Miracle, he says, "is simply the religious name for event. Every event, even the most natural and usual, becomes a miracle as soon as the religious view of it can be the dominant." He adds, "to me all is miracle." To the question "what is revelation?" he answers, "every original and new communication of the universe to man is a revelation." He describes prophecy as "every religious anticipation of the other half of a religious event, one half being given." The operation of grace becomes, in this new vocabulary of inwardness, "the common expression for revelation and inspiration, for interchange between the entrance of the world into man, through intuition and feeling, and the outgoing of man into the world, through action and culture." Schleiermacher's sharpest, most demanding redefinition is of belief. He makes a clear distinction between the secondhand acceptance of the belief of someone else and the firsthand experience of belief for oneself. "Belief . . . which is to accept what another has said or done, or to wish to think and feel as another has thought and felt, is a hard and base service. . . . It must be rejected by all who would force their way into the sanctuary of religion. To wish to have and hold a faith that is an echo, proves that a man is incapable of religion." These and other similar opinions made Schleiermacher the great champion—indeed the modern prophet—of personal active religious feeling as opposed to passive assent to formal and inherited doctrines.[8]

Schleiermacher was born in Breslau in 1768. He was sent to a Moravian boarding school and then to the Moravian seminary at Barby on the Elbe. At these schools, Schleiermacher attached himself to the simple, personal, experiential Christianity of the Moravians. This was in marked contrast to the Enlightenment rationalism of his pastor-father. Schleiermacher moved to Berlin in 1796 as pastor of the Berlin Charity Hospital. In Berlin he became part of the brilliant circle around Henriette Herz, in whose salon he also met Friedrich Schlegel. Schlegel and Herz together inspired Schleiermacher to undertake serious original work. His *Reden* appeared in 1799; his *Monologen* in 1800. In Berlin he also began, with Schlegel, his edition of Plato and, in 1808, he met and subsequently married Henriette von Willich. In 1810, when the University of Berlin was founded, Schleiermacher was appointed to teach theology there. Over the next ten years he lectured on hermeneutics, pedagogy, and theology, and he prepared his magisterial *Der christliche Glaube* (usually translated as *The Christian Faith*, hereafter referred to as the *Glaubenslehre*), which appeared in 1821.

The *Glaubenslehre* is Schleiermacher's great systematic work, a rigorous, exhaustive re-examination of the entire body of orthodox Protestant doctrine, a work on the scale of Calvin's *Institutes*. The Schleiermacher of the *Glaubenslehre* is quite different from the early Schleiermacher, despite strenuous attempts by him and others to reconcile the two ends of his life and thought. While the early work emphasizes the religious impulse in the human heart, the late work is a comprehensive attempt to demonstrate how every jot and tittle of standard Protestant dogma and church observance and biblical interpretation are authoritative not because the church or the Bible says so, but because it all derives from our human experience. Thus, what seemed at the start of his career to be a message about the primacy of individual religious feeling became, in the *Glaubenslehre*, a point-by-point defense of the standard, trinitarian, Protestant status quo. Schleiermacher's method was indeed consistent with his earlier work, when he declared in the *Glaubenslehre*, "all doctrines properly so-called must be extracted from the Christian religious self-consciouness, *ie* the inward experience of Christian people." But what was dismaying to some American liberals about the *Glaubenslehre* was that Schleiermacher found, with enormous learning and rigorous logic, that every doctrine of orthodoxy was a result of and sanctioned by the same human nature that had seemed so open to personal and therefore new religious experience in the *Reden* and the *Monologen*. To put it another way, the early Schleiermacher seemed to favor a liberal, personal, experiential approach to religion, while the later Schleiermacher seemed only to have found a new way to derive and justify the old standard dogmatic wall of Protestant orthodoxy. But if the liberals were dismayed by the *Glaubenslehre*, many of the orthodox also viewed it with alarm. It might reaffirm every single doctrine in the church, but it did so on the authority of human experience not on the authority of the Bible or the church. And because the *Glaubenslehre* thus amounted to a defense of orthodoxy, albeit on semipsychological grounds that clearly prefigure William James, it was the early Schleiermacher who was, far and away, most important for the Transcendentalists.[9]

Physically, Schleiermacher—whose name was a mouthful even for his friends, who called him "Schleier"—was very short and near-sighted, and he suffered from stomach pains all his life. He had a long face with a prominent chin and he wore a "slight expression of irony." He was physically active and made quick movements. He had a small lantern "constructed so as to admit of its being fastened in the button hole of his coat," and thus dressed he made his way every night through the empty and dark streets of Berlin on his way to the Herzes. When he botanized he wore a "green jacket and light colored trousers with a tin case slung across his back." His great feature was his eyes. A portrait of him as a young man shows a handsome, open face with enormous eyes. George Bancroft, who knew him well, said he had "an expressive countenance and an eye that flashes fire continually." Visitors also noted his characteristic gesture of laying his two forefingers on his left eye when engaged in deep reflection. He had a remarkable gift for friendship, without which, as he often said, he felt he had no existence. He was profoundly influenced by women, interested in women's points of view, and is indeed one of the few men on record as sometimes wishing he were a woman. He had a power of sympathy and a gift for phrase that reach us easily across time and language. To his sister he once wrote, "In dying, every living being deals out death, and he who has lost many friends by death dies at last by their hand, because excluded from all action upon those who constituted its world, and thrown back upon itself, the spirit consumes itself." He was a much-loved as well as an admired man, and when he died in 1834, the same year as Coleridge, newspapers as far away as America described his last hours in moving detail.[10]

Schleiermacher is a liberal Platonist. He believes that the world is as full as possible with the greatest possible number of different things and beings, that the key to the good life is reason, and that the invisible world reveals itself only in the visible. His deepest convictions go back to the *Timaeus*, "God gave the sovereign part of the human soul to be the divinity of each one"; to Proverbs 20:27, "The spirit of man is the candle of the Lord"; and to Luke 17:21, "For behold, the kingdom of God is within you." The temper of his mind is Arminian rather than Calvinistic, Erasmian rather than Lutheran. He draws heavily on Shaftesbury, not on Hobbes, and on Herder rather than Hume. Liberal Platonism, rooted in the *Timaeus*, the *Meno*, the *Phaedo*, and the *Phaedrus* rather than in the *Republic*, not only emphasizes the divine within, it also idealizes diversity (the world being as full as possible of different kinds of beings). Liberal Platonism also has a latent democratic ethos. The slave boy in the *Meno* has reason built into him; he does not need to be informed or instructed, merely educated. This proto-liberal, proto-democratic side of Plato held sway for the thousand years during which the *Republic* disappeared from sight. One can trace Liberal Platonism from Plutarch and other Middle Platonists through Numenius of Apamea (Fl 150 CE) and other Neopythagoreans to Plotinus, Porphyry, Iamblichus, Hypatia, Synesius, and Proclus. The liberal strain in Platonism survived into the Middle Ages via Olympiodorus, Boethius, and St. Augustine, who was a Platonist before he was a Christian. There is much Platonism in Dionysius the Aereopagite, who influenced in turn Peter Lombard, Albertus Magnus, Aquinas, Dante, Spenser, and Milton. The great mystics from Meister Eckert to Jakob Boeme are Liberal Platonists. In England the Cambridge Platonists Whichcote, Cudworth, Henry More, and John Norris revived liberal Platonism; it passed into the work of Shaftesbury and via him to Herder, Wieland, Goethe, Lessing, and Schleiermacher. From Schleiermacher and the Germans liberal Platonism passes to Emerson and the Transcendentalists, to Coleridge, Carlyle, and Sterling. It continues in the work of the Irish Renaissance, especially in W. B. Yeats, and in the work of William James, George Santayana, Dean Inge, Alfred North Whitehead, and Charles Hartshorne.

Just as liberal Platonism has always been a mediating activity—most often trying to show that Christianity and Platonism are compatible—so Schleiermacher had himself a genius for mediation. The school of theology which trailed after him is called "mediation (*vermittlungs*) theology," and his own work—from his early enthusiastic writings through his textual work with Plato and Paul and Luke to his writing on interpretation and his late work in systematic theology—is strongly marked by a style of argumentation in which competing or opposed viewpoints are fruitfully reconciled. Indeed, his own achievements are all the more impressive in the light of one another; his works mediate each other. The inaugurator of a hermeneutic that tends to deny the absolute authority of texts by historicizing them and by emphasizing the reader's contribution is also the accomplished textual scholar who spent much of his life trying to free the text of Plato from later accretions and rearrangements and "readings." The champion of living religious feeling based on the religious experience of the individual is also the hardheaded, logical constructor of the most impressive system of Christian dogmatics since Calvin, as well as the spokesperson for a religion of communication and community, which had important implications for George Ripley, as we shall see, and which continues to be one of the most appealing aspects of Schleiermacher's thought.[11]

A number of Schleiermacher's other interests still press for our attention. He was an early defender of the dialogue *form* as an essential part of Plato's message. He tried to include a dialogic element even in his own monologues: he thought of the dialogic not as theater or play-shape, but as an effort to capture the living human voice—the spoken voice prior to writing—and to capture the basic teaching or communicating situation, where there is a direct communication at all times on all points between teacher and taught. Schleiermacher came early to understand that religion arises in the inner life of the individual, and that it is each individual's obligation to celebrate and maintain his individuality, his difference, and to maintain and even increase the number of different individuals in the world. At the same time, Schleiermacher believes that any *expression* of religion necessarily involves communication ("The influence of Christ . . . consists solely in the human communication of the Word") and that communication is the indispensable basis of community: "If there is religion at all it must be social, for that is the nature of man, and it is quite peculiarly the nature of religion." Interested only in voluntary associations of people for purposes of communion or worship, Schleiermacher is therefore opposed to missionary activity, a state church, and Utopianism. "We must stop," he says, "at the affirmation that the world is good, and can make no sense of the formula that it is *the best*, and this because the former assertion signifies far more than the latter." Consistently enough, he also insists on the separation of religion from morality. He dislikes the Enlightenment's condescending assumption that religion, whether true or not, is useful to inculcate moral behavior. Schleiermacher insists that moral issues are one thing, and personal religious experiences and feelings another. An early modern voice against the idea that science and religion are locked in perpetual warfare, he argues, as will Emerson and Henry David Thoreau, that both religion and science are grounded in nature: "The general interests of science, more particularly of natural science, and the interests of religion seem to meet at the same point, *ie* that we should abandon the idea of the absolutely supernatural because no single instance of it can be known by us, and we are nowhere required to recognize it." Schleiermacher opposed the mythological expression of religious feeling. His is an early demythologizing position leading eventually to that of Rudolf Bultmann (1884–1976), the modern theologian who called for demythologizing the New Testament in order to arrive at its basic existential message. Schleiermacher is one of the first to announce the death of Satan: "The idea of the Devil, as developed among us, is so unstable that we cannot expect anyone to be convinced of its truth." One reads a long way in Schleiermacher before coming to the subject of sin. He is, in general, much more interested in creation and in preservation, two things he understands as basic and as bound closely together. "We know no divine activity except that of creation," he wrote, "which includes that of preservation."[12]

    Schleiermacher's work met a mixed reception in its own time. Writers admired his *Reden* and his *Monologen*. His great work, the *Glaubenslehre*, was received at the time, says one historian of German theology, with "a feeling of hostile stupefaction." Though he had numerous followers and disciples, some of the most important of them distanced themselves from him. A common difficulty was voiced by Octavius Frothingham, who noted in his history of Transcendentalism that Schleiermacher's work ended by making superfluous the very thing he had set out to defend.[13]

Schleiermacher's considerable importance for thought and religion in America in the first half of the nineteenth century is a complicated matter. He exerted, over time, a substantial influence on Emerson. Schleiermacher's writings were important—and acknowledged as important—for Orestes Brownson, Ripley, Parker, James Freeman Clarke, and Frederic Henry Hedge. Philip Gura has called for more attention to Schleiermacher, Leon Chai has convincingly shown Schleiermacher's centrality for Parker, and Julie Ellison has written at length on Schleiermacher and the interpretation of Romanticism in her volume *Delicate Subjects: Romanticism, Gender, and the Ethics of Understanding*. Schleiermacher was a central figure, a main bone of contention, in the miracles controversy in 1839 and 1840, and Ripley was his chief American spokesman.[14]

Schleiermacher figures in varying ways in the thought of Henry Thoreau, Mary Moody Emerson, Sarah Ripley, Sylvester Judd, Elizabeth Peabody, William H. Channing, and some of their friends and correspondents. His impact on English liberal religious thought—on Coleridge, Connop Thirlwall, the Hare brothers, Sarah Austin, and John Sterling—has not been fully explored, though Evelyn Shaffer has written on Coleridge and Schleiermacher's hermeneutics, and Anthony Harding has written about the importance of the religious opinions of Schleiermacher for Coleridge and Sterling. The question of Schleiermacher's influence is greatly complicated by the fact that he was an important figure not only for the Transcendentalists, but also for such mainstream Unitarians as Convers Francis and James Walker, and also for the opposition forces of Congregationalist Orthodoxy centered at Andover, including Moses Stuart, Edward Robinson, Edwards A. Park, and Bela Bates Edwards.[15]

Schleiermacher's influence on America began with Germaine de Staël's *Germany* (1810–1813), the book that first sparked wide public interest in German thought and culture, and that may be said to have launched the steady procession of American students who went to Germany to study. De Staël mentions Schleiermacher in her chapter on Protestantism, and her treatment of religion, which occupies a good fraction of her book, is based on Schleiermacher in a fundamental way. Her definition of religion as "the feeling of the infinite" is close to Schleiermacher's own sense of religion, in his early work, as a feeling for the infinite in the finite. What is noteworthy about this definition is not the easily mocked vagueness of the "Infinite" (by which De Staël means the divine), but the idea that religion is based not in books, leaders, and buildings, but in human experience, and in the human feelings rather than the mind.[16]

In 1818, eighteen-year-old George Bancroft set out to earn a German Ph.D. In his charge was Frederic Hedge, aged thirteen, bound for a German gymnasium. By 1819 Bancroft—though he was studying in Göttingen—had heard of Schleiermacher. In 1820 Bancroft took his degree, then moved on to Berlin, where he took a course with Schleiermacher on "the science of education" and became acquainted with the great man and his wife. Bancroft's letters to Harvard President John T. Kirkland during the fall of 1820 are full of warm, humorous, admiring glimpses of Schleiermacher. "A few evenings ago I was at his house," he wrote Kirkland on November 5. "A stupid German Professor, who had been to seek his fortune at St. Petersburg was there too, a perfect boor in his manners, and talking incessantly, though he did not know how to converse properly. As he went away Schleiermacher showed him to the door; but immediately on returning from lighting him out, the whole company fell upon the Doctor, to know how he could invite such a cub to a family supper. His wife seized him with strong hands by the collar, and began shaking the little philosopher most playfully. He cried for mercy and forbearance, jumped two feet high, demanding to be heard—and was at length heard and pardoned." In February 1821, when Bancroft was bound for home, he paid a final visit to Schleiermacher. "The last of all whose friendly hand was clasped in mine was Schleiermacher," wrote Bancroft. "He is the first pulpit orator in Germany, and besides that most learned scholar and acute Philosopher." The previous November he had written Kirkland, "I honour Schleiermacher above all German scholars." In 1823 Bancroft and Joseph Cogswell opened a school in Northampton, Massachusetts, where they put into practice the ideas of Johan Heinrich Pestalozzi and Schleiermacher.[17]

In 1825 William Emerson was in Germany, writing home to his brother Waldo that Schleiermacher was high on the list of reasons to study in Germany.[18] By this time, there was a second edition of the English translation of Schleiermacher's *Critical Essay on the Gospel of St. Luke*, and a copy soon found its way into Waldo Emerson's hands. This volume had a 154-page "Translator's Introduction" by Connop Thirlwall; it was a detailed survey of the biblical criticism of the preceding twenty-five years. Thirlwall began with the positions of Johann L. Hug (that the three synoptic gospel writers copied from one another) and Johann G. Eichhorn (that there was an earlier, now-disappeared gospel from which the existing ones descend).

Schleiermacher's gift for mediation and his disarming good faith can be seen in his opening claim that "the most pure, simple faith, and the keenest investigation are one and the same thing, inasmuch as no one who wants to believe what is of divine origin can wish to believe illusions, whether old or new, whether of others or his own." The tone, the comparative technique, and the historical positioning of both Schleiermacher and Thirlwall have a modern ring. Schleiermacher concludes, for example, that the first chapter of Luke was an "originally independent composition . . . written in all probability in Aramaic by a Christian of the more liberal Judaizing school," and the chapter "belongs to the period in which there still remained some disciples of John who had not yet come over to Christianity." This book was read and annotated by Coleridge in England and by Emerson in America.[19]

By 1827, Frederic Hedge, who was back in America, was reading Schleiermacher's *Predigten* (Sermons) in German. That same year, Schleiermacher himself noted that yet another American had arrived with a letter from Bancroft. This was probably Edward Robinson, of Andover and later of Union Theological Seminary, the first editor of the orthodox *Biblical Repository* started in 1831 and published at Andover, Massachusetts.[20]

The first strong evidence that Waldo Emerson's thought and faith were being shaped in a significant way by Schleiermacher came in 1829. Early that January, Emerson wrote to his aunt Mary Moody Emerson; he had fallen in love with Ellen Tucker and she with him. He felt extravagantly happy, happy "to the brink of fear" as he will later say. He told Aunt Mary about his new "felicity," and of "an apprehension of reverses always arising from success." His mind was already stamped with the habit of thought he would spell out in "Compensation." Happiness made him aware of fear— fear of losing happiness no doubt—and personal prosperity moved him to reflect not on independence but the opposite. This revealing letter goes on: "I cannot find in the world within or without any antidote any bulwark against fear like this; the frank acknowledgment of unbounded dependence. Let into the heart that is filled with prosperity the idea of God and it smoothes the giddy precipices of human pride to a substantial level, it harmonizes the condition of the individual with the economy of the universe." The striking phrase here is "the frank acknowledgment of unbounded dependence," because this is the definition of religious faith given by Schleiermacher in the *Glaubenslehre*. "The common element in all . . . expressions of piety, the self-identical essence of piety [*frommigkeit*] is this: the consciousness of being absolutely dependent, or, which is the same thing, of being in relation to God." The *Glaubenslehre* came out in 1821; a second edition appeared in 1830. There is no evidence that Emerson read the book, which existed—apart from selections—only in German until the twentieth century. But the similarity in phrasing is sufficiently striking to suggest that Emerson had at least heard of Schleiermacher's celebrated definition by 1829. Emerson would say, later on, that Schleiermacher had never been one of his great names. It is nevertheless true that from 1829 on there are threads—some of them important—of Schleiermacher running through Emerson's thought. It is also true that from 1829 on Emerson's religious thought runs parallel to Schleiermacher's in suggestive ways.[21]

In the early 1830s Schleiermacher's influence began to spread more widely in America. In 1830 Sarah Ripley was reading his German edition of Plato. In 1831, Emerson was coming to terms with Schleiermacher's work in biblical criticism, as Karen Kalinevitch and Elisabeth Hurth have shown in detail. George Ripley was reading Schleiermacher's *Reden*. James Freeman Clarke read it in 1833. They all read it in German since no complete translation of this book into English appeared until John Oman's in 1894.[22]

While those who would later be called Transcendentalists were thus trying to get at Schleiermacher's early inspirational work, and at his textual work on both Plato and the New Testament, a group of teachers and theologians at Andover Theological Seminary began what would become a long and important engagement with Schleiermacher's later theological writings. Andover represented Trinitarian Congregationalism, the parent stock from which the Unitarians had split off. Andover required its professors to sign an agreement to offer opposition "not only to Atheists and Infidels, but to Jews, Papists, Mahometans, Arians, Pelagians, Antinomians, Socinians, Sabellians, Unitarians and Universalists." The Unitarians tarred Andover as "orthodoxy" and enjoyed making fun of it as "an institution which would have disgraced the bigotry of the middle ages," as a place where "doctrine was hammered in, hammered down tight and the nail clinched on the other side," and where the students' free time was spent building coffins in the seminary workshop. Andover was, however, more complicated than that. While it did indeed stick to Trinitarian Congregationalism, it was home to a group of liberal theologians who were often at odds with their church leadership and who found in Schleiermacher and the mediating theologians in his wake a way to revolutionize Congregational theology and to re-found it on religious experience. This group included Edward Robinson, Moses Stuart (Channing's antagonist in the 1819 Unitarian Controversy), Edwards A. Park, Bela Bates Edwards, and the other Ralph Emerson (1787-1863), a distant cousin of Ralph Waldo Emerson, a minister, professor, and translator. They were all students or followers of F. A. G. Tholuck, who was in turn a student of J. A. W. Neander, the most eminent of Schleiermacher's disciples.[23]

In 1831 the periodical *The Biblical Repository* began publication. It was backed by Andover and edited by Edward Robinson, who had visited Schleiermacher in Germany and who now discussed Schleiermacher prominently in the three-part article on "Theological Education" with which the new journal opened. Many numbers of the *Biblical Repository* had material by or about Schleiermacher and his followers. A new edition of the *Glaubenslehre*—the most important of Schleiermacher's writings for the Andover group—was announced in the January 1831 number. The October 1831 number printed letters showing that Robinson's opinion of Schleiermacher was being sought by English theologians. In the number for January 1832, Professor Ralph Emerson translated a piece by Tholuck on "The Nature and Moral Influence of Heathenism." The issue for July 1832 had an article on "Theological Education and Literature in England" which noted that the English biblical scholar Daniel Veysie agreed with Schleiermacher.

By 1834, the year both Coleridge and Schleiermacher died, Schleiermacher's work was making itself felt in the thought of the Andover theologians, the emerging Transcendentalists, and in mainstream Unitarianism. Emerson reported that Hedge was reading him "good things out of Schleiermacher." The *Boston Recorder*, an orthodox religious newspaper, gave an extended notice of Schleiermacher's death, and James Walker's "The Philosophy of Man's Spiritual Nature" showed a profound grasp of Schleiermacher's main point. Walker observed "that the existence of those spiritual faculties and capacities which are assumed as the foundation of religion in the soul of man, is attested, and put beyond controversy by the revelations of consciousness," and that "from the acknowledged existence and reality of spiritual impressions or perceptions, we may and do assume the existence and reality of the spiritual world."[24]

During 1835 and 1836, Schleiermacher's influence in America moved from background to foreground. James Freeman Clarke wrote to Ralph Waldo Emerson in 1835 suggesting that the latter write something "about Schleiermacher the German Platonic, Calvinistic, Spinozaic, but wholly original theologian. De Wette says he is the greatest theologian since Calvin & Melancthon." Clarke went on at some length, urging Emerson's attention to this German defender of the "intellectual dignity" of "the religious principle." Schleiermacher divided everything into two categories, physics and ethics, that which is and that which ought to be. Emerson, writing to Carlyle a few months later, made a passing reference to Schleiermacher's distinction, which he had learned of from Hedge. The major event in Schleiermacher studies for 1835 was the translation into English of the section of the *Glaubenslehre* dealing with the doctrine of the trinity; "On the Discrepancy between the Sabellian and Athanasian Method of Representing the Trinity" was translated by Prof. Moses Stuart and printed in the *Biblical Repository and Quarterly Observer*. It consists of section 190 of the *Glaubenslehre* plus extensive commentary by Stuart. The whole piece runs 209 pages, and it represents Schleiermacher's effort to show not only that the doctrine of the trinity is grounded in human religious feeling, but that the Athanasian version—the view that the persons of the Trinity are all equal—most accurately reflects that feeling.[25]

The next year, 1836, saw the translation into English by William Dobson of a third important Schleiermacher text, his *Introduction to the Dialogues of Plato*. By June the book, which was published in London, was in America, as Elizabeth Peabody wrote her brother, on its way to John Pickering, a Cambridge classicist and linguist. Convers Francis's "Christianity as a Purely Internal Principle," published this year, shows how another mainline Unitarian had now more or less completely adopted the Schleiermacher position. Francis spoke of Christianity as "the first and only system which professed to build its kingdom wholly within the soul of man," and as "purely an internal religion." He also emphasized what he called "the spiritual principle in man." Another book published this year, Orestes Brownson's *New Views of Christianity*, explicitly referred its readers to Schleiermacher's *Reden* in its opening pages. Brownson's basic definitions at this point in his religious odyssey are pure Schleiermacher. "The religious sentiment," he says, "is universal, permanent, and indestructible; religious institutions depend on transient causes." As for the nature of that religious sentiment, he says, prefiguring Rudolph Otto, the modern Schleiermacherian and author of *The Idea of the Holy* (1923), religion is "the conception, or sentiment, of the Holy, that which makes us think of something as reverend, and prompts us to revere it."[26]

George Ripley was even more deeply involved with Schleiermacher's work. In 1836 he was reading Schleiermacher's *Grundlinien einer Kritik der bisherigen Sittenlehre* (*Outlines of a Critique of Ethics up to Now*) and *Predigten*, and Ripley's library, when it was sold in 1846, had come to include most of Schleiermacher's works, in German, as well as six volumes of German criticism and commentary on Schleiermacher. Ripley's *Discourses on the Philosophy of Religion Addressed to Doubters Who Wish to Believe* was published in 1836. It is not a polemical piece addressed to other theologians, so it does not mention Schleiermacher by name, but the title is clearly indebted to Schleiermacher's *Reden*, and the main point is one of Schleiermacher's main principles, "that the best understanding as well as the clearest evidence of Christianity is to be found in our own experience." This point is worked over in detail in Ripley's Discourse 5, which he calls "The coincidence of Christianity with the higher nature of man."[27]

The clearest expression of Ripley's views at this time is spelled out in an article for the 1836 *Christian Examiner* on "Schleiermacher as a Theologian." Ripley places Schleiermacher after Rationalism and after the so-called Higher Criticism, noting that because of these developments "the want of a more spiritual religion was distinctly and loudly expressed." A return to ancient supernaturalism was also out of the question. "Instead then of taking his stand in the written letter . . . [Schleiermacher] commenced with the religious consciousness of human nature." Ripley defines religion as something that "in its primitive element is neither knowledge nor action, but a sense of our dependence on God, and of our need of redemption from sin." With Schleiermacher, Ripley now recognizes, "in the nature of man, the same signatures of Divinity which authenticate the Gospel of Christ."[28]

On May 29, 1837, the Transcendental Club debated whether the essence of religion was distinct from morality, which is an important issue for the Schleiermacher of the *Reden*. Wanting to claim more for religion than the cool utilitarian calculations of the Enlightenment, Schleiermacher insists that "the fundamental intuition of a religion must be some intuition of the Infinite in the finite." Religion for Schleiermacher always means individual religious experience. In his early writings he is adamant that "the existing forms should not in themselves hinder any man from developing a religion suitable to his own nature and his own religious sense." For this reason, Schleiermacher completely separates church and state. He further says that religion resigns "all claims on anything that belongs either to science or morality." He is particularly scornful of "that common device of representing how necessary religion is for maintaining justice and order in the world."[29]

The central statement of Emerson's mature religious thought, a position which he never abandoned, is his "Divinity School Address," delivered on Sunday evening, July 15, 1838, and soon thereafter printed. Sidney Ahlstrom has observed that Emerson's "point of view resembled Schleiermacher's great romantic answer to the Enlightenment." Emerson's address is largely an attack on what he called "historical Christianity," and on what we call fetishizing the Bible. But the positive elements of the address are deeply congruent with the thought of Schleiermacher.

Emerson begins with the centrality and importance of "the moral sentiment," a concept and a phrase drawn from Scottish Common Sense, but now defined and used in ways Schleiermacher would have approved. Emerson sees the sentiment of virtue or the moral sentiment not just as the starting point for morality, but as the starting point for specifically religious feeling, the basis, so to speak, of *homo religiosus*. "The sentiment of virtue is a reverence and delight in the presence of certain divine laws," he wrote. A paragraph later, he begins again: "the intuition of the moral sentiment is an insight of the perfection of the laws of the soul." Emerson has by now come to understand that revelation *is* intuition: "It [revelation] cannot be received at second hand. Truly speaking, it is not instruction, but provocation, that I can receive from another soul. What he announces, I must find true in me, or reject: and on his word, or as his second, be he who he may, I can accept nothing." With such a personal, present-centered concept of revelation, it is no wonder that Emerson found it, as he says, "my duty to say to you that the need was never greater of new revelation than now." Later in the address Emerson says, in an often quoted sentence, "It is the office of a true teacher to show us that God is, not was; that he speaketh, not spake."[30]

Emerson's address is much concerned with the business of preaching, and perhaps the strongest parallel between Schleiermacher and Emerson is their common emphasis on the fundamental need to communicate one's religious feelings to other human beings. "It is very certain," Emerson says, with unusual emphasis, "that it is the effect of conversation with the beauty of the soul, to beget a desire and need to impart to others the same knowledge and love." It must never be forgotten that for Emerson as well as for Schleiermacher the crucial aspect of religion is that it is both found and communicated at the level of individual experience. "The test of the true faith," says Emerson, "should be its power to charm and command the soul."[31]

Emerson's views, as expressed in the "Divinity School Address," called forth a major public attack. On July 19, 1839, Andrews Norton delivered a "Discourse on the Latest Form of Infidelity" to the Alumni Association of the Divinity School at Harvard. Norton's ostensible target was Emerson's "Divinity School Address" of the year before, but Norton now went out of his way to specify Schleiermacher as one of his main targets. His opening gun is a defense of gospel miracles and an attack on the religious intuition of the individual.

"The latest form of infidelity," Norton says, "is distinguished by assuming the Christian name, while it strikes directly at the root of faith in Christianity, and indirectly of all religion, by denying the miracles attesting the divine mission of Christ." Norton is quite clear about what this means: "The denial of the possibility of miracles must involve the denial of the existence of

God." There is nothing left of Christianity if one removes its miraculous character: "Its essence is gone; its evidence is annihilated." Norton accepts the gospel miracles. Further, he explicitly rejects the possibility of individual religious knowledge or experience: "There can be no intuition, no direct perception, of the truth of Christianity."[32]

In a note ("Some Further Remarks on the Characteristics of the Modern German School of Infidelity") appended to the *Discourse*, Norton singles out Schleiermacher as an example. Noting that it is just forty years since the publication of the *Reden*, Norton says Schleiermacher "professes to have written it . . . through 'a divine call,' a 'heavenly impulse.'" Norton calls Schleiermacher a pantheist and notes disapprovingly his enthusiasm for Spinoza. "Religion, according to him [Schleiermacher], is the sense of the union of the individual with the universe, with Nature, or, in the language of the sect, with the One and All. It is a feeling: it has nothing to do with belief or action; it is unconnected with morality; their provinces are different; it is independent of the idea of a personal God. The idea of a personal God is pure mythology." Norton's case against Schleiermacher has become the standard one; it has been echoed most recently in the writings of Karl Barth, who holds that Schleiermacher has cut us off from the Bible and the Church as authorities. "Until better instructed," he writes, with belligerent humility, "I can see no way from Schleiermacher, or from his contemporary epigones, to the chroniclers, prophets and wise ones of Israel, to those who narrate the story of the life, death, and resurrection of Jesus Christ, to the word of the apostles—no way to the God of Abraham, Isaac, and Jacob and the Father of Jesus Christ, no way to the great tradition of the Christian Church."[33]

It was George Ripley who rose in 1839 to Emerson's and to Schleiermacher's defense with a series of three "Letters" to Norton. These letters, which together amount to 419 printed pages, have generally been taken as a defense of personal, intuitional Christianity, of Emerson, and of Transcendentalism. This is quite true, but the actual form Ripley's defense takes is a long, detailed exposition of the views of Spinoza and Schleiermacher. Eighteen pages of Ripley's first letter and 129 pages of the third letter are devoted exclusively to Schleiermacher. Ripley's "Letters" are the fullest exposition of Schleiermacher's religious views in English in the first half of the nineteenth century; they deserve to be much better known.[34]

In calling Schleiermacher a pantheist and in lumping him with Spinoza, Norton was repeating charges that had been made against Schleiermacher in Germany when the *Reden* first came out. Schleiermacher himself had replied in the second edition of the *Reden* to the charges of pantheism and of denial of a personal God, and, at great length, in the *Glaubenslehre*.

Most notably, Schleiermacher had taken the easily distorted definition of religion as a feeling of the Infinite as revealed in the finite and, by the time of the *Glaubenslehre*, had made it more specific—if less Platonic—by calling it a feeling of complete dependence. In the 149 pages he devotes to Schleiermacher, Ripley translates long passages from the *Reden*, from the *Glaubenslehre*, and especially from the *Predigten* (Ripley gives the reader almost 50 printed pages he has translated from Schleiermacher's sermons) in an effort to give a balanced and detailed account of Schleiermacher's mature views. Ripley was at pains to refute Norton's particular charges, of course, but he never lost sight of his main purpose, which was to present Schleiermacher as a deeply religious person, anything but the "infidel" Norton rashly called him. Ripley quoted prominently from the closing paragraphs of Schleiermacher's first speech in the *Reden*: "I maintain that piety is the necessary and spontaneous product of the depths of every elevated nature; that it possesses a rightful claim to a peculiar province in the soul, over which it may exercise an unlimited sovereignty; that it is worthy, by its intrinsic power, to be a source of life to the most noble and exalted minds."[35]

Schleiermacher's influence expanded in the late 1830s and early 1840s to most of the Transcendentalists. Thoreau's knowledge of Schleiermacher and his disciples came via one of the books cited by Ripley in his "Letters," a curious collection called *Selections from German Literature*, by B. B. Edwards and E. A. Park. Edwards and Park were two of Andover's leading liberals. This volume, which Thoreau recommended to Isaiah Williams when the latter requested a reading list on Transcendentalism, is a philosophical and theological volume, not a literary one. The selections are mostly by or about Tholuck and Carl Ullmann, both followers of Schleiermacher. There is also a translation of Tennemann's *Life of Plato* and a discussion, by Edwards, of recent Plato scholarship, in which Schleiermacher figures prominently. The entire volume is strongly Platonic and strongly Schleiermacherian. Presenting a sort of modern Christian Humanism, it seeks to ally modern religious studies in America with Plato and with modern German Idealism rather than with Aristotle and modern British Empiricism. Ripley's and Thoreau's uses of this book, suggest that by the late 1830s the Transcendentalists and the Andover Liberals stood—perhaps uneasily—together against the old-fashioned literalist Norton, who found himself more and more alone, as even the mainstream Unitarians such as James Walker came down on the side of Schleiermacher and Emerson.[36]

Schleiermacher turned up everywhere in the early 1840s. Hedge was reading the *Predigten* in 1840, Parker's April 1840 review of David

Strauss's *Life of Jesus* discussed Schleiermacher, Sylvester Judd was reading him, and Mary Moody Emerson reported that Louisa Payson was reading all of Schleiermacher's "system." Schleiermacher was represented in *Fragments of German Prose Writers* (1841), edited by Carlyle's friend Sarah Austin, and James Freeman Clarke's translation of W. M. L. De Wette's *Theodore* discussed Schleiermacher, as did De Wette himself in a letter to Clarke of March 13, 1841. Parker's *Dial* essay on "German Literature" of January 1841 mentioned Schleiermacher, and Charles Stearns Wheeler was reading the *Reden* this same year.[37]

In 1842 Theodore Parker published his *Discourse of Matters Pertaining to Religion*. Parker's concept of religion as developed in this volume is, as Leon Chai has ably shown, pure Schleiermacher. Parker called his opening chapter "The Religious Element." He claims that the "institution of Religion, like Society, Friendship, and Marriage, comes out of a principle deep and permanent in the constitution of man." Parker restates this with his customary clarity, saying, "there is in us a spiritual nature, which directly and legitimately leads to Religion." Not only is this element in us, but "we feel conscious of this element in us." Parker argues that philosophically we can examine the body, the understanding, the affections, and the moral sense, "and behind all these, and deeper down, beneath all the shifting phenomena of life, we discover the *religious element of man*" (Parker's emphasis). Pressing further, he finds "as the ultimate fact, that the religious element first manifests itself in our consciousness by a feeling of need, of want, in one word, by a *sense of dependence*" (Parker's emphasis). A lengthy footnote cites Schleiermacher and his commentators explicitly.[38]

At about the same time, Emerson found himself having to deal with Schleiermacher again. In addition to his early comments to Mary Moody Emerson about dependence, his use of Schleiermacher on Luke for his vestry lectures of 1831, Hedge's and Clarke's insistence that he look into or write about Schleiermacher, and the now-public centrality of Schleiermacher to his friends Parker and Ripley, he was himself now being compared to Schleiermacher on account of his "Divinity School Address." A comment in *Frazer's Magazine* for February 1841 classed Emerson's writing with Goethe's *Wilhelm Meister* and Schleiermacher's *Reden*, and Carlyle's friend John Sterling wrote to William Coningham that "in the rhetorical form with which he [Emerson] clothes his philosophy he resembles a little Schleiermacher in the beautiful *Reden*."[39]

In a journal entry titled "Facts" and dated July 1841, Emerson made one of his frequent attempts to face up to the reality and pressure of the past he so often raged against. He wrote:

All is for thee but thence results the inconvenience that all is against thee which thou dost not make thine own. Victory over things is the destiny of man; of course until it be accomplished it is the war & insult of things over him. He may have as much time as he pleases, as long as he likes to be a coward, & a disgraced person, so long he may delay to fight, but there is no escape from the alternative. I may not read Schleiermacher or Plato, I may even rejoice that Germany & Greece are too far off in time & space than that they can insult over my ignorance of their works. I may even have a secret joy that the heroes & giants of intellectual labor, say for instance these very Platos & Schleiermachers are dead & cannot taunt me with a look: my soul knows better: they are not dead: for the nature of things is alive and that passes its fatal word to me that these men shall yet meet me and shall yet tax me line for line, fact for fact with all my pusillanimity.

It is significant that when Emerson turned to face the past—the valuable past, the not-to-be-dismissed past—it consisted of Plato and Schleiermacher. Emerson's own best work is in that same tradition.[40]

It may be that Hedge and Clarke and the others persuaded Emerson to read more Schleiermacher, for we next find Emerson referring to him as though he had recently read him. "I have found a subject," he wrote in his journal in 1845, "*On the use of great men*; which might serve a Schleiermacher for monologues to his friends." And, indeed, *Representative Men* gains from its author's awareness of the dialogic element, the way in which Schleiermacher manages even in his so-called monologues or soliloquies to convey a sense that what matters in a text is what passes between speaker and hearer.[41]

By the late 1840s Schleiermacher had American followers in a variety of places and denominations. William Hall was translating part of the *Glaubenslehre* in the July 1849 number of the *Biblical Repository*. John Daniel Morell's *The Philosophy of Religion*, a book by an English disciple of Schleiermacher, was reprinted in New York in 1849. Morell's book had strongly influenced Horace Bushnell, the Hartford-based Congregationalist who had a two-page treatment of Schleiermacher in his own 1849 *God in Christ*. In the South, the Episcopalian John Warley Miles, who had been a student at the General Theological Seminary in New York, returned from his travels to settle in South Carolina, where he studied Schleiermacher and other mediating theologians and where in 1849 he published *Philosophical Theology*, a book that was at once translated into German by one of Neander's students.[42]

In New England, as Emerson was working on the lectures that would become *Representative Men*, George Ripley's translation of the fourth speech
from the *Reden* appeared in Hedge's *Prose Writers of Germany* (1848).
From the point of view of Transcendentalism, this is the central chapter
of Schleiermacher's most important book. The chapter, subtitled "On the
Social Element in Religion," aims "to submit the whole conception of the
church to a new examination, and from its central point . . . erect it again
on a new basis." The conception of religion put forward in Discourse 4 links
religion with criticism, with hermeneutics, and with communal life. It lays
the basis for a theology of community and communication. After the first
three discourses establish the foundation of religion in human nature and
in individual human experience, the fourth discourse extends the argument
to the social level. It is the crucial step from religious feeling to religious
community. "If religion exists at all," Schleiermacher says at the outset, "it
must needs possess a social character." This assertion is founded "in the
nature of man." Schleiermacher's real argument appears in the specifics. "It
is the disposition of man to reveal and to communicate whatever is in him."
The religious person "becomes conscious that he can never understand
his own nature from himself alone." And just as he is "urged by his nature
to speak" (a similar claim is made by Emerson in "The Poet"), it is "the same
nature which secures to him the certainty of hearers." A voluntary community, then, is the basic religious situation: "Mutual communications are
instituted . . . everyone feels equally the need both of speaking and hearing." This basic community of speaker and hearer is all that is needed.
Bibles are secondary, at best: "It is only when religion is driven out from the
society of the living, that it must conceal its manifold life under the dead
letter."[43]
     This voluntary community based on "reciprocal communication" must
remain voluntary and therefore should not, according to Schleiermacher,
go in for proselytizing. It must also refrain from the temptation to think it
has an exclusive hold on the truth. Schleiermacher further erased the usual
distinction between priest and layperson and gave his community a democratic basis, claiming that everyone is capable of being both speaker and
hearer by turns. One wonders if the social thought of Schleiermacher (as
well as that of Charles Fourier) might not lie behind Brook Farm itself.
     The Schleiermacher of the Transcendentalists is the early Schleierma-
cher of the *Reden* and the *Monologen*, not the later Schleiermacher whose
Glaubenslehre ultimately re-justified the church in all its dogmatic detail.
The early Schleiermacher confirmed Emerson, Brownson, Parker, and
Ripley in locating religion in personal religious feeling, in individual religious experience. He also confirmed for them the idea that religious

expression has a necessary communal or social basis, rooted, like individual religious feeling, in human nature—or as we might now prefer to say—in the human condition itself.

The perception that religion is basically an inward matter is not, of course, new with Schleiermacher. It can be traced back to Luke and to Plato's *Timaeus*. The tradition of Liberal Platonism running from the *Timaeus* to Whitehead and Hartshorne has kept it alive, as have the Quakers—especially George Fox—and the great religious mystics in many countries and ages. Schleiermacher's achievement—and that of American Transcendentalism—is to have recast these older traditions for modernity and to have done so with a philosophical, theological, and hermeneutic sophistication that still commands respect.

Indeed, in some respects, Transcendentalism and Schleiermacher have carried the day. Schleiermacher's work was the great precursor, the great rehearsal for William James, and Transcendentalism was a major step between Schleiermacher and James, recapitulating the one and prefiguring the other. More recently, Richard Niebuhr has emphasized the still vital center of Schleiermacher's concept of experiential religion. David Tracy has identified just what it was that enabled Schleiermacher to cut through morality and aestheticism to get at the central—and specifically religious—quality in human experience:

> As the aesthetic sensibility effectively distances itself from any claim to truth in the work of art, so too our own contemporary often religiously unmusical sensibilities may keep at a distance any claim to truth disclosed in the classic religious texts, events, images, rituals, symbols, and persons. Then we become the cultured among the despisers of religion—yet without the explosive romanticism of Schleiermacher's own contemporaries, but with the lowered temperatures, the reduced expectations and sometimes the pathos of a religious philistinism masked as a purely objective cultural sensibility.

And we find even Thomas Merton adopting some of Schleiermacher's central views. "It is a law of men's nature," Merton believed, "written into his very essence, and just as much a part of him as the desire to build houses and cultivate the land and marry and have children and read books and sing songs, that he should want to stand together with other men in order to acknowledge their common dependence on God, their Father and creator."[44]

American Transcendentalism can be regarded as the first flowering of Schleiermacher's ideas in America, ideas which are still alive despite—or perhaps even because of—the efforts of neo-orthodox theologians to argue them down. Indeed the very vigor and determination of his opponents— one thinks of Karl Barth—bear witness to the inner strength of Schleiermacher's thought, so perhaps it will be fitting to give the last scene here to Barth, a scene described by Keith Clements in a recent book. "In 1946 the University of Bonn, like so much else in Germany, lay in the ruins of war," Clements writes. "It was Barth himself, spending the summer semester there, who discovered the bust of Schleiermacher amid the rubble and restored it to a position of appropriate honor."[45]

<h1 style="text-align:center">NOTES</h1>

1. I am indebted to Charles Capper, Ernest Lowrie, and Conrad E. Wright for helping me think through this subject. One modern Transcendentalist—and by no means the only one—is Edward Hoagland; see his "Brightness Visible," *Harper's*, Jan. 1995.

2. Ralph Waldo Emerson, "The Divinity School Address," in *The Collected Works of Ralph Waldo Emerson*, ed. Alfred R. Ferguson et al. (Cambridge, Mass., 1971–), 1:71–93; Andrews Norton, *A Discourse on the Latest Form of Infidelity* (Cambridge, Mass., 1839); George Ripley, *A Letter to Mr. Andrews Norton* (Boston, 1839), *A Second Letter to Mr. Andrews Norton* (Boston, 1840), and *A Third Letter to Mr. Andrews Norton* (Boston, 1840). Ripley's comment on Schleiermacher is from a letter to Theodore Parker in 1852, printed in O. B. Frothingham's *George Ripley* (Boston, 1882), 229. Barbara Packer's comment on Hedge is in her superb "The Transcendentalists," in *The Cambridge History of American Literature*, ed. Sacvan Bercovitch (Cambridge, 1995), 2:498. The epigraph from Schleiermacher appears on the title page of Frederic Henry Hedge's *Reason in Religion* (Boston, 1865). An English translation of Schleiermacher's *Monologen* is *Schleiermacher's Soliloquies*, trans. H. L. Friess (Chicago, 1926).

3. The literature on Schleiermacher is vast. The indispensable guides are Terrence N. Tice, *Schleiermacher Bibliography* (Princeton, 1966); and Terrence N. Tice, *Schleiermacher Bibliography (1784–1984): Updating and Commentary* (Princeton, 1985).

4. Werner Jaeger, *Paideia*, trans. Gilbert Highet (New York, 1943), 2:383.

5. B. A. Gerrish, *A Prince of the Church: Schleiermacher and the Beginnings of Modern Theology* (Philadelphia, 1984), 20; Sidney E. Ahlstrom, *A Religious History of the American People* (New Haven, 1972), 590; Karl Barth, *Protestant Theology in the Nineteenth Century* (Valley Forge, 1973), 534–535; Hans Kung, *Christianity: Essence, History and Future* (New York, 1995), 694.

6. Friedrich Schleiermacher, *On Religion: Speeches to its Cultured Despisers*, trans. John Oman (New York, 1958), 13, 15, 18, 36, 45. Sidney Ahlstrom noted that James's *Varieties of Religious Experience* "can be understood as a twentieth-century version of Schleiermacher's *Discourses on Religion to its Cultured Despisers*." *Theology in America* (Indianapolis, 1967), 495–496.

7. Schleiermacher, *On Religion*, 76, 79.

8. Schleiermacher, *On Religion*, 89, 90–91.

9. The great biography still is Wilhelm Dilthey, *Leben Schleiermachers* (Berlin, 1870). Also useful are Frederica Rowan, *The Life of Schleiermacher* (London, 1860); Martin Redeker, *Schleiermacher: Life and Thought* (Philadelphia, 1973); and Jacksom Forstman, *A Romantic Triangle: Schleiermacher and Early German Romanticism* (Missoula, 1977). Schleiermacher's death was noticed in *The Boston Recorder* for Dec. 5, 1834, and in the York, Penn., *Messenger* for Jan. 1835.

10. Rowan, *Life of Schleiermacher*, 2:3, 4; George Bancroft to John T. Kirkland, Nov. 5, 1820, in *Life and Letters of George Bancroft*, by M. A. De Wolfe Howe (New York, 1908), 1:91; Rowan, *Life of Schleiermacher*, 1:251.

11. On Liberal Platonism, see Daniel Walker Howe, "The Cambridge Platonists of Old England and the Cambridge Platonists of New England," in *American Unitarianism, 1805–1865*, ed. Conrad Edick Wright (Boston, 1989), 87–120; and R. D. Richardson, "Liberal Platonism: Shaftesbury, Schleiermacher, and Emerson," *Symbiosis* 1(1997).

12. Friedrich Schleiermacher, *The Christian Faith*, ed. H. R. MacIntosh and J. S. Stewart (Edinburgh, 1928), 492; Schleiermacher, *On Religion*, 148; Schleiermacher, *The Christian Faith*, 241, 183, 161, 426.

13. F. Lichtenberger, *History of German Theology in the Nineteenth Century* (Edinburgh, 1889), 157; W. M. L. De Wette, in a letter to James Freeman Clarke printed in Clarke's translation of De Wette's *Theodore* (Boston, 1856), notes that De Wette was a student of Schleiermacher's, but that "the dialectic school of Schleiermacher has not been continued." O. B. Frothingham concluded his judicious account of Schleiermacher and Transcendentalism by saying "the transcendentalists, it is true, employed against the 'rationalists' the weapons that he put into their hands. At the same time they left as unimportant the theological system which his weapons were manufactured to support." *Transcendentalism in New England* (Philadelphia, 1972), 51.

14. Philip Gura, *The Wisdom of Words: Language, Theology, and Literature in the New England Renaissance* (Middletown, 1981); Leon Chai, *The Romantic Foundations of the American Renaissance* (Ithaca, 1987); and Julie Ellison, *Delicate Subjects: Romanticism, Gender, and the Ethics of Understanding* (Ithaca, 1990).

15. For Mary Moody Emerson, see *The Selected Letters of Mary Moody Emerson*, ed. Nancy Craig Simmons (Athens, Ga., 1993), 421; for Sarah Ripley, see K. W. Cameron, *Transcendental Reading Patterns* (Hartford, 1970); for Judd, see Richard D. Hathaway, *Sylvester Judd's New England* (University Park, 1981), 264, 269; for Elizabeth Palmer Peabody, see Elizabeth Palmer Peabody to George P. Peabody, June 18, 1836, and Rebecca Moore to Elizabeth Palmer Peabody, Apr. 2, 1861, Sophia Smith Collection, Smith College Library. These connections between Schleiermacher and Peabody were discovered by Megan Marshall. W. H. Channing mentions Schleiermacher in his introduction to the *Memoirs of Margaret Fuller Ossoli*. On Schleiermacher in England, see especially Anthony Harding, *Coleridge and the Inspired Word* (Kingston, Ont., 1985), as well as E. S. Shaffer, "The Hermeneutic Community: Coleridge and Schleiermacher," in *The Coleridge Connection: Essays for Thomas McFarland*, ed. Richard Gravil and Molly Lefebure (New York, 1990), 200–229. On Sterling, see Anthony Harding, "Sterling, Carlyle, and German Higher Criticism: A Reassessment," *Victorian Studies* 26(1983).

16. Germaine de Staël, *Germany* (New York, 1859), pt. 3, chap. 15, and pt. 4, chap. 1, 288.
17. Quoted in De Wolfe Howe, *Life and Letters of George Bancroft*, 1:90–91, 97; Harding, *Coleridge and the Inspired Word*, 141–142.
18. Karen Kalinevitch, "Ralph Waldo Emerson's Older Brother: The Letters and Journal of William Emerson" (Ph.D. diss., University of Tennessee, 1982), 14–20, 207. In some respects it was unfortunate that so many Americans went to Göttingen to study. The university was dominated by Eichhorn and his followers, who were friendly and attentive to their foreign students, but whose critical rationalism pretty well wrecked the faith of most of the young Americans. Had Bancroft, Cogswell, Everett, and William Emerson gone to Berlin and fallen under the spell of Schleiermacher it might have been different.
19. Friedrich Schleiermacher, *A Critical Essay on the Gospel of St. Luke*, trans. Connop Thirlwall (London, 1825), iv, 26, 27. Emerson owned a copy of this book. His notes appear in his *Journals and Miscellaneous Notebooks*, ed. William H. Gilmore et al. (Cambridge, Mass., 1960–1982), 8:486ff. Cited hereafter as *JMN*. Coleridge also owned and annotated a copy. See David Jasper, *The Interpretation of Belief: Coleridge, Schleiermacher and Romanticism* (New York, 1986), 59. Emerson's gospel lectures have been ably edited by Karen Kalinevitch in *Studies in the American Renaissance 1986*, ed. Joel Myerson (Charlottesville, 1986), 69–112, and have been discussed by Elisabeth Hurth in *In His Name: Comparative Studies in the Quest for the Historical Jesus* (Frankfurt, 1989).
20. Hedge's reading is recorded in K. W. Cameron, *Transcendental Reading Pattern*. The new American is announced in Rowan, *Life of Schleiermacher*, 2:308.
21. Ralph Waldo Emerson to Mary Moody Emerson, *The Letters of Ralph Waldo Emerson*, ed. Eleanor M. Tilton (New York, 1939–1990), 7:176.
22. The reading of George and Sarah Ripley and James Freeman Clarke is recorded in Cameron, *Transcendental Reading Patterns*.
23. Daniel Day Williams, *The Andover Liberals: A Study in American Theology* (New York, 1941), 6, 7, 13, 14. In order to appreciate the full influence of Schleiermacher and his followers on American religious thought, one needs a who's who of contemporaneous theologians. The following sketch is meant only to list the Schleiermacher party and to indicate something of their connections to the fountain. Schleiermacher's disciples included J. A. W. Neander, C. E. Nitzsch, A. D. C. Twesten, and Carl Ullmann. Neander's followers included Julius Muller and F. A. G. Tholuck. De Wette was commonly understood to be a prominent leader of the school of Schleiermacher, though he distanced himself from Schleiermacher in a letter to Clarke cited above, note 13. In Germany the School of Conciliation or School of Mediation (*vermittlungs Theologie*), which grew out of Schleiermacher's work, included Tholuck, I. A. Dorner, C. T. A. Liebner, J. P. Lange, H. L. Martensen, J. T. von Beck, C. A. Auberlin, C. B. Hundeshagen, K. P. Hagenbach, W. Beyschlag, Richard Rothe, C. J. Riggenbach, and F. Fabri. Tholuck's American students and admirers included Charles Hodge of Princeton Theological Seminary, Edward Robinson of Andover and later of Union Theological Seminary, Henry B. Smith and George L. Prentiss of Union Theological Seminary, Ralph Emerson of Andover, and Philip Shaff of Mercersburg Theological Seminary. Shaff and John Williamson Nevin (also of Mercersburg) were both "immensely indebted to

Schleiermacher and Neander," according to Sidney Ahlstrom, "Theology in America," in *The Shaping of American Religion*, ed. J. W. Smith and A. L. Jamison (Princeton, 1961). Shaff studied at Tübingen with Isaac Dorner, who was trained by Hegel and Schleiermacher. Moses Stuart of Andover, translator of part of the *Glaubenslehre*, had a string of influential students including James Marsh, Francis Wayland, and Calvin Stowe. Horace Bushnell, the Hartford minister who was sometimes called "the American Schleiermacher," came to his mature views through reading Marsh's edition of Coleridge's *Aids to Reflection* and "Schleiermacher on the Trinity." Ahlstrom, "Theology in America," 610. See also Walter Marshall Horton, *Realistic Theology* (New York, 1934), 27. Bushnell was also deeply impressed by the introduction to Richard Rolle's *Theologische Ethik* which was translated and presented in J. D. Morrell's *Philosophy of Religion* (New York, 1849). The Mediation or Conciliation theologians in America included, besides Bushnell, James Marsh, James Warley Miles, Edward Robinson, Philip Shaff, W. G. T. Shedd, and Henry Boynton Smith.

24. *JMN*, 4:360; *The Boston Recorder*, Dec. 5, 1834; James Walker, "The Philosophy of Man's Spiritual Nature," originally published as "Foundations of Faith," *The Christian Examiner* n.s., vol. 12(Sept. 1834):1–15; separately published by the American Unitarian Association in 1834 and quoted in Frothingham, *Transcendentalism in New England*, 120–121.

25. James Freeman Clarke to Ralph Waldo Emerson, Jan. 18, 1835, *Letters of Ralph Waldo Emerson*, ed. Ralph Rusk (New York, 1939), 1:425. Ralph Waldo Emerson to Thomas Carlyle, Mar. 11, 1835, in *The Correspondence of Emerson and Carlyle*, ed. Joseph Slater (New York, 1964), 120–121. Friedrich Schleiermacher, "On the Discrepancy . . . ," trans. Moses Stuart, *Biblical Repository and Quarterly Observer* 5(Apr. 1835):265–353 and 6(June 1835):1–116.

26. Elizabeth Palmer Peabody to George P. Peabody, June 18, 1836, Sophia Smith Collection, Smith College. Convers Francis, *Christianity as a Purely Internal Principle* (Boston, 1836), 7, 8, 10. Orestes Brownson, "New Views," in *The Works of Orestes Brownson*, comp. Henry F. Brownson (Detroit, 1882), 4:3.

27. George Ripley, *Discourses on the Philosophy of Religion Addressed to Doubters Who Wish to Believe* (Boston, 1836), 48, 50–69. Ripley's library (*Catalogue of a Select Private Library* [Boston, 1846]) contained *Der christliche Glaube* (Berlin, 1830), *Reden Uber die Religion* (Berlin, 1832), *Predigten* (Berlin, 1834), *Grundlinien der Sittenlehre* (Berlin, 1834), *Monologen* (Berlin, 1836), *Vertraute Briefe uber die Lucinde* (Hamburg, 1830), and *Kurtz Darstellung des Theologische Studiums* (Berlin, 1830). Ripley also owned H. Schmidt, *Uber Schleiermachers Glaubenslehre* (Leipsig, 1835); J. G. Ratze, *Erlauterungen in Schleiermachers christliche Glauben* (Leipzig, 1823); C. Rosenkranz, *Kritik der Schleiermachers Glaubenslehre* (Konigsberg, 1836); C. J. Brancis, *Uber Schleiermachers Glaubenslehre* (Berlin, 1834); and A. Schweitzer, *Schleiermachers Wirksamkeit als Predigten* (Halle, 1834).

28. George Ripley, "Schleiermacher as a Theologian," *The Christian Examiner*, 3d ser., no. 4(Mar. 1836):1–46. This is Ripley's translation of Friedrich Lucke's *Erinerungen an Dr. F. Schleiermacher*, with a preface by Ripley. See esp. 3, 4, 5.

29. Schleiermacher, *On Religion*, 237, 224, 24, 35, 18.

30. Sidney Ahlstrom, *Theology in America*, 294; Emerson, "Divinity School Address," 77, 80, 84, 89.

31. Emerson, "Divinity School Address," 84, 85.

32. Andrews Norton, *A Discourse on the Latest Form of Infidelity* (Cambridge, 1839), 11, 22, 32. Norton had opened the attack earlier in *The Boston Daily Advertiser* on Aug. 27, 1838.

33. Norton, *A Discourse*, 43; Karl Barth, *The Theology of Schleiermacher* (Grand Rapids, 1982), 271–272.

34. Ripley, *A Letter to Mr. Andrews Norton*, *A Second Letter to Mr. Andrews Norton*, and *A Third Letter to Mr. Andrews Norton*.

35. Kung, *Christianity*, 704; Ripley, *A Letter to Mr. Andrews Norton*, 135. The passage from Schleiermacher is Ripley's own translation. Lucke mentions the charge of pantheism in Ripley's "Schleiermacher as a Theologian," 18. Hans Kung still finds it necessary to defend Schleiermacher on this point.

36. See *The Correspondence of Henry David Thoreau*, ed. Walter Harding and Carl Bode (New York, 1974), 47–50. E. A. Park was a student of Tholuck. B. B. Edwards and E. A. Park, *Selections from German Literature* (Andover, 1839).

37. Parker's review of David Strauss's *Life of Jesus* appeared in *The Christian Examiner* for Apr. 1840 and was reprinted in *The Critical and Miscellaneous Writings of Theodore Parker* (Boston, 1843). Louisa Payson Hopkins discusses the acknowledgment of dependence in terms that suggest either a reading of or an openness to Schleiermacher in her *The Pastor's Daughter* (New York, 1835), chap. 11.

38. See Leon Chai, *Romantic Foundations of the American Renaissance*. Theodore Parker, *Collected Works of Theodore Parker*, vol. 1: *A Discourse of Matters Pertaining to Religion*, ed. F. P. Cobbe (London, 1863), 3, 5–6. Parker's library (MS catalogue in Boston Public Library) contained the following works by Schleiermacher: *Sammtliche Werke* (Berlin, 1835–1849), *Monologen* (Berlin, 1843), *Vertraute Briefe an Lucinde* (Hamburg, 1836), *Uber Die Religion* (Berlin, 1831), and three volumes of the *Theologische Zeitschrift*, ed. F. S., W. M. L. De Wette, and F. Lucke, (Berlin, 1819–1822).

39. John Sterling, *Correspondence between John Sterling and Ralph Waldo Emerson* (Cambridge, 1897), 37–38.

40. *JMN*, 8:18–19.

41. *JMN*, 9:188.

42. See Horace Bushnell, *God in Christ* (Hartford, 1849), 111ff. For Miles, see E. Brooks Holifield, *The Gentlemen Theologians: American Theology in Southern Culture, 1795–1860* (Durham, 1978), 66–71.

43. Friedrich Schleiermacher, "Discourse Four," trans. George Ripley, in *Prose Writers of Germany*, ed. Frederic Henry Hedge (Philadelphia, 1848), 442, 443.

44. Richard R. Niebuhr, *Experiential Religion: Schleiermacher on Christ and Religion* (New York, 1964); David Tracy, *The Analogical Imagination* (New York, 1991), 155; Thomas Merton, *The Seven Story Mountain* (New York, 1978), 13.

45. Keith Clements, *Friedrich Schleiermacher: Pioneer of Modern Theology* (London, 1987), 8.

Emerson and the Terrible Tabulations of the French

Barbara Packer

I N THE THIRD CHAPTER OF NATURE, ENTITLED "BEAUTY," RALPH
Waldo Emerson declares that a single day can be an epitome of history:
"Give me health and a day, and I will make the pomp of emperors ridiculous. The dawn is my Assyria; the sun-set and moon-rise my Paphos, and
unimaginable realms of faerie; broad noon shall be my England of the
senses and the understanding; the night shall be my Germany of mystic philosophy and dreams." France does not figure in this ideal day, though
Emerson's journals reveal the extent of his reading in French literature and
philosophy. What did Emerson think of the French nation, and what special
role did he understand it to play in the intellectual life of the human race?

Emerson learned French well enough in his boyhood to read it with
pleasure, though the spoken language eluded him.[1] But instruction in the
French language did not necessarily imply that the instructor always approved of French culture. George Ticknor, Emerson's teacher at Harvard,
combined Federalist distrust of French irreligion with Romantic disappro-
bation of French insincerity and artificiality. He began his survey of French
literature by announcing that alone of all the literatures of Europe, French
literature was the "confined literature of elegant society" rather than the
expression of a whole nation's character.[2]

Emerson dutifully copied Ticknor's depressing list of French literary
characteristics into his notebook:

1. Such a conventional regularity.
2. So little religious enthusiasm & feeling
3. Such a false character in the expression of love
4. So little deep sensibility
5. Such an ambition of producing a brilliant effect

6. So remarkable a restriction of success to those departments which will give some kind of entertainment.[3]

But Emerson was already an independent reader with tastes and opinions of his own. His early journals are full of quotations from French writers or allusions to their works. He admired French epigrams for their worldliness and malicious wit as well as for their generosity or magnanimity. He was moved by the religious intensity of Blaise Pascal and of François Fénélon, yet he could also enjoy the sly humor of Montesquieu, who remarked that if triangles were to make a god they would give him three sides.[4]

Emerson valued the French nation for another reason as well. He thought of modern France as above all the land of astronomy and mathematics, whose savants were equally skilled at devising formulae both to account for the motions of the heavenly bodies and to reveal regularity behind the apparent workings of chance. Three thinkers in particular attracted Emerson's notice at significant moments during his career. Pierre Laplace (1749–1827), mathematician and scientist, was for Emerson an emblem of the mind's pure power to solve the mysteries of the universe. Laplace, like the Newton whose work he supported and extended, believed in a universe governed throughout by laws. What we call "chance," he argued, was merely an event whose causes we could not yet discern. Laplace's gift for describing the serene, inviolable order of nature in prose that was itself lofty and beautiful made him venerable to the young Emerson, increasingly dissatisfied with historical Christianity but reluctant to abandon it without something permanent upon which to repose.

Charles Fourier (1773–1837), the visionary theorist who planned to replace the isolated households of competitive society with harmonic "phalanxes" of 1,620 inhabitants, came to Emerson's notice in the early 1840s. Fourier, who claimed that his discovery of the laws of "passional attraction" rivaled in importance Newton's discovery of the law of gravitational attraction,[5] hoped to see human life transformed by social structures that allowed full development of the passions instead of repressing them and that united men and women in communities where cooperation and benevolence had replaced the bitter strife of that state Fourier referred to with contempt as "Civilization."[6]

This melange of ideas was brought to Emerson's attention by his friend and fellow Transcendentalist George Ripley, who in 1840 resigned his position as pastor of the Purchase Street Church in Boston to lead a small group of men and women to found a new community in West Roxbury. In his planning for the community Ripley had read a book written by Fourier's chief

American disciple, Albert Brisbane's *The Social Destiny of Man* (1840), and though other theorists exercised an even greater influence on Ripley in these early stages, Fourier would come to play an increasingly large role in the life of the community Ripley founded.[7]

Emerson resisted Ripley's appeals to join the model community as he later resisted the proselytizing efforts of Brisbane himself. But he could not so easily dispose of the ideas Fourier represented, even though he suspected that Fourier's claims to mathematical inevitability belonged to the realm of pseudo-science rather than science. Still, Emerson was reluctant to dismiss Fourier's protest against the alienation and joyless labor of "civilized" societies; it resembled too closely what he himself had said in "The American Scholar" when he protested that the original divine Man has been reduced in the divided or social state to a grotesque fragment. Might Fourier not be right to calculate that it would take 1,620 modern individuals to form a perfect Man?[8]

The collapse of the various Fourierist experiments in America seemed to vindicate Emerson's conviction that paradise could not be achieved by social engineering, however complicated or mathematically ingenious. But Emerson survived Fourier only to be accosted by a variety of French thought less easy to dismiss, the new discipline of mathematical statistics. Adolph Quetelet (1796–1874), a Belgian who had studied astronomy and probability theory in Paris and who professed himself a disciple of Laplace,[9] applied to the analysis of a variety of natural and social phenomena the mathematical formula devised by Laplace for reducing error in astronomical observations.[10]

Laplace, it is true, had more than once suggested that the method he initially devised to determine the mean value among a number of astronomical observations might profitably be applied to the study of medical and economic questions, or even to questions of morality.[11] Quetelet went further; he argued that Laplace's formula could be applied to the study of any kind of variation in nature or society—the number of crimes and suicides every year in Paris, the height of French army recruits, the date of the lilac's flowering in Northern Europe, the age at which Belgian women first marry. He was convinced that the laws of probability would allow one to make accurate forecasts about the frequency of phenomena usually thought too eccentric to predict or too variable to comprehend. But predictive power was less interesting to Quetelet than the underlying regularity that made prediction possible. Societies, he believed, obeyed laws exactly as regular as those that governed the heavens. Other statisticians might be content to gather data; Quetelet wanted to analyze data to reveal permanent laws.[12]

The statisticical method, however, did not create in everyone the same sense of awe that the publication of Newton's laws had evoked. It was true that statistical analysis revealed impressive regularities in the frequency of even the most apparently random phenomena, but the regular recurrence of crimes, suicides, and mental illnesses hardly seemed cause for celebration. Worse still, statistics seemed to constitute a new form of determinism, uncanny because impersonal. It was bad enough to suffer because you were the victim of the Fates or the target of divine vengeance. What consolation was there in believing that your afflictions were the expression of inexorable statistical law?

To study Emerson's relation to these three very different savants—Laplace, Fourier, Quetelet—is to look at his intellectual development from a slightly different perspective than the one which places him in relationship to German or English or even Eastern thought. It suggests that in addition to a faith in intuition and spontaneity Emerson also felt an equal and opposite attraction to a world wholly impersonal, an order transparent to reason and impervious to individual desire.

Emerson's study of the severe beauty of the cosmic laws began early. Pierre Simon, marquis de Laplace, was undoubtedly the most important of the French scientists and mathematicians named in Emerson's early journals. Born in 1749, Laplace presented his first three papers to the Academy of Sciences in Paris when he was only twenty-one. He was still issuing volumes of his great compendium, the *Traité de mécanique celeste*, while Emerson was an undergraduate at Harvard.[13] During the course of his long life Laplace made substantial contributions to integral calculus, mathematical astronomy, cosmology, probability theory, optics, and the physics of heat. He helped to design the metric system adopted by the French Assembly in 1791; he served as examiner at the new École Polytechnique and as president of the Institute de France. During the brief life of the École Normale in 1795 he delivered lectures on mathematics to audiences of 1,200 pupils in the auditorium of the Jardin des Plantes.[14]

In addition to the many papers and books addressed to fellow scientists, Laplace wrote famous treatises on celestial mechanics and on the theory of probability that brought his ideas within reach of ordinary educated readers. The astronomer Sir John Herschel, writing in the *Edinburgh Review* in 1850, praised these two treatises—the *Exposition du système du monde* of 1796 and the *Essai philosophique sur les probabilités* of 1814—for their clarity and beauty of style.

There is in both a breadth and simple dignity corresponding to the greatness of the subjects treated of, a loftiness of style, the direct result of generality of conception, and which is felt as adding rather than detracting from clearness of statement, and a masterly treatment which fascinates the attention of every reader. Nowhere can be found so great a body of important discoveries, so consecutively enchained, and so distinctly and impressively announced. It is not too much to say, that were all the literature of Europe, these two essays excepted, to perish, they would suffice to convey to the latest posterity an impression of the intellectual greatness of the age which could produce them, surpassing that afforded by all the monuments antiquity has left us.[15]

Laplace, like Newton, demonstrated the mind's power over nature; he was a pure scientist who put his researches at the service of mankind; and he offered in his writings a credible modern version of the sublime. Emerson frequently includes the name of Laplace in honorific catalogues along with such names as Plato, Milton, Shakespeare, Newton, or Goethe. In 1823 he listed a review of Laplace's *Essai philosophique sur les probabilités* among a group of philosophical and religious writings about free will and necessity that he urged himself to consult as quickly as possible.[16]

Later the same year he entered in his journal a detailed precis of John Quincy Adams's 1821 report to the 16th Congress urging the adoption of the metric system.[17] Emerson began the first sentence of this journal entry with "La Place" but then crossed the words out, substituting "A French philosopher," possibly because he was unsure of how much of the 1791 report to the French Assembly Laplace had actually written. Emerson at least knew enough to connect Laplace's name with the metric system and particularly with its joyous promise of a world united under "the same laws, the same religion, & *the same system of weights & measures*."[18]

An English translation of the *Système du monde* had appeared in 1809; a heavily annotated translation of the first four volumes of the *Traité de mécanique celeste* by the American navigator and mathematician Nathaniel Bowditch (1773–1838) appeared in Boston between 1829 and 1839.[19] Certain passages in Emerson's journals, sermons, and early lectures suggest that Emerson was familiar with these works and that Laplace played an important part in helping to provide an intellectually and emotionally satisfying alternative to institutional Christianity at a time when Emerson's dissatisfaction with any kind of historical religion was increasing.

On June 2, 1832, Emerson noted in his journal the difference between his internal agitation and the chilly weather outside: "Cold cold. Thermometer says Temperate. Yet a week of moral excitement."[20] The "moral excitement" to which he refers is the letter he sent to the Second Church requesting that he be allowed to make changes in the administration of the Lord's Supper. Immediately preceding this entry is a passage dated May 26, 1832, which apparently served as the one of the germs of a sermon Emerson preached the following day. The May 26 journal passage reads as follows:

> Calvinism suited Ptolemaism. The irresistible effect of Copernican Astronomy has been to make the great scheme for the salvation of man absolutely incredible. Hence great geniuses who studied the mechanism of the heavens became unbelievers in the popular faith: Newton became a Unitarian. Laplace in a Catholic country became an infidel, substituting Necessity for God but a self intelligent Necessity is God.
>
> Thus Astronomy proves theism but disproves dogmatic theology. The Sermon on the Mount must be true throughout all the space which the eye sees & the brain imagines but St. Paul's epistles[,] the Jewish Christianity[,] would be unintelligible. It operates steadily to establish the moral laws[,] to disconcert & evaporate temporary systems. At the touch of time errors scatter[;] in the eye of Eternity truth prevails.[21]

What is noteworthy about this passage is not just its linking of Calvinism with Ptolemaism but the further distinction it draws between the Sermon on the Mount and local rites like the Passover supper. Emerson is willing to believe Jesus when he says, "Blessed are the poor in spirit, for theirs is the kingdom of heaven," because there Jesus is observing and recording the moral laws as objectively as Laplace had observed the laws of the universe. But when Jesus celebrates the Passover with his disciples he belongs to an archaic world of ritual, of tithe and priest, of "mystic sacrifice" and "atoning blood."[22]

Robert Richardson has argued that this "Copernican" sermon of May 27, 1832, with its "expressed preference for astronomy over conventional Christian theology," deserves to be seen as constituting Emerson's real break with the Church. It is easy to see why Emerson should turn to astronomy when he was looking for an alternative to biblical Christianity. The laws of celestial mechanics are not local or arbitrary; neither are they personal. The impartial Necessity that rules the universe rules every atom with equal force. One cannot imagine Laplace's Necessity speaking of the human race as Milton's predestinating God speaks: "Some have I chosen of peculiar grace / Elect above the rest; so is my will."[23] Toward the close of his sermon Emerson makes explicit the contrast between human text and celestial truth:

> The Scriptures were written by human hands. God intends by giving us access to this original writing of his hand to correct the human errors that have crept into them. Let us yield ourselves with a grateful heart to the instruction that comes from this source and not repine to find that God is a greater, wiser and more tender Parent than we were wont to worship.

The reverence Emerson felt for the great French savants like Laplace and the Comte de Lagrange disposed him initially to be respectful toward any French thinker who professed admiration for Newton and devotion to mathematics. This willingness to be impressed helps to explain in part the complexity of his response to the American disciples of Charles Fourier when they accosted him in New York in 1842. It was not a propitious moment to proselytize Emerson, who had recently lost his firstborn child, Waldo. He had been drawn to New York by financial need, an earlier lecturing trip to Providence having failed to garner more than "a small company & a trivial reward."[24] When Emerson reluctantly agreed to meet Horace Greeley and Albert Brisbane at a Graham boarding house for dinner on the last day of February in 1842 his spirits can hardly have been high.

He managed to survive the evening and even to write a humorous account of it to his wife Lidian. The letter makes clear how thoroughly out of place he felt at this temperance dinner with two determined ideologues.

> Yesterday I dined with Mr Horace Greeley & Mr Brisbane, the socialist, at a Graham Boarding House. Mr Brisbane promised me a full exposition of the principles of Fourierism & Association, as soon as I am once lodged at the Globe Hotel. Il faut soumettre: Yet I foresaw in the moment when I encountered these two new friends here, that I cannot content them. They are bent on popular action: I am in all my theory, ethics, & politics a poet and of no more use in their New York than a rainbow or a firefly.

Unfortunately for Emerson, Brisbane made good his promise to explain Fourierism in greater detail. On March 3 they had a meeting at the Globe Hotel during which Brisbane tried to indoctrinate Emerson in "the high mysteries of 'Attractive Industry.'"

> He wishes me "with all my party," to come in directly & join him. What palaces! What concerts! What pictures lectures poetry &

flowers. Constantinople it seems Fourier showed was the natural capital of the World, & when the Earth is planted & gardened & templed all over with "Groups" & "Communities" each of 2000 men & 6000 acres, Constantinople is to be the metropolis & we poets & Miscellaneous transcendental persons who are too great for your Concords & New Yorks will gravitate to that point for music & architecture & society such as wit cannot paint nowadays.

The indoctrination continued the next night at Brisbane's boarding house. It was an "animated" conversation, according to Emerson; he called it a skirmish in the "old war, Omnipotence of Arrangements versus Power of the Soul."[25]

There is no doubt which side Emerson took in the argument, but his defense of the soul's power might not have been quite as confident as has sometimes been supposed from the fact that he had published his famous first book of essays, containing "Self-Reliance," "The Over-Soul," "Circles," and "Spiritual Laws," only the previous year. By the time the book was published he was aware that the younger members of his own circle were beginning to regard his emphasis on the individual as anachronistic, even dangerous.

Some of Emerson's bemusement comes from the dramatically foreshortened nature of his career as a published author. A promising author at age thirty-three, a notorious heretic by thirty-five, Emerson found himself at thirty-eight in the position of elder statesman to a movement of younger idealists who found his individualism retrograde. To go from *enfant terrible* to *éminence grise* in three years would disconcert anyone; Emerson's comment about the difference between his own way of looking at things and that of the younger generation shows signs of annoyance. "The young people, like Brownson, Channing, Greene, E[lizabeth]. P[almer]. P[eabody]., & possibly Bancroft think that the vice of the age is to exaggerate individualism, & they adopt the word *l'humanité* from Le Roux, and go for '*the race*.' Hence the Phalanx, owenism, Simonism, the Communities."[26]

Still, Emerson remained more interested in communitarian schemes, and in Fourier's schemes in particular, than this passage might suggest. He could mock Fourier's imagined utopia, but at the same time felt constrained to acknowledge that "in a day of small, sour, & fierce schemes one is admonished & cheered by a scheme of such bold & generous air & proportion; there is an intellectual courage & strength in it which is superior & which is so much truth & destined to be fact [.]" In 1843 he copied into his journal biographical information about Saint-Simon and quotations from his works, including the final sentence from his 1814 tract, "Reorganization of European Society": "The golden Age is not behind but before us it consists in the perfection of the social order; our fathers have not seen it; our children will realize it; we must smooth the road for them."[27]

Dreams like these were too close to Emerson's own millenarian hopes to renounce outright. *Nature*, after all, had asserted that the axioms of physics translate the laws of ethics; its concluding chapter had prophesied the disappearance of spiders, snakes, prisons, and madhouses before a conquering influx of spirit. Was this really so different from Fourier's belief that his theory of "passional attraction" was the behavioral equivalent of Newton's law of gravity, or his cheerful prediction that the universal tillage of "Attractive Industry" will replace the noxious fluids that now impest the planet with healthy "imponderable fluids" and creatures useful to Man?[28]

Rejecting such visions meant that Emerson was renouncing the dreams of his youth and the still-living aspirations of many younger members of his loosely defined movement. On the other hand, he could neither share the young people's enthusiasm for "the race" nor accept the philosophical determinism that reduced each individual to stuff for social forces to shape. This kind of determinism Emerson associated with a certain pitiliess French mathematical spirit, a spirit he thought he could detect behind Fourier's elaborate schemes.

Emerson called the tendency to reduce reality to numbers "ciphering," and he thought of it as "specially French"; in a sour mood he could call the two great architects of the metric system, Laplace and Lagrange, nothing but "walking metres & destitute of worth."[29] The national tendency to heartlessness, however, makes Fourier's schemes all the more admirable:

> One is not to criticize the Fourier movement with too much severity, nor the genius of Fourier, but to rejoice on so favorable an indication. When in that godless French nation a genuine Frenchman appears, as national a Frenchman as Napoleon himself, and though, like the nation, devoid of all religion & morality, yet goes for philanthropy, solves the problem of human misery in a new & French way,—it is the same auspicious sign as this other, that Punch in London goes for philanthropy, and is a feather blowing the right way at last.[30]

Those who know only Emerson's mocking comments about Fourierism are likely to be surprised at discovering how strong were his hopes for its success, hopes at their most intense during 1843–1845, when Brook Farm was reorganizing itself into a model phalanx along explicitly Fourierist lines. The closing paragraph of the essay "Experience," published in 1844, draws back from a completely skeptical or despairing conclusion about the possibilities of successful reform just as Emerson's ridicule of Fourier's schemes had dissolved into appreciation of the spirit behind them. The paragraph from "Experience" begins in the accents of middle-aged skepticism, but at the crucial moment it recovers the voice of hope—or if not of hope, at least of the willingness to encourage others:

> I have not found that much was gained by manipular attempts to realize the world of thought. Many eager persons successively make an experiment in this way, and make themselves ridiculous. They acquire democratic manners, they foam at the mouth, they hate and deny. Worse, I observe, that, in the history of mankind, there is never a solitary example of success,—taking their own tests of success. I say this polemically, or in reply to the inquiry, why not realize your world? But far be from me the despair which prejudges the law by a paltry empiricism,—since there never was a right endeavor, but it succeeded. Patience and patience, we shall win at the last.[31]

Stanley Cavell remarked that the sentences about empiricism contain the true moral of the essay "Experience": "That is, what is wrong with empiricism is not its reliance on experience but its paltry idea of experience."[32] The sudden change of mood in the passage marks the point at which Emerson realized that he was drifting into the empiricism he has been condemning since his Harvard days and the terrific skepticism he found at the bottom of conservatism. Who was he to plant himself on the side of caution, cynicism, and mere sense?

Emerson had remarked in his journals in 1843 that Fourier's *Théorie de unité universelle* "is very entertaining, the most entertaining of French romances and will suggest vast & numerous possibilities of reform to the coldest & least sanguine." That word "romance" crops up again in the closing sentence of "Experience," in which Emerson, to the surprise and often disbelief of generations of readers, suddenly picks up his pilgrim's staff and sets out again toward the heavenly city: "Never mind the ridicule, never mind the defeat: up again, old heart!—it seems to say,—there is victory yet for all justice; and the true romance which the world exists to realize, will be the transformation of genius into practical power."[33]

Unfortunately, genius was not destined to be transformed into practical power in West Roxbury. The fire that consumed the half-built Phalanstery on March 1, 1846, accelerated the slow unraveling of Brook Farm. Emerson was more deeply affected by the ending of Ripley's brave experiment than he expected to be. He had always loved one of Fourier's central laws of passional attraction: "The attractions are proportional to the destinies."

It seemed intuitively true even if experientially false—in other words, a truth of the Reason rather than the Understanding. The Brook Farmers had displayed this slogan prominently when they celebrated Fourier's birthday. But now Fourier's radiant promise sounded bitter, just another of the hopes whispered by desire to men and women doomed to live in the world of limitation.

In the essay "Montaigne" Emerson makes clear how much he felt that the collapse of the Brook Farm experiment implicated him too. What is "reform" itself but desire? And what is the fate of desire but frustration?

> Charles Fourier announced that "the attractions of man are pro-portioned to his destinies;" in other words, that every desire predicts its own satisfaction. Yet all experience exhibits the reverse of this; the incompetency of power is the universal grief of young and ardent minds. They accuse the divine Providence of a certain parsimony. It has shown the heaven and earth to every child and filled him with a desire for the whole; a desire raging, infinite, a hunger as of space to be filled with planets; a cry of famine as of devils for souls. Then for the satisfaction;—to each man is admin-istered a single drop, a bead of dew of vital power, per day,—a cup as large as space, and one drop of the water of life in it. Each man woke in the morning with an appetite that could eat the solar sys-tem like a cake; a spirit for action and passion without bound; . . . but on the first motion to prove his strength, hands, feet, senses gave way, and would not serve him. He was an emperor deserted by his states, and left to whistle by himself, or thrust into a mob of emperors, all whistling, and still the sirens sang, "The attractions are proportioned to the destinies."[34]

The collapse of Brook Farm was a blow to the millenarian hopes of a generation and a sad measure of the gulf between the world of ideas and the world of things. In the years following, Emerson had to confront a pos-sibility even more sobering. What if desire itself did not emanate from the subject but rather manifested itself through the subject as the agent of some larger power? And what kind of power?

These questions began to obtrude themselves with particular force dur-ing Emerson's European trip of 1847–1848, and they grew even more urgent when he returned home to the sectional crisis surrounding the Com-promise of 1850. The Chartist movement in England, the failed revolution in France, the struggles between North and South over slavery, all inspired violent passions; and in these cases masses of human beings rather than individuals seemed the channels through which historical forces flowed.

For the first time in his life Emerson became seriously interested in trying to understand human beings in the aggregate. He came upon Quetelet's work at just the time when the strange new science of statistics seemed to promise a new way to understand the forces at work in human societies.

Emerson first mentions Quetelet in a letter to Lidian from London on June 28, 1848. "I breakfasted with Lord & Lady Lovelace, as Lord L. wished to read me a certain paper he has been writing on a book of Quetelet," Emerson writes. "We had quite a scientific time, and I learned some good things."[35] The next year he began copying into his journal passages from Quetelet's *Treatise on Man and the Development of his Faculties*.[36] One sentence in Quetelet that caught Emerson's eye was a saying of Napoleon's: "View man as we may, he is as much the result of his physical & moral atmosphere, as of his own organization." Another was an assertion Quetelet made himself: "Every thing which pertains to the human species considered as a whole, belongs to the order of physical facts."[37]

Emerson first thought of statistics as a new form of determinism, or, as he would later describe it, a new link in the adamantine bandages of Fate. Certainly Quetelet in the *Treatise on Man* remained supremely confident that, given the right formula and enough data, he could explain anything. At one point in the book he paused to offer a table plotting French dramas of the first, second, and third orders of merit against the ages of their authors when the works were composed. He concluded from this study that the years between thirty and forty are most propitious for the production of great French tragedy; those between forty and fifty, for that of great French comedy.

But Quetelet's main concerns were with larger social forces. He wished to bring to their study the methodological rigor associated with the physical sciences. Theodore Porter in *The Rise of Statistical Thinking, 1820–1900* explains it this way:

> Quetelet came to statistics from astronomy, and his commitment to the use of mathematics in the social sciences distinguished his approach from that of his reform-oriented statistical contemporaries. At the same time, his active interest in social policy and even in certain concrete reforms as well as the wide scope of his ambition for statistics separated his work from that of the various astronomers and mathematicians of his day who wrote demographic models and computed life tables. Quetelet was almost unique in the early nineteenth century in combining the characteristic concerns of the statistical movement with the technical tools of astronomers and probabilists.[38]

Porter thinks that Quetelet himself lacked the genius necessary to work out the mathematical techniques for analyzing statistical information of the kind he assiduously collected, and therefore adopted a dual strategy. In his practical work as a statistican he compiled statistical data as best he could "in order to learn something of the composition and perhaps the causes of the aggregate phenomena like natality, crime, and suicide." At the same time, in his published writings "he developed an extravagant system of metaphors and similes linking the social domain to the theories and even the mathematics of physics and astronomy."[39] He called this science "social physics," borrowing the term from Auguste Comte.

Quetelet's dream of a single, all-encompassing science of social physics never became reality. Interest in his theories nevertheless remained strong in Britain and America throughout the 1840s and 1850s. Sir John Herschel's 1850 review of a book on probability theory by Quetelet helped stimulate this interest. For Emerson Herschel's review was especially significant, since Emerson was already interested in Quetelet's ideas about the predictability of human behavior in large social groups. Herschel begins with a lengthy history of probability theory going back as far as Pascal, explaining the contributions made by Laplace to the subject and placing Quetelet's own work squarely in the Laplacian tradition. Toward the close of the review Herschel considers the fourth and last division of Quetelet's book, which deals with the relation between statistical method and social reality. Herschel agrees with Quetelet that the very regularity found in the annual march of statistical returns suggests an underlying regularity of causes operating within the social body. Even those human actions that seem "free as air" prove to be the effects of causes so determinate that only the intricacy of their mode of operation prevents making them a matter for fixed calculation.

> Taken in the mass, and in reference both to the physical and moral laws of his existence, the boasted freedom of man disappears; and hardly an action of his life can be named with usages, conventions, and the stern necessaries of his being, do not appear to enjoin on him as inevitable, rather than to leave to the free determination of his choice.

Emerson saw where such speculations led. In *Representative Men* he explored the comic side of statistical inference when he observed that "the terrible tabulations of the French statists bring every piece of whim and humour to exact numerical ratios. If one man in twenty thousand eats shoes or marries his grandmother, then in twenty thousand is found one man who eats shoes or marries his grandmother."[40] When the past can be used to predict the future with such precision, even in the realm of human eccentricites or aberrations, the freedom of the will evaporates.

But if Emerson found something amusing in statistics he also took its implications seriously. Quetelet's works reached Emerson just at the moment when his own need to think about the freedom or unfreedom of the will was intensified by the political crises of the early 1850s: the Compromise of 1850 and the Fugitive Slave Law that accompanied it; the deplorable cowardice of Massachusetts in enforcing the law; the rendition of the fugitive slave Thomas Sims by Justice Lemuel Shaw on April 12, 1851. Emerson responded to the rendition of Sims with a furious speech, "The Fugitive Slave Law," delivered first in Concord on May 3, 1851. But to stump for freedom was not enough; one must first decide whether freedom existed.

"Fate," the lecture Emerson delivered on December 22, 1851, in the Masonic Temple in Boston and later published in 1860 as the first essay in *The Conduct of Life*, is his attempt to harp on the string of fate long enough to learn its power. He marshals evidence from history, geology, and biology to prove the omnipotence of limitation. Then he adds: "One more fagot of these adamantine bandages is the new science of Statistics. It is a rule that the most casual and extraordinary events, if the basis of population is broad enough, become a matter of fixed calculation." This principle, basic to statistics, is known as the law of large numbers. The unfreedom of the will is one inference that can be drawn from the law of large numbers, but there are more cheerful inferences possible as well, and Emerson suddenly makes them explicit: "It would not be safe to say when a captain like Bonaparte, a singer like Jenny Lind, or a navigator like Bowditch would be born in Boston; but, on a population of twenty or two hundred millions, something like accuracy may be had."[41]

> Doubtless in every million there will be an astronomer, a mathematician, a comic poet, a mystic. No one can read the history of astronomy without perceiving that Copernicus, Newton, Laplace, are not new men, or a new kind of man, but that Thales, Anaximenes, Hipparchus, Empedocles, Aristarchus, Pythagoras, Oenipodes, had anticipated them; each had the same tense geometrical brain, apt for the same vigorous computation and logic; a mind parallel to the movement of the world. . . . As in every barrel of cowries brought to New Bedford there shall be one orangia, so there will, in a dozen millions of Malays and Mahometans, be one or two astronomical skulls.[42]

It has occurred to Emerson that the probabilistic curve, which looks inexorable when it is predicting suicides and crimes, predicts genius with just as much force. In a journal passage from the bleak year 1854 he links Fourier and Quetelet: "Fourier was right in his 1760 men to make one man. I accept the Quetelet statistics." Emerson had once thought of men as fragments and had found that thought depressing; now he sees them as parts of a mass large enough to support a percentage of superior individuals. The same idea lies behind a strange journal passage written in 1855, which blends statistics, Norse mythology, and a kind of proto-evolutionary theory into a grudging willingness to accept the universe:

> Most men are rubbish, & in every man is a good deal of rubbish. What quantities of fribbles, paupers, bed-ridden or bed-riding invalids, thieves, rogues, & beggars of both sexes, might be advantageously spared! But Quetelet Fate knows better; keeps everything alive, as long as it can live; that is, so long as the smallest thread of public necessity holds it on to the tree Igdrasil. . . . The mass are animal, in pupilage & near chimpanzee. Well, we are used as brute atoms, until we think, then we use all the rest. Nature turns all malfeasance to good. California gets peopled & subdued by the general gaol-delivery that pours into it.

Given this prediction of the conversion of evil to good, Emerson could hardly be surprised to discover that California, chief cause of the Compromise of 1850 and hence of the Fugitive Slave Law, would not only prosper but would one day elicit from him a hymn of praise that made the state sound like the paradise of Brisbane's Fourierist vision. In a letter written from Lake Tahoe on his return trip home in May of 1871 Emerson compared San Francisco's harbor to Constantinople's. Of the state's interior regions he wrote:

> There is an awe & terror lying over this new garden—all empty as yet of any adequate people, yet with this assured future in American hands,—unequalled in climate & production. Chicago & St. Louis are toys to it in its assured felicity. I should think no young man would come back from it.[43]

This power of seeing potential for redemption everywhere is what we mean by Emersonian optimism. It is reflected in the use he made of French thought. Although Emerson did not share the French love for mathematics he understood that only in mathematics could he hope to find an authority powerful enough to unseat the authority of tradition. He was attracted to astronomy because it revealed celestial realms whose apparent perturbations could be resolved into regularities, to statistics because it showed laws operating even in the realm of passions and crimes. But

Emerson quickly converted Laplace's atheistic Necessity into impersonal Theism. In a similar way he appropriated Fourier's phalanx as a symbol of the largeness of human possibility while he rejected it as a real solution to the problems of society. In the collapse of Brook Farm he found another use for Fourierism: it becomes a wistful symbol of the insatiability of human desire. Quetelet's statistical laws seemed to some observers to proclaim the inevitability of social evils. Emerson turned them into reassurances that genius can never be extirpated from the race.

NOTES

1. According to Gay Wilson Allen, the major subjects of the Boston Public Latin School that Emerson attended as a boy were Latin and Greek, but students could supplement this curriculum with private tutoring elsewhere. Beginning in the fall of 1815, when Emerson was twelve, he attended a Miss Sales's private school in French three days a week. "Ralph liked the language and was soon reading stories in a French anthology." *Waldo Emerson* (New York, 1981), 25, 34. But when Emerson visited Paris in 1848 he noted with regret that though the shop windows were full of toys to buy, "the only one of all which I really wish to buy is very cheap, yet I cannot buy it, namely, their speech. I covet that which the vilest of the people possesses." He notes that an American linguist who spoke fifty languages, Elihu Burrit, was "sadly mortified" to discover when he got to France that he could understand only a single word in any French sentence. *The Journals and Miscellaneous Notebooks of Ralph Waldo Emerson*, ed. William Gilman et al. (Cambridge, Mass., 1960–1982), 10:266–267. Cited hereafter as *JMN*.
2. Ticknor's words are quoted from one of Emerson's college notebooks, which he titled "Wide World 2." *JMN*, 1:54.
3. *JMN*, 1:54. It is worth remembering in view of Ticknor's final objection to French literature what Henry Adams said of literature in Boston and New York at the turn of the nineteenth century: "In default of other amusements, men read what no one could have endured had a choice of amusements been open." See his *History of the United States during the Administrations of Thomas Jefferson* (New York, 1986), 66.
4. In a journal entry dated Aug. 8, 1821, Emerson said of Montesquieu's book: "Of the *style* I am no judge but the book abounds with brilliant and touching thoughts." *JMN*, 1:268.
5. Jonathan Beecher, in his biography of Fourier, notes that Fourier always saw himself as the successor to Newton. "Newton had discovered the laws of material attraction, and Fourier those of passionate attraction." Fourier was not, of course, the first to claim a resemblance between the affective world and the laws of gravity. "During the century that followed the appearance of Newton's Principia numerous European philosophers and moralists attempted to generalize the Newtonian paradigm and to discover the principle of 'attraction' that governed life in society." See *Charles Fourier: The Visionary and His World* (Berkeley and Los Angeles, 1986), 108, 224. I am indebted to Conrad E. Wright for pointing out that

Francis Hutcheson, early eighteenth-century popularizers of Newton like William
Derham and William Whiston, and Adam Smith in *The Theory of the Moral Sentiments* all made similar comparisons between human sentiments and the law
of gravity.

6. See Carl Guarneri, *The Utopian Alternative: Fourierism in Nineteenth Century
America* (Ithaca, 1991), 18–19.

7. Guarneri points out that Saint-Simon was a more important influence upon Ripley
at the time of Brook Farm's founding than Fourier. Ripley initially found Fourier's
"numerical formulas and pseudoscientific prose" unappealing when he reviewed
Albert Brisbane's *Social Destiny of Man* for *The Dial* in October of 1840. But after
Brisbane's proselytizing visit to Brook Farm in May of 1843 Ripley became persuaded that "Fourierism was the logical culmination of Brook Farm's development." On Jan. 18, 1844, Brook Farm's new constitution announced the Brook
Farmers' intentions to transform their community into a model phalanx along
Fourierist lines. See Guarneri, *The Utopian Alternative*, chap. 2, esp. 44–59.

8. Maurice Gonnaud notes that Fourier remained a subject of sympathetic interest
to Emerson throughout the 1840s, and he notes several points of similarity between the two thinkers. "Its central postulate excepted, Fourierism seemed an
optimism similar to his own in the confidence of its approach. Its correspondences
here and there with certain doctrines of Swedenborg gave it a poetic dimension;
and its vindication of manual labor, which was the focus of Fourier's last works . . .
matched and perhaps extended the 'Doctrine of the Farm' Emerson had recently
preached." *An Uneasy Solitude: Individual and Society in the Work of Ralph
Waldo Emerson*, trans. Lawrence Rosenwald (Princeton, 1987), 311.

9. Theodore Porter, whose book *The Rise of Statistical Thinking, 1820–1900* (Princeton, 1986) is the source of my information about Quetelet, notes that Quetelet
claimed to have "enjoyed the lessons" of Laplace when he studied there in 1823.
But Porter thinks it unlikely that he actually received instruction from Laplace
himself. See *Rise of Statistical Thinking*, 43.

10. Charles Coulston Gillispie points out that Laplace's earliest work on the topic, a
memoir of 1774 entitled *"Memoire sur la probabilité des causes par les événe-
ments,"* takes up the subject of how to determine the mean value among a series of
astronomical observations in order to minimize the observational and instrumental
error incident to such observations. It was not until 1810–1811, however, that
Laplace derived the least-square rule for determining the mean value in a series of
observations from what is now called the central limit theorem. See Gillispie,
"Laplace," *Dictionary of Scientific Biography*, Supplement 1:282–283, 363.

11. Gillispie notes that Laplace's *"Memoire sur les probabilités"* of 1781, with its discussion of how to estimate causes through effects, "broke new ground in the field
of application. Indeed, it could be argued that social statistics as a mathematical
subject had its beginning in this memoir." And Gillispie points out that in the fifth
chapter of the *Théorie analytique des probabilités* of 1812 Laplace expressed-
confidence that probability theory could be applied to the study of medical and
economic questions, and even questions of morality, "for the operations of causes
many times repeated are as regular in those domains as in physics." Gillispie,
"Laplace," *Dictionary of Scientific Biography*, Supplement 1:303, 369. Porter argues that Quetelet and his successors took the decisive steps in reinterpreting the

probabilistic error function "as a law of genuine variation, rather than of mere error." Porter calls this "the central achievement of nineteenth-century statistical thought." See *Rise of Statistical Thinking*, 91.

12. Porter, *Rise of Statistical Thinking*, 44–55.

13. Gillispie lists three memoirs dated 1770 in his bibliography of Laplace's works; a fourth undated memoir may be from the same year. The five volumes of the *Traité de mécanique celeste* appeared between 1799 and 1825. See "Laplace," *Dictionary of Scientific Biography*, Supplement 1:388, 390. Emerson graduated from Harvard in 1821.

14. Gillispie, "Laplace," *Dictionary of Scientific Biography*, Supplement 1:334, 342.

15. [John Herschel], "Review of the *Lettres à S. A. R. le Duc regnant de Saxe-Coburg et Gotha sur la théorie des probabilités appliqué aux sciences morales et politiques, par M. A. Quetelet," *Edinburgh Review* 92(1850):11. Hereafter Herschel, "Quetelet on Probabilities."

16. *JMN*, 2:159. The review was published in the *Edinburgh Review* 23(1814): 320–340.

17. *JMN*, 2:367–368. Adams's "Report of the Secretary of State upon Weights and Measures" was presented to the House of Representatives on Feb. 22, 1821. According to Gillispie, although Laplace was probably responsible for the decision to make the new meter a fraction of a quadrant of the meridien, Talleyrand wrote the committee's famous report, with its joyous predictions of a union of mankind under the same laws, the same religion, and the same system of weights and measures. Laplace's aim in choosing this unit of measurement was to make linear and angular measurements convertible into one another, an aid in navigation. See Gillispie, "Laplace," *Dictionary of Scientific Biography*, Supplement 1:334–335. Emerson approved of the metric system but thought that men's inveterate prejudice for a pound and fear of the "barbarous kilometre" would doom the innovation to failure.

18. *JMN*, 2:367.

19. Gillispie says of this work, "Bowditch's commentary in the footnotes is an indispensable vade mecum for the study of Laplace, explaining and filling out the demonstrations, and containing a great body of historical as well as mathematical and astronomical elucidation." *Dictionary of Scientific Biography*, Supplement 1:388. Emerson couples the names of Laplace and Bowditch in his lecture on "The Uses of Natural History," delivered Nov. 5, 1833. See *The Early Lectures of Ralph Waldo Emerson*, ed. Stephen E. Whicher et. al. (Cambridge, Mass., 1966), 1:12. Emerson refers to research by Lagrange and Laplace on the periodicity of the errors in the orbits of the heavenly bodies in "The Naturalist," a lecture of May 7, 1834. And in "The Humanity of Science," delivered on Dec. 22, 1836, Emerson says: "Once we thought the errors of Jupiter's moons were alarming; it was then shown that they were periodic." See *Early Lectures*, 1:72 and 2:39 and similar passages in *JMN*, 4:34–35.

20. *JMN*, 4:27. The letter Emerson wrote to the Second Church does not survive, but a manuscript report in the archives of the Second Church from the Committee to whom Emerson's letter was referred is dated June 16. See *The Letters of Ralph Waldo Emerson*, ed. Ralph L. Rusk (New York, 1939), 1:351.

21. *JMN*, 4:26–27.

22. These phrases are from the sermon of May 27, 1832. See *The Complete Sermons of Ralph Waldo Emerson*, ed. Albert J. von Frank et. al. (Columbia, Mo., 1989–1992), 4:158. This sermon also contains a reference to the periodicity of error in the heavenly bodies.

23. Robert Richardson, *Emerson: The Mind on Fire* (Berkeley and Los Angeles, 1995), 125; John Milton, *Paradise Lost*, bk. 3, ll.183–184.

24. Emerson, *Complete Sermons*, 4:159; Ralph Waldo Emerson to William Emerson, Feb. 19, 1842, in *Letters*, 3:13–14. In an earlier letter to William, written on Jan. 24, 1842, a few days before Waldo's death, Emerson explains that his Boston course of lectures just finished has failed to meet his financial expectations and left him $200.00 short of needed income. He explains that he will be drawn to Providence by "the love of *paying debts.*" *Letters*, 3:5.

25. Ralph Waldo Emerson to Lidian Emerson, Mar. 1, 1842, in *Letters*, 3:18; Ralph Waldo Emerson to Lidian Emerson, Mar. 3, 1842, in *Letters*, 3:21; Ralph Waldo Emerson to Lidian Emerson, Mar. 5, 1842, in *Letters*, 3:23. A much longer record of what Brisbane said to Emerson in New York is to be found in *JMN*, 8:208–209.

26. *JMN*, 8:249.

27. *JMN*, 8:210, 329–330.

28. Ralph Waldo Emerson, *The Collected Works of Ralph Waldo Emerson*, ed. Alfred R. Ferguson et al. (Cambridge, Mass., 1971–), 1:21, 45. Cited hereafter as *CW*. Guarneri, *The Utopian Alternative*, 18. The account of the replacement of the earth's noxious fluids is from Emerson's record of Brisbane's talk. See *JMN*, 8:208–209.

29. *JMN*, 9:159.

30. *JMN*, 9:241.

31. *CW*, 3:48–49. His words here remind one of Thoreau's remark in *Walden* that if the old still have "some faith left" which belies their experience, "they are only less young than they were." *Walden*, ed. J. Lyndon Shanley (Princeton, 1971), 9. It was in 1845, the year after "Experience" was published, that Thoreau built his cabin on Emerson's land near Walden Pond and began an experiment of his own.

32. Stanley Cavell, *The Senses of Walden: An Expanded Edition* (San Francisco, 1981), 126.

33. *JMN*, 9:8; *CW*, 3:49.

34. *CW*, 4:103–104.

35. Ralph Waldo Emerson to Lidian Emerson, June 28, 1848, in *Letters*, 4:94.

36. This translation of *Sur l'homme et la développment de ses facultés, ou Essai de physique sociale* (Paris, 1835) was made by Dr. R. Knox (Edinburgh, 1842).

37. *JMN*, 11:67. The quotations are from pages 82 and 96 of Knox's translation.

38. Porter, *Rise of Statistical Thinking*, 42.

39. Porter, *Rise of Statistical Thinking*, 46.

40. Herschel, "Quetelet on Probabilites," 41–42; *CW*, 4:62.

41. Ralph Waldo Emerson, *The Complete Works of Ralph Waldo Emerson*, ed. Edward Waldo Emerson (Boston, 1903–1904), 6:17.

42. Emerson, *Complete Works*, 6:19.

43. *JMN*, 13:340, 440; *JMN*, 11:440; Ralph Waldo Emerson to Ellen Emerson, May 20 and 22, 1871, in *Letters*, 6:158. The temptation to stay in California seems to have been strong, for in an earlier letter (Apr. 27, 1871) Emerson wrote to his wife that

"if we were all young,—as some of us are not,—we might each of us claim his quarter-section of the Government, & plant grapes & oranges, & never come back to your east winds & cold summers,—only remembering to send home a few tickets of the Pacific Railroad to one or two or three pale natives of the Massachusetts Bay." See *Letters*, 6:152.

English Nature, New York Nature, and *Walden*'s New England Nature

NINA BAYM

THROUGHOUT HIS LITERARY LIFE, HENRY DAVID THOREAU depicted his quest for the ideal through metaphors of natural wilderness. From *A Week on the Concord and Merrimac Rivers*—"there is in my nature, methinks, a singular yearning toward all wildness"; through *Walden*—"Our village life would stagnate if it were not for the unexplored forests and meadows which surround it. We need the tonic of wildness"; to "Walking"—"in Wildness is the preservation of the World"—his textual surrogate looks for remote, untouched places in the universe signifying the promised land.[1] But, like countless nineteenth-century Americans of European ancestry, he also saw wilderness as the wasteland to which humans were consigned after the fall, a space to be redeemed through human toil, perfected by human civilization.[2]

In "Walking," for example, just a few sentences after he prefers swamps to pleasure grounds for spiritual re-creation, Thoreau writes without irony: "The weapons with which we have gained our most important victories, which should be handed down as heirlooms from father to son, are not the sword and the lance, but the bushwhack, the turf-cutter, the spade, and the bog hoe, rusted with the blood of many a meadow, and begrimed with the dust of many a hard-fought field."[3] Across the range of his writings, Thoreau, consistently inconsistent, constructs and dismantles polarities that are already internally conflicted: untouched nature (sometimes saving, sometimes vile) versus humanized landscape (sometimes salvific, sometimes despoiled).

These divisions are especially on display in *Walden*, which unlike most of Thoreau's published nature writings, is not shaped as an excursion in search of ideality; rather, it proselytizes on behalf of staying home and finding ideality in such nature as is ready-to-hand. As Steven Fink puts it, in this "excursion" Thoreau "does not *go* anywhere but builds himself a house," which is to say that *Walden* is no excursion at all.[4] A poem included in the first draft of *Walden* asserted: "My feet forever stand / On Concord fields, / and I must live the life / Which their soil yields."[5] These lines invite one to think of *Walden* as in some literal sense a work about living from and as a product of New England soil. And, as a book about the soil of New England, *Walden* shows nature to be historically and politically contingent as well as timeless. In *Walden's* New England, two centuries of Anglo habitation have both obliterated the original horrific wilderness and despoiled the sanctified virgin land. Now, a third kind of wilderness, testimony to human malfeasance, is reclaiming the terrain. With so many kinds of wilderness in textual circulation, Thoreau can make the concept signify ethical ideality and ethical failure simultaneously. But either way, the natural and the human are mutually constructed.

It can be argued that all Thoreau's representations of nature disclose the work of human history on the land. The fauna in his first published essay, "The Natural History of Massachusetts," are artifacts of back yards and roadsides, observed in orchards, gardens, on the roofs of deserted barns—deserted barns, staples of Thoreauvian description, represent the flight of New Englanders from the countryside—in the lofts of sawmills, and atop fences. The disappearance of the great quadrupeds is linked specifically to the appearance of (white) human beings. Even blocks of ice floating downriver in the spring thaw are anthropomorphized by skaters' tracks and holes from pickerel fishing; skeins of flax stretch across the river's shallows. A quick seasonal survey—*Walden* in a nutshell—recognizes fishermen, farmers, hunters, trappers, and town committeemen inspecting bridges and causeways after the spring thaw.[6]

Notations of the human presence in and impact on nature testify to Thoreau's literary ethic of observational fidelity: given that New England has in fact long been inhabited by white people, this ethic obliges him to produce natural descriptions replete with human political, historical, and economic activity. Such notations, however, also signify the writer's intention in *Walden* to advise New Englanders on improving their condition, especially their "outward condition or circumstances in this world, in this town" (W, 4). The author's impersonation of a barnyard chanticleer places Thoreau within his community as its chosen sentry. His concluding metaphor of extravagance—the cow kicking over the milk-pail (W, 324)—is similarly domesticated, and by making the farm animal rather than the wild buffalo represent true wildness, Thoreau makes wildness into an imaginative projection rather than the thing itself.

Walden, approached from this perspective, may be seen as a profoundly social book. The supposedly solitary Thoreau entertains constantly, some-

times twenty-five or thirty visitors at a time; he talks to his neighbors
through *Walden*, and they are constantly on his mind in *Walden*. The
meaning of the sojourn is arrived at through constant application to a range
of human activities subsumed under the name "Concord." Thus, although
nature in *Walden* registers a redemptive cycle of seasonal time, it also registers and speaks to Yankee history. The writer is a universal perceptual apparatus, intuitively connected to the spirit circulating through natural
forms; he is also formed by and attuned to local farms, crops, fences, wood
lots, orchards, barns, roads, and villages. Thoreau's specific experiment in
nature is, mainly, an experiment in farming, which involves both working
with the land and working against it to make it say something it would not
say by itself, that is, would not say "naturally." Whatever his reasons for
growing beans, Thoreau grows real beans.

Criticism holds that in each successive draft, and mainly in reaction to
the commercial failure of the *Week*, *Walden* became ever more inward
looking, increasing its seasonal symbolism and—according to the still
immensely influential reading of Sherman Paul—losing almost all of whatever communal intentions it might have had originally. Even Michael T.
Gilmore, who views *Walden* as a "nineteenth-century revision of the
agrarian or civic humanist tradition," thinks the book beats a private, anti-
historical retreat into the self. Yet J. Lyndon Shanley has shown how
Thoreau's revisions added "more and more of everything," including social
critique in "Economy," reflections on buying farms in "Where I Lived,"
and almost all of the chapter "Former Inhabitants and Winter Visitors."[7]
Thus, while the revisions do expand the spiritual allegory of the seasons,
they also increase *Walden*'s sociohistorical orientation. One can argue that
Walden never abandoned its public purpose; the published book, referring
to or addressing friends, neighbors, and society at large on virtually every
page, means to involve itself deeply in the lives of those it addresses: those
"who read these pages, who are said to live in New England" (*W*, 4).

New England's population in 1850 was around 80 percent rural, with
some 80 percent of this total directly engaged in farming and 20 percent
serving the farming population's needs. The region's economy was also
changing rapidly, with power and population converging in the city, merchants becoming industrialists, farmers becoming millhands, and agriculture itself mutating from relatively self-sufficient (but never completely
autonomous) small farms to market-oriented farming necessitating effi-
ciencies of scale like monoculture and large acreage. These changes played
out on a terrain whose rocky hillsides and lack of fertility had always made
farming difficult, and these difficulties were enhanced by the subdividing
practices of Yankee land tenure. By Thoreau's time Yankee farmers were in

full-scale flight from New England, moving through New York State to the midwest's more fertile, flatter lands, accelerating the pace of demographic shift.[8] Some of the industrial elite were setting up as gentlemen farmers like New Yorkers, thereby affiliating—it might be feared—with gentry values rather than their own yeoman origins.[9] Like so many New England books from this period, *Walden* speaks to these conditions: rural economic decline, depopulation of the countryside, Yankee out-migration, non-Anglo (specifically Irish) immigration, urbanization, railroads, mills, and generalized agricultural malaise. Like other books, *Walden* was obsessed with the issue of keeping Yankees at home on the land.

But why should Thoreau care if New Englanders stayed put or pulled up stakes? There are no doubt psychological explanations for his rootedness, but from a public perspective one might suggest that at least at the time he wrote *Walden* he cared as much for New England as for nature. There is nothing innovative about connecting nature to nation or region, especially for patriotic purposes: breathes there a man with soul so dead, O to be in England, and so forth. Moreover, progressive literary movements in England had been insisting from the mid eighteenth century onward that appreciation of nature as such was foundational to the uniqueness of English literature as well as to the English national character. Thoreau might assume that New Englanders, descended from the English people, would tend to love nature and appreciate nature writing. Here however was a problem: to love English nature writing would be, in effect, to love a specifically English nature as well, and thus encourage love of England not of New England.

Even worse than English nature writing from the perspective I am outlining here would be the imitation and adaptation of such writing (based in turn on imitative landscaping practices) of "New York nature writing," because nothing was worse for New England than New York values. By the revolutionary era if not before, conservative New England writers had defined New York as their moral antithesis, much as English writers contrasted their nation with France: New England as an upright, prudent, pious, ethical, land-based republican meritocracy, New York as a shifty, extravagant, infidel, commercial, sycophantic pseudo-aristocracy. *Walden*, thus, may be theorized as a specifically Yankee book of Yankee nature defined obliquely through and against these two other locospecific genres of nature writing. Thoreau's Yankee nature is a farmer's nature, not a nature of gentry *poseurs*, scientific or gentlemen agriculturalists, sportsmen, landscapers, tourists, weekend gardeners, or retired millionaires. It is about preserving the New England way. It exhibits an experiment in Yankee ingenuity: how to make do with a diminished thing—the never-fertile and now virtually exhausted New England soil—in order to rescue New England from the "restless, nervous, bustling, trivial Nineteenth Century" (W, 329).

To simplify and point his moral: the New England rural economy could be revived if New Englanders would lower their material expectations and raise their spiritual vision—if, specifically, they would stop thinking like New Yorkers and become again true Yankee yeomen as Thoreau exemplifies the type. This, however, is not a Jeffersonian expansionist so much as an austerely "Roman" Federal type, valorized in Revolutionary and early national conservative rhetoric, much of which cited the classical agricultural writers whose work Thoreau loved: Cato, Varro, Virgil, Hesiod.[10] "Civilization is a real advance in the condition of man," Thoreau writes, "but only the wise improve their advantages" (W, 31). The yeoman who attains to Roman virtue is the true gentleman, the wise and good representative of civilization—no simulacrum of inherited aristocracy, but the real, transcendent thing; not the noble savage, but nature's nobleman.

Thus, Thoreau's coincidental move to the pond on July 4 is at once personal and public, and in both senses it is political. It is a declaration of New England independence. In literary terms, it introduces a work that will represent the local terrain accurately rather than through the distorting lens of inapplicable imports, reminding New Englanders of the actual ground they must work if they are to persist as themselves. The basket-making, basket-selling passage in "Economy," typically read by critics as a parable of Thoreau's failure to sell the *Week* in the literary market, also narrates New England's failure, as a region, in the expanding, impersonal national market. The New Englander, like the American Indian, will be a vanishing species unless its people opt out of the market like Thoreau. The rush of American civilization toward market modernity, especially as signified by the railroad, threatens to pass New England by. Thoreau suggests that this very marginality might be New England's opportunity.[11]

The English nature writing that showed Thoreau how nature was specific to a political and economic way of life simultaneously showed him the limits of its usefulness for his own writing. "I look upon England to-day," he says, "as an old gentleman who is travelling with a great deal of baggage, trumpery which has accumulated from long housekeeping, which he has not the courage to burn" (W, 66). He writes in "Walking" that English literature "from the days of the minstrels to the Lake Poets" cannot serve his purposes because "it is an essentially tame and civilized literature," its wilderness a "greenwood."[12] Most of *Walden*'s literary allusions are to the classics and eastern sacred texts; yet an English network surfaces occasionally, as for example in the names of three English nature writers: John Evelyn (*Sylva: A Discourse of Forest Trees*—"According to Evelyn . . ." [*W*, 9]), William Gilpin (*Remarks on Forest Scenery*—"so admirable in all that relates to landscapes, and usually so correct" [*W*, 287]), and William Wordsworth (*Guide to the Lake Country*—the most oblique of these allusions, yet perhaps the most important: "this is my Lake country" [*W*, 197]).

All three of these cited works proclaim their nationalist aims of preserving, valuing, and where necessary constructing the English landscape to enhance English prestige and affirm the English national character. Evelyn, publishing in 1664 under the auspices of the Royal Society, inventoried the trees of England, praising their beauty, their usefulness, and above all their fundamental contribution to national power: the navy floated on timbered ships. His purpose was to foster forest preservation in a nation whose forests had virtually vanished. William Gilpin's theories of the picturesque adapted Burkean esthetic values of sublimity to the unpopulated or depopulated English countryside, promoting bourgeois internal tourism as an alternative to the aristocrats' Grand Tour. And—in Wordsworth's own words—his guide was designed to help "reconcile a Briton to the scenery of his own country."[13] Since Wordsworth also self-consciously brought literature into his project, it is especially when Thoreau sets his lakes against Wordsworth's that he most invokes the regional specificity of his own terrain and the writing accompanying it.

Many thousands of patriotic prospect and locodescriptive poems produced in England throughout the eighteenth century indicate the extent to which poetry figured in the endeavor to make England a country of nature, the English a nature-loving people, as well as to produce on the English terrain the nature implied in these formulations. One among many loci of such work—adduced here as illustrative of a huge archive—is the career of John Aikin (1747-1822), botanist, naturalist, geographer, and magazinist, who inventoried the terrain around Manchester for industrial purposes; published anthologies of English verse; edited the poetry of Milton, Spenser, Thomson, and Goldsmith; and celebrated the tendency of English poetry toward accurate nature description. In collaboration with his sister, Anna Laetitia Barbauld, Aikin also wrote juveniles like a *Farm-Yard Journal* and a *Calendar of the Natural Year* designed "for the instruction and entertainment of young persons." The popular *Calendar*, first published in 1785, was reissued in 1794, 1800, 1814, 1823, 1834, 1836, 1837, 1839, and 1850, and was incorporated in 1855 by Mary Howitt into her own illustrated anthology of poetry about nature and "Merrie England."

Mary Howitt was the spouse and partner of William Howitt, whose 1831 calendar, the *Book of the Seasons* (perhaps modeled on Aikin's), influenced Thoreau's habit of organizing his natural observations seasonally.[14] Howitt was an unabashed chauvinist; in the *Calendar*, e.g., he writes that turning "the eyes of those whose attention I may be so happy as to gain, on the loveliness and influence of Nature" is designed to promote national welfare by countering the "calculating spirit of trade." If not for nature appreciation and the correlated counterthrust of "our inestimable literature," he writes, trade would "long ago have quenched in the national heart those lofty sentiments which have borne it proudly in the eyes of an admiring world above all mean contamination." [15]

More than twenty years ago Raymond Williams summarized an already "well-known" English historiographical narrative about the "self-conscious development of landscape and what is called the 'invention' of scenery" in the eighteenth century: landowners returned from the Grand Tour with "new ways of looking at landscape." Helped by gardeners and celebrated by poets and painters, they created landscapes resembling those they had learned to see, in the form of "prospects" from their country houses. (Compare *Walden*'s self-consciousness about the "humble" scenery around the pond, which could not "much concern one who has not long frequented it, or lived by its shore" [W, 175]; or Thoreau's insistence that though his cabin had virtually no view, he "did not feel crowded or confined in the least" because—predictably—there was "pasture enough" for his imagination [W, 78–79].) This English esthetic work was bound up with locospecific effects of emergent agrarian capitalism like enclosure, rural impoverishment, and exodus to the cities, which had produced the unpopulated spaces required for large-scale landscaping. To Williams, the mystification, as he calls it, of the movement is its success in circulating such an obviously built environment as "a triumph of 'unspoiled' nature."[16]

Well in advance of the United States, therefore, England became the original "nature's nation." The concept, saturated with political and economic ideology, figured in internal political debates about the English future and contributed notably to the obsessive, overdetermined polarizing of England and France: English nature versus French artifice.[17] This opposition enters into American esthetic and literary politics in the antebellum years: on the one hand, lovers of rural life affiliate with England, urbanites affiliate with France; on the other, literary nationalists are keen to identify a way to distinguish "our" nature from "theirs," while still maintaining the English tendency to appreciate nature. As we know, the process of identifying an "American" nature did not come to rest until after the Civil War, when the opening of the West via railroads permitted public access to the nature of sublime spectacle. The scenery of *Walden*, of course, is nothing like this; the process had not yet achieved its goal, and it is certainly an irony that *Walden* became so centrally associated with its completion.[18]

Even as they praised unspoiled English nature, English nature writers called it the foundation of a traditional English way of life, thereby merging a back-to-nature movement with a "back-to-old-England" movement, wherein it was important to search out (or invent) and celebrate quaint customs among the rural folk, to populate the otherwise vacated scene with acceptable examples of the still-bucolic English heart. This demographic mystification is a picturesque politics by which selected types become unspoiled and natural at the moment they are prettified; if patronizing toward rural folk, this politics also distinguishes crucially between them and the urban proletariat, the much-maligned "cockney." American travelers beginning with Washington Irving contributed significantly to this movement, since they helped the English understand what was "Old World" about their rapidly industrializing country. The outcome was a landscape of happy tenants and magnanimous gentry: a squirearchy.[19] In the *Week*, the untraveled Thoreau already showed his knowledge of English landscape: "When we were opposite to the middle of Billerica, the fields on either hand had a soft and cultivated English aspect, the village spire being seen over the copses which skirt the river. . . . It seemed that men led a quiet and very civil life there."[20]

The so-called first generation of romantic poets worked within this eighteenth-century paradigm—Wordsworth, Coleridge, Leigh Hunt (who also published a calendar book, *The Months*—the genre was ubiquitous—in 1819), his sister-in-law Elizabeth Kent (author of a flora and a sylva, both of them botanical and poetical), the Howitts, Mary Russell Mitford, and numerous other writers of country life extolled each other's works and circulated them through extensive quotation. Wordsworth's *Guide* cited his own verses and invited readers to consult others of his poems for additional descriptions of lake scenery. Lines from Coleridge's 1798 anti-French poem, *Fears in Solitude*, are offered by William Howitt as preliminary to his chauvinistic *Rural Life of England*: "O native Britain! O my mother isle! / How shouldst thou prove aught else but dear and holy / To me, who from thy lakes and mountain rills, / Thy clouds, thy quiet dales, thy rocks and seas, / Have drank in all my intellectual life?"[21]

As well as quoting each other, these writers also uncovered esthetic merit in naturalist work originally published without literary ambitions— Evelyn's *Sylva*, e.g., or Gilbert White's *Natural History and Antiquities of Selborne*; their anthologies represented standard writers like Chaucer and

Shakespeare through extracts about nature. Anthologies proliferated. Segments of nature poetry appeared in tourist guides and travel books, manuals of natural history and natural science, books on farming, gardening, landscaping, and rural architecture. Diverse texts quoted each other until the source of a particular quotation became indeterminable, and readers on both sides of the Atlantic could tap into the whole reservoir with ease. It is not known, for example, if Thoreau read Wordsworth's *Guide*; but he did not need to. In an editorial of May 1847 in *The Horticulturalist*, Andrew Jackson Downing theorized about the appropriate colors of paint for a country home and cited Wordsworth on using local Portland stone for building in the Lake country. "An enterprise to improve the style of cottage architecture!" exclaims Thoreau. "One man says, in his despair or indifference to life, take up a handful of the earth at your feet, and paint your house that color. Is he thinking of his last and narrow house?" (W, 48).

Almost all this English writing is a literature about occasional refreshing visits to the country, a perambulatory, day-walking literature. If not written by tourists (Wordsworth was not a tourist in the Lake District) it was written for them. Even Mary Russell Mitford, in "our" village, was a city visitor, as these extracts (which represent the tenor of this kind of writing as a whole) will show: "It is a dull gray morning, with a dewy feeling in the air; fresh, but not windy; cool, but not cold;—the very day for a person newly arrived from the heat, the glare, the noise, and the fever of London, to plunge into the remotest labyrinths of the country, and regain the repose of mind, the calmness of heart, which has been lost in that great Babel." These remotest labyrinths—"delicious green patches, the islets of wilderness amidst cultivation, which form perhaps the peculiar beauty of English scenery"—are reached in short walks on footpaths or roads.[22] No wonder Thoreau saw English nature as "tame and civilized" and found its forms of civility unsuitable for his rustic purposes.

When Susan Fenimore Cooper looked back on her father's early landscape gardening and horticulture efforts, she remembered ideas about beautifying nature as English imports. In the 1820s, when the Coopers settled at Angevine, "some of the gentlemen in Westchester county were giving much of their attention to subjects of this kind; English books had led the way." In the same memoir she contrasted her father's urbane interest in farming with the common settlers', making her father out as a natural aristocrat, our country's finest. Throughout his life, she wrote, he delighted in the "peculiarly American process of 'clearing;' not in its ruder forms, of course, where the chief object of the colonist often appears to consist in felling a noble wood, and leaving the unsightly wreck—a lifeless array of half-charred stumps—to moulder slowly away."[23] Remains of just such "ruder" clearing are prominent in the scenery of *Walden*, where Thoreau hacked away at stumps for winter firewood. The absence of beautification around Walden is a sign that the landscape remains an ungenteel domain of subsistence farming. Certainly, Thoreau proposes to improve this landscape, but not by following the New York example.

The chief importer and popularizer of English landscape esthetics for New York consumption was Andrew Jackson Downing (1815–1852), the Hudson River entrepreneurial horticulturalist whose ideals of natural beautification meshed with his idealization of English refinement and—literally—class. New York commercial wealth, combined with the mobility made possible first by canals and then the railroad, increasingly launched genteel urbanites into the country for leisure, recreation, and retirement and gave new value to rural land. Downing's 1841 book on landscaping was "the best selling and most widely influential book of its type published in nineteenth-century America."[24] In all his writings, Downing eulogized England, where "the most intelligent and the wealthiest aristocracy in the world, have indeed made almost an entire landscape garden of 'merry England.' "[25]

> The cottage and villa architecture of the English has grown out of the feelings and habits of a refined and cultivated people, whose devotion to country life, and fondness for all its pleasures, are so finely displayed in the beauty of their dwellings, and the exquisite keeping of their buildings and grounds.
>
> It is this love of rural life, and this nice feeling of the harmonious union of nature and art, that reflects so much credit upon the English as a people, and which, sooner or later, we hope to see completely naturalized in this country.[26]

Downing understood and extolled the link between English landscape and a conservative class ethos:

> Much as we admire the energy of our people, we value no less the love of order, the obedience to law, the security and repose of society, the love of home, and the partiality of localities endeared by birth or association, of which it is in some degree the antagonist. And we are therefore convinced that whatever tends, without checking the energy of character, but to develope along with it certain virtues that will keep it within due bounds, may be looked

upon as a boon to the nation. . . . It is not difficult to see how strongly horticulture contributes to the development of local attachments. In it lies the most powerful *philtre* that civilized man has yet found to charm him to one spot of earth.[27]

Although Downing's solution is opposite to Thoreau's, both of them worried about the same problem: how to keep people at home. Downing's people, of course, are a different group, and his approach typifies the ethic of New York nature writing, a literature about taste, leisure, and nature appreciation for self-styled gentry who perceive the countryside as an opportunity to create a modified, somewhat democratized version of rural England. This is to make life into an upscale version of what Leo Marx calls the "middle ground," or what John Stilgoe calls the "borderland" of suburbia.[28] The scheme identifies New York City as the American equivalent of London, and the wilderness of the Adirondacks as a public sporting preserve, an American version of the great landowners' private parks. Books like Joel Tyler Headley's 1849 *The Adirondack, or Life in the Woods*, about camping in the Adirondacks, are saturated with this ambiance, and although passages on birds, animals, the sounds of the forest, and so on in Headley remind one strikingly of Thoreau, as does the literary habit of imposing spiritual or moral meaning on the scenery, the book is controlled by an urban dilettantism that *Walden* aggressively repudiates: "you cannot conceive the contrasts, nay, almost the shocks of feeling one experiences in stepping from the crowded city into the dense forest where his couch is the boughs he himself cuts, and his companions the wild deer and the birds; or in emerging again into civilized life, and listening to the strange tumult that has not ceased in his absence."[29]

In New York nature writing, country living is designed for people who want to appreciate artfully managed rural scenery without sacrificing the "pleasures and advantages of a city." This phrase is from an essay by Nathaniel Parker Willis in George Putnam's 1852 compendium, the *Home Book of the Picturesque*, which offers prose and illustration to show how the eastern railroads have opened a great variety of picturesque scenery to genteel travelers. Willis's essay, a pure sales pitch for the Highland Terrace area above West Point (where he himself built a country home, Idlewild), stresses how the railroad has made the site convenient to New York City, and yet far enough removed so as to avoid suburban "cockney annoyances." Far from a wilderness, Highland Terrace encompasses several villages and is divided into cultivated farms; with its "walls and fences in good condition, the roads lined with trees, the orchards full, the houses and barns sufficiently hidden with foliage to be picturesque," the whole

neighborhood is "quite rid of the angularity and well-known ungraceful-
ness of a newly-settled country."[30]

Willis presents himself as a gentleman farmer in his popular collection
Rural Letters, first published in 1849 (reissued 1850, 1851, 1853, 1854, and
1856). The sequence of letters written from "under a bridge" is so strikingly like and unlike *Walden* as to suggest that it was among Thoreau's chief
provocations, although there is no direct evidence of Thoreau's having
read it.[31] In this sequence, "Willis," like "Thoreau," has retreated to the
country to write, read, think, and benefit from a farmer's life; like him he
lives a mile or two from the nearest village, sermonizes and analogizes
from natural phenomena and rural activities; writes about books, visitors,
neighbors, country ways, local flora and fauna.[32] The series is loosely struc-
tured by the seasons and has transcendentalizing and moralizing passages
strikingly similar to Thoreau's.

But Willis is a gentleman farmer and a cosmopolite. His letters are
profoundly marked by his urbanity, as he comments on the latest books,
gossips about notables, entertains celebrities whom he regales with good
wine and cigars, alludes to his travels throughout Europe and Asia Minor,
and diversifies his routine with visits to New York City where he stays at
the Astor House. Even more important: his life in nature is represented by
a rhetoric of the esthetic picturesque that a writer like Thoreau would have
deemed hopelessly frivolous:

> It sounds easy enough to trim out a wood, and so it is if the object
> be merely to produce butternuts, or shade grazing cattle. But to
> thin, and trim, and cut down, judiciously, changing a "wild and
> warped slip of wilderness" into a chaste and studious grove, is
> not done without much study of the spot, let alone a taste for the
> sylvan.[33]

Willis eagerly anticipates the time when the area will have been recognized for its thousands of sites where the lawns were already made, "the
terraces defined and levelled, the groves tastefully clumped," and takes
pleasure in thinking "that by changes scarcely less than magical, these
lovely banks will soon be amply seen and admired, and probably as rapidly
seized upon and inhabited by persons of taste."[34] Above all, perhaps,
Willis's tendency to moralize is constantly ironized by a sophisticated
jocosity: "What a coverlet of glory the day-god draws about him for his repose! I should like curtains of that burnt crimson. If I have a passion in
the world, it is for that royal trade, upholstery."[35] A commentary on the
spiritual value of farming starts out like Thoreau but shifts its tone mid-
way through the passage:

The barrel of buckwheat not only cost me nothing, but I have had
my uses of it in the raising, and can no more look upon its value,
than upon a flower which I pluck to smell, and give away when it
is faded. I have sold some of my crops for the oddity of the sensation; and I assure you it is very much like being paid for dancing
when the ball is over.[36]

It is easy to think of Thoreau as knowing this work and distancing himself from it, just as he would know Willis as the leading magazinist of the
day and distance himself from *that* way of succeeding. When, in "Walking,"
Thoreau comments that although in his vicinity, "the best part of the land
is not private property," although "possibly the day will come when it will
be partitioned off into so-called pleasure-grounds . . . and walking over the
surface of God's earth shall be construed to mean trespassing on some
gentleman's grounds" he might have been speaking directly to Willis.[37] In
effect, *Walden's* exaggerations are in part a form of resistance to New York
gentility, just as the landscape he depicts rejects the gentrifying influences
of New York nature writing entirely. This writing, from his perspective,
regardless of the writers' sex, would be an emasculated, effete production—a lady's literature and a lady's way of being in nature.

In Susan Fenimore Cooper's work he had the lady herself. Always protective of her father's genteel pretensions, Susan Cooper was pleased to
occupy the ground he had cleared for her.[38] Her authorship of the successful *Rural Hours* (1850), though the book was published anonymously
"by a Lady," was widely known; the attribution served to draw attention to
the writer's gender and class. Cooper aimed to show how a "lady" whose
circumstances required her to pass a great deal of time in the country
might do so usefully and enjoyably. *Rural Hours* attempts to transplant
English village-based nature writing to the New York highlands. While
John Stilgoe seems overly severe—perhaps, even, Thoreauvian—when
he declares that Cooper "liked wilderness half erased by fields and agricultural spaces" and "liked agricultural spaces and activities only at a distance; she understood the country as scenery, as backdrop to her dreams
and aesthetic theories, not as an evolving artifact of agriculture," it is certainly the case that she conceived of the country as an evolving artifact of
New York money, and she walks among "the people" in *Rural Hours* as a
gracious lady of the manor.[39]

Rural Hours, currently enjoying renewed appreciation, is more scientific and more comprehensively observant than *Walden*. But its "natural"
observations merge in the English style with accounts of village activities,
kitchen gardens, cultivated flower gardens, farming rituals. The book has a

good deal of economic and political theorizing—most of which was deleted from the 1887 reissue—based on a hierarchical ideal of land proprietorship. The upper-class female persona contrasts tellingly to Thoreau's brusque yeoman, who, in the bean field chapter in *Walden*, is identified with the people, not the patrician: "A very *agricola laboriosus* was I to travellers bound westward through Lincoln and Wayland to nobody knows where; they sitting at their ease in gigs, with elbows on knees, and reins loosely hanging in festoons; I the home-staying, laborious native of the soil" (W, 157).

Thoreau's excursionary writing before *Walden* could not be a model for a book about staying home. Nor could New York or English literary examples serve for a book about New England. Within New England literary culture itself, there was virtually no formal precedent for a work like *Walden* (although there was considerable precedent for its political ideology—his traditional point was ultimately that luxury was the ruin of a people). Agricultural treatises and natural history surveys could provide resources and serve as benchmarks, however, and references to them abound in *Walden*. These inventories and reports had never aimed at "pure" science—if such an unmixed thing ever could exist—but always thought of nature in connection with a people's well being—the people here being the descendants of the original English settlers. They were locally specific and shared Thoreau's urgent convictions that New England's economic natural base was being permanently destroyed and a whole way of life was going down with it.

The "Natural History of Massachusetts" criticized the state natural history surveys for their mere facticity, but used the facts for transcendental moralizing. The botanies of Jacob Bigelow had long instructed him in local flora: where to look and when—June and July, in dry pastures, ditches, road sides and borders of woods at Woburn or Newton, in low grounds at Bridgewater, low situations at Brighton, or the salt marshes at Chelsea and Cambridge. And George B. Emerson's 1846 report on the trees of Massachusetts, which Thoreau first read in 1852, was especially important for its argument on behalf of preserving and revitalizing the forests.[40] George Emerson explicitly links New England survival with arboroculture. Thoreau had already used "the West" as a complicated but fundamentally positive symbol of American nationality; George Emerson saw "the West" as a concept inimical to New England, and Thoreau followed his example, redefining his ideal west as, precisely, an ideal, a habit of pure expectancy which actuality could only tarnish. Said Emerson:

There are millions of acres of land in the Western States far richer
than any in our State, which may be purchased for much less than
it will cost to render barren land productive. Why not go thither
and occupy the rich wild lands? For many reasons. This is our native land. . . . Every improvement in agriculture, in the management of the forests, and in the use of the other natural resources of
our State, makes it capable of sustaining a larger population, and
thus enables more of our young men and young women to remain
with us, rendering home dearer to those who would otherwise be
left behind. . . . There are still higher reasons. We live in a climate
and on a soil best adapted, from their very severity and sterility, to
bring out the energies of mind and body, and to form a race of
hardy and resolute men. . . . We are not willing to leave. We wish
that our children should grow up under the influence of the institutions which our forefathers have formed and left to us, and
which we have been endeavoring to improve. Here we wish to live
and to die; and when we die, we wish to be surrounded by those
who are most dear to us.[41]

When Ralph Waldo Emerson eulogized Thoreau for having so dedicated
"his genius with such entire love to the fields, hills, and waters of his native
town, that he made them known and interesting to all reading Americans,
and to people over the sea," he deliberately situated him in the English tradition of village-based nature writing, making Thoreau out to be an American Gilbert White, Concord an American Selborne. And although this
image certainly helped to popularize Thoreau in the postbellum era, it also
prettified him in, perhaps, just the ways *Walden* meant to reject. For if
George Emerson spoke about preserving forests to make New England
beautiful as well as prosperous again, *Walden* recorded the esthetic and
economic devastation of a terrain that nobody had—in several senses—
cared for. So that one of the book's great achievements—its own mystification—is its discovery of natural beauty in a ruined landscape.

As for persona, the puttering parson exiled to Selborne, eager to maintain connection with sophisticated, intellectual London, has little in common with the emphatic rawness of Thoreau's Yankee. Nor does White's
amateur scientism ("A valuable record and example how the leisure hours
of a country clergyman may be profitably and innocently employed," as
William Jardine puts it in his edition of *Selborne*, which Thoreau read)
have much in common with the fierce spirituality of *Walden*.[42] Indeed, a
close reading of *Walden* reveals much less naturalist detail than is commonly supposed. Extended recording of natural data is a trait of Thoreau's

later journals, which explains why so much contemporary criticism of Thoreau is journal-centered. In *Walden* we read that he "probably" heard a raccoon, "maybe" heard an otter (*W*, 227); hunters told him about foxes and he heard one at night, but all he ever saw were the hounds. Old-timers reminisced about vanished deer, wildcats, bear; Thoreau encounters squirrels, mice, rabbits, dogs, cows, a feral cat, a stray pig. What to make of a diminished thing: wasps and ants, toads and frogs, three kinds of fish (pout, perch, and pickerel), perhaps a dozen types of birds, a like number of tree and shrub species. There are numerous wild grasses, but all of them are weeds—wormwood, piper, millet grass (*W*, 157), pigweed, sorrel (*W*, 161)—demanding eradication for the sake of beans. There are few wildflowers—certainly nothing approximating the more than 250 species identified by Susan Cooper in *Rural Hours*.

But although it is true that a better-trained or more systematic eye like Cooper's might have produced a richer record of neighborhood biota, it is also true that *Walden's* sparseness of detail admirably conveys an ecologically damaged and esthetically unpleasing natural environment. The book allots more space to thawing clay, ice bubbles, the depth and shape of the pond as well as the color of its water than to organic natural phenomena, and indeed the transcendental point that "there is nothing inorganic" (*W*, 308) could hardly be demonstrated by inventories of living things. But in addition, the landscape of *Walden* is presented—deliberately I think— as a scene of wreckage, for such a landscape calls out for the project of reclamation that makes Thoreau's mission.

The New England landscape he depicts, therefore, is a panorama of partly cleared, derelict fields with stumps still standing, of abandoned or indebted farms, of roadsides lined with Irish immigrant shanties. The Hollowell farm, which he had hoped to purchase, is in ruins; the Flint for whom Flint's Pond is named has long since decamped after clear-cutting the shores and wearing out the soil; Baker Farm is untilled fields, a standing shack on the property appropriated by a family of immigrant—and ignorant—Irish.

Even *Walden's* scenery, and even as Thoreau testifies to the pond's immortality, registers decline: once "completely surrounded by thick and lofty pine and oak woods" (*W*, 191) its shores are now significantly denuded. Woodchoppers leveled the woods once to open a space for failed farming and are leveling again for the railroad and its fuel. There is a much-traveled cart road behind the cabin; a highway within earshot; a railroad causeway just across the water—the locomotive whistle penetrates Thoreau's "solitude" summer and winter (*W*, 115); the detritus of an abandoned hamlet a short walk away; a dead horse reeking in a nearby hollow; a Canadian woodchopper passing by daily and firing his pistol for sport throughout the day; stray dogs traversing the property; people fishing year-round; and for sixteen days one winter a hundred laborers skim the pond, leaving behind a mountain of melting ice. The compensatory wilderness here is not unprofaned nature but the rotting horse, along with "tortoises and toads run over in the road" (W, 318). The seasonal cycles of nature, promising resurrection from rot, offer only a second chance. Even Walden—the best, the purest, the fairest—shines only in the eyes of a redemptive lover: the brute facts are that "woodchoppers have laid bare first this shore and then that, and the Irish have built their sties by it, and the railroad has infringed on its border, and the ice-men have skimmed it" (W, 192-193).

This second chance is an occasion of mutual redemption, where the landscape is redeemed by human love, and the human lover by the responsiveness of the land to his vision. But this epiphany is not to be achieved by gentlemen farmers or builders of country houses, who would never place themselves in full view of a railroad causeway. In a dreadful irony, the "city people" flooding the region around Concord are Irish paupers. If this mess is to be redeemed spiritually by love, it is also to be redeemed materially through an agriculture that mediates between individual subsistence (or total self-sufficiency) and the market by producing for local trade. Thoreau did not try to grow everything he ate, and raised beans (which he did not eat) for cash and barter. Much as he inveighs against "trade" throughout Walden, his agricultural aim is limited scale, not full-blown repudiation of the market. His point is really what he says it is: the town assessors "cannot at once name a dozen in the town who own their farms free and clear" because the farmer is trying to "solve the problem of a livelihood by a formula more complicated than the problem itself. To get his shoestrings he speculates in herds of cattle" (W, 33). One could argue that far from advocating private withdrawal or radical individualism, Walden looks to a revitalized—a debt-free—community that has collectively overcome the fatal attractions of distant markets and superfluous goods.

Thoreau's recurring use of the word "experiment" for his enterprise sardonically invokes the many experiments in scientific—i.e., market-oriented—farming described in the agricultural journals (see e.g., W, 196). His unmanured field, he boasts, "was one field not in Mr. Colman's report" (W, 157), referring to the state agricultural surveys published by Henry Colman between 1837 and 1840. But his "experiment" is real enough, designed not to make the ridiculous argument that a farmer can live on parables (this formulation is part of the book's calculated extravagance of expression), but rather that true human material needs could be easily satisfied by New England farmers. He welcomes numerous visitors to his experiment because the more witnesses to its success, the better it will be for New England. At the pond he does not leave nature as he found it; he starts by chopping down trees and leaves a beaten path from cabin to pond behind him. His cabin is recycled from an Irishman's shanty, and his agricultural work permanently alters the scene's ecology, as it was meant to: "even I have helped to clothe that fabulous landscape of my infant dreams, and one of the results of my presence and influence is seen in these bean leaves, corn blades, and potato vines" (*W*, 156). Profanation and improvement are oddly one and the same; the contradiction remains unresolved but, on balance, the preference tilts towards improvement, towards making something productive from the inherently "lean and effete" soil, exhausted by long-extinct nations as well as more recent cultivators (*W*, 155, 156).

"Former Inhabitants" limns an entire hamlet whose disappearance from the locale constitutes an all-too-typical New England tragedy. If not for improvidence and shiftlessness—alchoholism, specifically—"the basket, stable-broom, mat-making, corn-parching, linen-spinning, and pottery business [might] have thrived here, making the wilderness to blossom like the rose, and a numerous posterity [might] have inherited the land of their fathers." And he continues—in two sentences rife with contradiction but devoid of irony—"Alas! how little does the memory of these human inhabitants enhance the beauty of the landscape! Again, perhaps, Nature will try, with me for a first settler, and my house raised last spring to be the oldest in the hamlet" (*W*, 264). Here, clearly, Thoreau offers his bean-farm and his whole experiment as an enhancement. Reclaiming the landscape cannot mean leaving it alone.[43]

Diatribes against luxury are common as rain in New England writing, and from the start of the national history New Englanders had contrasted themselves to luxury-loving, effeminate, Europeanized, commercial New Yorkers. Therefore, to interpret Walden as a brief for traditional New England lifeways is to place it within familiar regional traditions of literature and ideology; to contrast the prudent New England farmer with the extravagant, wannabe aristocrats of New York would be entirely conventional. The familiar problem is that New England farmers have been dazzled by New York; *Walden*'s innovation lies in its precise localism, and its approach to nature through this political, ideological scrim, its depiction of New England cultural morbidity in and through a representation of a ruined natural environment.

To be sure, this is not how *Walden* is read today. Now it works as an appeal for individual self-containment, for a withdrawn spirituality, for the value of solitary contemplation, and for the transcendent worth of untouched nature.[44] The book lends itself to this interpretation, of course. But it does so in part because the communal politics of the book has been occluded by utter historical defeat. The market revolution was under way, pushing New England in directions opposite to those Thoreau was advocating. The economic future of New England could not lie in small farms: manufacturing populations had to be provisioned by farmers selling beyond their local communities; the Irish were here to stay; industrialists were laying out country pleasure grounds on terrain vacated by emigrants to the west; summer tourists and upscale suburbs were on the horizon. Perhaps, even, the conviction that agrarianism had underlain New England's vanished prosperity was more myth than reality.

Yet, as the historical provocations to which *Walden* responded receded, divesting the book of its temporal, local referentiality, it became available as a model for national nature writing. Those who appropriated it for national purposes would never have thought to look to New York for what they wanted, and the gentrified, Anglophile writing of the New Yorkers would not have served their purposes. The afterlife of *Walden* constitutes one more example of the overdetermined, disproportionate influence of New England on American cultural history.

NOTES

1. Henry David Thoreau, *A Week on the Concord and Merrimack Rivers*, ed. Carl F. Hovde et al. (Princeton, 1980), 54; Henry David Thoreau, *Walden*, ed. J. Lyndon Shanley (Princeton, 1971), 317; Henry David Thoreau, "Walking," *Writings of Henry David Thoreau* (Boston, 1906), 5:224. Future parenthetical citations in the text to W will refer to this edition of *Walden*.

2. On European ambivalence toward wilderness, see especially Donald Worster, *Nature's Economy: A History of Ecological Ideas* (Cambridge, 1994); Clarence J. Glacken, *Traces on the Rhodian Shore: Nature and Culture in Western Thought from Ancient Times to the End of the Eighteenth Century* (Berkeley, 1967); John Stilgoe, *The Common Landscape of America, 1580 to 1845* (New Haven, 1982); Michael Williams, *Americans and Their Forests: A Historical Geography* (Cambridge, 1989).

3. Thoreau, "Walking," 227, 230.

4. Steven Fink, *Prophet in the Marketplace: Thoreau's Development as a Professional Writer* (Princeton, 1992), 243. See also Joan Burbick, *Thoreau's Alternative History: Changing Perspectives on Nature, Culture, and Language* (Philadelphia, 1987), 59–68.

5. J. Lyndon Shanley, *The Making of Walden* (Chicago, 1957), 143.

6. Henry David Thoreau, "The Natural History of Massachusetts," *Writings*, 5:119, 120.

7. Sherman Paul, *The Shores of America: Thoreau's Inward Exploration* (Urbana, 1958), 183; Michael T. Gilmore, *American Romanticism and the Marketplace* (Chicago, 1985), 36, 43; Shanley, *Making of Walden*, 25. For a reading of the *Week* as historical geography, see Ning Yu, "Thoreau's Critique of the American Pastoral in a Week," *Nineteenth-Century Literature* 51(1996):304–326.

8. For a general survey of agricultural conditions in the northeast, see Clarence H. Danhof, *Change in Agriculture: The Northern United States, 1820–1870* (Cambridge, Mass., 1969). For a larger overview of land use from Native American agriculture to modern farming practices in New England, see also Carolyn Merchant, *Ecological Revolutions: Nature, Gender, and Science in New England* (Chapel Hill, 1989).

9. See Tamara Plakins Thornton, *Cultivating Gentlemen: The Meaning of Country Life Among the Boston Elite, 1785–1860* (New Haven, 1989).

10. See Carl J. Richard, *The Founders and the Classics: Greece, Rome, and the American Enlightenment* (Cambridge, Mass., 1994), 123–168. See also Ethel Seybold, *Thoreau: The Quest and the Classics* (New Haven, 1951).

11. This argument parallels Leo Marx's influential discussion of Thoreau's objections to technological progress in *The Machine in the Garden: Technology and the Pastoral Ideal in America* (New York, 1964). But where Marx describes Thoreau's landscape as a form of moral allegory, I consider terrain as a recalcitrant actuality.

12. Thoreau, "Walking," 231.

13. William Wordsworth, *Wordsworth's Guide to the Lakes: The Fifth Edition (1835)*, ed. Ernest de Selincourt (New York, 1906), 106.

14. For the influence of William Howitt on Thoreau, see Robert Sattelmeyer, *Thoreau's Reading* (Princeton, 1988), 205; and Lawrence Buell, *The Environmental Imagination: Thoreau, Nature Writing, and the Formation of American Culture* (Cambridge, 1995), 399–402. The construction of nature by the calendar year goes back to antiquity, of course, and is inextricably connected to agriculture, making an "exploitive" relation to nature inescapably part of human categorization.

15. William Howitt, *The Book of the Seasons; or, the Calendar of Nature* (London, 1831), xvi–xvii.

16. Raymond Williams, *The Country and the City* (London, 1973), 122, 125.

17. For the picturesque in internal English politics, see Alan Liu, *Wordsworth, the Sense of History* (Stanford, Calif., 1989); for the construction of English national identity via contrasts with the French, see Linda Colley, *Britons: Forging the Nation, 1707–1837* (New Haven, 1992). But Colley does not discuss the nation-building uses of "nature."

18. Buell's *Environmental Imagination* gives a richly detailed narrative of *Walden's* elevation to the nation's paradigmatic nature text.

19. Recent discussions of the class-based implications of the English picturesque include Malcolm Andrews, *The Search for the Picturesque* (Aldershot, 1989); Ann Bermingham, *Landscape and Ideology: The English Rustic Tradition, 1740–1860* (Berkeley, 1986); Elizabeth A. Bohls, *Women Travel Writers and the Language of Aesthetics, 1716–1818* (Cambridge, 1995); Stephen Copley and Peter Garside, eds., *The Politics of the Picturesque: Literature, Landscape, and Aesthetics since 1770* (Cambridge, 1994). See also E. J. Hobsbawm and T. O. Ranger, eds., *The Invention of Tradition* (Cambridge, 1983); Liu, *Wordsworth*; Christopher Mulvey,

Anglo-American Landscapes: A Study of Nineteenth-Century Anglo-American Travel Literature (Cambridge, 1983). Washington Irving's *The Sketch Book* made an especially important American contribution toward constructing England as the "Old World," and its tropes recur in any number of American antebellum travel books.

20. Thoreau, *Week*, 53–54.

21. William Howitt, *The Rural Life of England* (Philadelphia, 1841), n.p.

22. Mary Russell Mitford, *Our Village: Sketches of Rural Character and Scenery*, 4th ed. (New York, 1828), 81, 82.

23. Susan Fenimore Cooper, ed., *Pages and Pictures, from the Writings of James Fenimore Cooper* (New York, 1861), 14, 347.

24. David Schuyler, *Apostle of Taste: Andrew Jackson Downing, 1815–1852* (Baltimore, 1996), 28.

25. Andrew Jackson Downing, *A Treatise on the Theory and Practice of Landscape Gardening, Adapted to North America; with a View to the Improvement of Country Residences*, 4th ed. (New York, 1849), 22.

26. Downing, *Landscape Gardening*, 352.

27. Downing, *Landscape Gardening*, 16.

28. John Stilgoe, *Borderland: Origins of the American Suburb, 1820–1939* (New Haven, 1988). Stilgoe uses "suburb" in a contemporary sense; in antebellum writing, the suburb was inhabited by workers—cockneys—who could not afford to live in the city itself.

29. J. T. Headley, *The Adirondack, or Life in the Woods* (New York, 1849), 53–54. The importance of Headley's book, as well as Nathaniel Parker Willis's *Rural Letters* (New York, 1849), was first noted in Hans Huth's *Nature and the American: Three Centuries of Changing Attitudes* (Berkeley, 1957).

30. Nathaniel Parker Willis, "The Highland Terrace, Above West Point," *Home Book of the Picturesque* (New York, 1852), 106, 110, 108.

31. But he had read at least one other book by Willis: see Sattelmeyer, *Thoreau's Reading*, 291.

32. The sequence originated at Willis's country seat, Glenmary, a farm of some 200 acres on a tributary of the Susquehanna some two miles from the village of Owego (in New York State near the Pennsylvania border), where he lived from 1837 to 1842.

33. Willis, *Rural Letters*, 97.

34. Willis, *Rural Letters*, 133.

35. Willis, *Rural Letters*, 59.

36. Willis, *Rural Letters*, 140. In his biography of Willis, Henry A. Beers contrasts him specifically to Thoreau as one who viewed nature "more as a landscape gardener than as a naturalist," and opposes the two as a cockney versus an elect spirit in nature—thus catching perfectly the class implications of Thoreau's transcendentalist meritocracy. *Nathaniel Parker Willis* (Boston, 1888), 225.

37. Thoreau, "Walking," 5:216.

38. For a view of Susan Cooper as oppressed and demoralized by her father's demands, see Lucy B. Maddox, "Susan Fenimore Cooper and the Plain Daughters of America," *American Quarterly* 40(1988):131–146.

39. Stilgoe, *Borderland*, 24. For a view of *Rural Hours* as the origin of a particularly

female, albeit also class-determined, way of relating to nature, see Vera Norwood, *Made From This Earth: American Women and Nature* (Chapel Hill, 1993).

40. Sattelmeyer, *Thoreau's Reading*, 173.

41. George B. Emerson, *A Report on the Trees and Shrubs Growing Naturally in the Forests of Massachusetts* (Boston, 1846), 36. In fact, this book's ecological argument goes well beyond Walden; some scholars may be crediting Thoreau for ideas he encountered in George Emerson's book.

42. Gilbert White, *The Natural History and Antiquities of Selborne*, ed. William Jardine (London, 1850), v. Jardine's edition, first published in London by Constable in 1829, by far the most widely circulated text of *Selborne* was revised and reissued several times. One of the leading English naturalists of his time, Jardine presented White as a model for ordinary folks who wanted to help science along, and was emphatic on the distinction between professional and amateur naturalists. His annotations mainly corrected White's errors and identified obsolete observations. Sattelmeyer, *Thoreau's Reading*, 289, identifies a Jardine edition as what Thoreau first read in 1853; the Bohn edition in Thoreau's library cited by Robert D. Richardson is Jardine's. I am disagreeing here with Richardson on the close resemblance of *Walden* to *Selborne*. *Henry Thoreau: A Life of the Mind* (Berkeley, 1986), 309. There is no attempt at a White-like completeness in Walden, and conversely no trace of Thoreauvian transcendentalizing, moralizing, or anthropomorphizing in White; it is precisely this absence of poetic, subjective overlay that Jardine praises.

43. For an extended discussion of the "Former Inhabitants" chapter, see chapter 6 of H. Daniel Peck's *Thoreau's Morning Work: Memory and Perception in* A Week on the Concord and Merrimack Rivers, The Journal, *and* Walden (New Haven, 1990).

44. The most impressive exposition of this approach is Buell's *Environmental Imagination*.

Concord Orientalism, Thoreauvian Autobiography, and the Artist of Kouroo

Alan D. Hodder

THE ROOTS OF MODERN AMERICAN FASCINATION WITH ASIAN religious traditions may be traced to eighteenth-century missionary and travel accounts, the beginnings of the East India trade, and the antiquarian interests of a few founding fathers. Prior to the Revolution, however, American knowledge of India and the Far East remained at best fragmentary. Cotton Mather had carried on an avid correspondence with Danish missionaries in Madras in the 1720s, but until well after the Revolutionary period much of what Americans thought they knew of the mysterious East came to them in the form of the stereotypical "Oriental tale," of which the "Arabian Nights" and Samuel Johnson's "Rasselas" were perhaps the most famous examples. With the inauguration of the East India trade in 1784, sailors' stories and a few articles of trade began to supplement the more fanciful information about Asian cultures available previously.[1] Concurrently, a few of America's more cosmopolitan Enlightenment thinkers began to evince a more studied interest in Chinese and Indian classical civilizations. Benjamin Franklin, for example, conceived an early interest in Confucianism and later established a close friendship with the British Orientalist jurist Sir William Jones. In 1794, Joseph Priestley, a transplanted English Unitarian, published the first serious study of Asian religious traditions in America, *A Comparison of the Institutions of Moses with those of the Hindoos and other Ancient Nations*, a book that helped shape John Adams's interest in these cultures. At the turn of the century, Hannah Adams included a thirty-page sketch of Asian religions in the third edition of her comparative survey of the world's religions.[2] Beginning as early as 1817, American Unitarians, including the young Ralph Waldo Emerson, were treated to some new insights about the religious and cultural life of

India in accounts provided in the Unitarian periodicals of the life and career of the Bengali reformer Rammohan Roy.[3]

Yet, notwithstanding these important earlier contacts, the formal inauguration of modern American interest in Eastern religions might be said to coincide with the belated arrival of the Bhagavad Gita in Concord in the summer of 1845. Here in its expectant reception by members of the Transcendentalist circle—chiefly Ralph Waldo Emerson, A. Bronson Alcott, and most notably Henry David Thoreau—we may locate the first collective manifestations of a tradition of American Romantic Orientalism that has strongly shaped subsequent American attitudes toward Eastern thought. Emerson included the formal announcement in a breezy letter he wrote on June 17 to family friend and townswoman Elizabeth Hoar: "The only other event," he wrote with not altogether disingenuous pomp, "is the arrival in Concord of the 'Bhagvat-Geeta,' the much renowned book of Buddhism, extracts of which I have often admired but never before held the book in my hands."[4]

With its, to us, surprising misidentification of the Gita as a Buddhist work, this fragment is as revealing for what it shows about the continued paucity of American knowledge of Asian culture as for what it suggests about then-current Transcendentalist enthusiasms. As he indicated, Emerson's appetite had been whetted for this long-postponed feast for years. In a piece of correspondence addressed late in life to F. Max Müller (1823–1900), Europe's premier nineteenth-century Orientalist and leading architect of the field of comparative mythology, Emerson dated his first exposure to the Gita to his reading many years previously of a sketch of Indian philosophy in Victor Cousin's *Cours de philosophie*. A letter addressed to his brother William on May 24, 1831, made reference to his reading of Cousin at this time.[5] It was not until 1845, however, when he borrowed a copy of Charles Wilkins's translation from his friend James Elliot Cabot, that Emerson saw a complete edition of the Gita.[6] And, by the time his own copy arrived from London some weeks later, the Gita had become the talk of the town, quickly assuming its pre-ordained position as the central exhibit in waxing Transcendentalist estimations of "the East."

Emerson's library was open, as usual, to his friends, and before long the Gita was making its rounds from one Transcendentalist reading room to another. By the next summer the journals of all three Transcendentalists resounded with accolades typical of early Orientalist fervor. To Alcott the Gita epitomized "oriental wisdom"; it was, he thought, the "Best of books," fully deserving of inclusion in "a Bible for Mankind."[7] Thoreau, whose reactions were conditioned by his appreciative reading of "The Laws of Manu" in 1840, apparently took his turn with the Gita while still ensconced at Walden Pond. Beginning in June of 1846, he began copying out long extracts from Emerson's copy, together with approving running commentary. Many of these entries he soon transferred to the "Monday" section of *A Week*, but *Walden* also proved a decided beneficiary, as Thoreau wished to make clear in its pages: "In the morning I bathe my intellect in the stupendous and cosmogonal philosophy of the Bhagvat Geeta, since whose composition years of the gods have elapsed, and in comparison with which our modern world and its literature seem puny and trivial."[8] Three years later the Concordians' enthusiasm had hardly abated. In 1848 Emerson could still write: "I owed,—my friend and I,—owed a magnificent day to the Bhagavat Geeta. It was the first of books; it was as if an empire spake to us, nothing small or unworthy but large, serene, consistent, the voice of an old intelligence which in another age & climate had pondered & thus disposed of the same questions which exercise us."[9]

While these were not the first reactions to Asian, or even Hindu, traditions in Transcendentalist literature, they signaled the start of an unselfconsciously ebullient phase of American Romantic Orientalism. At the same time, they inaugurated what was to become an influential wider consensus about the meaning of "India" in nineteenth-century America. Together, it may be argued, these three Transcendentalists of Concord set the basic terms of Romantic Orientalism, thus shaping all of their own, and their successors', subsequent readings of Asian literature and of Asia for some time to come. From this point on, the literature of Asia would serve Transcendentalists as a primary religious, intellectual, and literary touchstone. Among the Orientalists of Concord, however, the case of Henry David Thoreau proves especially revealing, as we shall see.

The Oriental Renaissance

Due recognition of the Transcendentalists' originating influence on subsequent American attitudes to Asian cultures should not obscure the fact that the profile of "the East" to which they contributed owed much to the views bequeathed to them by earlier European Orientalists, particularly as they arose in response to the re-establishment of Western contact with India in the early sixteenth century. The history of empire-building European contacts with Asia in the Age of Discovery is a long and involved story, but we may conveniently date the full flowering of European Orientalism from the 1784 founding of the Asiatic Society of Bengal, a scholarly association underwritten in its early years by the British East India Company. Established for the principal purpose of promoting the study of Indian laws, languages, and literatures, the Society sponsored the research of a small but gifted cadre of British scholar-magistrates who would make a lasting contribution to the Western study of India. Preeminent among these were Sir William Jones (1746–1794), the Society's first president and a polyglot linguist and scholar of extraordinary erudition; Charles Wilkins (1749–1836), also a magistrate in the colonial government and Jones's chief tutor in his early study of Sanskrit; Henry Thomas Colebrooke (1765–1837), a mathematician and linguist who exerted a decisive and lasting influence on Western interpretations of India; and Horace Hayman Wilson (1786–1860), who though arriving in Bengal only in 1808, soon became one of the most accomplished Sanskritists and prolific translators of his generation. In the English-speaking world of the nineteenth century, Wilson's reputation as an Indologist was surpassed only by that of Max Müller, Wilson's German-born successor at Oxford.

In 1788 the Society began publishing *Asiatic Researches*, a learned journal that went through twenty volumes before its final edition in 1839 and became the main conduit for transmission of information about India to the West. During the next fifty years, the work of these early British Orientalists issued in a series of translations of Hindu scriptures and classics, as well as learned monographs, that shed significant light on Indian civilization. Of special note are Wilkins's translations of the Bhagavad Gita (1785) and Hitopadeṣa (1787), a traditional collection of morality tales known to Emerson and Thoreau by 1841; Jones's translations of Kālidāsa's *Śakuntalā* (1789) and, importantly for Emerson and Thoreau, *The Institutes of Hindu Law* ("The Laws of Manu," 1794); Colebrooke's *Essays on the Religion and Philosophy of the Hindus* (1815) and his translation of the *Sāṁkhya Kārikā* (1837), a commentary on the Sāṁkhya system of Indian philosophy that Thoreau studied carefully in 1851; and Wilson's translations of Kālidāsa's *Megha-dūta* (1813) and the *Viṣṇu Purāṇa* (1840), a work also perused in Concord by 1845.[10]

As the work of these scholars began filtering into the learned centers of Europe in the last decade of the eighteenth and first few decades of the nineteenth centuries, it galvanized a movement of European cultural renewal inseparable from Romanticism generally. Among the first and most avid consumers of eighteenth-century reports about the Orient were German philosophers and poets. The proto-Romantic writer Johann Gottfried von Herder (1744–1803) viewed India as the cradle of civilization. For him and his Romantic successors, India was seen as a remnant of Europe's golden age and as the home of wisdom and philosophy, in which reason and feeling, art and religion, science and the imagination existed in harmony. Writing in the *Athenaeum* shortly after the turn into the nineteenth

century, Friedrich Schlegel, Germany's first Sanskritist and a leading exponent of Romantic Orientalism, found in this previously undisclosed literature a necessary sanction for his Romantic agenda, declaring, "We must
seek the supreme romanticism in the Orient."[11] By the mid nineteenth
century, Germany had already begun to assume the preeminent position in
the European academic study of Indian classical civilization that it would
maintain well into the next century. As the German, British, and French
universities began to absorb the windfall of translations and commentaries
of classical Hindu, Chinese, and Persian texts, European poets and scholars began to speak of an "Oriental Renaissance" parallel to and of as much
consequence as the Italian Renaissance of the fifteenth and sixteenth
centuries.[12] For such Romantic advocates and the historians who have
championed them, Orientalism was a movement that promised to bring
down the walls long separating East and West.[13]

    What many such Romantic accounts tended to gloss over, of course, were
the harsh political realities motivating and underlying much Orientalist
study.[14] However admiring Britain's colonial agents may have been of
Indian literature, art, or philosophy, they themselves could hardly lose sight
of the motives that prompted their studies or the conditions under which
they carried them out in Bengal. Colonialism was the enabling context in
which all of this brilliant work of European recovery, translation, and interpretation took place, as Sir William made clear in the preface to his translation of India's oldest and most venerated legal code, "The Laws of Manu"
(*mānava-dharmaśāstra*). Manu (or "Menu," as he was accustomed to trans-
literate it) was one of the first Hindu texts prepared for translation—
a choice that might seem odd today, until we recognize the role it was meant
to serve in the colonial government. In his preface, Jones's own motives, in
any case, were made entirely clear:

> Whatever opinion in short may be formed of Menu and his laws,
> in a country happily enlightened by sound philosophy and the only
> true revelation, it must be remembered, that those laws are actu-
> ally revered, as the word of the Most High, by nations of great im-
> portance to the political and commercial interests of Europe, and
> particularly by many millions of Hindu subjects, whose well di-
> rected industry would add largely to the wealth of Britain, and
> who ask no more in return than protection for their persons and
> places of abode, justice in their temporal concerns, indulgence to
> the prejudices of their own religion, and the benefit of those laws
> which they have been taught to believe sacred, and which alone
> they can possibly comprehend.[15]

Exposure of the colonialist agenda underlying the Orientalist project has been the main thrust of the new revisionist field of academic study that has grown up since the publication of *Orientalism*, Edward Said's now classic treatment of the subject in 1978. There Said construed Orientalism as Western Europe's way of conceptualizing the non-Western colonial world in order better to exploit and control it. It designates a style of thought and a mode of discourse concerning the peoples and cultures of the non-Western world—in particular Arabs and the Middle East—that arose in the eighteenth century to serve European, and later American, political and economic interests. Basic to Orientalist discourse was the penchant to collapse important cultural differences under the totalizing category of "the Orient" and oppose it invidiously to the equally artifical category of the Occident. The Orientalist, Said argued, willy-nilly subjected Arabs and Muslims to a process of stereotyping, homogenization, and often infantilization, in the service, inevitably, of his own cultural, political, and economic self-interest. While masquerading as a neutral and objective form of knowledge, Orientalism nevertheless grew out of a Western will to power. It was, in short, "a Western style for dominating, restructuring, and having authority over the Orient."[16] Orientalism was a designation that said very little about non-Western peoples themselves and a great deal about Europe and its colonialist agendas. Images of the Middle Eastern, African, or Asian "other" were constructed essentially out of European desires and projections. Believing that members of non-Western cultures could not speak or act adequately for themselves, the Orientalist scholar, magistrate, or missionary assumed that they must therefore be spoken for. In this way, Orientalist constructions of Eastern cultures were premised upon a certain privileged exteriority. In Said's handling, "the Orient" thus comes to be seen as a kind of open interpretive space, or, as it were, a mirror of the European self.

Few theories in contemporary cultural studies have received the kind of immediate and lasting acclaim accorded Said's treatment of Orientalism, but the book has not been without its critics. While most seem inclined to accept as just the basic implications of the anti-Orientalist critique, some have objected strenuously to this ostensible one-sidedness. In *Orientalism*, Said writes as if colonized peoples were bereft of their own voices and incapable of responding for themselves to the colonial challenge. According to this view, Said himself appears to have been coopted by Orientalist discourse in his own tendency to deny agency to colonized peoples. In effect acknowledging the justice of such criticism, Said has in his more recent work deliberately sought to give more free play to the reciprocal character of early European encounters with the Oriental "other." In *Culture and*

Imperialism (1993), in particular, he provides extended treatment of the culture of resistance that rose up everywhere in the colonial and post-colonial world in response to the threats of imperialist culture.[17] Such acknowledgement of the bilateral nature of colonial encounters provides a more complete representation of the history of cross-cultural encounters during the colonial period, including, as we will see further on, of Transcendentalist Orientalism. Yet Said's earlier insistence on the unilateral character of Orientalism cannot simply be passed off as a mere oversight, notwithstanding this somewhat belated correction. In fact, to a large extent, Said's original conception of Orientalism as a kind of one-way cultural and hermeneutical street simply reflects his epistemological belief that all knowledge, particularly knowledge of other cultures, is a product of self-revealing social construction. Orientalist depictions of the East are dangerous and incredible not only because they falsely assume the existence of some essential Oriental realities, but also because they falsely assume that knowledge of any sort is capable of transcending its own historical, linguistic, and ideological situation.[18] In his recent work, Said has sought to offer an account of colonial and postcolonial encounter more adequate to its dialectical complexities, but he has not apparently recanted the historicism of this basic hermeneutical assumption. Indeed, *Orientalism* offers a classic articulation of a kind of historicism that has come to be definitive of much contemporary cultural studies. Though Said and others continue to revise and debate his original thesis, *Orientalism* thus offers a representative statement of a certain way of conceiving intercultural understanding that still holds enormous sway in contemporary cultural and postcolonial studies. My purpose in invoking Said here is merely to highlight the differences between the conception of intercultural understanding that he represents and the view implied in the somewhat idiosyncratic brand of Romantic Orientalism that, as we will see, Thoreau himself espouses.

In *Orientalism*, Said focused almost exclusively upon Europe's treatment of Islam and the Middle East, but Indologists were not slow to realize the relevance of his critique to their own fields of study.[19] In the Oriental Renaissance extolled by European Romantics, India had taken center stage. In the familiar Orientalist caricature, India was a land of mystery and mysticism. The impression often left upon its European visitors—as in E. M. Forster's account of the booming Marabar caves—was one of sheer incomprehensibility. Yet such an impression resulted in part because of India's enormous complexity. Whether from the vantage of Boston or Berlin, Romantic Orientalists, in particular, conceived of India as a land of contradictions and thus in some sense a cipher of reality itself: childlike innocence, but unredeemable decadence; asceticism together with gross sensuality; the purest idealism and the most blatant idolatry; philosophic elevation yet the most depraved superstition. It was a place— for the Transcendentalists, a state of being, actually—predicated upon spatial and temporal distance. Travel accounts, early and late, excoriated what were conceived as India's bizarre religious practices, even as they dallied in her romance. Thus, defying all easy generalization, India became the perfect vehicle of European self-construction and the ideal object of European desire.

More, perhaps, than other parts of the non-Western world, India lent itself to the sort of European self-projection that Said has described. Europeans had of course lived in the shadow of the contiguous cultures of Islam and the Middle East for over a thousand years, but the re-establishment of European contact with the cultures of India and the Far East had to await the circumnavigation of Africa in the late fifteenth century and the eventual decline of the Ottoman Empire. To the first European merchants and colonists, India held out special fascination. In contrast to the civilizations of China and Japan, India seemed to retain some racial, cultural, and linguistic kinship with the European world by virtue of the Indo-European origins of Sanskrit and its cognate languages, and of Vedic culture itself. The India Europeans encountered in the sixteenth century thus represented a kind of amalgam of East and West, Europe and Asia, the strange and the familiar. To European observers, Indian culture seemed at once bizarre and somehow recognizable. Partly Indo-European in origin yet situated in an alien cultural setting of enormous antiquity, India offered to Europeans the perfect fusion of self and other, the familiar and the macabre.

Following the precedent set by many of Europe's first Orientalists, American Transcendentalists looked principally to the classical texts of Hinduism as the chief exhibit of Eastern wisdom. This was in part a simple consequence of the disproportionate scholarly attention that had been paid until that point in time to Hindu India under the aegis of the British royal government. By virtue of the concerted labors of British colonial agents, works of and about Hindu culture enjoyed a significantly wider publication and distribution in Western Europe throughout the first half of the nineteenth century than works involving other non-Muslim Asian cultures. For its part, Buddhism was poorly represented in the work of the first generation of European Orientalists, a fact that principally explains the Transcendentalists' tendency to conflate Hindu and Buddhist ideas in their earliest references to them. In fact, except for some early work of the French Orientalist scholar Eugène Burnouf—a portion of which Emerson and Thoreau included in translation in the January 1844 issue of the *Dial*— most Western readers had little real understanding of Buddhism until well after 1850, when the first European translations of the Pali and Mahayana canons and books about Buddhism began to be available in the West.[20] Emerson and Thoreau did not of course limit their Eastern readings to Hindu texts—they found much to admire in translations of Persian and Chinese texts also—but Hindu literature exemplified for them the contemplative values and the tradition of philosophical idealism they most prized. Thus, to the Orientalists of Concord, as to Europe's first Orientalists, it was Hindu India that initially offered the greatest revelations.

Orientalism in Concord

The image of India and the Orient we see refracted in the letters and journals of Concord's Transcendentalists in the mid 1840s obviously exhibits many of the features we have come to associate with European Orientalism generally. There is nothing surprising in this, since Emerson and his friends read the same books and relied on the same travel accounts as the Orientalists of Germany, England, and France. I want to complicate and problematize this relationship as we go along, but for now it is crucial to insist that, in its larger contours, Transcendentalist Orientialism represents essentially a somewhat belated, though provincial, recrudescence of Orientalist discourse. On the one hand, the Americans fully subscribed to Orientalist caricatures of Indian "superstition," idolatry, caste tyranny, and sloth. Earlier in his life, Emerson had scoffed at India's "immense 'goddery,'" while Thoreau was always ready to repudiate as "Hindoo tyranny" what he conceived to be India's conservatism and preoccupation with caste.[21] On the other hand, for these Transcendentalists, as for the German Romantics, French eclectics, and some British Indologists, India was also the "cradle of humanity" and a living relic of the Golden Age; she epitomized a benign and venerable conservatism reflecting the timelessness of human experience; her ancient scriptures—the Vedas, laws of Manu, and Purāṇas—exemplified better than any other literature their own favorite doctrines of literary organicism and romantic primitivism; her philosophers served as the virtual paragons of an uncompromising philosophical idealism; and her religion represented a pure type of contemplation and mysticism.[22] None of this was original to the Orientalists of Concord; indeed, most such formulations are immediately recognizable as reworked Orientalist stereotypes.

Notwithstanding this overlap, it is worthwhile to consider how different the Americans' cultural position was relative to that of most Europeans. One objection sometimes raised against the Orientalist critique is that it has tended to totalize the Orientalists much as it sees the Orientalists totalizing the Orient.[23] If Orientalist depictions of Hindus, for example, were indeed inextricably interwoven with British designs on Indian resources, then surely the romantic effusions of German philosophers, whose nation had as yet few vested colonial interests in South Asia, or the preoccupations of far-off American Transcendentalists would exhibit some important differences. The unorthodox view of American Romantic writing as a "postcolonial phenomenon" serves a useful purpose in this context as a necessary counterbalance to more conventional assumptions that this literature sanctioned incipient American expansionism.[24] It is true that by the 1840s American commerce had itself acquired a significant stake in the India and China trades, a fact witnessed in *Walden* in its various references to the Celestial Empire and, as I will note further on, Thoreau's extended discussion of ongoing trade in Walden ice.[25] But throughout most of the nineteenth century at least, American colonialist ambitions in Asia paled next to those of the great European powers. The ambiguous status of Americans in the arena of nineteenth-century European imperialism is suggestively illustrated in a letter Thoreau wrote from Concord on November 8, 1855, to his English friend Thomas Cholmondeley thanking him profusely for his generous gift of some forty-four volumes of mostly South Asian literature. Cholmondeley had sent the books to Thoreau from England shortly after returning from an extended visit to Concord and just before embarking for the war in the Crimea. In Thoreau's sincerely grateful but bantering letter, he expressed amazement at the sheer number of the Indian volumes of which he was the lucky beneficiary and then launched into a playful but pointed revisionistic parody of British imperialism:

> Have at them! Who cares for numbers in a just cause. England expects every man to do his duty. Be sure you are right and then go ahead. I begin to think myself learned for merely possessing such works: If here is not the wealth of the Indies, of what stuff then is it made? They may keep their rupees; this and the life of this is what the great company traded and fought for, to convey the light of the East into the West: this their true glory and success.[26]

In this cheeky fragment Thoreau makes it clear that as far as he is concerned the only Indian wealth worth getting out is that of a religious and literary sort. Thus, whether the position of a midcentury Massachusetts native was nearer to the colonizers, the colonized, or as seems more plausible, something in between, the presumption of a monolithic European Orientalism in which even Americans were complicit seems unwarranted.

It would make more sense to conceive of Orientalism as a kind of European familial tendency admitting of a variety of manifestations depending upon the facts of geography, history, and international experience.

Despite such American anomalies, some Transcendentalist writings on India and the Far East frequently do traffic in Orientalist stereotypes, as we have seen, and nowhere is this more evident than in the case of Emerson, whose mature engagement with India came only after a long and quite ambivalent courtship. Indeed, the progress of his acquaintance with India followed the general path of Europe's rediscovery of India generally: as a child in Boston, he encountered India in the form of the exotic merchandise—muslins, spices, and tea—flowing across India Wharf and the Boston Waterfront; as a senior at Harvard College, he encountered India again in the often fiercely bigoted images proffered by the missionary and travel accounts he read while researching his Exhibition essay on "Indian Superstition," and a few years after, in the news fielded by the *Christian Register* about the life and career of the Bengali reformer Rammohan Roy; and finally, as the Transcendentalist lecturer and published essayist, he encountered India again in the monographs and translations of the Hindu sacred texts that were finally making their way to New England. Emerson's own constructions evolved, consequently, from antiquarian curiosity and conventional bigotry to the enthusiastic endorsement typical of his middle and later years. Yet, while Emerson soon abandoned all traces of the old Christian-inspired prejudice and xenophobia, even his mature readings of India rarely departed far from the essentialist schema and typologies characteristic of Romantic Orientalism. His essay "Plato" in *Representative Men*, a classic formulation of Emersonian Orientalism, provides an apt illustration. Here the old Orientalist dichotomy between East and West is once more trotted out to illustrate Emerson's favorite doctrine of Polarity:

> The country of unity, of immoveable institutions, the seat of a philosophy delighting in abstractions, of men faithful in doctrine and in practice to the idea of a deaf, unimplorable, immense Fate, is Asia; and it realizes this faith in the social institution of caste. On the other side, the genius of Europe is active and creative: it resists caste by culture: its philosophy was a discipline: it is a land of arts, inventions, trade, freedom. If the East loved infinity, the West delighted in boundaries.[27]

Typologies of this sort governed much early Orientalist discourse, and Emerson never really extricated himself from their hold. In the final analysis, India served him passively as a kind of intellectual scaffolding over which to drape his own romantic vision. As Arthur Christy long ago demonstrated, Emerson embraced the Hindu teachings for the analogies they provided for his own conceptual system: in the Hindu doctrine of karma, he found the perfect analogue to his long-cherished doctrine of Compensation; in transmigration, he recognized his own belief in meta-morphosis; in the Upaniṣadic identification of *ātman* and *brahman*, he discovered an ancient sanction for his conception of the Oversoul and the God within; and through the Vedāntin's *māyā*, he found an image through which to elaborate his sense of nature's unlimited propensity for illusion.[28] Emerson approached the Hindu texts, as he did so much of his reading, as potential stimulants to his own philosophical and imaginative vision. His purpose in turning over the pages of these ancient texts was to locate those touchstones—"lusters," as he called them—that he could incor-porate into the body of his own work. Yanking them from their actual historical and literary contexts, he freely deposited them into the pages of the journals he could refer to blithely as his "savings bank," and he had no reservations about doing so. Insofar as it was directed primarily to Asian traditions, the sort of free-wheeling literary appropriation habitually practiced by the Transcendentalists might be conceived of as a kind of intellectual colonialism, as one writer has bluntly described it, in effect mimicking the general Orientalist attitude to its subject by subordinating the native integrity of these texts in order to serve an entirely Western purpose—but this was, after all, the way these writers exploited texts of every sort.[29] Needless to say, the Transcendentalists of Concord were not guilty, as some of their European predecessors had been, of rifling manu-scripts or ransacking ancient tombs and treasures in order to bring back the riches of the East.

Thoreauvian Orientalism

When viewed within the wider context of European Romantic Orientalism, Emerson's appropriation of Hindu classics appears more or less standard, even predictable, in view of this cavalier but distinctively Transcendentalist habit of lifting and appropriating his sources with little regard for their origins. Thoreau's work also reflects these reading habits, but his own reception of the Hindu texts evinces some striking departures from the more normative Orientalist line epitomized by Emerson. Thoreau's read-ings of Indian literature offer a revealing test case for contemporary critical theories of Orientalism, but they also shed significant light on Thoreau himself and the nature of his work.

In stark contrast to the protracted period of preparation and incubation that preceded Emerson's excited announcement in 1845 of the Gita's arrival in Concord, Thoreau's engagement with South Asian literature began quite suddenly with his reading of Emerson's *Manu* in 1840, and his response quickly became almost unreservedly enthusiastic. To judge from college reading lists, he read little from or about Asian traditions during his studies at Harvard, though he was no doubt familiar with some basic facts and the usual stereotypes.[30] His sporadic first references to India in his journals were, if anything, conventionally derogatory. In the first reference to Hinduism anywhere in his journals, he mourned the superficiality of New England church life with an analogy to Hindu temple worship: "One is sick at heart of this pagoda worship—it is like the beatings of gongs in a Hindoo subterranean temple." Later on the pages of his journals are punctuated with hackneyed references to the Indian juggernaut, Asian "serenity" and "indolence," or conventionally romantic images of "domes and minarets"—the familiar stock of eighteenth-century Oriental tales. Other early passages made it clear that Thoreau's attitudes had also been shaped by the usual polarities of the standard Orientalist grammar: "I cannot attach much importance to historical epochs—or geographical boundaries—when I have my Orient and Occident in one revolution of my body."[31] This last entry was made on August 14, 1840, and until this point in time, his depictions of Asian civilization consisted invariably of a kind of familiar Orientalist pastiche. Three days later, however, on August 17, he provided his cautious first assessment of a book he had recently borrowed from Emerson—Jones's translation of *The Laws of Manu*: "Tried by a New England eye, . . . they are simply the oracles of a race already in its dotage, but held up to the sky, . . . they are of a piece with its depth and serenity."[32]

Thoreau's reading that August marked the beginning of a devotion to Asian, especially Hindu, classics that continued for the next fifteen years. The next spring, he was immersed in *Manu* once again, and now flushed enthusiasm replaced his tone of qualified admiration:

> That title—The Laws of Menu—with the Gloss of Culucca— comes to me with such a volume of sound as if it had swept unobstructed over the plains of Hindostan, and when my eye rests on yonder birches—or the sun in the water—or the shadows of the trees—it seems to signify the laws of them all.
>
> They are the laws of you and me—a fragrance wafted down from those old times—and no more to be refuted than the wind.
>
> When my imagination travels eastward and backward to those remote years of the gods—I seem to draw near to the habitation of

the morning—and the dawn at length has a place. I remember the
book as an hour before sunrise.
  We are height and depth both—a calm sea—at the foot of a
promontory—Do we not overlook our own depths?[33]

During the next few years, Thoreau continued his Indological research,
supplementing Emerson's collection with texts drawn from the library at
Harvard College.[34] By the time he moved to Walden Pond in 1845, he had
probably also been introduced to Wilkins's translation of the Bhagavad
Gita, as we have seen. Into the "Sunday" and "Monday" sections of *A
Week*, he interpolated long extracts from the Gita, together with commentary upon them, as a vehicle as much of religious and social criticism as of
personal reflection. By the beginning of the next decade, he was familiar
with several other classical Hindu texts as well, including Wilson's translation of the *Viṣṇu Purāṇa*, William Ward's translations of excerpts from the
six systems of Indian philosophy, Rammohan Roy's translations of selected
Upanisads, and Colebrooke's translations of the *Sāṁkhya Kārikā*.[35] Besides English translations, Thoreau looked into French versions as well,
especially M. A. Langlois's French edition of the *Harivaṁśa*, an appendix
to the voluminous Indian epic the *Mahābhārata*. For reasons we can only
guess Thoreau himself prepared a partial translation of one episode from
Langlois's work.[36] References in the published writings confirm Miriam
Jesswine's view that of all these texts Manu, the Bhagavad Gita, and the
Sāṁkhya Kārikā were the most influential.[37] After the year 1850, references in the journals to Asian religions became less frequent. Thoreau's
journals and letters witness a renewed burst of enthusiasm in 1855, however, with the arrival of Thomas Cholmondeley's trunk of mostly Hindu
books, though this was an event more important for the further transmission of Oriental ideas than for their formative impact on Emerson and
Thoreau themselves.[38]
  In its first phase, then, Thoreau's representations of Hindu texts were
often indistinguishable from those of his mentor Emerson. Until 1841 or so,
his appreciation of this literature was clearly preconditioned by the various
romantic Orientalist platitudes that he and his friends more or less uncriti-
cally absorbed. Even much later, in the pages of *A Week* and *Walden*, Indian
cultural life occasionally became the butt of his satiric asides. But after
1841, the character of his references to Asian texts generally became more
studied, better informed, and quite deliberately implemented. In contrast
to Emerson, who remained throughout his life content to draw on Asian literature for mere embellishment and illustration, Thoreau studied it with a
care and scholarly diligence unrivaled to that point in American history.

And while Emerson remained locked within the prison-house of Orientalist constructions, Thoreau managed to supersede them with his own daring, and at times quite original, applications. This is not to suggest that
Thoreau's approach to his readings was any less self-serving than Emerson's; on the contrary, Thoreau clearly used this literature, perhaps at times
arrogantly, for his own distinctly personal and artistic aims. The point I wish
to emphasize here is that he used this material *differently* than any American had before him.

In order to dramatize the importance of this claim both for our understanding of Thoreau and for our understanding of early American Orientalism more generally, I would like now to point to three areas of Thoreau's
thought that offer suggestive illustration: his preoccupation with natural
sound, literary organicism, and bodily asceticism. Relative to other Transcendentalists, these themes are certainly characteristic of Thoreau's writings and, to a considerable extent, distinctive of his contribution.

One of the anomalous facts of Thoreau's life experience often duly noted
by his biographers but resistant to interpretation was his preoccupation
with natural sound. At times this preoccupation amounted almost to an
obsession. Meditations on natural sounds assume a prominent place in his
published writings: the "Sounds" chapter of *Walden* itself provides perhaps the most memorable example. But not until we begin leafing through
the journals do we realize what a crucial role they played in Thoreau's
interior imaginative life. Early and late, the journals witness repeatedly
Thoreau's extraordinary sensitivity to natural sounds. A dog barking dis-
tantly in the night, the notes of a whippoorwill, the singing of the local tele-
graph wire, or more famously, the faint rhythms of "some tyro beating a
drum" that, in the revelatory passage from *A Week*, marches the wakeful
heroes out into a mood of transport—all such sounds Thoreau pondered
with obvious fascination and delight. In his meditations they were quickly
assimilated to music, and the music to ecstasy. This acoustic rapture, as I
have called it in a previous essay, serves as a leitmotif in Thoreau's journals
and often provides the starting point or key ingredient to some of his most
searching reflections.[39] In several of his earliest journal entries, music
comes to be curiously associated with heroism, poetry, and war.[40] The
music that such heroes hear, however, is not the boisterous din of fife and
drum, but the subtler, barely audible, endlessly varied music of the natural
world itself, what Thoreau often likened to the music of the spheres.[41] Indeed, in his regular expeditions in the Concord environs, the most effectual sounds were those at a distance, sounds barely distinguishable from
the canopy of silence. In some notes for an essay on "Sound and Silence"
entered in his journals in December 1838 and later included in the con-

cluding passage of *A Week*, Thoreau wrote: "All sound is nearly akin to Silence—it is a bubble on her surface which straightway bursts—an emblem of the strength and prolifickness of the undercurrent."[42]

By the end of 1838, the imaginative complex described above—this idiosyncratic association of sound and silence with war and heroism, with poetry and music—had become a distinctive and generative component of Thoreau's imaginative vision. By this time it is already clear that his theory of sound had begun to serve the kind of literary rationale—a defense of literature as the propagation and publication of silence—that it did in the closing pages of *A Week*. The only thing lacking from this personal artistic vision was some sort of literary sanction, which is where the Eastern books came in. In August of 1838, in his first explicit reference to Asian texts, he associated ancient literature with music. But with his reading of *Manu* two years later, he made the connection more specifically to the Vedas: "A strain of music reminds me of a passage of the Vedas."[43]

At this point in time, Thoreau did not have access to translations of any Vedic hymns themselves—*Manu* itself is traditionally categorized as a legal text (*dharma-śāstra*), not part of Vedic revelation (*śruti*) per se. Nevertheless, *Manu* does provide a definitive statement of how Indian tradition conceived and understood "the Veda." Here Thoreau read that Veda was the attribution given to a compendium of sacred traditions believed to be uncreated, pre-existent, and universal. He discovered that the Veda was considered the archetype of the created world and that Hindus conceived of the creation and destruction of the world as the alternation between waking and deep sleep.[44] He found that the Veda was understood not only to be the charter of all human laws and traditions, but also the matrix of nature itself. Transcendental in nature, it yet manifested itself in the form of speech.[45] Indeed, elsewhere in the Vedic literature, Veda is sometimes personified as Vāk, or procreative "speech." Silent in its depths but manifest as sound, the Veda thus provided an exact analogue for Thoreau's developing philosophy of natural sound. When Thoreau wrote, therefore, that a strain of music reminded him of a passage of the Vedas, he might have meant not only that it reminded him of some passages from *Manu*, but also that a strain of music was analogous to, could be construed as, a passage from the Vedas. Like the Vedic hymns he was reading about, the sounds of nature arose, at first inaudibly, out of the wellspring of cosmic silence. In the months after his first reading of *Manu*, Thoreau elaborated on this important new association between Veda and music:

Music is the Crystallization of Sound. There is something in the effect of a harmonious voice upon the disposition of its neighbor-

hood analogous to the law of crystals—it centralizes itself—and
sounds like the published law of things. If the law of the universe
were to be audibly promulgated no mortal lawgiver would suspect
it—for it would be a finer melody than his ears ever attended to. It
would be sphere music.[46]

In this reflection, Thoreau made it clear that he did not accept Vedic self-
representations literally—Manu, too, stood in need of revision—but what
he conceived as the ancient Vedic philosophy of sound supplied the perfect
touchstone for his own developing Transcendentalist theory of literature
and a suggestive imaginative rationale for his experiences of acoustic delight. This identification of a Vedic analogue for his own private reflections
on the relationship between sound and silence was the product of
Thoreau's unique imaginative synthesis, but it also reflected a level of con-
versancy with Manu's text not shared by Emerson or Alcott.

This sort of close scrutiny of *The Laws of Manu* also encouraged him to
treat the Vedic literature as one of his earliest exemplars of literary organicism and a kind of romantic primitivism. "In Literature it is only the wild
that attracts us," he wrote in "Walking," and though he went on in this late
essay to despair of locating in any single tradition a purely naturalistic literature, his long-standing ideal of literary organicism appears to have owed
some of its earliest formulations to *Manu*.[47]

> I know of no book which has come down to us with grander pre-
> tensions than this, and it is so impersonal and sincere that it is
> never offensive nor ridiculous. . . . It seems to have been uttered
> from some eastern summit, with a sober morning prescience in
> the dawn of time, and you cannot read a sentence without being
> elevated as upon the tableland of the Ghauts. It has such a rhythm
> as the winds of the desert, such a tide as the Ganges, and is as su-
> perior to criticism as the Himmaleh mountains. Its tone is of such
> unrelaxed fibre, that even at this late day, unworn by time, it wears
> the English and the Sanscrit dress indifferently, and its fixed
> sentences keep up their distant fires still like the stars, by whose
> dissipated rays this lower world is illumined.[48]

This sort of literary organicism was by no means peculiar to Thoreau—
indeed, it is an important part of his Romantic inheritance—but he had
better reasons than other writers of the period for considering Indian literature in this way. In the creation story that opens Manu's account, the
lawgiver makes it clear that the three primordial Vedas—Rig, Yajur, and
Sāma—were themselves derived from a natural source: "milked out," as

the lawgiver puts it, "from fire, from air, and from the sun." In *A Week*, Thoreau quoted this verse with particular approval, adding "Nor will we disturb the antiquity of this Scripture; . . . One might as well investigate the chronology of light and heat."[49] In this fanciful appropriation of *Manu*, Thoreau exemplified the literary ideal to which he professed himself devoted. Thoreau's appropriation, though it required an at least imaginative acquiescence to the Hindu tradition's naturalization and therefore privileging of its sacred canon, in effect sanctioned his own programs of literary organicism.

While *Manu* was crucial for the development of Thoreau's reflections on natural sound and literary wildness, it left its deepest impression on his attitudes to the body and his ideas about personal asceticism. The best-known digest of Thoreauvian asceticism, the "Higher Laws" chapter of *Walden*, details his thoughts on the topics of vegetarianism, chastity, and human nature generally. It is fair to say that among professional critics "Higher Laws" has not been the most popular of *Walden*'s chapters, presumably because of its imputed preachiness and apparently overt moralizing. Here, it is thought, we encounter Thoreau at his most conventional. He began the chapter, for example, by drawing a sharp distinction between the higher and lower reaches of human nature, a distinction most of his readers would no doubt recognize as traditionally Pauline. And the rest of the chapter may strike us as a mixture of Victorian prudishness and Grahamite eccentricity.[50] "Higher Laws," we conclude, is Thoreau's concession to the reform-minded values of his times.

Most puzzling is the fact that Thoreau's flight to the Spirit in "Higher Laws" seems so much at variance with the downward or physicalist tendency evinced by the rest of the book. This is the same writer, after all, who ended his earlier chapter on the heavenly reflections of Concord's ponds with the memorably satiric quip: "Talk of heaven! Ye disgrace the earth," and who throughout *Walden* and his other writings seems so committed to opposing and counteracting the idealistic vaporizing of some Transcendentalist rhetoric.[51] The truth about "Higher Laws," however, is that it is neither a conventional temperance tract nor a paean to Thoreauvian primitivism but an odd combination of both. It begins with Thoreau's mock confession about his craving for raw woodchuck, but it quickly centers on the existential contradiction upon which the rest of the chapter, if not the entire book, is predicated: "I found in myself and still find, an instinct toward a higher, or, as it is named, spiritual life, as do most men, and another toward a primitive rank and savage one, and I reverence them both. I love the wild not less than the good."[52] The problem reserved for the rest of the chapter is how the two are to be reconciled. References elsewhere in

Thoreau's writing suggest that his attitudes to the body were intractably ambivalent. On the one hand, he could write: "I must confess there is nothing so strange to me as my own body—I love any other piece of nature, almost better," a sentiment that achieves haunting metaphysical elaboration in the account of Thoreau's vertiginous ascent of Mt. Katahdin.[53] On the other hand, he could conceive the body as a kind of temple of the spirit.[54] There was nothing apparently disingenuous about such pious affirmations, despite their biblical overtones; they clearly followed from his personal experience. In contrast to Emerson, who found his ecstasy on a bare common through the disembodied medium of a transparent eyeball, Thoreau's revelations regularly occurred in the woods through the medium of his physical senses, hearing above all. For him, at least, "higher" life depended on his physical health and the soundness of sense. The following journal passage, entered at age twenty, became a cornerstone of the mature Thoreauvian faith: "I never feel that I am inspired unless my body is also— ... The body is the first proselyte the Soul makes. Our life is but the Soul made known by its fruits—the body. The whole duty of man may be expressed in one line—Make to yourself a perfect body."[55]

This waggish reversal of the old catechism states this aspect of Thoreau's faith as well as anything could, but how and whether he could reconcile this affirmative sense of the value of the body in the construction of higher life with his felt sense of disgust for his own body remains a question for most readers.[56] Whatever the answer, a close consideration of his notes from *The Laws of Manu* suggests that here, once again, teachings from the Hindu tradition offered some perspectives to which he felt quite drawn. Thoreau found it particularly refreshing that Manu dwells as much upon the gross physical functions of human life—"how to eat, drink, cohabit, void excrement and urine"—as he does upon final beatitude—"however offensive it may be to modern taste."[57] Such comprehensiveness he admired for its own sake, especially since it was so conspicuously absent from official expositions of New England faith, but he also recognized that Manu's careful strictures on physical self-culture reflect a fuller and more adequate assessment of the crucial role played by the body in the religious life itself.

As his reading of Indian religious literature opened out to encompass other texts in the next several years, he must have seen that while superficially similar, the traditions of Indian and Western asceticism were built upon entirely different foundations. To be sure, India was the home of some of the world's most outlandish forms of physical austerity, as he wittily illustrates in the opening pages of "Economy." At the same time, however, the principles of yoga taught that spiritual growth depended upon the sedulous cultivation of the body through such practices as regular fasting, physical conditioning, and breath control. In some of these classical texts, at least, perfection of the body—not its mortification—was the central goal of religious asceticism, a fact Thoreau obviously understood, though it was nowhere a part of the standard Orientalist lexicon. But Thoreau's insight into Hindu thought went deeper. Citing an aphorism in "Higher Laws" from Roy's Vedic commentary, Thoreau went on to maintain: "Yet the spirit can for the time pervade and control every member and function of the body, and transmute what in form is the grossest sensuality into purity and devotion. The generative energy, which when we are loose, dissipates and makes us unclean, when we are continent invigorates and inspires us."[58] Here the transmutation of "generative energy," not its repression, comes to be seen as a driving force in the religious life. This idea, regularly illustrated in Hindu stories about saints and asceticism, apparently struck a chord of recognition. In this view, asceticism and sensuality were not so much opposing impulses as different expressions of the same generative energy. The ascetic life was attended by its own set of pleasures, a fact affirmed by Manu and verified for Thoreau by his own experience. Here again is Thoreau responding to his recent readings of Manu:

> The very austerity of these Hindoos is tempting to the devotional as a more refined and nobler luxury. They seem to have indulged themselves with a certain moderation and temperance in the severities which their code requires, as divine exercises not to be excessively used as yet.
>
> One may discover the root of a Hindoo religion in his own private history.—when in the silent intervals of the day or the night he does sometimes inflict on himself like austerities with a stern satisfaction.[59]

The Artist of Kouroo

Taken together, the three preoccupations considered above provide a good index of the character of Thoreau's appropriation of Hindu texts. His approach was clearly not scholarly in any modern sense of the term. He remained staunchly unconcerned with scholarly objectivity and with what these texts might signify in their own historical context. His was, to put it gently, a motivated reading. Like other Transcendentalists, he looked to the Asian literature for what it could illustrate, confirm, or suggest about his own thought or life experience. His examination was more searching and more thorough than most, but just as subjective. In the end, as with Orientalists of various stripes, India served as a mirror of his own interests and concerns. What distinguished his readings from those of Jones or Emerson or Alcott, of course, was that his method was often more self-consciously imaginative and his interests were more personal and distinctive.

I would like to offer one last illustration of Thoreau's appropriation of Hindu materials, since it epitomizes the deeper personal significance of this literature for him and his literary handling of it. Nowhere does *Walden* sustain the kind of extended interrogation of Hindu literature that we find in the "Monday" section of *A Week*, where Thoreau transcribed a string of his favorite passages appended with his own running commentary. What we find in *Walden*, rather, is that such references have undergone a thorough, imaginative assimilation in the service of his overarching artistic designs. Such allusions are not less momentous, however, and they often appear at crucial junctures in the book's unfolding development. Two such cases—the story of the king's son in "Where I Lived and What I Lived For" and the cryptic story of the artist of Kouroo in the penultimate sequence of the concluding chapter—take the form of teaching parables that effectively serve to frame the narrative of Thoreau's sojourn at the Pond. Like the anecdote about the mysterious bug hatched from a farmer's table after sixty winters, both of these narratives are stories of transformation, but unlike the Yankee yarn, Thoreau made it clear that these stories were derived from his Hindu sources. The former, the import of which is more or less self-explanatory, he copied out from his reading of the *Sāṁkhya Kārikā*, a philosophical text on yoga that Thoreau pored over in 1851.[60] The source of the Kouroo story, however, is a good deal more elusive.[61] For the sake of easy reference, I reproduce this vignette in its entirety below:

There was an artist in the city of Kouroo who was disposed to strive after perfection. One day it came into his mind to make a staff. Having considered that in an imperfect work time is an ingredient, but into a perfect work time does not enter, he said to himself, It shall be perfect in all respects, though I should do nothing else in my life. He proceeded instantly to the forest for wood, being resolved that it should not be made of unsuitable material; and as he searched for and rejected stick after stick, his friends gradually deserted him, for they grew old in their works and died, but he grew not older by a moment. His singleness of purpose and resolution, and his elevated piety, endowed him, without his knowledge, with perennial youth. As he made no compromise with Time, Time kept out of his way, and only sighed at a distance because he could not overcome him. Before he had found a stock in all respects suitable the city of Kouroo was a hoary ruin, and he sat on one of its mounds to peel the stick. Before he had given it the proper shape the dynasty of the Candahars was at an end, and with the point of the stick he wrote the name of the last of that race in the sand, and then resumed his work. By the time he had smoothed and polished the staff Kalpa was no longer the pole-star; and ere he had put on the ferrule and the head adorned with precious stones, Brahma had awoke and slumbered many times. But why do I stay to mention these things? When the finishing stroke was put to his work, it suddenly expanded before the eyes of the astonished artist into the fairest of all the creations of Brahma. He had made a new system in making a staff, a world with full and fair proportions; in which, though the old cities and dynasties had passed away, fairer and more glorious ones had taken their places. And now he saw by the heap of shavings at his feet, that, for him and his work, the former lapse of time had been an illusion, and that no more time had elapsed than is required for a single scintillation from the brain of Brahma to fall on and inflame the tinder of a mortal brain. The material was pure, and his art was pure; how could the result be other than wonderful?[62]

Those interested in Thoreau's Asian readings have long cited this story of the artist of Kouroo as an apparent instance of his at least oblique indebtedness to Hindu sources. To be sure, the designation "Kouroo" is Sanskritic; the allusion to "Brahma" and "kalpa" obviously situates the story in a Hindu context; and the reference to "Candahars" is, or at least sounds like, a Hindu designation as well. Nevertheless, the story of Kouroo's artist—of the artist's carefully conceived and endlessly persevering efforts to make the perfect staff and the astonishing transformation that results when after many eons it is finally completed—this story as such appears nowhere in the Vedic or any other literature, as far as I can discover. It is, rather, a kind of Orientalist bricolage: Thoreau peoples his imaginative setting with Hindu names and places, conjures up his plot out of related fables of transformation, but fashions his moral to convey a personal artistic vision. Like much of *Walden* generally, it is a meditation on time, self-determination, transcendence, and artistic creation. The artist of Kouroo is, of course, in some sense a representation of Thoreau himself, the artist of *Walden*. Both have undertaken a work of modest means, pursued it with unwavering devotion, and reserved for it only the most lofty ambition. Kouroo is mainly, perhaps, a parable about artistic work, about the importance of devotion, perseverence, and self-sacrifice. At no point does the artist pause to consider the results of his labors or their exorbitant personal costs. The real significance of the artist's work lies in the fact that it was *disinterested*—caring nothing for consequences, for costs, for self. The work is significant for its own sake and the discipline it requires and occasions.

Lyndon Shanley's reconstruction of the evolution of *Walden* indicates that Thoreau composed the story of the artist of Kouroo, along with much of the rest of the "Conclusion," during the sixth and final recensions of his manuscript, that is, sometime between 1853 and 1854.[63] During this same period, Thoreau wrote several of his more teacherly letters to his friend Harrison Blake. In one of these, dated December 1853, he digressed at length on the special transformative powers of devotion to work. One section of this letter bears a striking resemblance to the ostensible moral of the Kouroo story; indeed, it provides the best key I know of for its explication: "How admirably the artist is made to accomplish his self-culture by devotion to his art! The wood-sawyer through his effort to do his work well, becomes not merely a better wood-sawyer, but measurably a better *man*. Few are the men that can work on their navels,—only some Brahmins that I have heard of."[64] The sarcastic repudiation of brahmanical navel-gazing, seemingly gratuitous in context, represents a kind of authorial subterfuge: this facetious dismissal deflects a level of indebtedness that Thoreau seems unwilling here fully to concede. When the same advice is dressed up in parabolic form in *Walden*, however, its Hindu provenance is implicitly acknowledged.

On the face of it, there is nothing particularly noteworthy in the advice Thoreau tenders here to his friend Blake: it sounds Thoreauvian enough, if not typically Yankee. But what is the point of placing this same lesson in the Hindu framework in *Walden*? Actually, Thoreau's use of the identificatory tag "Kouroo" helps tip us off to the story's philosophical affiliations. The name Kouroo (or "kuru," as it would be transliterated today) occurs frequently in the Bhagavad Gita, a text Thoreau knew well, and in the *Mahābhārata*, the great epic of India, of which the Gita is a small part. In these works it designates a remote ancestor of the story's heroes and the family dynasty of which he was thought to be the progenitor. The Gita consists essentially of a dramatic dialogue between Arjuna, the chief warrior of his day, and his charioteer and guru, Krishna, considered by tradition to be an avatar or earthly incarnation of the great god Vishnu. The dialogue of Krishna and Arjuna takes place moments before the onset of a catastrophic fratricidal war between the two sides of India's great dynastic family in the no-man's-land between the two opposing forces. The field upon which their armies meet to join battle is designated significantly as "the field of the Kurus." Realizing that the impending battle spells certain destruction for his entire family, Arjuna resolves not to fight and appeals to Krishna for counsel. It quickly becomes apparent, however, that Arjuna's painful dilemma serves merely as a pretext for the fuller revelation of Krishna's wisdom. The ensuing teachings constitute the bulk of the Gita's narrative, and over the centuries, they have attracted a large body of commentary. Yet, like other wisdom literature, the teachings of the Gita have been interpreted in various sectarian, often inconsistent ways, in part because the Gita's teachings themselves seem so broadly eclectic and perhaps contradictory. Some commentators interpret Krishna as counseling primarily devotion to God (*bhakti*) as the best path to emancipation, others philosophical discernment (*jñāna*), and still others practical service (*karman*).[65] Thoreau offers his own fairly lengthy commentary on the Gita, both in his journals and in *A Week*, and it is interesting to see where his own commentary stands relative to this broader tradition.

In late June of 1846, after he had had some time to digest his reading of Emerson's Gita, Thoreau began to devote many pages of his journals to his transcription of and commentary on Gita verses. Reviewing these against Wilkins's translation, one is at first struck not so much by what he selected for comment as by how much he altogether ignored. Nowhere in these records did Thoreau acknowledge the central devotional or theological messages of the Gita or the famous theophany of Krishna that for many readers has been seen as the dramatic center of the work. The first verse Thoreau selected for citation in his journals, Bhagavad Gita 3.7, indicates the general concern and tenor of most of his readings: "The man is praised, who, having subdued all his passions, performeth with his active faculties all the functions of life, unconcerned about the event."[66] As the subsequent entries confirm, Thoreau focused almost exclusively upon those passages concerned with the analysis of right action (*karman*), particularly as they relate to the Gita's influential doctrine of disinterested action or *karma yoga*. These are the same passages that he selected for inclusion in "Monday" also: "Let the motive be in the deed and not in the event. Be not one whose motive for action is the hope of reward."[67] In this last verse, a translation of Bhagavad Gita 2.47, Wilkins rendered the Sanskrit *phalam*, or "fruit" (as in the fruit of an action), as "event," but the sense is clear enough in context.

Thus epitomized is the Gita's teaching of disinterested action—action, that is, in which the actor focuses entirely on the work at hand with no consideration for its results or rewards. This is, to be sure, one of the central tenets of the Bhagavad Gita. For Thoreau, however, it was apparently the only one of real significance. Not only was it the concern of his explicit Gita citations and commentaries, it was also the focus of his more oblique Hindu-inspired narratives, the story of the artist of Kouroo above all. Re-examination of this otherwise cryptic story in the light of these apparently related passages from his letters and journals indicates that the story's doctrinal pith, as it were, is Thoreau's personal appropriation of the Indian teachings about disinterested action. The account of Kouroo's artist, then, is not simply a story about the value of discipline and hard work; rather, it represents Thoreau's personal appropriation and understanding of the Gita's teachings about the value of disinterested action as a path (*mārga*) to self-transformation. While the story of the artist of Kouroo may be seen as yet another expression of Thoreau's tendency to construct a kind of personal mythology out of his readings, it rests upon a specific philosophical conviction for which the Gita verses catalogued in "Monday" and the journals supplied the necessary context.

Yet the story we encounter in *Walden*'s final pages is obviously less concerned with subtle points of philosophy or religious psychology than with artistic expression. The story may be also interpreted as an allegory of the creation of *Walden* itself, one which showcases Thoreau's own artistic credo. And here we begin to see more of Thoreau's personal appropriation at work. As early as 1842 he had written: "The artist must work with indifferency—too great interest vitiates his work."[68] Another note recorded fresh from a recent immersion in *Manu* similarly prefigures the story he composed ten years later: "A perfectly healthy sentence is extremely rare. Sometimes I read one which was written while the world went round, while grass grew and water ran."[69] Devotion, discipline, and the pursuit of perfection are certainly some of the central values that Thoreau's parable was intended to highlight, but the real key to the story is the impact on the artist himself of his persevering devotion to his craft. Artistic creation, or so the parable seems to say, is not an end in itself, but a discipline, a religious pursuit, whose value in the end accrues to the artist, not the finished piece for its own sake. At this point, the Gita's ideal of disinterested action and Thoreau's own ideals of artistic vocation can be seen to converge.

This application of the religious ideals of the Gita to artistic pursuits is a defensible elaboration of the Gita's doctrines, but it is somewhat idiosyncratic and surely Thoreauvian and Romantic in its emphasis on yoga as a model for artistic work. The story of the artist of Kouroo represents an image of India molded according to the pressures of Thoreau's own religious and artistic vision. The Kouroo story is thus less biography than it is autobiography, in a mode not entirely unfamiliar to us from other Orientalist presentations. When its sources are reconstructed, it provides a neat gauge of the character of Thoreau's Orientalism.

Just as from a literary standpoint *Walden* often succeeds where Thoreau's more ungainly first book does not, so the story of the artist of Kouroo succeeds in a way that the catalogue of Gita verses does not. But recognition of its link to the Gita draws our attention to the fact that the story is less fanciful, more philosophically invested, than we normally take it to be. It also prompts us to take another look at the Gita's doctrine of disinterested action in relation to Thoreau's work and to consider what, after all, it meant for him. A closer look at these verses and the story that they later inspired indicates that they all turn on a single paradox—the Gita's apparently esoteric identification of action and non-action. Several of the Gita's most notorious instances of this paradox Thoreau includes in his catalogue in "Monday": "He who may behold, as it were inaction in action, and action in inaction, is wise amongst mankind. He is a perfect performer of all duty"; and, "Wise men call him a *Pandeet*, whose every undertaking is free from the idea of desire, and whose actions are consumed by the fire of wisdom. He abandoneth the desire of a reward of his actions; he is always contented and independent; and although he may be engaged in a work, he, as it were, doeth nothing."[70]

Kouroo's artist labors through countless eons of time only to find in the moment of his awakening that all was a necessary illusion. Like the wise pandit, he also acts, as he later comes to find, without really having acted. Paradoxes like this were, we know, part of Thoreau's literary stock-in-trade. In *Walden* and elsewhere, he periodically resorts to puns, reversals, and paradoxes—literary shock tactics, as it were—in his efforts to wake his readers up to the deeper meanings of their own lives. Related antinomies— as between progress and rest, heroism and renunciation, sound and silence—run throughout his writings. But why he should lean so heavily upon this particular paradox between action and inaction at such a strategic point in *Walden* seems puzzling until we recognize how deeply founded it was in Thoreau's own life experience. It is but one more manifestation, I would submit, of the curious and often-noted bifurcated vision or "double consciousness"—as between understanding and reason, time and eternity, appearance and reality—that animates so much of his work.[71]

The classic example of this double-mindedness occurs in the "Solitude" chapter of *Walden*, which I cite in full below:

With thinking we may be beside ourselves in a sane sense. By a conscious effort of the mind we can stand aloof from actions and their consequences; and all things, good and bad, go by us like a torrent. We are not wholly involved in Nature. I may be either the drift-wood in the stream, or Indra in the sky looking down on it. I *may* be affected by a theatrical exhibition; on the other hand, I *may not* be affected by an actual event which appears to concern me much more. I only know myself as a human entity; the scene, so to speak, of thoughts and affections; and am sensible of a certain doubleness by which I can stand as remote from myself as from another. However intense my experience, I am conscious of the presence and criticism of a part of me, which, as it were, is not a part of me, but spectator, sharing no experience, but taking note of it; and that is no more I than it is you. When the play, it may be the tragedy, of life is over, the spectator goes his way. It was a kind of fiction, a work of the imagination only, so far as he was concerned. This doubleness may easily make us poor neighbors and friends sometimes.[72]

While Thoreau has naturalized this famous passage more completely than the story of the artist of Kouroo, the reference to Indra, king of the Vedic pantheon, once again betrays its Hindu affiliations. Thoreau worked up this passage from journal entries made in August 1852, not long after the period when he was reading avidly in Colebrooke's translation of the *Sāṁkhya Kārikā*, one of the definitive works of the Sāṁkhya system of Indian philosophy, and in Roy's translations of the Upaniṣads. In the *Sāṁkhya Kārikā*, in particular, Thoreau found a thoroughly elaborated philosophical basis for the odd experience of doubleness he describes in "Solitude." The Sāṁkhya school sets out a cosmological system based upon the foundational dualism of spirit (*puruṣa*), on the one hand, and nature or matter (*prakṛti*), on the other. Life and evolution result, it is thought, from the mingling and confusion of these two principles; while liberation, as in the case of the enlightened yogin, results from fully and finally distinguishing between them. The "spectator" (Colebrooke's own translation of the Sāṁkhyan *draṣṭṛ*) or "witness" (*sakṣin*), designates *puruṣa* in its embodied form as it witnesses to phenomenal experience. Its nature is consciousness, but it remains essentially separate from the world of action and experience. Read alongside Colebrooke's translation, this passage from "Solitude" appears to be a natural expression of the Sāṁkhya-Yoga system. Thoreau was obviously quite taken with this experiential and contemplative aspect of Indic tradition. In a famous letter written to his friend Harrison Blake, he had copied out a couple of passages from the *Harivaṁśa* to which he gives an explicitly autobiographical reference:

> "Free in this world, as the birds in the air, disengaged from every kind of chains, those who have practiced the *yoga* gather in Brahma the certain fruit of their works."

Depend upon it that rude and careless as I am, I would fain practise the *yoga* faithfully.

"The Yogin, absorbed in contemplation, contributes in his degree to creation: he breathes a divine perfume, he hears wonderful things. Divine forms traverse him without tearing him, and united to the nature which is proper to him, he goes, he acts, as animating original matter."

To some extent, and at rare intervals, even I am a yogin.[73]

This self-attribution has been over-interpreted by some commentators, but it does suggest that at some level Thoreau had taken the literature on yoga very much to heart. In introducing the Gita extracts that he includes in the "Monday" section of *A Week*, he quotes Warren Hastings's prefatory note to Wilkins's translation at some length:

To those who have never been accustomed to the separation of the mind from the notices of the senses, it may not be easy to conceive by what means such a power is to be attained; since even the most studious men of our hemisphere will find it difficult so to restrain their attention, but that it will wander to some object of present sense or recollection. . . . But if we are told that there have been men who were successively, for ages past, in the daily habit of abstracted contemplation, begun in the earliest period of youth, and continued in many to the maturity of age, each adding some portion of knowledge to the store accumulated by his predecessors; it is not assuming too much to conclude, that as the mind ever gathers strength, like the body, by exercise, so in such an exercise it may in each have acquired the faculty to which they aspired, and that their collective studies may have led them to the discovery of new tracks and combinations of sentiment, totally different from the doctrines with which the learned of other nations are acquainted; doctrines, which however speculative and subtle, still, as they possess the advantage of being derived from a source so free from every adventitious mixture, may be equally founded in truth with the most simple of our own.[74]

Thoreau was not, of course, in a position to practice yoga in any literal sense because the texts to which he had access do not explain the details of such practices. But the divine hearing which he mentions in the letter to Blake, and the repeated references to the separation between self and activity that occur in the Gita and the *Kārikā*, seem nonetheless to have found fertile ground in Thoreau's personal experience.

As in the case of Thoreau's fascination with natural sound, this odd experience of contemplative detachment receives significant attention in his writings, but usually only in the somewhat displaced form of his meditations on the reflecting properties of neighborhood lakes and streams. The reference to Indra in the passage from "Solitude," though more cryptic than most, links this passage to others of this sort. Time and again in Thoreau's writing, we find him enamored of the reflective characteristics of water, Walden Pond above all. In such reflections, the undisturbed surface of the pond serves as a kind of natural mirror—a "perfect forest mirror," as he puts it in *Walden*—of the pond's tree-lined banks, clouds drifting overhead, or even the figure of Thoreau himself.[75] At such moments, the glassy water becomes a kind of philosopher's looking glass, so vivid as to prompt a perceptual shift and, in turn, some psychological reorientation. The polarities and distinctions that defined normal experience are suddenly inverted or reversed—outside is now inside, upper is lower, sky settles onto water. It was perhaps significant to Thoreau that the mirror was sometimes used explicitly as a metaphor for the contemplative mind itself.[76] The familiar image of Thoreau lolling in his boat, gazing into the placid waters, provides ammunition for those who would see in such vignettes an updating of the Narcissus myth. Yet, as with other contemplative mirrors, what Thoreau found compelling about such self-mirroring was not that it simply reproduced the self, but that it recast the self as other. The Pond's reflections served, that is, as a natural type of religious ecstasy or personal transcendence.

The Brahmin's Well

The image of the mirror serves as an appropriate synoptic symbol, not only for this treatment of Thoreau and the other Orientalists of Concord, but for Orientalism generally. Whether the Orientalist sought justification for imperialist complicity, as did Jones; or correlates of cherished doctrines, as did Emerson; or confirmation of religious experience, as did Thoreau, India had a way of throwing into relief Western self-projections. To put it another way, the answers that Hindu texts provided depended on the questions posed. American Transcendentalists were not yet in a position to consider Hindu literature on its own terms, nor did they care to. They embraced this literature primarily for the precedents, sanctions, and illustrations it afforded for their own literary and religious agendas. To India, in particular, they looked for confirmation and explication of their own experience and ideology. They clearly read the texts of classical Hinduism completely out of context, but they read classical and European texts this way as well and, given their relative cultural isolation, they had little choice anyway. Consistent with their committed ahistoricism and perennialist idealism, they conceived these texts as universal expressions of human experience. But so qualifying this reading should not mitigate the significance of this literature for any of the Transcendentalists, particularly Thoreau. If they found in the literature of classical India confirmation of beliefs to which they were already disposed, as in the case of Thoreau's interest in literary organicism or personal asceticism, they also sometimes located exact and to them convincing representation of experiences and contemplative insights about which the literature of Europe seemed to say little. Thus, while Concord's Orientalism is more or less consistent with the characterization of European Orientalism proffered by the contemporary Orientalist critique— notwithstanding the important political, economic, and cultural differences between New England and Great Britain in the mid nineteenth century— the kind of closer consideration that Thoreau's decades-long preoccupation with Hindu texts affords also raises some noteworthy problems for the standard critique of Orientalism.

First of all, it must be noted that, contrary to the usual depictions of Orientalist self-mystification, the Transcendentalists were not in the least unconscious of the self-reflexive, if not overtly self-serving, character of their readings. While these Americans were no doubt also cozened by the romantic image of India diffused throughout Orientalist discourse, they nevertheless had few illusions about how "objective" their readings were. After a suggestive set of extracts on the topic of yoga, divine ecstasy, and final liberation that Thoreau entered into his journal in May 1851, he records the following revealing disclaimer: "Like some preachers—I have added my texts—(derived) from the Chineses (sic) and Hindoo scriptures—long after my discourse was written."[77] On one level, it appears that Thoreau is simply making a matter-of-fact editorial comment about his decision to embellish his manuscript of *A Week* with Asian extracts after it was substantially completed. On another level, however, he is making a frank assessment of the function such texts served in his life relative to his own prior experience. Compared to the rest of his readings, the Hindu texts provided a unique sanction for and clarification of experiences of spiritual euphoria to which he had apparently long been susceptible. Thoreau ransacked the Hindu texts for materials with which to construct his own, as it were, expanded, interior autobiography. Construed figuratively, the citation above is not the dismissive disclaimer it at first appears to be. The texts may have "been added" after the experiences had occurred, but they provided indispensable authentication, as the prominence of these texts

throughout his writings indicates. Thoreau was, in short, obviously aware
of the subjectivity of his readings of the Orient: good Transcendentalist
that he was, however, he deemed this a virtue, not a vice. Furthermore, on
philosophical grounds, he could hardly imagine how it could be otherwise.
In a set of reflections on the nature of historical knowledge recorded early
in his journals and then repeated elsewhere, Thoreau wrote that "Critical
acumen is exerted in vain to uncover the past—the past cannot be presented—we cannot know what we are not—but one veil hangs over past—
present—and future—And it is the province of the historian to find out not
what was but what is."78 This compact formulation of a kind of epistemological skepticism is especially instructive when considered in relation to
his readings of India and the Far East. Thoreau's transcendentalism obviously has little in common with Said's historicism, but this is one conclusion
at least on which they appear to agree.

It also seems appropriate to raise a caveat about facile comparisons
between the reflexivity of Orientalist and Thoreauvian readings of the Orient. Thoreau's literary representations of the Sāṁkhyan doctrine of contemplative witnessing prove instructive. Mediating, of course, between
Thoreau's lake-side reflections and the *Kārikā's* assertions about the contemplative witness is the metaphor of the mirror. But in neither case is the
mirror a mere agent of imitation or physical reproduction. Rather, as
Thoreau's meditative explorations of Walden's reflections make clear, the
value of such reflections is that they create the illusion of placing the onlooker outside and beyond the normal confines of his empirical self, thus
providing a perceptual illustration of an interior experience that did
not readily lend itself to description. This is where the image of Thoreau
leaning over his boat's gunwales differs so significantly from the mythical
Narcissus, or even from recent views of the composite European Orientalist: Narcissus was so enamored of his own image that he was driven to total
and unfortunate identification. For Thoreau, on the other hand, it was his
sense of *separation* from the objectification of himself, and the illusion of
self-transcendence it momentarily occasioned, that was most exhilarating.
A similar comparison might be drawn between Thoreau and the composite Orientalist of recent cultural studies. Where the self-reflexivity of the
Orientalists is seen to have closed off authentic communication between
East and West, Thoreauvian self-reflection sought to be emancipatory. To
put it more concisely, in Thoreau's meditations, Walden Pond could serve
as mirror and window both.

The two distinctions indicated above reflect the more obvious and
fundamental distinction between Thoreau's self-understanding and the
Orientalism classically described by Said. As we have seen, Thoreau boldly

acknowledged the circular character of his own Eastern researches, and in this respect could be said to anticipate the philosophical hermeneutics of the modern period. But in contrast to Said, for example, whose epistemology is grounded in a thorough-going historicism, Thoreau's epistemological views were predicated upon his idealism. The reason Thoreau could be so cavalier in his reification of India was that he assumed that his intuitions, if they were deep enough, must turn out to be valid for India as well, and vice versa. In other words, Thoreau's confidence in his Orientalist assertions was grounded in a flamboyant affirmation of the transpersonal self and a correlative denial of history. Thus he could write with a brashness only such unbridled idealist perennialism could countenance: "The Vedas and their Angas are not so ancient as my serenest contemplations."[79]

Nothing better illustrates the distinctive character of Thoreau's mature thinking about India than the Orientalist set piece with which he concluded his chapter "The Pond in Winter" in *Walden*. At its climax is the magniloquent eulogy of the Bhagavad Gita with which I opened this paper, but it begins with an extended and detailed account of Walden's seasonal participation in the American ice-cutting industry. During the winter of 1846–1847, his second in residence at the Pond, Thoreau observed carefully as a company of some one hundred Irishmen and their Yankee overseers came to Walden for the purpose of harvesting its ice. Cut into large blocks, hauled onto shore, and eventually loaded onto waiting wagons, the ice was then conveyed by train to the Charlestown docks, whence it was shipped to the tropics.[80] Having described the business of cutting ice in some detail, Thoreau then appends the following whimsical but revealing final paragraph:

> Thus it appears that the sweltering inhabitants of Charleston and New Orleans, of Madras and Bombay and Calcutta, drink at my well. In the morning I bathe my intellect in the stupendous and cosmogonal philosophy of the Bhagvat Geeta, since whose composition years of the gods have elapsed, and in comparison with which our modern world and its literature seem puny and trivial; and I doubt if that philosophy is not to be referred to a previous state of existence, so remote is its sublimity from our conceptions. I lay down the book and go to my well for water, and lo! there I meet the servant of the Brahmin, priest of Brahma and Vishnu and Indra, who still sits in his temple on the Ganges reading the Vedas, or dwells at the root of a tree with his crust and water jug. I meet his servant come to draw water for his master, and our buckets as it were grate together in the same well. The pure Walden water is

mingled with the sacred water of the Ganges. With favoring winds it is wafted past the site of the fabulous islands of Atlantis and the Hesperides, makes the periplus of Hanno, and, floating by Ternate and Tidore and the mouth of the Persian Gulf, melts in the tropic gales of the Indian seas, and is landed in ports of which Alexander only heard the names.[81]

Thoreau's contextualization of this passage indicates that he was fully cognizant of the commercial system that in some sense both underwrote and enabled his reading of the Bhagavad Gita. The East Indian consumption of Walden ice was not intended for Indians themselves, a fact convenient enough to ignore from far-off Concord. Moreover, as the ice trade taking place under his very nose made clear, Americans also profited from the British colonial presence in India. By contextualizing his own reading of the Bhagavad Gita in the Concord-to-India ice trade in this way, Thoreau called attention to the economic exigencies underlying Orientalist discourse, but any conclusions he might have drawn here about the ostensible complicity between knowledge and power he blithely abandoned in the interests of illustrating another, for him, more important set of lessons. In his juxtaposition of the well of Walden with the well of the Gita, in which he bathed his intellect, Thoreau insisted that the traffic between India and Concord was circular and reciprocal, not one-way or univocal. It was not so much, or necessarily, reciprocal at the level of material commodities, but it was and had to be emphatically reciprocal at the level of knowledge and experience. Thoreau and the brahmin's servant drew from the same transcendental well, and as they do so, distinctions of time and place evaporate. Here, in his fanciful account of the buckets of India and Concord knocking together in the same well, Thoreau offered a vision of the possibilities of union between East and West now virtually unthinkable in academic discourse.

NOTES

1. See Carl T. Jackson, *The Oriental Religions and American Thought: Nineteenth Century Explorations* (Westport, Conn., 1981), 3–13.
2. Jackson, *Oriental Religions*, 13–32; Hannah Adams, *A View of Religions*, 3d rev. ed. (Boston, 1801).
3. See Spencer Lavan, *Unitarians and India: A Study in Encounter and Response* (Boston, 1977); and Alan D. Hodder, "Emerson, Rammohan Roy, and the Unitarians," *Studies in the American Renaissance 1988*, ed. Joel Myerson (Charlottesville, 1988), 133–148.

4. Ralph Waldo Emerson to Elizabeth Hoar, June 17, 1845, in *The Letters of Ralph Waldo Emerson*, ed. Ralph Rusk (New York, 1939), 3:290.

5. Ralph Waldo Emerson to William Emerson, Apr. 1, 1844, and May 24, 1831, in *Letters*, 6:245–246, 1:322.

6. Ralph Waldo Emerson to James Elliot Cabot, Sept. 28, 1845, in *Letters*, 3:303.

7. Amos Bronson Alcott, *The Journals of Bronson Alcott*, ed. Odell Shepard (Boston, 1938), 178–181.

8. Henry David Thoreau, *A Week on the Concord and Merrimack Rivers*, ed. Carl F. Hovde et al. (Princeton, 1980), 135–143; Henry David Thoreau, *Walden*, ed. J. Lyndon Shanley (Princeton, 1971), 298; Henry David Thoreau, *Journal*, in *The Writings of Henry D. Thoreau*, ed. Robert Sattelmeyer (Princeton, 1981–1984), 2:253 ff. References to these three works hereafter abbreviated as *Week*, *Walden*, and *Writings*.

9. Ralph Waldo Emerson, *The Journals and Miscellaneous Notebooks of Ralph Waldo Emerson*, ed. William H. Gilman et al. (Cambridge, Mass., 1960–1982), 10:360. Cited hereafter as *JMN*.

10. Charles Wilkins, trans., *Bhagvat-geeta, or Dialogues of Kreeshna and Arjoon* (London, 1785); Charles Wilkins, trans., *The Heetopades of Veeshnoo Sarma* (Bath, 1787); Calidas, "Sakontala, or, The fatal ring: An Indian Drama," trans. William Jones (Calcutta, 1789); William Jones, trans., *Institutes of Hindu Law; or, the ordinances of Menu, according to the gloss of Culluca* (London, 1825); Henry Thomas Colebrooke, "Essays in the Religion and Philosophy of the Hindus" (London and Edinburgh, 1858); Ishvarakrishna, *The Samkhya Karika*, trans. Henry Thomas Colebrooke (London, 1837); Horace Hayman Wilson, trans., "The Megha duta; or Cloud Messenger" (Calcutta, 1813); Horace Hayman Wilson, trans., *The Vishnu Purana* (London, 1840).

11. "Im Orient müssen wir das höchste Romantische suchen." Cited in Raymond Schwab, *The Oriental Renaissance: Europe's Discovery of India and the East, 1680–1880*, trans. Gene Patterson-Black and Victor Reinking (New York, 1984), 13.

12. This phrase was first used as a chapter title in Edgar Quinet's *La Génie de Religion* (Paris, 1841). Cited in Schwab, *Oriental Renaissance*, 11.

13. See Schwab, *Oriental Renaissance*, 1.

14. Germany's leading role in European Indological research poses something of a difficulty for current views of European Orientalism, since German fascination with India was not motivated principally by the same sort of motives driving British and French Orientalist study. In the German case, scholarly and Romantic interest in Indic language and literature seems to have been stimulated more directly by a sense of recognition of and identification with the classical expressions of Indian culture. Parallels between German Romantic idealism and the philosophy of the Upanisads, for example, suggested important continuities in the Weltanschauung of these two removed but anciently related cultures.

15. Sir William Jones, preface to *Institutes of Hindu Law: or, the Ordinances of Menu, according to the Gloss of Culluca*, vol. 7 of *The Works of William Jones* (London, 1807), 89–90. Cited hereafter designated as *Manu*.

16. Edward Said, *Orientalism* (New York, 1978), 2–3.

17. Edward Said, *Culture and Imperialism* (New York, 1993).

18. Said, *Orientalism*, 21.

19. See Ronald Inden, "Orientalist Constructions of India," *Modern Asian Studies* 20(1986):401–406; Ronald Inden, *Imagining India* (Oxford, 1990); and Carol A. Breckenridge and Peter van der Veer, eds., *Orientalism and the Postcolonial Predicament: Perspectives on South Asia* (Philadelphia, 1993)—see especially the essays by Breckenridge, van der Veer, Lele, and Dharwadker.

20. *Dial* 4(Jan. 1844):391–401. See Jackson, *Oriental Religions*, 140–156; and, for the most complete history of Buddhism in America, Rick Fields, *How the Swans Came to the Lake: A Narrative History of Buddhism in America*, rev. ed. (Boston and London, 1986).

21. *JMN*, 2:195; Thoreau, *Writings*, 1:428; Thoreau, *Week*, 148.

22. Thoreau, *Writings*, 1:168–169, 177, 2:371; Thoreau, *Week*, 142–143.

23. Cf. Jayant Lele, "Orientalism and the Social Sciences," *Orientalism and the Postcolonial Predicament*, 45.

24. See Lawrence Buell, "American Literary Emergence as a Postcolonial Phenomenon," *American Literary History* 4(1992):411–442.

25. For a readable overview of the early American East-India trade, see Samuel Eliot Morison, *The Maritime History of Massachusetts, 1783–1860* (1921; Boston, 1961).

26. Henry David Thoreau, *The Correspondence of Henry David Thoreau*, ed. Walter Harding and Carl Bode (New York, 1958), 398. I have silently added punctuation to make this passage clearer.

27. Ralph Waldo Emerson, *The Collected Works of Ralph Waldo Emerson*, ed. Alfred R. Ferguson et al. (Cambridge, Mass., 1959–1987), 4:30. Cited hereafter as *CW*.

28. Arthur Christy, *The Orient in American Transcendentalism: A Study of Emerson, Thoreau, and Alcott* (New York, 1932).

29. Arthur Versluis, *American Transcendentalism and Asian Religions* (New York and Oxford, 1993), 4–5.

30. Kenneth Walter Cameron, "Books Thoreau Borrowed from Harvard College Library," in his *Emerson the Essayist* (Raleigh, 1945) 2:191–208; also Robert Sattelmeyer, *Thoreau's Reading: A Study in Intellectual History with Bibliographical Catalogue* (Princeton, 1988), 3–24.

31. Thoreau, *Writings*, 1:51, 142, 144, 169, 172.

32. Thoreau, *Writings*, 1:173–174.

33. Thoreau, *Writings*, 1:311–312.

34. For example, William Julias Mickle, "Inquiry into the Religious Tenets and Philosophy of the Bramins," which Thoreau encountered in Chalmers's anthology of English poetry on a visit late in 1841 to Cambridge. See Alexander Chalmers, ed., *The Works of the English Poets* (London, 1810), vol. 21. Cited in Thoreau, *Writings*, 1:387.

35. On Thoreau's first reactions to the Gita, see his *Writings*, 2:253 ff. See also Emerson, *Letters*, 3:290. William Ward, *A View of the History, Literature, and Religion of the Hindoos* (Hartford, 1824); and Rammohan Roy, raja, *Translation of Several Principal Books, Passages, and Texts of the Veds*, 2d ed. (London, 1832).

36. M. A. Langlois, trans., *Harivansa* (Paris, 1834–1835); Henry David Thoreau, *The Transmigration of the Seven Brahmans*, ed. Arthur Christy (New York, 1932). This translation is also included in Henry David Thoreau, *Translations*, ed. K. P. van Anglen (Princeton, 1986), 135–144.

37. Miriam Jeswine, "Henry David Thoreau: Apprentice to the Hindu Sages" (Ph.D.

diss., Univ. of Oregon, 1971), 28–29. Cited in Walter Harding and Michael Meyer, eds. *The New Thoreau Handbook* (New York, 1980), 94.

38. Thoreau, *Correspondence*, 387–388, 397–398. Franklin Sanborn discusses Thoreau's friendship with Cholmondeley in "Thoreau and his English Friend Thomas Cholmondeley," *Atlantic Monthly* 72(1893):741–756.

39. Alan D. Hodder, "'Ex oriente lux': Thoreau's Ecstasies and the Hindu Texts," *Harvard Theological Review* 86(1993):403–438.

40. Thoreau, *Writings*, 1:94, 124, 146, 149.

41. Cf. Thoreau, *Week*, 175–177; Thoreau, *Writings*, 3:323.

42. Thoreau, *Writings*, 1:61–62; Thoreau, *Week*, 391–393.

43. Thoreau, *Writings*, 1:52, 173.

44. *Manu*, 1:3, 21, 52; Thoreau, *Week*, 152.

45. *Manu*, 2:6–8, 76 ff.

46. Thoreau, *Writings*, 1:249.

47. Henry David Thoreau, "Walking," in *Great Short Works of Henry David Thoreau*, ed. Wendell Glick (New York, 1982), 313.

48. Thoreau, *Week*, 148–149.

49. *Manu*, 1:23; Thoreau, *Week*, 153.

50. Cf. Stephen Nissbaum, *Sex, Diet, and Debility in Jacksonian America: Sylvester Graham and Health Reform* (Westport, Conn., 1980). For a useful review of the range of attitudes represented by the body reformers of the antebellum period, see David S. Reynolds, *Walt Whitman's America: A Cultural Biography* (New York, 1995), 207–213.

51. Thoreau, *Walden*, 200.

52. Thoreau, *Walden*, 210.

53. Henry David Thoreau, *The Maine Woods*, ed. Joseph J. Moldenhauer (Princeton, 1972), 71.

54. Thoreau, *Writings*, 1:139; Thoreau, *Walden*, 221.

55. Thoreau, *Writings*, 1:137–138.

56. Eccles. 12.13. Cf. *Westminster Shorter Catechism*, Q. 1, 39.

57. Thoreau, *Walden*, 221.

58. Thoreau, *Walden*, 219.

59. Thoreau, *Writings*, 1:327.

60. Thoreau, *Walden*, 96; Iswara Krishna, *The Samkhya Karika*, trans. Henry Thomas Colebrooke (Bombay, 1887), 258–259.

61. There is still no consensus about the exact origins of this story or its proper interpretation. Arthur Christy construed it essentially as an allegory of Thoreau's own life and his pursuit of personal perfection. *Orient in American Transcendentalism*, 193–194. Sherman Paul provides a helpful but partially inaccurate gloss on the name Kouroo and supposes Thoreau may have run across it in his reading of *Manu. The Shores of America: Thoreau's Inward Exploration* (Urbana, 1958), 352–353. More recently, Kenneth Cameron has located a possible source in Chuang-tzu's story of the Woodcarver of Lu. "An Archetype for Thoreau's Fable of the Artist of Kouroo," *American Renaissance Literary Report* 5(1991):4–6. See also Walter Harding, ed., *Walden: An Annotated Edition* (Boston and New York, 1995), 317–318. All of these assessments contribute something to our appreciation of Thoreau's story. Cameron comes closer than most to identifying a specific

source, but even here the parallels between the stories of Chuang-tzu and Thoreau are only approximate, since several of the key details of Thoreau's story are clearly Hindu, not Chinese, in origin. The story of the artist of Kouroo exhibits what might best be termed a family resemblance to the Taoist story, just as it does to other related parables of transformation in the Hindu and Buddhist traditions.

62. Thoreau, *Walden*, 326–327.
63. J. Lyndon Shanley, *The Making of* Walden (Chicago, 1957), 68–73.
64. Thoreau, *Correspondence*, 311.
65. See Arvind Sharma, *The Hindu Gita: Ancient and Classical Interpretations of the Bhagavadgita* (La Salle, Ill., 1986).
66. Thoreau, *Writings*, 2:253–254.
67. Thoreau, *Week*, 139; Wilkins, *Bhagvat-geeta*, 40.
68. Thoreau, *Writings*, 1:391.
69. Thoreau, *Writings*, 1:219.
70. Thoreau, *Week*, 139.
71. The phrase is Emerson's. See "The Transcendentalist," in *CW*, 1:213. Cf. Joel Porte, "Emerson, Thoreau, annd the Double Consciousness," *New England Quarterly* 41(1968):40–50.
72. Thoreau, *Walden*, 134–135.
73. Thoreau, *Correspondence*, 251.
74. Thoreau, *Week*, 138.
75. Thoreau, *Walden*, 188. See also *Walden*, 98, 175, 177, 179, 186, 193; cf. *Week*, 45–46, and *Writings*, 1:128.
76. Cf. Wilkins, *Bhagvat-geeta*, 49.
77. Thoreau, *Writings*, 3:216.
78. Thoreau, *Writings*, 1:414–415.
79. Thoreau, *Writings*, 1:387.
80. On the rise and fall of the American ice trade, see Philip Chadwick Foster Smith, "Crystal Blocks of Yankee Coldness: The Development of the Massachusetts Ice Trade from Frederick Tudor to Wenham Lake, 1806–1886," *Essex Institute Historical Collection* 97(1961):197–232.
81. Thoreau, *Walden*, 297–298.

Transcendentalism
and Society

Transcendentalism and the
Spirit of Capitalism

John Patrick Diggins

AT THE POLITICAL FOUNDING OF THE AMERICAN REPUBLIC, in the drafting of the new Constitution in 1787, the question of who Americans were as a people received little attention. The new "science of politics" that the *Federalist* authors adopted drew from European sources, especially the Scottish Enlightenment, and the assumption was that the New World would replicate the collective behavior and produce the same social structures as the Old World. Although John Jay hailed the unanimity of the American people, Alexander Hamilton and James Madison regarded the people's divisiveness and diversity as irremovable, and they would cite European history to prove the inevitability of social conflict.

A half-century later, the New England Transcendentalists would question this reliance upon the "muses of Europe" and ask Americans to regard themselves as unique, exceptional, something new under the sun, and they questioned why the framers so distrusted human nature that they felt the need to devise political mechanisms to control the people themselves. Perhaps more than any other American *ism*, Transcendentalism comes closer to defining America in its own terms, bequeathing to us a country that we know all too well today, a country without reverence for government and the state and devoid of any theory of political authority.

Between American Puritanism and American Pragmatism lies Transcendentalism, the philosophy that set out to liberate the American people by advising us to turn inward, a move that George Santayana could well have called "the egotistic turn" in modern discourse, an anthropological conceit that reduced the universe to the categories of mind that thought about it. Santayana feared that Transcendentalism turned the mind too far inward, a self-preoccupation that could result in solipsism. Solipsists are convinced that nothing exists or is real other than their own selves. When a solipsist remarked to Bertrand Russell that she was surprised to find that she could

find no other solipsists, the philosopher replied that he was surprised that
she would be surprised by that discovery.

Santayana and the "Double Allegiance" of the Transcendentalists

Calvinism and Transcendentalism, Santayana wrote in his well-known
essay "The Genteel Tradition in American Philosophy," were once "living
fountains; but to keep them alive they required, one an agonized conscience, and the other a radical subjective criticism of knowledge." Both
disappeared, and the result was the American mind split in two, with one
half taking part in the becalmed spheres of respectable culture and the
other moving on to invention and industry and social organization. As
action replaced thought and organization replaced inspiration and revelation, a synthesis "could hardly be held in a single mind. Natural science,
history, the beliefs implied in labour and invention, could not be disregarded altogether; so that the transcendental philosopher was condemned
to a double allegiance, and to not letting his left hand know what his right
hand was making." This divided mind culminates, Santayana announced
in 1911, in the difference between the new, powerful, and masculine, and
the old, effete, and feminine. "The American Will inhabits the sky-scraper;
the American Intellect inhabits the colonial mansion. The one is the
sphere of the American man; the other, at least predominately, of the
American woman. The one is all aggressive enterprise; the other all genteel
tradition."[1]

Santayana had no trouble with an American character that combined
duty of work with liberty of spirit, but he worried about a people more
interested in changing the material world than in understanding it. Americans, Santayana complained, saw themselves as "idealists working upon
matter," and he attributed much of this conceit to the "poetic madness" of
the Transcendentalist assumption that actual thinking not only constitutes
reality but proudly spiritualizes it. The Transcendentalists made the self
the center of the mind's reflective capacities, particularly when asking
Emerson's question, "Where do we find ourselves?" A naturalist, Santayana was certain that nature is not simply a product of mind, a "social
construction," to use today's jargon, but instead part of the external world
which nourishes a mind willing to recognize and feed upon it. He saw in
the Transcendentalists a "systematic subjectivism" on the part of poets and
philosophers who seemed more devoted to following the rays that radiate
from the self than considering the conditions of experience that allow

objects of knowledge to have a separate status apart from the mind. Santayana's characterization may have been overdrawn, and he did acknowledge that such subjectivism could also provide the basis of the speculation essential to scientific inquiry, but he was one of the first to point out the ironies of Transcendentalism, particularly its exhortation to trust everything about the self except its own senses. Perhaps the Transcendentalist call to spiritual self-exaltation offered the only possible way to rescue America from an older Puritan angst of debilitating self-loathing.

In this rescue operation, the precious self had also to be delivered from a newer development that had less to do with sin and the temptations of the flesh than with society and the seduction of social relations. As Alexis de Tocqueville observed in *Democracy in America*, written in the early 1830s just as the Transcendentalists were coming upon the scene, the "democratic despotism" that proceeds from bourgeois society submerges the individual underneath the forces of uniformity. Tocqueville, together with Henry David Thoreau, Ralph Waldo Emerson, and other Transcendentalists, discerned a disturbing truth that seems to be somewhat neglected in the writings of our contemporary political and social theorists: Democracy, rather than enhancing diversity, purges society of differences and renders people more inclined to the comforts of cozy subordination than to the higher demands of civic virtue. Thoreau saw that in America it was not the State, which he dismissed as a dim-witted "imbecile," but society itself that posed a threat to the individual. The possible strangulation of the self by society haunted the intellectual imagination during the Jacksonian era. "Society as it is," wrote Orestes Brownson, "is a lie, a sham, a charnelhouse, a valley of dry bones."[2]

The Transcendentalists could have agreed with Tocqueville that democratic society brought about leveling and equalization that, without necessarily realizing freedom, threatened to erase the individual. Yet they seem to have paid less attention to the sources of their own freedom, which may in fact comprise an "inverted Calvinism," as Perry Miller remarked when noting how New England writers replaced God with nature and scriptural indoctrination with poetical inspiration.[3] But Tocqueville saw a direct relationship between religious liberty and political liberty. "For my part," he wrote, "I more easily understand a man animated at the same time both by religious passion and political passion than by political passion and the passion for well-being. The first two can hold together and be embraced in the same soul, but not the second two. It is religious passion that pushed the Puritans to America and led them to want to govern themselves." In Calvinism, obedience to God required resistance to tyranny. In much of today's political discussion, however, the assumption seems to be that the possibility of freedom depends upon the presence of free markets.[4] Tocqueville was convinced that freedom arose from convictions as much as conditions and that its origins lay in a religion that, paradoxically, had denied freedom of the will. It may have been the very uncertainty of one's state of the soul that required a life of strenuous striving to prove the unprovable. Tocqueville, steeped in Pascal, seemed to appreciate the paradoxes of Calvinism. "I have said before that I regarded the origins of the Americans, what I have called their point of departure, as the first and most effective of all the elements leading to their present prosperity. . . . When I consider all that has resulted from this first fact, I think I can see the whole destiny of America contained in the first Puritan who landed on those shores, as that of the whole human race in the first man."[5]

The German social scientist Max Weber also sought to discern the basis of American liberty and prosperity, and he, too, went back to the seventeenth-century Puritans. His seminal *The Protestant Ethic and the Spirit of Capitalism*, which was not published in English until 1930, appeared as a two-part essay in 1904–1905, the first section written before his trip to the United States, the second upon his return to Heidelberg. In his address presented in St. Louis, at a conference celebrating the arts and sciences of the world and held in honor of the centennial of the Louisiana Purchase, Weber spoke of the conditions that had shaped America's historical development. Like Tocqueville, Weber emphasized that America has been unburdened by a feudal past and a parasitic aristocracy, and he referred to the country's "democratic traditions handed down by Puritans as an everlasting heirloom."[6]

Thanks to the nurturing upbringing of his mother and especially his aunt, young Max Weber came to know the works of the New England Unitarian William Ellery Channing, a forerunner of Transcendentalism, and Theodore Parker, an indomitable mind steeped in German theology and philosophy. Weber's mother could never interest him in religion, but he was impressed with Channing's "unassailable height of convictions" as the fount of value and energy that compensated for humankind's infirmities. And while he had little use for Channing's antipolitical temperament and commitment to pacifism, he appreciated the joining together of theology and labor that gave American Protestantism an ingredient lacking in German religion: a steadfast temperament of "hardened asceticism." But like Perry Miller, Weber was more drawn to the earlier Calvinists than to the Transcendentalists who influenced his mother and aunt, and he traces the origins of capitalism to the very emotions that Unitarian Transcendentalism tried to purge from religion, not God's benevolence and humankind's excellence but quite the opposite: God's wrath and humankind's unworthiness, both of which combined to produce "a feeling of unpredecented inner loneliness" on the part of the Calvinist who desperately came to feel he could work his way out of the very situation of predestination into which God had willed him.[7]

Although this essay is no place to discuss the validity of Weber's thesis on the relationship of Calvinism to capitalism, it bears remembering that to explain America Weber returned to the very sources from which the Transcendentalists were trying to escape, a theology of fear and intimidation, and that he saw capitalism as born in defiance of God's will since it came into existence by the sweat and stress of human striving as well as self-denial. The term "capitalism" did not exist during the pre-Civil War era of the Transcendentalists, but Weber appreciated the Calvinists for much the same reason Perry Miller did: both saw them as tragic, existential, modern spirits who heroically assumed that alienated striving through the life of labor could redeem the world politically as well as spiritually.

Weber and Miller would probably have agreed with Santayana's estimate that intellectual life in America undergoes a progressive deterioration as the mind leaves behind the passionate intensity of New England and turns toward more practical matters in the world of business and polite society and stuffy academic circles. Where Weber saw intellect disappearing into organization and bureaucratic rationalization, Santayana saw it retreating into the academic cloister and settling for routine procedures and pragmatic compromise. Miller himself, one should note, scarcely regarded American Pragmatism with the same reverence with which he esteemed New England Transcendentalism, and in his anthology, *American Thought: Civil War to World War I*, he treated Pragmatism as a post-Darwinian outlook and made no effort, as do some contemporary scholars, to establish its roots in an older Transcendentalism. Perhaps Miller recognized, as did Weber, that the story of Calvinism and its relation to capitalism turns a Darwinian-oriented Pragmatism on its head: history may be the study not so much of the ascent of humankind as its descent, from spirit to matter.

Ralph Waldo Emerson and Max Weber

Santayana's notion of the Transcendentalists harboring a "double allegiance," wherein one part of mind remains unaware of what the other is doing, comes close to capturing Weber's idea of the irony of unintended consequences. The devout Puritans hardly set out to become Yankee materialists, yet the Protestant work ethic, and the strenuous imperatives of frugality, saving, and self-denial, produced the conditions of abundance that ended up sapping the fibre of the early settlers of the Massachusetts Bay Colony. The evolution of capitalism out of Calvinism, of material reality out of spiritual idealism, of experience out of consciousness, seems to have defied Emerson's sense of history as moving always from the lower to the higher, of moving onward and never backward:

> What is popularly called Transcendentalism among us, is Idealism; Idealism as it appears in 1842. As thinkers, mankind have ever divided into two sects, Materialists and Idealists; the first class founding on experience, the second on consciousness; the first class beginning to think from the data of the senses, the second class perceive that the senses are not final, and say, The senses give us representations of things, but what are the things themselves, they cannot tell. The materialist insists on facts, on history, on the force of circumstance and the animal wants of man; the idealist on the power of Thought and of Will, on inspiration, on miracle, on individual culture. These two modes of thinking are both natural, but the idealist contends that his way of thinking is in higher nature. He concedes all that the other affirms, admits the impressions of sense, admits their coherency, their use and beauty, and then ask the materialist for his grounds of assurance that things are as his senses represent them. But I, he says, affirm facts not affected by the illusion of sense, facts which are of the same nature as the faculty which reports them, and not liable to doubt; facts which in their first appearance to us assume a native superiority to material facts, degrading these into a language by which the first are to be spoken; facts which it only needs a retirement from the senses to discern. Every materialist will be an idealist; but an idealist can never go backward to be a materialist.[8]

Emerson is, of course, drawing upon Immanuel Kant to overcome the epistemological impasse of British empiricism which would have us believe that there could be nothing in the intellect that had not been previously experienced by the senses. But Emerson's passionate commitment to Idealism suggests why he disdains, or professes to disdain, the mundane activities of life that cannot be seen as emanating from spiritual intuition rather than from practical thought. The Transcendentalist, wrote Emerson, "does not respect labor, or the products of labor, namely property, otherwise than as a manifold symbol, illustrating with wonderful fidelity of details the laws of being; he does not respect government, except as far as it reiterates the laws of his mind."[9]

Yet Emerson's thinking was so dialectically rich that he would, as will be discussed shortly, respect wealth as a species of power. The Emersonian wing of Transcendentalism was more individualistic and more ambivalent about capitalism than was the communitarian wing, represented by Orestes Brownson, Bronson Alcott, George Ripley, and other utopian socialists who drew on the ideas of Henri Saint-Simon, Charles Fourier, and other European socialist thinkers to carry out their perfectionist zeal. The Brook Farmers were both anti-Whig and anti-Jacksonian, as skeptical of materialism as they were of majoritarianism. The communitarians believed that the lack of harmony everywhere in America was due less to the imperfections of the weak individual than to the conflicts and contradictions that originate in society itself.

The Transcendentalists left legacies that have perplexed the American scholar. Like Santayana, Van Wyck Brooks also saw the Transcendentalists as trying to educate Americans with "twin values" that are incompatible. Separating theory from practice and ethical ends from instrumental means, New England writers left the American character straddling a "middle place between vaporous idealism and self-interested practicality." Unable to relate the abstract to the concrete, the Transcendentalists failed to relate spiritual truths to social forces. The Calvinist residue still committed them to the life of the mind, and as a result the Transcendentalists could seldom engage the realities of existence as New Englanders lived it. "The experience of New England was an experience of two extremes—bare facts and metaphysics; the machinery of self-preservation and the mystery of life."[10]

Transcendentalists were aware of the "double consciousness" that had them observing the outward world of things only to rise to the inward world of thought. Emerson himself, financially successful in his writings and lecturing, felt the dualism of flesh and spirit. "The worst feature of this double consciousness is, that the two lives, of the understanding and of the soul, which we lead, really show little relation to each other; never meet and measure each other; one prevails now, all buzz and din; and the other prevails then, all infinitude and paradise; and, with the progress of life, the two discover no greater disposition to reconcile themselves."[11] Transcendentalists were also aware that, as Theodore Parker put it, "thought turns out a thing" just as ideas bear fruit. Herewith a riddle. If Calvinism turned out capitalism, if ideas precede facts as "the thought is the thing becomes," how did the Transcendentalists look upon the American economy as it was developing in the pre-Civil War era?[12] Did not capitalism proceed from the very idea of Calvinism that, according to Van Wyck Brooks, kept the Transcendentalists in a state of otiose, remote abstraction? Moreover, did the Transcendentalists themselves make the same mistake as the early Puritans in assuming that they could follow their calling, uphold the work ethic, strive to prove themselves, and somehow avoid the unintended consequences of their striving?

We are left with three fundamental questions when we study Transcendentalism in the second quarter of the nineteenth century. First, how did the Transcendentalists react to the rise of capitalism, or, more in keeping with the language of the time, to commerce and commercial society? The second question must be addressed in view of our contemporary historians informing us that democracy posed an obstacle to the advent of America's commercialization, that the "people" stood in deliberate and conscious opposition to the coming of the "market revolution." From the point of view of the Transcendentalists, did Jacksonian democracy really resist commercialism or did it actually reflect it? Finally, given that the "double consciousness" and "double allegiance" of the Transcendentalist mind continue unreconciled in American history, how is this legacy of Transcendentalism, this war between soul and society, the ascetic and the acquisitive, manifested in modern American literature?

Commerce and Wealth

At first glance it would appear that the Transcendentalists thoroughly repudiated the ethos of commerce that was overtaking the landscape in the 1830s and 1840s. The juxtaposition of the precious "garden" to the predatory "machine," the theme spelled out in Leo Marx's seminal book, was a leitmotif of the literature of the period.[13] Yet, as Marx noted, the idea that poetry and philosophy opposed science and technology in order to uphold a pastoral ideal reflects as much ambiguity as certainty. Not only did some writers extol the energy released by technology and equate invention with the power of the will to impose itself on nature and thereby extract its secrets, but both poetry and science had as their object the contemplation of nature and both drew value from the natural world, as did the Calvinist Jonathan Edwards.

Edwards also assimilated the philosophy of John Locke, or at least its epistemology. But perhaps even more than Calvinism it was Lockean political and social theory that sustained the capitalist ethos in America. It is now known that Locke wrote his *Second Treatise of Government* with America in mind, particularly a New World environment where claims to land had to be justified on the basis of some principle higher than greed. Locke's labor theory of value suited the colonies in their need to legitimate taking possession of land occupied by Native Americans. Locke himself sought to convert the Carolina Indians to productive land use rather than to dispossess them of their hunting grounds. But colonists ignored Locke's hopes and proceeded to expropriate land on the premise that whoever improves upon it by virtue of labor is the rightful owner. Thus the Lockean doctrine of labor reinforced an older Calvinist conviction that one has a duty to work upon the materials of earth.[14]

Many of the Transcendentalists felt compelled to repudiate Lockeanism together with Calvinism. In their critique, which was more epistemological than political, the Transcendentalists came close to presaging a Weberian sense that the modern intellect is giving itself over to "instrumental reason." James Marsh, acknowledging the earlier influence of Locke in America, was happy to report that Samuel T. Coleridge had "proclaimed the empire of Locke at an end." Now New England writers could shift from the external world, the sphere that they could methodologically analyze by the capacity of the understanding to relate means to ends, to the inner world of the faculty of reason, where feelings and intuitions lie waiting to be awakened by reflective self-consciousness. Locke confined his inquiries to what can be known and made useful, and thus America faced a temptation: "Give us Locke's mechanism, and we will envy no man's mysticism."[15] As did Weber at the end of the nineteenth century, the Transcendentalists recognized that a Lockean materialism that propelled commercial society would result in the "disenchantment of the world," the stripping of the universe of all that is magical, mysterious, and spontaneous. Both Weber and Emerson feared the rationalization of existence as first eliminating the intuitive and arbitrary and then confining the world to whatever is systematic and consistent. A society governed by the calculated application of rules is the nightmare of "The American Scholar" as well as "Science as a Vocation."

The commercial market requires laws protecting property and rules assuring the reliability of economic transactions. But the Transcendentalist critique of rule-bound human relations applied to politics as well as economics. Indeed to move from the *Federalist* authors to the Transcendentalists is to observe a shift in meaning in the metaphor of "mechanism." The framers of the Constitution relied upon the "machinery of government" to compensate for the "defect of better virtues" in humankind, and thus they tried to construct near-perfect institutions to control the "interests and passions" that rendered "fallen" people imperfect and incapable of civic virtue. The framers' political architecture rendered the Transcendentalists alienated from America's constitutional Republic for two reasons. First, the U. S. Constitution came to be conceived, in the words of James Russell Lowell, as "a machine that would go by itself"; second, such a self-perpetuating mechanism would require no role for the intellectual. When asked by Antifederalists why all the conflicts that were anticipated to emerge in the new Republic could not be mediated by leaders, James Madison replied that America could not count upon "enlightened statesmen to be at the helm." Although the *Federalist* reflected the skeptical "counter-Enlightenment," its authors followed the Enlightenment in its tendency to see society in the image of the impersonal machine. Thus the framers of the Constitution saw themselves as the last generation capable of using its intellect in order to devise a system of rule that would no longer need the services of the intellectual. Small wonder the Transcendentalists saw government as a "trick," politics as little more than "cunning," and democracy the "theatre of the demagogue."[16]

How did they see economics as it developed in Jacksonian America? Almost all the Transcendentalists valued labor over capital; many could agree with Channing that genuine character expressed itself in honest work; few shared the Lockean idea that the primary purpose of government is protection of property. The outstanding exception is, of course, Thoreau, the hermit of Walden Pond who made Americans feel, as Emerson put it, "the satire of his presence," and who today ought to embarrass Marxists who fail to see, as did Thoreau, how the fetish of labor and productivity confines socialism to capitalism's basic epistemes. (Taking Marxism out of nineteenth-century political economy is like, Michel Foucault wrote, taking a fish out of water.[17])

While many nineteenth-century intellectuals, including Karl Marx, distinguished capital from labor—with the former regarded as dominated by material forces and the latter carrying the potential means of overcoming human alienation—Thoreau saw no such saving distinction. Examining the "present mode of living" in his society, he could neither accept the capitalist idea of labor, which cast work as production and enterprise as generating the wealth of nations, nor the socialist idea, which cast labor as the humanizing and liberating activity in which the worker comes to know the world in the act of transforming it. From his youth, Thoreau had denounced "the blind and unmanly love for wealth," which he saw as driving the compulsion to work. "Trade curses everything it touches," he warned. Trade, credit, speculation, investment, brokering, supply and demand—all such activities Thoreau dismissed as a disguised form of gambling where the risk-taker wages the present against the future. "What differences does it make," Thoreau asked on reading of the California gold rush, "whether you shake dirt or shake dice?"[18]

Emerson, Thoreau's Concord compatriot, could have provided an answer. A pursuit of wealth that required exploration and discovery appealed to Emerson's romantic imagination. His series of biographical essays in

Representative Men celebrates heroic achievers, the movers and shakers of the world. The term "commerce" had a cramped meaning only in the Old World, Emerson advised; in the open American environment it allowed humanity to use its mind to acquire command over nature. Aware of the classical apprehensions about trade and commerce corrupting virtue, and aware as well that a society of conspicuous emulation meant a society of fawning dependency, Emerson nevertheless asked Americans to regard industrialization as liberating. "We rail at trade, but the historian of the future will see that it was the principle of liberty; that it settled America, and destroyed feudalism, and made peace and keeps the peace; that it will abolish slavery." It will also feed the poetic imagination:

> And what if trade sows cities
>   Like shells along the shore,
> And thatch with towns the prairie broad
>   With railways ironed o'er?—
> They are but sailing foam-bells
>   Along Thought's causing stream
> And take their shape and sun-color
>   From him that sends the dream.

Seeing the beauty and harmony of all things, Emerson saw commerce not so much as wasteful and acquisitive as circulatory and reproductive. "The merchant has but one rule, *absorb and invest*; he is to be capitalist; the scrape and filings must be gathered back into the crucible; the gas and smoke must be burned, and earnings must not go to increase expense, but to capital again. Well, the man must be a capitalist. Will he spend his income or will he invest?" Emerson trusted self-reliant individuals, and not government and its mechanisms, to provide the answer. "Wealth brings with it its own checks and balances. The basis of political economy is non-interference. The only safe rule is found in the self-adjusting meter of demand and supply. Do not legislate."[19] Marx remained absolutely convinced that capitalism liberated humanity from feudalism only to subordinate the human race to the chilling forces of the competitive market. Emerson remained convinced that the pursuit of wealth is itself liberating and that we can admire the rich not because we envy their possessions but because we value their independence and freedom of action. "Power is what they want, not candy," he wrote of the hustling entrepreneurs. The ability to be effective, to actualize thought and realize the ideal, is made possible by money. "Is not then the demand to be rich legitimate?"[20]

How does one answer Emerson's question in the face of recent historical scholarship?

Jacksonian Democracy and the Market Revolution

The period of American Transcendentalism represents a great divide in American social and political thought. A half century earlier, when the Republic was founded, it was assumed that a central government was necessary because people could not be trusted to govern themselves at the local community level. Imbued with this distrust, the framers, in contrast to Thomas Jefferson, remained skeptical of what would later be called "free market" economics, and Alexander Hamilton in particular looked to the authority of the nation-state to bring commercial activity under surveillance. But by the time Emerson and Thoreau appeared on the scene, the school of political economy moved away from regulatory mercantilism to advocate something approximating *laissez faire*, and this shift implied profoundly different notions of human action and its consequences.

The framers feared that an uncontrolled democracy posed a threat to property, but when manhood suffrage was widely adopted during the Jacksonian era, democracy and property turned out to be as compatible as milk and honey. One possible reason their fears proved unfounded is that few of the framers foresaw a strong work ethic developing in America. But a half century later political economists began to assume that the human spirit—even though characterized by an uncontrollable drive for the acquisition of wealth, and a drive extending far beyond the satisfaction of immediate needs—can be trusted apart from the watchful eye of government. The desire for wealth may be unlimited, but such desires drive people to work hard, and the search for gain will result in competition and honest production. As moralists, many Transcendentalists saw the drive toward wealth as petty and vulgar, and Emerson remained almost alone in seeing in it a proto-Nietzschean will-to-power. But here we confront a disparity between what the Transcendentalists saw and what our own present historians see, or think they see.

A long tradition of writing about the political environment of the Transcendentalist era has continued to insist upon one theme. Beginning more than a century ago in the writings of George Bancroft, especially in his address "The Office of the People"; continuing in Arthur Schlesinger's Pulitzer Prize-winning book *The Age of Jackson*; then amplified as "history from below" in Sean Wilentz's *Chants Democratic*; and, more recently, seemingly coming from above in Charles Sellers's *The Market Revolution*, readers have been told that the American people wish only to remain simple and virtuous and yet find themselves preyed upon by economic forces alien to their very being. Reduced to its simplest formulation, American history has no consensus, in contrast to what Tocqueville observed when he emphasized the attitudes and preferences shared among the people; instead our history is characterized by conflict and critical antagonisms among different classes, each of which holds different values. Such a formulation had been put forth in Vernon L. Parrrington's *Main Currents in American Thought*, which depicted America divided at its core, with Jeffersonian idealism opposed to Hamiltonian materialism, the moral majority against the rapacious few. Parrington portrayed Emerson as a Puritan moralizer transformed into a Transcendental seeker who warned America that "economic forces were in league against the ideal republic." As a social critic "the ideal he had drunk of was perennial condemnation of the material." Parrington quotes Emerson writing in his journals that democracy "must fall, being wholly commercial."[21] A Weberian formulation might go something like this: capitalism must fail, being wholly democratic.

Why must it fail? In democratic society people look to the state for favors and privileges, and as government agencies respond to political pressures apart from market forces, the state apparatus becomes bureaucratized and expands its reach of surveillance and control. The irony is that the greater the democratic participation of the people in the affairs of government the greater may be the domination of government over the people. Many of the Transcendentalists had a proto-Weberian sense of this possibility, as suggested in Emerson's critique of politics and specialization and the "cold-corpse" nature of institutions, and Tocqueville feared that democracy tends toward admininstrative centralization. Thus while the French writer looked to aspects of civil society in "voluntary associations," Emerson formulated the doctrine of self-reliance in opposition to the collective coercions of democratic politics. Despite these earlier insights, the historian Sellers sees democracy as innocent of irony and capitalism as guilty of sin.

Sellers's *The Market Revolution* contains provocative chapter titles such as "God and Mammon" and "Ethos vs. Eros," all of which are meant to drive home the point that such dualisms dispel "the mystifying relations of class, power, and culture, our historical mythology of consensual capitalism [that] renders incomprehensible the massive resistance that rallied around Andrew Jackson." Incomprehensible? Sellers would have us believe that those people who cheered Jackson's veto of the rechartering of the Bank of the United States were resisting the "market revolution" that was being imposed upon them against their democratic will: "Contrary to liberal mythology, democracy was born in tension with capitalism, and not as its natural and legitimizing expression."[22] Sellers seeks to persuade us of this desperate thesis by using the expression "radical democracy"—

as though capitalism itself cannot be considered, as Marx himself considered it, the most radical transforming phenomenon of the nineteenth century.[23] As Richard Hofstadter pointed out years ago, rather than juxtaposing democracy to capitalism, Jackson looked to what he called the "bone and sinew of the country," specifically the laborers, farmers, and mechanics, to take capitalism away from the capitalists by decentralizing it in the states and local communities.[24] In light of the financial speculation that afterwards spread like wildfire under Jackson's own scheme of "pet" banks, the historian Eric McKitrick was right to observe the parallels between the greed of a Jacksonian psyche that hated banks but loved money and the "Savings and Loan" crisis that followed Ronald Reagan's deregulation of monetary controls.[25] Today's historian may allow himself to be mesmerized by Jackson's slaying of the "Monster" Bank of the United States; Emerson knew better. "As soon as a man talks . . . General Jackson to me, I detect the coxcomb and charlatan. He is a frivolous nobody who has no duties of his own."[26]

Sellers quotes Bancroft dramatizing Jacksonian democracy as symbolic of the eternal "feud between the house of Have and the house of Want," only the historian acknowledges that in the end the Democratic Party followed the Whigs in accepting as inevitable the coming of a "bourgeois Republic." He then quotes a worker saying that it is clear that the Whigs were out to "make the rich richer and the poor poorer" and thereby serve their class interests. "But the Democrats," the worker lamented, "what shall we say of them?"[27] Actually, the question was answered almost perfectly by Theodore Parker, the Boston theologian who asked for proof of democracy as much as he did of divinity. The Whig organizes around the dollar and "sneers" at the lower classes, wrote Parker. And the Democrat?

> The Democrat party appeals to the brute will of the majority; . . . it knows no Higher Law. . . . There is . . . no vital difference between the Whig party and the Democratic party; no difference in moral principle. The Whig inaugurates the Money got; the Democrat inaugurates the Desire to get money. That is all the odds. . . . There is only a hand rail between the two, which breaks down if you lean on it, and the parties mix. . . . A Democrat is but a Whig on time; a Whig is a Democrat arrived at maturity; his time has come. A Democrat is a young Whig who will legislate for money as soon as he has got it; the Whig is an old Democrat who once hurrahed for the majority—"Down with money! there is a despot! and up with the desire for it! Down with the rich, and up with the poor!" The young man, poor, obscure, and covetous, in 1812 was a

Democrat, went a-privateering against England; rich, and accordingly "one of our eminent citizens," in 1851 he was a Whig.[28]

In contrast to many of our present historians of the period, the Transcendentalists saw America as rapidly becoming a middle-class society characterized by consensus rather than conflict. Parker's passage above presages John Stuart Mill's observation that in democratic politics what one party has in possession the other has in expectation.

With the advent of commercial society a consensualized capitalist culture played havoc with political definitions. The American character itself, as Tocqueville noted, would not stand still in order to come to terms with what it was. "Why Are Americans So Restless Amidst Their Prosperity?" is the title of one of his chapters. The French writer discerned in the American people the same unease and even anxiety and "quiet desperation" as did Thoreau and other Transcedentalists. Indeed when Parker notes that the difference between money and the desire to get money is only the difference between time and place, contingency and opportunity, and not character and virtue, Bancroft's distinction between "have" and "want" becomes a "feud" more rhetorical than real. "Down with money!" shout those who would incapacitate the wealthy so that they might replace them. Reinhold Niebuhr, drawing upon Nietzsche, noted that both the Christian and the radical are under the illusion that the "materialistic" forces of history "will automatically rob the strong of their strength and give it to the weak."[29] How can there be genuine class conflict when different classes aspire to the same things and thereby betray a consensus in doing so? Thoreau's imperative of "simplicity" protested an American society moving toward the snares of acquisitive consumption. What drove him to Walden Pond was the spectre of a deadening consensus overtaking capitalist culture.

Yet for all their efforts at transcendence, many New England Transcendentalists felt oppositions and dualisms within their own minds, and hence Emerson could struggle with freedom and fate and forever wonder whether wealth would be fulfilling or corrupting and whether knowledge would control power or submit to it. This Transcendentalist legacy continued in American literature and appears in Mark Twain's reverting to nature to escape the grip of society, William James's grappling with his "divided self," Thomas Wolfe's struggling between the craftsman and the celebrity, and F. Scott Fitzgerald's defining himself as trying to hold two contradictory ideas in his head at the same time while still functioning rationally. The rhapsody of its poetry aside, the Transcendentalists left a legacy of doubt and tension rather than cosmic serenity. "The New England temper distrusts itself as well as the world it lives in, and rarely yields to eccentricities of conduct," observed Henry Adams. "Emerson himself, protesting against every usual tendency of society, respected in practice all its standards."[30]

It could well be that at the base of Emersonian self-trust lies a distrust of the possibilities of reconciling dualisms and antinomies. Thus the Transcendentalist legacy juxtaposed freedom to possession, integrity to property, the ascetic to the acquisitive, the autonomy of the self to the subjection to the other, and the attractions of eastern innocence and acceptance to the restrictions of western experience and conscience. Reading the Transcendentalists one cannot be sure that they succeeded in ridding America of Calvinism and sin, and thus we sense that Emerson felt guilt and remorse just as we all do when we realize we have failed to live up to our own earlier ideals and those of our Republic. What hovered darkly over the New England mind was a conviction of betrayal, and nowhere was the burden of this Transcendentalist legacy better dramatized than in the theater of Eugene O'Neill, the playwright whose works were haunted, as was Emerson's poem "Threnody," by a loss that can be neither restored, forgotten, nor forgiven.

The Transcendentalist Temptation:
"Possessors Self-Dispossessed"

"Yes, I've read Henry Adams—some years ago but I remember it well," Eugene O'Neill wrote to his aunt of *The Education of Henry Adams*. "A great book! But so New England! And I've lived so much in New England in my past that all I want now is to forget it and be free of the Puritan pall."[31]

Several of O'Neill's plays took New England during the pre-Civil War era as their setting. And, of course, he could never forget what it meant to read Emerson and Thoreau (along with Europeans Schopenhauer, Strindberg, and Nietzsche, who called Emerson a "brother-*soul*"[32]) trying their best to escape the "Puritan pall." In his last years O'Neill planned an eleven-play cycle on the history of America from the colonial era to the period when he conceived the project, the 1930s. The cycle was to be titled "Threnody: A Tale of Possessers Dispossessed." Several of the scripts O'Neill ordered his wife to destroy (it was "like tearing up children," his widow, Carlotta Monterey, recalled[33]). One script, *A Touch of the Poet*, somehow escaped the fireplace and was published and performed; the fragments of another survived and later became *More Stately Mansions*.[34]

In such works O'Neill intended to portray the progressive decline of the

United States due to self-destructive greed driven by an unbounded desire on the part of Americans who sought to acquire and to own. Whether it be desire for property, love of a woman, or infatuation with new sources of energy in electrical generators (the theme of *The Dynamo*), O'Neill saw, as did the Transcendentalists, that in the urge to own one becomes owned by one's own desire. But O'Neill, in contrast to Santayana, avoids associating the dominance of the American will and "aggressive enterprise" with the American man and the refinements of American culture and passive gentility with the American woman. In *A Touch of the Poet*, it is a female who exhorts that "this is America not poverty-stricken Ireland where you are a slave! Here you are free to take what you want, if you have the power in yourself." The "possession of power is the only freedom," she declares, indifferent to Emerson's dictum that freedom requires relinquishing the heart's desires in order to see that "power ceases in an act of repose."[35]

In the pre–World War I years O'Neill read Emerson while recovering from tuberculosis in a sanitarium. He also read Thoreau, and some of his characters refer to the reclusive life of the poet. O'Neill's anarchist affinities also disposed him to Emerson and Thoreau. When working on the "Cycle" O'Neill became steeped in Transcendentalism and kept at his side Van Wyck Brooks's *The Flowering of New England*, which was published in 1936. In notes to a projected play fragment entitled "Thoreau in Simon," O'Neill jotted down excerpts from Thoreau's and Emerson's journals.[36] In *More Stately Mansions*, O'Neill has Simon Harford escaping periodically to live on a houseboat on a lake, and the dwelling replicated Thoreau's shack at Walden Pond. Appropriately, in these notes it is not the possession of power that brings freedom. On the contrary, O'Neill's characters are only truly autonomous when shipping out to sea, escaping into the woods, or living in one way or another apart from society and its conventions. In *Beyond the Horizon* the protagonist seeks solitude and simplicity, fearing bondage to the necessities of mundane existence, like mortgages and bank loans and the dreary realities of farm life that repelled Thoreau as much as O'Neill.

Drama critics share a widespread impression that O'Neill felt the "curse of the misbegotten" as he remained haunted by his father and mother, one an actor who forsook Shakespeare to achieve commercial success playing Monte Cristo, the other a morphine addict who played the piano in ghostly isolation from the rest of the family. "Everyman," wrote Emerson, "finds room in his face for all his ancestors."[37] But while O'Neill could scarcely shake off the shadowy presence of his jaded father and fragile mother, he also remained obsessed with the meaning of America. *A Touch of the Poet*, which takes place in New England during the Jacksonian era, captures

Theodore Parker's description of the Whig and the Democratic as representing little more than two acquisitive impulses that happen to arrive at different historical moments, one close to aristocratic affluence and leisure, the other conniving after it. *Desire Under the Elms* depicts lust, incest, and murder in an environment still feeling the long shadow of Puritanism. While the sons silently wish the father's death in order to inherit the land, the father grumbles: "God is not easy. . . . God's in the stone. . . . I'm making walls—stone atop o'stone—making walls till yer heart's a stone ye heft up out of o'the way o' growth onto a stone wall t'wallin yer heart!" The wall of stones walls him off from family and community.[38]

The Great God Brown, set in a more modern setting of the business boom of the 1920s, indicts the cult of commercial achievement celebrated during that era. The character Dion Anthony was a composite, O'Neill told the press, of Dionysias and Saint Anthony and his temptations. The antagonist to Dion the creator and poet is William Brown, a businessman-architect "heaven-bent for success" and driven by "the will of Mammon." Brown is, Travis Bogard observed in an ironic reference to Thoreau, "the secure God of a materialistic society, an assured possessor of all he surveys."[39]

The use of masks in the play enabled O'Neill to dramatize how the leading characters easily change roles, and this transferance of personality suggests two impulses within the same soul, the yearning to be the artist and the wish to be the success, the aesthetic visionary and the satisfied bourgeois, the Democrat and the Whig all in one. As did Emerson and Thoreau, O'Neill interrogated an American culture that left the poet wandering and the profiteer wallowing. In the theater of O'Neill as well as in the richly tense texture of New England Transcendentalism, one sees the "double consciousness," what Van Wyck Brooks described as mind straddling a "middle place between vaporous idealism and self-interested practicality," between creative aspirations and possessive impulses, patrician culture and peasant hunger, the lofty ideals that touch the dispensable poet and the immediate needs that drive the ascendent entrepreneur.

In O'Neill's America there is no trace of Puritanism and the spirit of capitalism in the Weberian sense, which at one time was understood to mean self-denial and moral duty. O'Neill shared the Greenwich Village generation's conviction that Calvinism repressed sexual drives that could only be sublimated in possessive acquisitiveness, and thus he saw liberty as providing the grounds for greed and aggression as much as freedom and escape from domination. In Jacksonian America "you are free to take what you want." Democracy, rather than standing in valiant opposition to capitalism, enthrones power and greed and ushers in a Nietzschean transvaluation of values. In a final scene in *More Stately Mansions*, the protagonist, his poetic ideals defeated, comes upon his avaricious wife and mother who have just agreed with one another, unaware of his presence, that somehow he is to blame for their rapacious ways. As they gasp in response to his entrance, he lectures them on truths that turn upside down the gender categories of the genteel tradition:

> You are mistaken, Mother. You are hiding from yourself again. . . .
> And Sara seems to have caught the cowardly habit from you. It is
> stupid of you to blame me. It is not in my head but in your hearts.
> I have merely insisted that you both be what you are—that what
> you are is good because it is fact and reality—that the true nature
> of man and woman, to which we have hitherto given the bad name
> of evil because we were afraid of it, is, in a world of facts domi-
> nated by our own greed for power and possession, good because it
> is true. And what is evil, because it is a lie, is the deliberate evasive
> sentimental misunderstanding of man as he is, proclaimed by the
> fool, Jean Jacques Rousseau—the stupid theory that he is naturally
> what we call virtuous and good. Instead of being what he is, hog. It
> is that idealistic fallacy which is responsible for all the confusion in
> our minds, the conflicts within the self, and for all confusion in our
> relationships with one another, within the family particularly, for
> the blundering of our desires which are disciplined to covet what
> they don't want and be afraid to crave what they wish for in truth
> [He smiles a thin tense smile.] In a nutshell, if you will pardon the
> seeming paradox, all one needs to remember is that good is evil,
> and evil, good.[40]

O'Neill himself, like many of the Transcedentalists, could hardly en-dorse such a nihilistic conclusion in which Christian values are abolished once the modern mind uncovers the forgery of their genealogy. If Emerson could convince himself of the unreality of evil, O'Neill as a dramatist had no choice other than to sustain conflict, convinced, as with that other Irish genius, William Butler Yeats, that life truly begins only when it is conceived as tragedy. Thus O'Neill leaves Van Wyck Brooks's "middle place" without resolution, hinting that if the desire to transcend desire could be fulfilled, the will to live may cease to assert its will to power. Seeing the temptations of Transcendentalism, O'Neill agreed with Nietzsche that it is better to be a satyr than a saint. "Life's all right," advises one of his characters in *The Great God Brown*, "if you leave it alone." Typical of O'Neill, the advice comes from the lips of a prostitute. The Transcendentalist can stoop as well as soar.

NOTES

1. George Santayana, "The Genteel Tradition in American Philosophy," "Emerson,"
and "Emerson the Poet," in *Santayana in America: Essays, Notes, and Letters in
American Life*, ed. Richard Colton Lyon (New York, 1968), 35–56, 258–283. See
also Joe Lee Davis, "Santayana as a Critic of Transcendentalism," in *Transcendentalism and Its Legacy*, ed. Myron Simon and Thorton H. Parsons (Ann Arbor,
1966), 150–177.
2. Alexis de Tocqueville, *Democracy in America*, trans. George Lawrence, ed. J. P.
Mayer (Garden City, N.Y., 1966), 690–693; Henry David Thoreau, *Walden and
Civil Disobedience* (New York, 1960), 222–240; Orestes A. Brownson, "The Everlasting Yes," in *The Transcendentalists*, ed. Perry Miller (Cambridge, Mass., 1950),
45–46.
3. Perry Miller, "From Jonathan Edwards to Emerson," *The New England Quarterly*
13(1940):589–616.
4. Tocqueville, *Democracy in America*, 279. The works of the Austrian economists
Ludwig von Mises and Friedrich von Hayek have long been known in America and
have been central to the free market theories taught at University of Chicago and
elsewhere, ideas that came to fruition in the Reagan presidency in the 1980s. After
the fall of communism in 1989, Hayek became the most influential theorist of political economy in eastern Europe. See, for example, the "Symposium on F. A.
Hayek" in the *Critical Review*.
5. Tocqueville, *Democracy in America*, 342; Alexis de Tocqueville to Louis de Ker-
gorlay, Oct. 17, 1845, in *Alexis de Tocqueville: Selected Letters on Politics and Society*, ed. Roger Boesch and James Toupin (Berkeley, 1985), 192.
6. See John Patrick Diggins, *Max Weber: Politics and the Spirit of Tragedy* (New York,
1996), 1–16, passim.
7. Diggins, *Max Weber*, 17–47; Max Weber, *The Protestant Ethic and the Spirit of
Capitalism*, trans. Talcott Parsons (New York, 1992).
8. Ralph Waldo Emerson, "The Transcendentalist," in *The Selected Writings of Ralph
Waldo Emerson*, ed. Brooks Atkinson (1940; New York, 1996), 81.
9. Emerson, "The Transcendentalist," 83.
10. Van Wyck Brooks, *America's Coming-of-Age* (1915; Garden City, N.Y., 1958), 18,
38.
11. Emerson, "The Transcendentalist," 93.
12. Theodore Parker, *The World of Matter and the Spirit of Man* (Boston, 1907).
13. Leo Marx, *The Machine in the Garden: Technology and the Pastoral Ideal in America* (New York, 1964).
14. James Tully, *An Approach to Political Philosophy: Locke in Context* (New York,
1993); Peter Hulme, "The Spontaneous Hand of Nature: Savagery, Colonialism,
and the Enlightenment," in *The Enlightenment and Its Shadows*, ed. Peter Hulme
and Ludmilka Jordanova (New York, 1990), 16–34.
15. James Marsh, "Preliminary Essay," in *The Transcendentalists*, 34–39. On "Mechanism" and "Mysticism," see Timothy Walker, "Signs of the Times," in *The Transcendentalists*, 39–43.

16. Jacob E. Cooke, ed., *The Federalist* (Middletown, Conn., 1961), see nos. 10, 37, 51, and 63; Michael Kammen, "*A Machine That Would Go By Itself*": *The Constitution in American Culture* (New York, 1986); Ralph Waldo Emerson, "Politics," in *The Portable Emerson*, ed. Mark Van Doren (New York, 1946), 187–204. See also Andrew Delbanco, *William Ellery Channing: An Essay on the Liberal Spirit in America* (Cambridge, Mass., 1981).

17. Ralph Waldo Emerson, "Thoreau," in *The Portable Emerson*, 567–589. Discussing Marxism in view of the theories of Adam Smith, David Ricardo, and other economic theorists, Foucault writes: "At the deepest level of Western knowledge, Marxism introduced no real discontinuity; it found its place without difficulty, as a full, quiet, comfortable and, goodness knows, satisfying form for a time (its own), within an epistemological arrangement that welcomed it gladly (since it was this arrangement that was in fact making room for it), and that it, in return, had no intention of disturbing and, above all, no power to modify even one jot, since it rested entirely upon it. Marxism exists in nineteenth-century thought like a fish in water; that is, it is unable to breathe anywhere else." Michel Foucault, *The Order of Things: An Archaeology of the Human Sciences* (New York, 1973), 261–262.

18. On Thoreau on work and alienation, see John P. Diggins, *The Lost Soul of American Politics: Virtue, Self-Interest, and the Foundations of Liberalism* (New York, 1984), 206–229.

19. On Emerson on wealth and power, see Diggins, *Lost Soul*, 192–205.

20. Ralph Waldo Emerson, "Wealth," in *The Complete Works of Ralph Waldo Emerson*, ed. Edward Waldo Emerson (Cambridge, Mass., 1903–1904), 2:85–127.

21. Vernon L. Parrington, *Main Currents in American Thought* (New York, 1927), 2:377–399; quotations from 392, 395.

22. Charles Sellers, *The Market Revolution: Jacksonian America, 1815–1846* (New York, 1991), 32, 268.

23. The advent of capital, wrote Marx, destroys everything in its way, including feudal restrictions and patriarchal relations, and its "ceaseless striving towards the general form of wealth drives labor beyond the limits of its natural paltriness" (*Naturbedurftigkeit*). Karl Marx, *Grundrisse: Foundations of the Critique of Political Economy*, trans. Martin Nicolaus (Baltimore, 1973), 325.

24. Richard Hofstadter, *The American Political Tradition and the Men Who Made It* (New York, 1948), 45–67.

25. Erik McKitrick, "The Great White Hope," *New York Review of Books*, June 11, 1992.

26. Ralph Waldo Emerson, *The Heart of Emerson's Journals*, ed. Bliss Perry (Boston, 1909), 284.

27. Sellers, *Market Revolution*, 340–341, 422.

28. Parker is quoted in Parrington, *Main Currents in American Thought*, 2:422.

29. Reinhold Niebuhr, *Moral Man and Immoral Society* (New York, 1960), 154.

30. Henry Adams, *The Life of George Cabot Lodge* (Boston, 1911), 50, 146.

31. Eugene O'Neill, *The Letters of Eugene O'Neill*, ed. Travis Bogard and Jackson R. Bryer (New Haven, 1988), 332.

32. Freidrich Neitzsche to Franz Overbeck, Dec. 24, 1883, quoted in Graham Parkes, *Composing the Soul: Reaches of Nietzsche's Psychology* (Chicago, 1994), 37. Elsewhere Nietzsche described Emerson as "one who instinctively nourishes himself

on ambroasia" and thereby sustains a youthful "lust" for life. *The Portable Nietzsche*, ed. Walter Kaufmann (New York, 1954), 522.

33. Quoted in Arthur and Barbara Gelb, *Eugene O'Neill* (New York, 1987), 938.

34. I am indebted to Martha Gilman Bower, who has worked on these remains in the Beinecke Library, Yale University. See the valuable "Introduction" to Eugene O'Neill, *More Stately Mansions: The Unexpurgated Edition*, ed. Martha Gilman Bower (New York, 1988), 3–17.

35. Eugene O'Neill, *A Touch of a Poet* (New Haven, 1957); Ralph Waldo Emerson, "Self-Reliance," in *Ralph Waldo Emerson: Selected Prose and Poetry*, ed. Reginald L. Cook (New York, 1966), 165–192.

36. See Bower's "Introduction," 12–14; see also Frederick I. Carpenter, "Eugene O'Neill, the Orient, and American Transcendentalism," in *Transcendentalism and Its Legacy*, 204–214.

37. Emerson, *Emerson's Journals*, 247.

38. Eugene O'Neill, "Desire Under the Elms," in *Three Plays of Eugene O'Neill* (New York, 1958), 7, 31.

39. Travis Bogard, *Contours of Time: The Plays of Eugene O'Neill* (New York, 1958), 275. See also Cynthia McCown, "*The Great God Brown*: A Diagnostic of Commercialism's Ills," *Eugene O'Neill Review* 17 (Fall 1993):53–59.

40. O'Neill, *More Stately Mansions*, 269–270.

The Celestial Village

Transcendentalism and Tourism in Concord

ROBERT A. GROSS

> O could I flow like thee, and make thy stream
> My great example, as it is my theme!
> Though deep, yet clear, though gentle, yet not dull,
> Strong without rage, without o'erflowing, full.
>
> —JOHN DENHAM, "Cooper's Hill" (1655)

WELL BEFORE THE AMERICAN RENAISSANCE, BEFORE EMER-son began selling big beyond New England, while Thoreau was storing unsold copies of *A Week on the Concord and Merrimack Rivers* in his room and revising *Walden* for publication, while the Alcotts were back in Boston, living miserably in shabby neighborhoods, Concord was already acquiring a happy reputation as a literary shrine.[1]

In 1852, the New York publisher George Palmer Putnam issued a handsome gift book for the Christmas season, *Homes of American Authors*, complete with engravings of the residences and "Anecdotical, Personal, and Descriptive Sketches" of the occupants. Designed to herald the coming of age of American authorship, the book was the pioneer of a now-familiar genre: the tourist guide to literary landmarks. In imitation of William Howitt's *Homes and Haunts of the Most Eminent British Poets*, published two years before by Harper and Brothers, *Homes of American Authors* gathered together essays by journalists and editors on New York's Grub Street to celebrate the makers of a national literature.[2] Seventeen figures comprise this Author's Row, and predictably, ten hailed from New England, five from New York, and only two from the South. More crucially, the Northerners resided mainly in antebellum America's leading vacation spots: Boston and Cambridge, the Hudson and Connecticut valleys, the White Mountains. Thanks to its situation as the home of Emerson and Nathaniel Hawthorne, Concord was granted admission to this select club.[3]

Sketching these two literary lions was George William Curtis, an erst-while Transcendentalist from a wealthy family in Providence and New York who had boarded as a student for a few seasons at Brook Farm back in 1842–1843 and then had sojourned in Concord for three years, living as a part-time laborer on local farms, taking in the sights, and befriending, as best he could, Emerson, Hawthorne, and Thoreau (whose Walden cabin, a future "home of an American author," he had helped to build one March day in 1845). After decamping for the Grand Tour of Europe, with a side-trip to Cairo and Jerusalem, Curtis returned to embark upon a literary career in New York. In 1852, a twenty-eight-year-old freelance writer, about to become associate editor of *Putnam's Monthly Magazine* and with national fame at *Harper's Monthly* ahead, he accepted the assignment to write about his former Concord friends for his imminent employer. No matter that he had not seen them or the town for six years, nor that Hawthorne, long since gone from the Old Manse, had only just moved back into Concord, right into Bronson Alcott's onetime residence on the Lexington Road, a home that would become renowned as the Wayside. Curtis was content to collect the facts by mail and trust to memory for local color. Indulging nostalgia for "one of those quiet country towns whose charm is incredible to all but those who by loving it have found it worthy of love," he portrayed Concord in the aesthetic language of the picturesque. Though it lacked the sublime prospects and variegated scenes of the Hudson Valley, the small town along the Concord River assumed, in the urbanite Curtis's gaze, a romantic aura all its own.[4]

Indeed, Concord took its character from "the sluggish repose of the little river" on whose banks it sat—or rather, dozed, "as if, loitering over the plain some fervent day, it had fallen asleep obedient to the slumbrous spell, and had not since awakened." Its current too indolent to turn a mill-wheel, its "languid" waters uninviting to navigation, the "dreaming idler" of a river, "belonging much more to the Indian than to the Yankee," provided safe harbor from the "rushing, whirling, bustling" progress of the age. Heedless of change, Concord's farmers, "sturdy, sterling men," carried on their seasonal rounds, growing corn and rye, the "tranquil" labor briefly pierced by the "rattle, roar, and whistle" of the trains that hurried by on trips back and forth to the city—"fleeting" reminders of a wider world and, Curtis intimated, convenient passage for curious tourists. Too far from Boston for market-gardens or summer homes, Concord preserved "a genuine country freshness and feeling, derived from its loneliness." A Rip Van Winkle of a town, it was sleeping through the Industrial Revolution—and all the happier for it.[5]

In this "dreaming, pastoral poet of a village," writers thrived. From the "broad river meadows" grew a harvest "of which the poet's thought is the sickle," in illustration of which Curtis invoked Emerson's verse. The "wide solitude" enchanted the poet with its beauty; the "placid scenery" matched the cool serenity of Emerson's mind. Even his house, though it had "a city air" and overlooked the highway, had a "bracing" atmosphere. "It is always morning within those doors." Stamped by the landscape, Emerson's writings expressed the spirit of the place. "The imagination of the man who roams the solitary pastures of Concord, or floats, dreaming, down its river, will easily see its landscape upon Emerson's pages," Curtis observed. ". . . If there be something oriental in his philosophy and tropical in his imagination," his texts "have yet the strong flavor of his Mother Earth—the underived sweetness of the open Concord sky, and the spacious breadth of the Concord horizon."[6]

Hawthorne derived a different advantage from the surround. His Muse stirred in the musty air of the "rusty, gable-roofed" Old Manse by "the dreaming river," in which he spent three years roughly overlapping with Curtis's Concord sojourn. Once an active parsonage, the Manse had become run down; its front gate, fallen off the hinges, no longer welcomed visitors to the door. That seclusion suited the unsociable tenant, who soon became "a phantom and a fable" to the neighbors. "'*Is* there anybody in the old house?' sobbed the old ladies in despair, imbibing tea of a livid green." Spared the intrusion, Hawthorne was free to brood over the ghosts of the ancient pastors who had inhabited the house, to contemplate the scene of the opening battle of the American Revolution—the famous "shot heard round the world" on April 19, 1775—that had taken place in his backyard, and to ply the waters of the river in his rowboat, like an ancient Indian, and dream. For Hawthorne, in this telling, the Old Manse evoked the romance of a fabled past in a solitary, natural setting. "The house, its inmates, and its life, lay, dream-like upon the edge of the little village," the sentimental Curtis suggested. "You fancied that they all came together and belonged together, and were glad that at length some idol of your imagination, some poet whose spell had held you, and would hold you for ever, was housed as such a poet would be."[7]

Reflecting on "the spectacle on which Hawthorne looked out, in his contemplative saunterings and reveries," Henry James lamented the meager materials with which the mid-nineteenth-century American novelist had to work: "no sovereign, no court, . . . no aristocracy, no church, no clergy, . . . no country gentlemen, no palaces, no castles, nor manors, nor old country houses, nor parsonages, nor thatched cottages, nor ivied ruins," to cite just a few of the cultural disabilities on James's now-famous list. *Homes of American Authors* expressed the poverty of that literary landscape in its very bid to conjure up romance, as is evident in Curtis's fanciful portrait of Concord. No "cloud of romance" surrounded Emerson's country house, a "plain" dwelling of recent vintage, occupying ground from which not even Thoreau could unearth an arrowhead. "Neither the Indians, nor Nature, nor Thoreau," Curtis was obliged to concede, "can invest the quiet residence of our author with the dignity, or even the suspicion of a legend." The Old Manse, at least, was a parsonage, enjoyed by two clergymen in succession, yet for all its "mosses," it dated back only seventy-five years, and it abutted the site of a well-known event, the Concord Fight, whose last local survivor, the eighty-seven-year-old Thaddeus Blood, was still walking around town when the newly wed Hawthornes took up residence. Symbolizing America's break with the past, the battle scene was memorialized by a monument, erected in 1836, that was, as we shall see, an emblem of modernity. To cast an antiquarian spell over such real estate required more legerdemain than the novice Curtis possessed.[8]

Actually, the charming fairyland Curtis dreamed up was not an original fabrication. His literary fancies were spun from materials furnished by the Concord writers themselves. It was Emerson, after all, who delighted in the environs and found refuge from care on the river or in the woods. Curtis merely borrowed the theme and quoted *Nature*. His indebtedness to Hawthorne was deeper but undisclosed. The "sluggish" river, the mysterious Manse, the dreamy atmosphere: these tropes came straight off the pages of *Mosses from an Old Manse*. Hawthorne's genius had transformed the old-fashioned, gabled house of the late Reverend Ezra Ripley into a Gothic "edifice," the departed pastor into a shadowy presence, the riverine setting into a scene out of John Bunyan—"the Enchanted Ground, through which the pilgrim travelled on the way to the Celestial City," falling into profound slumber owing to "the abundance of peace and quiet, within and all around us." Curtis took these immaterial images from Hawthorne's "Preface," treated them literally, and in a deft sleight of hand, extended them to Concord itself. Untainted by industry and trade, populated by plowmen and poets, associated with a fabulous past and eternal nature, the town belonged to the realm of the pastoral: a place apart from its own time, where an urban visitor might gain respite from the pressures of modern life. In Curtis's telling, Transcendentalism and tourism merged. A trip to Concord was a spiritual experience.[9]

Like the March girls on a lazy afternoon, Curtis built a pleasant castle in the air, light entertainment for the armchair traveler curious about the *Homes of American Authors*. This literary effervescence had a transient popularity; *Homes* was reprinted twice, in 1855 and 1857, before disappearing from view, until Elbert Hubbard retrieved the book in 1896 for the Roycroft Press, under the title *Little Journeys to the Homes of American Authors*.[10]

Curtis's perspective on Concord had more permanent influence in literary history. From his ornamental garden grew Van Wyck Brooks's *Flowering of New England*, which shaped a generation of criticism about Transcendentalism and society. Like Curtis, Brooks embraced Concord as an ideal writer's retreat, an antebellum Bread Loaf in Middlesex, where thought could be cultivated at an unhurried pace, without disruption by the demands of modern economic life. "Plain, low, quiet, the village had no obvious distinction," Brooks echoed Curtis. "The enterprising Yankees passed it by." In Concord, nature and man came together in rare harmony. "The village air . . . favoured meditation and contemplation. The hills and woods, not too exciting, afforded a gentle stimulus to genial and uninterrupted studies." Yet Concord was no cloister for Transcendentalists; in the small town lay social resources that enhanced the natural advantages. That insight gave sociological weight to literary criticism. Untroubled by the class divisions of an industrial city, the people of Concord, according to Brooks, came together in the daily life of the village. Emerson could mingle with the blacksmith, the grocer, the doctor and gauge their character on a universal scale. "Concord, indeed, was a school for the study of human nature," Brooks opined. ". . . The large mind in small conditions, the high mind in low conditions, everything in leasts: why should not Concord be one's Rome, one's world?"[11]

Perry Miller knew why not. The simple community was no place for a Romantic intellectual. Accepting the conventional description of Concord but disputing its implications, Miller endorsed Margaret Fuller's "taunt" to Emerson. "I trow the fates which gave this place Concord, took away the animating influences of Discord," she challenged. "Life here slumbers and steals on like the river. A very good place for a sage, but not for the lyrist or the orator." Fuller was well rid of Concord, Miller judged, when she engaged the leading events of her times in New York, Paris, and Rome. Back in his provincial backwater, Thoreau—"the Concordian Byron"— tilled the thin soil of small-town possibility and "wantonly" wore it out.[12]

Admiring or not, this prospect on Concord and its writers—"For at least a quarter of a century," Robert Spiller declared in the *Literary History of the United States*, "the idyllic town was the intellectual seed pod of the nation"—dominated scholarship down to the 1960s.[13] Like Curtis and James before them, twentieth-century commentators were ultimately captive to their Transcendentalist sources. In these historical accounts, spiritual ideals were conflated with social facts. No wonder Miller discerned so little tension in Concord. He, too, fell victim to the literary conceit of the torpid town by the sluggish river.

Ironically, the Concord writers were seldom lulled by such illusions. When he was not locked up in his study at the Old Manse, chasing down the phantoms of his imagination and putting them on paper, Hawthorne could be an acute observer of the neighbors. "I am not aware that the inhabitants of Concord resemble their native river in any of their moral characteristics," he confided to his notebook in August 1842; "their forefathers, certainly, seem to have had the energy and impetus of a mountain torrent, rather than the torpor of this listless stream—as was proved by the blood with which they stained their River of Peace." One prominent trait was a drive for wealth and comforts, which Thoreau exposed before the world in *Walden* with relentless fury at the distorted lives and desperate spirits it wrought.[14]

But George William Curtis was not noticing these sordid details when he decamped from Brook Farm in company with his brother Burrill and signed up for a schoolboy's holiday on a Concord farm. Drawn to the town by "a high and intense hero-worship" for Emerson, the idealistic youth, age twenty, was, like many reformers and intellectuals of the day, seeking to overcome the deepening division of labor in American society and to achieve, through his stint of agricultural work, a way to cultivate the "head" and the "hands" at the same time. Luckily for Curtis, he had the independence, financed by a wealthy banker-father, to negotiate his own terms. With a recommendation from Emerson, the brothers made a deal with a middle-aged farmer named Nathan Barrett: in exchange for room and board, each paid $1.50 a week and pledged to work five hours a day; normally, afternoons were their own. At a time when local youth were abandoning farm labor to immigrants from Nova Scotia and Ireland, the Curtis boys, descended from Puritans and eager for chores, may have offered an unexpected boon to Barrett, "a thoroughly skilled practical farmer." But one look at "the refined gentlemen" with shoulder-length hair parted in the middle prompted the canny employer to "test their metal." The first assignment was to shovel manure, a test they passed with flying colors. The boys soon became veterans of the potato patch, the apple orchard, and the hayfield, though George managed to cut his thumb on a scythe and put himself out of commission for a month at the very height of the harvest.[15]

Exhilarated by the "grand prospect" from Barrett's farm atop Punkatasset Hill, delighting in rural solitude—"so still a life after the city, and after the family at Brook Farm"—Curtis never perceived the swift economic changes happening around him, changes in which he was an unconscious participant. The Curtises arrived in Concord on May 11, 1844, part of an exodus from the troubled Brook Farm that would eventually bring twenty chastened souls to the town. Six weeks later, the Iron Horse made its dramatic appearance, its piercing whistle announcing the triumph of a new industrial order. Curtis was soon happily commuting into Boston for concerts and conventions and luxuriating in the new freedom to combine country living with city pastimes. He was evidently oblivious to the fact that his employer was equally quick to realize the advantages of the railroad. No gentleman-farmer despite his several hundred acres, Capt. Nathan Barrett had lost considerably on sheep-raising and cattle-butchering, but when the train pulled into Concord depot, the shrewd farmer seized his opportunity. Turning to dairying, he was soon selling milk to the city, delivering supplies to the station twice a day, as regular a sight on the road as "old 'Deacon Brown's accommodation stage.'" By 1850, Barrett owned twenty-five dairy cows, from which he derived "several thousand dollars a year." The railroad enriched Barrett not only as a farmer but as an investor. Along with sixty-three of his neighbors, Barrett owned stock in the Fitchburg Railroad, whose president was Francis Gourgas, a leading businessman-politician in town; among the shareholders were Ralph Waldo Emerson and John Thoreau, father of Henry David. Far from being invaded by the Iron Horse, as Curtis suggested in *Homes of American Authors*, the enterprising inhabitants had enlisted in the conquering horde. The privileged youth, in his carefree sabbatical on the farm, never grasped that his invigorating labors in Barrett's barn were an obscure but integral part of an economic transformation that was remaking the social landscape of New England. The same forces that made Concord a tourist's haven were deepening the commercial entanglements of the locals with the marketplace. Nathan Barrett could not complain. At his death in 1868, he had accumulated some 500 acres of land and over $30,000.[16]

It comes as no surprise that the Transcendentalists were embedded in the economic revolution of the times, whether they acknowledged it or not. Two generations of scholars, from the 1960s to the 1990s, have shattered Brooks's complacent image of the Concord writers as innocent philosophers of small-town democracy and have reinstalled them in the panorama of a society in change. Drawing on the insights of his mentor F. O. Matthiessen, Leo Marx showed us long ago how Emerson, Hawthorne, and Thoreau appropriated popular language and themes to expose the clash between the pastoral ideals of the republic and the unceasing engine of technological progress. Yet that interpretation, for all its power, sidestepped the persisting question: how were these intellectuals located in the society and culture they so compellingly engaged? In the new view from the

1990s, they emerge as avatars of the literary marketplace, formulating innovative careers at the lectern and in print; as critics of materialism and inequality, in search of alternatives to existing arrangements of property and work; as social reformers, anxious about masculinity and prepared to experiment with gender roles within and outside the family before settling, all too often, for conventional modes of Victorian domesticity; as political activists in the gathering antislavery movement, putting philosophies of individual freedom to practical tests; and, in the most hostile treatments, as apologists for capitalism and architects of its ascendent world view. "Exemplifying his advice to the American Scholar," Charles Sellers writes, "[Emerson] had planted himself indomitably on his bourgeois instincts, and the huge bourgeois/middle-class world came round to him. In the bourgeois cultural marketplace, insurgent intellectuals ended up building ... an ever more compelling bourgeois hegemony."[17]

The reaction against such root-and-branch revisionism has already set in. Even Thoreau, the vehement critic of "the curse of trade," once had hopes to succeed in publishing without tainting himself. How else, Richard Teichgraeber asks, could the Transcendentalists reach the people in whose democratic possibilities they profoundly believed? If they aspired to change the course of their countrymen, Teichgraeber explains, Emerson and Thoreau could not pretend to be superior souls, offering judgment from on high. It was imperative to "connect" with their fellow citizens, to enlist them in the task of self-criticism, to bring them to understand that the current ills of society were not inevitable, that they were at odds with the democratic purpose of the republic, and that with a revival of idealism, Americans could build a higher civilization, whose benefits extended to all. Such "connected critics," in complex dialogue with a popular audience, recall the engaged intellectuals of Matthiessen and Marx.[18]

Perhaps, then, it would be better to dismiss George William Curtis's sentimental portrait of Concord and its writers, notwithstanding its enduring presence in the "Travel" sections of the nation's press, and to move on to more serious business. Yet, three years after the publication of *Homes*, the disciple of Emerson, outraged at "Bleeding Kansas," was enlisting in the Frémont campaign and lecturing college students on "The Duty of the American Scholar to Politics and the Times." "Because we are scholars," Curtis asked, "shall we cease to be citizens?" It was time for a new generation of Minutemen to answer the alarm. "Brothers! the call has come to us. ... I summon you to the great fight of freedom." Activism and tourism were thus alternating, *not* opposing themes; they grew out of a common impulse and proved to be complementary vehicles of career. Like Emerson's "American Scholar," Curtis yearned to be both worldly hero and serene philosopher; in the great souls of the past and in the beauties of nature, he found allied resources for making the self.

Curtis was not alone. Nor was his vision peculiarly Transcendentalist. For many New Englanders in the middle decades of the nineteenth century, history and nature worked together both to inspire individuals and to strengthen community. And what better place to enact those roles than at a battleground by a river, in the backyard of an Old Manse? Curtis, Hawthorne, Emerson brooded over a scene congenial to romantics and conservatives alike and in such musings revealed the ties of Transcendentalism to the civic culture of the region. To comprehend these connections, there is no better route than to travel back to Concord and explore how the townspeople viewed their community, its place in history, its natural surround. That excursion will turn out, in the end, to be a tour of Concord Transcendentalism: a view of its articulation and its uses in local life.[19]

The trip takes as its focus a proud moment in local history: July 4, 1837, when the citizens, several hundred strong, gathered to dedicate the monument to the battle of April 19, 1775. Erected on land donated by the Reverend Ezra Ripley, the twenty-foot granite obelisk memorialized the noble event that had secured lasting laurels in the annals of the American Revolution. The opening clash of arms in the War of Independence—"the first forcible resistance to British aggression," as the inscription on the monument declared—was known far and wide as Concord Fight. Thanks to the heroism of the Minutemen, as the *Massachusetts Magazine* had predicted in 1794, someday the name of Concord would bear the luster of "imperial Rome." To honor the commanders who led that rendezvous with destiny, the Concord Artillery, the second-oldest militia unit in the Commonwealth (next to Boston's Ancient and Honorable Company), had the names of Maj. John Buttrick and Capt. Isaac Davis emblazoned on their cannon—a rare privilege granted by the state legislature in 1804, in recognition of "the beginning of a contest of arms that ended in American Independence." When Buttrick's son inspected the insignia at the unveiling of the cannon in 1804, he innocently declared, "I vum! it does look just like Dad!" That oft-repeated story added a light touch to the veneration.[20]

With such universal accolades, it should have been easy to raise a monument to the glorious day. It was not. If April 19 occasioned communal pride, its commemoration provoked considerable discord. For a half century, the townspeople had tried, time and again, to effect a proper memorial, but with no success. That failure was embarrassing to contemporaries but is revealing to the historian. The squabbles over the monument exposed the expansive ambitions, clashing interests, personal rivalries, and petty jealousies in a small New England town with two thousand inhabitants. Those contests were connected to the dynamic movements of the Jacksonian era: the advance of capitalism, the assertion of popular democracy, the disestablishment of religion. The tranquil scene of George William Curtis's imagining thus masked a second Concord Fight, smaller-minded and more vainglorious than its inspiration, but nonetheless a valuable cultural text. In that creation, Ralph Waldo Emerson and Transcendentalism would play a not insignificant part.

Inventing a nation out of a few million people, scattered over a broad territory, with little history in common, was no easy matter. It required new patriotic rituals to change popular consciousness, so that Americans would start thinking of themselves as citizens of the United States, rather than of, say, Massachusetts or Virginia. Unlike the French Revolutionaries, who replaced the traditional calendar after 1789 with new red-letter days to celebrate Festivals of Liberty, the Supreme Being, and the Unity and Individuality of the Republic, to note a few, the triumphant Patriots had a remarkably thin public life. Henry James could have added public holidays to his catalogue of American absence. There was the Fourth of July, to be sure, which the founders of the republic tried to make an annual exercise in civic virtue, but that venture foundered on partisan politics and private preoccupations. Concord commemorated the day in 1794 with "a truly Republican Oration" by a young Harvard graduate and apprentice lawyer named William Jones, who proclaimed that "The Fourth of JULY, 1776, will ever be an illustrious epoch in the history of man, as on that day, the declaration of our Independence was made, and tyranny in this country received the FIAT of expulsion." The event drew "a crowded audience from several towns," and local leaders were sufficiently pleased by the address to sponsor its publication. There is no record of a sequel. By 1806, one Concord resident was bewailing popular indifference to the annual date. Writing under the pseudonym "Peter Pencil" in a contribution to the *Boston Gazette*, he urged the farmer to take the day off from work—"suspend his scythe, wipe the sweat from his gladdened brow, and spend one day in festive gratitude, to those who have mitigated his task, by relieving from his hands the shackle of slavery." What was a day's loss of labor compared to the love of liberty?[21]

Concord Fight won even less recognition on the public calendar. It was seldom celebrated once the war ended, nor was it memorialized on the landscape. Training days for the militia were rarely scheduled to mark the event, and when the Concord Artillery or the Light Infantry met for drill, their parade ground was the village common, close by the local taverns.

Occasionally, a visiting unit like the Boston Fusiliers might camp out by the battlefield, but the site was more popular as a "fishing and boating ground."

There was good reason for the benign neglect. All over America before 1850, the landscape was as vacant of historical resonances as Henry James later lamented. Then again, daily life was replete with reminders of April 19 and the Revolution, what with all the aging veterans sitting around the stores and taverns rehearsing their "stories and traditions." An inhabitant was more likely to run into a survivor of the Fight than to visit the spot where Minutemen and Redcoats first exchanged fire. It was a little inconvenient to get there, for in 1792, at the initiative of the Reverend Ezra Ripley and others, the town endorsed a plan to pull down the North Bridge, reroute the main road that went over it, and use the planks for a new crossing a few hundred yards down river. With those changes, adopted after "much altercation," the field of combat was somewhat out of the way, and that suited parson Ripley, a forceful figure utterly unlike the unworldly "priest" of Hawthorne's Manse, just fine.

The new road shortened the trip to the village from farms in the north and so promoted attendance at Sunday meeting. But it carried another advantage for Ripley. The ancient way to the bridge passed straight through his property, from which his predecessor, the Reverend William Emerson, had witnessed the "memorable Day that . . . marked in plain though crimson Lines the Path of Duty for those to tread, that nobly scorned to wear the british Yoke." Though he occupied a central place in Concord as pastor of the church and minister of the parish, Ripley evidently wanted some privacy at home, without a steady stream of passengers by his door. He thus quietly appropriated what remained of the old road and incorporated it into his back pasture. In an unauthorized act of private enclosure, Ripley eliminated public access to the river and assumed title to the sacred ground. His proud proprietorship became legendary. Even George William Curtis heard about it and retailed the gossip in *Homes*. Whenever an out-of-town dignitary came calling, the parson liked to preen a bit; he would summon the hired boy into the Manse and talk over his private affairs. "Jeremiah or Nicodemus, the cow-boy, would deferentially approach and inquire, 'Into what pasture shall I turn the cow to-night, Sir?' And the old gentleman would audibly reply: 'Into the battle-field, Nicodemus, into the battle-field!'"[22]

Though the town lost partial access to the site, it did not forget entirely about a memorial. Local leaders tried fitfully to raise a monument. In 1792, they petitioned the legislature for state aid but were stymied by alert representatives from Boston, jealous lest Concord gain greater prominence

and thereby strengthen its recurrent bid to become the capital of Massachusetts. The town tried again during the War of 1812, to no avail. There
matters languished until 1824, when the aging marquis de Lafayette, on his
sentimental journey through the United States, came to Concord for a reception and touched off, as he did everywhere, a fresh wave of nostalgia for
the heroes and landmarks of the Revolution.[23]

On the eve of the fiftieth anniversary of April 19, town officials bestirred
themselves to push again for a memorial. This time Concord proved more
politic. Deciding not to compete with the Boston-area promoters of a vast
monument atop Bunker Hill, its representatives cut a deal. Instead of seeking state aid, they backed the Bunker Hill Memorial Association's request
for $10,000 from the legislature and invited its secretary, the Middlesex
Congressman Edward Everett, to deliver the address at the ceremony Concord set in motion for April 19, 1825. In return, the town was promised
$600 for its modest project.

There were two strings attached. The first obliged Concord to erect
a smaller scale version of the obelisk designed by Solomon Willard to ornament Bunker Hill—a provincial chip off the metropolitan block. The
second prescribed its location: the village center, paralleling the placement
of the monument in Charlestown. Nobody objected to the style require-
ment, but the site stirred angry protests. In principle, there was a good case
for the village over the battlefield. On April 19, 1775, the British had occupied the center all morning, taken over Wright Tavern for headquarters,
ransacked the area in search of provincial military supplies, seized and destroyed armaments and provisions, and made a bonfire of the liberty pole,
sparks from which spread to the courthouse and stirred alarm that the
British were burning the town down, prompting the Minutemen on the
high ground above the river to launch their fateful march toward "the middle of town to defend their homes, or die in the attempt." The resulting
skirmish at the bridge took but two to three minutes, and in its wake, the
Minutemen spent far more time and blood harassing the enemy's flight
from town, notably at Meriam's Corner. Measured by casualties, prisoners
of war, and property losses rather than symbolic "shots heard 'round the
world,'" the village could rightly claim recognition for its sacrifices.[24]

If anything, Concord center made common sense. Unlike most Puritan
settlements in Massachusetts Bay, the town had started out as a nucleated
village at its founding in 1636, and it had retained this core, even as population scattered to outlying farms over the years. Concentrated in the center were homes, shops, taverns, meetinghouse, courthouse, jail, and burial
grounds. Oriented around a common and milldam, the structures shared
no unity of style or well-defined boundaries. Still, this loose collection

stood out unmistakably on the landscape. With a strategic position on the road map, Concord served its rural neighbors as a hub of trade, a seat of courts, a meeting place for politicians, a staging ground and target for military expeditions. In 1825, commerce and manufactures were thriving amid an accelerating boom that ended only with the Panic of 1837. The village attracted leading agents of modern capitalism: two banks, an insurance company, newspapers, a post office. It was also something of an industrial park, with mills, craft shops, slaughterhouses, and tanneries jumbled close by private dwellings and public institutions. The sound of triphammers, the stench of offal, the mound of leather scraps in front of Deacon Tolman's shoe-making shop, the long teams of oxen lined up in front of stores and taverns: these were familiar conditions of village life. A public monument would add to this lively scene.[25]

So it appeared to the townsmen, who voted by a large margin—sixty-five to twenty-five—in favor of a village site near the town pump. Initially, the plan went off without a hitch. On the fiftieth anniversary of Concord Fight, the town celebrated with a parade, military exercises, the firing of cannon, Ezra Ripley's prayer, Edward Everett's oration, a twelve-piece band, and a dinner, at which thirteen toasts, one for each state in the original union, were made. "To Concord Fight," the participants raised their glasses, "an electric spark which for half a century has shaken the world." The centerpiece of the day was the solemn laying of the cornerstone, over which local Masons officiated with much pomp.[26]

The "huge granite block, some four feet cube," was a big hit with the boys at a nearby school. But other inhabitants seethed in discontent. One morning in the winter of 1825–1826 the villagers awakened to discover an unusual formation atop the cornerstone: a pile of tar barrels and boards, twenty feet high, raised in mockery of the site. "This monument is erected here," explained the inscription, "to commemorate the battle which took place at the North Bridge." The satirical display did not last long. The following night "some of the rowdy element," aggressively defending village honor, set the sham monument on fire. It was a "great illumination," one witness recalled years later. Unluckily for the assailants, their action proved self-defeating. The cornerstone was ruined. No shaft ever rose above the base.[27]

Nobody ever took credit for the mock monument or its destruction. Neither did the wits elaborate on their joke; for them, the absurdity of the village site was self-evident. But a few months later, the local paper, the *Yeoman's Gazette*, began running a series of pseudonymous essays by "Middlesex" on "the Monument at Concord," which set forth weighty objections.[28] Proponents of the center, it was charged, consisted of two groups, each preoccupied with narrow self-interest. One set comprised businessmen and homeowners who lived near the common; they had a lot to gain from a monument close by. "If the monument were of consequence . . . , would it not affect real estate, public houses, mercantile business, mechanic shops, &c?" The other was composed of "superficial" people who lived and worked on outlying farms, their days a constant round of chores. For them, the active village beckoned as an occasional relief. A trip to town, whether to trade at the store or go to Sunday meeting, would be improved by the chance "to see & gaze at a fine monument." These farmers had no interest in a memorial off the beaten track, no matter how suitable. In effect, both groups put pocketbooks over patriotism.

There were more arguments against the village. On April 19, 1775, many of its inhabitants fled the Redcoats, while those trapped in the center surrendered to superior power. Not a shot was fired against the invaders. "What claim then has the centre of town to the monument?" asked "Middlesex" rhetorically. A memorial there would be a testament to timidity.

Even if the center deserved a tribute, it was no place to put a shrine. To command notice in a busy village, a monument would have to tower over its surround; consequently, "it must be very costly & magnificent, or it will be no ornament, & will appear contemptible." The setting, too, defeated the purpose. It lacked the solitude and calm essential to a lofty scene. With the noise and the smells, the hubbub of commerce, the "teams [and] the dust," the area would be "very unpleasant" to tourists. As strangers in town, they would also attract attention from busybodies, suffer unsolicited "confusion, stares, & remarks," and be interrupted in their patriotic mission. Under these circumstances, the monument would be off-limits to women; no "lady" would expose herself to such insults. Instead of sacred space, the village was profane ground.[29]

This indictment of the noisy, dusty, crowded space raised the debate to a higher plane. At issue was the proper mode of consecrating and venerating the past. A patriotic pilgrimage, the essayist suggested, ought to be a liminal experience: a withdrawal from the everyday world, with its distractions and obligations, into the lofty realm of the spirit. The Concord monument, in this view, constituted a sanctuary into which worshipers would step in a spirit of reverence. It thereby resembled a Transcendentalist retreat—a walk in the woods, a sojourn at Walden Pond—but with a conventional twist. Visitors to the shrine would be imbued with gratitude for the sacrifices of the Minutemen and for the blessings of Providence. So inspired, they would rededicate themselves to the public good.

For this temple of freedom, the pious author proposed an unexpected location. The memorial should be erected not on the exact spot of the "first forcible resistance to British aggression" but on the high ground, north-west of the bridge, where the Minutemen held their "Council of War" and, detecting smoke rising from the town center, determined to "live free or die." As it happened, that site had practical advantages: a granite column above that hill would be "conspicuous" throughout town and readily acces-sible from the road. Guarded by a "handsome" fence, planted with "orna-mental and shady trees," providing seats on which visitors could rest, "the spot [would be] easily made one of the most inviting, delightful, & venera-ble." Its charms would attract the best type of tourists—genteel "persons of sentiment" and polite "parties of amusement," whose leisure would be purified by their presence on "almost holy ground." A pilgrimage to the monument would be a transcendent experience.[30]

"Middlesex" never revealed his identity, nor was it ever exposed. His pleading for the monument was overlooked in a larger controversy the series set in motion. Who deserved the glory of launching the armed re-sistance to British power: Lexington or Concord? "Middlesex" could not bear the recent claims that had been made on Lexington's behalf, and the bulk of his series was given over to establishing that Concord started the Revolutionary War. A cascade of polemics ensued, which would soon bring advocates of Acton, whose soldiers actually led the march to the bridge, onto the field, and it would occupy local partisans for generations. Even today Acton patriots like to quip that "Concord supplied the site and Acton the men."[31]

The pamphlet war had one unanticipated effect. Happily, it enables an identification of "Middlesex." He was none other than the Reverend Ezra Ripley, whose *History of the Fight at Concord, on the 19th of April, 1775, With a Particular Account of the Military Operations and Interesting Events of That Ever Memorable Day; Showing that Then and There the First Regular Forcible Resistance Was Made to the British Soldiery, and the First British Blood Was Shed by Armed Americans, and the Revo-lutionary War Was Thus Commenced* was issued by publisher Herman Atwell of the *Yeoman's Gazette* in 1827. That pamphlet mirrors "The Mon-ument at Concord," following the structure, rehearsing the details, and recycling the words of that newspaper series. Ripley acknowledged his debt to "Middlesex" but did not own up to that source. Was the parson a plagiarist? That suspicion is dispelled by the manuscript drafts of "Middle-sex's" letters to the editor, which have survived in obscurity at the Concord Free Public Library, along with numerous other Ripley documents. The handwriting is the same.[32]

Why did the man called "the Pope of Concord"[33] conduct this campaign for the monument secretly in the press, rather than make his case from the pulpit? Ripley had never been shy about his opinions, nor did he shrink at talking politics from the pulpit; in the early 1800s, he had alienated half the parish with his extreme Federalist preaching. In any case, this was no secular matter. Proper tribute to the Concord Fight was a sacred duty. One reason for the uncharacteristic circumspection may be the immediate circumstances of the First Church. For four decades the pastor had held the congregation together by sheer will, but now long-simmering discontent with his liberal theology was bursting forth. In the winter of 1826, members of the parish, longing for "a more active spiritual life" than Ripley furnished, gathered in private homes to pray together and to consider their religious needs. They were soon taking steps to organize an orthodox Calvinist church. By March, when "Middlesex" first appeared in print, the dissenters were acquiring land and hiring a contractor; in April, as the series continued, sixty-nine members of the parish established the "Second Congregational Society and the First Calvinistic Religious Society, in the Town of Concord." The parson did what he could to resist the Trinitarian declaration of independence, even as he was exalting Concord's decisive role in the break with Britain back in 1775. But it would surely do no good to announce his authorship. There was no point in stirring up new hornet's nests. And he might be accused of playing George III in the church dispute.[34]

The proud owner of the Old Manse may have also feared charges of bad faith. Who had pushed for tearing down the North Bridge in 1792? Who had cut off public access to the site where the Redcoats met their match? And who was now urging the erection of a monument conveniently across the river, on land owned by somebody else? Seventy-five years old in 1826, Ripley seldom doubted his own righteousness, but the Lord's servants, he knew, had many enemies. No sense exposing a vulnerable flank.

With two fights on his hands at once—the Trinitarian schism on one side, the misguided partisans of Lexington on the other—Ripley put aside the monument campaign. The cornerstone, damaged by fire, stood forlorn by the town pump, an embarrassment to local pride.

Ezra Ripley eventually got his way, but only by shifting course. In the winter of 1834, the minister resumed his initiative and submitted a new proposal to commemorate "the Great Events at Concord North Bridge on the 19th of April 1775." In order to break the logjam, he offered to donate the land for the monument. Scuttling the "almost holy" ground where "Middlesex" had earlier wanted the memorial—the hillside on which the Minutemen determined to "live free or die"—Ripley pledged a still more sacred space: the land behind the Old Manse, where the Redcoats first felt the force of American resistance. There were just a few conditions. The town had to fence the site with "a good stone wall" and to keep up the path leading to it, all at its own expense. There was also a deadline: if the work were not completed in three years, the parson would cancel the gift. At age eighty-three, he was in no mood to wait.[35]

While Ripley heard the clock ticking, he had other concerns tied to the immediate moment. In the mid 1830s, Concord was probably at its political and economic pinnacle. The central village was busier than ever; so promising were business prospects that an enterprising citizen drew up a commercial directory—the emblem of an urban future—and listed some nine stores, forty shops, four hotels and taverns, four doctors and four lawyers, a variety of county associations, a printing office and a post office, virtually all in the center. Manufacturing was humming, too, with a growing mill village in the west part of town, along the quick-running Assabet River, and rising producers of carriages and chaises, boots and shoes, bricks, guns, bellows, and pencils. In his *History of Concord*, a pioneering work that marked the town's bicentenary in 1835, Lemuel Shattuck noted that "the manufacturing and mechanical business of the town is increasing, and promises to be a great source of wealth."[36]

But not for everybody. Even as industrious businessmen and farmers like Nathan Barrett were getting rich, a great many people, native and newcomer alike, lost out and moved on. In what was still a farming town, 64 percent of adult males were landless, while the top tenth of taxpayers, some fifty men, controlled nearly half the wealth. The ties that bound neighbors together were fraying. On the farms, the old work customs—the huskings, roof-raisings, and apple bees—by which people cooperated to complete essential chores were dissolving. These were felt to be irksome and wasteful. Modern farmers who wanted work done hired it—and they paid only the going rate.

Rising inequality fueled resentments, which were played out in an assertive popular politics. Jacksonian democracy may have hailed the power of common men, but its mood was often rancorous and quick to detect signs of special privilege. In an atmosphere of growing antagonisms, longtime magistrates were accused of running the town for their personal advantage. The gala reception for Lafayette back in 1824 was a case in point; to critics, a self-styled elite had monopolized the event, crowding out the legion of common folk who had flocked to greet the "nation's guest," only to be turned away as if they were not good enough for the honor. By the early 1830s, such populist sentiments were widespread.[37]

At the very moment Ezra Ripley made his proposal for the monument, Concord seemed to be splitting apart. The parson could no longer boast that his community was a model of the New England way: one town, one church. It had been bad enough when the Trinitarians left the fold, but New Year's Day, 1834, introduced a new era of religious pluralism to Massachusetts. Through an amendment to the state constitution, citizens were no longer obliged to pay parish taxes, and sadly, in Ripley's view, even a majority of Concordians approved. Increasingly they were signing off; the fastest-growing denomination consisted of "nothingarians," who refused to support any religion.[38]

In local politics, Ripley discerned a growing threat. The *Yeoman's Gazette* was once a nonpartisan organ, run by his Masonic brother Herman Atwell, but in 1833, the printer turned coat and ferociously denounced the Corinthian Lodge, to which the parson had belonged since its founding for thirty-five years, as a bastion of illegal privilege. Ripley was Grand Chaplain of the Most Worshipful Grand Lodge of Massachusetts when Antimasonry took off in New England. In 1833, some 54 Concord voters joined a statewide petition campaign against the Order; the following year that number tripled to 152, comprising about half of the voters. Asserting their power, the townsmen threw Dr. Abiel Heywood, a pillar of church and state, out of the town clerk's office he had held for thirty-eight straight years. Not a Mason himself, Heywood became anathema for his friendships. He was ousted from power on March 3, 1834, the meeting at which Ripley made his offer of land.[39]

As it turned out, the minister's initiative overcame local divisions. Within a month, the town endorsed the idea and a year later took title to the land. In Ripley's patriotic plan divergent factions sank their differences, if only for a moment. To be sure, Antimasons did not want anything to do with Masons (and vice versa), but they readily cooperated on the monument committee with so-called "neutrals" in the dispute. That panel encompassed Unitarians, Trinitarians, and independents. And it moved forward with the work, even as the observance of the town's bicentennial of 1835 was being denounced by Herman Atwell's press as "Another Lafayette Celebration!"[40]

In May 1835, a small band of inveterate opponents of Ripley's monument—tavern-keepers and tradesmen in the village—called on the town to change its mind and spurn the gift. In an effort to line up votes before the town meeting, a contributor to the Antimasonic newspaper, styling himself "Old Concord," urged a return to the village site. Why should a monument be located in "the backside of Dr. Ripley's house?" he sneered. In 1775 the central village had won the right to primacy. "The town of Concord is the scene of events remarkable in the history of our Revolution; the first spilling of English blood is the most conspicuous—but other scenes of distress by the destruction of our property and the attempt to burn our public buildings in the centre of town render every spot in it of equal importance to the country at large." The words were wasted on the town, which dismissed the move to reconsider. With that out of the way, the majority resumed the crusade to purge Masons and their friends from public life.[41]

Why did Ripley's plan enjoy such smooth sailing? Its appeal may be that it cost the inhabitants nothing. The land was free; the costs of upkeep were paid by private donors; the fund set up in 1825 by the Bunker Hill Memorial Association financed construction. All the town had to do was authorize a change of venue. By this reliance upon private money to facilitate public ends, Ripley and his friends cleverly removed the issue from democratic give-and-take. If the town wanted a monument, here was a way to pay for it. Who could lose? Not the pastor, who burnished his reputation for public-mindedness. As a local patron, he gratified his whims and served the community.

On April 19, 1837, the minister went before the Concord Lyceum and, in a remarkable public lecture, addressed criticism of his charitable act.[42] Alarmed at the "agitated and unsettled state of society," Ripley, the doctor of divinity, diagnosed the symptoms: "bitter contention and discord among brethren . . . and the destruction of mutual confidence and harmony among the people." A house divided against itself cannot stand, he reminded listeners. Then, changing the metaphor, he likened "a well-regulated town or parish" to

> a swarm of bees, clinging together in one body, mutually sustaining and depending upon one another. Those which alight first and form the nucleus, the centre, support the adhering multitude, and confine the centre. If those in the centre let go their hold, the whole body fails; and if the surrounding multitude fly off, the whole swarm is broken up. So likewise, a town or other society; the centre collects and sustains the whole adhering body, and the more distant inhabitants confine and control the centre. Let either depart from mutual hold and connexion, and the whole is thrown into confusion and ruin.

Applying that apothegm, Ripley took up "jealousies and oppositions between the centre and the remote inhabitants of a town." Nobody could miss which town. It is inevitable, the parson observed, that in the course of time, "crooked roads must be straitened, narrow streets must [be] widened, new roads and bridges must be made, [and] public buildings must be erected and repaired." When improvements are brought forward, the only issue should be "the public good, that is, the good of the whole town." A gain for one section is a gain for all. Sometimes, progress requires personal sacrifices. Ripley pointed to the losses he had endured for the greater good. "Perhaps, no citizen has suffered more by the alteration of roads, than the present speaker," he claimed, "and yet he is convinced that those alterations were needful, and that the town is benefited." That statement must have astonished those in the audience with long memories, who recalled the minister's part in the removal of the North Bridge and his enclosure of once-public land into his pasture. "Vandalism," one townsman branded it, a land grab in disguise. Ripley saw things differently. He had paid a high price for rerouting the road. To compensate residents inconvenienced by the change, the town had laid out a bridle-way through his property near the Great Meadows, cutting off access to the river; he was obliged to sell land at a loss in order to remedy the situation. He did not like it, but that was his public duty.[43]

The minister pressed the point. With the fight over the monument clearly in mind, he brought up the common impression that "one portion of the town is benefited by handsome alterations and not other sections" and branded it wrong. Whatever honor or advantages a town gains from a public improvement—say, a monument—"belong to the whole of the town in common. The citizen 3 miles from the centre shares in honor and dishonor equally with him who is a mile or half a mile of the church." By the same token, every inhabitant suffers directly from conflict. Ripley compared peaceful to contentious towns and guessed that real estate values were "12 to 20 per cent" higher in the former. Nobody of "a quiet and peaceable disposition" wants to settle in a "contentious, divided, and quarrelsome town, and wealthy, respectable persons will leave such places even at a sacrifice."

Why, then, was there so much conflict in Concord? Ripley intuited the significance of recent social changes. "With more than a few, it has been too much the practice of neighbors and fellow citizens to live like strangers, and to cherish little or no sympathy for one another. One class of citizens hold themselves at a distance from another class,—one individual from another." In what is a familiar theme today, the patriarch who had presided over Concord for sixty years bewailed the loss of community. Neighbors used to know one another, share mutual interests, respect others' views. Now, with so little in common, they exaggerated "differences in opinion, on religion and politics" and polarized the community. Consider politics: "A thinks and says of B, he is a federalist, a whig, an opposer of government [that is, Jackson and Van Buren], and therefore ought to be opposed, though he professes to be a genuine Republican. B retorts and says of A that he is a tory, a friend of arbitrary government, and yet, a radical, a leveller." Similar enmities separate the classes:

> The professional man and the mechanic and manufacturer, the man of commerce and of civil office, should be sociable with the farmer, and the farmer, though he is acknowledged the nerve, the sinew, and the backbone of the country and the public welfare, should not pride himself in his importance and independence, and claim superiority to the mechanic, nor feel envy and unkindness towards men of profession, as though they were not working men and brothers.

This was a shrewd assessment of Concord in the 1830s. Attending different churches or none at all, their loyalties captured by one party or another, separated by widening gulfs, the townspeople needed new bases of unity. The monument for which Ripley had labored so long was clearly conceived to this end. It would pull Concord together in common devotion to the Revolution. It would highlight the blessings of Providence. It would crystallize a new civic identity. It consecrated a landscape of memory.

Ironically, that memorial was not in the village, close by the meetinghouse, the traditional focus of the Puritan hive. With disestablishment, the town center had lost that binding power. Thanks to Ripley's gift, the inhabitants would look elsewhere for symbolic unity. It would reside in the sacred ground behind the Old Manse. The Concord monument was not just a tribute to the Revolutionary fathers. It was also a testament to the pertinacity and ideology of Ezra Ripley.

On the Fourth of July, 1837, Concord played out Ripley's dream. At noon on "a very hot sunny day," bells rang out from the village churches summoning the inhabitants to patriotic worship. The center, one person recalled, became "as quiet as on a Sunday." Escorted by the militia companies, several hundred townspeople proceeded across the common, headed north up the old road to the bridge, passed the Old Manse, and turned into the path to the monument. The Reverend Barzillai Frost, Ripley's assistant and soon-to-be-successor, offered an opening prayer. The distinguished lawyer Samuel Hoar delivered a patriotic address. Only nine months before, he had been defeated for re-election to Congress by an Antimason-Democrat coalition. But on this day, his "commanding, eloquent, and impressive" speech was universally acclaimed. He was followed by the Reverend John Wilder, the Trinitarian pastor, with another prayer. Then little slips of paper, six inches square, were handed out. They contained the words to an ode composed specially for the ceremony. It

"Monument at Concord"
Engraving, John Warner Barber, reproduced from his
Historical Collections (Worcester, 1839), p. 385.

was Ralph Waldo Emerson's "Concord Hymn," and it consecrated the occasion in an elegaic poem that gave new language to his step-grandfather's
vision.[44]

   Sometime minister, recent author of the little volume *Nature*, which he
had written in the study of the Old Manse overlooking the battlefield, and
new resident of the town, Emerson could not be present for the event. But
he had proved his merit as the official speaker at the recent bicentennial
and as a member of the small group that produced the inscription for the
monument. The "Historical Discourse" Emerson delivered for the town's
200th birthday in 1835 celebrated the spirit of liberty in Concord's past and
tactfully avoided mention of the conflicts it was generating in the present.

The closing line he contributed to the inscription attested his religious reliability: "In gratitude to God and the love of Freedom this monument is erected A.D. 1836."[45] The "Concord Hymn" would do similar cultural work. Emerson was amused by the obsessiveness with which Ezra Ripley pestered Thaddeus Blood and other Revolutionary soldiers for details of Concord Fight—"The Doctor like a keen hunter unrelenting follows him up & down barricading him with questions"—but he was ultimately just as reverent about April 19.[46]

We remember the poem today for its opening lines about the "rude bridge," "the embattled farmers," and the "shot heard 'round the world.'" But the succeeding stanzas express a mood of meditation, not military bombast. The sounds of battle are long gone, the combatants in their graves. Nature has reclaimed the site. In a deft rewriting of history and landscape, Emerson evokes the "ruined bridge" lost to "the dark stream" rather than to the political agency of Ezra Ripley. For a rare moment, the Concord River was not sluggish. Through that theme of a natural world to which all things return in time, the poem poses its central dilemma: how to "redeem" Concord Fight from inevitable oblivion? That was the purpose of the "votive stone," the obelisk paid for by the Bunker Hill Memorial Association. Inscribed with a tribute to "heroes [who] dare[d] / To die, and leave their children free," the memorial would forge common bonds among a divided people. It would resonate "mystic chords of memory," in Lincoln's classic words, across the generations, from "sires" to "sons."[47]

The contemplative tone may seem unusual in the emerging age of "Young America," with its spread-eagled patriotism, but it was admirably suited to the aesthetic of memory embedded in the site. As the engraving widely circulated in John Barber's *Historical Collections* (1839) makes plain, the memorial resembled the romantic mourning scenes popular in the early republic. It was a secluded grove on a river's edge, shaded by stately trees, demarcated by a square fence, and focused on a tall obelisk, an icon widely used at the graves of high officials, but now extended to the deed of a people united in a common cause. That was exactly what Ezra Ripley as "Middlesex" had desired: a space apart from the intrusions of everyday life, where the pilgrim could enjoy the solitude of nature, commune with the forefathers, and renew commitment to the civil religion of the republic. Ripley's transcendentalism, if we may call it that, eschewed individualism. As with all his designs, its purpose was to strengthen established institutions.

On this occasion, nobody was prepared to dissent, certainly not Ripley's step-grandson. In the version of "Concord Hymn" that Emerson published in his collected *Poems*, the final stanza asks the "Spirit" that once emboldened the Revolutionary "heroes" to take on a final assignment. It should

> Bid Time and Nature gently spare
> The shaft we raise to them and thee.

That was a revision that suited the Transcendentalist muse in 1847. But on the hot July afternoon ten years earlier, the assembly invoked an orthodox God, addressed in the words "O Thou." Emerson was not yet the religious radical of the "Divinity School Address." On this occasion he was not even a "connected critic" of his countrymen. Putting his idealism to ceremonial ends, he composed an official "hymn" to be sung in unison by the patriotic worshipers, as in church, among whose voices could be heard that of Harvard College senior Henry David Thoreau. Interestingly, it followed the tune of "Old Hundred," a popular hymn from the Bay Psalm Book dating back to the Geneva Psalter of 1551. Upon its conclusion, Ezra Ripley delivered a solemn benediction, closing with the words: "And let the people say, Amen."[48]

Joining history and nature, Puritans, Minutemen, and Transcendentalists, the Fourth of July scene on the banks of the Concord River ends our tour. Restored from reverie, we may recall its lasting achievement: the creation of a tourist site.

George William Curtis bequeathed an enduring literary legacy, though, as we can see, it was hardly of his own making. A year into the Civil War, a few literary-minded friends got together in Concord to launch a periodical they called *The Monitor*. Dated May 3, 1862, it opened with a piece about "Concord" by an author whose subject and pseudonym were the same. On the extant copy of the magazine, he identified himself as S. R. Bartlett. The initials stood for Samuel Ripley, the minister-son of Ezra, in whose honor the writer was named. Born the very year the Concord Monument was dedicated, Bartlett was on the eve of his twenty-fifth birthday safe from the horrors of Bull Run. And he was in a puckish mood.[49]

Bartlett took it upon himself to introduce his native town. "You may, perhaps, have heard of the place before." It is the town where the Battle of April 19 took place and is commemorated every year. Describing the most recent celebration, "Concord" wrote, "It was a great day for the old town, and has given many an opportunity for its embryo writers and half-fledged poets to spread themselves upon."

But to know Concord truly, skip the festivities and make an expedition to its ponds, rivers, and woods. In familiar language, the piece noted that

"Concord air is not favorable for manufacturing"; its principal product is independent thought. In this peaceful town, writers and thinkers commune with nature, rather than fish or hunt. Adopting the tone of a tourist guide, "Concord" urged readers to visit the town and enjoy a refuge from care:

> Leave business behind—shake the dust off your feet as an evidence against it. Money, too, for there is nothing here that money will buy. Fashion, for it, alone, does not pass current here. Do not despise anyone you may meet in the woods, or up the river on account of their clothing.

It was essential to approach the natives of the woods politely, "for they will teach you much. Draw them out to talk if you can. Throw your philosophy to the winds,—they teach philosophy . . . they interpret notes of the birds . . . they explain the ideal republic of Plato." In sum, Concord offered a philosophical vacation: "Come and loaf about Concord a week; it will do you more good than a year's work or reading anywhere else;—that is, if you know how to enjoy. If not, stay away."

Well before Van Wyck Brooks, Bartlett had already captured the literary clichés about Concord and held them up to satire. Unfortunately, *The Monitor* lasted only three months, unknown to literary critics. Van Wyck Brooks never read it, nor did anyone else in his school. They were too busy dreaming about the Concord of the imagination to look the town plainly in the face. Then again, few of the natives ever did the same.

The author would like to thank the following persons for timely assistance: Rob Nelson for help in finding materials; Jim Whittenburg for computer analysis; Katherine K. Preston for her counsel on Protestant hymns; Margaret Cook in Special Collections at Swem Library; Chandos Brown, Richard Lowry, Steve Nissenbaum, and David Wood for general advice; Bob Richardson for suggesting the epigraph; and Ann Gross for criticism and patience from start to finish.

NOTES

1. William Charvat, *Literary Publishing in America, 1790–1850* (Amherst, 1993), 29–30; Joel Myerson, "Ralph Waldo Emerson's Income from His Books," in *The Professions of Authorship: Essays in Honor of Matthew J. Bruccoli*, ed. Richard Layman and Joel Myerson (Columbia, S.C., 1996), 121–134; Steven Fink, *Prophet in the Marketplace: Thoreau's Development as a Professional Writer* (Princeton, 1992), 252, 264–265; Madelon Bedell, *The Alcotts: Biography of a Family* (New York, 1980), 272–284.

2. *Homes of American Authors; comprising anecdotical, personal, and descriptive sketches, by various writers* (New York, 1853). Cited hereafter as *Homes*. Howitt's volume, *Homes and Haunts of the Most Eminent British Poets*, was first published by R. Bentley in London in 1849 and reprinted by Harper in 1851. It appears that Putnam's project continued (and recycled) an effort to promote "American scenery, art and literature" begun two years before. See *The Home Book of the Picturesque, or, American Scenery, Art and Literature* (New York, 1851); and Ezra Greenspan, "George Palmer Putnam: Representative American Publisher" (1997), 355–360. (I am grateful to Professor Greenspan for sharing his manuscript with me.) In *Homes of American Authors*, the anonymous contributors included such journeymen of the publishing trade as Charles F. Briggs, George S. Hillard, Rufus W. Griswold, and Parke Godwin. Receiving their tributes were not only monuments of the mid-nineteenth-century canon—Cooper, Emerson, Hawthorne, Irving, Simms—but also historians George Bancroft and William H. Prescott; the naturalist John James Audubon; novelists John Pendleton Kennedy, James Kirke Paulding, and Catherine Maria Sedgwick; poets William Cullen Bryant, Henry Wadsworth Longfellow, and James Russell Lowell; literary statesmen Edward Everett and Daniel Webster; and the reform-minded travel writer Richard Henry Dana.

3. Adam W. Sweeting, "'A Very Pleasant Patriarchal Life': Professional Authors and Amateur Architects in the Hudson Valley, 1835–1870," *Journal of American Studies* 29(1995):33–53; John F. Sears, *Sacred Places: American Tourist Attractions in the Nineteenth Century* (New York, 1989), 49–86; Dona Brown, *Inventing New England: Regional Tourism in the Nineteenth Century* (Washington, 1995). Of the New Yorkers, Audubon, Irving, and Paulding lived in the Hudson River Valley; Cooper in the eponymous town on Otsego Lake founded by his father; and Bryant, a native of western Massachusetts, on Long Island. The Yankees included the Bostonians Edward Everett and William H. Prescott, their Cambridge neighbors Longfellow and Lowell, Concord's Emerson and Hawthorne, Cape Ann resident Richard H. Dana, and the Marshfield Squire Daniel Webster (who also maintained "Elm Farm," close by his birthplace and within sight of the White Mountains). The peripatetic historian George Bancroft owned no permanent place. He summered in fashionable Newport, Rhode Island, and rented winter quarters in Manhattan. *Homes of American Authors* consequently featured his onetime residence in the Connecticut Valley town of Northampton, where Bancroft launched his history of America while teaching at the Round Hill School. It was not far from that site to the Berkshire County homeplace of novelist Catherine M. Sedgwick. The Southerners in the group were John Pendleton Kennedy, a Baltimore native with a summer home on Patapscot River, at the foot of Elk Ridge, and the South Carolinian William Gilmore Simms, who resided half the year on his father-in-law's plantation in Barnwell District, between Charleston and Augusta. This early canon of American writers was heavily weighted toward Putnam's literary stable: nearly half were house authors (Bryant, Cooper, Hawthorne, Irving, Kennedy, Lowell, Sedgwick, and Simms).

4. Gordon Milne, *George William Curtis & the Genteel Tradition* (Bloomington, 1956), 3–63; Gordon Milne, "George William Curtis—Inheritor of the Transcendental Mantel," *American Transcendental Quarterly* 18(1973):35–40; *Homes*, 233–234. Curtis's essay on "Emerson" appears on pp. 233–255 of *Homes*; the piece on "Hawthorne" covers pp. 291–313.

5. *Homes*, 234–236, 242.
6. *Homes*, 236, 241–242, 244, 249, 253–254.
7. *Homes*, 292, 294–295, 302–303.
8. Henry James, Jr., *Hawthorne* (New York, 1879), 42–43; *Homes*, 244–248; Paul Brooks, *The Old Manse and the People Who Lived There* (Concord, 1983); *Concord, Massachusetts, Births, Marriages, and Deaths 1635–1850* (Boston, 1895), 409.
9. Curtis, *Homes*, 241–242; Nathaniel Hawthorne, "Preface" to *Mosses from an Old Manse* (1846), in Hawthorne, *Tales and Sketches*, ed. Roy Harvey Pearce (New York, 1982), 1123, 1149; Leo Marx, *The Machine in the Garden: Technology and the Pastoral Ideal in America* (New York, 1967). At times, Curtis's paraphrases of Hawthorne border on plagiarism. The Concord River, Hawthorne wrote, "is certainly the most unexcitable and sluggish stream that ever loitered, imperceptibly, towards its eternity, the sea." Thanks to its "incurable indolence," the stream "idles its sluggish life away, in lazy liberty, without turning a solitary spindle" (1125–1126). Thoreau may also have been a progenitor of Curtis's prose. In the opening of his "Emerson" piece, the sentimental scribe evoked the "shriek" of the railroad penetrating the "virgin seclusion" of Walden Pond, employing one of Thoreau's enduring metaphors for his own touristic ends (*Homes*, 233–234). It is possible that Curtis read "The Iron Horse," a short extract from the *Walden* manuscript that Thoreau placed in *Sartain's Union Magazine* of July 1852, was captivated by its compelling metaphor of what Leo Marx has dubbed "the machine in the garden," and put it to work in his own piece for *Homes*, which he was composing during that very summer. On the other hand, during his days in Concord, Curtis composed a poem on "The Railroad," in which he evoked the noisy passage of the train through quiet country scenes:

> I rose,
> And stepping from the train, it glided on,
> Sweeping around the hill; the whistle shrill
> Raging through the stricken air. A moment more
> It rolled along the iron out of sight.

Fink, *Prophet in the Marketplace*, 259; the poem appears in *Early Letters from George Wm. Curtis to John S. Dwight, Brook Farm and Concord*, ed. George Willis Cooke (New York, 1898), 239–342.
10. The two reprints of *Homes* were issued by the New York publisher D. Appleton in 1855 and 1857.
11. Van Wyck Brooks, *The Flowering of New England* (1936; New York, 1952), 261–263.
12. Henry David Thoreau, *Consciousness in Concord: The Text of Thoreau's Hitherto "Lost Journal," 1840–1841*, ed. Perry Miller (Boston, 1958), 51–54.
13. Robert E. Spiller et al., eds., *Literary History of the United States* (1948; New York, 1953), 3:375.
14. Nathaniel Hawthorne, *The American Notebooks*, ed. Claude M. Simpson (Columbus, Oh., 1972), 319–320; Robert A. Gross, "'The Most Estimable Place in the All the World': A Debate on Progress in Nineteenth-Century Concord," *Studies in the American Renaissance 1978*, ed. Joel Myerson (Boston, 1978), 1–15.

15. Cooke, *Early Letters*, 1–2, 68–73, 195–198; Milne, *George William Curtis*, 21–23; Anne C. Rose, *Transcendentalism as a Social Movement, 1830–1850* (New Haven, 1981), 109–161; John Shepard Keyes, "Memoir of Nathan Barrett, Jr.," in *Memoirs of Members of the Social Circle in Concord. Second Series, from 1795 to 1840* (Cambridge, Mass., 1888), 266–272; Jack Larkin, "'Labor Is the Great Thing in Farming': The Farm Laborers of the Ward Family of Shrewsbury, Massachusetts, 1787–1860," *Proceedings of the American Antiquarian Society* 99(1989):189–226.

16. Cooke, *Early Letters*, 183–186, 198–201; Ruth R. Wheeler, *Concord: Climate for Freedom* (Concord, 1967), 178; Sterling F. Delano, "Brook Farm and Concord: Transit Between Celebrated Communities," *Concord Saunterer*, n.s. 4(1996): 23–44; Robert A. Gross, "Transcendentalism and Urbanism: Concord, Boston, and the Wider World," *Journal of American Studies* 18(1984):361–381; Keyes, "Memoir of Nathan Barrett"; 1850 Concord Town Assessment List. In 1850, 64 estates were assessed for shares in the Fitchburg Railroad, the great majority belonging to widows and minors, whose property was normally managed by men. On their own, 28 men held stock in the railroad company; they accounted for 5 percent of all 536 males on the annual assessment. Barrett possessed seven shares, worth $763; Emerson a dozen, at $1,308; Thoreau, a man of modest means, claimed but one share, valued at $109. Altogether, 65 men, comprising 12 percent of the whole, held stock in one or more corporations; 13 of them, including Nathan Barrett, owned shares in the Concord Bank.

17. Marx, *Machine in the Garden*; Rose, *Transcendentalism as a Social Movement*; Michael T. Gilmore, *American Romanticism and the Marketplace* (Chicago, 1985); Lawrence Buell, *New England Literary Culture: From Revolution through Renaissance* (New York, 1986); R. Jackson Wilson, *Figures of Speech: American Writers and the Literary Marketplace, from Benjamin Franklin to Emily Dickinson* (New York, 1989); Mary Kupiec Cayton, *Emerson's Emergence: Self and Society in the Transformation of New England, 1800–1845* (Chapel Hill, 1989); David Leverenz, *Manhood and the American Renaissance* (Ithaca, 1989); Charles Sellers, *The Market Revolution: Jacksonian America, 1815–1846* (New York, 1991), 380.

18. Fink, *Prophet in the Marketplace*; Richard F. Teichgraeber III, *Sublime Thoughts / Penny Wisdom: Situating Emerson and Thoreau in the American Market* (Baltimore, 1995).

19. Milne, *George William Curtis*, 92–93; George William Curtis, *The Duty of the American Scholar to Politics and the Times. An oration, delivered on Tuesday, August 5, 1856, before the literary societies of Wesleyan University. Middletown, Conn.* (New York, 1856). "GREAT MINDS LIVE ALIKE: Emerson, Hawthorne, Thoreau and the Alcotts shared homes and inspiration in Concord," the Sunday *New York Times* of May 4, 1997, proclaimed in its special Travel section on New England.

20. John Shepard Keyes, "Autobiography," 47–48, manuscript in Vault, A45, Keyes, Unit 2, Series I, v. 7, Concord Free Public Library (CFPL); *Concord Yeoman's Gazette*, Dec. 10, 1836; Robert A. Gross, *The Minutemen and Their World* (New York, 1976), 176; Lemuel Shattuck, *A History of the Town of Concord, Middlesex County, Massachusetts: From Its Earliest Settlement to 1832* (Boston and Concord, 1835), 228; Edward Waldo Emerson, "Centennial Celebration of the Organization of the Concord Artillery—1904," Vault A45, Emerson, Unit 2, CFPL.

21. David Waldstreicher, "Rites of Rebellion, Rites of Assent: Celebrations, Print Culture, and the Origins of American Nationalism," *Journal of American History* 82(1995):37–61; Len Travers, *Celebrating the Fourth: Independence Day and the Rites of Nationalism in the Early Republic* (Amherst, 1997); Albert Soboul, *The French Revolution 1787–1799: From the Storming of the Bastille to Napoleon*, trans. Alan Forrest and Colin Jones (New York, 1974), 594–595; William Jones, A.B., *An Oration Pronounced at CONCORD, the Fourth of July, 1794: Being the Anniversary of the American Independence* (Concord, 1794), 5–7; Joseph Lee, interleaved almanac-diary for 1794, entry for July 4, 1794, New England Historic Genealogical Society, Boston; *Boston Gazette*, July 3, 1806.

22. Wilbur Zelinsky, *Nation into State: The Shifting Symbolic Foundations of American Nationalism* (Chapel Hill, 1988), 186–187; Keyes, "Autobiography," 69; Gross, *Minutemen*, 171; Transcripts of Town Meeting Records, 1791–1793, vol. 6, CFPL; John Shepard Keyes, "Old Roads in Concord," paper read before the Concord Antiquarian Society, Feb. 4, 1889, and Keyes, "The Second North Bridge Battle," both at CFPL; Middlesex County, Court of General Sessions of the Peace, Records Book, Sept. 1790–Mar. 1801, and Petitions from Elisha Jones and others, Sept. 9, 1792, and from David Brown and others, Sept. 13, 1792, in Middlesex Court of General Sessions, File Papers, Mar. 1793 session, Massachusetts State Archives; William Emerson, *Diaries and Letters of William Emerson 1743–1776*, Amelia Forbes Emerson, comp. (Concord, 1972); *Homes*, 297–298. On the first anniversary of Apr. 19, 1775, the Rev. William Emerson did give a memorial sermon, but he was never able to make this an annual event, since he died in service as a military chaplain not long after. *Diaries and Letters*, 89–97.

23. Middlesex, "Monument at Concord," *Yeoman's Gazette*, Mar. 11, 1826.

24. "Middlesex," *Yeoman's Gazette*, Mar. 11 and 18, 1826; Gross, *Minutemen*, 120–129, 188–189; town vote to celebrate 50th anniversary of Concord Fight, Letter file 4, A-4, CFPL; Louis A. Surette, *By-Laws of Corinthian Lodge, of Ancient, Free and Accepted Masons, of Concord, Mass., . . . To Which Is Added a Historical Sketch* (Concord, 1859), 131–137; Edward Everett, *An Oration Delivered at Concord, April the Nineteenth, 1825* (Boston, 1825); George Washington Warren, *The History of the Bunker Hill Monument Association during the First Century of the United States of America* (Boston, 1877), 125–126. On Apr. 9, 1825, Solomon Willard, designer of the Bunker Hill obelisk, sent Edward Everett, secretary of the Memorial Association (BHMA), a sketch of the "little monument" intended for Concord. See records in custody of Bunker Hill Memorial Association. I am grateful to Thomas Brown of the University of Massachusetts for providing me copies of his notes on the collection.

25. Gross, "Transcendentalism and Urbanism," 369–370; Joseph S. Wood, *The New England Village* (Baltimore, 1997), 119, 139–140, 144–146.

26. Vote of town to celebrate 50th anniversary of Concord Fight, Mar. 7, 1825, Letter file 4, A-4, CFPL; town meetings of Mar. 7, Apr. 4 and 8, 1825, Concord Town Meeting Records, 7:237, 244–245; Committee on arrangements for Apr. 19, 1825, list of toasts, Vault A5, Unit C1, Folder 2, CFPL; *Concord Celebration: The Order of Proceedings, at the Celebration of the Nineteenth of April, 1825, of the Fiftieth Anniversary of Concord & Lexington Battles* (Concord, 1825); Surette, *By-Laws of Corinthian Lodge*, 131–132.

27. Keyes, "Autobiography," 7, Vault, A45, Keyes, Unit 2, Series I, v. 7, CFPL; Surrette, *By-Laws of Corinthian Lodge*, 131–133; Middlesex, "Monument at Concord," *Yeoman's Gazette*, Mar. 4, 1826; Edward Jarvis, *Traditions and Reminiscences of Concord, Massachusetts, 1779–1878*, ed. Sarah Chapin (Amherst, 1993), 222–223; Surette, *By-Laws of Corinthian Lodge*, 132–133.

28. The eight-part series ran every week from Mar. 4 to Apr. 29, 1826. Middlesex, "Monument at Concord," *Yeoman's Gazette*, Mar. 4, 11, 18, 25, Apr. 8, 15, 22, 29, 1826.

29. Middlesex, "Monument at Concord," Mar. 18, 1826.

30. Middlesex, "Monument at Concord," *Yeoman's Gazette*, Mar. 25, 1826.

31. The attack on Lexington's claims occupied the final four parts of the series. *Yeoman's Gazette*, Apr. 8, 15, 22, and 29, 1826.

32. The manuscript drafts of the newspaper series do not include numbers one and two. See Middlesex, "The Monument at Concord: Letters to the Yeoman Gazette concerning the erection of a Monument at Concord in 1835," CFPL.

33. *Homes*, 297.

34. John Wood Sweet, "The Liberal Dilemma and the Demise of the Town Church: Ezra Ripley's Pastorate in Concord, 1778–1841," *Proceedings of the Massachusetts Historical Society* 104(1992):88–92.

35. Town meetings of Mar. 3 and Apr. 7, 1834, and Apr. 6, 1835, CTM 8:2, 4, 10–12, 39; Petition from Ezra Ripley for warrant article, Concord Archives Box 12, 1834 file for Jan.-Feb.

36. Gross, "Transcendentalism and Urbanism," 369–372; Shattuck, *History of the Town of Concord, Massachusetts*, 218.

37. Gross, "Transcendentalism and Urbanism," 374–376. See also my essays "Lonesome in Eden: Dickinson, Thoreau, and the Problem of Community in Nineteenth-Century New England," *Canadian Review of American Studies* 14(Spring 1983): 1–17, and "Preserving Culture: Edward Jarvis and the Memory of Concord," introduction to Jarvis, *Traditions and Reminiscences*, xv–xliv.

38. Sweet, "Liberal Dilemma," 101–102. The amendment to Article III of the 1780 Massachusetts Constitution passed by a narrow margin in Concord: 75 in favor, 57 against. Concord town meeting, Nov. 11, 1832, CTM 7:443. In 1827, payment of the ministerial tax was near-universal: 97 percent of polls. By 1830, with the organization of the Trinitarian Church, it had fallen to 86 percent, and in 1834, the year disestablishment took effect, to 80 percent. Thereafter, townspeople would sign off the parish in droves: just under half were paying the tax in 1839, and the numbers kept falling, down to about one-third at Ripley's death in 1841. Sweet, "Liberal Dilemma," 103.

39. Surette, *By-Laws of Corinthian Lodge*, 158–162.

40. Gross, "Transcendentalism and Urbanism," 374.

41. "Old Concord," *Concord Freeman*, May 2, 1835; Concord Town Meeting Records, May 4, 1835; Petition from Joseph Meriam and others, Concord Archives, Box 13, May-Sept. 1835, CFPL. Ten men signed the request for the warrant article. Of this group, five were Masons, including tavernkeepers Thomas D. Wesson and Hartwell Bigelow, and one, Reuben Moore, was the son of the prominent Mason and local deputy sheriff Abel Moore. Of the remaining four petitioners, two were Antimasons.

42. Ezra Ripley, Lecture at Concord Lyceum, written Mar. 1837, delivered Apr. 19, 1837, in Samuel Ripley Sermons, Box 1 of 13, bMS Am 1835 (5), by permission of Houghton Library, Harvard University. The previous week Ripley spoke on the topic "Public and Private Interests." See "Early Records of the Concord Lyceum," 145.

43. For the taking of Ripley's land, see town meeting minutes for July 1, 1793, Transcripts of Town Meetings, 6:46a–46b, 48b. John Shepard Keyes, a future political leader and historian of Concord, was on the eve of entering Harvard College when he witnessed the dedication of the monument in 1837. A half-century later, he charted the events of the "Second Great North Bridge Battle," venting the suspicions of Ripley harbored by many in the town. Keyes undoubtedly enjoyed the opportunity to get even with the parson, who had upbraided him as a youth for his reckless ways. See his characterization of Ripley's "vandalism" in "The Old Roads of Concord." On Keyes, see Robert A. Gross, "Young Men and Women of Fairest Promise: Transcendentalism in Concord," *Concord Saunterer*, n.s. 2(1994):5–18.

44. Keyes, "Autobiography," 47–48; Surette, *By-Laws of Corinthian Lodge*, 134–137; William Stevens Robinson, *"Warrington" Pen-Portraits: A Collection of Personal and Political Reminiscences from 1848 to 1876*, ed. Harriet H. [Mrs. W. S.] Robinson (Boston, 1877), 15–17.

45. Gross, "Transcendentalism and Urbanism," 373–375; Keyes, "Autobiography," 47–48. Edward Jarvis later claimed credit for composing the inscription, after drafts were presented to the monument committee by Ripley, Lemuel Shattuck, and Emerson. According to this recollection, written 40 years after the event, each of the three submissions was too long—Emerson's was the best—so Jarvis, a Concord native and struggling doctor in his early thirties, measured the tablet, calculated the available space for text, and produced the winning draft. Jarvis, *Traditions and Reminiscences*, 223. But John Shepard Keyes, then a teenager who would become a major figure in local politics and devote himself from the 1850s on to beautifying and preserving the historical landscape, dismisses Jarvis's account as fanciful. I find Keyes's view, which is more concrete and informed by his lifelong presence in Concord, persuasive. Hence, my account is based on Keyes, "Autobiography," 47–48.

46. Ralph Waldo Emerson, *The Journals and Miscellaneous Notebooks of Ralph Waldo Emerson*, ed. Mertin M. Sealts (Cambridge, Mass., 1960–1982), 5:71.

47. Ralph Waldo Emerson, *Poems* (Boston, 1847); Phyllis Cole, "'The Quiet Fields of My Fathers': Emerson in Concord," paper delivered at the conference "Seeing New Englandly," Univ. of Southern Maine, Apr. 1980; Michael Kammen, *The Mystic Chords of Memory: The Transformation of Tradition in American Culture* (New York, 1991).

48. Keyes, "Autobiography," 47–48; *Grove Dictionary of Music*, 13:529; W. H. Havergal, *History of the Old Hundredth Psalm Tune* (New York, 1854); Walter Harding, *The Days of Henry Thoreau: A Biography* (1965; New York, 1982), 48.

49. *The Monitor*, May 3, 1862 (CFPL). The periodical appeared for eight issues, from Apr. 19 to June 21, 1862. It was published in Concord by Albert Stacy "for the proprietors."

"A Chaos-Deep Soil"

Emerson, Thoreau, and Popular Literature

DAVID S. REYNOLDS

W E HAVE BECOME ACCUSTOMED IN RECENT YEARS TO INTER-
sections between high culture and popular culture. This crossing of
cultural levels has a long history in American life. Some historians have
pointed to the thirty-year period immediately before the Civil War as a
time when little, if any distinction was made in America between high culture and popular culture. Although this argument is overstated, there were
significant examples of cultural intermerging, such as performances of
Shakespeare alongside of minstrels, farces, and burlesque shows.[1] We may
note that this carnivalized culture produced other phenomena as well: the
multivoicedness of *Moby-Dick*, in which "high" literary images are yoked
with a range of "low" devices, from street slang to frontier humor; the
publishing history of Edgar Allan Poe's and Nathaniel Hawthorne's tales,
which often appeared in popular periodicals or giftbooks; and the life and
work of Walt Whitman, the all-inclusive embodiment of every level of
American life.

On the surface, Ralph Waldo Emerson and Henry David Thoreau, self-
avowed individualists and critics of mainstream society, seem more
distanced from popular culture than do the others. It is perhaps understandable that much commentary on them has stressed their affinities with
a rather elite group of philosophers, reformers, and social commentators.
Recent observers, however, have been freshly situating them in the literary
marketplace and popular contexts.[2] The current article, which demonstrates the depth of their engagement with popular literature, is part of this
contextualizing enterprise.

The long-standing image of Emerson and Thoreau as alienated from
their contemporary popular literature was based on the mistaken notion
that this culture was staid, tame, and narrowly conventional. F. O. Matthiessen set the tone of much later criticism when he portrayed Emerson

and Thoreau as champions of self-reliance and literary iconoclasm railing against a culture of philistinism and conformity; he typically called Thoreau a "violent" imagist who tried to "startle his contemporaries out of their complacent dreaminess."[3]

Antebellum popular literature was not, however, uniformly complacent or dreamy. True, there emerged a large body of literature—religious tracts, sentimental poetry, Sunday School literature, ladies' magazines, and certain domestic novels—that enforced bourgeois values of domesticity, piety, and optimism. But popular culture, then as now, was multilayered, and the major writers of the time were fully aware of its richness. Even mainstream religion had its experimental aspects, evidenced particularly in a free-flowing sermon style that dispensed with theology and utilized imaginative and theatrical effects once considered sacrilegious. Moreover, with advancing print technology and rapidly expanding distribution networks, inexpensive forms of highly seasoned sensational literature appeared, ranging from penny newspapers, filled with crimes and other horrors, to spicy yellow-covered pamphlet novels, hawked on the street and in railway stations, to comic almanacs, often featuring a peculiarly American form of humor characterized by bumptious assertiveness, grotesque imagery, and the raw argot of the street and the frontier.

All American writers were aware of this sensational writing, but many snobbishly derided it and called for a national literature sealed off from popular idioms they saw as crude and violent. The editor Evart A. Duyckinck declared that American literature must remain "immune from democratic enthusiasms, and from the wildness of American life."[4] Cornelius Mathews, Duyckinck's associate in the Young America movement, similarly asked for "nationality in its purest, highest, and broadest sense," far above the rant of popular orators and barroom brawlers, a nationality that was as "majestic and assured as the action of [America's] institutions are calm and secure." Henry Wadsworth Longfellow demanded a literature "without spasms and convulsions," one that gained universality by being "the result and refinement."[5] James Russell Lowell argued that literature is universal only when it escapes provincial boundaries.

In contrast to these writers, Emerson and Thoreau determinedly opened themselves to popular idioms. In this opennesss they were not alone in the Transcendentalist group: one thinks of Theodore Parker, the orator whose speeches and writings incorporated a range of popular images, and Margaret Fuller, who, despite her well-known "aristocratic" views, was ambiguously attracted to democratic speech forms. Even more intently than Parker or Fuller, Emerson and Thoreau associated such idioms with democratic nationalism in their effort to forge a distinctly American literature. Emerson identified the "Representative Man" as the one who most successfully absorbed even the most common or trivial interests of his time and place. His own absorption in such interests enlivened his prose style with many indigenous images and enabled him to become a successful and widely publicized lecturer. Thoreau, more fully aware than Emerson of the sensational genres of antebellum popular literature, came to see a unique Americanness in these genres, which contributed much to the zest of his prose and its dissemination among his contemporaries.

Emerson's view of literature and people was based on the idea that greatness results from comprehensiveness of cultural vision. Genius in a vacuum could do nothing; its raw material came from what he called "the popular mind." "The poet," he wrote, "needs a basis which he cannot supply; a tough chaos-deep soil, or main, or continent, on which his art may work, as the sculptor a block of stone, and this basis the popular mind supplies: otherwise all his flowers & elegances are transcendental & mere nuisance."[6]

He arrived at this notion of the symbiotic relationship between the elite and the popular in the mid 1830s, just before his emergence as a major writer. In his Boston lectures delivered between November 1835 and January 1836 he concentrated on what he called "the popular origin of English letters." Crude popular tales of war and magic, he noted, had set the stage for Chaucer and writers of the British Renaissance. Chaucer was so heavily indebted to previous writers that his works led Emerson to declare, "There never was an original writer. Each is a link in an endless chain." He went on: "Every great man, as Homer, Milton, Bacon, and Aristotle, necessarily takes up into himself the wisdom that is current in his time." Citing several other writers and philosophers—Shakespeare, Bunyan, and Goethe among them—he insisted that "the man of genius must occupy the whole system between God or pure mind, and the multitude of uneducated men. He must draw from the infinite Reason on the one side and he must penetrate into the heart and mind of the rabble on the other."[7]

As time passed, he became almost obsessively preoccupied with accumulating historical instances of representative people whose imaginative reach spanned the highest and lowest levels of culture. Plato, he wrote, "absorbed the learning of his times," showing that "the inventor knows only how to borrow"; he "fortified himself by drawing all his illustrations from sources disdained by orators and conversers; . . . from cooks and criers; the shops of potters, horse-doctors, butchers, and fish-mongers." The "largely receptive" Napoleon, according to Emerson, possessed "the very spirit of the newspapers" and was notable for his "adaptation to the mind of the masses around him."[8]

For Emerson, it was Shakespeare who stood out as being particularly receptive to popular culture. "He soars indeed to [a] heaven of thought," Emerson wrote, but "returns instantly to the ground and walks and plays and rolls himself in hearty frolic with his humble mates." Emerson noted that Shakespeare's "fables were furnished to his hands" by a theatrical culture that "was low and popular; and not literary." The Avon bard "esteemed the mass of old plays, waste stock, in which any experiment could be freely tried," leading Emerson to reflect that genius "consists in being altogether receptive; in letting the world do all, and suffering the spirit of the hour to pass unobstructed through the mind."[9]

In associating genius with comprehensiveness, Emerson was interpreting cultural history from a democratic perspective shaped by Jacksonian America. What he saw as the effete and precious features of the Boston literary scene could be best counteracted, he thought, by the populist energies of his time. Although he was politically and sometimes socially hostile to the Jacksonian party, he wanted to instigate an *American* representativeness in aesthetics, and he felt that the party might provide leads in that direction. "We all lean on England," he complained in his journal. "I suppose the evil may be cured by this rank rabble party, the Jacksonism of the country, heedless of English & of all literature," embodying a spirit that "may root out the hollow dilettantism of our cultivation in the coarsest way."[10]

If writers like Duyckinck, Longfellow, and Bronson Alcott determinedly cut themselves off from the lowest manifestations of Jacksonian populism, Emerson actively sought them out. In his rides around Boston, he liked to frequent the rough North End areas of Ann Street, Charter Street, and Prince Street, where he could observe the unrestrained behavior of common workers, so different from the stiff elegance of Washington and Tremont streets. The "popular passions" Orestes Brownson came to loathe were precisely those that appealed to Emerson. Just as Vladimir Nabokov spent hours on upstate New York buses listening to the slang-filled conversations of teenagers as a way of preparing for *Lolita*, so Emerson thought that the writer's best school was the street. "If you would learn to write," he wrote in his essay "Society and Solitude," "'tis in the street you must learn it. Both for the vehicle and for the aims of fine arts you must frequent the public square." Not only slang but also swearing held an attraction for him: "I confess to some pleasure from the stinging rhetoric of a rattling oath in the mouth of truckmen & teamsters. How laconic & brisk it is by the side of a page from the North American Review. . . . [A]lways this profane swearing & barroom wit has salt & fire in it." It was such street-generated vigor, he believed, that genteel American writers lacked. "All the American geniuses," he generalized, "Irving, Bryant, Greenough, Everett, Channing, even Webster in his recorded Eloquence, all lack nerve & dagger."[11]

Repelled by such antidemocratic preciousness, Emerson in his own writings wished to prove himself the representative American genius who traversed every cultural level. He did not directly transcribe popular language; rather, he adapted it and transformed it by coupling it with elite ideas derived from a variety of sources, including Coleridgean poetic theory, Swedenborgian symbolism, and idealistic philosophy. Into such intellectual currents he infused what he saw as a unique, vibrant Americanness derived from popular culture. He scoured the popular scene and found many innovations occurring in the areas of religion, reform, humorous literature, and newspapers. Not only did he succeed in transmuting dynamic materials from these cultural arenas into artistic prose, but he also earned a surprising visibility in popular newspapers and on the lyceum circuit.

His flowering owed much to changes in American popular culture that were occurring in the 1830s. It was in this decade that American sermon style, which had long been moving to the imaginative and the secular, found its most innovative exponent in "Father" Edward Thompson Taylor, the popular minister of the Seaman's Bethel Church in Boston. The 1830s also witnessed the rise of key reform movements—Garrisonian abolitionism, the populist temperance movement, antiprostitution reform, and working-class radicalism—that ushered in a vitriolic rhetoric Emerson found bracing, though sometimes extreme. Even more rhetorically extravagant was the wild humor of the American frontier, which in the 1830s was widely disseminated in comic almanacs and popular stage melodramas. The same changes in print production that sped the publication of comic pamphlets also engendered the highly sensationalistic penny newspapers, which appeared in 1833.

The first of these popular phenomena to affect Emerson was the changing style of American sermons. From Puritan times through the late eighteenth century, American sermons generally followed a preordained, logical format of "Text," "Doctrine," and "Proof" (or "Application"). A truly informal, indigenous preaching style did not begin to emerge until the Second Great Awakening (1798–1815), initiated by frontier evangelists like Peter Cartwright and James McGready, who drove their unlearned congregations to religious frenzy with their emotional, illustrative sermons. Between 1805 and 1825 the new revivalism was brought to the Northern cities by immensely popular evangelists such as John Summerfield, Lorenzo Dow, and the entertaining "mechanick preacher" Johnny Edwards, all of whom greatly accelerated the general tendency from doctrinal to imaginative sermonizing. At the same time that sermon style was changing on the popular level, it was affected by intellectual currents, most notably European Romanticism, which gave rise to extemporaneous sermons based on intuition and secular exempla, and the Scottish Common Sense philosophy, which called for a simple "popular eloquence" using vivid examples instead of abstruse metaphysics.[12]

Emerson moved from an early fascination with the intellectual sources of change to a hearty interest in the kind of torrid popular evangelical preaching that his Brahmin colleagues dismissed as crude and chaotic. When he was a senior at Harvard, a small revolution in Unitarian sermon style was initiated by his teacher Edward Everett, who, having absorbed Romantic thought during a long stay in Germany, gave a sermon abounding, as Emerson later recalled, "in daring image, in parable," showing the young Emerson "the magic of form." At first dismayed by such a secular approach to the divine, Emerson lamented in his journal that "there is a danger of a *poetical* religion from the tendencies of the age" and that soon religion would "consist in nothing else than the progressive introduction of apposite metaphors." But soon he was expressing delight that "the preaching most in vogue at the present day depends chiefly on imagination for its success." By the time he became pastor of Boston's Second Church in the late 1820s, he was actually prepared to take imaginative flights beyond the sermon form altogether. Only 25 percent of his sermons at the Second Church were concerned with doctrinal issues, and his introduction of what he called "new forms of address, new modes of illustration" shocked even the informal Rev. Henry Ware, Jr., who criticized Emerson for using irreverent imagery in the pulpit.[13]

After Emerson left the Second Church's pulpit in 1832, the maturation of his literary consciousness owed much to the image-filled sermons of Father Taylor. Called by Whitman America's only "essentially perfect orator," Taylor became the prototype for the slang-whanging sermonizer Father Mapple in Herman Melville's *Moby-Dick*.[14] Although these writers' debts to Taylor are sometimes mentioned, what is neglected is Taylor's key role in the historic shift of American sermon style. An ex-sailor, cobbler, and tin peddler who became a Methodist preacher, Taylor introduced to the pulpit a secular, showmanlike style unmatched in imaginative vigor until the advent of post-Civil War pulpit performers like T. DeWitt Talmage and Dwight L. Moody. Taylor specialized in free-flowing sermons filled with striking metaphors and racy anecdotes, as when, in a sermon about a boy ruined by gambling and drinking, he lifted his hand and whispered, "Hush-h-h, he is cursing his mother—shut the windows of heaven, *shut* the windows." Taylor became a genuine friend of Emerson, whom he defended against all detractors even after Emerson abandoned formal Christianity. When asked by stricter religious types if Emerson was headed for hell, he

declared with characteristic jauntiness: "Go there. . . . Why if he went
there he would change the climate and the tide of emigration would turn
that way."[15]

Although Taylor became a celebrity, Emerson was alone among his contemporaries (Whitman and Melville excepted) in realizing the full significance of his stylistic innovations. Taylor's brash self-confidence pushed
Emerson toward his famous assertions of self-reliance. Believing that all
other preaching seemed "puny" and "cowardly" beside Taylor's, Emerson
said that when you see Taylor, "instantly you behold that a man is a Mover."
It was no great distance from Taylor's boast, "I am no man's model, no
man's copy," to Emerson's advice, "Trust thyself: every heart vibrates to
that iron string," or "Whoso would be a man must be a nonconformist."
More subtly, Taylor's oratory showed the possibilities of a new *stylistic* self-
reliance whereby emphasis in religion shifted from dogmatic content to
creative image and fluid poeticizing. Taylor's manner, Emerson noted,
showed that "form seems to be bowing substance out of the World,"
as "Taylor's Muse" is "a panorama of images from all nature & art." Calling
Taylor "the Shakespeare of the sailor & the poor," he wrote of a typical
Taylor sermon: "the wonderful and laughing life of his illustrations keeps
us broad awake. A string of rockets all night." Emerson declared that Taylor "rolls the world into a ball and tosses it from hand to hand."[16]

Having filled his journals and letters of the 1833–1836 period with enthusiastic remarks about Taylor's preaching, Emerson incorporated both
the creativity and humanism of the revival style into his major essays and
addresses, produced between 1836 and 1844. His comment on Taylor's
ability to roll the world in a ball and toss it from hand to hand was expanded
in *Nature*, in which he says that the imaginative person "tosses the creation
like a bauble from hand to hand, and uses it to embody any caprice of
thought that is upper-most in his mind." His demand in his 1841 lecture
"The Poet" for flexible form, passionate feeling, and native materials in
American poetry was linked directly to Father Taylor, for he declared that
poetic genius may be found "in some lowly Bethel by the seaside where a
hard-featured, scarred, and wrinkled methodist whose face is a network of
cordage becomes the poet of the sailor and the fisherman, whilst he pours
out the abundant streams of his thought through a language all glittering
and fiery with imagination."[17]

In the "Divinity School Address" (1838) Emerson applies the new
vibrant style of American sermons to the subversion of the doctrines and
forms of traditional Christianity. While preparing the "Address," he expressed disgust in his journals at the frigid sermons of an appropriately
named Unitarian colleague, Barzillai Frost, while he again commended

the warm homiletic style of Father Taylor. In the "Address" itself, he uses the daringly humanistic popular religious idiom to undercut the formal, elitist style represented by Frost. Emerson tells the memorable story of going one winter Sunday to hear a preacher whose sermon "had no one word intimating that he had laughed or wept, was married or in love, had been commended, or cheated, or chagrined. . . . The capital secret of his profession, namely, to convert life into truth, he had not yet learned." "The true preacher," Emerson stressed, "can be known by this, that he deals out to the people his life,—life passed through the fire of his thought."[18]

Throughout the "Address," Emerson enacts this enthusiasm for the new secular sermon style by using imagery from the natural world, popular literature, and his own experience. The rhetorical use of earthly imagery runs from the opening paragraph, in which Emerson rhapsodizes on "this refulgent summer," to the conclusion, in which he gives the metaphorical mandate, "now let us do what we can do to rekindle the smouldering, nigh quenched fire on the altar." At moments, Emerson arrestingly juxtaposes the grotesque and the lovely, as when he says, "the word Miracle, as pronounced by the Christian churches . . . is Monster. It is not one with the blowing clover and the falling rain." At other times, he dazzles us with a string of shifting images. At all points in the address, he takes the free-flowing sermon style and the humanized religion of his day to a new destination: the subversion of dogmatic Christianity and the joyous assertion of poetic creativity. It is this leap beyond Christianity that most differentiates him from Father Taylor. Taylor's images, however imaginative, had the clear goal of bringing about Christian repentance and conversion. Emerson's are meant to inspire a fluid, poetic apprehension of religion and the world. When he concluded the "Address" by defining the sermon as "the speech of man to men,—essentially the most flexible of all organs, or all forms," he was taking to a new extreme the imaginative ethos of American popular preachers. It is small wonder that the "Address" was denounced as "the latest form of infidelity" and that Emerson was not invited to speak to the Divinity School for nearly thirty years. He had been swept by the swelling wave of humanistic preaching toward new poetic revelations that temporarily alienated him from his more elitist Unitarian brethren but eventually earned him popular favor and enduring fame.

Closely allied to popular preaching were the many reform movements that led Emerson to declare in 1841: "In the history of the world the doctrine of Reform had never such scope as at the present hour." "[T]hese movements are on all accounts important," he wrote; they "are all preg-

nant with ethical conclusions."[19] Throughout his career, Emerson had
firsthand exposure to reform movements: in 1838 he became involved
in the protest against the maltreatment of the Cherokee Indians; in the
early 1840s he contributed money to the temperance movement and
wrote an essay on the Chardon Street convention of popular reformers; in
1844 he gave an address in Concord on West India emancipation; and
in the 1850s he was aroused to a white fury by the passage of the fugitive
slave law, which he denounced in the acidic rhetoric typical of popular
abolitionists.

Like Thoreau and Whitman after him, Emerson compensated for a certain temperamental stolidity and coldness by opening himself up fully to
the fiery, cutting rhetoric of popular reformers. He praised the abolitionists
as "wild men" who "reinforced the city with new blood from the woods and
mountains" and who "utter the savage sentiment of Nature in the heart of
commercial capitals." Reformers embodied the kind of assertive iconoclasm he valued, as he indicated when he declared that the person who
"has only a good intention is apt to feel ashamed of his inaction & the
slightness of his virtue when in the presence of active & zealous leaders of
the philanthropic enterprizes of Universal Temperance, Peace, & Abolition of Slavery."[20]

Developing a deep hatred for proper "goodies," Emerson in "Self-
Reliance" wrote: "Your goodness must have some edge to it,—else it is
none." This goodness "with an edge to it" was taught to him primarily by
the enthusiastic reformers of his day. "Without electricity the air would
rot," he wrote; "without a spice of bigot and fanatic, no excitement, no ef-
ficiency." When he asserted in 1841 that he owed much to "reformers of all
stripes and qualities," he was referring both to the linguistic fire and the
moral iconoclasm of popular reformers. He wrote that temperance, abolition, and other movements were all "fertile forms of antinomianism" that
provided "a keener scrutiny of institutions and domestic life than any we
had known."[21]

While he absorbed the verve of popular reformers, he did not sheepishly
imitate them; instead, he used reformist zeal to fashion reform anew. Noting the contradictions of reformers—their frequently sensational tactics,
their relapses, their sometimes gleeful fascination with the very vices they
denounced—he wrote that many rabid reformers use "outward and vulgar
means" and "affect us as the insane do. They bite us, and we run mad also."
Since he saw that "many a reformer perishes in his removal of rubbish," he
was eager to redefine reform as constant moral and intellectual self-
renewal.[22]

His shrewd recognition of the ambivalent nature of popular reforms and the pressing need for a rejuvenated reform is made clear in his essay "The Method of Nature," in which he writes:

> The reforms whose fame now fills the land with Temperance, Anti-Slavery, Non-Resistance, No Government, Equal Labor, fair and generous as each appears, are poor bitter things when prosecuted for themselves as an end. To every reform, in proportion to its energy, early disgusts are incident, so that the disciple is surprised at the very hour of his first triumphs, with chagrins, and sickness, and a general distrust. . . . [T]here is no end to which your practical faculty can aim, so sacred or large, that, if pursued for itself, will not at last become carrion and an offence to the nostril.[23]

The biting reform rhetoric of the day gave Emerson a tool for undercutting stale institutions, but he recognized that in adopting this rhetoric he had to transform it or redefine reform, which he realized quickly became "carrion and offence to the nostril." In his major essays we find a repeated dialectic of subversive dismissal of revered social norms followed by affirmations of self-reliance, aesthetic perception, and the symbolic imagination. Many of these essays can be called reform writings, since they expose errors and propose solutions. Unlike the genteel antebellum writers who sealed themselves off against popular culture, Emerson embraced the trenchant, militant spirit of contemporary reform. Unlike many reformers, however, he did not wallow in the perverse effects of vice; instead, he offered invigorating alternatives to the errors he perceived.

His overall effort to place reform in a larger philosophical context becomes explicit in his essay "Man the Reformer," which includes the following passage:

> What is man born for but to be a Reformer, a Re-maker of what man has made; a renouncer of lies; a restorer of truth and good, imitating that great Nature which embosoms us all, and which sleeps no moment on an old past, but every hour repairs itself, yielding to us every moment to a new day, and with every pulsation a new life?[24]

This passage says openly what virtually all of Emerson's essays say implicitly: man as reformer must not only be subversive ("a renouncer of lies") but also reconstructive ("a restorer of truth and good"), and his reconstructive powers should be recognized as organically linked to the ever-renewing powers of nature.

Just as Emerson redirected the energies of American reforms in his writings, so he transformed the language and spirit of popular humor. In the energetic humor and slang of the American masses, he discovered a rich source of creative imagery that reflected what he saw as the zest, the toughness, and the fluidity of his own culture. The main influence on him was frontier humor, which he warmly praised and incorporated in his pungent, ever-shifting imagistic writings. At the same time, he saw in much of this indigenous humor an excessive savagery and a linguistic abandon that he sought to enrich with larger themes.

Among his contemporaries Emerson was often regarded as a masterful American humorist. "Mr. Emerson is an inveterate humorist," wrote a reviewer for the *New Englander* in 1856. "He writes as if he were half quizzing and half in earnest. . . . He gathers up the widest analogies by the armful, and evokes at will the most striking illustrations from nature and history." Another reviewer remarked that one of his essay volumes was "enlivened by his well-known wit, running not infrequently into grotesque conceits, that are only saved from downright extravagance by the pithy and genial humor that relaxes the screwing lips of the critic into an irresistible smile, or a shouting peal of laughter." The qualities these reviewers noted in Emerson's style—grotesqueness, extravagance, unusual analogies—were those that distinguished the popular American humor Emerson admired.[25]

It was in the crucial period of the mid 1830s, just before his major creative period, that Emerson first recognized American popular humor writings as potent stylistic directives for American authors. The infiltration of backwoods idioms into the urban Northeast had a strong impact on Emerson as he searched for alternatives to a Unitarian style he considered tepid and a British style he viewed as earthbound. The 1830s marked the appearance of America's first purely comic almanacs (the first was published in 1831) and the sudden popularity of backwoods humor characters like Jack Downing, Davy Crockett, Nimrod Wildfire, and a host of other metaphor-spouting frontier screamers. More acutely than any of his liberal colleagues, Emerson recognized the significance of the linguistic invasion from the frontier.

Shortly before he wrote *Nature*, his first major work, he delivered a lecture, in November 1835, that indicates the impact of frontier discourse on his imagination. He made a paean to the frontier style that prefigured his later theories of language:

> Good writing and brilliant discourse are perpetual allegories. The imagery in discourse which delights all men is that which is drawn from observation of natural processes. It is this which gives that pi-

quancy to the conversation of a strong natured farmer or back-woodsman which all men relish. It is the salt of those semisavages, men of strong understanding, who bring out of the woods into the tameness of refined circles a native way of seeing things, and there speak in metaphors. "I showed him the back of my hand," said a backwoodsman, for *I broke friendship with him.* . . . The strong humor of Jack Downing's letters has not contributed so much to their popularity as the just natural imagery in which all thoughts are presented.

Having underscored the suggestiveness of backwoods humor and argot, Emerson in the next breath defined the poet as the one who through the power of imagination "converts the solid globe, the land, the sea, the sun, the animals into symbols of thought." What was new about this lecture was Emerson's eagerness to reinterpret standard Romantic outlooks, such as the nature of symbolic language, in terms of the linguistic strategies of the American backwoods.[26]

His enthusiasm for the frontier humorists remained unabated through the period, roughly between 1836 and 1844, during which he produced his most memorable and characteristic writings. In an 1842 essay for the *Dial,* he outlined the future of American writing as follows:

Our eyes will be turned westward, and a new and stronger tone in our literature will be the result. The Kentucky stump-oratory, the exploits of Boone and David Crockett, the journals of the western pioneers, agriculturalists, and socialists, and the letters of Jack Downing, are genuine growths, which are sought with avidity in Europe, where our Europe-like books are of no value.[27]

In the frontier genres Emerson discovered a native metaphor-generating procedure that reflected the unique fluidity of America democratic experience and that seemed the best available idiom for giving an indigenous flavor to his philosophy. When his notions about the creative imagination and individualism were expressed in the disjointed, kaleidoscopic style of American humor, the result was a dazzling imagistic pastiche whose linguistic fertility enforced the philosophical freedoms it heralded. For some of Emerson's contemporaries, particularly those devoted to English literary traditions, Emerson's typically American stylistic shifts compromised logic and consistency: Lowell famously called his style "a chaos of shooting-stars," the *English Review* said that his "grotesque extravagance becomes something more than a laughing matter," and Henry Giles charged that in Emerson things are "distorted, jostled, turned upside down in the giddy phantasmagoria of our borrowed vision, [and] are made to reel to and fro in a delirious and intoxicating dance."[28]

When compared with the wild, uncontrolled elements of much popular humor, however, his style may be seen as a notable enrichment of this humor. True, his essays are full of the sudden shifts and bizarre images that characterized native humor. When in *Nature* he talks of travelers trying to roast eggs on the cinders of a volcano or describes man as broken and in heaps; when in "The American Scholar" he says civilized people have become walking monsters amputated from the trunk or lined with eyes; when in "Self-Reliance" he calls consistency a hobgoblin and memory a corpse dragged about, he is using the kind of laughably grotesque images that made him known as an "inveterate humorist" in his day. But he departed from the popular humorists in constantly lending philosophical depth to themes that in the popular texts often pointed toward the superficial and amoral. The humorists' changeability was deepened by his notion of creative whim, their inconsistencies by his proclamation of nonconformity, their dizzying imagery by his poetic dissolvings of material reality in the name of idealism. All the subversive cultural phenomena they reflected he willfully adopted only to transform them into affirmations of poetic vision and the human spirit.

Given his incorporation of many contemporary themes and devices, it is perhaps not surprising that Emerson himself became a popular figure in American culture. Although none of his books were best-sellers, they stayed constantly in print and remained ready references for those who became aware of him through two immensely popular media: the newspaper and the lecture platform.

Other figures of his day had flash-in-the-pan popularity in individual areas. Writers like Lydia Sigourney, Susan Warner, Fanny Fern, Harriet Beecher Stowe, George Lippard, and their ilk produced works that had immense popularity but then quickly faded from view until they were resurrected by modern scholars. Lecturers like Wendell Phillips, Henry Ward Beecher, John Bartholomew Gough, and other lyceum stars reached immediate audiences in lectures that were sometimes reprinted but had little lasting appeal. Journalists like Horace Greeley, James Gordon Bennett, William T. Porter, and others reached tremendous readerships through ephemeral newspapers which now lie crumbling in rare book rooms.

Emerson, in contrast, had a triple visibility: as a publishing author, as a lecturer, and as a subject for newspaper columnists. These roles complemented each other. Typically his lectures were popular upon their first delivery, gained huge publicity when they were reported or reprinted in newspapers, and then became immortalized when they appeared in book form.

Did he covet popularity? There are indications that he did, and from a young age. In one of his earliest journal entries, written in 1820, he stated wishfully: "My talents (according to the judgement of friends or to the whispered suggestions of vanity) are popular, are fitted to enable me to claim a place in the inclinations & sympathy of men."[29] Seven years later he admitted, "I do not fully disclaim the vulgar hunger to be known, to have one's name hawked in the great capitals in the street." His turn from Unitarian preaching to more general lecturing can be partly attributed to a simple desire for popularity. Two years after leaving the ministry he mused, "Were it not a heroic adventure in me to insist on being a popular speaker?"

His emphasis on becoming a "popular speaker" reflects his desire to become more than just a publishing essayist; publication alone, he realized, did not insure wide appeal. "The good of publishing one's thought," he wrote, "is that of hooking to you likeminded men. . . . Yet, how few!" The main impetus behind his lyceum appearances was to reach the people, and he succeeded in doing so to a degree that is not sufficiently appreciated.

The popular interest in his lectures is indicated by the money he could command and by his durability on the lyceum circuit. In the 1840s and 1850s, when the average fee for a public lecture was around $15, he received between $40 and $75 per lecture. Although he never matched the annual lecture income of a figure like Wendell Phillips, who spoke on reform for free but on other topics for fees that earned him as much as $15,000 a year, his per-lecture fee in fact matched Phillips's and was roughly three times greater than what the typical lyceum commanded. Like all lecturers, Emerson had his off nights of thin turnouts and tepid receptions. But he frequently attracted sizable crowds who appreciated him. When in 1850 the journalist Nathaniel P. Willis went to hear Emerson speak in New York's spacious Mercantile Hall, he found the room so crowded that he was pressed against a wall by the mob and had no view of the speaker.[30] A decade later the *Atlantic Monthly* could assert: "It is a singular fact, that Mr. Emerson is the most steadily attractive lecturer in America. . . . Mr. Emerson always draws" (*Log*, 148). Even as late as 1871, when the likes of Henry Ward Beecher and Mark Twain were captivating lecture audiences, the *Springfield Republican* could state that Emerson "is the most widely known, the greatest, and the most attractive of all the present lecturers" (*Log*, 244).

His lasting appeal as a lecturer can be largely explained by the fact that his name was kept constantly before the public in newspapers. Emerson had ambivalent feelings about the popular press. On the one hand, he was disgusted by the notorious sensationalism of America's penny papers. "What sickening details in the daily journals!" he wrote, noting that "family newspapers" such as the *New York Tribune* had superseded crime sheets like the *Newgate Calendar* and the *Pirate's Own Book* "in the freshness as well as the horror of their records of crime." "To what base uses we put this ineffable intellect!" he lamented. "To reading all day murders & railroad accidents." Nonetheless, he knew well enough that, in his words, "Newspapers are the proper literature of America," and he understood their potential for enhancing his own popularity. He wrote in his journal:

> Cheap literature makes new markets. We have thought only of a box audience, or at most a box & pit; but now it appears there is also slip audience, & galleries one, two, three; & backstairs, & street listeners, besides. [Horace] Greeley tells me the Graham's Magazine has 70,000 subscribers. And I might write a lecture, if I will, to 70,000 readers.[31]

His very disgust with the sensationalism of popular newspapers fueled his eagerness to appear in these newspapers, since his presence might have an uplifting effect. This phenomenon was noted in 1852 by an essayist for the *Home Journal* who, quoting Emerson to the effect that he intended his lectures as an antidote to depraved popular newspapers, pointed to the fact that the lectures of Emerson and others were reported so often in the press that the newspapers spread the antidote far and wide. Noting the paradox of the situation, the essayist remarked, "There goes the diseased newspaper, with the corrective pustule—the 'report of last night's lecture'— inserted by the reporter's quill, and (irrelevant, but professionally interesting) nothing to pay for the virus," so that "by the very circulation of the disease itself, the healing principle is carried to the extremities of the land" (*Log*, 69-70).

In Emerson's case, the antidote was carried widely, for American newspapers of every variety were eager to report his lectures. The *New York Tribune*, the newspaper he singled out for its horrors, proved a strong and consistent publicist. Beginning in March 1842 and through the remainder of the decade, the *Tribune* regularly carried multicolumn reports of his lectures, often with lengthy excerpts. By the 1850s, his name seemed to be appearing everywhere, in all grades of newspapers. An 1850 article in the *Christian Inquirer* noted his ubiquity in the press:

> The reviews, magazines, newspapers, foreign and domestic, have made it no small part of their business these few months past, to

say their say about Mr. Emerson. The entire range of criticism upon him, we judge, would cover the whole ground, from Shakespeare down to the latest Lunatic, the Massachusetts Quarterly, representing the beginning, and the New York Herald, at the end of the scale. . . . Mr. Emerson seems to be used in a good many places, as the wagon full of chain cables is used on board our steamboats, to trim ship (*Log*, 54).

It might seem unlikely that a philosopher with a staid personality would be viewed as good press, but Emerson developed a democratic public persona that made him seem both wise and entertaining. A Boston paper typically reported his lecture on the Anglo-American as follows: "It was sententious and piquant, abounding in humor, and underlaid with a vein of the deepest thought and *Emersonian* sense" (*Log*, 97). Not restricting himself to elite lecturing venues, he made efforts to appear among average Americans. In 1858, for instance, he appeared at the annual Middlesex County Fair in Concord, where "a very large assemblage" of countryfolk, after holding a competition for swine, bulls, and other animals, heard his luncheon lecture about the virtues of the farmer (*Log*, 129).

Although listeners and readers of Emerson tended to simplify his message, there are indications that he actually took steps to accommodate to the mass audience in order to maintain visibility. What some today see as a falling off in the quality of his essays as time passed is connected to his effort to tailor his style for the masses. Most of the pieces in *English Traits* and all of the ones in *The Conduct of Life* were originally given as lectures. If these volumes seem less profound than the first and second series of *Essays*, it is because their contents reflect changes in Emerson's style toward the diverting and the secular. In 1867 *Fraser's Magazine* noted: "His method . . . has become more practical. . . . This has given his later style a more popular and, so to speak, iconographic character; and it has also developed his humor,—witty he always was" (*Log*, 170).

Scholars have often pointed out that he could befuddle his audiences. But even the obscure moments of his lectures were not out of line with popular taste in an age when traveling trance lecturers, animal magnetists, and phrenologists palmed off their mystical pseudoknowledge to gaping audiences. Looking back on his lyceum success in the 1850s, the *Saturday Review* generalized, "He managed to write what the crowds which throng American lecture rooms appear, for some strange reason, to relish; and he contrived to put it in unintelligible form. By these two facts he secured a popularity which there is no other way of explaining" (*Log*, 146).

The final explanation for his success in reaching people, in the short and

long run, can be explained by the extraordinary reach of his vision. In trying to account for the fact that he was America's "most steadily attractive
lecturer," the *Atlantic* asked, "What, then, is his secret?," pointing to his
comprehensiveness:

> Is it not that he out-Yankees us all? that his range includes us all?
> that he is equally at home with the potato disease and original sin,
> with pegging shoes and the Oversoul? that, as we try all trades, he
> has tried all cultures? and, above all, that his mysticism gives us a
> counterpoise to out super-practicability? (*Log*, 148)

Like those past geniuses he admired for embracing the popular culture of
their day, Emerson fully incorporated the popular idioms of antebellum
America and, as a result, came closer to reaching the people than any other
contemporary philosopher.

In 1853, Emerson discussed popular culture with Thoreau. Indulging his
penchant for antisocial crustiness, Thoreau declared that anything that
succeeded with the popular audience was suspect. Objecting to this attitude, Emerson said, "Who would not like to write something which all can
read, like Robinson Crusoe?" Shortly after this conversation, Thoreau was
approached by a girl who had heard he was giving a lyceum talk that
evening. She asked him if his lecture would include a "nice interesting
story" that would entertain her and her brother. Thoreau pondered the
girl's request, trying to think of a diverting anecdote to put in his lecture.[32]
    These interchanges reflect Thoreau's ambivalence about the popular
culture of his day. As the age's chief attacker of materialism and conformity,
Thoreau stood for a spiritual-minded individualism that in some senses
stood in opposition to popular culture. "If you would get money as a writer
or lecturer," he wrote, "you must be popular, and that is to go down per-
pendicularly. Those services which the community will readily pay for, it is
most disagreeable to render."[33] On the other hand, few observed antebellum culture as attentively as he, and few responded to the popular
concerns of his day as eagerly as he. The man who in one breath dismissed
the popular in front of Emerson and in the next catered to it in response to
the girl instinctively rejected herd mentality even as he wished to exploit
popular styles and themes.
    Despite his reputation as a philosopher distanced from popular culture,
Thoreau was strongly attracted to popular language because of its usefulness as a tool of communication. "Perhaps the value of any statement," he
wrote in 1852, "is its susceptibility to be expressed in popular language.

The greatest discoveries may be reported in the newspapers." Like Emerson, he saw energetic popular speech as a refreshing alternative to lifeless aristocratic language. "Anything living is easily and naturally expressed in popular language," he explained. "I cannot help suspecting that the life of these learned professors has been almost as inhuman and wooden as a rain-gauge or self-registering magnetic machine."[34]

Also like Emerson, he scoured history and contemporary life for examples of writers who creatively used popular language. Classic literature, he stressed, was equally accessible to the many and the few, what he called "the hasty and the deliberate reader." The Bhagavad Gita, the Laws of Menu, and the Bible stood out for him in this regard. Great writers, he pointed out, absorbed their times: Dante was weaned on popular stage plays depicting hell; Shakespeare inherited most of his plots and much of his language from popular culture; and the young Milton was influenced by romances and the drama. Among contemporary writers, Thomas Carlyle struck him as particularly responsive to popular idioms. Arguing that Carlyle "has plucked the ripest fruit in the public garden," Thoreau called his style "eminently colloquial. . . . It resounds with emphatic, natural, lively, stirring tones, muttering, rattling, exploding, like shells and shot, and with like execution."[35] Because of his popular-based language, Thoreau went on, Carlyle's essays are "sermons to kings, and sermons to peasants, and sermons to all intermediate classes."

Thoreau's own efforts toward comprehensiveness of cultural vision contributed to his sometimes surprising interest in common speech and mundane literary genres. In 1850 he met a drunken Long Island oysterman whose searing wit impressed him as Shakespearian. Between snores and vomits, the man would occasionally awake and blurt forth what Thoreau called "some happy repartee like an illuminated swine. It was the earthiest, slimiest wit I ever heard." Thoreau added laconically, "He was one of the few remarkable men I have met."[36] So insistent was Thoreau about the creativity of common speech that in *Walden* he apportioned far more space to blunt-spoken illiterates like the Canadian woodchopper and the almshouse half-wits than to educated visitors like Ellery Channing.

His reading habits were also democratic. So much has been written about his debts to classic sources, from the Asian scriptures through the Romantics, that we are apt to forget that he was also intimately aware of the American popular press and, in particular, of the new audiences for sensational literature. In an 1836 article on American literature, he recognized the importance of popular literature: "The question with us is whether a book will take—will sell well, not whether it is worth taking or worth selling. . . . The press is daily sending forth its thousands and tens of

thousands, for the publisher says 'tis profitable." He was especially cognizant of the immense power of newspapers with the advent of the penny
press. "We do not care for the Bible," he wrote in "Slavery in Massachusetts," "but we do care for the newspaper. . . . The newspaper is a Bible
which we read every morning and every afternoon, standing and sitting,
riding and walking. It is a Bible which every man carries in his pocket,
which lies on every table and counter, and which the mail, and thousands
of missionaries, are constantly dispersing."37

Second only to newspapers in popularity, he knew, were the cheap, sensational novels that were issued by the tens of thousands in the form
of paper-covered pamphlets with brightly colored jackets, melodramatic
illustrations, and alliterative titles printed in bold, black lettering. His
knowledge of this literature dates from at least the fall of 1846, when during a hike in Maine he stopped at taverns and houses, where he entertained
himself by reading pamphlets of crime and adventure. At one house he
found "Flash novels manufactured in N Y and Boston expressly for these
markets . . . by Prof [Joseph Holt] Ingraham and others—all printed as it
were in colored ink red and yellow & with engravings interspersed—'The
Belle of the Penobscots' and other thrilling stories." Later, on the parlor
table in a backwoods home, he encountered "the Wandering Jew cheap
Edition and fine print The Criminal Calendar—& Parish's Geog—& Flash
novels 2 or 3."38

Although he lamented the excesses of popular sensational literature, he
came to associate the thrills and savagery it embodied with a distinct Americanness. He complained about the "startling and monstrous events as fill
the daily papers" and compared reading the average newspaper to rooting
in a sewer. Nonetheless, antebellum America, with its Barnumesque freaks,
frontier slang, crime-filled penny papers, and yellow-covered flash novels,
was known worldwide as a culture of sensationalism, and he wished to coin
literary capital from its perceived wildness. "In literature it is only the wild
that attracts us," he wrote. "Dullness is only another word for tameness."
British literature, in his view, had no "wild strain. It is an essentially tame
and civilized literature, reflecting Greece and Rome. . . . There was need of
America." "America is the she wolf to-day," he declared. Elsewhere he
wrote, "We must look to the west for a new literature," predicting that popular expressions "which now look so raw slang-like and colloquial when
printed another generation will cherish and affect as genuine and American
and standard."39

Thoreau developed his mature writing style in response to an American
popular audience that feasted on sensations and hungered for curiosities.
He lived at Walden in the same decade that saw the emergence not only of

pamphlet novels but also of P. T. Barnum, the so-called Prince of Humbug, who displayed in his famous museum on Broadway a razzle-dazzle line-up of freaks and oddities, including bearded ladies, mermaids, dwarves, two-headed calves, and so on. Thoreau, the hermit who lived on beans, was perceived by some as one more American oddity. When *Walden* appeared in 1854, the *Knickerbocker* compared Thoreau and Barnum in an essay titled "Town and Rural Humbugs." *Graham's* made a similar point by saying of Thoreau's volume: "Sometimes strikingly original, sometimes merely eccentric and odd, it is always racy and stimulating." For James Russell Lowell, Thoreau was little more than a publicity hound who used the odd and the paradoxical to gain attention and arouse controversy. "He seeks, at all risks," Lowell wrote, "for perversity of thought. . . . It is not so much the True that he loves as the Out-of-the-Way. As the Brazen Age shows itself in other men by exaggeration of phrase, so in him by exaggeration of statement."[40]

Thoreau actually made similar comments about his own work. Shortly before *Walden* appeared, he confessed to his friend Harrison Blake, "I trust that you realize what an exaggerator I am,—that I lay myself out to exaggerate whenever I have an opportunity, pile Pelion on Ossia, to reach heaven so." After completing a draft of *Walden*, he scribbled in his journal:

> My faults are:—
> Paradoxes,—saying just the opposite,—a style which might be imitated.
> Ingenious.
> Playing with words,—getting the laugh,—not always simple, strong, and broad.
> Using current phrases and maxims, when I should speak for myself.[41]

Indeed, what chiefly distinguishes Thoreau's prose from other antebellum writing about philosophy and nature is the intentionality with which it devotes itself to "getting the laugh" and "using current phrases and maxims" in an effort to satisfy the public's attraction to sensations.

His experience in writing *Walden* showed him responding directly to this popular attraction. *Walden* was initially impelled by the public's curiosity about his strange hermitage. The idea for the volume came to him when he learned that the audience at one of his lyceum lectures (probably the one on Carlyle on February 4, 1846) had expected to hear about his life in the woods. About the same time, people on the street and in stores were asking him such questions as "What do you eat?" and "Aren't you lonesome?"[42]

From this source in the public's curiosity, *Walden* evolved over several years as a response to public interest in the sensational. The most popular novel of the 1840s, George Lippard's *The Quaker City; or, The Monks of Monk Hall*, had set the stage for *Walden* and other reform works by delivering trenchant social criticism in sensational, often freakish imagery. Whether or not Thoreau read *The Quaker City* along with the other "flash novels," he learned the Lippardian technique of coupling the reformist and the odd. *Walden* would become his most popular work *because of*, not *in spite of* its caustic, nettlesome attacks on American conventions.

It was not the optimistic, benign chapters of *Walden* but rather the subversive ones that were the most popular when they were first presented as lyceum lectures. When in November 1848 Thoreau gave his biting "Economy" lecture, his audience was not offended or dismayed, as we might expect from its satirical tenor, but titillated and amused. The *Salem Observer* noted that the lecture "was done in an admirable manner, in a strain of exquisite humor, with a strong undercurrent of delicate satire against the follies of the times. Then there were interspersed observations, speculations, and suggestions upon dress, fashions, food, dwellings, furniture, &c., &c., *sufficiently queer to keep the audience in almost constant mirth*. . . . The performance has created '*quite a sensation*' amongst Lyceum goers" (*Log*, 37; italics mine). If "Economy" was "sufficiently queer" to create "a sensation" with the public, a tamer lecture, which would become the chapter "Where I Lived, and What I Lived For," bored the audience with its quiescent accounts of nature's beauty and classical learning. This lecture, noted the *Observer*, was "less successful than the former one in pleasing all," because it was "rather too allegorical for a popular audience" (*Log*, 37).

Evidently aware of this popular preference for the sensational, Thoreau made sure to heighten this quality in his various revisions of *Walden* between 1847 and 1853. His description of the way his neighbors did penance was relatively bland in the original version, as he listed in his journal their self-inflicted problems. In the final version, he filled in the gory details of these penances, comparing his neighbors to torture victims suspended over fire, or chained for life to trees, or looking at the sky over the shoulder until only water passed down their twisted throats, and so on. As he was expanding his manuscript in 1852 and 1853, he added such dark or weird items as the battle of the ants, the hooting owl in "Sounds," the thawing sandbanks in "Spring," and the pursuit of the loon. Perhaps influenced by the Lippardian, Gothicized dark-reform rhetoric that blossomed in the late 1840s, his attacks on conventional, do-good reformers took on vitriol and grotesqueness in the later versions: among the added images was that of philanthropy as human and divine carrion, that of his fear of getting some reformer's virus mingled with his blood, and that of the Indians who mock the Jesuits by demanding that they increase their tortures.

Needless to say, Thoreau does with sensational images what no popular writer of the day did: he determinedly points them toward an affirmation of contemplative individualism and aesthetic perception. When he describes the news of Princess Adelaide's whooping cough coming by cable to the broad, flapping American ear, or people saluting a scarecrow wearing the latest shift, or American monkeys dutifully imitating the head fashion monkey in Paris, he is exploiting the kind of grotesque effects that insured the popularity of a Barnum or a Lippard; but he is using them in original ways, to endorse self-reliance and deep thinking.

Because he simultaneously used the sensational and redirected it, his prose lent itself to quotation in the popular press either for its sheer entertainment value or its philosophical import, or both. There were several other individualist anarchists of the day—Josiah Warren, Ezra Heywood, William B. Greene, and Benjamin Tucker—who held views quite similar to his but who received nowhere near the visibility he gained in popular periodicals, mainly because their prose was not as divertingly quotable as his. "We might easily fill a page," wrote the *Graham's* reviewer of *Walden*, "with short, sharp, quotable sentences, embodying some flash of wit or humor, some scrap of quaint or elevated wisdom, some odd or beautiful image. . . . Even its freaks of thought are full of suggestions. . . . If he has the wildness of the woods about him, he has their sweetness also."[43] This reviewer captured the dual nature of Thoreau's prose: its bizarre, sensational quality (registered in the words "wit or humor," "odd," "freaks of thought," "wildness"), which connected it to Barnumesque popular culture; and its idealistic quality ("elevated wisdom," "beautiful," "suggestions," "sweetness"), linking it to philosophy.

For several popular newspapers, it was the sensational Thoreau that proved particularly quotable. Among the strange or wild passages excerpted from his writings by contemporary newspapers were his fantasy of standing in a swamp "lulled by the minstrelsy of gnats and mosquitoes"; his confessions of savage instincts, such as "There is in my nature, methinks, a singular yearning toward all wildness" and "I grow savager and savager every day, as if fed on raw meat"; his intimations of perverse thoughts within all people, including "Nothing is ever so unfamiliar and startling to a man as his own thoughts"; and his humorously strange images, such as his comparison of a man with one idea to a hen with a chicken and of another with a thousand ideas to a centipede that makes you "crawl all over."[44]

If we study the arc of Thoreau's career, we find suggestions of his continuing interest in connecting with the popular audience—an interest that met with more success than is usually acknowledged. In his first effort at professional writing, when he was in New York in 1843 after having published only in the intellectual journal *The Dial*, he tried hard to become a popular periodical writer. He offered articles to *Democratic Review*, the *New Mirror*, the *Brother Jonathan*, and other periodicals but found that they were overwhelmed with contributions that cost nothing. "Literature comes to a poor market here," he wrote Emerson, "and even the little that I write is more than will sell." "*The Knickerbocker*," he reported, "is too poor, and only *The Ladies' Companion* pays," but, as he later told his mother, "I could not write anything companionable." He vented his frustrations with the popular press: "My bait will not tempt the rats,—they are too well fed." Altogether, his New York experience chastened his expectations of popular success.[45]

In time, however, these expectations were fulfilled in ways he could not have then anticipated. True, he had setbacks. His first volume, *A Week on the Concord and Merrimack Rivers*, sold so poorly that it provoked his defensive quip that after the publisher had sent him the unsold copies he owned a library of nine hundred volumes, over seven hundred of which he wrote himself.

But he approached popularity with the publicity surrounding *Walden*. Reports of his lectures about his pond years appeared not only in local papers like the *Salem Observer*, which described his making "quite a sensation," but also ones with much larger circulation. One of the Walden talks was noticed by the *New York Tribune*, which in April 1849 reported that Thoreau "has been lecturing on 'Life in the Woods,' in Portland and elsewhere. There is not a young man in the land—and very few old ones—who would not profit by an attentive hearing of that lecture" (*Log*, 41). Soon a public battle was raging over the value of Thoreau's hermitlike lifestyle. Shortly after defending Thoreau, the *Tribune* published an angry letter from a reader, calling himself Timothy Thorough, who lambasted Thoreau as "a good-for-nothing, selfish, crab-like sort of chap" who shirked life's normal duties. Other papers jumped into the fight (*Log*, 42). The Philadelphia *North American and Gazette* denounced the *Tribune* for endorsing Thoreau, asking, "What is such a solitary life, after all, but a voluntary abandonment of civilization and return to barbarism?" (*Log*, 44) This negative piece was reprinted in the Washington, D.C., *Daily National Intelligencer*, and the *Tribune* felt compelled to defend itself by insisting that Thoreau was a model for "a large class of young men who aspire to Mental Culture through Study, Reading, Reflection, &c." (*Log*, 42).

The controversy contributed to the visibility of *Walden*, which enjoyed a first-edition sale of two thousand copies. This figure was of course not close to that of best-selling novels such as Lippard's *The Quaker City*, which sold some 210,000 between 1845 and 1851, or Harriet Beecher Stowe's *Uncle Tom's Cabin*, which sold in the millions, but was respectable for a nonfiction volume. The newspaper squabble and the increasing sensationalism of the successive drafts of *Walden* were not the only factors behind its appeal. In 1852, as Thoreau was revising certain sections in the volume, he asked a fellow naturalist about examples of effective writing. He requested specifically for him "to direct me to those works which contained the more particular *popular* account, or *biography*, of particular flowers, from which the botanies I had met with appeared to draw sparingly" [Thoreau's italics]. At about the same time, he reported enjoying the very homeliest writings about rural life, as indicated by his declaration: "After having read various books on various subjects for some months, I take up a report on Farms by a committee of Middlesex Husbandmen [about bogs and cornfields] and I feel as if I had got my foot down to the solid and sunny earth, the basis of all philosophy, and poetry, and religion even."[46]

Several of his contemporaries noticed popular techniques in *Walden*. One reviewer stated flatly, "He coveted readers, and believed that he should have them," and another explained that he wrote *Walden* to satisfy "an inquiring public" and that "in the whole course of the book he keeps this audience in mind, goes out to meet it, and by a most conspicuously popular style adapts himself to it."[47]

Not only the relative success of *Walden* but, in a larger sense, Thoreau's whole posture as a writer and lecturer made him a more popular figure than is generally recognized. As an antislavery speaker he was considered a sufficiently lively crowd-pleaser to be asked once to stand in for the popular Frederick Douglass. Thoreau's impassioned speech on John Brown had obvious appeal for the mass readership, for it was chosen by James Redpath to be reprinted with other popular antislavery writings in *Echoes from Harper's Ferry* (1860), which speedily sold more than thirty thousand copies.

In spite of his early failures as a professional writer, in time he had signal success in placing his work with popular periodicals. Sections of the volume that would become *The Maine Woods* were originally published in the *Union Magazine* and the *Atlantic Monthly*. The first four chapters of *Cape Cod* appeared in *Putnam's*, chapters 5 and 8 in the *Atlantic*, and one segment was included in a popular giftbook, *Tales and Sketches from the Fire-Side. By the Best American Authors*. The majority of pieces later collected as *Excursions and Poems* and *Anti-Slavery and Reform Papers* had first appeared in periodicals that included the *Boston Miscellany*, *Graham's*, and the *Democratic Review*.

It would not be until the early twentieth century that he would appear in the literary canon, but his association with Walden Pond kept his name before the public eye. A series of travel articles describing Concord began appearing in popular newspapers in 1856, increasing in frequency as time passed. Although Concord's rich history, quiet beauty, and diverse literary community were mentioned, Thoreau was often the main pretext for these articles. In a front-page piece on September 5, 1856, a correspondent to the *National Intelligencer* wrote: "Near Concord is a beautiful pond called Walden. If the reader has not yet read Thoreau's 'Walden' he had best stop reading this letter now, and go and get it" (*Log*, 112). Thoreau's death in 1862 prompted a rash of enthusiastic articles, and by the end of the 1860s Walden had become a popular spot for picnickers and tourists. In 1866, the *National Anti-Slavery Standard* reported the tenth annual "Walden Pond Picnic," which attracted many from Boston and elsewhere who flocked in railroad cars for a rural outing. The next year's picnic featured a lecture by Alcott on Thoreau. In 1868 one paper called Walden "a famous place for pic-nics," and another reported: "Walden Pond seems to have lost nothing of its popularity as a summer resort. We learn that it is engaged for parties for every week day until the first of October, and if we mistake not an excursion train runs regularly from Boston for their accommodation" (*Log*, 187, 196). Swimming, boating, and swinging were favorite pastimes, and, in one reporter's words, "The bath houses resounded with scream and splash" (*Log*, 196).

Although the noisy activity doubtless made Thoreau roll in his grave, he would have derived some satisfaction in seeing Walden become what one reporter called "this American Mecca" (*Log*, 233). The pond's fame was increased in 1869 by a series of articles in the *New York Times* about Edmond S. Hotham, a would-be Thoreau who built a cabin near the spot where Thoreau's had stood and who lived there on a diet of boiled corn mush. Using boards from Thoreau's old family home in Concord, which was being torn down, Hotham built a cabin for just over $15 and survived there on just $1 a month—almost twice as cheaply as Thoreau had two decades earlier. Inside the cabin, Hotham had a modest stove, a rough cupboard, a couple of stools, a few utensils, and a straw-covered wooden bed that doubled by day as a desk. Not only the *Times* but other papers took note of Hotham, who in 1870 disseminated advice through the *Tribune*: "Mr. Hotham, whose cabin now stands where Thoreau built his cottage, recommends the young men of New York, through the columns of the Tribune, to follow his example, and, when their money is little and daily growing less, to betake themselves to the woods to live by their own labor, and without running to the tailor or the hotel-keeper" (*Log*, 223).

But if Hotham, like Thoreau, wanted to appeal to a mass audience, he failed to use Thoreau's main device for doing so: prose that absorbed popular images and that lived for future generations to enjoy. Shortly after Thoreau's death, a newspaper essayist predicted that Thoreau would "probably, by means of the press, become more familiar to the generation that succeeds him than he was to those in whose neighborhood his life was past" (*Log*, 156). This prediction proved accurate. Thoreau's writings were the subject of regular newspaper commentary throughout the 1860s and 1870s. In 1870 it was reported: "Certainly, Thoreau is the representative American hermit, and perhaps the richest character that ever lived in Concord. . . . Thoreau's books are fast gaining in popular favor" (*Log*, 235).

"Representative hermit": an oxymoron that neatly captures the spirit of the arch-individualist who, on a deep level, wanted to represent the American masses.

NOTES

1. See Lawrence Levine, *Highbrow/Lowbrow: The Emergence of Cultural Hierarchy in America* (Cambridge, Mass., 1988).
2. See especially Richard F. Teichgraeber III, *Sublime Thoughts/Penny Wisdom: Situating Emerson and Thoreau in the American Market* (Baltimore, 1995); Leonard Neufeldt, *The Economist: Henry Thoreau and Enterprise* (New York, 1989); Steven Fink, *Prophet in the Marketplace: Thoreau's Development as a Professional Writer* (Princeton, 1992); and David S. Reynolds, *Beneath the American Renaissance: The Subversive Imagination in the Age of Emerson and Melville* (New York, 1988).
3. F. O. Matthiessen, *American Renaissance: Art and Expression in the Age of Emerson and Whitman* (New York, 1941), 98.
4. Quoted in Michael Paul Rogin, *Subversive Genealogy: The Politics and Art of Herman Melville* (New York, 1983), 73.
5. Quoted in *The Native Muse: Theories of American Literature*, ed. Richard Ruland (New York, 1972), 1:302, 305.
6. Ralph Waldo Emerson, *Emerson in His Journals*, ed. Joel Porte (Cambridge, Mass., 1982), 344.
7. Ralph Waldo Emerson, *The Early Lectures of Ralph Waldo Emerson*, ed. Stephen E. Whicher and Robert E. Spiller (Cambridge, Mass., 1966–1972), 1:284, 285, 2:62.
8. Ralph Waldo Emerson, *Essays and Lectures*, ed. Joel Porte (New York, 1983), 634, 641, 728.
9. Emerson, *Early Lectures*, 1:300, 316; Emerson, *Essays and Lectures*, 712, 711.
10. Ralph Waldo Emerson, *The Journals and Miscellaneous Notebooks of Ralph Waldo Emerson*, ed. Alfred R. Ferguson et al. (Cambridge, Mass, 1960–1982), 4:297. Hereafter cited as *JMN*.
11. Ralph Waldo Emerson, *The Complete Works of Ralph Waldo Emerson* (New York, 1968), 7:11; Emerson, *Emerson in His Journals*, 240–241, 218.

12. See George Campbell, *The Philosophy of Rhetoric* (1776; Carbondale, Ill., 1963), 111, and Hugh Blair, *Lectures on Rhetoric and Belles Lettres* (1783; Philadelphia, 1860), 314.

13. Emerson, *Complete Works*, 10:333; Emerson, *Emerson in His Journals*, 38, 43, 46; Ralph Waldo Emerson, *Young Emerson Speaks*, ed. Arthur C. McGiffert (Boston, 1938), 28.

14. Walt Whitman, *Prose Works, 1892*, ed. Floyd Stovall (New York, 1964), 2:549.

15. Quoted in Robert Collyer, *Father Taylor* (Boston, 1906), 49, 55.

16. *JMN*, 7:360; Collyer, *Father Taylor*, 51; Emerson, *Essays and Lectures*, 260, 261; Ralph Waldo Emerson to William Emerson, Jan. 7, 1835, in *The Letters of Ralph Waldo Emerson*, ed. Ralph L. Rusk (New York, 1939–), 1:431; *JMN*, 5:255, 287, 9:236.

17. Emerson, *Essays and Lectures*, 34–35; Emerson, *Early Lectures*, 3:362.

18. The quotations in this and the following paragraph are from the "Divinity School Address," in *Essays and Lectures*, 84, 85, 75, 91, 80, and 91.

19. Emerson, *Essays and Lectures*, 135, 158, 159.

20. Emerson, *Complete Works*, 7:95; Emerson, *Emerson in His Journals*, 169.

21. Emerson, *Essays and Lectures*, 262, 549; Emerson, *Early Lectures*, 3:259, 257.

22. Emerson, *Essays and Lectures*, 162.

23. Emerson, *Essays and Lectures*, 127.

24. Emerson, *Essays and Lectures*, 146.

25. Quoted in *Emerson among His Contemporaries: A Harvest of Estimates, Insights, and Anecdotes from the Victorian Literary World*, ed. Kenneth Walter Cameron (Hartford, 1967), 106, 115.

26. Emerson, *Early Lectures*, 1:224.

27. Emerson, *Essays and Lectures*, 1250.

28. James Russell Lowell, *Literary Essays* (Boston, 1892), 353; *Emerson among His Contemporaries*, 28, 43.

29. Emerson, *Emerson in His Journals*, 6. The subsequent quotations in this and the following paragraph are on 58, 127, and 140.

30. See Kennth Walter Cameron, *Transcendental Log: Fresh Discoveries in Newspapers Concerning Emerson, Thoreau, Alcott and Others of the American Literary Renaissance, Arranged Annually for Half a Century, from 1832* (Hartford, 1973), 51. Hereafter cited parenthetically in the text as *Log*.

31. Emerson, *Complete Works*, 7:165; Emerson, *Emerson in His Journals*, 433, 39, 301.

32. Emerson, *Complete Works*, 10:457.

33. Henry David Thoreau, *The Writings of Henry David Thoreau* (New York, 1982), 6:138.

34. Henry David Thoreau, *The Journal of Henry David Thoreau*, ed. Bradford Torrey and Francis H. Allen (New York, 1962), 356, 726.

35. Thoreau, *Writings*, 1:154; Henry David Thoreau, *Early Essays and Miscellanies*, ed. Joseph J. Moldenhauer and Edwin Moser (Princeton, 1975), 226, 234.

36. Thoreau, *Journal* (1962), 157.

37. Thoreau, *Early Essays*, 39; Thoreau, *Writings*, 6:33.

38. Henry David Thoreau, *Journal*, ed. John C. Broderick et al. (Princeton, 1984), 2:293, 301.

39. Thoreau, *Journal* (1962), 467; Thoreau, *Writings*, 5:231; Thoreau, *Journal* (1962), 144, 182; Thoreau, *Journal* (1984), 1:481.

40. Quoted in *The Recognition of Henry David Thoreau: Selected Criticism Since 1848*, ed. Wendell Glick (Ann Arbor, 1969), 5, 40.

41. Thoreau, *Writings*, 6:220; Thoreau, *Journal* (1962), 7:7–8.

42. J. Lyndon Shanley, *The Making of* Walden *with the Text of the First Edition* (Chicago, 1957), 18.

43. Quoted in *Recognition of . . . Thoreau*, 5.

44. These and other quoted passages are summarized in Kenneth Walter Cameron, *Literary Comment in American Renaissance Newspapers: Fresh Discoveries Concerning Emerson, Thoreau, Alcott* (Hartford, 1977), 37–49.

45. Thoreau, *Writings*, 6:107, 107–108.

46. Thoreau, *Journal* (1962), 3:280, 327.

47. Quoted in *Recognition of . . . Thoreau*, 149, 131.

Transcendentalism in Print

Production, Dissemination, and Common Reception

RONALD J. ZBORAY AND
MARY SARACINO ZBORAY

"THIS DAY HAS PASSED AWAY WITH LITTLE TO DISTINGUISH IT
from other days," Mary Pierce wrote in 1838 during a stay at her sister's home in Bangor, Maine, "save that I have been reading some dozen
pages in Mr Emerson's 'Nature,' which I know not how sufficiently to admire. If this be transcendentalism," she continued, as if entranced, "may I
have my heart and head embued with so bewitching a philosophy."[1] As this
otherwise mundane letter reveals, *Nature* had wended its way from the
Frederic Henry Hedge household into Mary's hands and transformed her
potentially unremarkable day into a memorable one. This teenaged daughter of the Reverend John Pierce, a Unitarian more conservative than the
Transcendentalist Hedge, might not have so easily happened upon Emerson's work while at her father's home in Brookline, Massachusetts.[2] Without
venturing her interpretation of the text, perhaps in deference to Pierce,
Mary went on to ask "Has father read it?" Despite her hesitancy to expound,
she nonetheless felt moved to document her enthusiasm for the book. In so
doing, she left a small, but significant record of the production, dissemination, and common reception of Transcendentalism in print in antebellum
New England.[3]

This example represents only one of many encounters with Transcendentalist texts among antebellum New England readers. Some New Englanders, like Mary Pierce, crossed paths with Transcendentalists and
offered comments; others, who never traveled within such circles, also had
something to say. Though generally not so eloquent or receptive to this
"new philosophy" as Pierce, a diverse set of New Englanders remarked
upon Transcendentalist texts in the letters they habitually wrote and in the
blank-book journals they routinely filled. While these observations laced
through correspondence and diaries of the time period, they vied for space

with other matters that often overwhelmed the text of personal accounts. As Pierce observed, "little" did "distinguish" one day from another when people filled the pages with concerns of everyday life: occupations, religion, education, families, and friends.[4] At times even reading became routine and habitual, leading New Englanders to the Bible, "useful" texts like spellers, and the classics. As such, the printed word seldom challenged tradition and often reaffirmed beliefs. Little wonder that specific references to Transcendentalism bury themselves, like needles within haystacks of personal testimony. But every now and then people came across something disturbing or, conversely, "bewitching," by writers such as Ralph Waldo Emerson, Henry David Thoreau, Margaret Fuller, or Theodore Parker. At times, these readers felt moved, like Mary Pierce, to write about their experience. It is to these experiences that we devote this essay. Before we turn to discussing their accounts of textual reception, dissemination, and production, however, we will explain our methodology and introduce these readers of Transcendentalism.

Methods

Our approach to studying Transcendentalism in print begins with readers and not with authors or publishers. Texts and the circumstances of their production provide the usual starting point for analyses of print culture.[5] Indeed, most scholarship on Transcendentalism centers on the authorial biography of canonical writers, like Emerson or Thoreau, and close textual analysis of their published work.[6] Information about publication and dissemination usually remains relegated to footnotes, bibliographies, or articles in scholarly journals specializing in the topic or period.[7] The small body of reception studies seldom pursues the text to the ultimate reader, but tends to stop at reviews or other notices in periodicals.[8] Studies on influences from within Transcendentalism (and from British and Continental Romantics upon it) are more numerous.[9] Insofar as these provide intellectual context for possible readers of Transcendentalist works they hint at the general nature of the potential reading public but give little conclusive evidence to connect specific texts and readers.[10] A few researchers, inspired by developments in literary theory and the history of the book, have addressed the reader (or reading) in their interpretation of Transcendentalist texts and authorial intention; however, these constructions of readership principally depend on internal textual evidence.[11]

While we acknowledge the great value of these authorial or textual inquiries for shedding light on Transcendentalist writing, we venture here a reader-centered approach to Transcendentalism in print. Instead of analyzing Transcendentalist books, poetry, essays, or sermons, we consulted manuscripts authored by common readers[12] in the hope of discovering the meaning of Transcendentalism within the context of the person's everyday life.[13] Our methodology, which entails transcribing significant biographical events, along with any and all references to the reception, dissemination, and production of printed material, allows for this contextualization. Thus, the end product of our research transcends analysis of mere rosters of titles wrenched from personal meaning. This approach offers an opportunity to relocate the site of the cultural production of meaning from the text itself (and all that implies about authorship, publishing, and marketing) to the interaction between text and reader.[14] The evidence, of course, is but a self-representation of that interaction, but it is the closest we can come to understanding the significance for readers, short of interviewing them.

As we read through about 320 sets of these personal manuscripts authored by New Englanders living between 1830 and 1861, we extracted whatever is mentioned about Transcendentalism within the everyday context of getting books (or other printed items) and reading them.[15] We discovered readers of Transcendentalism appearing in just under half of the thirty manuscript repositories we visited, mostly throughout New England (Table 1).

This larger project, a book-length study of popular literary experience in antebellum New England, entails developing a geographically and socially representative selection of manuscript personal records of encounters with the printed word. We transcribe verbatim every record of such an encounter and its context. More than 800 "informants" report on their own reading patterns and those of family and friends—roughly two thousand people who have contributed collectively over 100,000 separate encounters with print.[16] While diaries and letters provide our principal source (736 and 2,669 items, respectively), we are also looking at lists of books read, postmaster's subscriptions, amateur newspapers (in manuscript and print), general store accounts, and library charge records (Table 1). Evidence of literary encounters has appeared in 3,546 separate manuscript items from throughout the first six decades of the nineteenth century, with 32 percent and 40 percent respectively concentrated in the 1840s and 1850s (Table 2). Almost 60 percent of the documents originating from New England come from the Boston region (the eastern Massachusetts counties, including eastern Worcester County, as well as Rockingham County, New Hampshire), where in 1850, about 31 percent of New England's population resided.[17] Within the Boston region we have data from all counties and most of the 219 cities and towns. In fact, relevant documents originate from all 64 counties in the rest of New England, with the exception of Piscataquis County in Maine; Coos and Strafford counties in New Hampshire; Bennington, Grand Isle, and LaMoille counties in Vermont; and Washington County in Rhode Island. Our documentation does not stop at New York's eastern border, however, for we follow antebellum New Englanders in their characteristic roamings across the United States to California and around the world, from China to Persia to England (and a little over 1 percent comes from informants at sea). About 20 percent of our documents originate from outside of New England.

Rampant horizontal mobility conspires with the ups and downs of social mobility that attended New England's antebellum industrialization and intensifying agricultural commercialization to frustrate any attempt to place our informants into tidy socioeconomic niches in a solid wall of social structure.[18] That informants of very different social positions can report on the reading of others further complicates matters. And occupations may change over time, as may, particularly, women's wealth and status after marriage, spousal abandonment or disability, or widowhood.[19] In the face of this complexity, we have striven to represent the broadest occupational range permitted by the type of sources we employ, meaning personally written accounts. This limits our informants to those with the reading and writing skills, minimal disposable income, cultural predisposition, and leisure time to keep diaries or engage in the type of correspondence that registers reading patterns. Though this wide net can include just about every New Englander but indigent illiterates, in reality our sample is not "from the bottom up"; rather, "from just above the bottom and to the top and everywhere in between" more accurately characterizes it.[20] We have testimony from captains and seamen, housewives and servants, schoolchildren and teachers, factory operatives and owners, apprentices and masters, hardscrabble and gentry farmers, clerks and storekeepers, businessmen and bankers, petty and grand politicians, former slaves and newly transplanted masters, impecunious and well-to-do clergymen, Irish immigrants and nativists, toddlers holding their first book and octogenarians their last. Every major religious denomination active in the region at the time is represented, as are even many minor ones, like the Swedenborgians. Whigs, Democrats, Republicans, Free-Soilers, partisans of every other stripe, and the seemingly apolitical are here, too.

Needless to say, with this scope and depth of coverage, our Transcendentalist subset represents but one stream in an ocean of information, perhaps less than 1 percent of our total universe of literary encounters. Below, we offer some observations about the relationship between our larger set

TABLE 1. Sources of Manuscript Materials Consulted in Which Reading Occurs

Abbreviation[1]		Repository	Diaries+	Letters+	Other=	Items>	Collections
AAS	1	American Antiquarian Society	50	282	8	340	25
	2	American Jewish Historical Society[2]	0	0	1	1	1
	3	American Textile History Museum	1	18	0	19	6
	4	Andover Historical Society	0	35	0	35	3
	5	Archives, College of the Holy Cross	1	0	0	1	1
	6	Archives of the Archdiocese of Boston	2	20	2	24	1
FCCS	7	Archives, First Church of Christ, Scientist	0	0	1	1	1
	8	Beverly Historical Society	10	25	3	38	8
BPL	9	Boston Public Library	28	123	4	155	3
CHS	10	Connecticut Historical Society	86	15	4	105	39
	11	Connecticut State Library	17	7	4	28	13
	12	John J. Burns Library, Boston College	2	34	1	37	1
	13	Lexington Historical Society	6	0	0	6	3
	14	Library of Congress	0	60	0	60	1
	15	Lynn Historical Society	15	0	0	15	4
MeHS	16	Maine Historical Society	32	61	10	103	9

17		Marblehead Historical Society	1	4	4	9	6
18	MHS	Massachusetts Historical Society	79	64	9	152	21
19		New England Historic Genealogical Society	19	49	1	69	10
20		New Hampshire Historical Society	157	3	7	167	29
21	OCHS	Old Colony Historical Society	6	0	1	7	7
22	PEM	Peabody Essex Museum	24	49	1	74	15
23		Providence Public Library	0	9	0	9	4
24	RIHS	Rhode Island Historical Society	70	39	4	113	13
25	SL	Schlesinger Library, Radcliffe College	43	1,050	38	1,131	35
26	SC	Sophia Smith Collection, Smith College	6	587	11	604	7
27	SCHS	South Carolina Historical Society	0	25	1	26	1
28	VHS	Vermont Historical Society	70	85	21	176	15
29	YU-B	Yale University, Beinecke Library	1	24	5	30	2
30		Yale University, Sterling Memorial Library	10	1	0	11	3
		TOTAL	736	2,669	141	3,546	320

[1] Abbreviations are given only for archives containing manuscript material that reports reading of Transcendentalist texts. All of these repositories with abbreviations are cited in our notes.

[2] The hundreds of books we examined for inscriptions in this collection have been counted as one item in order to avoid inflating overall figures.

TABLE 2. Decadal Distribution of Manuscript
Items in Which Reading Occurs

Decade	Diaries+	Letters+	Other=	Items
Before 1830	48	153	10	211
1830s	178	557	29	764
1840s	201	888	51	1,140
1850–1 May 1861	309	1,071	48	1,428
After 1 May 1861	0	0	3	3
TOTAL	736	2,669	141	3,546

and the Transcendentalist subset, but since our analysis of the whole is ongoing, what we say is necessarily suggestive and preliminary—and subject to future revision. In any case, such quantitative dimensions provide but the backdrop for our study, for our method is qualitative insofar as it depends upon a close textual reading of the common readers' testimony in manuscripts.

We consult manuscript rather than printed diaries and letters because much of the latter was written by prominent figures who might not represent the experiences of more common readers. Moreover, the most useful personal accounts contain repetitive entries of daily reading, which discourage publication of the entire document. Even handwriting and page formatting contain important clues about a writer's state of mind when recording acts of reading; transcription for publication often obscures this evidence, while we can take note of these features if they seem significant.

By confronting manuscripts in this manner, we are, in essence, treating our diarists and correspondents as "dead informants" and ourselves as participant-observers.[21] We not only observe people reading, but participate in the informant's own literary self-representation through our reading of the diary or letter. Although we are amassing much information about who read what when and where, our primary goal is to understand how these people read and, above all, what it meant to them. In short, we are employing the "dual strategy," recommended by Robert Darnton, "which . . . combine[s] textual analysis with empirical research." We depart, however, from Darnton and many reader-response practitioners, such as Wolfgang Iser, in that our close readings are applied not to "implied" readers in print, but to texts created by readers themselves. Indeed, as we will show, the rich and varied responses of readers of Transcendentalism give us particular occasion for textual analysis.[22]

TABLE 3. Materials Bearing Testimony of Reading by Place of Origin[1]

Origin	Number	Subtotal	% of All	% U.S.	% New England
Boston Region[2]	1,670		47.09	51.94	59.37
Other New England	1,143		32.23	35.53	+40.63
All New England		2,813			100.00
Other Northeast[3]	185		5.22	5.75	
South[4]	163		4.60	5.06	
West[5]	56		+1.58	+1.74	
States Beyond New England		+404			
All U.S.		3,217	90.72	100.00	
Other countries[6]	256		7.22		
At sea	40		+1.13		
Non-U.S.		296	8.34		
Unknown	+33	+33	+.93		
All	3,546	3,546	100.00		

---

[1] For diaries written in several locations, only the principal place of origin is used.

[2] Includes the Massachusetts counties of Barnstable, Bristol, Essex, Middlesex, Norfolk, Plymouth, Suffolk, and the eastern half of Worcester, as well as Rockingham County, New Hampshire. Francis X. Blouin, Jr., *The Boston Region, 1810-1850: A Study of Urbanization* (Ann Arbor, Mich., 1980), 23.

[3] Includes material from Delaware, New Jersey, New York, and Pennsylvania.

[4] Includes material from Alabama, District of Columbia, Florida, Georgia, Kentucky, Louisiana, Maryland, Mississippi, Missouri, North Carolina, South Carolina, and Texas.

[5] Includes material from California, Illinois, Indiana, Kansas, Michigan, Ohio, and Wisconsin.

[6] Includes Argentina, Australia, Austria, Azores, Canada, China, Cuba, Egypt, England, France, Germany, Greece, Haiti, Hawaii, Ireland, Italy, the Netherlands, Palestine, Persia, Portugal, Scotland, Spain, and Switzerland.

In pursuit of these readers' testimonies, we faced one final methodological hurdle. Works specifically deemed "Transcendentalist" required
identification within the mass of imprints we located. In scouting out that
nebulous set of titles, authors, and publishers which frustrates attempts to
contain its boundaries, we avoided both an overly inclusive (and virtually
limitless) roster as well as a narrow focus upon the most indisputably Transcendentalist works. While we approached the manuscripts with some
definition of Transcendentalism in mind,[23] we ultimately allowed the
antebellum New England reader to determine the boundaries between
the movement and other literary expressions. Although the readers were
likely to mention the prominent authors—Emerson, Thoreau, Margaret
Fuller, and Theodore Parker—rather than more obscure ones—contemporaries struggled to apply concrete definitions and meaning to Transcendentalism as they tussled with its ambiguities or sought to know more
about its producers.

The Readers

The few readers of Transcendentalist texts among our 822 historical informants were in some ways different and in others exemplary of the whole.
Some of the more persistent readers were relatively obscure people of various professions and income levels, who professed Unitarianism (or with
leanings in that direction) and had familial or social ties to Transcendentalists, like Mary Pierce, whom we have already met. As the daughter of a minister, she lived comfortably, but certainly not luxuriously. She eventually
married a lawyer and editor of *The American Railroad Journal*, Henry Varnum Poor; the union allowed her to lead a more affluent, domestic life in
Bangor, Maine, and New York City. Separated from her family, she
nonetheless maintained an affectionate relationship with her father until
his death in 1849, and kept peace within a family riven by religious faction-
ing: her mother's Tappan kin pulled two of Mary's sisters toward orthodoxy,
while another sister became a Baptist. Mary herself hovered between her
father's beliefs and even greater religious liberalism. She explored Universalism and Spiritualism during the 1850s as a vehicle for reaching the
deceased Pierce.[24] Another reader of Transcendentalism who fits the above
description was Daniel Franklin Child, an upwardly mobile clerk who lived
in his widowed sister's house in Boston with his wife and children. Child, a
more radical-leaning Unitarian than Poor, belonged to Theodore Parker's
Twenty-eighth Congregational Society in Boston; he was so familiar with
the works of his pastor and others that he might justifiably be called a "Tran-

scendentalist consumer" of literature. A dedicated abolitionist, he joined Parker's Vigilance Committee, following the reformist minister's lead to free the "fugitive slave" Anthony Burns on May 26, 1854.[25] In Worcester, John Park, after sixty-one years of leading an exciting life as a surgeon in the U.S. Navy, a publisher of the Boston *Repertory*, and founder of the Boston Lyceum for Young Ladies, resumed his literary diary in 1836 following decades of neglect. In it, he wrestled with the very Transcendentalist philosophy that captivated his former pupil, whose death he solemnly recorded on July 23, 1850: Margaret Fuller Ossoli. Having so much leisure time, Park devoted most of his days to reading and discussion with his family, friends, and fellow congregants at Aaron Bancroft's (later, Alonzo Hill's) Second Parish.[26] Finally, Elizabeth Dwight, who belonged to Ephraim Peabody's congregation at King's Chapel (*i.e.*, Stone Chapel), Boston, where she was married in 1857, had her own thoughts on the Transcendentalist friends of her husband James Elliot Cabot, a lawyer and editor, who let Emerson borrow his copy of the Bhagavad Gita in 1845 and eventually became his literary executor and biographer. Elizabeth recorded her response to Transcendentalism in copious letters, and she mailed pieces of Transcendentalist literature to Ellen (Dwight) Twisleton who lived, much to her devoted sister's chagrin, in England with her husband, Edward.[27]

For these and a few others, literary encounters with Transcendentalism were relatively extensive; however, within our pool of reader informants, most of those who read Transcendentalist works dipped into them only once or twice. The social nature of reading in antebellum New England accounts for much of this. By the outbreak of the Civil War, reading was still mostly a communal activity. Women listened to neighbors read while they sewed, fathers read out loud to wives and children, and benevolent organizations sponsored social occasions in which reading provided entertainment while people handcrafted items for charity. Furthermore, frequent gift giving and book borrowing brought New Englanders into a social network of reading, much in the way that Cabot connected with Emerson over the Bhagavad Gita.[28] If people shied away from a foray into Transcendentalism or failed to sustain a reading diet of such works, their social groups were perhaps not ripe for such ventures. It is not surprising that many of those who rarely read a Transcendentalist work, or came across one unexpectedly, lived well outside the Boston area and were not even tangentially part of the Transcendentalist circles that flourished there and in Concord—the very relations that often nourished people's reading of Emerson, Parker, and Fuller.

Insofar as people read Transcendentalist texts in shorter formats ranging from mere fillers in periodicals to thin pamphlets, it discouraged a systematic engagement with the full philosophical import of the movement.[29] Rather, readers often became acquainted with Transcendentalism in a piecemeal manner that did not preclude an enjoyment of decidedly non-Transcendentalist material. For many people outside of the literary networks that encouraged reading Transcendentalism, periodicals or daily newspapers with book reviews and accounts of public lectures acted as agents of the movement. Subscribers "accidentally" encountered pieces by and about Emerson or Thoreau and then often read or passed on these writings to others. Indeed, New Englanders subscribed to many periodicals that occasionally published Transcendentalist literature and they referred to specific reviews or other pieces in such journals as the *Dial*, the *Christian Examiner*, the *Atlantic Monthly*, and the New York *Tribune*. No doubt these fragments, fillers, excerpts, sermons, newspaper columns, and pamphlets contributed to a composite image of Transcendentalism in the minds of readers. As we will see, these readers in their letters and diaries recognized Transcendentalism as its own distinct stream in the manifold course of their literary encounters.

Whatever the means by which readers of Transcendentalism procured their texts, they, as a subset of our larger population of New England readers, remain difficult to characterize as sociologically unique among their well-read contemporaries. They worked in various occupations, as domestic laborers, clerks, and mill operatives; some were professionals, like teachers and lawyers, and some had lives of relative leisure. As we have seen, the more persistent readers intersected with social circles exposed to Transcendentalists. These readers also had a tendency to espouse liberal Protestant creeds, particularly Unitarianism. But, here again, the boundaries dissolve into the larger universe of New Englanders who left documents of their reading experiences in general. We have found that most of the prolific, open-minded, vocal, and lively readers (and, consequently, useful as informants), hailed from urban areas, especially the Boston region and that they, too, professed liberal Protestant, if not always Unitarian, creeds. This impression, based upon our larger work in progress, conforms to Daniel Walker Howe's insight that "Liberal Christians were among the leaders in that campaign to develop an American literary culture. . . . It is safe to say that no other religious denomination in the country devoted so large a proportion of its energies to literary activity, or reposed so much confidence in belles lettres."[30] Therefore, if we draw any conclusions about religion and the reading experience of New Englanders in general, and readers of Transcendentalism in particular, we draw from the same pool.

But any fixed generalizations about religious affiliation and reading

Transcendentalism are liable to crumble under close scrutiny. First of all, readers of Transcendentalism were not unique for their tendency to read about and embrace liberal creeds, nor were their lives entirely untouched by orthodoxy. Although they, along with an ever increasing number of Congregationalists, rejected orthodoxy throughout the first half of the nineteenth century, many were brought up in such a climate.[31] "The truth was," John Park, a Unitarian for most of his life, disclosed, "I had been educated in the dogmas of Calvinism, as essential points of Christian belief." For him, as no doubt for others, "Reading and reflection had induced me to abandon them as shocking to reason, and incompatible with our notions of the attributes of Deity."[32] But Sarah Smith Browne, a Salem, Massachusetts, matron who admired Theodore Parker, saw her own abandonment of Calvinism within the greater evolution of Congregationalism towards liberalism, not as the result of a program of study. In 1855 she could presume: "Dr. [Samuel] Hopkins would have *now* but few disciples. Heaven be praised for so much progress! In childhood, I played with the 'History of the Devil,' yet I came out, *intuitively*, on the *liberal side*."[33] Sometimes those who abandoned conservative doctrine still read conservative productions. Park, for example, reviewed, no doubt with a critical eye, his copy of Jonathan Edwards's *Freedom of the Will* in 1847 and lent it out a few times to other interested neighbors.[34] By and large, however, it was the more conservative Congregationalists, but also ministers, who still read the "New Divinity Men" (alongside other works, of course) during the period under study here.[35]

Further complicating any notions of religious determinism in defining readership of Transcendentalist works is the nagging presence of exceptions to the rule. Although most of these readers tended toward Unitarianism or were Unitarians, not all were, of course. For example, J. Edwin Harris, whom we will meet, worked as a factory operative in Biddeford and Saco, Maine, and was a Methodist who frequented Evangelical camp meetings with his sisters. He lost much of his devotion after a favorite minister left the area: "I shall not go [to the Methodist vestry] again very soon—I hate every one that goes there except Mr Sanderson who I respect, reverence, admire, and Love— . . . . now he is going away and I will stay at home—'I will bury myself in my books and the Devil may pipe to his own.'"[36]

The ecumenical spirit with which many New Englanders approached the practice of religious beliefs further complicates matters, making it often impossible to assign religious affiliation. Some of this openness was due to necessity, for in frontier areas New Englanders were often happy to have any regular clergyman at all. As one Unitarian reader (albeit not of

Transcendentalism) living in Dixfield, Maine, said of the "Orthodox Minister" engaged by her congregation: "He is better than no minister." Some New Englanders availed themselves of diverse meetinghouses and concurrently attended services of different denominations.[37] Christopher Keith attended several churches in or around Providence, sometimes for unexpected reasons. "Went to meeting . . . at Seekonk, having gone there for that purpose, and the walk," he recorded on Sunday, August 30, 1857. During the next year he "Attended the Central Baptist Church," but also "went to meeting . . . at the Quaker Church" and "attended Union Prayer Meeting for the first time." A month after he "Attended the Rev Mr Richards church," Keith listened to a spiritualist lecture on a Sunday evening. Despite Keith's general adherence to organized religion, he confessed on May 23, 1858 to a streak of pantheism:

> Sinful though it may be, I like to be in the quiet stillness of the woods on Sunday, for I feel that God is there as well as in the church. Where the soul is in the right frame and spirit, God will be with it, whether on the mountain, in the desert, in the woods or on the stormy ocean.

Keith's reading list (promiscuous, but no more so than that of many antebellum readers) further frustrates attempts to encapsulate his religious practices. After opening his journal with excerpts from Emerson's essays, he recorded regular reading of chapters in the Bible, Peter Bayne's *The Christian Life*, Andrew Jackson Davis's *The Great Harmonia*, Philip Doddridge's *The Rise and Progress of Religion in the Soul*, Henry Duncan's *Sacred Philosophy of the Seasons*, Edmund H. Sears's *Athanasia*, Jeremy Taylor's *Rules for Holy Living*, and James Walker's *The Philosophy of Skepticism*. Within this amorphous roster of religious titles Keith also grappled with Edwardsian orthodoxy while composing his thoughts on man's moral nature: "Dr [Timothy] Dwight says 'The human character is never depraved to the full extent of the human powers.'"[38]

This hunger for multifarious religious reading matter hardly denoted readers of Transcendentalism, for it characterized many of New England's literary enthusiasts, who embraced the work of Archbishop François de Salignac de La Mothe Fénelon, Francis Wayland, as well as Judaica and Swedenborgian and Spiritualist writings. But these well-versed New Englanders were eclectic in their reading anyway, religious or otherwise. Many savored British and German Romantics (*e.g.*, Carlyle, Coleridge, and especially Goethe) as much as or more than the American authors they inspired. Consequently, learning German and writing translations occupied much reading time. Conversely, readers of Transcendentalist texts sometimes showed little interest in German (or only indirectly, such as through Philip James Bailey's *Festus*, a verse-drama inspired by Goethe's *Faust*) and, of course, not everyone who read German literature was led to American Transcendentalism.[39] A similarly broad contextual pattern exists for literature at the opposite end of the scale: cheap pamphlet novels and sensationalistic literature that lay "beneath the American Renaissance." Elite and working-class New Englanders read Eugene Sue's crime novels, including the *Mysteries of Paris* (John Park remarked that "though the characters are many of them low and disgusting, virtue has some recompense"), and Joseph Holt Ingraham's yellow-cover romances, for example, alongside Transcendentalist texts.[40] And, Emerson and Thoreau derived inspiration from the same well of popular culture that entertained their reading audience.[41]

The eclecticism that allowed New Englanders to read popular novels, European Romanticism, and a variety of theological writings also led them to Eastern texts, although not always in the self-reflexive way in which Transcendentalists embraced "Orientalism."[42] Caroline Sturgis, a Transcendentalist author, called upon such writings almost therapeutically: "I wish I had an Eastern Book to read," she implored of her friend Ralph Waldo Emerson, "—a new publication by an old Hindoo. Perhaps you will send me one or two to keep until the birds sing again. I will promise to read them, homeopathically—three drops of this essence in one tumbler of cold water."[43] But most common interest registered through travel books on South and East Asia, missionary reports, and philosophical works that all fell into New Englanders' hands; furthermore, lectures on the topic attracted several people who otherwise might not have read about the Orient.[44] After reading Howard Malcom's *Travels in South-Eastern Asia*, Louisa Waterhouse, who satirized Emerson in her diary, took copious notes on "Boodhism *in my own words*," but mysteriously crossed them out, writing: "No one wants to know Boodhism." Ellen Wright, a student at Mrs. Sedgwick's Academy in Lenox, Massachusetts, found Joguth Chunder Gangooly's *Life and Religion of the Hindoos* "very interesting . . . written in a style so quaint & clear." Enoch Hale, a Newburyport printer, borrowed *The Hindoos* from the Newburyport Atheneaum in 1843. Curiously, the religious affiliation of Raja Rammohun Roy, translator of several Hindu texts, led to a discussion one evening that left Harriet Low, a devout Salem Unitarian who took an interest in accounts of India, quite disturbed. When it was finally determined at a dinner party made up principally of British guests (Low lived in Macao, China, for three years) that Roy "was a *Unitarian*; he was not a *Christian* he was a *Deist*," Low confided to her diary: "It is rather galling to one to hear that you are not ranked among

Christians. ... I long to put Mr. Channing's Sermons into all their hands and open their understanding that they may understand."[45]

The somewhat surprising juxtaposition of Channing and Asian religion also settled upon the mind of John Park, who would later read Channing's works in six volumes. Commenting upon his sermon at the dedication of a Unitarian church in Newport, Rhode Island, Park detected a touch of eastern philosophy:

> the Doctor presses his favorite theme of the divinity of the human soul too far. His doctrine is nearly if not identically that of the ancient Brachman school, which represented the spiritual nature of man as an emanation of the Deity. The principal difference appears to be that the Eastern philosopher taught that at the death of the body the soul is reabsorbed into the Deity, becoming again one essence; whereas Dr Channing considers it as possessing an eternal individuality.[46]

Park, both well versed in theological debates and unusually prolific in his reading habits, stands out in this regard. Needless to say, however, some of those who engaged a Transcendentalist work ignored Eastern religions and indeed limited their religious readings altogether.

Within this universe of religious texts, the works of William Ellery Channing graced the reading lists of many New Englanders, including those who explored Transcendentalism. Few who read or heard him speak, even those who felt he strayed too far from moderation, failed to admire his eloquence. John Park, ever on the lookout for taints of Transcendentalist philosophy within Unitarianism, thought that "all the productions of [Channing's] pen" including the Newport sermon he criticized, were "able and impressive." Another Unitarian reader of Channing remarked that "It is the height of my ambition to write like him," and yet another that "The only fault one can find with his Sermons is they are not suited for vulgar minds." But Mellen Chamberlain, a Congregationalist who hoped to win the hand of a conservative Trinitarian could not fail to be swayed by his words:

> I hope she has no good reason to suspect that I am heterodox on the great articles of religious belief. If ever I find myself inclined to Unitarianism, it is that I am influenced by the practical piety of Channing and disgusted with the Intellectual pride of Andover. But I am not Unitarian.[47]

While Channing's works often became part of people's self-conscious attempts to adhere to a rigorous program of reading, few commented upon *Self-Culture*, the printed lecture delivered in Boston as part of the Franklin lectures (September 1838), or self-culture as a concept—"the care which every man owes to himself, to the unfolding and perfecting of his nature." Part of this perfection, according to Channing, depended upon reading habits. "Let every man, if possible, gather some good books under his roof, and obtain access for himself and family to some social library." The author and Democratic politician Alexander Hill Everett, who put Channing's words into practice by consulting a wide range of books, read "Dr Channing's lecture on Self-Culture aloud to wife" and deemed it "one of his best productions." Hannah Lowell Jackson, a friend of the Channing family, discussed self-culture with Channing himself during a visit to his Newport home: "what a delightful place this world would be, if people would be disinterestedly devoted, to self culture," she told him after he explained "that true self improvement is perfectly disinterested[;] it consists in a perfectly impartial love of truth & virtue in others as well as ourselves." Jackson was advised on how to put self-culture into action; Channing counseled her "to be reading some book wh. obliges me to think deeply & seemed to think that with the aid of a little method I could find an hour a day for such reading." But such good intentions were not always feasible for those who worked all day. One young man, engaged in setting up a time-consuming business of his own, wrote at the end of 1850: "I never saw so much as now, the importance of early self-culture and discipline." Exhausted by daily demands upon his energy and time, he wrote the next year: "too tired to read or hardly think. I dispair of self improvement."[48]

But reading was not the only way to self improvement. The venerable New England tradition of the Lyceum and public lecture introduced a variety of authors, including Transcendentalists, to those who might not read their works. Because this topic deserves its own treatment, we will not pursue it here, but certainly, many of those who recorded books they read also attended lectures. And clearly, more New Englanders recorded their responses to Transcendentalists' lectures than to their writings.[49]

With the above characteristics and qualifications of the New England readers of Transcendentalism in mind, we will now move on to their specific experiences with Transcendentalist texts. Below we discuss three different aspects of Transcendentalism in print: reception, dissemination, and production. In a reversal of the usual sequence and in keeping with our reader-centered approach, we begin with reception; from readers' remarks about a text, we discern some of their socioculturally constructed patterns of response. We then trace, in certain cases, the dissemination of texts from the reader to the source of distribution. For example, we find that many readers borrowed Transcendentalist texts from neighbors or family members. We conclude with the production of Transcendentalism as seen through the lens of the reader.

Reception

New England common readers responded to Transcendentalist texts in much the same way as they did other printed matter such as novels, travel accounts, religious works, art books, and history. They called upon a common discourse of response that developed within the literary conventions of letter writing, diary keeping, and published reviews to discuss the works of Emerson, Parker, Fuller, and Thoreau. The range of reactions encompassed a simple registering of titles read or borrowed; extracts of text copied in commonplace books; terse expressions of interest or disregard; judgments of verisimilitude and usefulness; invidious or favorable comparisons; curiosity about authors' lives; a text's instrumentality; opinions about writing style, readability, and language use; and, less often, imaginative discursions and philosophical ponderings about "meaning." This discourse of response, though generally universal for antebellum New England common readers, differed regarding Transcendentalist texts in two ways: first, readers usually augmented any quick declarations of interest with further explanation or more complex contradictory statements; second, readers seldom referred to verisimilitude or "usefulness." While readers overall applied these terms liberally to other works they read as a compliment to an author for imparting knowledge or supplying new information, common readers of Transcendentalist texts seldom found them to be particularly "useful" (*i.e.*, practical) or amenable to study. This comes as no surprise given the non-utilitarian nature of most Transcendentalist works and their departure from emulation of "real life."[50]

Within this range of responses, readers of Transcendentalism often called upon the simplest way to react in writing, which is noting a specific title—an elementary, but enduring testament to the text's impression upon the person's life. By recording a title (often in shortened form) and sometimes the author's name, frugal people could reserve space in their relatively expensive blank books for other everyday matters while creating a memory bank of reading. One schoolteacher, forced by necessity to borrow and excerpt books rather than buy them, explained: "But I must stop or I might transcribe [passages from texts] till my little book were filled, but this is not the purpose of my *Diary*, though I think it well that these beautiful things be interwoven into the texture of our daily lives."[51] Daniel

Child, who seldom missed a day of record keeping in his diary, apparently followed this example, for he rarely used space to quote or comment upon texts he read, although he did sometimes expound at length about the sermons he heard delivered on Sunday by Theodore Parker and his guests at the Melodeon (or Music Hall) in Boston. For about twenty-two years, Child recorded the names of articles, periodicals, or books he read and whether he read them out loud to other family members. Of about 300 titles read over this period, including novels, travel accounts, biographies, and history, at least 55 were religious, with nearly half that number by Theodore Parker (*e.g.*, *The Transient and Permanent in Christianity*, *A Sermon of Merchants*, *A False and True Revival of Religion*, and *A Sermon of Immortal Life*). He also listed a number of sermons and theological works authored primarily by Unitarians, including James Freeman Clarke, Ezra Stiles Gannett, William Ware, and John Turner Sargent. Given Child's radical stance against slavery, he favored abolitionist pieces such as Parker's essay on "John Brown's Invasion" in the *National Anti-Slavery Standard*, Thomas W. Higginson's speech "on the courage of the African race" in the *Liberator*, and James Freeman Clarke's *Slavery in the United States*, but the family also read some works by more moderate reformers, such as William Ellery Channing's *Emancipation*. Daniel sometimes silently perused texts, such as Andrew Jackson Davis's spiritualist tome, *Principles of Nature*, and sections of Lydia Maria Child's *Progress of Religious Ideas* (a comprehensive historical overview of world religions), which he may have thought too controversial. Tellingly, he also refrained from a family reading of "Compensation" and other of Emerson's essays until after consulting his pastor, Theodore Parker, for his views on "The Writings of Ralph Waldo Emerson." For the Child family, such Transcendentalist leanings were ultimately guided by Parker's example.[52]

Others who read Transcendentalist works followed Child's title-listing practice, even if they were accustomed to writing complex discussions on literature. Elizabeth Dwight, who often went on at length about books read, only reported to her sister, "I have been at home very quietly & reading a great deal in all sorts of books from Robertson's 'Charles V.' to Mr Emersons, 'Representative Men.'"[53] J. Edwin Harris entered little else in his diary at times but the items he read and purchased, at great detriment, no doubt, to his savings. Harris's lengthier responses to literature were reserved for a close friend to whom he once wrote about Longfellow ("the greatest Poet that I have ever read") and the other writers who filled his hours of daily reading. Given his irreverence toward church services—a sharp contrast to the Childs' piety—the only religious book he engaged was John Adams's *The Life of "Reformation" John Adams*, read on a Sunday while still within the Methodist fold. While sustaining this steady reading habit between 1856 and 1861, Harris came upon, but did not deliberately seek out Transcendentalism in print. Because he read most editions of the *Atlantic Monthly* published between 1857 and 1861, often at the mills, he also necessarily was exposed to works by Emerson and Thoreau, but he only named a few. Harris noted in September 1860 that he read Emerson's "Illusions" and "Solitude and Society." He also tersely reported in 1860 a Sunday literary rendezvous with a piece by Thoreau: "Have read from the Atlantic Monthly for June July and August a fine serial sketch entitled 'Chesuncook,' by H.D. Thoreau." No doubt Harris's appetite for Transcendentalism was whetted by these "accidental" encounters. The author Lucy Larcom, herself once a "mill girl," worried that the public was not ready for such wide circulation of Transcendentalism: "Emerson is 'coming out' in the Atlantic, isn't he? Poor 'Brahma!' . . . I doubt whether in the nature of things, the world can become philosophic enough to appreciate Philosophers." She probably erred in her assessment; this popular periodical that presented Emerson and Thoreau to thousands contributed to their lasting reputation among a broad readership.[54]

The practice of jotting down titles of Transcendentalist works read in periodicals, such as the *Atlantic Monthly*, or elsewhere was linked to another popular way of registering response: the excerpt. New Englanders preserved in scrapbooks or commonplace books the passages of text that they found most memorable from otherwise perishable or impermanent sources: magazines, newspapers, and borrowed books. Augusta King, for example, kept a scrapbook of newsclippings and short pieces, given her by her uncle Ellis Gray Loring, a Boston lawyer and abolitionist who befriended Emerson and Caroline Sturgis. These included "Mr Emerson's Letter to Mr Van Buren" (an 1838 protest against Cherokee removal), a poem from the *Western Messenger*, clips from Thomas Carlyle, Bailey's *Festus*, and Eliza Buckminster Lee's life of Jean Paul Richter. Mary Baker Eddy, as a young woman, also kept a scrapbook book full of clippings. "'Other men are lenses through which we read our own minds.—Emerson,'" read one piece of newsprint from an unidentified source. An account of "James Freeman Clarke / Essentials and Non-Essentials in Religion. Third Lecture in the Music Hall . . ." also found a place in Eddy's compilation, among poetry and an article about the malpractice of a mesmerist. She preserved a periodical excerpt from *Self-Reliance*: "There is a time in every man's education when he arrives at the conviction that envy is ignorance." Other readers saved not only snippets, but excerpted favorite works, as in the case of a Connecticut schoolteacher who copied from the October 1843 and January 1844 issues of the *Dial*.[55]

Christopher Keith, who borrowed books from the Providence Athenaeum, probably charged out Emerson's *Essays, Second Series*, in November 1854. Over a period of three days he transcribed in his blank book sections (not always verbatim), paraphrased portions, and inserted some key words in the margins of his extractions, as a kind of index to these notes. He read "Manners," "Gifts," "Nature," and "Politics" with enough enthusiasm to transcribe pages of quotations, but he commented upon a single line from "Manners." A clerk of modest means, with an insecure position as a plat maker that left him unemployed during the Panic of 1857, Keith found enduring wisdom in the line from "Manners," "Without the rich heart, wealth is an ugly beggar," which he expounded on and refashioned: "This is very true, he that has wealth is poor unless he has a heart that can appreciate its use and make it yield him its full value. Wealth can make one rich, if he uses it so that [it] counts up charitable actions; but it is not wealth absolutely, only so relatively." Keith appropriated Emerson's line "For, fashion is not good sense absolute, but relative," to create an analogy to wealth. Keith favored other passages on the relative nature of wealth; for example, he quoted from "Nature": "The stars at night stoop down over the brownest <,> ^and^ homeliest common, with all the spiritual magnificence which they shed on the Campagna." But he lavishes attention on "Gifts," Emerson's counsel against ostentation in acts of human exchange. He transcribed the lines "Flowers and fruits are always fit presents; flowers, because ^it is always^ <they are> a proud assertion that <a ray of> beauty ^outweighs^ <outvalues> all the utilities of the world." Keith also copied Emerson's words "Rings and other jewels are not gifts<,> but apologies for gifts. The only gift is a portion of thyself< .... > <Therefore> the poet brings his poem, the shepherd<,> his lamb." After duplicating more of Emerson's words, Keith composed two paragraphs of paraphrase, an exercise in contemplating the author's voice:

> A boquet of flowers is better than jewelry, because the selection and arrangement of the flowers is your own and the receiver can see somewhat of your own skill and talent in it, and thus really gets at your mind and heart. ... The article reminds you as much of the giver as of the artifice.

The significance that Keith assigned to Emerson's other words in the opening pages of his diary/commonplace book remains a mystery, for he did not comment on them. In the future, he would seldom mention the author again. Yet Keith's encounter with this Transcendentalist was the start of a seventeen-year habit of inscribing, digesting, and pondering printed materials in these blank books devoted to reading. It is fitting that he copied words from "Nature" that called upon the journal as a metaphor: "Each young and ardent person writes a diary, ^upon^ <in> which<,> when the hour<s> of prayer <and penitence> arrive^s^, he inscribes his soul."[56]

Many readers went beyond rostering titles or inscribing authors' words to recording (for instance) their personal reactions to the Transcendentalist books they read. The short, one-sentence verdicts—usually a declaration akin to "I found this book very interesting/satisfying/amusing," which are ubiquitous to the discourse of literary response in antebellum New England—are lacking for Transcendentalist texts. Yet readers did find such works "interesting," albeit in a more ambiguous way. Statements of interest cannot always be dismissed as testaments to a critically shallow mind, for as Nina Baym explains, "interest" denoted "a powerful human experience"; with interest came the possibility of "enchantment, absorption, or fascination."[57] Apparently, New England readers of Transcendentalism seldom felt the same kind of clear, unqualified pleasure they frequently experienced in other contemporary works; furthermore, the new philosophy did not lend itself to the kind of engagement that sustained "interest"—being swept up in an entertaining story, gaining useful information, or receiving sheer inspiration.

While a few New Englanders responded in quick, unqualified bursts of enthusiasm, more, curiously, contradicted statements of interest. Martha Osborne Barrett, a worker in a milliner's shop in Danvers, Massachusetts, for example, found Theodore Parker's autobiographical *Experiences as a Minister* "intensely interesting" but, she added, "at times pathetic," a qualification apparently elicited by the tragedies of ill health in his later years. Lucy Larcom also began her review of Emerson on a positive note. She wrote to her friend William Robinson, who had loaned her some texts: "I have read your books with much satisfaction; Emerson particularly." She went on to qualify her enjoyment: "but he seems to be very much like the old heathen philosophers. How such a head grew up among Yankee cabbages, I don't understand." She explained the negativity in terms of her religious conservatism: "I shall never get over my *Puritan penchants*, and I don't want to." Mary Pierce followed a similar pattern. She asked her fiancé, Henry Poor, in 1841, "Have you read much of Mr Cranch's poetry? I have seen some piece that I liked very much." Her gesture of enthusiasm preceded the negative note: "but his Endymion in the January number of the dial strikes me in a rather ludicrous light."[58] Here the qualification reflects not only a judgment on Cranch's absurd imaginative flights, a typical antebellum negative response to any kind of literature, but also the cat-and-mouse games of courtship; wishing to impress Henry, a lawyer more versed in the works of Lord Coke than the Transcendentalists, with her sobriety, Mary was ever cautious about revealing her preferences in reading—especially those items that might be deemed "ludicrous" or of unconventional literary style.[59]

Pierce's expression of qualified "interest" echoed in the response of another woman, S. W. Goddard of Providence, who revealed in 1852 a similarly ambivalent attitude that implied both enthusiasm and repulsion for the unconventional. She prefaced her thoughtful estimate of Margaret Fuller's *Memoirs* with the typical registration of response. "I have been reading of late the Life of Margaret Fuller, and have been very much interested in it," she confessed, despite being "prejudiced against it." Although Fuller "was truly a wonderful creature and had some of the noblest elements of character," she continued to a friend in South Carolina, there were "many things which I could not wholly approve" in the book. Goddard, like other readers, after proclaiming interest, even awe, conceded discomfort with Fuller's erudition: "It is an affecting illustration of the evil of *overtasking* the mind in early life, and a useful lesson may be drawn from it, in conducting the education of girls." Despite her reservations concerning Fuller, a woman who challenged the gender prescriptions of her age by cultivating her intellect, Goddard recommended the memoir, partly because of its potential to engross. "Mrs Holbrook might dissent from many of Margaret Fullers views" as well, but "*she* could not fail to read the history of such a mind, with interest."[60]

Statements of interest about Fuller's *Memoirs* were voiced by other New England women who supplemented their initial expression of engagement with her life story with critical sentiments about the Transcendentalist who astonished contemporaries with her brilliance, but also her arrogance, competitiveness, egotism, and sarcasm.[61] Louisa Gilman Loring, who took part in Fuller's "Conversations," reacted with bittersweet recollections to her former friend's life story. "I have read it, with deep interest," Loring explained, but then went on to relay the heartache she experienced when portions of the book summoned painful memories:

> Mr Emerson's part affects me exactly as Margaret herself always did; notwithstanding my entire faith in her superiority of intellect, & perfect willingness to sit at her feet & receive crumbs from her affluence, she always oppressed me, by requiring *more* admiration than *even* I could give. I remember when we lived in the Winter St. house, after some hours listening to her (for *conversation* it could not be called) she left me in a rather antagonistic state; thus Jesus's words came soothingly to me, 'I am meek & lowly in heart

& will give *peace* unto your soul'—& strange that I was reminded
of that time, by finding myself repeating those very words as I laid
down Mr Emerson's account of Margaret.

Loring went on to empathize with Fuller's mundane life, but also her
reformist spirit—facets of a life that no doubt allowed Loring, who led a
primarily domestic existence but also shared her husband's abolitionist
zeal, to identify with the Transcendentalist thinker: "Dear Emelyn's account of her is charming & comes in quite another spirit. As a wife &
mother, as a sympathizer & nurse to those poor soldiers, she is so much
more human, loveable & noble." Loring regretted the loss of the woman so
affectively defined more than that of the writer and thinker: "I wish I could
have known her [thus], filling so beautifully those relations." Loring concluded by merging the literary and biographical: "On the whole the book
gives a very impressive idea of Margaret, & she has certainly been very fortunate in the numerous gifted contributors to her fame."[62]

Mary Pierce Poor, like Loring, found herself engrossed in the memoirs
of Fuller in a way that transcended simple interest allotted to enjoyable
books. "The most absorbing thing I have seen lately is Margaret Ossoli's
life," she wrote to her sister-in-law Laura Stone. "Have you read it?" In
June 1851, well before its publication in February 1852, Poor anticipated
reading it in a utilitarian way, as a guide for editing and publishing her father's own memoirs. Expecting that Fuller's *Memoirs* might help her walk
the tightrope between honesty and discretion, Poor conceded: "Father was
a man who said little to hurt the feelings of any one, but he wrote freely &
discharged himself in these memoirs by way of letting off the steam. I have
not quite decided what to do. I long to see the life of Margaret Fuller."
Upon finally reading about Fuller she felt unexpectedly taken with the
book's ability to enthrall, but she also perceived a mixture of the unflatter-
ing with the remarkable, and that balance, for her, made the book laudable:
"It is the most honest candid memoir I ever met with. You see Margaret
with all her faults & all her genius, &, (what all did not know before), her
warm woman-heart."[63]

A genuine fascination with the character of an author, as in the case of
Margaret Fuller, defined the response of many New Englanders who, in
this fashion, contributed to the pool from which authorial celebrity was
created.[64] Reverence at a distance satisfied most New Englanders. "Concord is a sort of mecca to me; I dont know that I should dare to meet any of
the 'Celebrities,' though," Lucy Larcom confessed in 1854 to her friend
Harriet Robinson, a neighbor of Emerson and Thoreau. Although she published her own first book of prose-poems that same year, she remained

timid in the face of these authors: "I'd like to peep in at their sitting room windows some dark night when they wouldn't see me." Other readers veiled their admiration in anonymity when they took to jotting down notes, usually biographical, about authors they read about in newspapers. Abby Clark Stimson, the wife of a Providence businessman, for example, recorded in July 1850 the sad circumstances of Fuller's death: "Ship Elizabeth from Gibralter wrecked on Fire Island 4 miles from Long Island Lighthouse—Margaret Fuller Ossoli perished with her husband & child." Mellen Chamberlain, a law student and librarian at Harvard University, scribbled in his diary: "Emerson lives at Concord & has a very pretty fortune." William Lloyd Garrison, Jr., while a clerk in Lynn, Massachusetts, wrote little about the content of the lecture he heard by Thoreau ("extremely fine") but ventured more on biographical details: he "is a friend and neighbor of Emerson," he reported to his brother Wendell. But he continued with a typically New England response to authorship—the comparison, invidious or otherwise, with other writers: "and is thought by many to be an imitator of the great Ralph Waldo."[65]

Some unremarkable New Englanders met Transcendentalist authors and spoke from experience. Giles Waldo, a schoolteacher and administrator from Scotland, Connecticut, who had the good fortune actually to meet Emerson while working in Washington, D.C., was pumped for mundane details by his brother George—even after the latter had received a long letter about Emerson's "spiritual" qualities and "goodness." In the initial letter, Giles had gushed: "He made me feel that we *belonged* to each other.—Emerson is a better, more spiritual man than even I had anticipated. He is all goodness without pretending to goodness." To slake his brother's thirst for down-to-earth particulars, Giles surrendered this information: "You want to know Emerson's history.—I cannot tell you a great deal." He went on, however: "save that he graduated from the theological school at Cambridge in 1826 I think or thereabouts—preached a little while in Boston—indeed continued his connection with the Unitarians—very slightly however—until a very few years since, and now he inclines to find good every where; but especially worships with the more spiritual who are found among all sects & classes." Giles embellished his sketch with a crumb of information on the author's appearance: "Emerson *looks* about 30 years old—but is, I suppose, nearer 40." Giles defended Emerson against his detractors: "His views are his own and his style also.—He has been called an imitator of Carlyle—but with no shadow of truth.—I am inclined to think that the style of no two writers is more dissimilar." Giles on another occasion referred to the authorial relationship as "one of *attraction*, see if you can *attract* & *be attracted*, as R.W.E. & Carlyle are to each other."[66]

The underside of authorial celebrity that Giles Waldo evaded—the comparisons and unkind gossip about personal traits and appearance—at times
surfaced from face-to-face encounters with celebrated Transcendentalists,
much as it did with other authors. Such comments might arise despite little engagement with authors' publications. Harriet Robinson, who led a
domestic life in Concord, Massachusetts, assessed Thoreau against Emerson and considered both as men rather than authors; the works of both
took a backseat to the historical biographies she preferred. Emerson "is a
most divine man, besides being so great a genius," she concluded. After
making a call to his home, she reported that "There never was a better husband, father or family man, no doubt, besides being a most excellent
townsman and public spirited withal." Although she averred that Thoreau,
whom she also met, "was quite eloquent," she remarked that "He is considered to resemble Mr Emerson, but I do not think he does. Mr E. is a
god by the side of him." Robinson's acid reports about Thoreau's seclusion
at Walden entertained her shy friend Lucy Larcom: "Your account of
Thoreau quite amuses me. I dont think I shall 'fall in love' with him; certainly not, if he looks to me as he does to you. Perhaps he caught the
resemblance to the birds you speak of, from living out in the woods, like
'Jeminy Jed.'" After Larcom finally visited the site of Thoreau's experiment
in August 1856, she felt moved to read *Walden* and despite the prior bad
press from Robinson admitted: "I like him better since I saw and read
Walden. He's a curiosity, any way."[67]

The invidious distinction that Robinson summoned up about authors
was also leveled, albeit more gently, at literary productions. Sarah Alden
(Bradford) Ripley, a friend of Emerson's who later lived in the Old Manse,
the dwelling place for several New England authors, employed this device
with regard to his biographical writings. In 1845, she wrote: "Mr Emerson
has lately written a lecture on Buonaparte considered as the expression of
material force, and is about writing others on Plato, Swedenborg and I dont
know who else." Ripley divulged: "I liked his old biographical lectures better than any he has written since." Elizabeth (Dwight) Cabot likewise compared works of Emerson, revealing that she found *Conduct of Life* "very
interesting, more so to me than anything he has published." Its pious spirit,
not its basis in any familiar theology, won Cabot's favor: "It seems to me
brimful of Faith, though he has no Creed & never uses any religious phraseology." Mary Pierce Poor compared periodicals that published Transcendentalist writings; she passed by issues of the short-lived *Spirit of the Age*
because it did not measure up to expectations generated by its predecessor,
The Harbinger. "We [Henry and I] did not think it equal to the Harbinger
& we have not made so strong an effort to get it," she explained to a friend.

Pierce added a note of optimism, however: "I hope it is improving & that the old friends of the Harbinger will try to make it equal to that paper."[68]

Instead of quibbling about the relative merits of authors or their publications, some New Englanders drew deeper lessons from Transcendentalism and often contemplated the consequences of such writings upon the lives of others. They might, for example, note the instrumental effect on relatives and friends. Giles Waldo, estranged both geographically and in spirit from some family members, hoped Emerson's writings would bridge the intellectual gaps. He reported being "most of all pleased with . . . the influence of Emerson's works upon Uncle Sam. It is as I could not but hope it would be." Giles went on to explain (though not lucidly) the essence of the influence in metaphysical terms: "This spirit is positive, not satisfied with destroying . . . it would engraft the new; it must construct; most especially must it believe, as well as deny." Elizabeth (Dwight) Cabot's favorite book of Emerson's, *Conduct of Life*, not only gave her pleasure; it also offered succor in times of national strife. Given the context of her response to the book—she brought it up in a letter, just after a long, fretful discussion about the "family quarrel" of the sectional crisis—Cabot apparently hoped Emerson's "faith" would act as a healing force to a generation about to be riven by war: "Every one who has the element of Faith strongly developed in them becomes helpful to their fellow-creatures it seems to me sooner or later & where it is united in [Emerson] with such strength & delicacy of perception & so much poetical insight it creates something that will abide in the hearts & lives of his generation."[69]

Sometimes instruction drawn from a Transcendentalist work was directed inward, as readers pondered their own physical and intellectual existence. Christopher Keith, contemplating the passing years of his life, hoped to emulate some issues of the *Dial* he read nearly twenty years after their initial publication: "they are like wine—they improve by age," he mused. "So may I grow wiser and better as life wears away." John Townsend Trowbridge, a world-weary writer who spoofed the Boston cheap publishing industry in his *Martin Merrivale*, called upon Theodore Parker as an antidote to his own malaise: "Walked in woods, to find spiritual tho't, but I am dull, lethargic, worldly, full of mean & groveling tho'ts. Read Parker's sermons, which were of some help." Lucy Larcom received similar mental benefits from Emerson. Although she averred that she "was never wholly converted to [Emerson or],—his ideas," she admitted "that he always sets you a thinking." After reading Emerson's unsigned essay on "Persian poetry" in the *Atlantic*, she tried to identify the author by the prose's intoxicating essence: "I think its spirit is very much like Emerson's, that same sort of *liquor*, but the way of serving it, the style in Emerson is his own." But the lessons drawn from Transcendentalism were not always so benign nor the effects so positive. They could distill to a simple adverse emotional or physical reaction, such as the one Elizabeth (Dwight) Cabot expressed after reading one of Emerson's works: "miserable in consequence." John Park, who wrestled with the "German mysticism" that invaded Unitarianism, felt "exceedingly nervous" so that "I *could not sl*eep all night," after reading in 1852 "a long article in the Christian Examiner by [O. B.] Frothingham, of Salem, of 'the Christ of the Jews & the Christ of St. Paul.'"[70]

Much of the response to Transcendentalist texts departed from the personally instrumental to center upon language and style, with at least a few readers finding it, in Christopher Keith's words, "beautifully written." Annie (DeWolf) Middleton simply remarked "very beautiful" of one of Emerson's poems. Isabel Morgan, an academy student at Lenox, Massachusetts, recorded in 1845 having heard her teacher read "a portion of Mr Parker's beautiful writings." One pious normal school teacher in Framingham, Massachusetts, remarked upon the affinity of "Parkerism, spiritualism, Emersonianism—all systems, beautiful systems in the makers' eye," but added the warning that "'God shall try every man's work, of what cost it is.'"[71] Such judgment of beauty was often reserved for religious works, but also occasionally the depictions of nature by European Romantics.[72] This attribution of beauty underscores the significance, for some common readers, of both the religious and European Romantic context of the movement.

The analysis of Transcendentalist prose through the lens of European Romanticism usually went deeper than mere apprehension of beauty. Some readers dissected word choice and stylistic patterns. For example, Mary Pierce recognized in Fuller's translation of Johann Eckermann's *Gespräche mit Goethe* that the very practice of translating ineluctably transformed the translator's own prose style in his or her native tongue. The result was a "hybrid" language in word selection and order, as well as in sentence length and syntax. Pierce, in her analysis, triangulated Fuller, Eckermann, and Carlyle: "It [*i.e.*, Fuller's *Conversations with Goethe*] is written in a very animated and easy style though at times it seems to be a close imitation of Carlisle—perhaps this is owing to the fact that both have translated Goethe's writings and may have acquired that similarity by intimate acquaintance with the same author."[73]

Other commentators on Transcendentalist prose style appreciated the writer's creative deployment of words to convey intuitive knowledge. They thus seemed to some extent attuned to (or at least aware of) the movement's hermeneutic practices and epistemological distinctions. Hannah Lowell Jackson, for example, turned to *Nature* during an 1839 visit to the William Ellery Channing home in Newport for insight into the language of intuitive understanding. After a pleasant walk to the seashore with her friend Mary Channing and other family members, Hannah's thoughts took a philosophical turn. William Ellery Channing's son William Francis engaged her in private conversation about the limitation of words in the conveyance of meaning:

> Wm walked home with me & talked about the analogy between thoughts & words; he seemed to think that there is a mysterious analogy between thoughts & words, between all spirit & matter, but then said that language being an artificial symbol is not a good example, but certain looks & gestures always belong to certain feelings; to which I agreed but I do not feel sure that I understand him exactly & he says there is a chapter in 'Nature' about it which I am going to read.

Giles Waldo, who professed a similar detachment from logical structures of language, celebrated writings inspired by intuition. His uncle, he hoped, would not study Emerson; "if he really imbibes the spirit which moved the writer, all is well." Elizabeth (Dwight) Cabot, who was sometimes, as we have seen, made "miserable" by Emerson, nonetheless enjoyed the "poetical insight" and even savored his "writ[ing] as a heathen might who was unconsciously imbued with the spirit of Christianity, but had never heard of its name." Even amateur writings inspired by Carlyle's *Sartor Resartus* (one reader called it "eloquent and deeply penetrating— . . . greatly decried . . . in the eyes of those to whose senses every thing must be palpably addressed to be understood"), such as those penned by Nathaniel Middleton, were discussed with a consciousness of intuitive import. S. W. Goddard, a family friend, commented upon his amateur poems:

> To a certain class of minds, I should think they could not fail to be interesting. *They* would p[e]rceive their connection[?] and *feel* their deep import. To such, the history of a human soul has a profounder interest than all material[?] circumstances, disconnected with thi[s?], but *these* are the *few* the *very* few. But why, you may say, when these minds are of the highest order, being more awakened to unseen realities, why not address your self to them . . . ?

Goddard further proclaimed that the "poems are . . . rich in profound sentiment and power of expression save in some few instances, the meaning is not sufficiently obvious."[74]

While Goddard tolerated Transcendentalism's occasionally obscure prose as it tried to communicate via intuitional grasp, other readers admitted that the movement's language was inherently difficult, if not impossible to comprehend. As Sarah Alden (Bradford) Ripley explained in a letter discussing George Bancroft's Transcendental idioms, "I attempted to interpret but did not succeed well. What do they mean by 'Weltgeist?' We people of the understanding are not satisfied with an intuition darkly felt. We ask for definitions, for something that can be grasped."[75] Kitty Bigelow Lawrence, for example, referred in 1849 to the obtuse "proverbial philosophy" of Martin Farquhar Tupper to make a point about Transcendentalism. "We both in vain tried to understand it. It sounds very much like Ralph Waldo Emerson's poetry." Her sister, Annie Lawrence, held the same views and agreed with Francis C. Gray, who in an 1840 lecture made a "capital hit at the Transcendentalists; or rather who here profess it, & know not what is their object, to grasp at something great & inconceivable." So strong was the link between the intuitive grasp of meaning and Transcendentalism among antebellum New Englanders that even a conservative Congregationalist could stand accused if he acknowledged extra-verbal communication. When Thomas Hyde, the son of Reverend Lavius Hyde (educated at Andover), successfully challenged during a debate at Williams College the thesis that "it was impossible to think without language—that even reasoning & reflection could not proceed without the use of words," a fellow student pronounced him "guilty of a tendency to transcendentalism." John Park, however, voiced the most articulate and, perhaps, most intractable dissent over the language of Transcendentalism. "I derive great pleasure from perusing the speculations of able, logical writers," Park recorded a year after *Nature* was published. "Only spare me Transcendentalism—give me something that can be distinctly comprehended, and I am willing to study hard."[76]

For Park, Transcendentalism had its own "style" that not only was incomprehensible, but that attacked the very rational foundations of his religious belief. A devoted member of Aaron Bancroft's Second Parish in Worcester, Park in 1837 heartily engaged contemporary printed debates over David Strauss's *Life of Jesus* and miracles.[77] Park approached these issues with firm grounding in theology and philosophy, especially Lockean empiricism. While he often wrote page upon page refuting arguments put forth by Friedrich Schleiermacher, William Henry Furness, and Theodore Parker, Park reduced much of his criticism to an author's ability to write lucid prose. Transcendentalist infidels, to Park's mind, erred inexcusably because they did not write clearly.[78]

Not surprisingly, Park was especially disturbed if he suspected that "Transcendentalist language" was being adopted by a Unitarian minister. When "Reverend Mr [Edward] Hall, of Providence" made a call, Park exclaimed, "I always rejoice, in these days, to find a clergyman untinctured by the verbiage of Transcendentalism." Park charged those ministers who adopted it in writing with obfuscation: "Read James Freeman Clarke's Tract, called the History of the Atonement. A thousand such Tracts would not be of the least use to the Christian community.—it is but a series of obsolete, theological trash, clothed in transcendental idiom." Park concluded that "modern German philosophy" with its "senseless jargon of words, without any distinct and intelligible meaning" was responsible for infecting Unitarianism. After completing a memoir of philosopher Johann Gottlieb Fichte, Park contemptuously credited the subject with being "the father of the 'new philosophy,' so zealously propagated among us of late, by R. W. Emerson, Parker and some others of the same school. On this pitiful system of philosophy," Park continued, "I am inclined to pen some comments, for it appears to me to be absurd and contrary to our experience." While the Germanic influence upon some American Transcendentalists seemed extreme to Park, it was not always contaminating, as in the case of George Ripley. "I read a sermon by the Rev. George Ripley, preached at the Ordination of Mr Dwight, at Northampton," he wrote in 1840. "I am gratified to find by this production, that though too deeply tinged with a partiality to some of the German theologians, for my taste, he is very far from the extravagant transcendentalism of Mr Emerson." Park's toleration failed to extend, however, to the authors represented in his cherished *Christian Examiner*; stressing the abundance of "citation[s] of German mysticism" in the periodical, he found "every article" in the January 1839 issue "tinctured with the transcendental phraseology, recently so current in Boston productions."[79]

Park's antidote to German confusion was British clarity. "I think it bad to acquire the habit of reading what I do not understand," Park explained. He concluded that "For satisfactory reasoning give me an Englishman or a Scotchman." Among his favorite authors was John Locke, whom he read in five volumes, just as Theodore Parker (that sometime foe of Lockean sensationalism) rose in the mid 1840s to prominence and notoriety in Boston. On another occasion, Park compared the British and Germans to the latter's discredit: "in perusing the productions of the most profound English or Scotch philosophers, written in the good old Saxon idiom I find them *intelligible*, whether I can assent to all their views or not. Thus I console myself when perplexed by a passage in Richter, or Kant or Fichte, by a persuasion that my author's mind was misty—not mine."[80]

Predictably, Park favored the "Unitarian Moralists" as well. Of Francis Bowen, he said in 1839: "His idiom is English and his Intellect, sane"; of James Walker: "one of the most lucid, efficient writers of our day." But Andrews Norton was perhaps Park's favorite and most comforting author— one who Park might concede was "seeking a living religion that would stir the hearts of men." "Mr. Norton is one of the most learned and logical writers we have in the United States," he wrote in 1837 after reading the first volume of *On the Genuineness of the Gospels*, hot off the press. Norton's writing was so philosophically relevant for Park that after a fire nearly destroyed his library of "two thousand volumes" in 1845 he considered selling some charred works to finance insurance of his favorite books. "Norton's volumes, and all works of that description, I will keep as long as I have eyes to read and remaining sense to understand them," he wrote to his daughter, in a letter filled with dismay over Theodore Parker's dispute with the Boston Association of Congregational Ministers. "In the present prevalence of skepticism, seemingly tolerated and almost countenanced in high places, I must not only review, but study the Evidences of Christianity, that they may be clear and uppermost in my mind."[81]

Park sought reinforcement of his theology—and, perhaps more importantly, interchange about books that would have otherwise been contemplated in isolation—from the community of readers who gathered at the Second Congregational Society of Worcester and the homes of Aaron Bancroft, Alonzo Hill, and other congregants. "Mr Kendall [called] in the evening," Park remarked in 1838, "We discuss Mr Emerson's infidel sermon."[82] When readers together analyzed "Mr. Hurlbut's Review" of Furness's *Remarks on the Four Gospels*[83] and decided it was "an able and very complete refutation of Mr Furness's position . . . [on] miracles," they influenced one another's reception of the text. Moses Stuart's "Review of Schleiermacher," it was agreed, proved to be "among the most powerful refutations of the doctrine of the Trinity that has been published though the Professor still maintains that he believes in the Trinity." Orestes Brownson's novel, *Charles Elwood*, elicited a debate over "whether the deaf, dumb and blind have any notion of a Deity." The liveliest response occurred in 1841 during Park's absence, but he recorded the controversy nonetheless. The subject was Parker's *Discourse on the Transient and Permanent*; Park reported the respondents as having "considerable zeal—some palliating, if not defending, and some censuring."[84] His reading group thus had become to some degree a microcosm of the range of reception of Transcendentalism in print.

Dissemination

In March 1845, about the same time that John Park in Worcester was fashioning himself a protector of rational religious tradition by insuring his most precious books, Daniel F. Child was reading to his family "aloud,

Rev. J. T. Sargent's farewell Sermon at the Suffolk Street Chapel," a discourse occasioned by that minister's resignation due to exchanging pulpits
with Theodore Parker.[85] A week later Child recited "Rev. Theodore
Parker's letter to the association of Congregational Ministers of Boston,"
with its references to Sargent's "expulsion" and Parker's heterodox position
in relation to Unitarianism. Having read these and several other productions spawned by religious controversy, Child and his family not only continued to read Parker's printed works, they also became devoted members
of the Twenty-eighth Congregational Society.[86]

Child's oral rendering of Transcendentalist-inspired texts was not an unusual way to disseminate the literature. For many—if not most—people in
antebellum New England, reading was a social act. Reading out loud was
a form of entertainment, especially for women burdened with tasks that
required their visual attention, such as minding children, cooking, and
sewing. For example, in 1856, during one of Annie Middleton's coveted
annual summertime visits from Charleston to see her Rhode Island family,
her cousin "came and partook with us just as we were, Baby and all . . .
[and] repeated a poem of Emerson's." Lucretia Bancroft performed the
same function for the industrious women of her father's parish when she
read to them Parker's *Discourse on the Transient and Permanent in Christianity* during an afternoon meeting of their charitable sewing society.
"Very edifying!!" John Park exclaimed upon hearing all about the recitation
from his wife, a member of the circle; he knew well that Bancroft's "humorous and witty" delivery could keep "young, and old, in a constant burst
of laughter" and that she did justice, at least for Park, to the notorious
ordination sermon.[87]

Women burdened with domestic labor were not the only ones who listened as others read Transcendentalism. When Mellen Chamberlain,
a Harvard Law School librarian teetering on the verge of poverty and
chronic malnutrition, was invited to nightly dinners by the generous Harvard Law Professor William Kent (1802–1861), he was not only seated one
night in 1847 with Charles Sumner, but was treated to his reading "from
Emersons poems, some of which [Sumner] thought quite fine tho' he
did'nt go with [Emerson] entirely." When Ellis Gray Loring hosted dinner
parties, he often read out loud to his guests as part of the evening's entertainment. One time he "read a little while in Ripley's Introduction to his
Selections from Cousin" to an audience including Transcendentalist author Caroline Sturgis and his niece Augusta King. On another occasion he
"read aloud to L. Mrs Child, C. Sturgis & Augusta K., Mr Emerson's 1st
lecture on human culture.—Afterwards, Noctes Ambrosiana."[88]

When New Englanders did not read aloud as part of a face-to-face relationship kindled by mutual enjoyment of a text, they found other ways to disseminate printed materials to absent friends and family. They sent clippings from newspapers and loaned books, sometimes with the goal of influencing the borrower's reception. As we have seen, Giles Waldo sent home his cherished copy of Emerson's *Essays* in hopes of strengthening relations while influencing his kinfolk's receptivity toward the "new philosophy." "Write me soon,—" Waldo wrote to his brother George, "telling me your experiences & c." Not content to influence kin alone, Waldo also requested that "when all the folks get through with Emerson's Essays, & c., I wish you would *carry* them to Julia Wells," a faithful correspondent from Southold, Long Island. Thus the *Essays* passed from Giles to his brother George, to their uncle, and then to a "wonderful" friend.[89]

Personal distribution of Transcendentalism in print cemented community ties while insuring the dissemination of cherished ideals. When Theodore Parker's "The Life of Webster" appeared in the *Commonwealth*, Daniel Child visited three neighbors, "Mrs. Rice's, Mr. Otis Everett's, and Mr. Brigham's taking to each a copy of Mr. Parker's discourse." By distributing this sermon, Child not only brought Parker's words to those who may not have heard him at the Melodeon just the day before, he also propagated the ardent abolitionism he shared with his pastor. The multifunctionality of dissemination appears as well in Child's formalized gift giving. In presenting Parker's "Public Function of Woman" to John Pierpont, who was mourning his wife's death, Child attempted both to console and to humor a saddened spirit: "clergymen probably liked to know what others of their profession were doing," he recorded having said as he presented the gift.[90]

Not all personally disseminated texts had the intended effect of pleasing, humoring, consoling, or influencing, for some people merely ignored what they were given or gave them passing notice without incorporating the tenets contained in the text into their intellectual life. This dismissiveness occurs, for example, in the diary of Frances Jocelyn, who distributed pamphlets for the American Tract Society and who was being courted by David Peck, a divinity student at Yale University. Jocelyn mentions receiving, but not actually reading "a book by Emmerson" (the only Transcendentalist-authored book named in her eighteen-year-long diary) "brought" to her by the new superintendent of her Sunday School, "Mr. Patterson," when he came to call. Although she attended one of Emerson's lectures on "Power" with her suitor and had the leisure hours to read, this volume (and others like it) failed to change the course of her reading habits.[91]

Similarly, the Transcendentalist texts given to Carroll Norcross, a Waterville (Maine) College student and sometime schoolteacher, apparently did little to influence his reading habits. Committed with consumptive symptoms to a water cure establishment during the fall of 1853, and thus relieved for a time of *"everlasting* Latin and Greek," he had occasion to dip into "one of Mr. Parker's sermons, [in] a couple of volumes," after a "lady patient" let him borrow it. Still, Norcross's consciousness that day betrayed more of a concern for his physical recovery than intellectual challenge when he wrote immediately after mentioning the texts: "Took a 'wet-sheet'—right from the cold water at three P.M." His diary reveals no further engagement with the movement.[92]

John Park was similarly immune. Always eager to battle Transcendentalism and the German literature that inspired it, he remained unimpressed with Goethe's *Egmont*, which had been translated and loaned to him by his friend Francis Boott. "I write again to Mr Frank Boott, thanking him for Egmont, and making some objections to Goethe's plot, particularly to the introduction of such a character as Clara, in preference to the Countess Egmont." After finishing the book, however, he reassured Boott that "the perusal of Egmont had produced in me a more just feeling of candour towards German literature than I had formerly cherished." Encouraged by Park's less severe assessment, Boott induced Park to try one other piece of German literature, Sarah Austin's "Fragments from German Writers." Although Park judged it "a work well worth reading—and one that has satisfied me that Germany produces other minds than mystics—" still, there were "too many of *them.*"[93]

When Francis Boott loaned his books to Park, he used a courier, a mutual friend who made periodic trips between Worcester and Boston, but for people living at great remove, especially overseas, such a method was not feasible. Though costly, mail or shipping might be the only way to disseminate materials.[94] "I am glad you received May [*sic*] newspaper & read Mr Emerson's lecture," Elizabeth Dwight wrote to her sister in England in 1855. "We got a Bangor paper from Lucy giving an account of Mr Hedges sermon," Abby Pierce wrote from Brookline, Massachusetts, to her sister Mary in Bangor, Maine, in 1848. "It was quite flattering, tho I do not suppose, any more so than it deserved." Likewise, Samuel May, Jr., mailed in 1848, "a copy of Theodore Parker's *Letter on Slavery*, just published," to Dr. John Estlin, a regular correspondent. Sending papers sometimes assuaged book owners' guilt over withholding their latest purchases from immediate circulation. While making up one of her "bundle[s] to send to Lancaster," Sarah P. E. Hale complained in 1838 that "Oliver asked me for the second volume of Bancrofts Hist. but we have only had ours a couple of days and have not done our duty by it yet. I shall send some English papers." Sometimes it was impossible to locate a text a relative living abroad desired. When Ellen Twisleton wanted a back issue of the *Atlantic Monthly* sent to her in England for an essay by "Ralph Waldo on Culture," her sister Elizabeth thought it might be difficult to secure the number published only two months prior. "It is sometimes difficult to get an old number of the Atlantic, but I think I can," Elizabeth comforted her sister. In performing the work of maintaining family ties, she extended the discussion of book exchange to acknowledging mutual opinions about Emerson. "I agree with your views about him *word for word*, & am glad I know what they are." Dwight then went on to share her anticipation of Emerson's forthcoming work. "He is about to publish a new book called the 'Conduct of Life' which I expect to find good things in," she wrote. As we have seen, she did.[95]

Despite the prevalence of personal exchange of books and periodicals in correspondence, readers in their letters or diaries seldom identified what books they borrowed from libraries. Evidence for such borrowing, however, is abundant in library charge records, although not necessarily for Transcendentalist titles.[96] For example, only fourteen people (some of them apparently sharing the same household) among 279 patrons charged Emerson's essays, poems, or miscellanies from the Taunton Social Library between May 7, 1856, and March 3, 1859 (Table 4). Of 15,561 charges recorded, those of Emerson's works (including *English Traits* and *Representative Men*) accounted for a mere .43 percent—the waiting list was obviously not a long one. Conversely, a long one could testify to a book's popularity. Sarah P. E. Hale, for example, described in 1837 her pursuit of a copy of Goethe's *Faust* for her son's German class: "I may possibly get it from the Atheneum but there is such a rage for German now prevailing that it is next to impossible to get such a thing from a public library. The alternate of buying is one to which I am loth to resort."[97] Patrons like Hale had to exercise considerable patience to get a popular work from a library. In Taunton between May and December 1856, for example, Furness's translation of *German Tales* was often charged out by one patron shortly after it was returned by another (Table 5). Common knowledge was that if a book was easily gotten off the shelves in a library, it was out of fashion.[98]

As with their library charges, readers seldom elaborated upon their experiences with subscribing to periodicals, Transcendentalist or otherwise.[99] In rural New England, subscriptions to periodicals with Transcendentalist content were probably a rarity. Our own search through lists for periodicals subscribed to by residents near Waitfield, Vermont, from 1857 to 1860 yielded evidence of the circulation of only one relevant periodical, the New York *Tribune*, which accounted for 166 out of 893 recorded subscriptions in the local postmaster's records.[100] Similar records suggest that

TABLE 4. Borrowers of Emerson's Essays, Poems, and
Miscellanies in the Taunton Social Library

Charged	*Returned*	*Title*

4.A.: CHARGES OF C. E. BARTON

58/07/16	58/07/23	Nathalie
58/07/23	58/08/17	White Lies
58/07/23	58/07/26	Gold Mines of [the] Gila
58/07/26	58/08/02	Last of the Mohicans
58/08/02	58/08/20	Doniphan's Campaign
58/08/17	58/08/19	Emerson's Poems
58/08/26	58/09/17	Camp Fires of [the] Red Men
58/08/30	58/09/01	[Father] Henson's Story
58/09/06	58/09/10	Whittier's Poems 1 & 2
58/09/10	58/09/14	Redwood
58/09/14	58/09/25	Hagar
58/09/17	58/10/12	Pathfinder

4.B.: CHARGES OF MORTIMER BLAKE

57/12/14	57/12/28	Mallet's Northern Antiquities
57/12/28	58/01/27	"
58/01/27	58/02/23	"
58/03/19	58/03/26	Wild Northern Scenes
58/03/23	58/04/05	Moss-Side
58/03/27	58/04/05	Emerson's Poems
58/04/05	58/04/12	Knickerbocker Mar
58/04/24	58/05/07	Ran Away to Sea
58/04/24	58/05/03	Glimpses of Nineveh
58/05/03	58/05/24	Habersham's Explorations
58/05/07	58/05/18	Plant Hunters

4.C.: CHARGES OF FRANCES DEAN

56/12/20	56/12/26	Pictures of Olden Times
56/12/20	56/12/26	Gertrude
56/12/26	57/01/10	Italian Sights, &c
57/01/10	57/01/14	Physician's Vacation
57/01/17	57/01/28	At Home and Abroad
57/01/17	57/01/28	Emerson's Essays
57/01/28	57/02/07	Early History of N England
57/02/07	57/02/14	Napoleon & Josephine Corr.
57/02/14	57/02/21	Hampton Heights
57/02/21	57/02/28	Greenwood Leaves 1.
57/02/21	57/02/28	Goodrich's Rems. vol. 1.

TABLE 4 (*cont'd*)

4.D.: CHARGES OF J. H. DEAN

56/05/31	56/06/14	Peg Woffington
56/06/30	56/07/25	Plurality of Worlds
56/07/25	56/07/26	Recs. in Astronomy
56/08/02	56/08/19	Grace Lee
56/08/23	56/09/23	Recs. in Astronomy
56/09/23	56/10/22	Emerson's Essays
56/11/29	56/12/27	Story on the Constitution, 1 & 2
56/12/06	56/12/30	De'Tocqueville, 1-2
57/01/31	57/02/28	Past & Present, Chartism
57/02/10	57/02/25	Aurora Leigh
57/03/06	57/04/04	Arabian Nights

4.E.: CHARGES OF WILLIAM COBB

57/11/12	57/12/11	Queechy
58/02/04	58/02/18	Denmark Norway and Sweden
58/02/18	58/03/03	Motley vol. 1
58/10/09	58/10/11	Aspenwold
58/10/09	58/10/11	Ran away to Sea
58/11/12	58/11/24	Emerson's Poems
58/11/24	58/12/21	History of King Philip
58/11/24	58/12/21	Emerson's Essays 1.
59/01/08	59/01/24	Mallet's Northern Antiquities
59/01/08	59/01/24	Northmen in N. England
59/01/27	59/01/29	Gibbon 1-2

4.F.: CHARGES OF JOHN W. HART

58/04/10	58/04/28	Anna Hammer
58/04/10	58/04/28	Deerslayer
58/04/28	58/05/18	Yemassee
58/04/28	58/05/08	Characteristics of Women
58/05/08	58/05/20	Vivia
58/05/20	58/05/29	Emerson's Miscellanies
58/05/20	58/05/29	Ernest Linwood
58/05/29	58/06/07	Soyer
58/05/29	58/06/07	Locke Amsden
58/06/07	58/06/16	Australian Crusoes
58/06/07	58/06/16	Nothing to Wear

4.G.: CHARGES OF G. G. HEWINS

57/12/25	58/01/12	Charlotte Bronte 1-2
58/01/02	58/01/12	Atlantic Monthly (Nov)

TABLE 4 *(cont'd)*

58/01/14	58/01/29	Daisy Chain 1-2
58/01/16	58/01/25	One of Scott's Novels 1-2
58/01/29	58/02/04	Daisy Chain 1-2
58/02/02	58/02/10	Emerson's Essays
58/02/11	58/02/19	Queechy
58/02/13	58/02/16	Married not Mated
58/02/16	58/02/27	Here and Hereafter
58/02/19	58/02/27	Daring Deeds of Am. Heroes
58/03/11	58/03/18	Great Commanders

4.H.: CHARGES OF Z. L. HODGES

58/01/11	58/01/22	David Copperfield
58/01/22	58/02/06	Goodrich's Rems. 2d.
58/01/25	58/01/29	Daisy Burns
58/01/29	58/02/15	Boat Life
58/02/06	58/02/22	Tent Life
58/02/15	58/02/23	Emerson's Essays
58/02/23	58/02/27	Robinson Crusoe
58/03/06	58/03/15	Quits
58/03/06	58/03/15	Moss Side
58/03/15	58/03/26	Charlotte Bronte vol. 1 & 2
58/03/26	58/03/27	Irving's Washington vol 3d

4.I.: CHARGES OF H. B. HUBBARD

58/06/08	58/06/10	Debit and Credit
58/06/12	58/06/14	Agnes Sorel
58/06/12	58/06/14	Two Guardians
58/06/14	58/06/28	Lamartine's Celebrated Charctr 3d
58/06/16	58/06/28	Baked Head
58/06/28	58/07/01	Emerson's Miscellanies
58/07/01	58/07/02	Blackwood June
58/07/01	58/07/03	Swain's Poems
58/07/01	58/07/03	Aurora Leigh
58/07/03	58/07/06	Castle Avon
58/07/09	58/07/12	Lord Montagu's Page

4.J.: CHARGES OF WILLIAM JONES

58/05/01	58/05/07	Foresters
58/05/07	58/05/12	New England Stories
58/05/07	58/05/25	Reed English History
58/05/12	58/05/19	Atlantic May
58/05/19	58/06/02	Life of Burr
58/05/25	58/05/28	Emerson's Essays 1. series

TABLE 4 *(cont'd)*

58/05/28	58/06/02	White Lies
58/06/02	58/06/21	Life of Burr
58/06/02	58/06/11	Emerson's Poems
58/06/11	58/06/16	Redwood
58/06/16	58/06/25	Woman's Thoughts about Women
58/06/21	58/06/30	Life of Burr
58/06/25	58/06/30	European Acquaintance
58/06/30	58/07/09	Harper July

4.K.: CHARGES OF MRS. P. R. LEONARD

57/11/21	57/12/03	Bancroft vol. 4
58/01/14	58/01/20	Atlantic Monthly Jany
58/01/20	58/01/29	Atlantic Monthly Dec
58/05/04	58/05/29	Livingstone's Africa
58/06/08	58/07/01	New Biographies
58/07/01	58/07/27	Emerson's Miscellanies
58/07/17	58/08/13	History of King Philip
58/08/03	58/08/09	Confidential Disclosures &c
58/09/09	58/09/21	Atlantic Monthly
58/09/09	58/09/21	Confidential Disclosures
58/09/21	58/09/22	Atlantic Aug
58/09/21	58/09/29	Emerson's Poems
58/09/30	58/10/25	Atlantic July
58/10/27	58/10/28	Emerson's Poems
58/10/28	58/11/05	Bayne's Essays 2d.
58/11/15	58/11/27	Indiana Sketches
58/11/15	58/11/27	Bancroft 6
58/11/30	58/12/27	DeQuincy's Mis. Essays
58/12/17	58/12/29	Hertha

4.L.: CHARGES OF E. S. LOTHROP

57/08/03	57/08/15	Blackwood July
57/09/26	57/10/23	Grote 3
57/09/26	57/10/23	Coleridge 1
58/01/20	58/02/04	Grote's Greece 8th.
58/01/20	58/02/04	Grote's Greece 7th.
58/07/19	58/07/28	Emerson's Poems
58/07/21	58/07/28	Jerrold's Wit
58/08/11	58/08/17	Blackwood Mar. Apr. May
58/08/11	58/08/17	Two Millions
58/08/17	58/09/03	Ruskin's Elemt of Drawing
58/08/17	58/08/19	Atlantic June & July

TABLE 4 (*cont'd*)

4.M.: CHARGES OF ERWIN REED

58/02/16	58/02/27	Athanasia
58/04/08	58/04/20	Bayne's Essays
58/04/20	58/05/04	Whittier's Poems 1-2
58/05/03	58/05/08	Swain's Poems
58/05/03	58/05/08	Knickerbocker Apr
58/05/08	58/05/14	Emerson's Poems
58/05/14	58/05/29	Lowell's Poems 1-2
58/05/29	58/06/05	Henson's Story
58/06/05	58/06/26	Sydney Smith's Sketches
58/06/05	58/06/09	Three Days in Memphis
58/06/09	58/06/23	Fudge Doings 1-2
58/06/23	58/07/06	Taylor's Northern Travel

. . .

58/08/30	58/09/07	Atlantic Aug
58/09/07	58/09/18	Trifleton Letters
58/09/07	58/09/18	European Acquaintance
58/09/18	58/10/08	Life &c of S. S. Prentiss 1-2
58/10/08	58/10/23	Titcomb's Letters
58/10/08	58/11/03	Emerson's Miscellanies
58/11/16	58/11/26	Rems. of Shelley & Byron
58/11/26	58/12/11	Cosas de Espana
58/11/26	58/12/11	Allston's Lectures on Art
58/12/18	58/01/01	Miles Standish's Courtship
58/12/18	58/01/03	Empress Josephine

4.N.: CHARGES OF WILLIAM REED

57/12/02	57/12/03	Testimony of the Rocks
57/12/08	57/12/21	Queens of Scotland 3 & 4
57/12/30	58/01/20	Motley's Dutch Republic 1
58/03/11	58/04/10	Motley's Dutch Republic 3d
58/09/07	58/09/17	Shelley & Byron
58/09/07	58/09/17	Emerson's Poems
58/11/20	58/12/10	Women of the Revolution 1-2-3
58/12/23	59/01/01	Life of King Phillip
58/12/23	59/01/01	Life Thoughts
59/01/01	59/01/11	Richard 2d
59/01/08	59/01/26	Andromeda

NOTE: The five charges immediately preceding and following the Emerson charge are shown. Emerson's *English Traits* and *Representative Men* are not included.
SOURCE: Taunton Social Library, Record of Books Circulated, May 7, 1856-March 3, 1859, OCHS.

TABLE 5. Borrowers of Furness's *German Tales* in the Taunton Social Library
September 1856–May 1857

Charged	Returned	Patron
56/09/27	56/10/03	Mrs. Corey
-0-		
56/10/03	56/10/20	J. W. Crossman
-0-		
56/10/20	56/11/03	George F. Champney
-0-		
56/11/03	56/11/08	Dr. Ebenezer Dawes
-2-		
56/11/10	56/11/11	H. L. Danforth
-0-		
56/11/11	56/11/24	Erwin Reed
-4-		
56/11/28	56/12/08	C. F. Wilbur
-5-		
56/12/13	56/12/15	C. I. H. Bassett
-5-		
56/12/20	57/01/10	James A. Sproat
-3-		
57/01/13	57/01/27	Nathan Carver
-11-		
57/02/07	57/02/21	E. H. Reed
-14-		
57/03/07	57/03/17	W. W. Fairbanks
-2-		
57/03/19	57/03/21	H. Tweed
-2-		
57/03/23	57/03/25	F. H. Wilbur
-2-		
57/03/27	57/04/11	C. J. Reed
-5-		
57/04/13	57/04/17	William Thomas Leonard
-8-		
57/04/25	57/05/08	Mrs. George L. Wilmouth

SOURCE: Taunton Social Library, Record of Books Circulated, May 7, 1856–March 3, 1859, OCHS. William Henry Furness, ed. and tr., *Julius and Other Tales from the German.*
-N- = Number of days intervening between when the book was returned and the next charge.

TABLE 6. Periodicals Lent by John Park

Loaned	Borrower and Title (As Recorded by Park)[1]	Returned
02/14/40	"Mr[.] Thom[a]s 4 English Reviews & Christian Examiner"	
0?/0?/42	"Mr Thomas Christian Examiner for Jan[.]"	03/07/42
0?/0?/42	"Mr Haven Christ[.] Examiner for May[.]"	06/06/42
0?/0?/42	"Mr Fischer Christ[.] Examiner for July"	07/0?/42
10/01/46	"D[itt]o. 4 volumes bound in two, of Norton's Cambridge Review"	
0?/21/47	"Mrs F. Merrick Christian Examiner for March"	
0?/06/47	"Hasbrouk Davis the Christian Examiner for May"	
05/06/48	"Mrs Burt Christian Examiner for May '48"	
06/28/48	"Lemuel Williams Esq. T. Parker's Sermon on J.Q. Adams"	
07/19/48	"Mr Wm S. Brazer 3 Tracts 1 vol Tracts, 1 No Christian Examiner"	
07/04/49	"Rev N. Bent Christian Examiner for Ma[y]"	
04/08/50	"Mrs FT Merrick Christian Examiner for March"	
05/07/50	"Mrs F.T. Merrick Christian Examiner for May"	

SOURCE: John Park, list of books at the unpaginated end of vol. 4 of Diary, by courtesy of the Trustees of the Boston Public Library.
[1] We use Park's own words in order to exemplify the precision of his recordkeeping (despite its formal inconsistency).

subscribers in Bridport, Vermont, seldom, if ever, took a Transcendentalist journal (January 1839 to December 1841), even though the records roughly coincide with the *Dial*'s early years.[101] Diary literature shows, however, that readership of the *Christian Examiner*, the *Atlantic Monthly*, and the *Tribune* was extensive in urban areas. As with books, these periodicals circulated via loan, as John Park's diary documents (Table 6). And, as evidence of periodicals' long-term value people often had them bound. Even working-class J. Edwin Harris did this for his *Ballou's Pictorial Drawing Room Companion* and *Waverley*, among other magazines.[102]

As in the case of periodical subscriptions, most readers did not describe their book-buying experiences, but only tersely recorded the titles and, sometimes, the prices paid for them. Titles of purchases most frequently appear among rosters of other items in account books. Such documents, however, give few clues as to what motivated purchases or what bookstores were like. They do hint at gift giving, especially during the holidays. While many New Englanders bought books—particularly Romantic poetry (*e.g.*, Byron), art books, biographies, and Bibles—as gifts, they seldom chose Transcendentalist books (although some writers like Emerson might see pieces appear in literary annuals).[103] Sarah Browne of Salem, Massachusetts, however, on one of her January excursions to Boston did purchase "Parker's book of Essays [for] $1.25." More typical seasonal gifts included "Carlyle's Hero Worship for new years gift" at "1.12 1/2," "Undine for Rebecca," and "Milton & book [for] 1.00."[104] These titles registered in the manuscripts of some of our most prolific letter writers and diarists are mere traces of the full, but unrecorded shopping experience.

People apparently saw shopping as a chore and buying books was no exception, so the failure to record such tiring excursions is not surprising. "Wife too much fatigued to write this evening," Daniel Child wrote in March 1840, "having been shopping both A.M. & P.M." Other young women referred to "the tiresome task of 'shopping'" in their diaries; "Have been out shopping to-day and returned Home very much fatigued," Cornelia D. Jocelyn recorded of a spree in New Haven. Shoppers may also have failed to record their bookstore experiences because they were brief ones. They wished to limit these encounters because the danger of overspending for the budget-minded was always lurking; the chaotic arrangement of books forced buyers to browse (and therefore risk impulse buying) or to require assistance from sales-hungry attendants. John Patton, for example, successfully "Resisted the wish to buy Head's Handbook of Painting $6.50 Stones of Venice 3 vols $32!, Lessing's Laocoon, Eckerman's Conversations with Goethe" at Appletons in New York; he managed to go home only with some good bargains.[105]

The complex social networks nurtured within bookstores may have also been off-putting for common readers who made quick business of visiting bookstores. For the literati, a bookstore probably served as a place for gossip when they pitched ideas to publishers and promoted their own works. K. A. Wilson noted in a letter to his friend Joshua Lawrence Chamberlain the shop's social function for authors such as Edward Everett and Henry Wadsworth Longfellow who "congregate[d] daily" at Ticknor and Fields during the 1850s. Mellen Chamberlain, the law librarian, used Boston area bookstores in a businesslike fashion to meet with autograph auctioneers and collectors, old friends, and professors. Margaret Fuller's "Chat in Boston Bookstores," published in 1840 in the *Boston Quarterly Review* gives a more humorous account of a professor and a clergyman who gossip about various publications and authors while they browse through the disorderly stacks.[106]

No matter how readily available books may have been, especially in urban areas, people could not always afford all the books they wanted. Impecuniousness or frugality often dispelled hopes of ownership. J. Edwin Harris, for example, recorded seeing a notice in the *Atlantic Monthly* for *Conduct of Life* during a period in which irregular factory employment, low wages in the wake of the Panic of 1857, and chronic illness coincided with the disappearance of diary entries showing book purchases. John Park, much more financially comfortable than Harris, lamented in 1837 his inability to purchase George Ripley's forthcoming *Specimens*. "I receive Mr Ripley's Prospectus for printing a series of translations of valuable German works," Park recorded months before the publication of the first volume. "I want them—but can I afford to take them?" The most aggressive sales techniques could not seduce the unwilling buyer, as newlywed Crawford Nightingale made clear to James Munroe, the publisher who was a co-partner in the firm that brought out such Transcendentalist works as Emerson's *Nature*. Nightingale wrote:

> You mention some new books—I should be glad to have them if I had the money to pay for them, but I have married a wife & gone to housekeeping within a couple of years, and in order to do it was obliged to anticipate my income. Meanwhile I have stopped buying books, & depended on borrowing, wh I must continue to do, until I have paid my debts, which will take a year longer, & perhaps somewhat more. But I have not forgotten my old and tried friends in the book line, and when I am in funds again will come back to them.

As these testimonies show, "getting the books out" apparently was one thing; getting readers to buy them was quite another.[107]

In an effort to learn about works they might not be able to afford or find, readers often turned to reviews. When the fictional "Prof. P." of "Chat in Boston Bookstores" was asked, "What is read . . . ?," he replied, "Newspapers, Reviews, Travels, Sermons, and controversy, especially theological controversy." We found, like the "Professor," that both reviews and religious controversy were popular—and that reviews of controversial religious authors were even more so. These sometimes forced a reader to take notice of a book that she or he might have otherwise avoided. "I was unfair enough to read Mr Morrison's review of Mr Parkers book, in the Examiner, without any intention of reading the work itself," Feroline (Pierce) Fox wrote to her sister Mary Pierce Poor in 1842. She went on to delineate the reasons why she could never have read Parker's *A Discourse of Matters Pertaining to Religion*:

I cannot bear [Parker's] spirit, or rather his want of reverence for things I esteem holy, and though the book may abound in eloquent passages I care not to read them, if Jesus is lightly esteemed and his mission disregarded. Do you feel as I do? Tell me when you write. Christ is in my view as near as God as possible, without being God himself, and if this comfort and hope is taken from me I am forlorn and alone, for how could I know God excepting through this perfect manifestation of his character and this express image of his person[?]

John Hopkins Morison's critical assessment of Theodore Parker's theological position satisfied Fox's curiosity about an author without her having to buy his work, but it also gave her intellectual ammunition against a viewpoint that she found untenable. To her mind, Morison presented her with a satisfying review, negative as it was.[108]

Most New England readers, like Pierce, inadvertently reviewed the reviewer, either confirming expert opinion when it conformed to their own or disparaging criticism with which they disagreed. For example, disappointed that a writer for the *Foreign Quarterly Review* could not adequately debate David Strauss's *Life of Jesus*, Park sighed, "it is to be regretted that the reply was not by an equally powerful hand." Conversely, readers might dismiss vicious attacks: "Today I read a long insidious article in the 'New Englander' an Orthodox Periodical, issued at New Haven," Park complained in 1845. "[T]he Article is headed 'Theodore Parker and Liberal Christianity.' Such unjust attacks disturb my feelings, perhaps too much—but I trust that in the end, the denomination to which I belong, will by their Christian character and conduct live down the aspersions of their assailants." Of course, not all reviews were religious in nature, and, at times, people simply enjoyed them as substitutes for books themselves. As we have seen, Daniel Child, a subscriber to the *Massachusetts Quarterly Review*, there read Parker's "The Writings of Ralph Waldo Emerson" in 1850. He also perused in that journal James R. Lowell's review of Thoreau's *A Week on the Concord and Merrimack Rivers*, but he probably did not read the book itself. Child called the review "A shrewd article," apparently for its deceptively mild tone.[109]

Child's encounter with a book he never read or purchased underscores a fundamental difference between reader-centered and author/publisher-centered approaches to studying literary dissemination. Many of the transactions described above—oral recitation, personal exchange, library borrowing, reading of reviews or excerpts—were not accompanied by a direct exchange of money for a given textual experience, the nexus naturally so important for publishers and authors seeking a market. Indeed, for producers, brisk and broad sales usually defined success.[110] The publisher's market, the author's public, and the reader's experience were not identical.

Production

Publishers', authors', and readers' experiences seemingly converged, however, when economic panic struck in 1857, alerting all three to the dread of financial loss and instability within the industry. "Books are low stocks are low, every thing but money is low," Christopher Keith noted after buying Laurence Sterne's works "half price." The conditions that for once encouraged him to purchase instead of borrow, alas, adversely affected his employment. In the midst of this uncertainty, Keith's thoughts once again focused upon the relative nature of wealth, a topic introduced to him through his reading of Emerson's essays three years prior, in November 1854. By November 13, 1857, he wrote "if I come out of this crisis with as much money as before it began I shall consider myself fortunate. But this I cannot expect. However, it does not make much difference whether I have little or much when I leave the world." Keith read more than ever, quoted passages from the Bible, digested large segments of newspaper articles, and recorded extensive response to *Experience of Life*. He soon encountered Emerson again, this time through the *Dial*, and once again he pondered those things that transcended earthly value:

> I have been reading the Dial published some few years ago by the transcendentalists. It is beautifully written and contains some very fine literary pieces. It was a good publication in its day but did not have a long life. It was edited by Emerson and a few others of the same stamp. It is a very good volume to read now although it has attained some considerable age. But that is the case usually with works of real merit; they are like wine—they improve by age. So may I grow wiser and better as life wears away.

Nearly twenty years after its demise, the *Dial*, a periodical of the early 1840s, still breathed life for Keith as he thought about the nature of its production. He recalled its famous editor and recognized the collaboration ("a few others of the same stamp") involved in conducting the journal, although he did not record their names. With businesses failing all around him, he emphasized the transitory nature of this publishing venture, which as he noted "did not have a long life." In judging the *Dial*, he also pointed out its enduring features, the beauty of its contributions. For him, the editing and writing quality combined to guarantee its timeless value long after it failed.[111]

When New Englanders thought about the physical object of the book, periodical, or essay, they seldom noticed the production process which, due to rapid local industrialization and commercialization, provided them with an unprecedented number and variety of imprints.[112] Readers took an interest in production primarily when it became tangible to them: when they held in their hands a piece of print or spoke to others directly involved, or when they found some personal element in a printed artifact— just as the *Dial* prompted Keith to muse upon his own aging.

In their letters and diaries, readers seldom allude to a publisher or print shop, unless they were themselves authors or knew authors or booksellers personally. Understanding full well the risks entailed in publishing, John Park (a former editor) could only guess that his acquaintance "Mr. Sullivan," who in 1839 "purchased the subscription list of the Christian Monitor . . . which he will edit & publish," would "find, but too soon, that his calculations will be subject to many deduction." Similarly, Ellis Gray Loring was concerned about his friend Emerson, who, unable to make a firm living on publications alone, was forced to deliver lectures. On the day of the first lecture in the "Conduct of Life" series in 1851, Loring worried:

> It is now said that Emerson is poor, & finds it necessary to lecture for a support. I am sorry for this, for I do not think he needs poverty either as a stimulus to his genius or to soften his character. He really has so much to say that he does not need to have it ground out of him. You know they say the first spontaneous runnings of the wine-press are the most rich & flavorous. Doubtless this is most true, where the vintage is most delicate.

Alexander Hill Everett agonized over the sluggish sale of his book *Critical and Miscellaneous Essays*. Revealing a sober consciousness of how publishers might make or break a sale, Everett griped to his brother-in-law in 1846:

> Munroe did not seem to me to be doing quite so much as he might to get my book into circulation. Would it not be wise to have some placards placed at the windows of shops where it is sold, and perhaps have it advertised more freely? Munroe told me, I think, that he had about 300 copies left. I should like to get rid of them as

soon as possible and prepare for another enlarged edition in two volumes.

Everett's sister, Sarah P. E. Hale, often corresponded with her brother, serving as a college president in Louisiana, about various local publications, including her own. After mentioning how "very handsomely" the third volume of Bancroft's *History* appeared, she noted in 1841 that "My little books for [Christmas] season are out, and have received the usual quantity of puffs from newspaper Editors who have not apparently read them." Authors like Hale were painfully aware of the seasonal sale of their books. "The summer business in books of this kind is very small," Charles S. Francis reminded Caroline Sturgis in 1852 (via her father) of the sales of *Rainbows for Children.*[113]

Such are the perennial concerns of writers. Common readers, by comparison, took notice most often of the publication process when pamphlets, periodicals, and newspaper accounts—especially those espousing theological positions—were to appear soon on the market or were just hot off the press. "Rev. Ralph W. Emerson lately preached, on the Lord's day, at East Lexington. . . . [H]e offered no prayer, during the exercise, and had no text to his sermon," a disgusted John Pierce recorded in 1840. "I shall be hardly less surprised, if in the 'Harbinger,' of which he and Miss Fuller are to be joint editors," Pierce mused, "it should be maintained, that prayer is a relic of barbarism, superceded by the light of modern times." John Park likewise complained of the propagation of infidel ideas, but went further to doubt the propriety of publishing them. After reading James Freeman Clarke's *History of . . . Atonement* (1845), he remarked: "What could have been a motive to the Association Committee to publish such a time-wasting pamphlet, I am at a loss to imagine." Similarly, Park in 1847 saw "no striking reason why" "Mr Furness's Sermon, delivered at Cambridgeport, May 30th" should have been "printed by request."[114]

Despite these censorious attitudes, readers more commonly took a timely interest in current religious developments and its controversies. The speed at which pamphlets or news columns delivered the words of clergymen helped readers keep abreast of the debates. Daniel Child, for example, could acquire during the early 1840s some pamphlets within weeks of the sermons that inspired them. With the popularization of phonography (a method of recording words shorthand by their sound) people interested in what clergymen had to say but not able to attend a Sunday meeting could read a more-or-less exact transcription the next day in the newspaper. Child noted the importance of phonography in the rapid dissemination of Theodore Parker's discourses (as a testament to their reputations, he recorded the name of the phonographer as well). "Evening, husband reading Mr. Parker's sermon, of yesterday, in memory of John Quincy Adams," Child entered in his diary in 1848, "phonographically reported for the Chronotype by Henry M. Parkhurst." Listening to a sermon that was being recorded meant watching a performance that would reach many times the number seated within the church. When "the music hall was filled to its utmost capacity—while vast numbers must have left for want of either sitting or standing room" as it was when Parker spoke ("full hour and a half of rapid delivery") on Anthony Burns in June 1854, those present felt privileged. It "is to be given, in print, to the public tomorrow," Child wrote on June 4, 1854, and expressed amazement at the sermon's length when he read the newspaper version of "Mr. Parker's discourse" the next day in the *Commonwealth*: "more than seven columns." Seeing a text in creation—as one did in witnessing the delivery of a sermon to be printed within hours—gave it an exhilarating immediacy. Perhaps for this reason, Andrew Jackson Davis's *Principles of Nature*, supposedly delivered under trance to an amanuensis, attracted Daniel Child's attention, as it did that of other New England readers.[115]

Readers' interest in the performance-to-print sequence needs to be measured against the relative lack of it in the nuts-and-bolts of production. Certainly publishers struggled against this indifference with often vainglorious newspaper columns or advertisements pointing out "new dress" (usually upgraded typography or paper). Gleason's *Pictorial Drawing Room Companion* also printed several depictions of the industrial process behind the illustrated weekly. The Harpers in New York even recruited the New England children's writer Jacob Abbott to write an illustrated primer on their manufactory, with room-by-room descriptions of each stage of book production.[116] These and similar attempts simply did not register in readers' diaries and letters; even what little attention was given to the look of the book did not concern Transcendentalist texts, which were often published in unexceptional formats. Instead, for readers Transcendentalism in print wore the face of the author—not of the publisher, printer, bookbinder, paper and type maker, or bookseller—a human visage in keeping with readers' own use of literature for everyday social ends.

Transcendentalism and Everyday Life

Sometimes, however, it became difficult to imagine real faces behind literary production if texts fashioned by the industry were not mimetic, not "useful," if they seemed ludicrous, vague, morally offensive, or breached rules of logic—in short, if they seemed out of touch with the everyday experiences of life. For these reasons, Louisa Waterhouse, the wife of physician Benjamin Waterhouse, had little regard for Transcendentalist works within her more conventional (at least among New Englanders) literary diet. She feasted upon Shakespeare, Charles Lamb, Laurence Sterne, Henry Wadsworth Longfellow, Walter Scott, and Samuel Pepys. But she also imbibed practical texts such as spellers, Greek and Latin grammars, histories, and multifarious religious writings, including both the Koran and Channing. Waterhouse developed the habit of recording her imaginative response to literature, often in the form of fanciful dialogues, plays on words, and parodies. In confronting the challenge to say something witty in her diary about Transcendentalism, she chose to lampoon it. She noted its segregation from the material concerns of everyday life and framed it within abstract rules of grammar laid out by John Horne Tooke in his *Diversions of Purley*. "Tooke speaks of a *Transcendental Particle* (see 2 vol. Chap. 7. of Participles.)," Waterhouse wrote. "There is a *Transcendental Emerson* which is about the same." By equating Emerson with a transformative part of speech which turns a verb into an adjective while potentializing its original active qualities, Waterhouse conceived of him converting occurrence into latency. Conversely, she envisioned herself eliciting a flurry of domestic activity:

> I was going to say something of *Transcendentalism*, but it is Monday morn, Butcher would know what we shall have for dinner, a new Butter man. Would you have some Honey? The Merchants ask Shall I measure off the quantity of dimity you want & take back the remainder? The Grocer, Mrs. W. shall I send a Barrel of Flour? [W]e have some new. *Wiffee* has Edward come down in town? Do these Oct[avo] Vols go into this library this morning . . . ? Wiffee Here's the news-paper full of nonsense.[117]

These harried, yet productive spaces of domestic life contrasted sharply with the "Ideals of Every-Day Life" as set forth in an essay of that name in the *Dial* by John Sullivan Dwight insofar as he warned against "letting little economies draw the mind wholly off from the contemplation of anything interesting and inspiring." Waterhouse, like many antebellum New England women, nevertheless found stretches in which to read and think despite less than ideal conditions, "the petty or contradictory details of daily experience."[118] She, in fact, thrived in such an environment.

Sophia Ripley, a producer of Transcendentalism, also remarked upon the incongruities of the literary and everyday life that so intrigued Waterhouse and Dwight. Like Waterhouse, she saw little relevance in molasses and flour for literary genius, as evidenced in a letter to Caroline Sturgis:

> [Margaret Fuller] dropped in to dinner, & then we walked together to the Chelsea boat—talking of all manner of things except those immediately around us, & stood waiting among flour & molasses barrels for half an hour, into whose unholy presence we drew Mr Allston, Coleridge & Goethe, without once thinking how we were profaning these sacred names.[119]

For her, earthly materials "profane" greatness. Embarrassed to be caught among "those things immediately around" while discussing lofty matters, Ripley deprecated the commonplace setting in which her own reception of Goethe and other literary luminaries was being formed—settings that for Thoreau, who asked "What shall I learn of beans or beans of me?" might be inspirational.[120]

Antebellum common readers self-consciously incorporated Transcendentalism in print into their everyday lives, even if they belittled themselves for it. Reception crystallized in quotidian spaces: in factories, in water-cure establishments, while visiting relatives, in the calling rooms of friends. They listened to others reading out loud while caring for their children or performing other domestic duties; in doing so, these readers/listeners socialized the very texts, ironically, that exalted the individual. In the same vein, communities of readers sometimes formed in private homes to assay Transcendentalism's challenge to doctrines definitive of their congregations. Predictably, the conversation in such settings wandered, to the chagrin of some readers like John Park, toward the mundane: "stoves and furnaces—persons going to destruction by drunkenness—the licence law—the scarcity of wood—and on eating onions!!—all very intelligible topics, suited like certain elementary books 'to the meanest capacity.'"[121]

Transcendentalist texts became entrenched in the everyday as they were disseminated. The interpersonal circulation of books—those relatively expensive items within a world of consumer necessities—outside of the market not only helped people practice frugality, it also fostered relationships as social networks were forged through lending and borrowing. Sending books via courier involved still other middlemen (and women) in the sociability of exchange. Although we found little extensive information on the experience of library borrowing or book purchases, such excursions to shops and repositories invariably drew people into a community of readers.

Given the everyday context of reading, it comes as no surprise that common readers seldom commented upon production, except as it became concretized through the people who produced the initial text. Readers simply were curious about authors, but seldom abstracted these Transcendentalist producers as supra-human; nor did readers engage a text without imagining the mediation of a person with the pages of text. They followed the course of authors' lives in the newspaper and gossiped about them at times. They watched them preach to crowds, only to see the speech reproduced in the columns of newspapers the next day. No wonder the lyceum and public lecture attracted so many of our informants—or that the spoken words of Transcendentalists inspired antebellum New Englanders to fill more lines in their letters and diaries than did the printed word.

Probably because they valued the human dimensions of literary production and its dissemination, people often became alienated by the inability of Transcendentalist authors to speak to them in a "coherent" fashion that was so necessary to make a reading experience "interesting." An inability to locate the meaning in the often confusing lexicon of Transcendentalism broke the "flow" that made reading pleasurable. But the intuitive logic of Transcendentalism defied "study," and try as they might, readers found that time and effort did not always produce results. No wonder Christopher Keith became frustrated quickly in his attempts to comment upon Emerson's words as he transcribed fragments from "Nature" and other essays.[122] He, like some other readers, resigned himself merely to quoting rather than digesting Transcendentalism. Similarly, Mary Baker Eddy exemplified many Victorian scrapbook and commonplace book makers in her assemblage without commentary of newsclipped Transcendental aphorisms.

Little wonder that, dripped out in such manner, Transcendentalist texts became almost lost within the larger texts of people's lives. An entry from Elizabeth (Dwight) Cabot's diary was not unusual in its weave of a Transcendentalist thread through a dense, everyday texture:

Saturday Jan. 3 [1857]. Splendid snow-storm. Arranging presents, flowers, & photographs. Visit from Mr Heard. Charles & Arthur to dine, Ravelles in the afternoon, with the children. Mr & Mrs Dabney & Miss D.—to tea, read Mrs Stowe[,] wrote to Ellen & read Thoreau in the evening.

Yet, at times, readers like Cabot experienced a union of the sacred and the profane and professed an empathy with those "connected critics" who wanted so desperately to reach them: "Teaching Nellie, settling accounts, reading newspapers [and] Mr Emerson. A blessed quiet morning."[123]

However rare those momentary encounters with Transcendentalism in print are within the thousands of extant antebellum New England diaries that discuss reading, they are, nevertheless, "blessed" ones, indeed.

ACKNOWLEDGEMENTS

Since the larger project from which this essay is drawn has been ongoing since 1992, we have accumulated too many debts to list them all here. However, we must acknowledge the generous contribution of funds from a National Endowment for the Humanities-American Antiquarian Society six-month resident Fellowship (1992); a Study Grant from the Schlesinger Library, Radcliffe College (1993); and the Benjamin F. Stevens Fellowship from the Massachusetts Historical Society (1994). A 1998–1999 Fellowship for University Teachers awarded by the National Endowment for the Humanities provided a year's time off from university duties to complete our book manuscript on the experience of reading in antebellum New England, based upon research from which this essay has drawn—and the Schlesinger Library at Radcliffe College granted both authors Honorary Visiting Fellowships for the same purpose. From 1995 through 1997 the Georgia State University (GSU) Department of History supplied a Graduate Research Assistant, Dale Vanderhorst, who helped us transcribe the John Pierce reading list and the Taunton Social Library Records. An Outstanding Junior Faculty Award from the College of Arts and Sciences at GSU and a History Department Summer Research Leave together provided funds for about six months of travel to collections throughout New England during 1996. A GSU Research Inititation Grant funded yet another expedition north to complete our research in the fall of 1997, and the History Department provided essential release time to do so. In these and many other ways, the GSU History faculty has encouraged our collaboration in research and publishing since our 1992 arrival in Atlanta. Also, we are deeply grateful to Margie Patterson and the other Interlibrary Loan Officers at GSU who secured for us a stream of diverse materials. Too numerous, as well, are the many acknowledgments due to the participants in the M.H.S. conference from which this volume springs, but we must single out for special thanks our two commentators, Leo Marx and Alan Trachtenberg, along with Dean Grodzins, Philip Gura, Mary Kelley, and Joel Myerson. Finally, we wish to thank Richard D. Brown and Kenneth Silverman for their constant encouragement of our work.

NOTES

1. Mary Pierce to John and Lucy (Tappan) Pierce, Nov. 16, 1838, Poor Family Papers, Schlesinger Library, Radcliffe College (see Table 1 for library abbreviations in subsequent citations). For background on Mary Pierce, see James R. McGovern, *Yankee Family* (New Orleans, 1975); Janet Farrell Brodie, *Contraception and Abortion in Nineteenth-Century America* (Ithaca, 1994), chap. 1; Ellen K. Rothman, *Hands and Hearts: A History of Courtship in America* (New York, 1984);

and Ronald J. Zboray and Mary Saracino Zboray, "Whig Women, Politics, and Culture in the Campaign of 1840: Three Perspectives From Massachusetts," *Journal of the Early Republic* 17(1997):277–315.

2. John Pierce did not own (nor did he record having borrowed) a copy of *Nature*; see John Pierce, "Book Lists," 1814–1849, Poor Family Papers, SL. Pierce listed 1,389 books in his roster, which is noticeably lacking in Transcendentalist texts. This comes as no surprise, given Pierce's discontent with other of Emerson's productions. McGovern, *Yankee Family*, 23. On Mary's brother-in-law Hedge, see 45–46.

3. The region was an important Transcendentalist locus, probably the most significant one in the United States. Still, Octavius Brooks Frothingham's contention that "there never was such a thing as Transcendentalism out of New England" ignores the movement's national dimension. *Transcendentalism in New England: A History* (1876; New York, 1959), 105. Yet the reception-centered model we present here works better with a narrower regional focus, especially since so much of what was read was produced within the region.

4. Our use of the phrase "everyday life" is influenced by the theoretical concerns expressed in the essays in *The History of Everyday Life: Reconstructing Historical Experiences and Ways of Life*, ed. Alf Lüdtke, trans. William Templer (Princeton, 1995); see especially Lüdtke's essay "What Happened to the 'Fiery Red Glow'? Workers' Experiences and German Fascism," 198–251, for use of a diary to understand everyday experience.

5. Roger Chartier and Daniel Roche, "New Approaches to the History of the Book," in *Constructing the Past: Essays in Historical Methodology*, ed. Jacques Le Goff and Pierre Nora (New York, 1985), 189–214; Roger Chartier, "Texts, Printing, Reading," in *The New Cultural History*, ed. Lynn Hunt (Berkeley, 1989), 154–177.

6. This holds even when authorship is emphasized. Stephen Adams and Donald Ross, Jr., *Revising Mythologies: The Composition of Thoreau's Major Works* (Charlottesville, 1988); Steven Fink, *Prophet in the Marketplace: Thoreau's Development as a Professional Writer* (Princeton, 1992); Lawrence Rosenwald, *Emerson and the Art of the Diary* (New York, 1988).

7. We mean not to diminish the value of this work, for indeed we rely quite heavily upon it, but to underscore the relative (and unfortunate) lack of "mainstreaming" that might allow the wealth of information about publication, marketing, and reception to stand on its own. Perhaps this is because the opinion William Charvat voiced in 1959—despite the development of the so-called history of the book since then—remains all too true: "Publishing is relevant to literary history only in so far as it can be shown to be, ultimately, a shaping influence on literature." *Literary Publishing in America, 1790–1850* (1959; Amherst, Mass., 1993), 7.

8. Richard F. Teichgraeber III, *Sublime Thoughts/Penny Wisdom: Situating Emerson and Thoreau in the American Market* (Baltimore, 1995), esp. part 3; William J. Sowder, *Emerson's Reviewers and Commentators: A Biographical and Bibliographical Analysis of Nineteenth-Century Periodical Criticism* (Hartford, 1968); Gary Scharnhorst, *Henry David Thoreau: An Annotated Bibliography of Comment and Criticism Before 1900* (New York, 1992).

9. Kenneth Walter Cameron, *Emerson's Transcendentalism and British Swedenborgianism* (Hartford, 1984); Kenneth Marc Harris, *Carlyle and Emerson, Their*

Long Debate (Cambridge, Mass., 1978); Stanley M. Vogel, *German Literary Influences on the American Transcendentalists* (1955; Hamden, Conn., 1970); Robert Weisbuch, *The Atlantic Double-Cross: American Literature and British Influence in the Age of Emerson* (Chicago, 1986).

10. One line of inquiry pursues the Transcendentalists' own reading; the findings, however, are usually put to the service of textual interpretation with the implication that such information provides "keys" to unlock esoteric references in the canon. See, for example, Kenneth Walter Cameron, *Emerson and Thoreau as Readers: Selected Chapters from the Transcendentalists and Minerva* (Hartford, 1958); and Kenneth Walter Cameron, *Transcendental Reading Patterns . . .* (Hartford, 1970). Robert Sattelmeyer draws upon this research in his *Thoreau's Reading: A Study in Intellectual History with Bibliographical Catalogue* (Princeton, 1988).

11. For examples of a range of scholarly constructions of the Transcendentalist reader, see Stephen Railton, *Authorship and Audience: Literary Performance in the American Renaissance* (Princeton, 1991); Alan D. Hodder, *Emerson's Rhetoric of Revelation: Nature, the Reader, and the Apocalypse Within* (University Park, Pa., 1989); Christina Zwarg, *Feminist Conversations: Fuller, Emerson, and the Play of Reading* (Ithaca, 1995). Two edited works point the way for historicizing the reader: Cathy N. Davidson, ed., *Reading in America: Literature and Social History* (Baltimore, 1989); and James L. Machor, ed., *Readers in History: Nineteenth-Century American Literature and the Contexts of Response* (Baltimore, 1993).

12. Here we present primarily the "common reader" or those who were not professional writers or prominent as literary figures. Although we did read papers of Transcendentalist writers such as Elizabeth Peabody and Caroline Sturgis, we avoided focus upon their perceptions except insofar as they comment upon the common reader's experience. The term "common reader" is conventional in readership studies; see, for example, Richard D. Altick, *The English Common Reader: A Social History of the Mass Reading Public* (Chicago, 1957). Of course, common readers range from those of uncommon means to relatively poor ones.

13. Others, of course, have used the personal records of historical readers to describe the reading experience: inscription and marginalia in books is analyzed in Cathy N. Davidson, *Revolution and the Word: The Rise of the Novel in America* (New York, 1986), 5, 6–9, 69–79, 264–266; Mary Kelley, "Reading Women/Women Reading: The Making of Learned Women in Antebellum America," *Journal of American History* 83(1996):401–424; Marilyn Ferris Motz, "The Private Alibi: Literacy and Community in the Diaries of Two Nineteenth-Century American Women," in *Inscribing the Daily: Critical Essays on Women's Diaries*, ed. Suzanne L. Bunkers and Cynthia A. Huff (Amherst, Mass., 1996), 189–206; Barbara Sicherman, "Sense and Sensibility: A Case Study of Women's Reading in Late-Victorian America," in *Reading in America*, 201–225; Barbara Sicherman, "Reading and Ambition: M. Carey Thomas and Female Heroism," *American Quarterly* 45(1993):73–103. Richard D. Brown effectively uses diary literature to understand social processes surrounding reading—especially the drive for upward mobility—in his *Knowledge Is Power: The Diffusion of Information in Early America, 1700–1865* (New York, 1989).

14. A reader-centered approach has, of course, its own advantages and limitations. It should not supplant but augment those that center on authors or texts. It rounds out the perhaps needlessly complex flow chart of "The Communications Circuit" posited by Robert Darnton in his seminal essay, "What Is the History of Books?" reprinted in *The Kiss of Lamourette: Reflections in Cultural History* (New York, 1990), 110. See also Roger Chartier, "Texts, Printing, Reading." The chief advantage of the reader-centered approach is its avoidance of often imprecise abstractions like "the market" or "the reading public" applied to the specifics of cultural transmission through print. It also encourages a finer appreciation of overall relationships between various titles and of the multivalency of printed artifacts. For a fuller discussion of multivalency, see Ronald J. Zboray and Mary Saracino Zboray, "Books, Reading, and the World of Goods in Antebellum New England," *American Quarterly* 48(1996):588–589.

15. Although Transcendentalism has roots before 1830, most of the major defining events, such as Emerson's pastoral resignation, his "Nature" and "Divinity School Address," the founding of the Transcendentalist Club, the Ripley-Norton debate, and the start of Brownson's *Boston Quarterly Review*, took place in the 1830s. The 1861 terminus is more problematical, of course, for some species of Transcendentalism (or at least the reputation of some writers associated with it) remained strong through the war and postbellum years, but it can be argued that this is a distinct, more mature, and perhaps more institutionalized phase. As Lawrence Buell has written, "The Civil War . . . marks the approximate point beyond which the energy of the New England Renaissance began to abate." *New England Literary Culture from Revolution through Renaissance* (New York, 1986), 12. In any case, we have here followed convention with our terminus.

16. We borrow the term "informants" from cultural anthropologists, some of whom have come to appreciate the value of written personal accounts. Although it is an unusual tool, one anthropologist introduced diary keeping to her informant in order to study village culture in Tanzania; see Pat Caplan, "Spirits and Sex: A Swahili Informant and His Diary," in *Anthropology and Autobiography*, ed. Judith Okely and Helen Callaway (New York, 1992), 64–81. Caplan discovered that diaries allowed her informant to categorize knowledge about his culture rather than being cued by the anthropologist. As Caplan explains, "he was the one to choose the topics contained in [the diary], not I" (66). The historical diary (or letter) removes the problem inherent in the interview with living informants that Kirsten Hastrup notes: "What we listen to are the informants' own voices, but what they speak are not 'cultural truths'; they are circumstantial responses to the ethnographer's presence and questioning." "Writing Ethnography: State of the Art," in *Anthropology and Autobiography*, 121. James Clifford, "Introduction: Partial Truths," in *Writing Culture: The Poetics and Politics of Ethnography*, ed. James Clifford and George E. Marcus (Berkeley, 1986), discusses these problems.

17. On the definition of the boundaries, see Francis X. Blouin, Jr., *The Boston Region, 1810–1850: A Study of Urbanization* (Ann Arbor, 1980), chap. 2. The 1850 U.S. census gives 2,728,116 as New England's population, with 837,933 for the Boston region. Aggregate population figures derive from J. D. B. DeBow, *Statistical View of the United States . . . Being a Compendium of the Seventh Census* (Washington, D.C., 1854), 114; with county data from J. D. B. DeBow, *The Seventh Census of*

the United States: 1850 (1853; New York, 1990), 4–7, 20–21, 34–36, 50–52, 67, 78–79. The moderate bias toward information from the Boston region must be understood in light of a phenomenon long recognized by historical geographers who trace the relationship of information flow to city systems: dominant cities tend to send much more correspondence than they receive and much more than even secondary cities. For example, northern rural districts in 1856 sent only 3.5 letters per capita while Boston sent 40.8. Ronald J. Zboray, *A Fictive People: Antebellum Economic Development and the American Reading Public* (New York, 1993), 72, based on figures in Allan Pred, *Urban Growth and City Systems in the United States, 1840–1860* (Cambridge, Mass., 1980), 225. Our data confirm that this bias emerges from correspondence, for when letters are subtracted, the remaining figure yields nearly the same proportions as seen in the aggregate population figures: the Boston region, 34.33 percent, and the rest of New England, 65.67 percent.

18. We do not reject class as an analytical concept in this time and place, but only the blunt determinism that attempts to link a particular title to a specific socioeconomic group. Rather, insofar as class more significantly influences overall reading patterns and experiences, it is better understood in terms of likelihoods, not certainties, expressed through specific historically grounded life trajectories—another reason for the centrality of the biographical dimension in our research method.

19. For a keen discussion of class in antebellum New England, see Karen V. Hansen, *A Very Social Time: Crafting Community in Antebellum New England* (Berkeley, 1994), 30–35. See also Peter R. Knights, *The Plain People of Boston, 1830–1860: A Study in City Growth* (New York, 1971); and Peter R. Knights, *Yankee Destinies: The Lives of Ordinary Nineteenth-Century Bostonians* (Chapel Hill, 1991). Of our 822 informants, about 391 or 47.56 percent are women and 431 or 52.43 percent are men. The women, however, more than redress the slight imbalance by their generally more extensive accounts.

20. Classic discussions of "history from the bottom up" and "the inarticulate" appear in Jesse Lemisch, "The American Revolution Seen from the Bottom Up," in *Towards a New Past: Dissenting Essays in American History*, ed. Barton Bernstein (New York, 1968), 3–45; and Jesse Lemisch, "'Listening to the Inarticulate': William Widger's Dream and the Loyalties of American Revolutionary Seamen in British Prisons," *Journal of Social History* 3(1969–1970):1–29. Our informants, by definition, are thus not the "inarticulate," but, indeed, can be at times highly articulate and even revelatory about their experiences, literary and otherwise.

21. For uses of "dead informants," see Zboray and Zboray, "Books, Reading, and the World of Goods," 588–589; Karen V. Hansen and Cameron L. MacDonald, "Research Note: Surveying the Dead Informant: Analysis and Historical Interpretation," *Qualitative Sociology* 18(1995):227–236.

22. Darnton, "First Steps Toward a History of Reading," in *The Kiss of Lamourette*, 181; Wolfgang Iser, *The Implied Reader: Patterns of Communication in Prose Fiction from Bunyan to Beckett* (Baltimore, 1974).

23. We used these works to help us set limits: Frothingham, *Transcendentalism in New England*; Perry Miller, *The American Transcendentalists, Their Prose and Poetry* (Garden City, N.Y., 1957); Paul F. Boller, Jr., *American Transcendentalism, 1830–1860: An Intellectual Inquiry* (New York, 1974); Barbara L. Packer, "The

Transcendentalists," in *The Cambridge History of American Literature*, ed. Sacvan Bercovitch (Cambridge, 1993), 2:329–604; Wesley T. Mott, ed., *Biographical Dictionary of Transcendentalism* (Westport, Conn., 1996); Clarence L. F. Gohdes, *The Periodicals of American Transcendentalism* (Durham, N.C., 1931); William R. Hutchison, *The Transcendentalist Ministers: Church Reform in the New England Renaissance* (New Haven, 1959).

24. On Lucy (Tappan) Pierce, see McGovern, *Yankee Family*, 12–13; on the religious strife within the extended and nuclear family, 23–25; on the sisters, 40–49; and, on Mary's beliefs, 75–76.

25. Ronald J. Zboray and Mary Saracino Zboray, "Reading and Everyday Life in Antebellum Boston: The Diary of Daniel F. and Mary G. Child," *Libraries and Culture* 32(1997):285–323; for his reading list, 1839–1861, see 304–314.

26. John Park, Diary, 1791–1852, 5 vols., by courtesy of the Trustees of the Boston Public Library. Margaret Fuller died on July 19, 1850, but Park registered it days later. See Mar. 25, 1837, for Park's own digestion of his life up to that point. On Park, see Charles Capper, *Margaret Fuller, An American Romantic Life: The Private Years* (New York, 1992), 56–63; Edward H. Hall, "Reminiscences of Dr. John Park," *Proceedings of the American Antiquarian Society*, n.s. 7(1892):69–93.

27. For information on Elizabeth (Dwight) Cabot, see *The Letters of Elizabeth Cabot*, [ed. Richard C. Cabot?] (Boston, 1905). James Elliot Cabot met Emerson for the first time in 1845 coinciding with when Emerson had his copy of *Bhagvatgeeta, or Dialogues of Kreeshna and Arjoon*, trans. Charles Wilkins (London, 1785)]; on the event, see Eleanor M. Tilton, introduction to *The Letters of Ralph Waldo Emerson*, ed. Eleanor M. Tilton (New York, 1990), 7:37–38.

28. On the social nature of reading in antebellum New England, see Zboray and Zboray, "Books, Reading, and the World of Goods." On reading in benevolent societies, see Lori D. Ginzberg, *Women and the Work of Benevolence: Morality, Politics, and Class in the Nineteenth-Century United States* (New Haven, 1990), 149–152.

29. Transcendentalism might variously be described as, among other things, a trend, influence, fashion, or movement. The latter downplays the individualism of Transcendentalists but highlights their social consciousness, institutional critique, and, among themselves, community life. See Anne C. Rose, *Transcendentalism as a Social Movement, 1830–1850* (New Haven, 1981), viii–ix. On the importance of social and communal considerations, see Packer, "The Transcendentalists."

30. Daniel Walker Howe, *The Unitarian Conscience: Harvard Moral Philosophy, 1805–1861* (Cambridge, Mass., 1970), 174. Howe's chapter on "Genteel Letters" outlines some of the favorite authors. Our own research among common New England readers also shows a similarly high regard for William Wordsworth, Walter Scott, Maria Edgeworth, Felicia Hemans, Thomas Reid, Hugh Blair, and Thomas Gray. A relish for romantic novels, cheap fiction, and especially Byron among the population overrode the Unitarian Moralists' attempts to discourage such reading. See Howe, *Unitarian Conscience*, chap. 7, *passim*, and 192, 200–201. According to Lawrence Buell, the "intimate connection between the American Unitarian movement and the so-called American literary renaissance has been long known and loudly proclaimed." See his "The Literary Significance of the Unitarian Movement," in *American Unitarianism, 1805–1865*, ed. Conrad

Edick Wright (Boston, 1989), 163, and throughout for the complex nature of this relationship. That Unitarians also outnumber other denominations for being the most "powerful, influential, prestigious and wealthy" in Boston naturally registers in the output of more detailed personal accounts and in the access to more books. On wealth, see William H. Pease and Jane H. Pease, *The Web of Progress: Private Values and Public Styles in Boston and Charleston, 1828–1843* (New York, 1985), Table A-5, 237.

31. On the liberalizing trends within Congregationalism prior to 1805, see Conrad Wright, *The Beginnings of Unitarianism in America* (Boston, 1955). For an enlightening essay on the relationship of Samuel Hopkins and Jonathan Edwards to William Ellery Channing, see Conrad Wright, "The Rediscovery of Channing," in his *The Liberal Christians: Essays on American Unitarian History* (Boston, 1970). Wright elsewhere is quick to point out, however, that "the conflict between liberals and orthodox within the churches of the Standing Order was not the only reason for such changes" (*i.e.*, institutional restructuring, religious pluralism, improved transportation, technological change); Conrad Wright, "Institutional Reconstruction in the Unitarian Controversy," in *American Unitarianism*, 5.

32. John Park, Diary, May 19, 1794, BPL. Of course, liberal readers might read such works to their aging parents who held onto conservative beliefs. Sarah P. E. Hale, for example, read Jonathan Edwards's *The Great Christian Doctrine of Original Sin Defended* to her father, who was too ill to go to church; Diary, vol. 2, May 27, 1860, Hale Papers, The Sophia Smith Collection, Smith College, Northampton, Mass.

33. Sarah Smith (Cox) Browne to Albert Gallatin Browne, June 29, 1855, Browne Family Papers, SL. Browne is probably referring to Daniel Defoe, *The Political History of the Devil* (1726), later simply entitled in various editions *The History of the Devil*.

34. John Park, Diary, Oct. 5, 1847, BPL; vol. 4 [n. pag.]: "Mr[.] Burnside[,] Edwards on the Will & Grimshaw's History of the United States" (Nov. 7, 1842); "John C. B. Davis[,] Edwards on the Will" (July 15, 1845); "Mr[.] Burnside[,] Edwards on the Will" (Oct. 14, 1847). Another liberal who confronted orthodox texts was John Pierce, who read his library copy of Ezra Stiles Ely, *A Contrast Between Calvinism and Hopkinsianism*, on Aug. 22, 1815, and a review of *Freedom of the Will* from H. P. Tappan on June 28, 1839. "Book Lists," Poor Family Papers, SL.

35. Elizabeth Pierce, Mary's conservative sister, read Edwards's *A History of the Work of Redemption*. "I may depend upon the general correctness of his sentiments, because he was a man of prayer & humility with exalted views of God. Such qualities prepare a person to receive & communicate truth." Notebook, c. July 1828, Poor Family Papers, SL. Elizabeth Jocelyn is a good example of a well-read conservative Congregationalist. She belonged to Samuel William Southmayd Dutton's North Church, in New Haven. According to her diary (Jocelyn Boxes, Connecticut Historical Society, Hartford), she read Jonathan Edwards's *Sinners in the Hands of an Angry God* (Mar. 2, 1851), *The Treatise on Religious Affections* one Sunday when she remained at home (Mar. 10, 1851), and *The Life of David Brainerd* (May 11, 18, and 25, July 6, 1851). But she also read Jacob Abbott, *The Young Christian*; Catharine Maria Sedgwick, *The Poor Rich Man and the Rich Poor Man* (Mar. 17 and 19, 1839); Fénelon's "very interesting" *Lives of*

the Ancient Philosophers (n.d., 1841); John Gillies, *Memoirs of Rev. George Whitefield* (Sept. 12, 1847); Thomas Cogswell Upham, *Principles of the Interior or Hidden Life* (Nov. 5, 12, and 21, 1848); Thomas Dick, *The Philosophy of a Future State* (Mar. 5, 1849); Horace Bushnell, *God in Christ* (May 6, 9, and 13, 1849); Edward W. Hooker, *Memoir of Mrs. Sarah L. Huntington Smith* (May 5, 1850); Ichabod S. Spencer, *A Pastor's Sketches* (Mar. 4 and 6, 1851); George Gilfillan, *The Bards of the Bible* (Feb. 17 and Mar. 2, 1851); and William Nevins, *Practical Thoughts* (n.d., 1851). Rev. Jonas Perkins, who catalogued his "Books on Divinity" (BPL), read Edwards's *Freedom of the Will* and Samuel Hopkins's *The System of Doctrines*.

36. J. Edwin Harris, Diary, Apr. 17, 1858, J. Edwin Harris, Diaries and Letterbooks, 1856–1870, Maine Historical Society. On Wednesday, June 16, 1858, he recorded: "Like a damned fool as I am, went to church tonight—ships and porridge—Hell and Damnation."

37. Persis (Sibley) Andrews, Diary, Apr. 16, 1843, MeHS. Karen V. Hansen found similar behavior recorded in her set (primarily working-class) of antebellum New England diaries. Approximately two-thirds of these diarists attended services at "more than one church." *A Very Social Time*, 151 and Table 2, 152.

38. Christopher Keith, Diary, Aug. 30, 1857, Jan. 24, 31, May 23, June 13, May 21, 1858, Miscellaneous Manuscripts Collection, Rhode Island Historical Society, Providence. On Dwight as an example of Edwardsian "reassertion of the freedom of the will," see Wright, *Beginnings of Unitarianism in America*, 92.

39. The starting point for considerations of the German impact is Henry August Pochmann, *German Culture in America: Philosophical and Literary Influences, 1600–1900* (Madison, 1957); see also Stanley M. Vogel, *German Literary Influences on the American Transcendentalists* (1955; Hamden, Conn., 1970).

40. John Park, Diary, Oct. 17, 1845, BPL. Daniel Child, for example, consumed much of the popular literature mentioned in David S. Reynolds, *Beneath the American Renaissance: The Subversive Imagination in the Age of Emerson and Melville* (New York, 1988). See Zboray and Zboray, "Reading and Everyday Life in Antebellum Boston," 304–315. Child also delved into longer works, such as Lockhart's *Life* of Walter Scott. Harris, conversely, favored genteel and Romantic poetry, especially Byron, Thomas Moore, and Longfellow. On the antebellum New England middle-class audience for Eugene Sue's famous tome, see Ronald J. Zboray and Mary Saracino Zboray, "The Mysteries of New England: Eugene Sue's 'Imitators,' (1844)," *Nineteenth-Century Contexts* 22(1999), forthcoming.

41. As David Reynolds reminds us in his contribution to this volume, "'A Chaos-Deep Soil': Emerson, Thoreau, and Popular Culture," Emerson and Thoreau were more in tune with the popular culture surrounding them than previously supposed, because that culture was not as conventional as commonly assumed.

42. Alan D. Hodder, "Concord Orientalism, Thoreauvian Autobiography, and the Artist of Kouroo," elsewhere in this volume. Arthur Versluis points out that Transcendentalist interest in Asian religions was primed by the Unitarian perspective, as well as the influx of information about East and South Asia. *American Transcendentalism and Asian Religions* (New York, 1993), 6–8.

43. Caroline Sturgis Tappan to Ralph Waldo Emerson, Nov. 1850, Sturgis/Tappan/Prout Papers, SC.

44. See, for example, Frances Jocelyn, Diary, 1852–1853, CHS: "Elizabeth [Jocelyn] and Susan attended Mr [Henry Richard] Hoisington's Lecture in the Court St Church [New Haven, Connecticut] on the Hindoos" (Jan. 27, 1852); "Mr [David] Peck accompanied Cornelia, Sue, & I, to hear Mr. Hoisington lecture on '*Hindoo Temples*'" (Jan. 28, 1852).

45. Louisa Lee Waterhouse, Journal, c. Apr. 19, 1840, Massachusetts Historical Society; Ellen Wright to Lucy McKim, Feb. 16, 1861, Garrison Papers, SC; Enoch Hale, Diary, 1839–1849, Feb. 1, 1843, Phillips Library, Peabody Essex Museum, Salem; Harriet Low, Diary, Nov. 27, 1833, typed transcript, PEM, original in the Low-Mills Family Papers, Library of Congress, Manuscript Division. Raja Rammohun Roy, *The Precepts of Jesus: The Guide to Peace and Happiness* (Calcutta, 1820). Low found (July 21, 1829) much useful knowledge in a review (*Quarterly Review*) of Reginald Heber's missionary account, *Narrative of a Journey through the Upper Provinces of India* (London, 1829). Low had been reading Channing's sermons regularly during her stay in China, especially on Sundays, often when she could not attend church services. See her diary, Feb. 19 and 20, Apr. 15 and 23, June 10, and July 8, 1832. "After Church read some of Mr. Channing's works. Oh what a mind!" (July 8, 1832); "Came home [from Church] and read two excellent sermons. One of Dr. Channing's which I would advise you to read, it is the 'Liberal Preacher'" (Mar. 31, 1833). See also Sept. 7, 8, 15, 22, and 29, Nov. 10 and 24, and Dec. 1, 1833.

46. John Park, Diary, May 12, 1848, and Jan. 22, 1839, BPL.

47. John Park, Diary, Jan. 22, 1839, BPL; Cyrus Parker Bradley, Diary, Oct. 4, 1836, New Hampshire Historical Society, Concord; Harriet Low, Diary, Sept. 7, 1833, PEM; Mellen Chamberlain, Diary, Nov. 3, 1844, by courtesy of the Trustees of the Boston Public Library.

48. William Ellery Channing, *Self-Culture* (1839; New York, 1969), 42; Alexander Hill Everett, Diary, Jan. 1, 1839, Hale Papers, SC; Hannah Lowell (Jackson) Cabot, Diary, Sept. 4, 1839, typed transcript, carbon copy, 1839–1842, pages 3, 12, Almy Family Papers, SL; George Foster Allen, Papers and Diaries, 1850–1871, Aug. 2, 1851, PEM. He considers self-culture at the undated end of his diary for 1850. On self-culture, see David Robinson, *Apostle of Culture: Emerson as Preacher and Lecturer* (Philadelphia, 1982).

49. Donald M. Scott, "The Popular Lecture and the Creation of a Public in Mid-Nineteenth-Century America," *Journal of American History* 66(1980): 791–809; Carl Bode, *The American Lyceum: Town Meeting of the Mind* (Carbondale, Ill., 1956); Mary Kupiec Cayton, "The Making of an American Prophet: Emerson, His Audiences, and the Rise of the Culture Industry in Nineteenth-Century America," *American Historical Review* 92(1987):597–620.

50. On the range and categories of antebellum common readers' response in the Boston region to a variety of texts, including fiction and nonfiction, see Ronald J. Zboray and Mary Saracino Zboray, "'Have You Read . . . ?': Real Readers and Their Responses in Antebellum Boston and Its Region," *Nineteenth-Century Literature* 52(1997):139–179. Nina Baym's work in this area is, of course, foundational; many of our findings about categories of response—such as a respect for verisimilitude and usefulness, as well as a desire for a book to sustain interest while being morally sound—reflect those in *Novels, Readers, and Reviewers: Re-*

sponses to Fiction in Antebellum America (Ithaca, 1984). On the discourse of reviewers, see also James L. Machor, "Fiction and Informed Reading in Early Nineteenth-Century America," *Nineteenth-Century Literature* 47(1992):320–348.

51. Martha Osborne Barrett, Diary, Dec. 22, 1854, PEM.

52. For a complete listing of the Childs' reading, including works by the ministers
named in the text, and for a treatment of the controversial topics and Parker's relationship to Spiritualism, see Zboray and Zboray, "Reading and Everyday Life in
Antebellum Boston." Daniel F. and Mary D. Child, Diary, 1839–1876, D. F. Child
Collection, MHS. On the range of antislavery reform activity among Unitarian
ministers, including Bellows and Dewey, see Conrad Wright, "The Minister as
Reformer: Profiles of Unitarian Ministers" in *The Liberal Christians*, 62–80.

53. Elizabeth Dwight to Ellen (Dwight) Twisleton, May 14, 1854 [*i.e.*, 1855], Cabot
Family Papers, SL.

54. Harris made about $17 a month but managed to purchase volumes of poetry and
issues of magazines; on his salary, see his Diary, MeHS, Jan. 15, 1856, Apr. 2, 29,
June 30, 1857, Mar. 4, Apr. 29, 1858. Among the books he purchased were collec-
tions of poems by Charles Swain (June 5, 1857), Alfred Tennyson (June 8, 1857),
Gerald Massey (Aug. 1, 1857), Robert Burns (Nov. 6, 1857), Henry Wadsworth
Longfellow (Jan. 11, 1858), and Leigh Hunt (Feb. 5, 1858). On his response to
Romantic poets, see J. Edwin Harris to George A. Callahan, Apr. 4, 1858, vol. 7,
Letterbook; on reading *"Reformation" John Adams*, Diary, Apr. 13, 1856; on reading the Transcendentalist works mentioned, Sept. 1 and 4, Mar. 28, and Sept. 16,
1860. Harris aspired to be a poet; one of his creations, written on "Sunday eve"
(i.e., Jan. 29, 1860) and called "'The Witches Sacrament,'" betrays further his dis-
illusionment with religiosity (Diary, Jan. 31, 1860). Our findings add another dimension to the assertion that the *Atlantic Monthly* under the editorship of James
Russell Lowell was primarily read by the middle class. Ellery Sedgwick, *The Atlantic Monthly, 1857–1909: Yankee Humanism at High Tide and Ebb* (Amherst,
Mass., 1994), 40–41. Lucy Larcom to Harriet Hanson Robinson, Dec. 18, 1857,
Papers of Harriet Jane Hanson Robinson and Harriette Lucy Robinson Shattuck,
SL. Larcom was reacting to the many parodies of the poem, as her letter states;
see [Charles Godfrey Leland], "[A Defense of 'Brahma']," in *Critical Essays on
Ralph Waldo Emerson*, ed. Robert E. Burkholder and Joel Myerson (Boston,
1983), 164–169.

55. Augusta King, undated, newsclippings, etc., vol. 5, Ellis Gray Loring Papers, SL;
access to photocopy of Mary Baker Eddy's Scrapbook, circa 1830–1860, courtesy
of Church History Department, The First Church of Christ, Scientist, Boston,
Mass.; Ralph Waldo Emerson, "Self-Reliance," in *The Collected Works of Ralph
Waldo Emerson*, ed. Alfred R. Ferguson et al. (Cambridge, Mass., 1971–), 2:27;
Caroline Bowen, Diary and Commonplace Book, 1841–1855, commonplace book
within diary, n.d., CHS.

56. Keith, Diary, scattered entries, Nov. 12–14, 1854, RIHS. He quotes or paraphrases
passages from Emerson's "Manners," "Nature," and "Gifts" in the *Collected
Works*, 3:90, 82, 103, 93, 94, 109. Words between "^ ^" denote Keith's additions to
Emerson's text, and words between "< >" denote deletions. Keith was irregularly
employed by Sept. 15, 1857.

57. Baym, *Novels, Readers, and Reviewers*, 272, 42.

58. Martha Osborne Barrett, Diary, July 31, 1859, PEM; Lucy Larcom to William
    Stevens Robinson, Jan. 13, 1853, Robinson-Shattuck Papers, SL; Mary Pierce to
    Henry Varnum Poor, Apr. 3, 1841, Poor Family Papers, SL. See Joel Myerson, *The
    New England Transcendentalists and the Dial: A History of the Magazine and Its
    Contributors* (Rutherford, N.J., 1980), 291, on Cranch, 133–139, and the typically
    more favorable reactions to the *Dial* from Bostonians, 49–50. See also Joel Myer-
    son, "The Contemporary Reception of the Boston *Dial*," *Resources for American
    Literary Study* 3(1973):203–220.

59. For an enlightening analysis of how reading played a similar role in courtship, see
    Susan K. Harris, *The Courtship of Olivia Langdon and Mark Twain* (New York,
    1996), 93–105, chap. 4; see also the consideration of courtship and fiction in Ron-
    ald J. Zboray and Mary Saracino Zboray, "The Romance of Fisherwomen in Ante-
    bellum New England," *American Studies* 39(1998):5–30. In her courtship letters,
    Mary repeatedly assured Henry of her conventional disposition. For example, she
    distanced herself from Marianne Jackson after discussing with her Sophia Dana
    Ripley's "Woman" in the *Dial* 1(Jan. 1841):362–366. Mary wrote: "When last
    [Jackson] was here we talked about a number of the dial we had both been read-
    ing. She has some strange opinions about woman's lot and woman's sphere and
    seemed to agree with Mrs Ripley who wrote an article for the Dial upon the social
    position and intellectual sphere of our sex." Mary Pierce to Henry Varnum Poor,
    Apr. 17, 1841, SL. On this incident, see Ronald J. Zboray and Mary Saracino Zbo-
    ray, "Political News and Female Readership in Antebellum Boston and Its Re-
    gion," *Journalism History* 22(1996):6.

60. S. W. Goddard to Annie (DeWolf) Middleton, June 9, 1852, N. R. Middleton
    Family Correspondence, South Carolina Historical Society, Charleston. *Memoirs
    of Margaret Fuller Ossoli*, ed. Ralph Waldo Emerson, James Freeman Clarke, and
    William Henry Channing (Boston, 1852), was, after Barnum's autobiography, the
    best-selling American biography published during the decade. Joel Myerson,
    Margaret Fuller: A Descriptive Primary Bibliography (Pittsburgh, 1978), 39.

61. Capper's *Margaret Fuller* points out these among Fuller's "Personality and Traits";
    see index, 412–414. The editors of the *Memoirs*, however, "had to repress her sex-
    uality, her quarrelsomeness, her brooding sense of incompleteness, and her in-
    creasingly radical political point of view." Robert N. Hudspeth, "The Sources,"
    The Letters of Margaret Fuller, ed. Robert N. Hudspeth (Ithaca, 1983), 1:61.

62. Louisa Loring to Anna Loring, Feb. 8, 1852, Ellis Gray Loring Papers, SL. On the
    generally positive experiences of those who took part in the "conversations," see
    Capper, *Margaret Fuller*, 298–306, and for information on Louisa Loring, 292–
    293. She refers to Emelyn Story's contribution to the volume. According to Hud-
    speth, "The Sources," 60: "The Storys sent a long account of their days with
    [Fuller] in Italy" to the *Memoirs*' editors.

63. Mary Pierce Poor to Laura Stone, Mar. 18, 1852; Mary Pierce Poor to Lucy Pierce
    Hedge, June 17, 1851; Mary Pierce Poor to Laura Stone, Mar. 18, 1852, Poor
    Family Papers, SL. The book had been in the works since at least November 1850.
    Hudspeth, "The Sources," 59–61. Mary W. Pierce Poor, *Memoir of John Pierce,
    D.D., Communicated by Charles Lowell* (Boston, 1852).

64. Response to authorial celebrity is considered in Andrew Elfenbein, *Byron and the
    Victorians* (New York, 1995), chap. 2; Susan Barerra Fay, "A Modest Celebrity:

Literary Reputation and the Marketplace in Antebellum America" (Ph.D. diss., George Washington University, 1992).

65. Lucy Larcom to Harriet Hanson Robinson, Dec. 16, 1854, Robinson-Shattuck Papers, SL; Lucy Larcom, *Similitudes: From the Ocean and the Prairie* (Boston, 1854); Abby Clark Stimson, Diary, July 23, 1850, Diman Family Papers, Manuscript Collection, RIHS; Mellen Chamberlain, Diary, Mar. 27, 1847, BPL; William Lloyd Garrison, Jr., to Wendell P. Garrison, Jan. 16, 1858, Garrison Papers, SC.

66. Giles Waldo to George Waldo, Jan. 15, Mar. 1, and July 18, 1843, George Waldo Papers, The Yale Collection of American Literature, Beinecke Rare Book and Manuscript Library, Yale University. Little information has been compiled on Waldo. William Ellery Channing called Waldo "a dull man, a very dull man." William Ellery Channing II to Ralph Waldo Emerson, Dec. 19, 1844, in "The Letters of William Ellery Channing," ed. Francis B. Dedmond, *Studies in the American Renaissance 1989*, ed. Joel Myerson (Charlottesville, 1989), 215; for background, see 212 n. 2. See also Myerson, *The New England Transcendentalists and the Dial*, 87–8, 92, 208, 284 n. 3; Ralph L. Rusk, ed., *The Letters of Ralph Waldo Emerson* (New York, 1939), 3:165; Martin K. Doudna, "An Emersonian in the Sandwich Islands: The Career of Giles Waldo," *Hawaiian Journal of History* 21(1987):42–57; Martin K. Doudna, "Thoreau and the Sandwich Islanders," *New England Quarterly* 61(1983):432–439.

67. William S. Robinson and Harriet Hanson Robinson, Diary, June 9, 1856, May 31, 1855; Lucy Larcom to Harriet Hanson Robinson, Apr. 25, 1855; Robinson Diary, Aug. 26, 1856, in Nov. 25, 1856; Lucy Larcom to Harriet Hanson Robinson, Nov. 21, 1856—all in Robinson-Shattuck Papers, SL.

68. Sarah A. Ripley to George F. Simmons, Jan. 9, 1845, Sarah Alden Bradford Ripley Papers, SL; Elizabeth (Dwight) Cabot to Ellen (Dwight) Twisleton, Dec. 16, 1860, Cabot Family Papers, SL; Mary Pierce Poor to Martha L. Talbot, Dec. 23, 1849, Poor Family Papers, SL. She is referring to *The Spirit of the Age* (New York, 1849–1850) and the Associationist *The Harbinger* (New York, 1845–1849). The lectures Ripley mentions became parts of *Representative Men*, which "seems to have been more consciously intended for a book from the start." Albert von Frank, *An Emerson Chronology* (New York, 1994), 194; for the lectures on "Napoleon" delivered during 1845–1848, see 194, 196, 200, 202, 204, 205, 209, 221–228. For a stimulating discussion of *Conduct of Life*, see David M. Robinson, *Emerson and the Conduct of Life: Pragmatism and Ethical Purpose in the Later Work* (Cambridge, 1993), chap. 7.

69. Giles Waldo to George Waldo, Feb. 6, 1843, YU-B; Elizabeth (Dwight) Cabot to Ellen (Dwight) Twisleton, Dec. 16, 1860, Cabot Family Papers, SL. As Waldo made clear to his brother in a July 18, 1843, letter, Giles apparently had a strenuous relationship with his uncle Samuel. "I cannot give over hoping good from Uncle Saml.," Giles wrote, "on the principle laid down by Carlyle that 'the Dunce is the *only fatal* person.' Where there is intellect there is certainly good ground for hope."

70. Keith, Diary, Feb. 16, 1858, RIHS. John Townsend Trowbridge, Diary, 1853–1856, Aug. 14, 1853, by courtesy of the Trustees of the Boston Public Library; Lucy Larcom to Harriet Hanson Robinson, Apr. 2, 1858, Dec. 18, 1857, May 14, 1858,

Robinson-Shattuck Papers, SL; Elizabeth (Dwight) Cabot, Diary, Sept. 25, 1859, Cabot Family Papers, SL. John Park, Diary, Jan. 3, 1852, BPL. On Trowbridge, see Ronald J. Zboray, "Cheap Publishing in Antebellum Boston: John Townsend Trowbridge's *Martin Merrivale: His 'X' Mark*," *Dime Novel Round-Up* 60(1992): 78–83.

71. Keith, Diary, Feb. 16, 1858, RIHS; Annie (DeWolf) Middleton to N. R. Middleton, Sept. 1, 1856, in *Life in Carolina and New England during the Nineteenth Century as Illustrated by Reminiscences and Letters of the Middleton Family of Charleston South Carolina and of the De Wolf Family of Bristol, Rhode Island* (Bristol, R.I., 1929), 89; Isabel Morgan, Journal Kept at School at Lenox, Mass., June 22, 1845, Journals, Rotch Family Papers, MHS. Frances Merritt Quick, Diaries, Sept. 20, 1858, Frances Merritt Quick Papers, SL. Annie Middleton was unusual in her tastes, for Emerson's poetry "was never highly appreciated by his contemporaries," according to Joel Myerson, because of its "departure from the more traditional forms of a Longfellow or a Holmes." "Introduction," *Emerson and Thoreau: The Contemporary Reviews*, ed. Joel Myerson (Cambridge, 1992), xiv.

72. An example of response to the Romantics occurs in the diary of Cyrus Parker Bradley, a student at Dartmouth. He wrote of Wordsworth's "lesser pieces": "I admire them—they harmonize well with my own feelings. So childlike, so pure, so innocent.... These were lines which strongly reminded me of my own early childhood, when, brought up in the woods of Northwood..., found company in everything—in the birds, in the old cat, the cow, the inanimate objects." School Diaries, Sept. 12, 1835, Cyrus Parker Bradley Papers, 1830–1838, NHHS.

73. Mary Pierce to Henry Varnum Poor, July 27, 1839, Poor Family Papers, SL.

74. Hannah Lowell (Jackson) Cabot, Diary, Sept. 4, 1839, typescript carbon copy, 1839–1842, page 6, Almy Family Papers, SL; Giles Waldo to George Waldo, Feb. 6, 1843, George Waldo Papers, YU-B; Elizabeth (Dwight) Cabot to Ellen (Dwight) Twisleton, Dec. 16, 1860, Cabot Family Papers, SL; Fanny [Webb?] to Sarah Watson, Feb. 12, 1838, Dana Family Papers, SL; S. W. G[oddard] to Annie (DeWolf) Middleton, 25 [?] 1852, N. R. Middleton Family Correspondence, SCHS.

75. Sarah Alden Bradford Ripley to George F. Simmons, Feb. 12, 1844, in Feb. 29, 1844, Sarah Alden Bradford Ripley Papers, SL. Bancroft is not often seen as a Transcendentalist, yet various scholars place him within those circles. On Bancroft as "the only one among the Transcendentalists who was prepared to sully his hands by actual party politics," see Perry Miller, *The Transcendentalists: An Anthology* (Cambridge, Mass., 1950), 422–423. See also Rose, *Transcendentalism as a Social Movement*, 106–107, for the relationship between Transcendentalism, political reform, and the Democratic party. On Bancroft's belief in man's "intuitive 'faculty' to transcend his sensate nature" as part of his political philosophy, see John Patrick Diggins, *The Lost Soul of American Politics: Virtue, Self-Interest, and the Foundations of Liberalism* (New York, 1984), 178–179; and Elisabeth Hurth, "Sowing the Seeds of 'Subversion': Harvard's Early Göttingen Students," *Studies in the American Renaissance 1992*, ed. Joel Myerson (Charlottesville, 1992), 98.

76. Katharine Bigelow ("Kitty") Lawrence, Journal [ts. transc.], Oct. 31, 1849, Lamb Family Papers, MHS; Annie B. Lawrence, Diary, Jan. 11, 1840, Lamb Family Pa-

pers, MHS; Thomas Hyde to Lavius Hyde and Abigail (Bradley) Hyde [n.d.]
[1846?], Hyde Family Papers, [MSS 920 H992] State Archives, Connecticut State
Library; John Park, Diary, Mar. 8, 1837, BPL. Park's reading list is a model for
those who would understand the intellectual life of a socially prominent antebellum Unitarian. On the value of reading lists for studying intellectual influences
upon theologians like William Ellery Channing, see Wright, *The Liberal Christians*, 26–27. On the debates among theologians between 1820 and 1850 over the
origin and meaning of language, and these debates' effect upon literary developments, see Philip F. Gura, "The Transcendentalists and Language: The Unitarian
Exegetical Background," *Studies in the American Renaissance 1979*, ed. Joel Myerson (Boston, 1979), 1–16.

77. Park addressed the issue in his diary, Feb. 16, 1837, when he first saw a literary notice of Strauss's work, and on Mar. 20, 1837: "Part of the forenoon with Dr Bancroft. . . . I mentioned likewise to the Doctor the reported publication, in Berlin, of
a work by an eminent scholar and divine by the name of Straus, bracing a learned
argument to prove that there was no such historical character as Jesus Christ—
that his mission, & whole biography were but Christian Mythology, in which there
was a good moral!" As we discuss below, Park later read a review in *Foreign Quarterly Review* of David Friedrich Strauss, *Das Leben Jesu, Kritisch Bearbeitet*
(Tubingen, 1835–1836). Translations of *Das Leben Jesu* would appear, including,
for example, *The Life of Jesus; or, a Critical Examination of His History* (London,
1838?–1842), but Park did not apparently read the book itself.

78. On Feb. 14, 1837, after "studying Schleiermacker's discussions on the Trinity,"
Park wrote: "more impracticable still to comprehend the views of modern Trinitarians. I know what they *say*. Their words are intelligible words, but when
arranged by them into positions, I am confounded."

79. Park, Diary, Feb. 24, 1840, Dec. 3, 1845, Jan. 20, 1842, Feb. 14, 1846, Aug. 12,
1840, Jan. 5, 1839, BPL. While theology was certainly important in his assessment of an author, Park could admire a comprehensible theologian with whom
he disagreed: "Engaged, today, principally, in reading Mr Furness's 'Remarks on
the Four Gospels.' As a literary production, it does great credit to the talents of
the author; but as a theological work, to me, it is in many points far from satisfactory." Diary, Jan. 12, 1837. Park refers here to the Worcester Lyceum: "In the
evening, we attend a lecture, by Mr Weiss at the Lyceum—his object was to
explain the philosophic theories of Kant and other Germans—but I was none the
wiser. I know no more what their theories are than I did before." Diary, Jan. 20,
1842. Park's biographer, his son-in-law, recognized this antipathy toward the Germans: "[H]e had little patience with the religious mysticism which was creeping
into Unitarian pulpits fifty years ago, imported straight, as he thought, from
the German mystic philosophers whom he detested." Hall, "Reminiscences of
Dr. John Park," 69–93, 92. Even translations from German perplexed him and
after reading Eliza Buckminster Lee's translation of *Life of Jean Paul Frederic
Richter* (Boston, 1842), he reported, "I find many persons of distinguished mental acumen boldly confessing their inability to seize, satisfactorily, a German's
meaning" (Feb. 28, 1844). J. H. Allen, "The Conflict of American Unitarianism
and German Thought," in *Unitarianism: Its Origin and History* (Boston, 1898),
97–115.

80. Park, Diary, Oct. 14, 1851, May 23, 1839, Feb. 28, 1844. He began the first volume of Locke on Dec. 7, 1846, and finished the fifth on Mar. 13, 1847. Cameron Thompson, "John Locke and New England Transcendentalism," *New England Quarterly* 35(1962):435–457. See also Gura, "The Transcendentalists and Language," esp. 4, 12–13; and Frederick C. Dahlstrand, "Science, Religion, and the Transcendentalist Response to a Changing America," *Studies in the American Renaissance 1988*, ed. Joel Myerson (Charlottesville, 1988):1–25. For background, see Wendell V. Harris, *The Omnipresent Debate: Empiricism and Transcendentalism in Nineteenth-Century Prose* (DeKalb, Ill., 1981).

81. Park, Diary, Mar. 6, 1839, Mar. 26, 1837, June 24, 1837. See Howe, *The Unitarian Conscience*, 12–20, for a definition of "Unitarian Moralists" and a discussion of relevant names; and, on "living religion," Conrad Wright, *The Liberal Christians*, 40. Park read Norton on June 24 and 27, 1837. He began the second volume on Apr. 5, 1844, and noted its controversial declarations. On Apr. 16, 1844, he commented: "It will bring a host of assailants upon him; but his views of the Jewish Scriptures are very much those I have entertained for, at least, fifteen years." The third volume he quickly read between Apr. 17 and 21, 1844. He read other works by Norton: see, for example, the entry for Oct. 1, 1839, in which he peruses *A Discourse on the Latest Form of Infidelity, Delivered at the Request of the Association of the Cambridge Theological School* (Cambridge, Mass., 1839). John Park to Louisa (Park) Hall, Feb. 5, 1845, inscribed in Diary, under entry for Feb. 6, 1845. After Park rails against Parker his train of thought moves him to write, "these considerations lead me, by a rather obscure connexion, to speak of my books. It is my intention, in a favorable season, if there should be a prospect of getting anything for them, to dispose of a parcel of the rubbish—enough at least, to repay the expense of insuring the rest—for insure I must." See also Jan. 11, 1845.

82. Park, Diary, Oct. 21, 1838. On reception through historical reading communities, see James L. Machor, "Historical Hermeneutics and Antebellum Fiction: Gender, Response Theory, and Interpretive Contexts," in *Readers in History*, 54–84.

83. For a discussion of Furness's *Remarks on the Four Gospels* (1836), see Elisabeth Hurth, "That 'Grand Model of Humanity': William Henry Furness and the Problem of the Historical Jesus," in *Studies in the American Renaissance 1995*, ed. Joel Myerson (Charlottesville, 1995), 101–126. Park, like others, objected to what Hurth describes as Furness's departure from "traditional 'proofs' of the life of Jesus narratives. . . . Furness devalued the traditional argument for miracles" and declared "'that all men are endued with miraculous powers'" (105). Park, on Mar. 5, 1837, sketched the reception of Martin Luther Hurlbut's review of "Furness's Remarks on the Gospels" in the *Christian Examiner* 22(Mar. 1837):101–124. "The male members of the second Church meet at Dr Bancroft's in the evening. Dr Bancroft in the chair. . . . Mr. Hurlburt's Review in the Christian Examiner was mentioned as an able and very complete refutation of Mr Furness's position that miracles, so called, are merely *wonderful* facts, not deviations from the established laws of nature, and are only manifestations of that commanding control which mind, the human mind may attain over matter."

84. Park, Diary, Mar. 5, 1837, May 3, 1840, and Aug. 1, 1841. Parker's essay particularly disturbed Park, who read it twice and discussed it with several people at his or their homes. He also accepted "two anti-Theodore Parker sermons" distributed

by Alonzo Hill and enjoyed sermons by George Edward Ellis, delivered in Worcester on Aug. 15, 1841. Park declared these sermons, apparently aimed at Parker, "very much to my taste; especially that of the afternoon, which had a pointed reference to Parker's Ordination Sermon on 'The Permanent and Transient in Christianity.' I like Ellis much." Diary, July 5, Aug. 1, 4, 8, and 15, 1841. On Aug. 8 he has a discussion with a visitor: "Principal subjects, the new-fangled theory of consciousness being the revealer of all important religious truth—and the rather critical state of our Parish."

85. Child, Diary, Mar. 12, 1845, MHS; John Turner Sargent, *Ministry at Suffolk Street Chapel: Its Origin, Progress, and Experience* (Boston, 1845). On the exchange controversy, see Dean Grodzins, "Theodore Parker's 'Conference with the Boston Association' January 23, 1843," *Proceedings of the Unitarian Universalist Historical Society* 23(1995):66–101, and his essay in these pages.

86. Child, Diary, Mar. 24, 1845, MHS. For example, according to their diary, the Childs read Emory Washburn's *Argument of Hon. Emory Washburn, Before an Ecclesiastical Council* on Sept. 11, 1841; John Turner Sargent's *The True Position of Rev. Theodore Parker* on Jan. 11, 1845, and Feb. 19, 1845; Ezra Stiles Gannett's "Mr. Parker and His Views" on Mar. 20, 1845; William Ware's *Righteousness before Doctrine* on Apr. 26–27, 1845; and *Letter of the Boston Association of Congregational Ministers to Rev. John Pierpont with His Reply* on Jan. 31, 1846. On the controversy surrounding John Pierpont, the Childs' pastor until 1845, see Jane H. Pease and William H. Pease, "Whose Right Hand of Fellowship?: Pew and Pulpit in Shaping Church Practice," in *American Unitarianism*, 195–199, and 205 n. 26; and Hutchison, *The Transcendentalist Ministers*, 118–119.

87. Annie (DeWolf) Middleton to Nathaniel Russell Middleton, Sept. 1, 1856, in *Life in Carolina and New England*, 89. On July 7, 1841, Park wrote in his diary about Bancroft's hilarious "auction" of the goods nobody wanted to buy of the charitable organization at a recent local ladies' fair. Lucretia apparently performed for the society again, this time reading Parker's *Discourse*, on Aug. 4, 1841. On oral reading practices within patterns of household work, see Zboray and Zboray, "Books, Reading, and the World of Goods," 598–603.

88. Mellen Chamberlain, Diary, Mar. 27, 1847, BPL; Ellis Gray Loring, Diary, Mar. 17 and 23, 1838, vol. 4, Ellis Gray Loring Papers, SL.

89. Giles Waldo to George Waldo, Jan. 15, 1843, George Waldo Papers, YU-B.

90. Child, Diary, Nov. 1, 1852, and Oct. 18, 1855, MHS.

91. Frances Jocelyn, Diary, 1852–1853, Mar. 10 and Feb. 12, 1852, CHS. Jocelyn kept a diary between 1839 and 1857; the five surviving volumes that contain fairly regular entries for most years (except 1846 and 1847) record over 300 titles she read.

92. Carroll Norcross, Diary, Apr. 7, 1852, Oct. 28, 1853, Cargill-Knight-Norcross Families Papers, 1807–1870, MeHS.

93. Park, Diary, Dec. 31, 1841, Feb. 27 and May 20, 1842, BPL.

94. For discussions of newspaper exchanges, see Zboray, *A Fictive People*, 119–121; Brown, *Knowledge Is Power*, 232; Richard Burket Kielbowicz, *News in the Mail: The Press, Post Office, and Public Information: 1700–1860s* (New York, 1989); and Thomas C. Leonard, *News For All: America's Coming-of-Age with the Press* (New York, 1995), 2–19, 118–124.

95. Elizabeth Dwight to Ellen Twisleton, Mar. 19, 1855, Cabot Family Papers, SL; Abigail L. Pierce to Mary Pierce Poor, July 4, 1848, Poor Family Papers, SL; Samuel May, Jr., to Dr. John Bishop Estlin, Jan. 13, 1848, courtesy of the Trustees of the Boston Public Library; Sarah P. E. Hale to Edward Everett, May 4, 1838, Hale Papers, SC; Elizabeth (Dwight) Cabot to Ellen Twisleton, Nov. 11, 1860, Cabot Family Papers, SL. May is discussed throughout his cousin's biography by Donald Yacovone, *Samuel Joseph May and the Dilemmas of the Liberal Persuasion, 1797–1871* (Philadelphia, 1991).

96. For some examples of the analysis of library charges, see Zboray, *A Fictive People*, chap. 11 and appendix 2; Mark Olsen and Louis-Georges Harvey, "Reading in Revolutionary Times: Book Borrowing from the Harvard College Library, 1773–1782," *Harvard Library Bulletin* 4(1993):57–72. A related source of evidence can be found in the papers of reading clubs. For example, one such club in Worcester purchased Emerson's *Representative Men* on Feb. 5, 1850, for $.80 and *Memoirs of Margaret Fuller* on Feb. 27, 1852, for $1.60; see Worcester Reading Club, 1849–1928, octavo vol. 5, Worcester (Mass.) Book Clubs Collection, 1844–1977, courtesy American Antiquarian Society. In the same collection, The Worcester Book Club, List of Books, 1845, contains Emerson's *Essays, Second Series* and Fuller's *Woman in the Nineteenth Century*.

97. Sarah P. E. Hale to Edward Everett, Feb. 16, 1837 [?], Hale Papers, SC.

98. "I hope to miss Shakespeare from the library soon; forlorn is the youth that has not made an oratory for him"—Dahlia [*i.e.*, Margaret Fuller], "Chat in Boston Bookstores," *Boston Quarterly Review* 9(1840):326. On Fuller as the author, see Capper, *Margaret Fuller*, 313. Traveling could also mean delay in getting a book, as John Patton wrote to his "niece" Caroline W. H. Dall that "[Marianne] is most anxious to read Margaret Fuller's Life, which I intend to get for her before I leave [for home]." John Patton to Caroline W. H. Dall, Aug. 1, 1852, Caroline Wells Healey Dall Papers, SL.

99. In the case of Transcendentalism, this paucity of mention may relate to the low numbers of subscribers. So few subscribed to the *Dial*, for example, that Emerson lamented in 1843: "Perhaps we shall print no more Dials for the subscription list does not quite support it, and yet it has warm friends. I think for friendship & hope's sake we must cherish the blameless journal a little longer." Ralph Waldo Emerson to Giles Waldo, Apr. 3, 1843, excerpted in Giles Waldo to George Waldo, Apr. 14, 1843, George Waldo Papers, YU-B. See also Emerson to Margaret Fuller, Apr. 20, 1843, in *Letters of Ralph Waldo Emerson*, 4:165–166. Joel Myerson estimates that "for the April 1843 number the publisher printed at least seven hundred and seventy copies: a minimum of five hundred for sale in Boston, two hundred and twenty for subscribers, and fifty for English sales." "A Union List of the Dial (1840–1844) and Some Information About Its Sales," *Papers of the Bibliographical Society of America* 67(1973):322–328, quotation on 326. "The regular income of the *Dial* does not pay the cost of its printing & paper." Elizabeth Palmer Peabody to Henry David Thoreau, Feb. 26, 1843, in *The Letters of Elizabeth Palmer Peabody, American Renaissance Woman*, ed. Bruce A. Ronda (Middletown, Conn., 1984), 261. Compare the *Dial*'s circulation with that of the contemporaneous *Boston Miscellany* (Bradbury, Soden, & Co.), which Nathan Hale, Jr., struggled to make a viable literary monthly in the face of his publisher's

desire to turn it into a ladies magazine. Hale's mother wrote: "The Miscellany so far has succeeded I believe as well as its publishers expected. They printed of the Specimen number 4500 and this being exhausted they have printed a second edition of it." Sarah P. E. Hale to Edward Everett, Dec. 14, 1841, Hale Papers, SC. The initial success did not prevent the magazine from failing in February 1843, shortly before Emerson wrote his letter to Waldo. The limited circulations of Boston literary journals need to be set in context of those of other types of literary periodicals of the early 1840s, such as Boston's *Uncle Sam*, a story paper (circulation 7,000); Philadelphia's *Godey's Ladies Book* (an estimated New England circulation 6,000); and Park Benjamin's *New World* (circulation 25,000). See Mary Noel, *Villains Galore: The Heyday of the Popular Story Weekly* (New York: Macmillan, 1954), 16, 19; on *Godey's* in New England, see Sarah P. E. Hale to Alexander Hill Everett, June 10, 1841, SC.

100. Waitfield, Vt., MS book containing 399 names of subscribers to 112 periodicals (893 subscriptions in all), Jan. 1, 1857–Jan. 1, 1860, Vermont Historical Society, Montpelier.

101. [F. P. Fletcher, Postmaster?], "Newspapers & Pamphlets Recievd [*sic*], Bridport Jany 1 1839 Post Office"; F. P. Fletcher, Postmaster, Bridport, "Post Office Book Commence Oct. th31[*sic*]/41" to Dec. 31, 1841, VHS. The documents report 386 subscribers to about 295 different periodicals for a total of 3,318 subscription records. An earlier survey of New Boston, N.H., postal records also failed to turn up Transcendentalist titles, even though several Boston story papers appeared in the lists. See Ronald J. Zboray, "Technology and the Character of Community Life in Antebellum America: The Role of Story Papers," in *Communication and Change in American Religious History*, ed. Leonard I. Sweet (Grand Rapids, Mich., 1993), 204.

102. J. Edwin Harris, Diaries 1856–1876, MeHS. See, for example, Dec. 9, 1856. "Evening, Call at Bookbindry for my Pictorial[.] Read—write &c"; Feb. 9, 1857, and July 24, 1857: "Make a call—on the Pepperell folks. Evening. leave my Waverleys at—the Bindery." That binding meant preservation was recognized; for example, Bronson Alcott wrote: "I wish to put the few books and papers that I possess, into a form more worthy of preservation." Jan. 28, 1836, Joel Myerson, ed., "Journal for 1836," *Studies in the American Renaissance 1978*, ed. Joel Myerson (Boston, 1978), 28.

103. Ralph Thompson, "Emerson and the Offering for 1829," *American Literature* 6(1934):151–157.

104. See Sarah Browne, Account Book, Jan. 10, 1843, Jan. 1, 1842, Dec. 31, 1856, Browne Family Papers, SL. On Milton, see Elizabeth Ellery Dana, Account Book, Jan. 5, 1855, Dana Family Papers, SL. On the other hand, Browne purchased "Memoirs [of] Margaret Fuller [at] $2" and "Parker on Webster [for] 75cts.," in the spring season of the yearly publication cycle, perhaps for personal use. See Sarah Browne, Account Book, Apr. 11, 1852, Apr. 10, 1853, Browne Family Papers, SL.

105. Child, Diary, Mar. 19, 1840, MHS; Helen M. Warner, Diary [MS Cb 1084], Apr. 22, 1851, New England Historic Genealogical Society, Boston; Cornelia Jocelyn, Diary, Apr. 23, 1855, Jocelyn Boxes, CHS; John Patton to Caroline W. H. Dall, Oct. 24, 1854, Caroline Wells Healey Dall Papers, SL. On shopping as a chore that was second only to child care and sewing in the time it consumed for women, see

Jeanne Boydston, *Home and Work: Housework, Wages, and the Ideology of Labor in the Early Republic* (New York, 1990), 78, 82–88. On the interior chaos of an antebellum New York City bookstore, based on an analysis of the contents of one store's inventory, see Zboray, *A Fictive People*, chap. 10.

106. K. A. Wilson to Joshua Lawrence Chamberlain, Mar. 30, 1856, Chamberlain-Adams Family Papers, SL; Mellen Chamberlain, Diary, Aug. 19, 1843, Jan. 7 and 9, Nov. 23, 1847, Aug. 30, 1848, BPL; Fuller, "Chat in Boston Bookstores," 323–331.

107. J. Edwin Harris, Diary, Jan. 25, 1861, MeHS (his recording of book purchases ends on Apr. 30, 1858); Park, Diary, Mar. 18, 1837, BPL; Crawford Nightingale to James Munroe & Co., Dec. 18, 1847, James Munroe & Company, Correspondence, courtesy American Antiquarian Society. We are here referring to Michael Hackenberg, ed., *Getting the Books Out: Papers of the Chicago Conference on the Book in 19th-Century America* (Washington, D.C., 1987).

108. Fuller, "Chat in Boston Bookstores," 326; Feroline (Pierce) Fox to Mary Pierce Poor, Aug. 12, 1842, Poor Family Papers, SL.

109. Park, Diary, Dec. 23, 1838, and Feb. 7, 1845, BPL; Child, Diary, Jan. 5, 1850, MHS.

110. Ronald J. Zboray, "Literary Enterprise and the Mass Market: Publishing and Business Innovation in Antebellum America," *Essays in Economic and Business History* 10(1992):168–181; Susan Geary, "The Domestic Novel as a Commercial Commodity," *Papers of the Bibliographical Society of America* 70(1976):365–395.

111. Keith, Diary, Oct. 30 and Nov. 13, 1857. On his reading patterns, see Dec. 7, 1857, Jan. 26 and 31, Feb. 4, 7, 11, and 14, 1858; on the *Dial*, Feb. 16, 1858, RIHS.

112. On the boom in local publishing, see Ronald J. Zboray and Mary Saracino Zboray, "The Boston Book Trades, 1789–1850: A Statistical and Geographical Analysis," in *Entrepreneurs: The Boston Business Community, 1700–1850*, ed. Conrad Edick Wright and Katheryn P. Viens (Boston, 1997), 210–267. W. S. Tryon, *Parnassus Corner: A Life of James T. Fields, Publisher to the Victorians* (Boston, 1963). On Boston publishers in the national context, see John Tebbel, *A History of Book Publishing in the United States*, vol. 1: *The Creation of an Industry, 1630–1865* (New York, 1972).

113. John Park, Diary, Jan. 13, 1839, BPL; Ellis Gray Loring to Anna Loring, Dec. 22, 1851, Ellis Gray Loring Papers, SL; Alexander Hill Everett to Edward E. Hale, Jan. 6, 1846, Hale Papers, SC; Sarah P. E. Hale to Alexander Hill Everett, Nov. 29, 1841, Hale Papers, SC; Charles S. Francis & Co. to William Sturgis, Apr. 26, 1852, Sturgis/Tappan/Prout Papers, SC.

114. John Pierce to Lucy (Pierce) Hedge, Apr. 16, 1840, Poor Family Papers, SL; Park, Diary, Dec. 3, 1845, and July 4, 1847, BPL. On the reference in the *New York Evening Post* and *New-Yorker* to the forthcoming *Dial* as "*The Harbinger*," see Myerson, *New England Transcendentalists*, 44.

115. Child, Diary, Mar. 6, 1848, June 4 and 5, 1854, MHS. Child read Davis's book on 41 scattered evenings from Oct. 9, 1847, shortly after it appeared, to Oct. 21, 1848. On Davis, see Zboray and Zboray, "Reading and Everyday Life in Antebellum Boston," Appendix A, and on Davis, 309–310.

116. Frederick Gleason's *Flag of Our Union*, for example, throughout the late 1840s and early 1850s constantly alerted readers to the paper's "new dress." One such

editorial ran: "Well, gentle reader, here we are, with our clean new summer clothes on, and very happy to greet you. The type in which the FLAG is printed to-day, is very beautiful and clear, and its mechanical execution is unrivalled.— Though our last suit had been worn but six months, it was already getting a little seedy, owing to our immense edition, and we don't intend anything shall remain in that state about our paper" (July 1, 1848). Jacob Abbott, *The Harper Establishment; or, How the Story Books Are Made* (New York, 1855). The book is discussed in Zboray, *A Fictive People*, chap. 1.

117. Waterhouse, Journal, June [c. 14], 1840, MHS; John Horne Tooke, *Eptea Ptopoenta; or, Diversions of Purley* (1805; Menston, Eng., 1968), 2:495. "Wiffee" apparently was Benjamin Waterhouse's pet name for his wife.

118. John Sullivan Dwight, "Ideals of Every-Day Life," *Dial* 1(Jan. 1841):307–311 and 1(Apr. 1841):446–461; quotation from 451, 461.

119. Sophia W. Ripley to Caroline Sturgis, Oct. 3, [1845?], Sturgis/Tappan/Prout Papers, SC.

120. Henry D. Thoreau, *Walden*, ed. J. Lyndon Shanley (Princeton, 1971), 155.

121. Park, Diary, Feb. 2, 1840, BPL. He prefaces this comment with: "The male members of the Church were notified to meet, this evening, at Deacon Kettell's. The proposition was made, a month or two ago to revive the meetings, which we held in the early part of 1837. It died away, then, and I have understood the reason was, that several of the members said the discussions were on subjects so abstruse, they did not understand them!!"

122. On "flow" see Mihaly Csikszentmihalyi, *Flow: The Psychology of Optimal Experience* (New York, 1990).

123. Elizabeth (Dwight) Cabot, Diary, Jan. 3 and Mar. 3, 1857, Cabot Family Papers, SL. On the Transcendentalists as "connected critics," see Teichgraeber, *Sublime Thoughts/Penny Wisdom*.

Transcendentalism
and American Reform

Mrs. Brackett's Verdict

Magic and Means in Transcendental Antislavery Work

ALBERT J. VON FRANK

> Emersonian transcendentalism and political activism in mid-nineteenth-century America were inherently incompatible.
>
> —JOHN CARLOS ROWE[1]

ONE DAY IN 1841, MRS. SAMUEL E. BRACKETT, WIFE OF A prosperous Boston dry-goods merchant, declared to Ralph Waldo Emerson that she would as soon hear that her friends were dead as that they had become Transcendentalists, because, she explained, Transcendentalists "are paralysed & never do anything for humanity."[2] In the reform environment of that period, it was clear what "doing something for humanity" meant. It certainly did *not* mean publishing an important book of essays, as Emerson had just done, nor retreating to a utopian community in West Roxbury, as had several of Emerson's friends. It meant, of course, taking up the cause of the slave—or perhaps of temperance or prison reform or peace. It meant being "political."

Mrs. Brackett's notion that the mark of a serious person is to be up and doing, to be perpetually busy in the work of the Lord, has appealed irresistibly to generations of Emerson's doubtful readers, whose first and last test of an idea has often been whether it is apt to put reformers immediately into motion against some particular abuse. Even so sympathetic a reader as Thomas Carlyle applied this test, which was to become a persistent point of disagreement between the two writers. On reading Emerson's second volume of *Essays* (1844), Carlyle professed to find in it

> a *Soliloquizer* on the eternal mountain-tops only, in vast solitudes where men and their affairs lie all hushed in a very dim remote-

ness . . . whom, so fine a fellow seems he, we could perpetually
punch into, and say, "Why won't you come and help us then?" . . . .
To which he answers that he won't[,] can't, and doesn't want to (as
the Cockneys have it): and so I leave him, and say, "You Western
Gymnosophist! Well, we can afford one man for that too."[3]

One cannot suppose that Carlyle, author of "The Nigger Question," here
regrets the loss of Emerson to antislavery agitation, but the point is well
made that too much thinking of a certain sort is going to be at the expense
of action. Carlyle's choice of the word "afford" is a revelatory appropriation
of the values of the marketplace and signals his belief that the cash value of
an intellectual is determined by his occupation with the practical means of
reform.

Emerson's reply lumps Carlyle together with Mrs. Brackett:

> But of what you say now & heretofore respecting the remoteness
> of my writing & thinking from real life, though I hear substantially
> the same criticism made by my countrymen, I do not know what it
> means. If I can at any time express the law & the ideal right, that
> should satisfy me without measuring the divergence from it of the
> last act of Congress.[4]

To hesitate, thoughtfully, before the call of so clear a duty as that of agitating for reform (or antislavery in particular) is simply to bring thought itself
into disrepute. Accused of playing Hamlet, Emerson cuts a comic figure by
making the defense of thought and observation seem an eccentric alternative to the available modes of realized engagement. "The genius of the
day," he said in 1841, "does not incline to a deed, but to a beholding."[5] Historians have concluded from such remarks (it may be a little hastily) that
Transcendentalism must be a philosophy of sitting on the sidelines. This, as
we shall see, has been a major premise in the most popular and influential
line of historical interpretation; its unfortunate cultural work has been, by
and large, to impugn the value of ideas.

Historians' critiques of Transcendental reform, going back at least as far
as 1945 and the publication of *The Age of Jackson* by Arthur M. Schlesinger,
Jr., have tended strongly to assume that effective reform operates not on
individuals but on the political process and through institutional channels.
Reform, in this view, seeks to change laws for the purpose of altering institutional structures; arguments that are principally moral or that arise
from romantic notions of human perfectibility are therefore apt to be discounted, pertinent only to whatever extent they can rally voters on particu-

lar issues. This critique, echoed by Stanley M. Elkins, George Fredrickson, and others, is thoroughly pragmatic; as in Carlyle's approach, it conceptually defines and organizes the relevant field of behavior (what counts and what does not count as "real" reform) from the endpoint of specific political objectives. It therefore pays more attention to tactics and to making judgments about them than to the ideas that may have prompted the tactics in the first place. This pragmatism rests on certain vulnerable assumptions about what produces political change in a democratic society and seems (especially in Schlesinger's case) to be an effect of projecting backward a familiar, normative model of party politics. Historians who reject Transcendental reform as "irresponsible" for avoiding conventional political instrumentalities do not, as a rule, go on to suggest that the freedom of the slaves was eventually procured by the devices of shrewder, more worldly politicians. Indeed, it would be easier to argue that emancipation required, before anything else, the collapse of politics.

Mrs. Brackett would clearly have been better satisfied had Emerson spent less time thinking and writing and more time working in organized philanthropy. As Anne C. Rose has pointed out, this was a popular choice among the Unitarian leadership: Henry Ware, Jr., for example, Emerson's erstwhile senior colleague at the Second Church, belonged to the Cambridge Anti-Slavery Society, the Massachusetts Temperance Society, and the Massachusetts Peace Society; Ezra Stiles Gannett, who favored the Colonization Society, pursued a similarly demanding agenda. Both men demonstrated the seriousness of their social engagement by destroying their health—without producing any other visible result.[6]

Emerson nowhere comments directly on this spectacle of fruitless yet energetic self-immolation, but it is reasonable to suspect that it seemed to him of a piece with the characteristic Unitarian devotion to the reified externals of life at the expense of spirit—a tendency of which he famously complained in the "Divinity School Address." Indeed, Emerson's main objection to the way in which reform was being constructed as a public venture centered less on its cooperative nature than on a related issue: the undue value it granted to circumstance. "Very trivial seem the contests of the abolitionist," he wrote in 1841, "his objects trifling whilst he aims merely at the circumstance of the slave."[7] Physical meliorations were not a thing, in Emerson's view, on which to spend a life. The doctrine that says they are is simply a distributed and disguised form of the personal desire to be rich.

Emerson hesitated in the 1830s and early 1840s because, while he shared the reformers' conviction that life was not what it could and should be, he was convinced that their understanding of the problem and the methods they adopted were implicated in the contamination they opposed. That contamination was not slavery or intemperance; it was not the oppression of women or the mistreatment of imprisoned criminals or any of the hundred other abuses loudly complained of, but rather what Emerson was apt to call the skeptical doctrine of materialism—what is perhaps now more often referred to as commodification—aggravated in unprecedented ways by the market revolution of Jacksonian America. The active question between the Transcendentalists and other reformers was whether the social distortions brought on by the marketplace could be adjusted piecemeal by materialist strategies or whether a root solution might instead be found in a principled critique of materialism. The former solution was predominantly political, the latter predominantly philosophical. In practice they were linked dialogically.

As has already been suggested, historians have taken Mrs. Brackett's opinion to heart ever since Arthur Schlesinger, Jr., gave it a prestigious endorsement in *The Age of Jackson*:

> From their book-lined studies or their shady walks in cool Concord woods, they found the hullabaloo of party politics unedifying and vulgar. . . . [F]or the typical Transcendentalist the flinching from politics perhaps expressed a failure they were seeking to erect into a virtue. The exigencies of responsibility were exhausting: much better to demand perfection and indignantly reject the half loaf, than wear out body and spirit in vain grapplings with overmastering reality.[8]

It is quite impossible to say specifically what these objectionable demands for perfection were or why Schlesinger chose to associate them more with Transcendentalism than with abolitionism. The formulation seems to be a way of defending compromise and a sort of concessive realism in moral questions (erecting these failures into virtues) against the propositional validity of categorical imperatives.

Despite the good work that *The Age of Jackson* has done, it needs to be remembered that the book was not merely an affirmation of the sufficiency of politics, but an apologia for the Democratic party—that it was composed during Franklin Roosevelt's third term while the country was at war and under the inspiration that a right view of party politics could be the saving of a nation. The book represents a remarkable confusion of the

Democratic party with the idea of democracy itself and sins most egregiously in offering a preference for hullabaloo over thinking and thoughtfulness. If Schlesinger's discussion of Emerson and the Transcendentalists does not amount to a wholesale rejection of the intellectual, it is only because the author is concerned to redefine that figure as, very specifically, a wielder of power high in the ranks of the Democratic party. If one prefers democracy to the reign of wealth and privilege or sides with labor against capital, one must work immediately for the Democrats; not to do so is simply to fail to draw conclusions from premises and to shirk public responsibilities. The democrat, therefore, who is not a Democrat must be timid and softminded.

   This tends to Emerson's disparagement, of course, and makes a sort of hero, in Schlesinger's view, of Orestes Brownson, the only Democrat among the attendees at the Transcendental Club meetings. Brownson is lauded for coming into the party from a concern for the working class, but he soon noticed that John C. Calhoun was also a Democrat. Before long, without needing to leave the party, Brownson was attacking the Transcendentalism of Emerson and Theodore Parker and supporting slavery—a coordination of allegiances and defiances that Schlesinger does not go out of his way to comment on.

   Indeed, the anti-abolitionism of the Democrats is a fundamental embarrassment to Schlesinger's thesis. He is constrained to confess that in the 1830s, the Jacksonians were uniformly hostile to antislavery and generally took it out on the Whig John Quincy Adams. This ought to have been enough by itself to insinuate a nuance into Schlesinger's schematic sense that the Democracy fought the good fight and that Whigs were an oligarchy of capitalists. Had it been that simple, Emerson would obviously have been culpable (he was a Whig during most of that party's lifetime), but where slavery is the test issue (as it was not for Schlesinger), party identities break down and believers in the social logic of democracy become hard to locate by party affiliation.

   The main tradition of historiography on the subject of Transcendentalism and antislavery, following Schlesinger, has been significantly blinkered by a liberal postwar consensus about the inestimable beauty and efficacy of American democratic institutions. Schlesinger allows that Emerson "recognized . . . the inevitable drift of transcendentalism toward the democratic position," yet because he did not become a Locofoco candidate for Congress or engage social issues in any hearty, cooperative way, the conclusion must be that "politics represent his greatest failure." After all, as Schlesinger points out, "a man of Emersonian principle should follow his principle." The condescending attitude toward organized politics developed by "the wisest man of the day" is a tough pill for the historian to swallow, inclined as he is to see no problem in the practical connivance of the intellectual in power politics. That Emerson was suspicious about politics—at a time when neither party was much against slavery—was apparently no part of what made him "wise" but was evidence rather of "the headlong escape into perfection [that] left responsibility far behind for a magic domain where mystic sentiment and gnomic utterance exorcised the rude intrusions of the world."[9] Unfortunately, this not very helpful summary of Transcendentalism was adopted pretty much intact by subsequent historians, who, like Schlesinger, were apt to invest all their hopes for social progress and for the triumph of justice in the ordinary machinery of America's institutional life.

In *Slavery* (1959), Stanley M. Elkins reproduced Schlesinger's emphasis on the "irresponsibility" of the Transcendentalists, concluding that if one is not working by the ordinary rules of political engagement, one simply is not working at all. "Not only did these men fail to analyze slavery itself as an institution, but they failed equally to consider and exploit institutional means for subverting it. . . . Their relationship with abolition societies was never anything but equivocal."[10] The restriction of legitimacy to "institutional means"—as unimaginative as it is arbitrary—belongs to the liberal consensus of the 1950s. Then, too, the notion that one can measure an individual's civic responsibility, depth of commitment, and weightiness of moral engagement by determining whether he belongs to the Pine Street Antislavery Society would be laughable were it not a standard so universally resorted to. The implication seems to be that any kind of visible allegiance to a worthy institution—whether a political party or an association for reform—must of course weigh more in the balance than any activity that might conceivably constitute one an intellectual.[11] Thus the tautological title of Elkins's chapter on the Transcendentalists: "Intellectuals without Responsibility."

One interesting irony is that the Transcendentalists gave rather more thought than have the historians to the concept and theory of responsibility. To be responsible is to offer a personal and appropriate act in "response" to the call of duty and not to put it off on someone else. The more thoroughly personal and the more thoroughly appropriate the responsive act, the more "responsible" we customarily say the actor is. Conversely, if the call of duty is not received as personal but as essentially generic or social, placing identical demands on everyone, and if the responsive act is therefore constructed as a collective gesture, displacing the burden of producing an effect statistically and actually onto others, then we would be justified in regarding such behavior as relatively irresponsible and evasive, a deliberate lightening of the individual burden. Such is Emerson's meaning in "Self-Reliance" when he insists that "It is only as a man puts off from himself all external support, and stands alone, that I see him to be strong and to prevail." Such is Thoreau's meaning in "Civil Disobedience" when he says that "Even voting for the right is doing nothing for it."[12]

The only agent that *can* be responsible, in other words, is a self-reliant one; all others act not for themselves, not as the authors of their acts, but merely as some group scripts and permits. In an 1840 lecture on "Reforms," Emerson made this point very strongly:

> If you take the reform as the reformer brings it to you he transforms you into an instrument. It behoves you to receive into a willing mind, every trait, every bold stroke which is drawn. Let the Age be a showman demonstrating in picture the needs and wishes of the soul: take them into your private mind; eat the book and make it your flesh. Let each of these causes take in you a new form, the form of your character and genius. Then the Age has spoken to you, and you have answered it: you have prevailed over it.[13]

Reform, says Emerson, needs true volunteers, not conscripts or ideological clones: if mere numbers avail nothing in moral matters, as the Transcendentalists consistently declared, it is a service to the cause to see that its force derives instead from free and responsible individuals capable, by virtue of their freedom, of shaping what is to be re-formed. Emerson's reluctance to sacrifice the individual to the agenda, which looks cold and selfish on a superficial examination, is in fact offered as a means of preserving to the triumph of reform its best resource. Hence, he contends: "the temptation is always great to lend himself to these movements and as one of a party accomplish what he cannot hope to effect alone. But he must resist this degradation of a man to a measure."[14] The question is not whether one ought to be a force for justice but how one can actually and authentically become such a force. Can slavery be defeated by a party of men who are willing to be commodified into tools and instruments, who have so little regard as that for their own freedom and independence? Should not the force opposing slavery consist rather of men and women than of numbers? If so, then perhaps reform should rely on the likelihood that a radical and general cultivation of freedom, quite apart from any particular goals, would practically exclude the toleration of slavery so common in 1840 in New England.

Is this all moonshine, as the historians allege? Is the Slave Power *only* to be brought to its knees when a majority consent to sign the registry of the

Antislavery Society? If one reinserts the discomfortingly individualistic
statements of Emerson and Thoreau into the political environment of the
1840s, they become more credible. The diagnosis arrived at by Transcendentalists and abolitionists alike assumed that injustice was an effect of the
arrogant selfishness appealed to by the marketplace with its promotion of
"secondary" desires.[15] What then was the main prop of slavery? Was it not,
then and always, the incapacity of the "responsible" members of society—
those, especially, privileged and empowered and dehumanized by the marketplace—to think for themselves? Was it not their unwillingness to rely on
their own private judgment of slavery that led them to defer instead to
some Constitutional argument or to the current proslavery policies of the
Whigs or the Democrats? What led any man at that time to consent to the
cruelty and injustice of human bondage but some alien force of rhetorical
or pecuniary influence warping him away from a natural revulsion? Who
could doubt, if this were true, that the encouragement to resist influence,
to suspect the primacy of the material, to question institutions, and to think
for oneself would be anything but helpful to antislavery? Indeed, it would
be emancipatory in itself.

Modern critics of the Transcendentalists will perhaps say that the moonshine in all this is the notion that people have "private judgments" or opinions on issues like slavery that were not put in their brains by the culture—
that no position is less cultural or more natural than another. Emerson
would say, I think, that a wealthy man who embraces a policy of greed and
exploitation is not just behaving wrongly, but also unnaturally, and that he
could be said to be "thinking for himself" in constructing his oppressive
acts only on the false assumption that his "self" *is* the thoroughly trained-
up, amoral capitalist it seems to be. Certainly it belongs to the definition of
Transcendentalism that its proponents believed in an intuitive moral sense
by virtue of which we are repelled by ugliness, cruelty, and injustice on
the one hand and attracted to beauty, kindness, and equity on the other—
responses stemming not from some painstaking education but rather from
having eyes and consciences and being human. Whether one believes that
this is objectively true or merely that a philosophy that encourages us to
define good as natural and evil as artificial does useful cultural work, the
effect is favorable to freedom and justice, not unfavorable.

The problem with the old historical critique, then, is its flat failure to
understand Emerson's position combined with its strange disbelief in the
capacity of "abstract" thought to move things forward. The routine political
context in which the historiography of American reform has been carried

out makes a fetish of the very thing that Emerson was most critical of: tactics. His desire to do away with tactics (a point examined further below) deeply offends an axiomatic position of majoritarian politicians and reform agitators alike and is quite enough in itself to attract charges of irresponsibility. One way, therefore, to rehabilitate Emerson as a credible antislavery voice would be to survey overlooked evidence that he really *was* tactical, and show that Hamlet was no Hamlet after all. Len Gougeon took this approach in his 1990 monograph *Virtue's Hero,* an important, deeply informed study that, together with concurrent work by others on Transcendentalism and the marketplace, goes far toward dissolving the critical impasse created by Schlesinger's dismissive portrayal. Yet the approach fails to challenge (indeed it accepts) the worrisome assumption that Emerson's thoughtful and principled position against tactics has no value. It recoups Emerson, but at the peril of representing him not as a distinctive thinker—that is, not as a Transcendentalist—but, in the end, as the run-of-the-mill abolitionist he had earlier been faulted for not being.

The major turning point in Gougeon's narrative is the 1844 "Address on West Indian Emancipation," which displays Emerson's new "willingness to consider . . . collective rather than . . . individualistic" methods. "There can be no doubt," Gougeon writes, "that in August 1844 Emerson made the transition from antislavery to abolition, and his association with organized abolitionists would continue to grow from this point forward."[16] The implication is that Emerson has seen the error of his ways and signed on to a movement of which he had previously been critical. Yet because "abolitionism" was very much a moving target, it is not altogether clear where the concessions truly lay. In 1842 and 1843 William Lloyd Garrison had made a point of emphasizing moral suasion over political maneuvering in connection with his application of Christian perfectionism and his renunciation of the Constitution. His redefinition of the issues, constructively a move toward Emerson's position, may indeed have made it easier for Emerson to speak out, there being less need now to foreground his differences. The West Indies address, moreover, while it clearly embraced abolitionist aims, need not (indeed should not) be read as an endorsement of collective strategies or tactics. Although it was well received by the abolitionists (as it should have been), there is some question whether, in their eagerness to have Emerson for an ally, they felt any pressing need to understand his views precisely.[17]

These views emerged from an earlier belief that, as Emerson said in *Nature* (1836), "The problem of restoring to the world original and eternal beauty is solved by the redemption of the soul."[18] The fundamental method of reform, in all its myriad manifestations, is the preservation of symbolism:

the bringing of the outer world into conformity with the inner—or submitting objective reality to the control of thought. Thus, love and justice, not a selfish rush for material advantage, should be what the relations of human beings express. This the reformer acknowledges, but too often without an operant faith in the power of the regime for which he contends. The abolitionist, with his strategies and tactics, his desire to appear forcible by leaguing himself with others, illustrates his belief that love and justice somehow need to be led, by his interfering assistance, his subterfuges, into a commanding position. Conversely, Transcendentalism, a "Saturnalia of faith," conducts itself on the assumption that ideas like love and justice have formidable attractive powers of their own and assemble their constituencies without need of means. This is the "magic" in terms of which Emerson always understood true reform. Character, about which he was speculating much at just this time, was the sign of individuality and self-reliance; it was the principal locus of reform and something that, as he said, accomplished its renovations "directly by presence, and without means."[19] The flourishing of means, on the other hand, inevitably signals an attention to circumstance, qualifies and subverts the authenticity of the reform, and sells the ideal short. Thus, for example, in examining the Brook Farm experiment, Emerson found that while he shared the reformers' hopes and aims, he had, in Sacvan Bercovitch's nice phrase, "to protect the ideal against their attempts at its realization."[20]

If Emerson had somehow been against realization itself, as the Schlesinger line of historians appears to have assumed, it would clearly be impossible to find a definition of reformer that would fit him. Yet the immense significance that Emerson placed on self-reliant character makes sense only if it is seen as the distinctive business of character to conform real life to higher and highest principles. This happens privately and individually; it does not and cannot happen in the marketplace, where "Things are in the saddle / And ride mankind." Because Transcendentalism devalues the material circumstance and redirects attention to ideas as causes—because, in short, it *begins* in ideas and not in conditions—it is supposed by unsympathetic critics to be incapable of regarding as real, much less of then engaging and counteracting, a matter so solid as slavery. John Carlos Rowe has recently advanced this version of Mrs. Brackett's complaint in a study significantly entitled *At Emerson's Tomb*, a work that disputes Gougeon's thesis that Emerson, as a Transcendentalist, did actually abet the abolitionist cause. Conceding what Gougeon thoroughly proves (that Emerson was a major antislavery force between 1844 and the Civil War), Rowe argues that this somewhat tardy commitment confers no distinction on Transcendentalism because it was entered into against the logic of Emerson's most character-istic thought. Had Emerson been consistent, Rowe implies, he would have taken warning from his hesitations and never involved himself at all; as Rowe puts it, "Emerson either must abandon the fundamentals of tran-scendentalism or the principles of political activism."[21]

This proposition is perhaps true or false depending on what we suppose the terms mean. If the contention is that Transcendentalism is ideolog-ically indifferent or unfriendly to the cause of the slave and has nothing essential to contribute to the political success of the antislavery movement, then it is certainly false. If, however, the suggestion is that Transcendental-ism does not construct the problem as a political one in the first place and is not logically committed to engage it with ordinary political tactics, then the proposition is as certainly true. Can a political end like the abolition of American slavery be served by a non-political program like Transcenden-talism? The question is tricky because if that is what Emerson seems to have accomplished, we are forced to conclude that his approach, by virtue of *having* a political effect, becomes political after all. As an intellectual, as a writer and speaker, indeed as a man of acknowledged independence and character, he had influence and was effective, yet without recourse to the means that, in our common reckoning, mark the presence of the reformer. This is what Emerson's detractors, from Mrs. Brackett on down, have failed to see with sufficient clarity.

Rowe's discussion of Emerson's stance sets off as a category unto itself the texts that are important to Gougeon's case for Emerson's social com-mitment. Beginning with the "Address on Emancipation in the British West Indies" in 1844 and culminating with "The Fortune of the Republic" in 1863, there are a great many occasional statements on public affairs, most of which Emerson never collected into a volume during his lifetime. These Rowe calls "political writings" and rightly observes that they have not been much studied until recently. Yet designating them as "political writings" grossly prejudices the case, easing the burden of the argument by assuming almost everything that is proposed to be demonstrated: namely, that these writings are inconsistent with Emerson's (mostly earlier) "Tran-scendental" statements. It ought to be a simple matter to show that ab-stract, otherworldly writing is on a different track from pragmatic, socially engaged writing, but in fact, in Emerson's case, both kinds—in this alleged distinction—make very nearly the same claims about the causative role of ideas in the world and both urge the duty of action.

If it were true, as Rowe asserts, that "More often than not, transcenden-talism works to rationalize present wrongs rather than bring about actual social change," it would have to be because it is altogether too trusting of the Oversoul, "Who marries Right to Might" and "Knows to bring honey / Out of the lion"—or because it just does not care enough about the phenomenal world.[22] And yet, what are we to make of the historical fact that Transcendentalists were far more likely than the general population to be involved in the most radical forms of antislavery work? Theodore Parker, Henry Thoreau, Franklin B. Sanborn, Thomas Wentworth Higginson, and Emerson had two things in common: Transcendentalism and a positive eagerness to support John Brown. Bronson Alcott, a member of the Boston Vigilance Committee, put his life in danger to help liberate the fugitive slave Anthony Burns. Thoreau ran a lesser risk to help runaways on to Canada. Parker literally worked himself to death in his opposition to slavery. Not a single individual identifiable as a Transcendentalist but was an active, vociferous supporter of the antislavery cause. When Orestes Brownson wanted to support slavery, he had first to break his ties with the Emersonians. When Harriet Martineau complained that Margaret Fuller's circle of women were self-absorbed society matrons, Higginson set the record straight, pointing out that they were in fact all staunch abolitionists. If it were somehow the business of Transcendentalists to rationalize present wrongs, they would seem to have missed a spectacular opportunity here. In fact, the record of the Transcendentalists on slavery is so good, taken all in all (Schlesinger to the contrary notwithstanding), that one might reasonably wonder what it was about their peculiar beliefs that made them so uniformly conscientious. The charge of aloofness or disengagement has no obvious relevance to the Transcendentalists as a group: it is a misgiving—an enduring doubt—about the movement's central figure, about Emerson himself.[23]

The impression prevails that the thinker's whole value is and must be as a tactician; let him go behind stratagems for practical success, let him visit the primary questions instead, and he is straightway a nuisance. This is the difficulty that remains after conceding that Emerson could be an effective agitator when he chose to be: that he must have left his own proper thought behind in exchange for the chance to produce an impression in the real world. In other words, as in Rowe's argument, he is either a Transcendentalist or someone who makes a difference. At any given time, Emerson has the option of talking about means or magic, the material or the spiritual, the real or the imaginary, and in the nature of things the two cannot be related or conjoined in symbolism, but each rejects the other.

Thus, for example, there is the "curious association," as Rowe calls it, of the abolition of the Atlantic slave trade together with other "miracles" in a passage from Emerson's early manifesto, *Nature*:

> There are not wanting gleams of a better light,—occasional examples of the action of man upon nature with his entire force,—with reason as well as understanding. Such examples are, the traditions of miracles in the earliest antiquity of all nations; the history of Jesus Christ; the achievements of a principle, as in religious and political revolutions, and in the abolition of the slave-trade; the miracles of enthusiasm, as those reported of Swedenborg, Hohenlohe, and the Shakers; many obscure and yet contested facts, now arranged under the name of Animal Magnetism; prayer; eloquence; self-healing; and the wisdom of children. These are examples of Reason's momentary grasp of the sceptre; the exertions of a power which exists not in time or space, but an instantaneous in-streaming causing power.[24]

Rowe cites this passage to argue that its mysticism is in contradiction to Emerson's explanation, in the West Indies address eight years later, of the mechanism (Parliamentary debate) by which the slaves of Jamaica were emancipated. The implication is that Emerson can ascribe the triumph of good to mysterious supernatural powers and be a Transcendentalist or in the alternative he can flip around and give credit, realistically, to the mundane working of a very human institution.

And yet Emerson's discussion of the history leading up to the act of emancipation is not without its attentiveness to a magic above means:

> Other revolutions have been the insurrection of the oppressed; this was the repentance of the tyrant. It was the masters revolting from their mastery. The slave-holder said, I will not hold slaves. . . . Out it would come, the God's truth, out it came, like a bolt from a cloud, for all the mumbling of the lawyers. One feels very sensibly in all this history that a great heart and soul are behind there, superior to any man, and making use of each, in turn, and infinitely attractive to every person according to the degree of reason in his own mind.[25]

Rowe cannily points out, what Emerson also mentions, that if emancipation had the blessing of "a great heart," it was helped along as well by a sizable cash payment in compensation to the slaveholders. Yet this scarcely diminishes the miracle, for if some West Indian slaveholders got paid, a greater number of English slaveholders did the paying. Emerson is clear on this point, that the miracle mainly happened in England, where for the

ALBERT J. VON FRANK

first time in history the freedom of some 300,000 black people was worth more to a culture of profit-driven merchants and shopkeepers than twenty million pounds sterling. This is a surprising development, even if one knows it was talked about beforehand. What had come over them? What light was brightening in England? The advancement was in the value of freedom; the gaugeable headway it was making against purely mercantile or capitalist values was a sign of the times, a sign of a finer, self-reforming civilization, and surely, as well, of more victories to come.

So, while there were agents made use of, the miracle of conversion remains central. If the Transcendental faith lay in an ultimately irresistible force of moral progress, such force still works, if not by means then by agents, by the efforts of men and women who align themselves with it and who contribute as their several characters determine. As with other theoretical inevitabilities, as predestined grace comes, or as the dictatorship of the proletariat comes, so progress comes without excusing any from action. Rowe assumes that Emerson contradicted himself by asserting on the one hand that a kind of miracle had occurred when men voluntarily forswore the unrighteous but profitable and self-gratifying use of power and on the other that a grindingly slow political process had borne fruit. Rowe is willing to understand that the first assertion is a Transcendental one, but under the impression that Transcendentalism can have nothing to do with this real and present world, he is unprepared to grant that the second is driven by the first, that the long-drawn-out dance in English courtrooms and in the House of Commons is but the phenomenal form that the miracle takes. Men act who are possessed by an idea; the world is re-formed to match a new clarity about the nature of justice.[26]

The sudden, intense interest in reform at this period seemed to Emerson sufficiently motivated by the spiritually deracinating effect of the marketplace. The most responsible acts of protest and healing would therefore aim at restoring spiritual power and insight, to the end of resacralizing everyday life.[27] What the history of the English parliamentarians revealed was that no action was more necessary—especially for Emerson—than the education of the will, than leading the will back through the contaminations of selfishness to find in original thought the source of authentic action. "We know that the ancestor of every action is a thought."[28]

One way to assess the significance of the West Indies address of 1844 is to observe that the occasion fell shortly before the American election season of that year, during which the Liberty party made tremendous gains in voter support. If the delivery of the address can be construed as political activism, it would be of that Transcendental kind that is less concerned with parties and their agendas than with the vindication of abstract right, in this instance through the action of voters. It was a sign of progress that such abstract right had shown its power by commanding the votes to abolish slavery in the West Indies; Emerson's point in the address was that the same moral revolution, the same miracle, was bound to occur, as a political event, in America. Over the next twenty years, in a way to suggest that Emerson was picking his spots, all of his most notable statements on slavery would bear close relation to current political developments, including his first address on the Fugitive Slave Law (1851), which he used as a stump speech for John Gorham Palfrey's Free Soil campaign for Congress, and the second Fugitive Slave address, delivered on the seventh of March, 1854, with an eye to the Kansas-Nebraska Act and its repeal of the Missouri Compromise. The presumption of Emerson's disengagement has obscured from us the extent to which he becomes vocal on the slavery question out of a desire precisely to affect the political behavior of his audience. His approach to this task was remarkably different from that of his hotter, more confrontational friends (many of whom had left off voting), yet one could argue that his characteristic attention to the philosophical motives for political action finally made Emerson's appeal more radical than theirs, not to say more effective with a thoughtful audience.

As Emerson took the platform that first of August, 1844, he knew that his audience had already framed his performance as a kind of coming out; it was to be the delivery of a belated word of encouragement to the antislavery vanguard. His introductory remarks allude to the drama of that circumstance by rehearsing some of the reasons why, as he said, he "might well hesitate" to address this audience. He observes, in the first place, that he comes "from other studies" (7), indicating that this present engagement is apart from his own proper work (he had in fact interrupted his labors on *Essays: Second Series* to write and deliver the address) and implying at the same time that to speak well on slavery requires its own separate study (though in fact he had done a great deal of research for the address and would do yet more to prepare it for publication).

The second of his motives for hesitation was that he had not, he said, "the smallest claim to be a special laborer in this work" (7). Emerson thus lists among his disqualifications the very point that, for his immediate audience, gave particular interest to his declaration. In so doing, he also acknowledges that such an address as the occasion seemed to call for had already a history of specialist treatment—belonged, that is, to a genre firmly established by orators with credentials of a decidedly certain sort.

Emerson makes use of this pretense of hesitation to locate himself,

independently, outside the group he seems to be joining. He had used a
similar manoeuvre at the very outset of his lecturing career in 1833, when
he prefaced his remarks on "The Uses of Natural History" with a disclaimer of any special license to speak on the topic, apart from the strong
interest in it that all people felt. On both occasions it seemed vitally important not to surrender the topic to professionals or indeed to cater to expectations created by a tradition of specialist treatment. The list of reasons
why he "might well hesitate" is in fact a ground-clearing statement of his
qualifications for speaking, ironically presented, from the perspective of
tradition, as disqualifications.

    Although I do not wish to belabor this point, it nevertheless seems to
me that the address is deeply preoccupied with the personal conditions of
its production, the question of speaking or not speaking, the history of
Emerson's own silence on the subject, the decision to speak now, and
finally and above all, the nature of proper and effective speaking on public
or political matters. For Emerson to have given just the kind of address the
abolitionists looked for would have required his total concession to the
prevailing mode of antislavery oratory; this is perfectly evident in their response to the address, which focused strictly on the "news" that Emerson
was now one of them. It is equally evident in the form of Emerson's resistance to making his speech a "performance."[29]

    The conclusion of the first paragraph nicely illustrates this posture of
resistance: if the typical abolition speech assumes the effectiveness of
bearing forceful personal witness, Emerson insinuates a doubt: "In this
cause," he declares, "no man's weakness is any prejudice: it has a thousand
sons; if one man cannot speak, ten others can; and whether by the wisdom
of its friends, or by the folly of the adversaries; by speech and by silence; by
doing and by omitting to do, it goes forward" (7). Given Emerson's history,
one might construe such a statement (as indeed many have) as a rationalization for past and even future silence—an exculpation; as an introduction
to a *speech*, however, it functions rather to state a position on the problem
of leadership and the cult of personality in reform movements. If the purpose of giving antislavery speeches is formally and ritualistically to constitute a certain class professional antislaves, then opposition to slavery can
and will be ceded to a minority, indeed to a priestly caste, quite as though
mankind were not involved and could not move independently in the
matter. Thus there is an important issue at stake for Emerson in the preservation of his amateur standing; his unwillingness to be subsumed formally
by the ranks of the hot contenders is equivalent to opening the movement
out to humanity in general, understood not as an audience to be addressed
but as veritable authors of the moment's speech.[30]

This resistance to co-optation is abetted by Emerson's philosophical and literary misgivings about the normative abolition speech, the bloody rhetoric of its litany of horrors, its stirring appeals to anger and outrage, as though the cause had nothing to do with the better world that slavery denies and postpones. "The blood," Emerson said, "is moral: the blood is anti-slavery: it runs cold in the veins: the stomach rises with disgust, and curses slavery" (10). There is evidence in this address that Emerson was susceptible to the power of such visceral images: to such an extent, indeed, that he came to mistrust them. They seemed to challenge and even to pass beyond language; the effort to realize and reproduce the savage cruelties of slavery—for an audience that had, literally, no sense of them—is an effort against the inherently symbolic nature of language:

> if we *saw* the whip applied to old men, to tender women; and, undeniably, though I shrink to say so, pregnant women set in the treadmill for refusing to work; when, not they, but the eternal law of animal nature refused to work;—if we *saw* men's backs flayed with cowhides, and "hot rum poured on, superinduced with brine or pickle, rubbed in with a cornhusk, in the scorching heat of the sun;"—if we *saw* the runaways hunted with bloodhounds into swamps and hills; and in cases of passion, a planter throwing his negro into a copper of boiling cane-juice,—if we *saw these things with eyes*, we too should wince. (10; emphasis added)

Emerson continues:

> It became plain to all men, the more this business was looked into, that the crimes and cruelties of the slave-traders and slave-owners could not be overstated. The more it was searched, the more shocking anecdotes came up,—things not to be spoken. (10)

But why "not to be spoken"? It was, after all, just the ordinary business of the abolitionist speaker to publicize the extremest outrages of the Slave Power. Here the omission to speak does not seem to be a euphemistic cover for sex crimes, since Emerson mentions these. One suspects that he is consciously declining the usual gambit of the antislavery orator, that he is refusing the appeal to blood, having sensed what is problematic and manipulative in the ordinary stump eloquence of such occasions. Emerson observes how it had become proverbial in Massachusetts that "eloquence is dog-cheap at the anti-slavery chapel" (28). Meaning, ambiguously, both that the case speaks for itself and that it is all too dangerously easy, given such a topic, to rouse the emotions.

Though he recognizes the physical plight of the slaves, Emerson does not "aim" at it but seems rather to recoil from constructing slavery for his audience as an affair of whips, hard labor, and short rations, as though to do so (as custom required) were to adopt the owner's view of the slave as a body, as a material object. In the address, it is not the physical suffering of the slave that Emerson exploits or that captures his attention; surprisingly (and to some disappointingly), it is instead the moderate way in which, on the first of August, 1838, the ex-slaves celebrated their emancipation. Emerson quotes several sources, including a statement by Queen Victoria, that commend the ex-slaves' conduct in setting aside the day of liberation for thanksgiving and prayer, civilly declining the riot and murder that opponents had predicted and friends feared. "The manner in which the new festival was celebrated," Emerson said, "brings tears to the eyes" (18).

As a rhetorical unit within the address, the discussion of this event precisely mirrors the discussion of the political debate in England which had resulted, after many long years, in the act of emancipation. Emerson had marveled at the civil and dispassionate reasonableness that had made heroes of Thomas Clarkson, William Wilberforce, Charles James Fox, Edmund Burke, and William Pitt, and which had made the first of August, as he said, "a day of reason; of the clear light" (7). Genuine emancipation, which in Emerson's view was not to be distinguished from the advance of civilization, required the two events that he chose here specially to commemorate: slaveholders ceasing to act as slaveholders and slaves ceasing to act as slaves. The liberation of England's leading citizens from the commercial values of their shopkeeper's culture, allowing them to move beyond a paltry model of the world as commodity, was strictly analogous to the introduction of a new political force in the West Indies, where, Emerson said, "A man is added to the human family" (29). If the slaves, ceasing to be slaves, were free now to lead a more human life, so, too, were the emancipators, each a closer approximation, as Emerson said elsewhere, "to the right state of every man."[31]

The prospect that Emerson's abolitionism envisioned was not paternalistic, interventionist, or protective, but something that looked to the gathering of forces, political, economic, and otherwise, that promoted freedom and self-determination. Every action undertaken in service to these principles, everything done to make them credible and attractive, participates in the historical progress that Emerson refers to at the end of the address as a "blessed necessity" (33). Its meliorative operation is seen as evolutionary, inexorable, and assured. It is assured because power, including human power as expressed in beautiful actions, favors it; people *will* assert their humanity as they come to feel a regard for it, and will regard it most truly, Emerson supposed, as they evade the traps of a skeptical materialism and see humanity subsisting more in justice than in luxury, more in expansion than in limitation, more in connection to an ideal life than in fretfulness over food and clothes.

Emerson believed that the "better life" promised by reform had to have reference (and indeed did have reference when properly understood) to his underlying Unitarian/Transcendental construction of "life" as an empowering spiritual progress. What made one life better or more worthy of emulation than another, he supposed, was the degree of its adherence to truth; he also believed that to these various degrees of authenticity power was awarded in proportion—the very power that excited the emulation. "Who has more obedience than I, masters me, though he should not lift his finger."[32] Within this understanding of the relation of life and power, significant victories had to be moral and ideal ones; yet Emerson did not figure these as won privately or "in the abstract": he understood that a world and real life were given as the place in which to gain them, as all his heroes had done.

Faith, then (or a belief that power rather than circumstance is controlling), is required to act largely and heroically in the cause of freedom, though such faith had not been indispensable, Emerson found, to antislavery as it was commonly carried on. In a contention between "brute force" and an idea, the reformer had to be faithful and affirmative, his allegiance undivided between the parties. At one point in the address, Emerson speaks of a setback in the historical process when it looked as though West Indian emancipation might not actually occur; he speaks of this turn as if it invited a religious doubt, a kind of despair, about the efficacy of divine ideas: "There have been moments in this, as . . . in every piece of moral history, when there seemed room for the infusions of a skeptical philosophy; when it seemed doubtful, whether brute force would not triumph in the eternal struggle" (32). It was Emerson's main objection against popular antislavery that it relied in its indictments and in its remedies on a materialist construction of reality and thereby lost the integrity of its motive to the skeptical philosophy it opposed. "It has been," he noted, "in all men's experience a marked effect of the enterprise in behalf of the African, to generate an overbearing and defying spirit" (8). It may be that this kind of mild rebuke, ordinarily received as a piece of timidity or a misplaced aestheticism, is in fact a complaint about the willingness of abolitionists to break faith with the value of what is contended for and to become contaminated by the enemy's love of force.[33]

A more faithful reading of history would not be sidetracked by those particular, authentically attested episodes of cruelty that were the staple of agitation. They were the chaff of history, symbols that refused to be read as symbols, each in itself a skeptical argument that selves could be taken for physical bodies after all, the Not-Me of the world. Compared with the coming-to-be of emancipation, these episodes were "not to be spoken of." At the close of the address, Emerson said, "I am sure that the good and wise elders, the ardent and generous youth, will not permit what is incidental and exceptional to withdraw their devotion from the essential and permanent characters of the question" (32).

A proper and effective political response requires a steadier attention to essential principles: as, for example, that if slavery is wrong it is only wrong because some good is thereby denied, temporarily, against the world's need of it. Emerson argued specifically that

> if the black man carries in his bosom an indispensable element of a new and coming civilization; for the sake of that element, no wrong nor strength nor circumstance can hurt him: he will survive and play his part. So now, the arrival in the world of such men as Toussaint, and the Haitian heroes, or of the leaders of their race in Barbadoes and Jamaica, outweighs in good omen all the English and American humanity. The anti-slavery of the whole world is dust in the balance before this,—is a poor squeamishness and nervousness: the might and the right are here; here is the antislave: here is man: and if you have man, black or white is an insignificance. (31)

While such a statement is clearly a critique of the antislavery crusade, it does not amount to a declaration of the irrelevance of either politics or reform agitation. It merely says that whatever is to be saved must have merit and virtue in itself, and that it is ultimately saved for and by the power of that virtue. Those on both sides of the question are too apt to think, in their skepticism, that virtue is helpless, always a needy victim. Reform is not a ministering to powerlessness, but, rightly seen, a cooperation with power itself.

The abolitionists may have believed, after the first of August, 1844, that Emerson was now "one of them," a joined member in a collective protest, his assent finally and clearly given to their aims. Yet it might be closer to the truth to say that they had joined him, to the extent that they could now see themselves working, not by their own poor power—alone *or* together— but under the sponsorship of an idea that could not lose. Is it the act of a political activist to embolden the troops, to give them reasons which they themselves would feel were "higher" and more worthy? This Emerson did not only in his "political writings" but equally in his Transcendental ones— if, that is, we can tell the difference.

Notes

1. John Carlos Rowe, *At Emerson's Tomb: The Politics of Classic American Literature* (New York, 1997), 21.
2. Ralph Waldo Emerson, *The Journals and Miscellaneous Notebooks of Ralph Waldo Emerson*, ed. William H. Gilman et al. (Cambridge, Mass., 1960–1982), 8:120. Cited hereafter as *JMN*. Emerson's "Mrs. B." is conjecturally identified by the editors.
3. Thomas Carlyle to Ralph Waldo Emerson, Nov. 3, 1844, in *The Correspondence of Emerson and Carlyle*, ed. Joseph Slater (New York, 1964), 371.
4. Ralph Waldo Emerson to Thomas Carlyle, Dec. 31, 1844, in *Correspondence of Emerson and Carlyle*, 373.
5. Ralph Waldo Emerson, "Introductory Lecture [On the Times]," in *The Collected Works of Ralph Waldo Emerson*, ed. Alfred R. Ferguson et al. (Cambridge, Mass., 1971–), 1:179. Cited hereafter as *CW*.
6. Anne C. Rose, *Transcendentalism as a Social Movement, 1830–1850* (New Haven, 1981), 31–33.
7. *JMN*, 8:119.
8. Arthur M. Schlesinger, Jr., *The Age of Jackson* (Boston, 1945), 382.
9. Schlesinger, *Age of Jackson*, 382–385. The assumption that Transcendentalism is allied to "the democratic position" is a fair inference from Emerson's affirmations about "the infinitude of the private man," yet he and Thoreau were sharp critics of the (selfish) Jacksonian individualism fostered by the market revolution. Any thinking about this issue will benefit from the contemporary distinction between "individualism" and "individuality" usefully surveyed by Sacvan Bercovitch in "Emerson, Individualism, and Liberal Dissent," *Rites of Assent: Transformations in the Symbolic Construction of America* (New York, 1993), 307–352, and George Kateb, *Emerson and Self-Reliance* (Thousand Oaks, Calif., 1995).
10. Stanley M. Elkins, *Slavery: A Problem in American Institutional and Intellectual Life*, 3d ed., rev. (Chicago, 1976), 168. Elkins settles quite amazingly on Theodore Parker as an example of the failure to "analyze slavery . . . as an institution": had Parker analyzed it, as he was well informed enough to have done, he might have agitated for the legality of slave marriages rather than attack slavery in toto. His Transcendental "obtuseness," as Elkins calls it, to "piecemeal reform" in fact saved him from the guilt and infamy of making slavery that much more politically acceptable.
11. For example, Aileen Kraditor, in *Means and Ends in American Abolitionism: Garrison and His Critics on Strategy and Tactics, 1834–1850* (1969; Chicago, 1989), 8, makes membership in a society part of the definition of the term "abolitionist," which would seem not only to leave Emerson and Thoreau out of the picture, but to preempt discussion of all other ways of contributing to the antislavery cause. The historians' fascination with antislavery societies as the inevitable site for people determined to make a difference further overlooks a point nicely made by Debra Gold Hansen: that the abolitionists' attachment to freedom and opposition to coercion meant that their societies had difficulty enforcing discipline, were never

perfect models of cooperative (as opposed to individualistic) behavior, and were often, as Maria Weston Chapman put it, "not really organizations." *Strained Sisterhood: Gender and Class in the Boston Female Anti-Slavery Society* (Amherst, Mass., 1993), 104.

12. *CW*, 2:50; Thoreau, "Resistance to Civil Government," *Reform Papers* (Princeton, 1973), 69.
13. Ralph Waldo Emerson, "Reforms," in *Early Lectures of Ralph Waldo Emerson*, ed. Stephen E. Whicher and Robert E. Spiller (Cambridge, Mass., 1959–1972), 3:260. Cited hereafter as *EL*.
14. *EL*, 3:265.
15. On the abolitionists and the marketplace, see Paul Goodman, *Of One Blood: Abolitionism and the Origins of Racial Equality* (Berkeley, 1998). On the Transcendentalists, see Michael Gilmore, *American Romanticism and the Marketplace* (Chicago, 1985); Bercovitch, *Rites of Assent*; Richard F. Teichgraeber III, *Sublime Thoughts/Penny Wisdom: Situating Emerson and Thoreau in the American Market* (Baltimore, 1995); and Anita Haya Patterson, *From Emerson to King: Democracy, Race, and the Politics of Protest* (New York, 1997).
16. Len Gougeon, *Virtue's Hero: Emerson, Antislavery, and Reform* (Athens, Ga., 1990), 84–85.
17. For the reception of the address, see Len Gougeon, "Historical Background," *Emerson's Antislavery Writings* (New Haven, 1995), xxx, and *Virtue's Hero*, 84–91.
18. *CW*, 1:43. Compare Garrison: "Moral reformation is necessary to produce an enlightened, conscientious, impartial political action. A man must first be abolitionized before he will be able or willing to burst the shackles of party, and give his vote for the slave." *Liberator*, Aug. 16, 1839.
19. *CW*, 3:53. Emerson made the same point in "Walter Savage Landor" (1841), in *The Complete Works of Ralph Waldo Emerson*, ed. Edward Waldo Emerson (Boston, 1903–1904), 12:345 (hereafter cited as *W*), and in the late lecture on "Character": "Its methods are subtle, it works without means." *W*, 10:120.
20. Bercovitch, *Rites of Assent*, 329. In discussing the subject of Brook Farm, Bercovitch suggests that Emerson had an instinct for socialism but dissented, once again, on the question of means.
21. *W*, 9:78; Rowe, *At Emerson's Tomb*, 21. What Gougeon shows is the record of Emerson's multifarious engagement in the antislavery cause: the extent to which this activity is "Transcendental" is often not dealt with directly, thus giving Rowe his opening.
22. Rowe, *At Emerson's Tomb*, 40; *W*, 9:79.
23. Thomas Wentworth Higginson, *Margaret Fuller Ossoli* (1884; New York, 1981), 126–129. See also Albert J. von Frank, *The Trials of Anthony Burns: Freedom and Slavery in Emerson's Boston* (Cambridge, Mass., 1998), which argues at length that the antislavery activism of these men followed directly from their Transcendentalism.
24. Quoted in Rowe, *At Emerson's Tomb*, 21, from *CW*, 1:43.
25. Ralph Waldo Emerson, "An Address . . . on . . . the Emancipation of the Negroes in the British West Indies," in *Emerson's Antislavery Writings*, 26–27. Further citations from this text will be given parenthetically.
26. In his 1840 lecture on "Politics" (the basis for the essay of the same title), Emerson

indicates the utter subordination of politics to the power of ideas: "The vice of young politicians . . . is the belief that the laws make the city and the people: that the gravest modifications of the policy, the modes of living, and the character of the population may be accomplished by voting them: that commerce, education, religion, may be voted in or out and that any measure, though it were absurd, may be imposed on a people if only you get sufficient numbers to make it a law. But the wise know that . . . the state must follow the character and progress of man and does not lead it, that the state goes not by will but by fate, . . . that the form of government that prevails is always the expression of what cultivation exists in the population which permits it, that the Law is therefore always only a memorandum." *EL*, 3:241. Thus, unless Emerson contradicts himself, the credit for West Indian emancipation cannot belong very specially to Wilberforce, who nevertheless deserves all admiration for having the enlightenment, civilization, and self-reliance to have filled his sails in just the way he did.

27. See Goodman, *Of One Blood*, 81, for the argument that this was the project also of the abolitionists. The "Divinity School Address" is a major instance of Emerson's concern to domesticate the idea of the miraculous—that is, of the production of effects without means.

28. *EL*, 3:267.

29. See Gougeon, "Historical Background," xxx.

30. I take it that Emerson's defense of the amateur stance is an application of the distinction he makes in "The American Scholar" between "Man Thinking" and the mere thinker.

31. *CW*, 1:65.

32. *CW*, 2:40.

33. "But whilst [reforms] have this high origin it must be confessed that they do not retain the purity of an idea. They are presently organized in some low inadequate form and present no more poetic image to man than the tradition which they reprobated. They mix the fire of the moral sentiment with personal and party heats, with measureless exaggerations, and the blindness that prefers some darling measure to justice and truth." *EL*, 3:259.

Woman Questions

Emerson, Fuller, and New England Reform

PHYLLIS COLE

The female Greek, of our day, is as much in the street
as the male to cry, What news?

— MARGARET FULLER, "The Great Lawsuit"[1]

I N 1876, DESCRIBING THE REFORM TENDENCIES OF TRANSCEN-
dentalism, Octavius B. Frothingham began with Brook Farm but found
his exemplary case in the movement for women's rights. "To a man and a
woman," he claimed, the Transcendentalists had in some measure advocated freedom for women, and with almost equal unanimity their opposers
had also opposed enlarging the female sphere. "More definitively than any
other, this reform can trace its beginnings and the source of its inspiration
to the disciples of the transcendental philosophy." Frothingham did not
elaborate his thinking at length, only quoting Margaret Fuller and concluding broadly that moral idealism had produced social discontent throughout
the movement. Still, he advanced a thesis about the importance of women's
issues to the Transcendentalists—and of Transcendentalism to the women's
movement—that no twentieth-century surveyor has taken up. When Perry
Miller introduced Fuller's "Great Lawsuit" in his 1950 anthology, he settled
for a glance at the wider field, finding Fuller a pioneer of feminism, the
movement's activists (Theodore Parker, W. H. Channing, George and
Sophia Ripley) all substantial supporters, and Ralph Waldo Emerson a
benign onlooker. Now Barbara L. Packer, representing a new generation
of scholars, places both Fuller and reform nearer the center of Transcendentalism. Amidst detailed attention to antislavery and communitarian
thought, however, she does not take up feminism beyond the work of
Fuller.[2]

In what terms did male and female Transcendentalists claim new possibilities for women, and in what relation to the women's rights ideology

simultaneously generated by other American reformers? Eventually a history needs to be written that extends from originating moments through the public, often New England–based women's rights conventions and parties of the 1850s and 1860s. Smaller-scale studies of such cultural interaction are needed first, however. My essay focuses on the two leaders Emerson and Fuller, in the crucial years of the late 1830s and early 1840s when their "New Views" were first meeting antislavery and communitarian views in the embattled, still church-dominated culture of eastern Massachusetts.

Both writers approached the "woman question" through conversation, private at first but with a public audience never far from mind. In the summer of 1838, Emerson told Fuller and their close mutual friend Elizabeth Hoar of his desire to write on topics that would provide "telescopes into the Future," and the women objected to his list of male poets and politicians. "E. H. says, add the topic of the rights of Woman," Emerson noted in his journal; "& Margaret Fuller testifies that women are Slaves."[3] From such casual remarks and notations grew a longer dialogue through Fuller's publication of "The Great Lawsuit" (1843), her first version of *Woman in the Nineteenth Century*, and Emerson's of *Essays: Second Series* (1844). These were years of growing ethical engagement for all the major Transcendentalists, as recent scholars have been emphasizing.[4] My aim is to follow the posing of various "woman questions"—for there were of course more than one—within that ethical discussion.

Both Emerson and Fuller first asked not about women's rights but about women's "genius": Could the female mind discover and act upon the godlike capacity of consciousness enabling the highest cognition and creativity? For the Transcendentalists genius was a key to all larger questions of resisting conformity, cultivating spirit, and transforming culture; and with differing degrees of hesitation, both of these leading thinkers invited women to claim its inspiration. A recently discovered manuscript summarizing Fuller's first conversations with women shows the subject of her series in 1839–1840 to be a mythic typology of genius, with Apollo its male avatar and Minerva a complementary female "wisdom." After extended discussion of intellectual differences between men and women, the group united in commitment to "the formation of the Apollo within us." A year later, in the spring of 1841, Emerson joined Fuller's only conversation to include men, which similarly took up consideration of mythic archetypes. One of several male participants who consistently sidetracked her agenda, he still may have been led to consider anew the female mind's potential. In a journal entry that May, he illustrated internal "genius" as opposed to external "talent" through the case of a woman—neither Minerva nor Margaret Fuller, but his own aunt Mary Moody Emerson:

> Aunt Mary, whose letters I read all yesterday afternoon, is Genius always new, subtle, frolicsome, musical, unpredictable. . . . She is embarrassed by no Moses or Paul, no Angelo or Shakspeare, after whose type she is to fashion her speech: her wit is the wild horse of the desart who snuffs the sirocco & scours the palm-grove without having learned his paces in the Stadium or Tattersall's. What liberal, joyful architecture, liberal & manifold as the vegetation from the earth's bosom, or the creations of frost work on the window![5]

Emerson was celebrating a woman's capacity to generate language that both owned the (male) cultural past and reflected nature's wildness. The critical term "genius" had had a long European history of association with male sexuality, very much to the disparagement of women. Even the Romantic masters from Rousseau through Coleridge, newly embracing knowledge based upon the female-identified traits of emotion and sympathy, recognized its power only in men.[6] But the heritage of European Romanticism included women's appropriations of genius as well. Most notably, French critic and novelist Germaine de Staël had responded directly to Rousseau in *Corinne* (1807), imagining a heroine whose rhapsodic speech could win the crowds of Rome to chant, *"Long live genius! Long live beauty!"* De Staël was a novelist of vast influence, "benefactress" (as Fuller later put it) even to New England schoolgirls unfamiliar with her name.[7] She offered powerful terms for imagining inspired womanhood: ravishing beauty, association by dress and speech style with the pre-Christian sibyl, poetic improvisation worthy of a laurel crown. Expressing her own internal conflict, De Staël also saw the story of this sibylline woman as doubly tragic; in the novel, Corinne dies no longer capable of brilliant speech, spurned by a lover who feels he cannot subdue her to domestic life. Mary Moody Emerson drew the novel's lesson while her nephew was still an adolescent, lamenting Corinne's inability to remain "sufficient to herself."[8] In Mary's mind, romantic entanglement could only spell the demise of female brilliance.

Margaret Fuller and Ralph Waldo Emerson shared an interest in the Corinne type, but each came to it separately—Waldo through the direct influence of his unmarried, self-taught aunt Mary. His tribute to her genius points to genuine intellectual power in this woman, as well as to her own Romantic style and preoccupations. As I have argued elsewhere, Mary served as both precursor and mentor to her nephew in defying institutions, claiming intuitive knowledge, and valuing a frolicsome style. In the early 1820s she had recommended Wordsworth, Milton, Price, Plato, and Hindu poetry to the young Harvard man, as well as quoting de Staël on the ancient goddess mysteries of Eleusis.[9] In fact Mary sent him a cryptic characterization of herself *as* de Staël, storing up ideas for a son instead of publishing them. He gladly accepted the role of son to de Staël, later urging her to continue such generosity.[10]

Most important for his own developing patterns of thought about women, Waldo also characterized Mary, with comic hyperbole and genuine awe, as a priestly or prophetic figure, "sibylline" in fragmented prose style and revelatory power if not (like Corinne) in beauty or public visibility. He recorded her letters in his journal as the work of "Tnamurya," an anagram converting the name "Aunt Mary" to divinatory mystery; marveled over her as "the weird woman" of her religion, able to read the fates; implored her in 1826 to continue writing the "secret oracles" that his imminent license to preach would need. Employing most directly the Romantic tropes of de Staël, he gave pagan names to her spiritual power. No New England woman could speak directly from a pulpit, but perhaps she might from the sibyl's cave. By defining her letters as "secret oracles," Waldo was crediting his aunt with divine knowledge and a poet's gift for language, but limiting her audience to himself. More powerful than a "muse"—they rarely used that term—she still served as his private inspiration.[11]

Emerson has often been characterized as the archetypal male individualist of American literature, but any such characterization must take into consideration the depth of his exchange with women and interest in characterizing them. Christina Zwarg has recently claimed that the fourteen-year (1836–1850) correspondence between Emerson and Fuller reveals his most antihierarchical, implicitly feminized character; my research compounds the case for a feminized Emerson, bracketing the Fuller dialogue with an almost half-century (1812–1858) conversation by letter and journal with Mary Moody Emerson.[12] The two women hardly met each other, Mary abandoning residence in Concord just a few months before Margaret first visited in 1836, but Waldo's characterizations of them sounded common themes for years thereafter. Margaret, he remembered retrospectively, appeared upon first meeting a "new Corinne, . . . more variously gifted, wise, sportive, eloquent, who seems to have learned all languages, Heaven knows when or how,—I should think she was born to them,—magnificent, prophetic, reading my life at her will, and puzzling me with riddles."[13] Like Mary she seemed spontaneously learned, at once playful and divinatory—and, with a power at once flattering and disconcerting, able to read *his life*. In this characterization, individualism gives way once more here to hyperbolically praising a power outside the self, though finding in it at last a gift to self.

But in 1836, unlike Mary Moody Emerson, Fuller clearly entertained ambitions wider than private conversation and influence. At the time of their meeting, Fuller was already deep into correspondence with Cambridge Unitarians W. H. Channing and James Freeman Clarke, as well as advanced in reading the European authors who would elicit many of her most important ideas and symbols. From these backgrounds she shared Emerson's interest in the intellectual woman of prophetic power, but with a new immediacy and implication of finding personal authority. At sixteen, asking whether a former teacher preferred "the brilliant De Stael or the useful Edgworth," she had immediately expanded on her own choice by characterizing de Staël as "useful, too, . . . on the grand scale, on liberalizing, regenerating principles." Wishing increasingly to be such an agent of public renewal, she had laid no claim as yet on behalf of herself or other women. "I have greatly wished to see among us such a person of genius as the nineteenth century can afford . . . ," she wrote to James Freeman Clarke in 1830, "a centre, round which asking aimless hearts might rally,— a man fitted to act as interpreter to the one tale of many-languaged eyes!"[14] Emerson later drew a portrait of female genius apprehending the world without harboring designs upon it; Fuller was imagining, but not yet claiming, such designs herself.

The nature of genius often preoccupied both Emerson and Fuller in their early conversations. Emerson already counted Michelangelo and Raphael on his list of artists who possessed it most purely when, in the summer of 1838, Fuller arrived with Samuel Ward's portfolio of their engravings. Both connoisseurs especially valued Raphael's and Michelangelo's representations of sibyls, Emerson commenting that one by Raphael presented "a higher style of beauty than we live in sight of" (*JMN*, 7:160, 46-47). His house even today is hung with prints of these figures. But Fuller was seeking immediate models in the rich images offered by the Italian artists. "The Sibyl I understood . . . ," she wrote after viewing copies of Raphael at the Athenaeum. "What apprehensiveness in the eye! Such is female Genius; it alone understands the God. The Muse only sang the praises of Apollo; the Sibyls interpreted his will."[15] As critics of art, both Emerson and Fuller looked for ideal human types more than formal achievement, but Fuller sought ideals of divine mediation for women, necessarily in the female figures represented rather than the male artists themselves. Her study of Italian Renaissance art in 1838–1839 enabled conversion of an older delight in classical mythology, first derived from childhood reading of Ovid, into a gendered vocabulary of the soul (*MHF*, 30). In one of her later public conversations she claimed that all her knowledge of the myth of Psyche had come from Raphael (*MHF*, 118).

Emerson, though willing to converse in depth with women and reflect on ideal types of womanhood, did not fully endorse the aspirations of those in his milieu. His first years of conversation with Fuller coincided with the most ecstatic affirmations of his early rhetoric; the pleasure of viewing Michelangelo and Raphael with Fuller, for instance, came just five weeks after the "Divinity School Address." But in the private record of his journal he meanwhile recorded darker thoughts about women. Their trouble was a tragic sense of life, he wrote just after his entry on Raphael, so that earnest conversation revealed even the grandest lady as "some stricken soul with care & sorrow at her vitals." Not referring explicitly to either Fuller or the women nearest him—aunt Mary, wife Lidian, friend Elizabeth Hoar—he could still generalize so as to include all of them. A week later, declaring his inability really to "hear" one particularly tragic woman, he added, "Were she my sister, I should sail for Australasia & put the earth's diameter between us."[16]

Emerson looked for a "newborn bard of the Holy Ghost" among the women around him and at the same time raised standards resulting in their ineligibility. No doubt he was capable, as Christina Zwarg writes, of a "trial feminism" toward Fuller; but I would argue that his opening of possibility for women characteristically moves back to closure.[17] A long journal passage of October 1837 illustrates the pattern. "In conversing with a lady," he began, "it sometimes seems a bitterness & unnecessary wound to insist as I incline to, on this self-sufficiency of man." He had told his female "friend" that there could be no society in the future; and she responded, "Very true but very mournful." Women could not abandon social bonds and embrace individuality, so his paths were shut to them; "and the fine women I think of who have had genius & cultivation who have not been wives but muses have something tragic in their lot & I shun to name them." The assumptions about female "genius" here are stunning: that wives, wholly embedded in the lives of others, could never join this highest rank of mind; that single women ("muses," not poets or oracles) were marred by the sorrow of their very state, so that he wanted only to avoid further reflection upon them.

Resisting that impulse, however, Emerson went on to consider the "new woman" of his time, explicitly separating her from the perceived failure of his aunt and her *alter ego* de Staël:

> Therefore I think a woman does herself injustice who likens herself
> to any historical woman, who thinks because Corinna or De Stael

or M.[ary] M.[oody] E.[merson] do not satisfy the imagination and the serene Themis, none can, certainly not she. It needs that she feel that a new woman has a new as yet inviolate problem to solve[:] perchance the happiest nature that yet has bloomed is hers[;] let it not [be] ruined beforehand on despair grounded on their failure; but let the maiden with erect soul walk serenely on her way, accept the hint of each new pleasure she finds, try in turn all the known resources, experiments, pleasures that she may learn from what she cannot as well as what she can do, the power & the charm that— like a new dawn radiating out the Deep of Space—her new born being is. (*JMN*, 5:410)

The final clauses here offer a fully Emersonian rhetoric of possibility, endorsing the mind's active engagement with the world and envisioning its new birth in ways consonant with "The American Scholar," *Nature*, and the "Divinity School Address." But their invitation is hedged around with impossibly constricting negatives, in particular with a brutal judgment of the "historical" woman, a composite figure of Mary, Corinne, and the pre-Apollonian earth goddess of Delphi. For all, he implies, their despair was personal failure, inability to see the "new dawn" serenely enough rather than a legitimate response to circumstance, let alone a resource for wisdom. And again the passage ends by generalizing, effectively excluding all women from visionary power. "Tears are never far from a woman's eye," he observes, even the eye of "the loveliest maiden on whom every grace sits." Apparently "new" women shared their forebears' sense of tragedy, thus excluding themselves after all from serene, solitary vision. Granted, Emerson did not endorse the misfortune that he diagnosed in these words. Rarely, however, did he speak so fatalistically in his early prose.

Fuller, the leading "new woman" of Emerson's personal and cultural world, may have heard such words from him in person, but neither of them explicitly confronted gender questions in their letters. She wrote more confidingly to other male friends. W. H. Channing heard of the aspiration, as she quit teaching girls in Providence, now to educate women in ways that "any spiritual thinker" would understand (*FL*, 1:354); George Davis, onetime object of her love, received the emotional testimony of her willingness to forego women's common experience for the "destiny of the thinker, and (shall I dare to say it?) of the poetic priestess, sibylline, dwelling in the cave, or amid the Lybian sands."[18] Few women would have so risked appearing ridiculous, even in private, by directly claiming that high Romantic role. Her most direct communication, however, went to female friend Sophia Ripley in August 1839, proposing weekly conversations for "thinking women" of Boston. Fuller now remained silent about her own role and its prototypes, instead proposing a democratically inclusive forum in which women could both "systematize thought" and "state their doubts and difficulties." At stake, however, were the high questions of spiritual thinkers: "What were we born to do? How shall we do it?" (*FL*, 2:86-87).

In this group, much more than through dialogue with Emerson and other male Transcendentalists, Fuller began to develop a distinctive body of feminist thought. Such a dimension emerged immediately in the first of five seasons of conversations, extending from November 1839 to May 1840. Fuller devoted only six weeks directly to mythology, the "playful as well as deep" topic first proposed; then her interest expanded from Minerva to "beauty" as a general aesthetic principle, proceeded through Coleridge's classifications of philosophy and the arts, and focused three weeks explicitly on the intellectual differences between men and women, before offering two final discussions of inspiration and art.[19] The theme throughout this sequence was creativity as a goal of life for women as well as men, from Fuller's opening emphasis on women's inability to "reproduce" rather than merely "display" knowledge, through its closing affirmation of genius as a principle to be discovered within.

More than previously available records of the conversations, Elizabeth Peabody's full transcript shows that Fuller shared responsibility throughout for developing ideas. Each of the conversations on mythology began with her synopsis, but then the floor was open. Fuller first told of Apollo as Genius, son of Creative Power and Latona, apparently without commenting on this markedly masculine idea of human origin. Immediately someone asked the obvious woman's question, "What is *Latona*?" Fuller conceded, "[T]he Greeks did not care much about the *mothers*." Likewise, when she interpreted Apollo's pursuit of Daphne as the love of genius for variety, a participant objected that such genius could never be bound to the "domestic hearth," and Fuller admitted the inference as true ("BC," 205). Clearly none of these women wanted to admit polygamous variety into even imaginative marriages. Without pressing for radical reinterpretation of gender roles, however, they unselfconsciously allegorized the myths from female perspectives.

The heroine Psyche, topic of the fifth conversation, offered Fuller's central image of woman as pilgrim and aspirant. Neither a goddess nor a mortal of divinatory power, Psyche lost her elusive husband, Cupid, by seeking to know his face and name, but she regained him and won immortality through a series of heroic tasks. Fuller interpreted Psyche's frail humanity as "stimulated by what was forbidden," and others present soon joined her in pursuing an allegory of the fall. Responding to questions about Psyche's understandable desire to know her spouse, Fuller saw the fault as lack of self-trust, attention to the skepticism of wicked sisters who represented circumstance rather than soul. At ease with a leveling of Greek and Hebrew "fable," they found that, in both Psyche and Eve, "Analysis instead of faith makes the origin of evil." But when challenged—"Is the *desire* of knowledge *sin?*"—Fuller declared Psyche's travails a necessary development from simplicity through suffering to restoration. "[I]f happiness is to be measured by its quality we are gainers still," she concluded, "—for when at last the purification is complete, we have our happiness & are conscious of it" ("BC," 206–207).

The personal identification signaled by Fuller's "we" continued despite her greater philosophical abstraction in the conversations following. Turning eleven weeks later to the definition of "Woman," Fuller was asked whether she thought any faculty belonged only to masculine or feminine mind:

> Margaret said no—she did not—& therefore she wished to see if the others fully admitted this. Because if all admitted it, it would follow of course that we should hear no more of repressing or subduing faculties because they were not fit for women to cultivate. She desired that whatever faculty we felt to be moving within us, that we should consider a principle of our perfection & cultivate it accordingly. ("BC," 215)

The moment represents both her style of leadership, at once strongly directing and seeking consent from the group, and her central exhortation to mental enfranchisement. Following a method she had first introduced in discussing "Beauty," Fuller devoted this set of conversations to reading and commenting on papers by members of the group. All agreed, as Ellen Hooper put it, that women "had spontaneously what men have by study reflection & induction"; and they began to explore the power in that spontaneity. Might not women rather than men therefore have the greater genius? Coleridge had remarked "that every man of great poetical genius had something feminine in his face." But the sexes differed in proportion rather than kind: a woman could emulate Napoleon, a man Corinne. Even while insisting on difference only in degree, Fuller believed men to possess genius, "the fire caught from heaven," more easily than women. She was met with a chorus of objections, then by Sally Gardiner's written argument for difference as only "accidental or arbitrary." If women would develop their power of concentration, Gardiner proposed, the future might "manifest itself in forms beautiful as poetry & art, permanent as empires, all emanating from her home— . . . a beauty & a power which shall bless & heal the nations. Then the progress of the race will be harmonious & universal; the Hebrew seer said truly, 'Men shall learn war no more.'" Of this most visionary utterance in the transcribed conversation, Fuller commented that it was "the aspiration which is prophecy" ("BC," 214–216). Whether or not she learned from Gardiner, this short essay articulated a vision later central in her own writing.

Particularly in dialogue with Elizabeth Peabody, Fuller explored the relationship between such creativity and the circumstances of women's lives. Motherhood, she assumed, prevented the "isolation" needed by artists, but what of unmarried women? Peabody suggested that too often they either spent their lives mourning the lack of a husband or, following society's dictates, continuing to seek one. "This caused some lively talk all around," Peabody added to the transcription of her own remarks. A week later Peabody directed another question to Fuller: Was it not an illusion that women of genius suffered most acutely? Did not more ordinary mortals need to bear what Emerson would call the "tragedy of *limitation*"? Fuller's answer confirmed the lessons she had taught from Psyche's story. A young soul desiring "to reform society—to know everything—to beautify every thing & to have a perfect friend" would of course suffer more acutely than an individual who remained undeveloped. Consciousness was pain, but also "the pledge of immortality" ("BC," 215, 218).

In developing her own redemptive myth of the female soul in process, Fuller was responding to both de Staël and Emerson. The suffering she affirmed had a much higher value than Corinne's, which amounted to the mere obstruction of genius through an unworthy man's rejection. So, consciously or unconsciously, were she and her colleagues engaging the very issues that Emerson had named in his 1837 journal entry on women. Unmarried women might resist the circumstances rendering solitude a matter of despair. The tears in a woman's eye were warranted, and they did not prevent vision. Women might be poets, not muses, to the enrichment or even transformation of the world. Emersonian concepts of self-trust and idealism were surely in play here, but also undergoing revision. "I went into the woods and read a little book called 'Nature' through for the first time," Fuller wrote to Emerson a month before ending the first series of conversations. "I was pleased to feel how more truly I understood it now than at first. . . . The years do not pass in vain. If they have built no temple on the earth they have given a nearer vi[ew] of the City of God." This new understanding resulted from her own active production of thought that season; and it included resistance as well as agreement to the visionary millennium of *Nature*; for Fuller went on to claim a desire to be Pericles rather than Anaxagoras, one who practiced "thought living, [rather] than living thought" (*FL*, 2:128). As well as affirming her desire for agency, the very statement claims her right as a woman to choose between two male identities.

Fuller's confidence in a Periclean self was both shaken and transformed later in 1840, following news of impending marriage by her friends Samuel Ward and Anna Barker, both of whom she loved. Feeling abandoned by human friends, she experienced a new self-discovery that amounted, she felt, to revelation. "All things I have given up to the central power, myself, you also," she wrote to Emerson. Yet this passivity to spiritual power resulted as well in feeling "at home," able to be claimed by others: "I need to be recognized," she added. If Fuller was ingenuously admitting emotional need, she was also claiming her ideal of a decade earlier, to be a genius "round which asking aimless hearts might rally." Later that fall Fuller began her second series of conversations by relating the changes within her, asking for new understanding, and discovering an audience "melted into one love" (*FL*, 2:158–160, 183). She was finding a new vocational center in women.

Simultaneously, however, Fuller sought authority to consider gender questions in a male-dominated cultural world; so she invited both men and women to a new series of conversations on mythology in the spring of 1841. As eighteen-year-old transcriber Caroline Healey saw, the experiment proved a failure and a frustration to Fuller. Indeed, greater knowledge of the previous series sharpens our sense of missed opportunities in the 1841 conversations. Fuller was both more ambitious than the previous year and facing greater odds. A systematic overview of Greek mythology began the series rather than an invitation to "playful" discussion, and now the men present talked around the subject of myth itself rather than agreeing to interpret particular myths. William White asked the orthodox question whether Biblical revelation was not necessary to complete human knowledge, and Fuller hotly defended her most fundamental premise, that God had left no age or culture without revelation. Amidst Fuller's attempt to present the great goddess Ceres, Emerson asked why the present age should not create myths as great as the Greeks'; and from this digression Fuller could not return to the archetype of loss and painful searching that Ceres represented.

Much less did a real discussion of gender difference or women's potential ever develop, even when the question arose "why Genius was masculine and Wisdom feminine" (*MHF*, 33–34, 45, 41, 78). The group had its most coherent discussion of Cupid and Psyche, which they again heard as a fable of temptation and contrasted to the Biblical history. A year later and in the presence of Emerson, Fuller gave Psyche's actions a less Emersonian reading than she had with the women's group. The heroine's need to look at Cupid's face had come from within herself rather than from circumstance, Fuller asserted; Emerson, on the other hand, felt it was the soul's privilege to notice only its inner good and "not to look!" Fuller leaped back with a defense of evil as necessary in the scheme of good. Redemption rather than fall, she insisted, was the point of Psyche's story (*MHF*, 112–114, 118).

Then Elizabeth Peabody, as Healey recorded, "got into a little maze trying to introduce Margaret and R.W.E. to each other, a consummation which, however devoutly to be wished, will never happen!" (*MHF*, 118–119). This was a brash judgment of all parties concerned, but it recognized genuine differences between Emerson and Fuller. Despite a common interest in women's power of knowledge, their conclusions about women differed as widely as their conclusions about evil. Emerson was not finally seeking independent authority by women of vision. When he went home later that spring and reread Mary Moody Emerson's letters, he found genius there, brilliance of language akin to Shakespeare's and Paul's, but he did not ask why this woman had never become a preacher or poet. Instead he projected the possibility of an "interior or spiritual history of New England" that he might write, drawing his own picture of Mary's influence on her nephews (*JMN*, 7:446).

In her first series of conversations, Fuller imagined a young female soul seeking "the *Universe*," wanting "to reform society—to know everything" ("BC," 218). "Reform" belonged to her Transcendentalist vocabulary as a term of desire for interior and total regeneration, and she saw such desire as destined to run sorrowfully into the world's imperfections. But in November 1840, attending the Chardon Street Convention in Boston, Fuller and Emerson both had their most extended meeting to date with another sort of reformers, the abolitionists, who combined visions of universal regeneration with organized activism for change. This convention officially gathered to debate the legitimacy of sabbath, church, and ministry in future religious practice, but embedded in such issues was also the question of "woman's sphere." Octavius Frothingham later judged with good cause that "transcendental philosophy" had generated a language of discontent for women; but women abolitionists had taken much more direct responsibility for speaking in public, claiming rights, and forging a movement. For rather different reasons, Transcendentalists and abolitionists were both challenging religious orthodoxy and its prescriptions for women. Chardon Street might be taken as a symbol of their meeting: before the year ended abolitionist Maria Weston Chapman was asking Fuller to enlist support for the cause from her conversation group.

When first founded in October 1833, the Boston Female Anti-Slavery Society had maintained informal ties to the orthodox churches of New England, with Congregational minister's wife Charlotte Phelps its president, attention to charitable work and private lectures its whole aim. Soon, however, Phelps invited Lydia Maria Child, author of the controversial *Appeal in Favor of That Class of Americans Called Africans*, to join the group; in turn Child brought in Chapman, her sisters, and their friends from the intellectually and economically elite circles of Unitarian and Quaker Boston. Newly autonomous ventures began shortly thereafter. Child initiated a highly successful annual fundraising fair in 1834, then, supported by personal donations from the BFASS, began researching and writing her *History of the Condition of Women, in Various Ages and Nations*. As this book appeared in 1835, Chapman and her set were making headlines by facing down an angry Boston mob and defending their own freedom to meet with British abolitionist George Thompson. Unitarian reformer Harriet Martineau was also visiting Boston from England, and, when she publicly offered sympathy with the women, she found herself vilified along with them by the press. Her narration of these events in *Society in America* (1837) had all the more resonance because it was situated amidst her double critique of slavery and the "Political Non-Existence of Women" in the United States. Martineau's praise of the abolitionist women confirmed a change already underway in the BFASS: despite resistance by more conservative members, by 1837 Chapman, Child, and their colleagues had indirectly claimed a political existence, sponsoring lawsuits for the freedom of several former slave women, coordinating the first petition drives among New England states, and organizing the first national Anti-Slavery Convention of American Women in New York City. As recording secretary, Chapman published this history in annual volumes entitled *Right and Wrong in Boston*.[20]

The books of Child, Martineau, and Chapman laid a foundation for future arguments about women's sphere, but the issue exploded after BFASS members at the New York Convention forged an alliance with Angelina Grimké. Immediately they persuaded this former slaveholder, Quaker, and author of *An Appeal to Christian Women of the South*, along with her sister Sarah, to lecture under their sponsorship. The Grimkés found a bold vocation and wide audience in Massachusetts. Over six months in 1837 they conducted eighty-eight meetings in sixty-seven towns. Not the first female lecturers in American history, they still forged new roles in ambition and earnestness, as well as in the scandal of carrying their antislavery message to "promiscuous audiences" of men and women. Finally in February 1838 Angelina Grimké addressed the Legislative Committee of the Massachusetts legislature, forthrightly declaring her own elevation to public stature as a supplicant for slave women. "I stand before you," she repeated three times for rhetorical emphasis.[21]

Such public courage was contagious, soon translating to women's advocacy for themselves. As Grimké wrote to a friend, Chapman and Child in particular agreed "that it is time our fetters were broken." The counter-response was equally vigorous, drawing the lines of battle over woman's sphere for the entire antebellum era. Not only did Catharine Beecher counter Angelina's *Appeal* with her own published argument, restricting woman's influence to the home. In addition, the Congregational ministers of Massachusetts formally declared their churches closed to women who would "so far forget themselves as to itinerate in the character of public lecturers and teachers"; and the New England Anti-Slavery Society and its women's auxiliary, the BFASS, themselves split internally. William Lloyd Garrison, the radical abolitionist leader with whom Child, Chapman, and Grimké had always found alliance, now threw the whole force of his organization and journal, *The Liberator*, behind their claim to voice and authority. But a group of clergy who were all husbands of conservative BFASS members—the founding president's husband, Amos Phelps, chief among them—opposed both Garrison and the women, limiting the contribution of female abolitionists only to private and segregated roles. In an "Appeal of Clerical Abolitionists on Anti-Slavery Measures," they warned that by "overthrowing slavery" radicals would also "overthrow government, civil and domestic, the Sabbath and the church and ministry."[22] Anticlericalism, always implicit in Garrisonian attacks on proslavery ministers, now waxed stronger. Both in her prose reports and in satiric verse, Chapman turned a scathing eye on male "Lords of Creation" who would deny women the liberty offered them by Jesus and Paul. When a more conservative member of the female society quoted Chapman's own minister, William Ellery Channing, in defense of her point, Chapman retorted, "You know I never consider Dr. Channing an authority."[23]

In the early years Emerson, Fuller, and the other Transcendentalists took no active part in either the antislavery movement or its controversy over women. But there were many social and discursive connections between these elite Boston-area groups, especially through Unitarianism. Maria Chapman may have felt no awe for Channing, but her radical abolitionism was in league with his moderate and more individualized position in *Slavery* (1835), which all the Transcendentalists respected. When Garrison shook hands with Channing at one legislative hearing, Chapman whispered to her neighbor, "Righteousness and peace have kissed each other!" Among other Unitarian clergy, abolitionist Samuel May maintained the closest of ties to his sister Abby and her Transcendentalist husband Bronson Alcott; and Convers Francis, initiating member of the Transcendentalist Club, was brother to Lydia Maria Child. In the Emerson family, Waldo's aunt Mary and brother Charles had been converted by Garrison's agents to abolitionist principle by the spring of 1835, and Charles in turn offered a public defense of Harriet Martineau amidst the "hubbub" against her. Soon thereafter Martineau visited at the Emerson house, Waldo noting the folly of her critics, and when *Society in America* appeared, he even more warmly endorsed the defense of "a good cause which has been trampled on." Chapman later remembered Emerson's direct praise of Martineau: "Joy that you exist," he had declared during the Boston controversy. "Honor to your spirit, which is so true and brave."[24]

But approbation for Martineau was probably not enough to put a copy of Chapman's *Right and Wrong in Boston* in the Emersons' library. Most of all, Waldo was married to Chapman's cause in the person of his wife Lidian. She took pleasure in conversation with Martineau, talked and corresponded about the cause with Aunt Mary, and joined the Concord Female Anti-Slavery Society. When the Grimké campaign came to Concord in September 1837, just days after her husband's "American Scholar" address, Lidian hosted them for dinner and declared to a niece, "I shall not turn away my attention from the abolition cause till I have found whether there is not something for me personally to do and bear to forward it."[25] Soon Waldo was complaining in his journal about Lidian's perpetual grief for "the wretched negro in the horrors of the middle passage." She was simply acting upon the Grimkés' Biblical motto, "Remember them that are in bonds, as bound with them." But neither husband nor wife made any record of the even more personally unsettling issue brought to Concord by the Grimkés. In the very days of their visit, both sisters were publishing newspaper series claiming the prophetic power and social equality of women. Just the week before, Angelina's article in the *Liberator* had claimed "The Sphere of Woman and Man as Moral Beings the Same," especially urging women to engage in the political process by petition. Sarah datelined from Concord the twelfth of her *Letters on the Equality of the Sexes*, setting forth "The Legal Disabilities of Women" and claiming the right of property ownership.[26] These were opening shots in the public campaign for women's rights, and they must also have been audible in the Emersons' dining room.

Margaret Fuller visited Emerson the same week as the Grimké dinner, but if she heard this talk she was not at first impressed. Several weeks later

Emerson recalled a recent line of Fuller's that may have referred to the Grimkés: "Who would be a goody that could be a genius?" She had little patience with moralism unrelieved by imagination or wit.[27] Rather than defending Martineau and winning the long-term approbation of Maria Chapman, like Emerson, Fuller wrote directly to Martineau that fall criticizing *Society in America* as a monotoned "abolition book," and years later Chapman edited the *Autobiography* in which Martineau reciprocated by savaging Fuller's conversations. "While Margaret Fuller and her adult pupils sat 'gorgeously dressed,' talking about Mars and Venus, Plato and Goethe," Martineau wrote, "the liberties of the republic were running out as fast as they could go, at a breach which another sort of elect persons were devoting themselves to repair."[28] Martineau, of course, had not actually attended the conversations; she visited Boston four years too soon and was only embroidering details from the 1852 *Memoir* of Fuller. But Martineau's image of a politically indifferent, pedantic female Transcendentalist has endured.

So has this image obscured the extent of Fuller's association with the feminist abolitionists of Boston. An old friendship with Child, dating from the mid 1820s, provided at least a distant relationship to the BFASS, one which Child renewed by attending the 1839–1840 conversations. Abolitionists Caroline Sturgis, Louisa Loring, Maria White, Sarah Shaw, and Anne Greene Phillips—as well as Lidian Emerson—would at one season or another join Fuller's group as well. Chapman apparently did not attend, but lived two doors from Elizabeth Peabody's bookstore and knew Fuller socially. Whether sincerely or ironically, her sister Anne Weston described Fuller on one such occasion as "more magnificent than usual." Most of all, Fuller's falling out with Martineau was only the sad sequel to a friendship begun when the two women met in 1835 at Eliza Farrar's house in Cambridge. Fuller had expected to join the two women on Martineau's return voyage to England the following summer, but she was prevented by her father's death. Instead Martineau appealed to her friendship with Emerson—forged amidst the controversy that winter—and recommended that Fuller be introduced in Concord. Fuller did not like the antislavery principle of *Society in America*, but she revealed her distaste only when Martineau asked and still valued friendship with a woman who might prove, as she had written, "an intellectual guide."[29]

Fuller responded to the new questions about women much more warmly than to the antislavery politics generating them. She asked in 1837 about the relative merits of a "goody" and a "genius," Emerson recorded, while "talking of Women." As she had implied years before, her own deeper hope was to overcome that very opposition between womanly types, proving like de Staël "useful too, . . . on liberalizing, regenerating principles" (*JMN*, 5:407; *FL*, 1:154). Conversation with Emerson in the fall of 1837 was by no means her only opportunity to speculate anew about these possibilities for women. Memorializing Channing in "The Great Lawsuit," Fuller later recalled how his social circle had enabled opposing parties on the woman question to come together candidly: "when the progress of Harriet Martineau through this country, Angelina Grimké's appearance in public, and the visit of Mrs. Jameson, had turned his thoughts to this subject, he expressed high hopes as to what the coming era would bring to Woman" ("GL," 41). She clearly took a part in this exchange too, from Martineau's visit in 1835 through Jameson's departure late in 1837.[30]

The next summer, back in Concord, Fuller told Emerson that "women are Slaves." She had come to this abrupt formulation in relatively short months of hearing from and about antislavery women—a formulation remarkably close to what she had rejected in Martineau. Now, on the same visit as her sharing of Raphael's sybils with Emerson, she must have been full of such testimony. He noted Fuller's remark just a day after recording his own discovery that conversing with women was an entry into "remediless evils" (*JMN*, 7:48).

A larger spiritual crisis, however, would soon forge bonds between the Transcendentalists and the advocates of slaves and women. Both were "come-outers" from established churches, investing hope for religious renewal in the rejection of traditional clerical authority. In the "Divinity School Address" that summer, amidst his critique of a clerical establishment unable to preach the soul, Emerson had quoted the words of "a devout person, who prized the Sabbath": At present it seemed "wicked to go to church Sundays." The person in question was Lidian Emerson, who had made this remark amidst the previous year's controversy between ministers and women.[31] Though she never permanently left the church, Lidian was in effect agreeing with Maria Chapman's position in *Right and Wrong in Boston . . . 1837*: "As church members, we have been hindered by the ministry:—as women, we are hindered by the ministry:—as abolitionists, still comes a 'clerical abolitionist', to prevent as far as in him lies, the vigorous prosecution of our efforts." In the same years, one clerical establishment was labeling Emerson a heretic and defending the legitimacy of Scriptural "miracle" as the only ground for faith, while another clerical establishment was using Scripture to exclude women from abolitionist leadership. Controversy between pro and anticlerics consumed the antislavery movement between 1837 and 1839. By the spring of 1840 the BFASS dissolved its formal organization as a result. Chapman and Child, along with Lucretia Mott and Abby Kelley, then won places on the executive committee of the national, Garrison-controlled American Anti-Slavery Society; in response clerical conservatives again departed to form a separate organization.[32]

Why would any woman go to church Sundays? Yet where was the spiritual grounding for ethical commitment without it? The abolitionist feminists answered in a kindred spirit to the Transcendentalists: The spirit lay within and deserved expression. When Chapman submitted her remonstrances against the clergy in a BFASS report, the officers objected that no antislavery society should "discuss the affairs of the Free Church." They referred especially to one particular come-outer Congregational group in Boston, but there were other models for a woman-empowering church as well. In *Letters on the Equality of the Sexes*, Quaker Sarah Grimké urged women "to think for themselves, to take the volume of inspiration in their hand, to enter into their closet, and ask wisdom." The Bible, she promised, would offer ample evidence, in "prophetesses" like Miriam, Deborah, and Huldah, that "women are now called to that office as well as men." Priestcraft had ended, but prophecy just begun.[33] Tapping a quite different Romantic philosophy of the spirit and a wider vein of revelation than the Bible, Fuller extended Grimké's point by seeking an intuitive ground for wisdom and prophecy.

Though Fuller presented her conversations in the fall of 1839 as an experiment in education, she always focused on questions of religious knowledge and meaning. Her mode of self-presentation as a "poetic priestess" was remarkably nonconfrontational; declining to follow Grimké (or Emerson) onto the lecture podium, she gathered women in parlors or in Elizabeth Peabody's bookstore. Such meetings constituted no obvious violation of woman's sphere, yet her class ranged freely through the marketplace of ideas. Similarly, she made no anticlerical or antiscriptural remarks, just ignored orthodox religious authority altogether and expounded an alternative mythological and moral understanding. Referring to none of Boston's current controversies, she spoke to the crisis of all come-outers. When Sturgis and Child presented their respective ideas about the relation between goodness and beauty ("BC," 210–211), these BFASS members were reaching for a positive vision beyond Chapman's satiric naysaying. In the same months Child was attempting unsuccessfully to mediate among abolitionists through columns in the *Liberator*: "Is there no way of avoiding a recurrence of such disagreeable, mortifying, and discreditable collisions?" She sought a more personal wholeness from the Transcendentalists, whether "merrymaking" to Emerson's lectures or joining Fuller's group.[34]

Child may also have relayed information between the leader of conversations and the abolitionist naysayer, for although Chapman never expressed interest in Fuller's conversations, Fuller wanted to investigate Chapman's thinking. When Chapman requested support in December 1840, Fuller declined, but she also admitted that she had attended the Chardon Street Convention explicitly to hear Chapman's ideas about "religious institutions and the social position of women" (*FL*, 2:197–198). Fuller's letter encapsulates her attitude toward feminist abolitionism. "The Abolition cause commands my respect," she wrote, "as do all efforts to relieve and raise suffering human nature." Yet she objected to the movement's "partizan spirit," its attention to enfranchising "the African only," and most of all its particular "measures" (*FL*, 2:197). One need only look at Chapman's records to realize what Fuller meant by "measures," the week-to-week business of hosting lectures, undertaking lawsuits, and organizing petition drives. Most of all, Chapman had written to her hoping to find support for the annual fair, which now, in the first Christmas season without the BFASS to back it, needed a new constituency. Cerebral Fuller felt no interest, but mildly commented, "my own path leads a different course."[35] In fact she rather than Chapman was entertaining the wider, philosophically and mythically grounded, transformation of relations between the sexes. Fuller was drawn to Chapman for the single, crucial reason that the abolitionists were defending women's public leadership. Though the conversations so far had not focused explicitly on this issue, they had clearly drawn Fuller to Chardon Street.

The Chardon Street Convention, whose first three-day meeting lasted from November 17 to 19, 1840, has never been known by historians as a forum for debating the woman question; but its constituents brought such debate inevitably into the consideration of sabbath, church, ministry, and scripture. Organized by Garrisonians, with Chapman as its secretary, the Convention easily embraced the radical wing of the women's antislavery movement. Tallying the obviously incomplete list of participants in the *Liberator* shows about one in every six to be a woman, but those who signed the official call include twice that proportion, eight of twenty-four. These were largely feminist abolitionists; their female opponents, of course, would have abstained from participating on principle. If any of Fuller's conversationalists joined her there, the records do not include their names; even hers was unlisted, suggesting more of an onlooker's than a participant's role. Emerson's article on this heterogeneous assembly for the *Dial* mentions the female presence several times: Chapman among its most eminent members, "madwomen" as well as "madmen" among the eccentrics, and "no want of female speakers" contributing to the occasion's extemporaneous oratory. He alluded to the controversial acceptance of women's public voice with mixed grace and irony, naming Mrs. Little and

Lucy Sessions for their "pleasing and memorable part in the debate," but also "that flea of Conventions, Mrs. Abigail Folsom, . . . but too ready with her interminable scroll."[36]

Since no proceedings of the Convention were ever published, we cannot know how or if the women and their male supporters approached the question of women's position in religious institutions. One glimpse of characteristic rhetoric, probably a sequel to the Convention, was an essay the following spring in the *Liberator* by Chapman's sister Caroline Weston in defense of "Female Praying, or Speaking, in Promiscuous Assemblies." Weston argued that Paul's apostolic rule of silence for women in church was designed only for a particular moment and reflected his still incomplete apprehension of Christian liberty; against that often-quoted injunction she weighed the actual presence of prophetesses in the New Testament and Paul's definitive declaration that in Christ there was "neither male nor female." Perhaps such arguments about Biblical texts, clearly aimed at the orthodox, made Fuller comment on the Convention to Chapman, "I heard nothing that pleased me." Like the other Transcendentalists present—Emerson, Parker, Ripley, Thoreau, Very—she would not have been bound to this single revelation of divine principle in any case. But the Transcendentalists would all have agreed with Weston's conclusion that inspiration continued from the Bible into the present: "Does not the Spirit still influence the minds of men, and guide, warn, admonish, and instruct them?"[37]

In fact, Fuller admitted to Chapman, she had heard not only an unsatisfying case for women's prophecy, but "no clear statement from any one." The maneuverings of mutually antagonistic men perhaps silenced many women, indeed almost brought consideration of the sabbath to a halt. Most of the Convention's first day was given over to a protest by religious perfectionists against following formal rules of order, then to an orthodox resolution declaring the Bible "the only rule of faith and practice." This latter move, as the orthodox press openly declared, aimed to exclude from the meeting the very people who had called it, the "Come-outists, and Transcendentalists, [who] . . . wished to have the privilege of ranging the universe for evidence, and desired that each one might be his own Standard of religious faith for himself." The orthodox attempt to dominate continued. On the second day, after Garrison, Alcott, and Parker among others offered their criticisms of the sabbath, chief "clerical abolitionist" Amos Phelps—Chapman's old adversary in BFASS politics—seized the floor for four hours in its defense. One news report declared him victorious and mentioned no women participants at all. Emerson told a different story, emphasizing the effectiveness of Little, Sessions, Alcott, and an unlettered man from South

Marshfield, while alluding to the conservative filibuster only as "a great deal of wearisome speaking." At least, he concluded, "men and women" had been able to discover the value of a "lofty reliance on principles, and the prophetic dignity and transfiguration which accompanies, even amidst opposition and ridicule, a man whose mind is made up to obey the great inward Commander."[38] Facing a common opposition, abolitionists and Transcendentalists of both sexes had publicly come together in this affirmation for the first time.

Ironically, Emerson found more to praise than Fuller in the women at Chardon Street. He seems even to have amended his dark view of 1837 that the potential "new woman" was disabled by sorrow, for here were women discovering principle and voicing it. But Fuller, following out the year's "mighty changes," was reaching toward a mighty empowerment of women. The Chardon Street Convention showed genuine cleavages in New England religious culture, but its participants responded to them in power struggle rather than productive dialogue.

The real result of the Convention for Fuller, Emerson, and their friends lay outside the event itself in their own burgeoning reform ideas, now at least tentatively allied with a broader range of New England radicalism. This crossing of ideas mattered as much for future writing about women as about slavery, church, and state. The Transcendentalists first joined the Garrisonians on Chardon Street in the midst of their agony of decision over George Ripley's proposal to found a community at Brook Farm. Attending the Convention in mid November himself, Ripley no doubt pursued the talk begun a month before when he and his wife Sophia had met with Emerson, Fuller, and Alcott in Concord to invite their participation. Two days before the Convention, Emerson shared jokes about sabbath-keeping with his own vacationing wife and warned her to come home soon: "[T]he 'Community' question is in full agitation . . . & if you wish to have a voice in it & not to find your house sold over your head or perhaps a troop of new tenants brought suddenly into it you must come & counsel your dangerous husband" (*JMN*, 7:407–408; *EL*, 2:360). The feminist abolitionists promised to free the house—woman's sphere—by taking her out of it into public voice and influence, but the community question promised transformation of houses and marriages from within.

Even in 1840 Fuller referred to the Brook Farm debate as "Phalanx talk," and Emerson more clearly indicated knowledge of Charles Fourier, the French philosopher and visionary who had conceived of a community of 1,620 people as the social unit for a utopian world. Life's dilemmas, he wrote to Fuller shortly after meeting with Ripley in Concord, could only be solved by a "strong passion or a fit work. . . . The first will never come to such as I am; the second I do not absolutely despair of, especially in these days of Phalanx" (*FL*, 2:163; *EL*, 2:349). Fourier's theory of "passional attraction" determined his structuring of both work and love. Labor could be organized by offering individuals activities suiting their passions, and all could equally act upon passions in choosing and ending sexual partnership.[39] As Fuller later declared in *Woman in the Nineteenth Century*, and by implication knew in 1840, Fourier placed "Woman on an entire equality with Man," giving to each "that independence which must result from intellectual and practical development."[40]

Fuller, Ripley, and Emerson, however, all suppressed from their public statements the extent of sexual independence, especially for women, in Fourier's theory. Even in their later days of explicitly adopting the Fourierist model, Brook Farmers avoided all implication of condoning free love. Only in retrospect did Emerson portray Fourierism as a source of sexual havoc. The reformers, he recalled in "Historic Notes of Life and Letters in New England," had been "gentle souls . . . casting sheep's-eyes on Fourier and his houris," while Fourier himself had taught the principle "Indulge," securing "the greatest amount of kissing that the infirmity of human constitution admitted." Even then Emerson emphasized his disagreement with Fourier's falsely sensual notion of women and separated French theory from New England experiment. At Brook Farm the confusion of gender roles had been only benignly comic. Women sawed their own wood and men hung out the wash, so that when the men danced in the evening, "clothespins dropped plentifully from their pockets."[41]

It was not so certain that only comedy would ensue in 1840. As Emerson debated the prospects for Brook Farm and planned to convene with abolitionist women, as his wife remained on her independent vacation, the potentially most dangerous siege of their household came from Margaret Fuller. This was the season of Emerson's and Fuller's much-discussed crisis in friendship.[42] She had expressed a "need to be recognized" after her experience of spiritual illumination and now apparently was seeking further freedom in her friendship with this married man. Her now-lost letter to Emerson that October was probably not attempting seduction; besides, his letters to her had invited daring in their own wit and passion, and he rather than she may have confused this passion with sexuality. "You would have me love you," he wrote in his journal to an unnamed other. "What shall I love? Your body? The supposition disgusts you" (*JMN*, 7:400). On the day of the Brook Farm discussion, Emerson and Fuller had attempted, as he later wrote, to bring "things to speech" even "in a cold room at abrupt & stolen moments" (*EL*, 2:349); her letter came soon after. "I think I could wish it unwritten," Emerson responded. Whatever the letter's content,

Emerson was now calling a halt to conversation about their relationship: "Do not expect it of me again for a very long time" (*EL*, 2:352-353). Urging Lidian home in mid November as he prepared to attend the Chardon Street Convention, he seems to have wanted the pace of social experimentation slowed considerably.

About a month after the Chardon Street Convention, Emerson recorded a remarkable dream that also amounted to a parable of reform:

> A droll dream last night, whereat I ghastly laughed. A congregation assembled, like some of our late Conventions, to debate the Institution of Marriage; & grave & alarming objections stated on all hands to the usage; when one speaker at last rose & began to reply to the arguments, but suddenly extended his hand & turned on the audience the spout of an engine which was copiously supplied from within the wall with water & whisking it vigorously about, up, down, right, & left, he drove all the company in crowds hither & thither & out of the house. Whilst I stood watching astonished & amused at the malice & vigor of the orator, I saw the spout lengthened by a supply of hose behind, & the man suddenly brought it round a corner & drenched me as I gazed. I woke up relieved to find myself quite dry, and well convinced that the Institution of Marriage was safe for tonight. (*JMN*, 7:544)

Emerson's wonderfully comic dream overlays the recent Chardon Street Convention with the Fourierist proposal and the challenge from Fuller. At first only an observer of the reformers' denunciations of marriage, he is "astonished & amused" at the performance of the conservative orator, then suddenly implicated, sighted, and drenched by his hose. The dream shows intriguing parallels to actual events at Chardon Street, where the speech of radical men and women was followed by a four-hour rebuttal by Reverend Phelps. Perhaps more than he had expected, Emerson came under attack along with them. In his dream the marriage question has taken over from the sabbath question as the day's agenda. Historically these questions had arisen together, with Phelps and his colleagues warning against an attack on "government, civil and domestic," as well as "the Sabbath and the church and ministry." But it is Fourier and his houris, as well as Margaret Fuller, who so sexualize the dream scene. Implicitly, his male orator is silencing and scattering provocative women with his spout of malicious, ejaculatory words—and Emerson, though soaked along with them, also wakes up glad to be dry in the safety of marriage. His loyalties are divided in this dream, but in the end he does not wish to withstand the opposition of his ostensible foe, the male conservative.

. . .

"We are all a little wild here with numberless projects of social reform," Emerson wrote to Thomas Carlyle that fall.[43] In a sense the wildness ended before the year was over for him and Fuller. He resisted her effort to discover deeper or freer friendship, she refused to use the conversations to proselytize for Chapman's cause, and both declined Brook Farm. But for each, refusal led to definition of a positive reformer's role. In lectures beginning immediately and extending through 1844, Emerson articulated possibilities for individual amendment of life significantly different from either the reformers or the conservative in his dream. Fuller wrote to Chapman, "[Woman] needs new helps I think, but not such as you propose"; and though Anne Weston answered Fuller's letter with little encouragement, claiming that the abolitionists had only a "collateral & not direct" interest in women's rights, Fuller began proposing her own "helps."[44] Out of the next three seasons of conversations, public and private, would come her 1843 *Dial* essay "The Great Lawsuit," the original version of *Woman in the Nineteenth Century*. Both Emerson's and Fuller's ethical engagements grew from and contributed to the broader culture of reform in Boston, but with very different results for the question of women's status: Emerson contained and suppressed gender questions as he assumed a reformer's role, whereas Fuller made them a new center of mythic and political inquiry.

Emerson projected a new idea even while explaining to Ripley that December why he could not join Brook Farm. Instead of creating a community, he would recreate the private home: "I am already in the act of trying some domestic & social experiments which my present position favors. . . . I think that all I shall solidly do, I must do alone" (*EL*, 2:370). The masculine individualism of this domestic reform jars in a way that his more famed stances of solitude do not. Where in it is Lidian, the domestic partner whose opinion on Brook Farm he had so recently been seeking? In fact she expressed reluctance but not a veto in the "experiments" which followed at the Emerson house; it was Abby Alcott who flatly said no to the prospect of sharing the Emerson house, and the servants who refused to sit with the family for dinner. But most important is Emerson's rhetorical continuity from his letter to the lecture "Man the Reformer," presented in January 1841 and printed in the *Dial*. Declaring a young man's independence false because supported by the labor of slaves and workers, he recommended that each man take up the world's manual labor, at least in his own garden.[45] Recent contact with both antislavery and communitarian reform is obvious in this idealizing of male work at home, but nowhere does it consider either how a woman's domestic labor might be redeemed or how it contributes to the young gardener's welfare. Neither Brook Farmers nor abolitionists so wholly ignored women's work.

Likewise, Emerson's reform essays from 1842 to 1844 mediated between Transcendentalism and social agency by proposing individual conscience as the foundation for change, but he largely suppressed women of conscience and the critical questions they had raised. One exception is "Chardon Street and Bible Conventions," which he wrote for the first issue of the *Dial* under his own editorship in 1842; but this was a light, semi-satiric piece, and even here he mentioned particular women rather than women's issues. In a companion essay, he described Fourierism without reference to its theory of sexual equality. Two years later in "New England Reformers," which Linck C. Johnson calls his "most sustained effort to define his proper relation to reform and the reformers," women had disappeared even more substantially. Their invisibility is especially notable since Emerson made this presentation in March 1844 as part of the Amory Hall lecture series, surrounded by both the issues and the company that he had previously met on Chardon Street. Garrison began the series with the same three-part critique of sabbath, church, and priesthood—and ended with "The Condition and the Rights of Women"; meanwhile Ernestine Rose, a feminist and socialist soon to be affiliated with Elizabeth Cady Stanton, addressed "Social Reform."[46] But Emerson, recalling New England's recent turn from formal religion and its movements of abolitionists and socialists, mentioned no women as participants or subjects of debate, only affirmed the self-reforming conscience of "one man" (*CW*, 2:149, 150, 156). If that one man could be a woman, the rhetoric of "New England Reformers" did not so imply.

At least for a moment Emerson did extend the invitation to women that summer when the Concord Female Anti-Slavery Society hosted his "Address on Emancipation in the British West Indies." His first unequivocal statement of support for the antislavery movement proceeded through a history of British campaigning to an indictment of racial injustice in present American society without naming women among the heroic activists. But in finally offering singular, miraculous intellect as the greatest source of change, greater than "money-subscription and vituperation," he addressed all those in his audience who carried out those characteristic antislavery activities: "I say to you, you must save yourself, black or white, man or woman; other help is none" (*W*, 11:145).

Given that bold, unusually hortatory moment, it is all the more striking that the same summer Emerson gathered his thoughts on reform into *Essays: Second Series* in a pattern thoroughly divided about the nature and duty of women. Printing "New England Reformers" as an appendix, he also included a brief disquisition on the woman question in his essay "Manners." Rather than urging ethical awareness on women in the direct manner of his recent antislavery speech, Emerson conceded new status while defining manners as an expression of their traditional sphere. Whereas the open air belongs to Man, he explained, the house is primarily Woman's:

> Our American institutions have been friendly to [Woman], and at this moment I esteem it a chief felicity of this country, that it excels in women. A certain awkward consciousness of inferiority in the men may give rise to the new chivalry in behalf of Woman's Rights. Certainly let her be as much better placed in the laws and in social forms as the most zealous reformer can ask, but I confide so entirely in her inspiring and musical nature, that I believe only herself can show us how she can be served.[47]

This sequence equivocates in several respects, not only granting rights in the name of chivalry and its elevated, truly unequal valuation of women, but also barring them figuratively from the out-of-doors even amidst apparent emancipation. Further, confidence in women's "inspiring and musical nature" allowed Emerson to stand at a distance from the justice demanded by reformers, implying that women themselves would not ask for it. He was framing the question of rights with a statement of women's mental difference, attributing divinatory power to the female mind in such a way as to undercut rather than enhance a rights argument.

For now Emerson expanded on women's "inspiring and musical nature" in a way that drew upon both his conversation about female archetypes with Fuller and his even longer meditation on Mary Moody Emerson: Actual women, he asserted, verify the ancient pictures of Minerva and "make good in our imagination the place of muses and of Delphic Sibyls." Genuine power resided in such a conception of women, as it always had for Emerson, but in an equally familiar pattern he derived no poetic or prophetic authority from it for the woman herself. Like Persian Lilla, her nature tended to sympathy with "intellectual persons" (i.e., men) rather than intellect of her own: "Are there not women who fill our vase with wine and roses to the brim . . . ; who unloose our tongues and we speak; who anoint our eyes and we see?" (*CW*, 3:88–89) Despite the independent intellects of both of the women who had most contributed to his own speech and vision, Emerson could not derive from Romantic myth or reform ideology a primary rather than secondary role for women. Finally, his "we" defined an all-male rather than inclusive readership.

This pattern of political generosity undercut by Romantic androcentrism explains how, eleven years later, Emerson could both be willing to address

the Boston Woman's Rights Convention and, when he did so, define for
them a "relative" life of embellishing "trifles" in society and the family. Now
committed to antislavery politics in a way that his 1844 oration had only
hinted, Emerson found room in his lecture "Woman" to celebrate the
movement's role as a university and "metaphysician" to women, as well as
to defend the still quite radical idea of women's suffrage (W, 11:408, 416,
420–422). But beginning with belief in women's "oracular nature," recalling the Greek, Hebrew, and Saxon faith in the prophetess, he soon relegated them to a life of affection and manners. No external change affected
women's "organic office in the world," and that office was mediatory (W,
11:405, 415, 407).[48]

   Lydia Maria Child already saw Emerson's internal contradiction in 1843,
when she devoted one of her *Letters from New York* to clarifying her own
position on women's rights. She found in him an example of how even the
most refined of men could barely acknowledge "individual responsibility"
as a need for women. Once she had heard Emerson urge the women of his
lecture audience explicitly to "be" rather than "seem," telling them that labored forms and etiquette charmed much less than living as "God made
them." Child appreciated the advice but flushed angrily at the motive.
"Men were exhorted to be, rather than to seem, that they might fulfil the
sacred mission for which their souls were embodied . . . but women were
urged to simplicity and truthfulness, that they might become more pleasing."[49] Ironically, by the mid 1840s and beyond, even as Emerson acknowledged the women's rights movement, he was exhorting women toward
rather than away from the "seeming" of genteel manners—even more distant, in effect, from his characteristic self-reform by "one man."

   Fuller expressed similar reservations about Emerson. In May of the
same year, even as she wrote to him of progress on "The Great Lawsuit" for
July's *Dial*, she also bristled at his expression of regret that Samuel and
Anna Ward's new child had not been a son. "Why is not the advent of a
daughter as 'sacred' a fact as that of a son[?] I do believe, O Waldo, most
unteachable of men, that you are at heart a sinner on this point. I entreat
you to seek light in prayer upon it" (*FL*, 3:124). The joke made an ideological as well as personal point. In "The Great Lawsuit," she did not name her
editor as a sinner against women. But her essay laid down the indictment
that even men of culture spoke disparagingly of women, "in no light sally
of the hour, but in works intended to give a permanent statement of the
best experience," further, that "not one man in the million, shall I say, no,
not in the hundred million, [could] rise above the view that woman was
made *for man*" ("GL," 13). Emerson had been an intellectual source for
her claim to primary being, but not its application to women.

The development of Fuller's feminist thinking must have been rapid between her conversations of spring 1841 and the writing of "Great Lawsuit" in spring 1843, but it is not well documented. The sequence of ongoing conversations charts her direction: fine arts and mythology in 1840–1841, ethics in 1841–1842, religion, education, and the position of women in 1842–1843. She began her essay before the last series had ended, drawing upon a fund of knowledge and authority from all. Considerable new reading went into it, not only reading of thinkers from the past but, as she wrote to Frederic Hedge, "contemporary spirits [who] call to us in crowds" (*FL*, 3:108). The best evidence of such reading is the "Great Lawsuit" itself, whose argument employs or alludes to Child's *History of the Condition of Women*, the current literature of women's protest, the "little treatises" delimiting woman's sphere, and the press, both mainstream and reformist.[50] Her 1843 essay provided what she had asked for from both Emerson and Chapman, a meditation on the slavery of women and an account of their religious status. Though she developed both the contemporary implications and the cultural depth of her work when, after moving to New York, she revised it as *Woman in the Nineteenth Century*, almost three-quarters of the final book and the core of its argument originated in 1843. I emphasize the achievement of the *Dial* essay rather than the revision here so as to make a case for Fuller's feminism as the direct expression of Boston's reformist culture, not the rejection of Boston which some critics have seen in it.[51]

"The Great Lawsuit" is free religious discourse, a sermon for come-outers seeking spirituality and ethical grounding in themselves and in all scriptures of the past and present. The female archetypes of Greece and Rome that Fuller explored in her conversations now recur in transformed patterns of meaning, often alongside Biblical archetypes. Instead of Psyche's redemptive search for Cupid, Fuller imagines Eurydice calling for Orpheus, thereby following the Christian directive "Seek and ye will find" and creating a new Eden ("GL," 7, 4, 3). Her ideals of equality are the gender-balanced Olympus of Greek mythology, the angelic state portrayed by Swedenborg, and "the heaven where there is no marrying nor giving in marriage" ("GL," 24). In the searching and pilgrimage necessary to reach these ideals, female as well as male prophets point the direction. Fuller never names herself as a sibyl, but alludes to Cassandra and the priestesses who "told the oracle of the highest god," offers Michelangelo's Persican Sibyl as the image of a single woman who is no "old maid," and situates the contemporary Seeress of Prevorst alongside "ancestresses at Delphos." Again Biblical images are interwoven. Even the "severe nation" of Hebrews "greeted, with solemn rapture, all great and holy women as heroines, prophetesses, nay judges in Israel; and, if they made Eve listen to the serpent, gave Mary to the Holy Spirit" ("GL," 21, 37, 38, 18). Without pausing to argue against the Bible's "severe" aspects, she draws from it a redemptive female typology.

The oracular nature of women provides one pole, now renamed "Muse," in Fuller's androgynous theory of mind. As in the conversations, she works within the cultural tradition distinguishing women's feeling from men's rationality, now extending the Romantics' complication of this polarity in such a way as to empower women. Just as Shelley, "like all men of genius, shared the feminine development," so the Muse woman can complete herself by partaking of masculinity, figured for her as the goddess Minerva: "Male and female . . . are perpetually passing into one another. . . . There is no wholly masculine man, no purely feminine woman." Though Fuller held such a conviction from her first season of conversations, she has refined a mythic vocabulary for conceptualizing it. Then "genius" was masculine and a woman's goal to bring the "Apollo within." Now Fuller sees male and female forms of genius, each incomplete within the psyche without growth toward the other. As in Emerson's essay a year later, oracular femininity alone is dependent, but Fuller makes this point by way of warning, calling women "rather to the Minerva side" out of "love for many incarcerated souls, that might be freed could the idea of religious self-dependence be established in them" ("GL," 42–44). The sympathetic quality that Emerson would celebrate as wine and roses is precisely what must be liberated.

Even more than developing her classical mythos and its consonance with Biblical redemption, however, Fuller has now developed a legal and political component of argument wholly lacking in the early conversations. While charting a quest, her essay also presents a "Great Lawsuit." This title, which she later omitted from *Woman in the Nineteenth Century* but devoted her preface to defending, structures the entire original version. The opening paragraphs propose that an "inheritance" has been lost to humanity and must now be claimed in ever higher courts, and the closing asserts that woman must "assume her inheritance," "vindicate [a] birthright for all women." Originally Orpheus was a "lawgiver by theocratic commission," but now Eurydice calls for him, pleading their common cause as Fuller the author also pleads ("GL," 1, 47, 6–7). Fuller's interpreters ever since Thomas Wentworth Higginson have insisted that the title does not mean what it appears to, a suit by women against men.[52] Indeed Fuller restates her more complex meaning in the subtitle, "Man *versus* Men, Woman *versus* Women": The lost inheritance is ideal human nature, which neither sex has sufficiently claimed. But Fuller's metaphor of a lawsuit has multiple resonances, and one surely is the grievance of women against male prerogatives. Her opening pages intertwine metaphors from myth and law, introduce Orpheus and Eurydice, then at last turn to "the principle of liberty" and its resulting "protest . . . in behalf of women." "The Great Lawsuit" is also a protest, measuring American injustice toward women, as well as toward the red and black races, against the "golden certainty" of an ideal American law that guarantees freedom and equality. "It is not surprising," she soon claims, "that it should be the Anti-Slavery party that pleads for woman, when we consider merely that she does not hold property on equal terms with men; so that . . . the wife . . . inherits only a part of [her husband's] fortune, as if she were a child" ("GL," 8, 11). Fuller's suit to restore the lost inheritance has universal mythic resonance, but also alludes to women's actual pursuit of property rights in American courts.

As this sentence indicates, Fuller was forging a rhetorical if not organizational alliance with feminist abolitionism in "The Great Lawsuit."[53] Since declining Chapman's request for assistance in 1840 she had gained extensive familiarity with the cause at least by reading. Her political indictment of the American republic suggests a second look at Harriet Martineau, her analogy of woman to slave an acquaintance with the Grimkés' writing; likewise, knowledge of property questions may have derived from Sarah Grimké, of legal actions from Chapman's reports on the BFASS. Perhaps most of all she was simply reading the antislavery press, which she now refers to as a banner of freedom amidst the puffed-up patriotism of other newspapers, consistent in championing both African slaves and women. She echoes the abolitionist analogy between slavery and women's disinheritance throughout the essay, putting words of complacent supremacy into the mouth of a "trader" and husband, then complaining of men's universal "tone of feeling towards women as towards slaves" ("GL," 9–12). Two Quaker abolitionist women, Angelina Grimké and Abby Kelley, provide the key examples of present-day religious prophecy: both women, in Fuller's estimation, appeared in public out of conscience and sacred commitment ("GL," 40).

Fuller declines full identification with these partisans, preferring instead a more distant view of the battle—from a "high house-top" if no hill or cathedral spire is available ("GL," 11). Yet she persistently raises questions in common with the feminist abolitionists. Given the disparagement of women by men, she argues, the wishes of women must be "publicly represented" by women themselves ("GL," 12). She refers to both political and cultural representation, but says much more about the latter, endorsing the public appearance of actresses and Quaker preachers as well as the particularly luminous Grimké and Kelley ("GL," 12–13, 40). She herself chose a semi-private forum for speaking in 1839 but now strongly links her work as a writer with the appearance of women on stage. Conservatives would have women communicate only by writing at home, but she finds the pen, "that help to free agency," just as public and confrontational as the lecture rostrum or the pulpit. Female authorship can influence the times, "[b]ut how to get this platform, or how to make it of reasonably easy access is the difficulty" ("GL," 12, 18–19). She seems to be rearing her own platform on that metaphoric housetop—at once domestic, farsighted, and in the open air. Indeed, like the feminist abolitionist, Fuller breaks down the specious boundary between private home and public forum. To the trader who imagines his aimiable wife entirely content in her "own sphere," she points out that no woman really spends time in her house, but rushes out to balls and theaters, meetings for revival and for missions, seeking as much as her husband to hear the news in the street. The difference between governing a state and governing a ladies' fair is one of power, not public presence ("GL," 13). Directly from such "signs of the times" Fuller declares principles of political as well as ethical weight: "We would have every arbitrary barrier thrown down. We would have every path laid open to woman as freely as to man" ("GL," 14).

Similarly, Fuller supports her case for the independent spiritual authority of women with social if not explicitly political analysis. Having represented wisdom as Minerva, celibate and armed, she now defends single life as a fact of contemporary America, a condition potentially not of despair (as she and Peabody once agreed) but of independence and creativity. Miranda, the fictional alter ego with whom she discusses education and vocation, particularly represents this "self-reliance," an Emersonian term now converted to mean independence from male support ("GL," 16). Fuller offers no endorsement of Fourieristic free love but implicitly maintains Fourier's contention that the liberation of humanity will be measured according to the liberation of its women. Celibacy rather than passional freedom appears the means to a future, more ideal union with men, for "[u]nion is only possible to those who are units" ("GL," 44) The mythic image of this separatism is an Indian maiden "betrothed to the sun," but at last Mary, virgin mother of the Biblical tradition, symbolizes a messianic future when the inheritance will be regained and union restored ("GL," 37, 47).

If even Fuller's earliest conversations spoke to a crisis of spirit for those who were abandoning clerical authority in Boston, now she has assumed authority herself to prophesy a millennial future arising out of sexual equality. In the tradition of American jeremiad, her sentences move swiftly from indictment to vision and from politics to spirit. Were "every barrier thrown down," she writes, "we believe that the Divine would ascend into nature to a height unknown in the history of past ages." Caution and internal conflict, as well as audacity, can sometimes be felt in these proclamations. She enacts the part of a female law-giver by stating, "There is one law for all souls," but then reverts to masculine language in describing both divinity and prophecy: A "son of God," not a daughter of Minerva, will be the law's true interpreter ("GL," 14). Nonetheless, she envisions female selfhood as the key to millennial peace and does so in sentences that claim alliance with the abolitionists' cause:

> For woman, if by a sympathy as to outward condition, she is led to aid the enfranchisement of the slave, must no less so, by inward tendency, to favor measures which promise to bring the world more thoroughly and deeply into harmony with her nature. When the lamb takes place of the lion as the emblem of nations, both women and men will be as children of one spirit, perpetual learners of the word and doers thereof, not hearers only. ("GL," 42)

Fuller's logic moves from outward to inward, slavery to women. She is still not taking up the abolitionists' cause, but grounding a new argument in theirs. Most of all, she shares with them both a millennial vision and an activist's standard for measuring its fulfillment. If "inward tendency" is the key to a better society, its reunited women and men will be, in Biblical terms, "*doers* of the word." Painful discrepancy between ideals and actions will have disappeared.

Fuller's strategy in 1843 was not to proclaim this transformation complete but to "sue" for it. As much as "The Great Lawsuit" shared Emerson's belief in social change as hinging upon inward and individual principle, it also spoke of external, redressable inequities and embraced collective action. Fuller had learned from the abolitionists and wanted to plead and agitate as well as envision. Ellen DuBois suggests that the most important connection between the abolitionist and women's rights movements was not merely the analogy of women to slaves, but a political framework that opened critique of large institutions and provided a theory of social change including both inward and outward dimensions.[54] "The Great Lawsuit," while still proceeding from Transcendentalist principles, learned and disseminated these lessons. Fuller's education as a reformer surely continued after 1843. Her revision eighteen months later added both a protest against the Mexican War and an inquiry into the marketplace of marriage and prostitution, and she directly exhorted readers to act on both issues. Though now leaving Boston, she still wrote as a Boston reformer. "It is a *bold* book," Child commented to fellow abolitionist and Fullerite Louisa Loring.[55]

Fuller and Emerson both embraced reform in the course of the 1840s, but in quite different styles of partisanship and different response to the "woman questions" around them. Of course the simple fact that one was a woman and the other a man goes some distance toward explaining their differing stances on women's rights, but equally important is the way that each read the nature of women within a surrounding culture. Fuller did not simply filter Romantic philosophy through female experience and inevitably become a feminist, but sought out past and present authorities to assist her in creating a mythology and politics. Emerson was a radical, not conservative, male cleric, but his particular reading of the Romantic feminine did not well serve radical argument. In a sense he never got over being the favored "son of de Staël." He could personally hail Fuller's "Great Lawsuit" as "a piece of life" and "an important fact in the history of Woman." Over the long run, however, his male feminism remained at best permissive toward women's rights, much less directly engaged than that of his associationist friend W. H. Channing, let alone his younger colleague Thomas Wentworth Higginson, who had come of age under the double influence of the Transcendentalist and antislavery movements.[56]

Subsequent women's rights activists recognized both Emerson's and Fuller's influence. Frothingham substantially overstated the role that Transcendentalists played as the defining source of the American women's movement, but he drew an important line of thought in its complex history. Even as feminists resisted Biblical and ministerial prescriptions, they sought to enfranchise souls, finding in their movement a liberal religious awakening as well as a political protest. Despite his concessions to conservatism, Emerson stood among significant prophets of this free religion and individual conscience; and Fuller, with her "*bold* book," was a founder. Emerson served as a source in part for what he said about women, but much more for what he provoked them to say for themselves. Herself responding to Emerson, Fuller also generated in her own terms an ideology and transformative vision for later American feminists. Elizabeth Cady Stanton was no Transcendentalist, but in differing proportions she acknowledged the value of both thinkers. Her decision to call the 1848 convention at Seneca Falls, she later claimed, was a direct product of Emerson's "healthy . . . discontent." But in her history of women and men in the wider movement Emerson held only a peripheral role, while Fuller was listed on the dedicatory page, described as an intellectual and social critic, and declared "the precursor of the Woman's Rights movement of the last thirty-three years."[57]

Such an estimate is confirmed from much closer perspective, moreover, by Caroline Healey Dall, transcriber of Fuller's 1841 conversations and quintessential daughter of reform Boston. Her private and public writing over the decades following offers one of the vital passages from the forma-

tive period of Transcendentalist thinking about women to the longer and
wider history of which it is part. As Helen R. Deese writes elsewhere in this
volume, Dall not only came of age learning from Peabody and Parker,
Emerson and Fuller, but turned in old age to memorializing their accomplishment. In the intervening years, before and after the Civil War, Dall
was a women's rights activist. She valued Emerson enough to arrange the
1855 Boston Convention so as to insure his presence, thanking him for the
address "Woman" even though "some of the papers thought it doubtful,
whether you were for us or against us." But when four years later she
composed her own women's rights history as an address for a national convention, she paid tribute to Fuller as the American Wollstonecraft—and
called her essay by Fuller's title, "The Great Lawsuit."[58]

NOTES

1. Margaret Fuller, "The Great Lawsuit," *Dial* 4(1843):13. Cited hereafter as "GL."
2. O. B. Frothingham, *Transcendentalism in New England: A History* (1876; New York, 1959), 175; Perry Miller, *The Transcendentalists: An Anthology* (Cambridge, Mass., 1950), 457; Barbara L. Packer, "The Transcendentalists," in *The Cambridge History of American Literature*, ed. Sacvan Bercovitch (New York, 1995), 2:329–604. Thirteen years later, in *Margaret Fuller, American Romantic* (Garden City, New York, 1963), Miller was considerably more dismissive of his subject, perhaps distancing himself from women's insurgency of that day: "Her 'feminist' propaganda is actually a slight contribution to the campaign for 'women's rights'" (xii).
3. Ralph Waldo Emerson, *Journals and Miscellaneous Notebooks of Ralph Waldo Emerson*, ed. William H. Gilman et al. (Cambridge, Mass., 1960–1982), 7:48. Cited hereafter as *JMN*.
4. Among studies that have influenced my thinking on Transcendentalist ethics are David M. Robinson, "Margaret Fuller and the Transcendental Ethos: *Woman in the Nineteenth Century*," *PMLA* 97(1982):83–96; Len Gougeon, *Virtue's Hero: Emerson, Antislavery, and Reform* (Athens, Ga., 1990); Julie Ellison, *Delicate Subjects: Romanticism, Gender, and the Ethics of Understanding* (Ithaca, 1990); Charles Capper, "Margaret Fuller as Cultural Reformer: The Conversations in Boston," *American Quarterly* 39(1987):509–528, and *Margaret Fuller: An American Romantic Life* (New York, 1992); and John Carlos Rowe, *At Emerson's Tomb: The Politics of Classic American Literature* (New York, 1997).
    Two previous studies of Emerson and Fuller in dialogue have been especially important, though I differ from both by setting this dialogue in the context of New England reform. Larry J. Reynolds emphasizes the personal dynamics of an elite circle of Boston friends as the source of Fuller's thinking in "GL," claiming a distinct focus on women's rights only for her revised book. "From Dial Essay to New York Book: The Making of *Woman in the Nineteenth Century*," in *Periodical Literature in Nineteenth-Century America*, ed. Kenneth Price and Susan Belasco Smith

(Charlottesville, 1996), 17–34. Along with Christina Zwarg, I trace the feminist "agency" of Fuller and Emerson in their dialogue itself. But for Zwarg "feminism" refers to an antihierarchical, deconstructive theory of "absolute doubt," prompted in both Fuller and Emerson by their reading of Charles Fourier, whereas I focus on the historical development of an American women's rights movement as a setting for their conversation. Christina Zwarg, *Feminist Conversations: Fuller, Emerson, and the Play of Reading* (Ithaca, 1995).

5. Nancy Craig Simmons, "Margaret Fuller's Boston Conversations: The 1839–40 Series," *Studies in the American Renaissance 1994*, ed. Joel Myerson (Charlottesville, 1995), 204–206, 208, 222 (cited hereafter as "BC"); Caroline Healey Dall, *Margaret and Her Friends, or Ten Conversations with Margaret Fuller on the Mythology of the Greeks . . . Beginning March 1, 1841* (Boston, 1895; cited hereafter as *MHF*); *JMN*, 7:442.

6. See Christine Battersby, *Gender and Genius: Towards a Feminist Aesthetics* (Bloomington, 1989) for the androcentric tradition and its Romantic permutations, as well as Ellison, *Delicate Subjects*, on the feminine-associated powers of sympathy and divination in Schleiermacher, Coleridge, and Fuller.

7. Germaine de Staël, *Corinne, or Italy*, trans. and ed. Avriel Goldberger (New Brunswick, 1987), 21; "GL" 34. See also Madelyn Gutwirth, "Woman as Mediatrix: From Jean-Jacques Rousseau to Germaine de Staël," in *Woman as Mediatrix: Essays on Nineteenth-Century Woman Writers*, ed. Avriel H. Goldberger (Westport, Conn.,1987), 13–29; and Battersby, *Gender and Genius*, 98–100.

8. Mary Moody Emerson, *Selected Letters of Mary Moody Emerson*, ed. Nancy Craig Simmons (Athens, 1993), 108.

9. Phyllis Cole, *Mary Moody Emerson and the Origins of Transcendentalism: A Family History* (New York, 1998); Mary Moody Emerson, *Selected Letters*, 217–218 (Wordsworth), 182 (Milton), 144 (Price), 185–188 (Plato), 157 (Hindu poetry), 139, 143 (de Staël).

10. Almanac entry sent as a letter, Mary Moody Emerson to Ralph Waldo Emerson, 1821?, bMsAu 1280.226 (822) Houghton Library, Harvard University; Ralph Waldo Emerson, *Letters of Ralph Waldo Emerson*, ed. Ralph L. Rusk (New York, 1939), 1:138. Cited hereafter as *EL*.

11. *JMN*, 1:49; *EL*, 1:171. RWE's transcriptions of letters from "Tnamurya" are in *JMN*, 1–3.

12. Zwarg, *Feminist Conversations*, chap. 1. Cases for Emerson's misogyny include Joyce W. Warren, *The American Narcissus: Individualism and Women in Nineteenth-Century American Fiction* (New Brunswick, 1984), chap. 2; and David Leverenz, *Manhood and the American Renaissance* (Ithaca, 1989), chap. 1.

13. Quoted by Miller, *Margaret Fuller*, xix. Emerson most definitively linked the two women in a journal of 1871 that amounts to his private history of women's writing: "I pass over my own list of thinkers & friends, as I have counted some of them a few pages back, and only add, that I believe our soil yields a few good women, too, as England or France, though we have not a book from them to compare with [de Staël's] 'Allemagne.' Yet M.M.E.'s journals shine with genius, & Margaret Fuller's Conversation did." *JMN*, 16:259.

14. Margaret Fuller, *The Letters of Margaret Fuller*, ed. Robert N. Hudspeth (Ithaca, 1983–1993), 1:154, 166–167. Cited hereafter as *FL*.

15. Ralph Waldo Emerson, James F. Clarke, and W. H. Channing, *Memoirs of Margaret Fuller Ossoli* (Boston, 1852), 1:190.
16. *JMN*, 7:56, 48. On the personal sorrows as well as Romantic impulses of Lidian and Elizabeth, see Cole, "'Men and Women Conversing': The Emersons in 1837," in *Emersonian Circles: Essays in Honor of Joel Myerson*, ed. Wesley T. Mott and Robert E. Burkholder (Rochester, 1996), 127–159.
17. Zwarg, *Feminist Conversations*, 39.
18. Quoted in *Memoirs*, 1:99. See Capper, *Margaret Fuller*, 289, for the identification of Davis as the recipient.
19. "BC," 204, 209. The ninth through fifteenth conversations are missing from the transcript, but their Coleridgian subjects are outlined in *FL*, 2:118–119. On Fuller's mythography, see Robert D. Richardson, Jr., "Margaret Fuller and Myth," *Prospects* 4(1979):169–184. Jeffrey Steele illuminates Fuller's female archetypes and goddess-mysticism in *The Representation of the Self in the American Renaissance* (Chapel Hill, 1987), chap. 5. Without access to Peabody's transcript of the 1839–1840 conversation, however, he traces the development of such thinking all to the fall of 1840 (105ff).
20. Debra Gold Hansen, "The Boston Female Anti-Slavery Society and the Limits of Gender Politics," in *The Abolitionist Sisterhood: Women's Political Culture in Antebellum America*, ed. Jean Fagan Yellin and John C. Van Horne (Ithaca, 1994), 46–52; Carolyn L. Karcher, *The First Woman of the Republic: A Cultural Biography of Lydia Maria Child* (Durham, 1994), 220–221; Harriet Martineau, *Society in America* (1837; New York, 1966), 1:168–172 (cf. chap. 3, secs. 6 and 7); Harriet Martineau, *Retrospect of Western Travel* (1838; New York, 1969), 2:159–165; Maria Weston Chapman, *Right and Wrong in Boston: Report of the Boston Female Anti-Slavery Society* (Boston, 1835–1837).
21. Gerda Lerner, *The Grimké Sisters of South Carolina* (Boston, 1967), 137–138, 227; Jean Fagan Yellin, *Women and Sisters: The Antislavery Feminists in American Culture* (New Haven, 1989), 40–41 (Grimké quotation 41).
22. Grimké letter quoted by Hansen, "Boston Female," 53; Lerner, *Grimke Sisters*, chap. 12; "Pastoral Letter of the General Association of Massachusetts (Orthodox) to the Churches under their care," quoted in Elizabeth Cady Stanton et al., *History of Woman Suffrage* (1881; New York, 1970), 81–82; "Appeal of Clerical Abolitionists," quoted by Hansen, "Boston Female," 53–54.
23. Chapman, "The Times that Try Men's Souls," quoted in Stanton et al., *History of Woman Suffrage*, 1:82–83; Chapman quoted by Hansen, "Boston Female," 55.
24. Chapman on Channing quoted by Debra Gold Hansen, *Strained Sisterhood: Gender and Class in the Boston Female Anti-Slavery Society* (Amherst, 1993), 86; *JMN*, 5:113, 154; Chapman, "Memorials of Harriet Martineau," in Martineau, *Autobiography* (London, 1877), 3:160. For the antislavery sentiments of Mary, Charles, and Lidian Emerson, see Cole, "'Men and Women Conversing,'" 149–154.
25. Gougeon, *Virtue's Hero*, 30–31; Ellen Tucker Emerson, *The Life of Lidian Jackson Emerson*, ed. Delores Bird Carpenter (1980; East Lansing, Mich., 1992), 62; Lidian Emerson, *The Selected Letters of Lidian Jackson Emerson*, ed. Delores Bird Carpenter (Columbia, Mo., 1993), 60–61.
26. *JMN*, 5:382; Sarah Grimké and Angelina Grimké, *The Public Years of Sarah and*

Angelina Grimké: Selected Writings, 1835–39, ed. Larry Ceplair (New York, 1989), 188–194, 231–237. On the Grimkés' and other feminist abolitionists' identification with slaves, conveyed in motto and emblem as well as formal rhetoric, see Yellin, *Women and Sisters*, chaps. 1–2.

27. *JMN*, 5:407. Fuller may have been merely contrasting genius with "goody" in the New England sense of "goodwife," conventional woman. But another journal passage by Emerson, following shortly after his critique of abolitionists as "men & women of one idea," suggests how the term was more likely used in his conversations with Fuller: "I hate goodies. I hate goodness that preaches" (*JMN*, 7:30–31).

28. *FL*, 1:309; Martineau, *Autobiography*, 2:381–383.

29. Capper, *Margaret Fuller*, 94–95, 153–155, 187; Karcher, *First Woman of the Republic*, 677n.; Anne Weston quoted in Hansen, *Strained Sisterhood*, 86. Yellin lists Fuller's intimate friend Caroline Sturgis among members of the BFASS in *Women and Sisters*, 128 and 153; none of Fuller's many letters to Sturgis, however, takes up antislavery issues.

30. Capper, *Margaret Fuller*, 239, on the timing of Jameson's departure.

31. Ralph Waldo Emerson, *Collected Works of Ralph Waldo Emerson*, ed. Alfred R. Ferguson et al. (Cambridge, Mass., 1971–), 1:88 (cited hereafter as *CW*); cf. *JMN*, 5:382.

32. Hansen, "Boston Female," 54–56 (Chapman quotation, 55); Ruth Bogin and Jean Fagan Yellin, introduction to *The Abolitionist Sisterhood*, 18; Aileen Kraditor, *Means and Ends in American Abolitionism: Garrison and His Critics on Strategy and Tactics, 1834–1850* (New York, 1967), chap. 3.

33. Hansen, "Boston Female," 55; Hansen, *Strained Sisterhood*, 84; Sarah Grimké, *Public Years of Sarah and Angelina Grimké*, 258, 248. Cf. Blanche Glassman Hersh, *The Slavery of Sex: Feminist-Abolitionists in America* (Urbana, 1978), 142–145, on Quakerism and Transcendentalism as the two forms of liberal religion of interest to the greatest number of nineteenth-century feminists.

34. Karcher, *First Woman of the Republic*, 260, 258.

35. See Lee Chambers-Schiller, "'A Good Work among the People': The Political Culture of the Boston Antislavery Fair," in *The Abolitionist Sisterhood*, 249–274. A year later, however, Fuller enjoyed shopping for beautiful, European-imported gifts at this same fair (*FL*, 2:261).

36. Wesley T. Mott, "The Chardon Street and Bible Conventions," *Encyclopedia of Transcendentalism*, ed. Wesley T. Mott (Westport, Conn., 1996), 227–228; *The Liberator*, Nov. 27 and Oct. 16, 1840; Emerson, "Chardon Street and Bible Conventions," *Dial* 3(July 1842):100–112. Reprinted in part as "The Chardon Street Convention," *The Complete Works of Ralph Waldo Emerson*, ed. Edward Waldo Emerson (Boston, 1903–1904), 10:373–377 (cited hereafter as *W*). Describing the same events, Garrison did not mention women's presence except to deplore Mrs. Folsom's interruptions; Abigail Folsom, probably insane and surely out of control, proved a genuine trial to the abolitionists through these years. *Letters of William Lloyd Garrison*, ed. Walter M. Merrill and Louis Ruchames (Cambridge, Mass., 1971), 1:725, 727n.

37. Mott, *Encyclopedia of Transcendentalism*, 27–28; Caroline Weston, "Female Praying, or Speaking, in Promiscuous Assemblies," *The Liberator*, Apr. 2, 1841.

38. "Anti-Sabbath and Anti-Ministry Convention," *The Christian Journal*, reprinted in *The Liberator*, Dec. 11, 1840; Emerson, "Chardon Street and Bible Conventions," 102.

39. On the relationship between Fourier and feminism, see Carl J. Guarneri, *The Utopian Alternative: Fourierism in Nineteenth-Century America* (Ithaca, 1991), 130–132, 244–247, 354; on Fuller's and Emerson's debt to Fourier, Zwarg, *Feminist Conversations*, 24–28, esp. 27n. on the their actual reading of Fourierist literature.

40. Margaret Fuller, *The Essential Margaret Fuller*, ed. Jeffrey Steele (New Brunswick, 1992), 315.

41. *W*, 10:346, 356, 366–367.

42. See for instance Steele, *Representation*, 106–109, and Zwarg, *Feminist Conversations*, 48–52.

43. Ralph Waldo Emerson to Thomas Carlyle, Oct. 30, 1840, in *The Correspondence of Emerson and Carlyle*, ed. Joseph Slater (New York, 1964), 283–284.

44. *FL*, 2:198; Weston quoted by Capper, "Margaret Fuller as Cultural Reformer," 528n.

45. Barbara Ryan, "Emerson's 'Domestic and Social Experiments': Service, Slavery, and the Unhired Man," *American Literature* 66(1994):485–508; Ralph Waldo Emerson, "Man the Reformer," *Dial* 1(April 1841):523–538.

46. Ralph Waldo Emerson, "Fourier and the Socialists," *Dial* 3(July 1842):86–96; Linck C. Johnson, "Reforming the Reformers: Emerson, Thoreau, and the Sunday Lectures at Amory Hall, Boston," *ESQ* 37(1991):278, 239–240.

47. *CW*, 3:87–88, in T. Gregory Garvey, *The Emersonian Dilemma: Essays on Emerson and Social Reform* (Athens, forthcoming).

48. Zwarg interprets this essay more favorably, as does Armida Gilbert in "'Pierced by the Thorns of Reform': Emerson on Womanhood." Zwarg, *Feminist Conversations*, 257–269.

49. Lydia Maria Child, "Women's Rights," *Letters from New York, Second Series* (New York, 1843), 249.

50. "GL," 7, 9, 11. See Karcher, *First Woman of the Republic*, 225–226, on the relationship of Fuller's text to Child's.

51. On the relation between Fuller's two versions, see Reynolds, "From *Dial* Essay to New York Book," as well as Marie Urbanski, *Margaret Fuller's Woman in the Nineteenth Century : A Literary Study of Form and Content, of Sources and Influence* (Westport, Conn., 1980), 129–130. Bell Gale Chevigny presents an influential anti-Boston argument in "Growing Out of New England: The Emergence of Margaret Fuller's Radicalism," *Women's Studies* 5(1968):65–100; David M. Robinson relates her work to Channing, Emerson, and others in "Margaret Fuller and the Transcendentalist Ethos."

52. Thomas Wentworth Higginson, *Margaret Fuller Ossoli* (Boston, 1887), 200; cf. Urbanski, *Margaret Fuller's Woman in the Nineteenth Century*, 129, and Robinson, "Margaret Fuller and the Transcendentalist Ethos," 86.

53. On Fuller's "platform logic" within a feminist tradition including Grimké and Kelley, see Annette Kolodny, "Inventing a Feminist Discourse: Rhetoric and Resistance in Margaret Fuller's *Woman in the Nineteenth Century*," *New Literary History* 25(1994):355–382.

54. Ellen DuBois, "Women's Rights and Abolition: The Nature of the Connection," in

Antislavery Reconsidered: New Perspectives on the Abolitionists, ed. Lewis Perry and Michael Fellman (Baton Rouge, 1979).

55. Lydia Maria Child, *Lydia Maria Child: Selected Letters, 1817–1880*, ed. Milton Meltzer, Patricia G. Holland, and Francine Krasno (Amherst, 1982), 219.

56. *EL*, 3:183. Stanton's *History of Woman Suffrage* reveals Emerson as a signer of calls for the 1850s Women's Rights Conventions and once a speaker, but Channing as an office-holder and organizer, Higginson as a writer and orator of long-term commitment. See for instance 1:820, 227, 256 on Emerson; 1:129–131 and 226 on Channing; 1:131–132, 249–252, 656–661 on Higginson. Stanton does not reprint Emerson's 1855 address as she does many others; Theodore Parker, though not an active partisan either, is represented by a full sermon, "The Public Function of Woman" (1:277–282). Cf. Emerson's oration within a longer tradition in *Against the Tide: Pro-Feminist Men in the United States, 1776–1990, A Documentary History*, ed. Michael S. Kimmel and Thomas E. Mosmiller (Boston, 1992).

57. Elizabeth Cady Stanton, *Eighty Years and More: Reminiscences 1815–1897* (1898; New York, 1971), 148; Stanton, *History of Woman Suffrage*, 1:3, 801–802.

58. Dall quoted in Helen R. Deese, "'A Liberal Education': Caroline Healey Dall and Emerson," in *Emersonian Circles*, 248; Dall, "The Great Lawsuit," in *Historical Pictures Retouched* (Boston, 1860), 249–264. Cf. Stanton, *History of Woman Suffrage*, 1:673–674, for the origins of this essay in the 1859 Convention.

Brook Farm, Fourierism, and the Nationalist Dilemma in American Utopianism

Carl J. Guarneri

THE NEW ENGLAND FOURIER SOCIETY'S ANNUAL MEETING OF January 1845 was an occasion for festive congratulations and ambitious plans. The Brook Farm community, begun in 1841 as a Transcendentalist experiment in cooperative individualism, had recently officially proclaimed itself the "Brook Farm Phalanx" and pledged allegiance to the utopian socialist doctrines of Charles Fourier. Now, as the Brook Farmers met with Albert Brisbane and other national Fourierist leaders, they hatched plans to take over the rapidly growing communitarian movement's weekly journal, *The Harbinger*, and to concentrate American Associationists' efforts on transforming the modest settlement at West Roxbury into a successful phalanx (or model Fourierist community) that would approximate Fourier's grand specifications.

Brisbane and William Henry Channing, who gave the convention's keynote addresses, aired distinctly nationalistic themes. Recently returned from a trip to France, Fourier's first American disciple listed the obstacles to radical social movements presented by the European monarchical and class system, and by contrast the advantages that the democratic and open society of the United States gave to reformers intent upon the peaceful, voluntary reconstruction of society. Channing, Brook Farm's unofficial pastor, extended Brisbane's theme by linking Brook Farm, Fourierism, and the national mission in a stirring call to realize the social millennium on American soil. Foregoing the rhetoric of self-culture and spiritual renewal that pervaded Brook Farm's early years, Channing redirected the Transcendentalists toward a national communal project. America's "peculiarly favorable opportunities," he reminded listeners, imposed "responsibilities and duties, the fulfilment of which can neither be evaded nor postponed." From its

447

founding, the United States was a beacon of democracy in a dark, monarchical world. Now, presented with "the true solution to the social problem" in Fourier's blueprint, it had been "commissioned by Providence" to "manifest before the Nations of the Earth . . . the possibility of human brotherhood" in social relations.[1] The Brook Farmers' role in this holy undertaking was to become a model for other communal experiments and, even more important, to indoctrinate the nation in the sublime truths of Fourierism. Channing's speech signaled how far, in rhetorical and practical terms, Brook Farm had leaped by 1845 beyond the insular confines of Transcendentalist Boston and plunged into the broad channel of American utopianism.

"Nothing could be more absurd," wrote the historian Daniel Boorstin in the 1950s, "than to try to make of the isolated utopian communities in American history anything like a great tradition of utopianism in the mainstream of our thought. . . . We have, of course, had our New Harmonys, our Brook Farms, and our Oneidas; but these have been, at most, minor tributaries of our thought."[2] Boorstin worked from a consensus model, prominent among historians and literary scholars in the Cold War decades, which denied the influence of ideology among Americans and glorified instead their pragmatic "national character." Yet even a passing acquaintance with the literary and cultural-history scholarship of the forty years since Boorstin wrote is enough to suggest how central the idea of utopia was to American self-conceptions long before Transcendentalist Brook Farm was founded in 1841 or the community converted to Fourierism in 1844. Boorstin in fact got it backwards: communal experiments like Brook Farm—and indeed the Transcendentalist movement from which it sprang—did not create (or purport to create) a native utopian tradition; they defined themselves in relation to powerful, pre-existing American utopian ideals and rhetoric.

Influenced by theories of social constructionism and chastened by critiques of Eurocentrism, Americanists of recent decades have recognized that the New World was "invented" by Europeans rather than discovered by them and that utopian notions decisively shaped—and at times obscured—this historical process. Once the American continents entered Europeans' consciousness in the sixteenth century, they served as repositories for the dreams, fantasies, visions, and hopes of Old World cultures teetering between righteous self-confidence and chiliastic despair. Whichever version of the utopian dream Europeans embraced—fantasies of a faraway Eden or ancient Golden Age, the notion of America as a blank slate upon which the social contract could be written anew, hopes that civilization would reach its climax at its western terminus, or the belief that a spacious refuge for religious dissenters might become the millennial ground—such ideas were imposed on the New World landscape, and upon its aboriginal population, with little regard for stubborn facts.[3]

Like the New World, the "imagined community" of the United States was itself a utopian invention. In the timespan of the generation framing the Revolution, national independence was codified with foundation documents, Founding Fathers, and a republican civil religion that appropriated Protestant eschatology for the state. After the Revolution, persisting utopian dreams and images became attached to the fledgling United States with such rapid and pervasive effect that it became the referent of various terms, including Jefferson's "last best hope" for humanity, the evangelicals' "redeemer nation," expansionists' "manifest destiny," and immigrants' "promised land."[4]

The symbolic merger of these two utopian inventions—New World and nation—was "America," a name expressing the effective absorption of Western utopian assumptions and ideals by the enterprise of the United States. The word itself, contracting to exclude the rest of the hemisphere yet capable of seemingly boundless allusion, inhabited that powerful space that lies between fact and metaphor. America became simultaneously a trope and a home for utopian longings, a connection strengthened in the century after 1776 by a national career of economic success, massive immigration, and geographic expansion.

Far from being marginal to this process by which utopia became Americanized, Fourierist Brook Farm contended for a central role in shaping it at a time when a fierce public debate raged over the nature and future of the young United States. Like other antebellum spokesmen with idealistic programs, from abolitionists and women's rights advocates to their Transcendentalist friends Ralph Waldo Emerson and Henry David Thoreau, the Brook Farmers drew energy and inspiration from popular notions of the mission and promise of America. During an era when the nation was expanding and its modern capitalist institutional matrix was crystallizing, they espoused Fourierism as an alternative, "true" version of the American dream, contrary in some fundamental ways to dominant social practices yet also faithful in essence to national ideals. In arguing for their version of the American utopia the Brook Farmers took their place as competitors among a broad spectrum of American dreamers. And the course they charted as loyal American dissenters was followed by many utopian groups thereafter. For one legacy of the marriage of utopia and America is that recurrent patterns of community dreaming and building have woven themselves into the fabric of American culture. Frances Fitzgerald is the most recent observer to note that a common sensibility links twentieth-century communes to mainstream groupings such as planned suburbs and retirement communities, and that both kinds of communities trace their roots to nineteenth-century millennialism and, deeper still in the past, to the Puritan "city on a hill."[5] The history of the United States *is* in some respects the chronicle of a contest of overlapping, competing perfectionist experiments. Some have been official, some not; some have been enduring, most not; some are professedly mainstream, others oppositional. Virtually all have claimed a unique ability to realize, reform, criticize, or supplant the one big utopia: America itself.

But just how oppositional, how "subversive," can utopian theories be in such an environment? If the symbolic lexicon of the United States is itself utopian, how can alternative utopias maintain the critical distance required for true dissent? Has the nation's dominant discourse pre-empted the language of utopia? The abstract, pervasive, future-oriented idealism of American culture lends legitimacy to utopian ideas and movements, but it also presents them with unforeseen problems of absorption and co-optation. The inability of communities like Brook Farm to become more than what Boorstin called "minor tributaries" in the course of American social thought may have much to do with their derivative relationship to American utopianism. Despite their attempts to demonstrate their Americanness—or rather in large part *because* of it—utopian and communal experiments have had a difficult time establishing themselves as enduring presences in American life.

In a series of books exploring the ideological dimensions of Transcendentalism, Sacvan Bercovitch has sharply etched the constricting boundaries that the rhetorical legacy of Puritanism set upon Transcendentalist discourse, and by implication upon American dissent as a whole. By grafting Antonio Gramsci's concept of cultural hegemony onto a wide-ranging analysis of Puritan biblical imagery and rhetorical forms such as the jeremiad, Bercovitch illustrates the power of American discourse to absorb and co-opt dissent. With revolution and nationhood, in Bercovitch's telling, the Puritan vision evolved into the myth of America, a national cultural field that has harnessed utopia (in the abstract, a potentially liberating dream) to the demands of ideology (maintenance of the socioeconomic status quo and its official culture).

A crucial juncture in this dynamic, according to Bercovitch, was the point at which Ralph Waldo Emerson, the Transcendentalist high priest of the "American self," came to grips with the mid-nineteenth-century socialist challenge to America's rhetoric and social practice. First, through sources as diverse as Alexis de Tocqueville, the English journals, and Fourier, Emerson encountered the socialist critique of "individualism" and absorbed it into his idealist challenge to northern society. A genuine, liberating individualism would not fragment but leaven society, Emerson insisted, but it had not yet been tried. Then, increasingly through the 1840s as he ruminated critically on the Brook Farm experiment, Emerson began to identify his utopian dream of individualism with the invisible workings of American society. When Emerson publicly declared in 1844 that the utopian "union" the communitarians sought "must be ideal in actual individualism," he crossed an important line. For the first time in his thought, according to Bercovitch, "the dream of self-reliance was organic to a certain society, in a certain place, as a tendency toward perfect union inherent in its laws, customs, assumptions, and institutions." Here was a "breathtaking" leap of nationalist faith, "a wholesale appropriation of utopia, all the hopes of reform and revolution nourished on both sides of the Atlantic by the turmoil of modernization, for the American Way."[6]

By and large, Bercovitch's readings of other American Renaissance writers follow parallel tracks; they suggest that by the 1850s an American consensus had effectively reduced dissent to a form of liberal, mostly individualist, nationalism that sustained the culture even as it purported to reform it. While the "office" of Hawthorne's *Scarlet Letter* remained complex and ambiguous, the "cultural work" of such oppositional writers as Whitman and Thoreau was clear: to obviate true alternatives to capitalism by "redefining injustice as un-American, revolution as the legacy of '76, and inequities of class, race, and gender as disparities between the theory and the practice of American-ness."[7] When they invoked a better or alternative American idea, utopians like Thoreau and reformers like Frederick Douglass, according to Bercovitch,

> miscalculated not just the power but the nature of rhetoric. They had thought to appropriate America as a trope of the spirit, and so to turn the national symbol, now freed of its base historical content, into a vehicle of moral and political renovation. In the event, however, the symbol had refigured the moral and political terms of renovation—had rendered freedom, opportunity, democracy, and radicalism itself part of the American Way.[8]

I hesitate to endorse the ruthless single-mindedness of this outlook, which threatens to reduce literature to ideology and at times appears insensitive to the profound ambiguities of literary forms. The spectre of symbols manipulating people rather than vice versa suggests that Bercovitch risks taking the "linguistic turn" around the bend toward a denial of human agency. Among the most serious reservations about Bercovitch's approach is its tendency to reify hegemony into a monolithic fact rather than a multi-faceted process that takes place in real historical time. As Gramsci himself portrayed it, the establishment of hegemony is a constant struggle, a give-and-take process through which dominant and subordinate groups share and contest social meanings; it is not the one-time, one-sided, Jonah-and-the-whale story Bercovitch tends to favor, where the prevailing system of thought simply "ingested competing forms of radicalism."[9] American dissent and what Bercovitch calls "the American Way" have evolved dialectically and simultaneously in mutually influencing ways. Elsewhere I have tried to show, for example, how the utopian-socialist critique of northern society, incarnated in such diverse forms as Brook Farm's attack on American individualism and the proslavery writer George Fitzhugh's indictment of northern "free society," evoked powerful new ideological defenses of the northern social order. As Bercovitch's own essays imply, Emerson's "self-reliance" and Lincoln's celebration of "free labor" were not the products of some abstraction called "American ideology" but the outcome of an antebellum debate over the meaning and future of an evolving American society.[10]

Nevertheless, in his exploration of the American "rites of assent" Bercovitch offers a powerful and sobering dose of realism for those who have turned to the rich and fertile ground of mid-nineteenth-century American culture to find "roads not taken," utopian counterproposals and counternarratives to what was at that very time emerging as dominant social discourse and conventional social practice. His work, along with that of recent critics of American "exceptionalism," compels us to consider the ways that nationalist ideology pervaded and often vitiated the quest for alternative structures of thought.[11] With our ears attuned to the lexicon of national symbols and the rhythms of national-utopian rhetoric, we can hear clear echoes of the ritual of national consensus in the Brook Farmers' ideals and plans. In its original European formulations socialism may have "repudiated the very rhetoric of America," as Bercovitch asserts; it may well have "tended toward a total, unequivocal dissociation of the ideal not only from the United States but also from the meaning of America."[12] Yet when adopted, interpreted, and transformed by its advocates at Brook Farm, the Fourierist brand of socialism became so infused with American nationalism and the assumptions of American middle-class culture that its challenge to American ways dissolved easily into acceptance and then affirmation. In the course of the antebellum debate over the meaning of America, the communitarian wing of Transcendentalist reform, no less than the Emersonian individualist one, evolved toward utopian affirmation of the culture of competitive capitalism and its merger with American national destiny.

To place Brook Farm in the context of American ideology and a national communitarian movement is to break with a tradition of scholarship that has considered the community only as a variant of New England Transcendentalism—and a problematic one at that. For a long time, the fact that Transcendentalists supported such a communal venture struck historians as a "curious paradox."[13] Even when historians of Transcendentalism such as Octavius Frothingham and Perry Miller acknowledged the emergence of an "associative" or "fraternity" wing of the movement represented by George Ripley, Theodore Parker, Orestes Brownson, and W. H. Channing, they seemed unsure whether Brook Farm took that faction beyond the blurry boundaries of Transcendentalist philosophy. How could religious nonconformists who generally paid homage to spontaneity, intuition, and personal freedom submit to a community experiment? One answer, hinted at by Miller and then developed in a series of articles by Charles Crowe, was that Ripley and the Brook Farmers did not abandon generally held Transcendentalist ideals such as self-expression and personal integration, but built a miniature society in which to realize them. Cooperative living would eliminate the obstacles to spiritual growth presented by an acquisitive, unequal, compartmentalized society and would make the means of Transcendentalist self-culture available to more individuals.[14]

This interpretation linked the early years of Brook Farm to broad Transcendentalist ideals, but it failed to account for the Brook Farmers' direct and visceral reaction against Emersonian individualism and, consequently, their promotion of a near-mystical communal ethos. Parker, Brownson, and other reform-minded Transcendentalists emphasized the egalitarian and social rather than the individual and heroic implications of humanity's "likeness to God." Ripley and the Brook Farmers took this embryonic collectivism one step further. "The doctrine they taught above all others," John Codman recalled, "was . . . that the human race was one creation, bound together by indissoluble ties," and thus that society should reflect "one heart, one brain, one purpose."[15] This notion of the "solidarity of the race," borrowed by Channing and John Dwight from the French Saint-Simonian Pierre Leroux, moved the powerful self of Emersonian Transcendentalism offstage and substituted an ideal of organic community as the Brook Farmers' Christian-socialist aim. Nor did the interpretation of Brook Farm merely as individualism in a group context explain its eventual conversion to Fourierism. Perry Miller was mystified. Why, he asked, did

George Ripley transform Brook Farm "from a Transcendental picnic into a regimented Phalanx"? "It must have been," Lindsay Swift surmised in a passage Miller quoted approvingly, "that he came to lay more stress on the method by which individual freedom was to become assured, than on the fact of personal liberty itself." Insisting that the real Brook Farm was a carefree Transcendentalist idyll, both Swift and Miller abruptly broke off their histories when the community converted to Fourierism and entered what Miller labeled its "socialistic and totalitarian" phase.[16]

How, then, to explain the "unnatural union" of Brook Farm and Fourierism? As Miller suggested, the Brook Farmers were struggling to get a living and were indeed attracted by the more systematic organization of production and distribution in Fourier's scheme. But it is clear that a host of additional, complementary motives brought about the conversion. Among them were Brisbane and Horace Greeley's earnest proselytizing, Ripley's desire to diversify the community's class membership, and the Brook Farmers' need to attract outside capital to expand the community's workshops. The variant of "social" Transcendentalism that had influenced Brook Farm's founding created affinities between the young community's arrangements and specific features of Fourier's phalanx blueprint, such as its "integral education" of body and mind, its guarantees of maintenance for the sick and aged, and its division of ownership into joint-stock shares. On the more theoretical level of "social science," Fourier's affirmation that the beneficent divine law governing the universe could be extended to social relations corresponded to the Transcendentalists' "mystical intuition of a patterned world."[17] Where Fourierism differed dramatically from the Brook Farm Transcendentalist faith, in its reliance upon social mechanics rather than spiritual reform to harmonize interests, it could be Christianized to fit better. Since community members were engrossed in everyday affairs, much of this task was left to their revered friend Channing. In his sermons at Brook Farm, his speeches at reform conventions, and his writings in *The Present*, Channing interpreted Fourierism as a "science of unity" to reconcile individual initiative and communal bonding, and he attempted to add moral agency and an ethic of self-sacrifice to Fourier's mechanistic plan. Channing's explorations in the winter of 1843–1844 became—to use Zoltan Haraszti's happy image—"the bridge on which the Brook Farmers crossed over to Fourierism."[18]

That bridge was lined with American flags. As early as September 1843, as Channing was thinking his way toward Fourierism in *The Present*, he issued a "confession of faith" that joined "the unity of the human race" and "the kingdom of Heaven on earth" with "the duty of this nation to establish united interests." When Channing recommended Fourierism to Brook

Farm he infused it with America's "providential mission to fulfill the law of love." Brisbane, too, during frequent visits to the West Roxbury community impressed upon members his conviction that the United States was destined to realize Fourier's dreams and, conversely, that the Fourierist blueprint culminated the American national genius.[19]

At each stage in Brook Farm's development its perspective widened. Begun as a modest and largely unpublicized local experiment, it evolved into an important public cause linked to the national communitarian movement. At the outset, Ripley had privately voiced the hope that Brook Farm could become "a light over this country and this age."[20] By 1844 he and the other Brook Farm leaders became convinced that despite their precarious finances they had proved it possible to live a better life than that afforded by competitive institutions. With interest in communitarianism spreading nationwide due to the Fourierist craze, the time had come to escalate Brook Farm's ambition into a full-fledged challenge to the existing society. And this task of transforming America, Brook Farmers were convinced, was actually the way to fulfill the nation's destiny. Far from rendering Brook Farm "something foreign and forlorn in West Roxbury," as Perry Miller claimed, the community's conversion to Fourierism culminated its growing claims to Americanness.[21]

Once they took the helm of the national Fourierist movement, the Brook Farmers also took the lead in remapping Fourier's secular and universalist views onto the Protestant-nationalist rhetorical field of American discourse. To be sure, Ripley and his Transcendentalist colleagues had, for their time and place, strong cosmopolitan leanings, as was evidenced by their earlier borrowings from German idealists and French eclectic philosophers and, more generally, their interest in foreign ideas and movements. In a sense, Brook Farm's adoption of Fourier culminated this widening of intellectual horizons beyond the confines of Anglo-American Protestant culture. *The Harbinger* featured pioneering translations of George Sand's novels, reviews of books from the European continent, and incisive analyses of the Revolutions of 1848. But these foreign interests and importations were fundamentally grounded in domestic concerns. The Brook Farmers' move toward socialism, John Dwight attested, "did not take its first impulse from France or Fourier" as much as from the "liberal movement in theology" and the dislocations of an unbridled capitalist economy.[22] They welcomed Fourier's theory because it offered a "science of unity" that their theology forecasted and a communal blueprint that the young nation needed to follow. Given the urgent sense during the antebellum years that the nation's future was at stake and its role in human history would be unique, it is no wonder that advocates of new political, social, and cultural programs framed such projects as promoters of national identity or destiny. As westward expansion, the spread of slavery, and the takeoff of industrial capitalism prodded Americans to reexamine inherited social ideals, the public debate that resulted became not simply a dispute between differing diagnoses of social problems but a contest over the meaning of America. Communal experiments like Brook Farm which were established as model colonies became exhibits, and at times voices, in this debate. So did essays by Emerson such as "The American Scholar" and "Self-Reliance." It was no coincidence that the Brook Farmers' attempt to identify utopian socialism with the national mission occurred at the same moment that Emerson was linking the emergence of individualism to the course of American development. The pervasive language of Americanness inspired, shaped, and constrained both projects.

Beyond the nationalistic assumptions of antebellum public discourse, the Brook Farm Fourierists had special reasons to insist upon their doctrine's consistency with true American ideals. One was their intent— virtually unique among antebellum communitarians—to convert large numbers of ordinary Americans. The Shakers saw themselves as a permanent beleaguered minority among what they called "the world's people"; the Oneida Community was a one-of-a-kind experiment; and the Mormons, although they harbored expansionist dreams, imposed a rigorous creedal test which put *de facto* limits on recruitment. Unlike these groups, the Fourierists aimed to build settlements that welcomed all religions and classes, harmonized differences through cooperative social mechanisms, and duplicated themselves throughout the land. Theirs was the purest and most radical version of the communitarian faith that, as the nation expanded, successful pilot communities would be everywhere imitated and quickly supplant existing social and economic structures.[23] A revolution that was voluntary had to be presented as improvement rather than disruption, familiar rather than foreign.

Ironically, the very alienness of Fourier's system also seemed to compel its translation into a language middle-class Americans understood. Fourier's "theory of universal unity" was in actuality a disorganized compendium of ideas that began with a psychology of the human "passions" and exploded almost without warning into precise community specifications, detailed indictments of contemporary civilization, sexual and epicurean fantasies, "proofs" of theological doctrines, and speculations on the beginning and end of history. From this vast and idiosyncratic system Brisbane and the Brook Farmers pared down Fourier's system to a flexible and persuasive community blueprint—taking special care to weed out Fourier's predictions that strange new animal species would emerge in "Harmonic" society and his evident delight in listing future varieties of sexual liberation. The vocabulary of "passions" and "attractions" was transcendentalized into the realm of "the soul"; Fourier's neologisms such as "series" and "phalansteries" became "work groups" and "unitary dwellings." Rather than rest their doctrine upon an erratic and potentially subversive foreign genius, the Brook Farmers called it "Association" or "social science," not Fourierism.[24]

Most important, the Brook Farmers sensed that their audiences required reassurance that, despite its grounding in the universal and secular categories of the European Enlightenment, the Fourierist vision fit with the noblest aspirations of evangelical Christianity and American nationhood. Fourier's theory, like the "scientific" socialism that followed it, repudiated the idea of national uniqueness. Its critique of competitive "Civilization" indicated the web in which the developed countries were enmeshed and toward which the entire world was evolving; its solution, the phalanx, was based upon an abstract, universalist analysis of human nature rather than national or regional cultures. By contrast, Brook Farmers not only found a special place for the United States in Fourier's scheme; they argued insistently that far from repudiating American values, utopian socialism was merely a more effective way to realize the consensual goals of republicanism, democracy, Protestant Christianity, and missionary nationalism. In its American guise Fourier's strange and wonderful utopia became, in short, the loyal opposition.

Brook Farm's Fourierists were especially adept, for example, at assimilating the rhetoric of millennial Christianity. Much like the prevalent liberal-Protestant teleology, the American edition of Fourier's theory envisioned a centuries-long reign of love at the climax of human history. The utopia to be brought by phalanxes became identical in Fourierist minds to the biblical millennial kingdom. "Our ulterior aim," wrote Charles Dana, "is nothing less than Heaven on Earth."[25] Lectures and tracts cast the Fourierists as prophets heralding a New Jerusalem where instincts would be guided to cooperative harmony and become truly divine. Christ's second coming would take the form of a redeemed society. By grafting the progressive eschatology of utopian socialism onto Christian salvation history, the Fourierists transferred to their movement some of the breathless urgency, prophetic power, and inspiring optimism of the antebellum evangelical awakening.

Yet in contrast to the universal kingdom implied in scripture, the utopians forecast an emphatically American millennium, commenced and climaxed on American soil. In expounding their critique of American society

CARL J. GUARNERI

the Fourierists ventured to the verge of repudiating exceptionalism. With unusual decisiveness and clarity, their manifestoes denied the fundamental uniqueness of American social and economic institutions, insisting that competitive capitalism, here as in Europe, was heading toward a new feudalism that would place workers in bondage to banks, corporations, and machines. "The civilization[s] of Europe and of the United States are of one and the same stock," Ripley declared. Channing elaborated: "the tendencies of society here are identically the same with those which have brought, or are rapidly bringing, every nation in Europe to the dizzy verge of revolution.... This Republic of the United States [has] exactly the same struggle between Capital and Labor, between Aristocracy and the Working Classes, which the monarchies of the Old World are shaken with."[26] But when they switched from diagnosing social ills to promoting the Fourierist antidote, utopians retreated to the national mythology of uniqueness. Thanks to its late discovery and vast domain, the United States, they claimed, had been granted a crucial grace period before the onset of neo-feudal oppression. If the public acted quickly, while the young nation's institutions were still malleable and class antagonisms not yet hardened, America could lead the way to Harmonic bliss. Indeed, by declaring that Europe had already capitulated, Fourierist spokesmen could conclude that it was up to America alone to save the world for a cooperative future. The United States was humanity's second chance, the "social savior of the enslaved, degraded and suffering millions throughout the world," the utopian-socialist Promised Land.[27] (It is not surprising that in 1844 French Fourierists, disturbed by such exceptionalist rhetoric, broke off discussions with their American counterparts that were meant to lead to transatlantic cooperative ventures.[28])

Once welcomed into Fourierist ideology, messianic nationalism brought along familiar markers of America's beneficent uniqueness which were supposed to guarantee communitarians' success: the pragmatic cast of mind necessitated by the frontier, the advantages of cheap land and middle-class mores, the participatory spirit encouraged by representative government. Republican habits and institutions would play a supporting role as communitarian experiments matured and spread.

For all its talk of replacing "the whole system" this utopia had not severed its ties with the grand national utopia. Far from subverting "America," the Fourierist revolution was meant to realize its promise. A national landscape planted with phalanxes became the "true" version of American utopianism. To Brisbane and Ripley, Fourierism was simply "the continuation, the completion of our great political movement of 1776" by which Americans would "consummate the great work of Reform commenced by their noble ancestors." The principles of liberty and equality given political form in the Declaration of Independence and Constitution would now be extended to America's social system. The result would be "the organization of human rights in social institutions."[29] By linking small and relatively self-sufficient cooperative "townships" the Fourierist plan would complement the Founders' decentralized system of government. Channing, John Dwight, and the Brook Farmers envisioned a utopian-socialist substructure peacefully inserted beneath the federal political system and grounding its national motto of "many made one."[30]

Such rhetoric tied Fourierism to an alternative conception of America's mission. Like mainstream nationalists the New England Fourierists declared that the New World's discovery was "providential" and reminded hearers that the nation's "peculiar opportunities" imposed exacting "responsibilities." But instead of—or in addition to—material prosperity and republican institutions, the United States was, they believed, summoned "to manifest before the Nations of the Earth, the possibility and reality of a brotherhood of Freemen, united by Justice, and of multitudes made One by Love."[31] Onto this new claim for the "City on a Hill" Fourierist spokesmen transferred the covenant rhetoric of their Puritan forebears. "Acknowledging, as we do, our providential mission to fulfill the law of love, and professing . . . to encourage each and every member of our communities in the exercise of their inalienable rights, we stand before the face of God and fellow-nations, as guilty of hypocrisy and a breach of trust," Channing scolded during the depression of the early 1840s.

> [W]e deserve the retributions, losses, disgraces, which our savage robberies of the Indians, our cruel and wanton oppressions of the Africans, our unjust habits of white serfdom, our grasping national ambition, our eagerness for wealth, our deceitful modes of external and internal trade, our jealous competitions between different professions and callings, our aping of aristocratic distinctions, our licentiousness and sensuality, our profligate expenditures, public and private, have brought, and will continue to bring upon us.[32]

Here was the Brook Farm Fourierists' jeremiad, their version of the exhortatory Puritan sermon, which Bercovitch claims became identified for three centuries with conceptions of America's mission and which limited dissent to a lamentation of departure from American ideals.[33] To be sure, the Fourierists' commitment to nationalism was an endorsement of America's potential rather than its present, inspired by communitarianism not individualism. But the rhythms of the Fourierist appeal were precisely those of millennial nationalism, with its litany of advantages and responsibilities and its alternating visions of impending judgment and heavenly promise. The jeremiad effectively synchronized utopian socialism with American nationalism.

But in doing so it brought the summons to dissent into the ritual of consensus. "A dominant culture takes root," T. J. Jackson Lears has suggested, "not by imposing ideology, but by addressing utopian longings."[34] The Brook Farmers' vocabulary of American ideals couched in Protestant-nationalist rhetoric harnessed their program to the historical project of "America," that utopian dream that effectively channeled challenge into confirmation of the dominant order. By invoking national "destiny" and the social millennium these New England Fourierists joined a respectable native tradition of dissent, one that had reached a kind of crescendo in the spirit of "boundlessness" infecting antebellum political ideologies and the perfectionist dreams of middle-class reform.[35] It was as easy to hear the rhythms and rhetoric of the nation's utopian venture within Fourierist rhapsodies as within other antebellum manifestoes, such as the *Democratic Review*'s jingoistic essays promoting Manifest Destiny, the Washingtonians' declaration that "all men are created *temperate*"—or for that matter, Emerson's assertion that radical individualism was America's unique contribution to Anglo-American thought.[36] This kind of recognition cut two ways, functioning as revision but also as reassurance. As long as "special utopias" echoed the national one, little that was fundamental was being questioned.

Granted, the Fourierists' utopia was the phalanx, not the family farm, business enterprise, or the self-reliant individual. The Brook Farmers' attack upon individualism and Brisbane's claim that social equality was "far more precious" than political liberty carried potentially subversive implications for competitive capitalist institutions and even for American nationalism.[37] Yet the revolution the Brook Farmers proposed never took them far from the American mainstream. The material premises of the Fourierist utopia, much like its rhetorical structure, were interpreted in ways that harmonized communitarian aims with an idealized version of American practice.

Within its community frame American Fourierism incorporated many of the assumptions, arrangements, and promises of liberal capitalism. While Fourier based the elaborate guarantees for individual expression in his phalanxes on an uncompromisingly radical "passional psychology," his American followers defended phalanx individualism on economic grounds as a semicapitalist alternative to free competition that stopped well short of the "tyranny" of "communism" (the abolition of private property). Members retained shares in the Brook Farm Phalanx as private property, which was deemed "inviolable," and investors were promised a healthy return on their capital. An elaborate accounting system was set up to administer a modified wage plan with differential rewards for skill and type of work. Again, where Fourier prescribed frequent rotation of tasks and division of labor into specialized groups in order to gratify a basic human desire for fulfillment in work, the Americans praised them for raising productivity and wedding each member's interests to the others'. The phalanx economy was supposed to run as smoothly as a self-regulated machine, replicating the natural order of society. "In Association," Brisbane wrote, "*Selfishness will be rendered Social* and be made to serve the interests of the whole."[38] Presented this way, Fourierist arrangements functioned as a "visible hand" analogous to the invisible one that laissez-faire capitalists believed guided free-market competition to the common good.

As for the bourgeois family, which Fourier had lambasted as the font of hypocritical morality and the seed of selfishness, it would be left unchanged in the American phalanx, but now purified because affections would be freed from "domestic cares and anxieties." The real problem, Ripley and John Dwight reassured readers, was the economically inefficient "isolated household," not the middle-class family or monogamous marriage.[39] By socializing domestic chores the Fourierist "revolution" would renovate the kitchen but stop well short of the bedroom.

To hear these assurances is to sense Marx and Engels's frustration that utopian socialists were "compelled to appeal to the feelings and purses of the bourgeois" and to recognize some truth in the *Communist Manifesto*'s claim that "although the originators of these systems were, in many respects, revolutionary, their disciples have . . . formed mere reactionary sects."[40] Not quite; but as presented by the Brook Farmers and their colleagues Fourierism proved so close to conventional American ways that it was less an alternative *to* them than an alternative version *of* them. Their utopia was framed not as an irreconcilable enemy of American society but as an attractive rival for the allegiance of Americans and the destiny of their nation.

Seeing Fourierism as a rival Americanism not only allows us to watch it squander its subversive ideological potential; it helps explain its meteoric rise and fall as a social movement. In the emotionally charged atmosphere of antebellum debate, the Brook Farmers' and Brisbane's formulation had instant appeal for thousands of northerners who were drawn to communitarian reform but were reluctant to depart from old allegiances. Yet Fourierism's structure of accommodation-within-dissent also played a crucial role in the failure of the movement. In his penetrating essay on the concept of cultural hegemony, one that complements Bercovitch's ap-

proach, Lears points out that radical movements contesting a ruling
group's authority could be undermined by such ideological ambivalence,
which Gramsci called "divided consciousness": "Subordinate groups could
identify with the dominant culture—often for sound reasons—even as
they sought to challenge it. And that challenge could be undermined by
such identification."[41]

As young ministers and incipient professionals, Brook Farm's Fourierist
spokesmen qualified less as a "subordinate group" than as leaders of a "historical bloc," Gramsci's term for a cross-class coalition bound by religious
or ideological ties as well as economic interests, an alliance that then seeks
to achieve cultural hegemony or wrest it away from its dominant voices.[42]
But Lears's basic point still holds: beneath their manifestoes and critiques,
the Fourierists' fundamental commitment to the ideals and values of the
American consensus diluted their social criticism and undermined the
movement. Their belief in property rights, Protestant morality, and peaceful progress gave legitimacy to mainstream American culture even as they
attempted to supplant its society. Externally, accommodations to individualism and capitalism left the phalanxes vulnerable to market pressures and
profit-seeking shareholders; internally, the retention of private property
rendered each phalanx a "house divided against itself," as one Fourierist
veteran complained.[43]

For Brook Farmers, the boost in capital, morale, and social relevance
that came from joining the national movement proved short-lived; it was
undermined by the national leaders' determination to achieve quick economic success. Richard Francis, echoing Lindsay Swift, notes that Brook
Farm's conversion to Fourierism "took the participants away from their
local sustenance, that tightly knit and highly focused cultural scene that
provided them with so much of their energy and idealism."[44] Local sympathy did not translate into adequate material support, but the endorsement
of Fourierism's national and New York leaders proved little better. Brisbane's suggestion early in 1845 that Fourierists nationwide concentrate
their efforts on turning Brook Farm into the movement's "model phalanx"
was retracted by the year's end. Brook Farm's agricultural and workshop
operations had expanded slowly and failed to turn a profit, and the New
York Fourierist leaders preferred the North American Phalanx in New Jersey or a fresh start elsewhere. "Fifteen thousand dollars might do a great
deal at Brook Farm," Brisbane told Ripley unfeelingly, "but would it do the
thing effectually—would it make a trial that would impress the public?" He
now suggested "bringing Brook Farm to a close, and making preparations
for a trial under more favorable circumstances."[45] Left to themselves, the
Brook Farmers continued their expansion and stretched their resources to

the limit until a fire in March 1846 destroyed their nearly completed central dwelling, or "phalanstery," making their dissolution inevitable.

Similar conflicts between anxious investors and committed community members occurred in the other miniature American phalanxes, and most communities compounded these problems with internal conflicts over Fourier's modified wage structure or the degree of communal living required of members. As a result, they suffered brief and troubled lives: of the twenty-four Fourierist communities founded between 1842 and 1846, only five survived for as much as three years.[46] Many were the victims of internal disputes over "whether the infant Association should . . . be Civilisee [i.e., conventional] or Phalansterian," and none attained a material standard of living as prosperous as middle-class life outside them.[47] As the conflicts and disappointments lingered, the communitarian promise of freedom, harmony, and abundance appeared increasingly hollow; it was, at any rate, too close to prevailing ideals to compel lasting commitment once the depression of the early 1840s lifted and economic prospects brightened.

To make matters even worse, Brook Farmers developed in *The Harbinger* an evolutionary version of cooperation that enabled them to see utopian-socialist ideals in such solidly mainstream institutions as "benevolent associations, railroads, steamboats, and especially . . . large manufactories."[48] As the movement faded, in increasingly compensatory fashion this misty optimism merged the Fourierist future, faith in progress, and American social trends into a benign and indistinguishable whole. With one foot in the dominant culture, these Fourierists were unable to stand apart from the ideological consolidation of the 1850s, in which the emerging free-soil and free-labor version of Americanism sanctified northern capitalism and unified the section against the southern threat. Not surprisingly, Brook Farm's erstwhile utopian-socialist leaders became enterprising journalists, private businessmen, Republican Party spokesmen, and—eventually—Union heroes in the Civil War. It was only fitting that Brook Farm ended its days as a Union camp where soldiers were trained to defend the free-labor society against its Southern enemies.[49]

For the Brook Farm Fourierists as for other antebellum idealists, the problem of agitating for an alternative utopia in America proved to be a dilemma: absorbing the rhetoric of American nationalism risked losing the very identity of dissent; ignoring it—if it was possible—risked sectarian marginalization. When the Brook Farmers adopted Fourierism they linked their local experiment to an alternative version of the national project; when they translated utopian socialism into native idioms they made it persuasive and popular, but they also left it fatally vulnerable to absorption. In the end, their promotion of Fourierism turned out to be much like what

Bercovitch has called "the Americanization of utopia," a "ritual recycling of
the energies of radical change into structures of continuity" that affirm the
American system even as they challenge it, and thus dilute utopian dissent
into loyal opposition.[50]

Could it have been otherwise? Did the rhetoric of utopianism inevitably
transport its nineteenth-century American practitioners to the United
States of Utopia? A radical critique of cultural complicity and co-optation
implies that one can be *in* a culture but somehow not *of* it; more specifically in this case, it implies that dissenters could hope to effect social
change by advocating ideas or programs truly alien to whatever held
together the society at large. One cannot ask critics to transcend their culture—the very expression is probably oxymoronic. To frame judgments
this way would be to ignore much of what we know about the thick atmosphere in which human societies evolve and from which they draw their
life. Indeed, to expect "transcendence" is to be swayed by the same false
promise of self-reliance and a mystical relation to everyday social reality
that the Brook Farmers and later social activists criticized in Emersonian
individualism.[51]

Nonetheless, a posture of critical distance from national symbology
can be demanded if not expected. While acknowledging the conformist
pressures of American culture, we should notice that the Brook Farmers
increasingly *chose* to mine the storehouse of national myth. Like abolitionists, feminists, and other antebellum reformers—indeed like their nemesis
Emerson—these utopians faced the decision of whether to translate their
programs and ideals into the discourse of Americanism or to ignore or resist that symbolic universe. By the late 1840s Emerson chose the former
and was well on his way to harmonizing Transcendentalist self-culture with
the invisible hand of American capitalism. Among communitarian groups
there was a range of responses, from the Shakers' relative isolation from
cultural debates about America, with their resulting survival as a small
sect, to the Fourierists' immersion in the national symbolic, with their consequent evanescent popularity. Somewhere between stood the Mormons,
who in a sense reinvented the Puritan "errand into the wilderness" but only
got away with their parallel utopia until national expansion caught up with
them in the 1880s.

A half-century after the Brook Farmers nationalized their utopia, Edward Bellamy penned the most popular utopian fantasy of the entire
century, *Looking Backward* (1888). Bellamy had traveled a route from
Transcendentalism to a diluted, Americanized socialism that was remark-

ably similar to the Brook Farmers'. As a young idealist raised in western Massachusetts, Bellamy absorbed Emersonian conceptions of self-culture, the poet-seer, and the Over-Soul into his imaginary glimpses of an ideal world. In the early 1870s he turned, as had Channing and the Brook Farmers, to the concept of the "solidarity of the race" as justification for collective reform. *Looking Backward* merged the impulse toward solidarity with urban-industrialism. When its hero, Julian West, awoke in Boston in the year 2000 he encountered a bureaucratic and technological utopia that would have seemed oppressive to antebellum communitarians, although Bellamy saw it as the heir of "the Brook Farm Colony and a score of phalansteries," and although he, too, proclaimed his utopia "'the new heavens and the new earth . . .' which the prophet foretold."[52]

Bellamy deliberately set out to make socialism respectable in America by separating it from subversive cultural ideas, including foreign theories, "an abusive tone about God and religion," and "all manner of sexual novelties." He called his doctrine Nationalism to emphasize that capital and labor needed to be nationalized peacefully by the voting public. Bellamy preferred the term to socialism because of its ties to the American consensus: "Socialist is not a good name for a party to succeed in America. No such party can or ought to succeed which is not wholly and enthusiastically American and patriotic in spirit and suggestions."[53] In *Equality* (1897), the sequel to *Looking Backward*, and in his movement's journals Bellamy set out to show that the Nationalist "Great Revolution" was only the fulfillment of the promise of equality embodied in the Declaration of Independence; perhaps it was even a conserving "counter-revolution," aiming for the "maintenance of republican institutions against the revolution . . . being effected by the money power."[54]

Well into the twentieth century, American socialists consciously and unconsciously tried to overcome their private and public alienation by "putting themselves in some kind of proper relationship with the Americanism of the era," as Warren Susman noted.[55] After a shrewd examination of such attempts and their co-optation, Susman asked plaintively:

> Why have we [socialists] allowed sentiment and rhetoric to replace the good hard work of analysis and deep thought? Why have we so often found ourselves playing the Americanization game ending up ironically reinforcing the order we propose to change[?] . . . Have we really been wise in our pursuit of Americanism in an effort to capture it for socialism, or has that very Americanism ended up capturing us because we have not been sufficiently self-aware or self-critical? . . . Must Americanism win?[56]

466   CARL J. GUARNERI

Lauren Berlant, at the end of her admirable charting of Nathaniel Hawthorne's complex maneuvers within the symbolic field of utopia, suggests that it is about time for the historical nation, the United States, to shed its utopian "A"—that "scarlet letter" at the beginning of "America." Today's utopians must "develop tactics for refusing the interarticulation, now four hundred years old, between the United States and America, the nation and utopia." Feminist, ecological, and other radical agendas, she contends, should be advocated "without reference to the national frame, which has been sullied by its long exploitation of the dream of political happiness it has expressed."[57]

Can American radicals become post-nationalist utopians? *Should* they? A recent profusion of ecological and feminist utopias, which at their most ambitious seek to transcend patriarchal or exploitive practices that have been tied to nationalism, may betoken a more cosmopolitan direction to American radicalism.[58] Perhaps feminist or planetary consciousness can become viable candidates for the non-national identities Berlant invokes. An alternative, localistic path would be to cultivate particularist ethnic, racial, and sexual identities against the claims of the liberal nation-state, as some multiculturalists currently urge—though not as yet in the language of utopianism. Beset by the threat of fragmentation that such "identity politics" poses, some leftists have sought to revise the "American dream" to make it more inclusive. Indeed, the rhetoric of America remains alluring as a rousing way to frame—and to contain—reform energies: witness, for example, Richard Rorty's recent call for the American left to revive its national pride and to fight for political and economic changes that will "achieve our country."[59] Whichever new directions American dissenters explore, they will have to face the resilient tradition of American exceptionalism and will have to cope with the dilemma of nationalism that the Brook Farmers' faced. As alternative utopias strive to reach a popular audience and to shape the development of a post-industrial, post-patriarchal, multicultural United States, it would not be surprising if the perils and promises they foresee were still couched in the rhetoric of the jeremiad and the symbolic vocabulary of the American experiment.

NOTES

1. William Henry Channing quoted in "Convention of the New England Fourier Society," *The Phalanx* 1(Feb. 8, 1845):310, 315, 309.
2. Daniel Boorstin, *The Genius of American Politics* (Chicago, 1953), 173–174. In responding to Boorstin's claim, this essay draws upon evidence from my history of American Fourierism, *The Utopian Alternative: Fourierism in Nineteenth-Century*

America (Ithaca, 1991), and subsequent research. A preliminary version appeared as "The Americanization of Utopia: Fourierism and the Dilemma of Utopian Dissent in the United States," in *Utopian Studies* 5(1994):72–88; portions of that essay are reprinted here by permission.

3. For European utopian visions of America, see Howard Mumford Jones, *O Strange New World: American Culture—The Formative Years* (New York, 1967), 1–70; Mircea Eliade, "Paradise and Utopia: Mythical Geography and Eschatology," in *Utopias and Utopian Thought*, ed. Frank E. Manuel (Boston, 1966), 260–280; Edmund O'Gorman, *The Invention of America: An Inquiry into the Historical Nature of the New World and Its Meaning* (Bloomington, 1961); and Hugh Honour, *The New Golden Land: European Images of America from the Discoveries to the Present Time* (New York, 1975).

4. On the appropriation of utopia by American nationalism, see Charles L. Sanford, *The Quest for Paradise: Europe and the American Moral Imagination* (Urbana, 1961); Ernest Lee Tuveson, *Redeemer Nation: The Idea of America's Millenial Role* (Chicago, 1968); and Lawrence Friedman, *Inventors of the Promised Land* (New York, 1975). For the more general point that modern nations such as the United States are "imagined political communities" that employ technology to popularize "invented traditions," see Benedict Anderson, *Imagined Communities: Reflections on the Origins and Spread of Nationalism* (London, 1983); and Eric Hobsbawm and Terence Rogers, eds., *The Invention of Tradition* (Cambridge, 1983).

5. Frances Fitzgerald, *Cities on a Hill: A Journey through Contemporary American Cultures* (New York, 1987), 23–24.

6. Sacvan Bercovitch, *The Office of the Scarlet Letter* (Baltimore and London, 1991), 142. For the quotation from Emerson, see "New England Reformers," in *The Complete Works of Ralph Waldo Emerson*, ed. Edward Waldo Emerson (Boston, 1903–1904), 3:267.

7. Sacvan Bercovitch, *The Rites of Assent: Transformations in the Symbolic Construction of America* (New York and London, 1993), 19.

8. Bercovitch, *Rites of Assent*, 19.

9. T. J. Jackson Lears, "The Concept of Cultural Hegemony: Problems and Possibilities," *American Historical Review* 90(1985):571; Bercovitch, *Rites of Assent*, 19. See Walter L. Adamson, *Hegemony and Revolution: A Study of Antonio Gramsci's Political and Cultural Theory* (Berkeley and Los Angeles, 1980), 174.

10. Guarneri, *Utopian Alternative*, 381–382; Bercovitch, "Emerson, Individualism, and Liberal Dissent," *Rites of Assent*, 307–352. For a fuller exposition of how "individualism" crossed the Atlantic and entered American dialectics, see Yehoshua Arieli, *Individualism and Nationalism in American Ideology* (Baltimore, 1966).

11. For example, Dorothy Ross, *The Origins of American Social Science* (New York, 1991), uncovers the "deep structure" of exceptionalism that provided the foundation for American social scientists' response to socialism from the 1870s onward. For recent contributions to the debate over exceptionalism in American history, see Michael Kammen, "The Problem of American Exceptionalism: A Reconsideration," *American Quarterly* 45(1993):1–43; Byron E. Shafer, ed., *Is America Different? A New Look at American Exceptionalism* (New York, 1991); and Ian Tyrrell, "American Exceptionalism in an Age of International History," *American Historical Review* 96(1991):1031–1055.

12. Bercovitch, *Office*, 138.

13. Charles R. Crowe, "Transcendentalist Support of Brook Farm: A Paradox?" *The Historian* 21(1959):281.

14. See Perry Miller, ed., *The Transcendentalists: An Anthology* (Cambridge, Mass., 1950), 464; Crowe, "Transcendentalist Support of Brook Farm"; and Charles R. Crowe, "'This Unnatural Union of Phalansteries and Transcendentalists,'" *Journal of the History of Ideas* 20(1959):495–502.

15. John Thomas Codman, *Brook Farm: Historic and Personal Memoirs* (Boston, 1894), 227.

16. Miller, *The Transcendentalists*, 469; Lindsay Swift, *Brook Farm: Its Members, Scholars, and Visitors* (New York, 1900), 135.

17. Richard Francis, *Transcendental Utopias: Individual and Community at Brook Farm, Fruitlands, and Walden* (Ithaca, 1997), 71.

18. Carl J. Guarneri, "The Associationists: Forging a Christian Socialism in Antebellum America," *Church History* 52(1983):36–49; Francis, *Transcendental Utopias*, 115–136; Zoltan Haraszti, *The Idyll of Brook Farm* (Boston, 1937), 27.

19. W. H. Channing, "A Confession of Faith," *The Present* 1(Sept. 1843):6, 9; Marianne Dwight, *Letters from Brook Farm, 1844–1847*, ed. Amy L. Reed (Poughkeepsie, N.Y., 1928), 55.

20. George Ripley to Ralph Waldo Emerson, Nov. 9, 1840, in Octavius Brooks Frothingham, *George Ripley* (Boston, 1883), 310.

21. Miller, *The Transcendentalists*, 464.

22. John S. Dwight, "Another 'Latest Form of Infidelity,'" *Boston Daily Chronotype*, Sept. 4, 1849.

23. Arthur Bestor, Jr., *Backwoods Utopias: The Sectarian Origins and the Owenite Phase of Communitarian Socialism in America, 1663–1829*, 2d ed. (Philadelphia, 1970), 1–19.

24. Guarneri, *Utopian Alternative*, 93–98. For the most complete account of Fourier's wide-ranging theory, see Jonathan Beecher, *Charles Fourier: The Visionary and His World* (Berkeley and Los Angeles, 1986), 193–352.

25. Charles A. Dana, "A Lecture on Association, in Its Connection with Religion," in *Association, in Its Connection with Education and Religion* (Boston, 1844), 26.

26. George Ripley, "Tendencies of Modern Civilization," *The Harbinger* 1(June 28, 1845):35; W. H. Channing, "The Philadelphia Riots," *The Phalanx* 1(May 18, 1844): 31.

27. John S. Dwight, "Democracy versus Social Reform," *The Harbinger* 5(Oct. 16, 1847):302; Albert Brisbane, "The Question of Slavery," *The Harbinger* 1(June 21, 1845):31.

28. Guarneri, *Utopian Alternative*, 250–251.

29. Albert Brisbane and Osborne Macdaniel, "Exposition of Views and Principles," *The Phalanx* 1 (Oct. 5, 1843):8, 4; George Ripley, "The Fourth of July," *The Harbinger* 1(June 21, 1845):32.

30. "Convention of the New England Fourier Society," 315; W. H. Channing, "Many United in One," *The Harbinger* 1(July 26, 1845):111; John S. Dwight, "E Pluribus Unum," *Boston Daily Chronotype*, Sept. 24, 1849.

31. "General Convention of the Friends of Association in the United States," *The Phalanx* 1(Apr. 20, 1844):105; "Convention of the New England Fourier Society," 309.

32. Channing, "Confession of Faith," 9.
33. Sacvan Bercovitch, *The American Jeremiad* (Madison, 1978), 132–210.
34. T. J. Jackson Lears, "Power, Culture, and Money," *Journal of American History* 75(1988):139.
35. John Higham, *From Boundlessness to Consolidation: The Transformation of American Culture, 1848–1860* (Ann Arbor, 1969); John L. Thomas, "Romantic Reform in America, 1815–1865," *American Quarterly* 17(1965):656–681.
36. *A Second Declaration of Independence; Or, the Manifesto of All the Washington Total Abstinence Societies of the United States of America* (Worcester, Mass., 1841), 3; Emerson, *Complete Works*, 5:287.
37. Brisbane and Macdaniel, "Exposition," 4.
38. Albert Brisbane, *Association; or, a Concise Exposition of the Practical Part of Fourier's Social Science* (New York, 1843), 35.
39. George Ripley, "Influence of Association upon Women," *The Harbinger* 3(Sept. 27, 1846):253; John S. Dwight, "How Stands the Cause?" *The Harbinger* 3(Nov. 7, 1846):350.
40. Karl Marx and Friedrich Engels, "Manifesto of the Communist Party," in *Basic Writings on Politics and Philosophy*, ed. Lewis S. Feuer (Garden City, N.Y., 1959), 39.
41. Lears, "Concept of Cultural Hegemony," 576.
42. Lears, "Concept of Cultural Hegemony," 571.
43. Alcander Longley, "Life in the North American Phalanx," *Social Record* 1(Sept. 1858):31.
44. Francis, *Transcendental Utopias*, 136.
45. Albert Brisbane to George Ripley, Dec. 9, 1845, reprinted in Codman, *Brook Farm*, 144–146.
46. Guarneri, *Utopian Alternative*, 153.
47. John Humphrey Noyes, *History of American Socialisms* (Philadelphia, 1870), 454.
48. John Gray, quoted in Noyes, *American Socialisms*, 480. See also George Ripley, "Rail Road to the Pacific," *The Harbinger* 4(Dec. 19, 1846):30–31.
49. Guarneri, *Utopian Alternative*, 344–345, 382–383.
50. Sacvan Bercovitch, "Investigations of an Americanist," *Journal of American History* 78(1991):983.
51. Brook Farm's Charles Dana, for example, saw Emerson's Transcendentalism as "the poetical and mystical expression of the Ego-ism which makes modern life so mean." Dana, "Review of *Studies in Religion*," *The Harbinger* 1(Nov. 15, 1845): 362.
52. Edward Bellamy, "Progress of Nationalism in the United States," *North American Review* 154(June 1892):743; Bellamy, *Looking Backward, 2000–1887*, ed. John L. Thomas (1888; Cambridge, Mass., 1967), 226.
53. Edward Bellamy, quoted in Michael Fellman, *The Unbounded Frame: Freedom and Community in Nineteenth-Century American Utopianism* (Westport, Conn., 1973), 123.
54. Edward Bellamy, *Edward Bellamy Speaks Again!* (Kansas City, Mo., 1937), 59.
55. Warren I. Susman, "Socialism and Americanism," in his *Culture as History: Transformations in Twentieth-Century American Culture* (New York, 1984), 78.
56. Susman, "Socialism and Americanism," 84–85.

57. Lauren Berlant, *The Anatomy of National Fantasy: Hawthorne, Utopia, and Everyday Life* (Chicago, 1991), 217.

58. See Frances Bartkowski, *Feminist Utopias* (Lincoln, Neb., 1989); and Boris Frankel, *The Post-Industrial Utopians* (Cambridge, 1987).

59. Richard Rorty, *Achieving Our Country: Leftist Thought in Twentieth-Century America* (Cambridge, Mass., 1998).

Beyond Transcendentalism

The Radical Individualism of William B. Greene

Philip F. Gura

EMEMBERED TODAY ONLY FOR HIS EARLY PUBLISHED ASSESS-
ment of Transcendentalism, William Batchelder Greene once stood
in the vanguard of America's Party of Hope, one of those young men whom
Ralph Waldo Emerson later remembered as having "knives in their brain,"
so intent were they on dissecting all inherited systems of belief. Indeed,
in the 1840s Greene had made so strong an impression in Boston and Concord that even so severe a judge as Margaret Fuller described him as "the
military-spiritual-heroico-vivacious phoenix of the day."[1] As we seek to understand Transcendentalism and its legacy more fully, Greene, as well as
others in his cohort, warrants attention, particularly as an example of what
exotic fruit the "New Thought" bore in its second generation and beyond.

Graduating from the Harvard Divinity School in the mid 1840s, Greene
shortly thereafter brought Transcendentalism to the hinterlands by assuming a Unitarian pulpit seventy miles west of Boston and there set about
modifying and extending the principles of "liberal" religion.[2] His religious
beliefs eventuated in a sharp critique of America's burgeoning economy.
An early association with Orestes Brownson, for example, had led to an interest in and the subsequent adoption of the principles of Pierre Leroux
and Philippe Buchez; from there he found his way to the "mutualism" of
Pierre-Joseph Proudhon, an intellectual odyssey indicative of how Transcendentalism's centripetal force might push individuals in ever more
radical directions.[3] Thus, by the late 1840s, in an elaborate program for
economic and social reform based in Leroux's and Proudhon's ideas, and
leavened by a profoundly catholic spirituality, Greene eclipsed even Brook
Farm's Fourierists in his challenge to America's market economy.[4]

One of Greene's eulogists noted that he "could not but wonder at the
fatality which prevented [Greene] from making that mark on the public

mind which he made on all the individual minds that came within the sphere of his influence." "He was intended for a great man," this writer continued, prefiguring Emerson's problematic assessment of Henry David Thoreau, "but some subtle element in his nature prevented him from realizing the distinction to which his powers evidently pointed." Greene should be judged more charitably, for his unique spiritual pilgrimage and the reform activity it engendered are worth detailing as examples of how Transcendentalists took with utter seriousness Emerson's counsel to live as "Man Thinking." More than just another dreamy youth oscillating in Emerson's rainbow, from his pulpit and with his pen, Greene contributed significantly to the ferment of antebellum reform. As the Concord sage himself put it after he first met the young man, Greene seemed nothing less than "a special answer to a special prayer."[5]

Greene was born in Haverhill, Massachusetts, April 4, 1819, the son of Nathaniel Greene and Susan Batchelder. His father was a newspaper editor who eventually established the *Boston Statesman*, a leading Democratic journal, and whose prominence in party politics secured him the position of Boston postmaster between 1829 and 1849.[6] In addition to his political interests, Nathaniel had a strong literary bent, writing for various periodicals and publishing in book form translations of tales in French, German, and Italian, activities that would resonate strongly in his son.

Evidently believing that a sure way to preferment lay in military service, early in 1834 Nathaniel wrote to Lewis Cass, secretary of war, requesting his son William's admission to the United States Military Academy at West Point. Testimonials appended to the application indicate the young man's preparation at several academies in Massachusetts and also, in 1833, a stay of several months in Paris with a relative and a tutor, a signal experience given William's subsequent interest in French social thought. The application was successful, and Greene attended West Point from July 1, 1835, until November 15, 1837, when he withdrew because of poor health.

He returned to Boston to convalesce but within a year restarted his military career by volunteering for duty in the Seminole War (1835–1842), then being waged in Florida. His commission supported by no less a personage than Sen. Daniel Webster, Greene was made second lieutenant and sent in July 1839 to Florida, where he served until November 1841. He abruptly resigned, again ostensibly due to ill health; but his own testimony, as well as that of his friend Elizabeth Peabody, indicates that during this time he went through a profound spiritual crisis, the resolution of which pushed him toward a career in the ministry.[7]

Upon leaving the army Greene joined the Charles Street Baptist Church—he had been raised "in the Calvinistic faith"—but at about this same time, perhaps at the prodding of Orestes Brownson, a family friend, he also stepped boldly into the world of the Transcendentalists, visiting at Brook Farm, for example, and browsing at Elizabeth Peabody's West Street bookstore where, the *grande dame* of Transcendentalism later recalled, he sought an edition of Kant in some language other than German. Peabody was enough impressed—she was struck, she recalled, by "a different cast and method of thought" from that to which she was accustomed—to introduce him to her mentor, the Reverend William Ellery Channing. Soon enough Greene was visiting Emerson himself. Taken under the latter's wing like so many other promising youths, by January 1842 Greene had published in *The Dial* an essay on "First Principles" and was encouraged to attend various of the "conversations" then so central to Transcendentalism's development.[8]

Later that spring Greene again visited Emerson, probably to ask for advice about the ministry. He decided to study at the Newton Theological Institution, a Baptist seminary. Newton's records indicate, however, that while Greene felt it "his duty to be making some preparation for the ministry," he was "not settled in regard to the particular course which he ought to pursue." Fortunately, the Institution was willing to offer him the freedom to work through his faith, and for a year and a half he remained essentially a special student, taking courses of interest and examining "some of the proof texts in favor of the doctrine of a tri-personal Godhead." After studying such passages "in their connections, and in the light of the original language in which the New Testament is written," Greene later wrote, he found that their supposed Trinitarianism "vanished like the morning mist before the rising sun." Thereupon, he went to the president of the Institution and bluntly "told him I was a Unitarian." Thus, in 1844 Greene decided to cross his Rubicon, the Charles, and successfully applied to Harvard's divinity school where, given his theological sophistication, he was enrolled as a senior and quickly made his mark. Thomas Wentworth Higginson, for example, recalled that during that period Greene was one of the "most interesting men in the Divinity School."[9]

We have little information about these years, but clearly throughout his time at Newton Greene remained abreast of Transcendentalist currents. In 1843, for example, he published his first book-length effort, *The Doctrine of Life*, a revision of the essay he had brought out in *The Dial*. In November 1842 Emerson noted that "Lieutenant Greene preached for Brownson a week or more since, with tolerable success," and from Methuen, on August 24, 1842, Greene himself reported to Brownson that he was "getting along famously with the people."[10] Further, two essays that Greene published in the *American Review* in 1845 (and which formed the core of his subsequent evaluation of Transcendentalism) indicate his continued interest in Emerson and the revolution that he had wrought in theological matters. With newfound resolve, Greene threw himself into his studies in Cambridge and graduated in the summer of 1845.

Shortly thereafter he married Anna Shaw, the daughter of Robert G. Shaw, one of Boston's merchant princes. By autumn he was preaching on trial to a small Unitarian church in the rural Massachusetts community of West Brookfield, twenty miles west of Worcester. His liberal Christianity evidently pleased the parish, and in October he accepted its offer of a position. He requested that James Freeman Clarke preach his ordination sermon and that Dr. Francis Parkman, one of the state's stalwart Unitarians, be given a part in the service. Greene was ordained early in November and remained in that pulpit until 1850, when he requested (why is not clear) an end to his pastoral relationship.

Whatever the reason for his request for dismissal, Greene spent his time in West Brookfield productively. In addition to his small book on Transcendentalism, he published two sermons in defense of the Unitarian interpretation of scripture, a refutation of Jonathan Edwards's treatise on the freedom of the will, a lengthy autobiographical account of how he had come to find his liberal faith, a tract on "Equality" in which he proposed solutions to the imbalance that he saw between the worlds of capital and labor, and a treatise on "mutual banking," these last two derived, as we shall see, from his immersion in French social thought. Nor did he neglect his Boston connections, for the "Town and Country Club" that Emerson and others had started claimed as a member this emissary from western Massachusetts, the group's records indicating that Greene was active in its discussions.[11]

After his resignation from the West Brookfield pulpit, Greene joined his father in Paris, where since 1849 he had pursued his literary interests. First-hand acquaintance with French attempts to solve the mid nineteenth century's economic problems led the younger Greene to publish, in Boston in 1857, another economic critique, *The Radical Deficiency of the Existing Circulating Medium and the Advantages of a Mutual Currency*, but other details of his decade abroad remain sketchy. Returning to the United States with the outbreak of the Civil War, Greene once more entered military service. Given his previous experience, he was commissioned a colonel in the First Massachusetts Heavy Artillery and served in various forts around Washington, D.C. By the fall of 1862, though, he again had resigned, evidently because of what he considered uncalled for interference with his command. At the least, from this last exposure to military service Greene acquired the military rank subsequently associated with him.

Greene's marriage into Boston's financial gentry had freed him from quotidian concerns, and after this final military interlude he retired from any conventional profession to spend time in further cogitation and writing, activities that occupied him until his death. In particular, he continued to engage both theological and economic subjects, taking on such new thinkers as Herbert Spencer on the matter of "consciousness" and exploring the mysteries of the Jewish Kabbala. In 1875 he published a collection of his fugitive pieces under the title *Socialistic, Communistic, Mutualistic, and Financial Fragments*, a work whose topics ranged from his favorite hobbyhorse, the mutual bank, to the plight of the working classes, to the issue of free love and the institution of marriage.[12] He gave time, too, to politics. He became vice-president and chairman of the executive committee of the Labor Reform League and was involved with the anarchist platform proposed by E. H. Haywood, to whose journal *The Word* he frequently contributed. Greene spent his last years in England and died at Weston-super-Mare on May 30, 1878, receiving, as "Colonel Greene," lengthy obituaries in all Boston's major papers.[13]

As this brief outline suggests, Greene's life was full and fascinating, in part because of his association with some of America's most well-known intellectuals and reformers, but also because of his own contributions to freedom's ferment. I wish now to look more closely at his publications in the 1840s and early 1850s, when he was most engaged with Transcendentalist thought, for Greene's chief interest is twofold. First, he provides an example of how Transcendentalist thought affected the beliefs and careers of young clergymen reared in conservative rather than liberal Christian churches. Second, Greene allows us to understand better how second-generation Transcendentalists received and modified the ideas of the movement's first exponents.

In this decade two major influences marked Greene's theological development. First—from his very first effort, in *The Dial* in 1842, through his publication by 1850 of essays on the atonement and "remarks" on Edwards's treatise concerning the freedom of the will—Greene strove to reconcile his interest in the "New Thought" with conservative Trinitarian theology in general and with the doctrine of predestination in particular. Indeed, more than any other second-generation liberal Christian minister—and like James Marsh in the 1830s, so important an influence on Emerson and other members of the Transcendental Club—Greene illustrates the continued power of predestinarian theology to shape a liberal understanding of religious reform.[14] Throughout Greene's years as a divinity student and clergyman he struggled to refigure the conservative theological principles in which he had been raised such that they would better agree with the ideals of the religious and social radicalism that he subsequently adopted.

Second, from an early point in Greene's religious development (at the latest, upon his return from the Seminole War) and probably as a result of his contact with Brownson, "an old friend" of his father, the young man had drunk deeply at the well of French social thought. In the 1840s, he admired particularly Buchez's *Introduction à la Science de l'Histoire* (1812, 2d ed. 1842) and Pierre Leroux's *De l'Humanité* (1840).[15] Both Greene's *Dial* essay and his first separate publication, *The Doctrine of Life*, for example, depended heavily on Buchez's elaborately schematized notions of mankind's moral and spiritual development and, concomitantly, on his belief that human progress was predicated on certain spiritual revelations—progress recapitulated in the spiritual development of each individual.[16]

In both authors, Greene found a strong animus against the class divisions that seemed to epitomize nineteenth-century society and that were based primarily in inequalities of property. From Leroux's analysis and discussion of such artificial distinctions among men Greene obtained his sense that human happiness could be attained only through solidarity with the whole race—that is, through a profound identification with and commitment to a classless society. To Leroux and Buchez, acquisitive capitalism, rather than marking the height of civilization, illustrated mankind's capitulation to its baser instincts.[17]

Greene was brought to such ideas by a conversion experience, one which he later reported in detail to Elizabeth Peabody and described autobiographically in his remarks on the atonement (1848) and again in scarcely veiled terms in his *Remarks on the Science of History; Followed by An A Priori Autobiography* (1849). His dark night of the soul occurred in the spring of 1839, when he was still in Florida. Greene had become disenchanted with a war he considered "unjust." Then "one evening," as he told Peabody, "I was walking, about a hundred yards in front of the house in which I lived, when suddenly upon turning to go back, I fell—I felt no pain, no sickness of any kind, and immediately rose again to my feet." He continued:

> I fell again, though still without pain or sickness, and this time I found it difficult to rise. I then crept, as well as I could, on my hands and feet, into the house, and got into bed, and went to sleep. In the

morning I began to feel very ill, and sent my servant for assistance. The doctor came soon, and bled me in my arm, informing me that I had a remittant fever [i.e., malaria]. I grew quite ill afterward, and remained several days confined to bed, with my energies, both physical and mental, completely prostrated. During this time, I was too unwell to think at all, and almost too unwell to remember anything.

After a while, I recovered, and walked about a little in the fresh air. This motion enlivened me, and I began to feel the operation of the vital forces, so that I felt almost well. I immediately began, with my renovated strength, to carry on that education of the will which was now the main occupation of my life. I endeavored to imagine myself suffering the torments of hell, and rising superior to them through the forces of spiritual energy; I endeavored to put myself in the position of unflinching defiance. But it was all in vain, my mental energies were still prostrated by the remains of my fever. . . . I still thought God to be a tyrant, but all my opposition to him was prostrated. I could no longer carry on the war. These reflections then passed through my mind:—Fever depends on the state of the body, no effort of will can save any man from it: *what if God should first give me a remitting fever,* AND THEN DAMN ME IN MY STATE OF CONSEQUENT PROSTRATION, would he not then conquer both body and soul? The empire of my soul is then not mine;—God rules there as well as in the body. I, who acknowledge no right but prevailing might, am then conquered by might—I am driven from my last strong hold. I can defy even, only by permission, and only by strength given me by the superior power whom I defy. What a mockery of my Supreme Sovereignty in my own self-subsisting essence is this. . . . I have no independent action. . . . [18]

Given this description, it is also worth noting, as Peabody later recalled, that Greene's illness and subsequent confrontation with divine omnipotence were paralleled by events in his military command that only exacerbated his fragile self-esteem. He reported to Peabody, for example, that the ill behavior he encountered in soldiers under his command made him realize that "these brutal men are not governed by the complex of my thoughts, nor by the complex of laws of Nature, of which they know nothing, but by *me,*—a self-determining force, a free spirit, a *person.*" "At once it flashed like lightning upon him," Peabody wrote. "'And God is behind the complex of the laws of Nature,—a self-acting, free, supreme, infinite Person, to whom all finite persons are responsible,'" he told her.

Thereupon, Peabody reported, Greene flung to the ground his copy of
"Queen Mab," which had been "his gospel," rushed to his valise, and took
out the Bible "that his mother had put into it when he left home." No
longer, he declared, would he follow Shelley's theology, "namely, that God
is merely a complex of the laws of Nature." His experience in Florida, he
told Peabody, "had brought him to deeper truth," to an acknowledgment of
the sublime majesty of God, and his "problem" thereupon became "the
discovery of the means whereby [he] might obtain communion with the
FATHER." From this time he considered himself a "free man."[19]

Greene's obsession with his own helplessness in the face of God's power
indicates why when he first began to travel in Brownson's and Peabody's
circles he gave so much attention to the problem of the will. To that he
turned as well in his contribution to *The Dial* and in the book subsequently
published from it. What Greene worked toward in these writings was his
own understanding of the complex interplay between what Emerson (in
his great essay, "Experience," from this same period) understood as the
balanced forces of *power* and *fate*. As Greene put it in 1842, "In every
human action there is an element of Liberty, and an element of Destiny.
Liberty modifies destiny, and destiny modifies liberty." Man is thus neither
wholly free nor wholly enslaved and has the power, Greene postulated, "to
throw off, one by one, the bands which fasten him to earth." "The fool is
driven before his destiny," he concluded, "but the man of understanding
rideth thereon."[20]

More surprising was Greene's rumination on the extent of man's freedom, for, though arguing for it, he treated the subject through terminology
that derived in large measure from Jonathan Edwards's treatise on the will,
which for almost a century had been considered unassailable in New England's conservative theological circles.[21] Commencing this section of his
essay with a surprising quotation, Gov. John Winthrop's famous distinction
between "natural" and "civil" liberty, Greene observed that "there is no
self-determining power of the will," for "always the will obeys the emotions of the sensibility, as modified by the dictates of the intelligence." In
other words, he continued, "the precise conduct of a man may be known,
if we have given, the *precise character* of the man, and the motives which
are to act upon that character." Man thus "is not accountable for the
motive, neither is he accountable for the action; but he is accountable for
the *character*." Or, as he put it a few years later in his *Doctrine of Life*,
"nothing is manifested in our character, the germ of which was not already
in our nature."[22]

I do not wish to make too much of Greene's understanding of the relation between action and motivation, uncannily like Edwards's notion that

"the will always is as the greatest apparent good is." Rather, I only note that even though much of Greene's early work demonstrates a struggle with his Calvinist legacy, his exposure to Transcendental thought allowed him to modify such theology through his insight that a person's actions, his attempts to put himself in line with what he believes to be the higher Ideal, finally constitute the spiritual life. As he put it, glossing Buchez, "there is no soul which does not *desire, think,* and *act*: in other words, there is no soul without *sensibility, intelligence,* and *power.*" Thus, if man always has before him the proper idea of what he wants to be, Greene concluded, "he will ascend toward it," as a good Transcendentalist should.[23] Whether at this point Greene intended an analogy to Emerson's famous notion, articulated in "The American Scholar," of "Man Thinking" is moot; but surely Emerson, by presumably concurring in Margaret Fuller's acceptance of Greene's work for their *Dial,* understood that, wherever the young man had started, he had come very near the Transcendentalists' notion of the centrality of the self.

One twentieth-century reader has pointed out (unflatteringly) that Greene's youthful efflorescence in *The Dial* reads a bit like Bronson Alcott's "Orphic Sayings," which also had found a home therein.[24] After Greene entered the Newton Theological Institution, however, he began to organize his theological notions more systematically, and he published the results in 1843 in *The Doctrine of Life,* a seventy-four page booklet. Herein Greene directly addressed such topics of interest to Emerson and his circle as "Consciousness" and "The Transcendental World." More significantly, Greene still felt compelled to address his own conservative religious background and thus devoted the last half of his book to an exploration of such cardinal doctrines as the Trinity, the Fall, and the Atonement.

After declaring (with a footnote to Leroux's *De l'Humanité*) that "*All life is at once subjective and objective,*" because the subject can only be known by what he is not, that is, by "that which is furnished by the object in which he lives"; and further, that "*the transcendental world, the world of ideas, is objective,*" Greene attempted to square such notions with the Christian mysteries as understood by a Trinitarian. Dismissing as erroneous commonly understood notions of the Trinity, he claimed that he could accept the term only if, after positing that "God is self-living," one understood that "there can be no life in strict unity." "The being that lives," he went on,

> the object in which he lives, and the relation between the two, are necessary to every fact of life; always, therefore, (if to the word we may attach any meaning) a triplicity is necessary.

> If, then, we assert that God lives, we at once assert a triplicity.
> If we assert that God is self-living, we assert that he has the ob-
> ject of life in himself; in other words, we assert a TRIPLICITY
> IN UNITY.[25]

This, then, was how one might preserve the centrality of the Trinity as a
Transcendentalist!

In his treatment of the Atonement Greene similarly rejected the validity
of the more well-known mediatorial schemes, emphasizing instead "not
that Jesus was himself made perfect through sufferings, but that through
sufferings he was made a perfect captain of salvation" who "was enabled
to transmit the influence which was what entered from him into the life
of his disciples." This cleared the way for Greene to conclude that "We may
... in this world, become connected with the new Adam, which is Christ,"
by keeping him in mind as "the ideal man," an idea that Brownson had
championed. Thus, in striving to emulate Christ, men found that "conformity with God" which as moral beings they always sought. Peabody later
recalled that as early as the winter of 1841–1842 Greene had been reflecting on this idea, for he had praised a passage in Dr. Channing's sermon
"Likeness to God" (1828) as having the "whole Transcendental movement"
in New England "wrapped up" in it.[26] Unlike Emerson, however, who by
this time had left his formal ministry far behind and conceived of Christ
primarily in metaphorical terms, Greene continued to understand and
explicate the Son's mission in an overtly theological way.

Greene took this theology to Harvard's divinity school, where the Unitarian principles of Convers Francis and George Noyes, the two chief faculty, appealed to him. Here he penned two important essays—one on
Emerson's recently published *Essays: Second Series* (1844), the other on
"The Bhagvat Geeta, and The Doctrine of Immortality"—for the *American
Review*, both of which he later incorporated with little change into his
important pamphlet on Transcendentalism. Before we turn to these efforts,
however, it is worth considering Greene's standing among the Transcendentalists in this period. For despite his many friendships in this group,
over the next five years he would grow increasingly critical of Transcendental philosophy, even as its major premises continued to liberate his theology.
As much as he may have been influenced by Brownson, who by this time
himself had severely criticized Transcendentalism as he walked the road to
Rome, the evidence suggests that Greene's increasingly judgmental attitude was related as well to some personal matters.

For one thing, Greene had never been reticent about voicing his opinions of others. Higginson, for example, remembered him as "Mercilessly

opinionated," and Peabody had been struck by his "unexpected and oracular remarks, often quite *piquant* in their expression."[27] Greene's presence at the various "conversations" around Boston thus enlivened what at
times could seem rather ethereal experiences. As Ednah Dow Cheney
(present at a session in which Greene got the better of Bronson Alcott)
observed, he "almost rivaled Socrates in winding an adversary up into a
complete snarl."[28]

Greene's forthrightness often made people uncomfortable. He sharply
criticized the orthodox clergy, for example, for eliminating all that was
transcendental in their creeds, "which are now only logical *fetiches*," but he
found most Unitarians no better. "They have no life," he observed, "for
they mistake manifestation for principle . . . and are the only Christians
who *idolize a man*."[29] As much as such comments might have been welcomed by some of Greene's associates, his outspokenness in criticizing by
name certain Transcendentalists, even some of his staunchest advocates,
raised eyebrows—and tempers.

Peabody, for example, recalled hearing Greene claim that "The Transcendentalists of Boston are the extreme opposite of Kant; they do not see
the transcendental objective (except Mr. Emerson, who names it *Over-
soul*); but it is they themselves who transcend."[30] To be sure, this indictment
of the Transcendentalists' egotism was shared by both Peabody, who had
criticized them on similar grounds, and Brownson, whose devotion to the
lower classes set him apart from most of the Transcendental Club.[31] Greene
obviously had come to see that the Transcendentalist movement as a whole
was too elitist. As much as he admired Emerson, for example, he received
the "Divinity School Address" cooly, for he found in it a "gospel addressed
to the philosopher and the theologian" and not "to the poor, for that must
address the heart and will rather than the intellect." Greene also had doubts
about the morality engendered by Transcendental egotism, for, as Peabody
recalled, in speaking of the tendencies of the movement he "lump[ed]
together the errors of pure mind—with the base passions of *modern french
novels* and the moral indifference of a *Goetheism*."[32]

Greene's animus could be even more personal, as it was in the case of
Theodore Parker. At one point, for example, Parker evidently had criticized some of Greene's theological views, a slight that deeply troubled the
young theologian. Greene already had thought Parker a "rotten conservative" on social issues and now went so far as to impugn his marriage, suggesting that the *"certain coldness* with respect to individual relations"
which characterized the Transcendentalists—that is, his sense that they
"approached one another for purely intellectual purposes"—had made for
alienated affections.[33]

Besides indicating that Greene's derogatory comments were widely known and upsetting to all involved, a remarkable (but unfortunately undated and incomplete) letter from Peabody to Brownson (probably written during the lecture series Parker subsequently published as *A Discourse of Matters Pertaining to Religion* [1842]) reveals much about her young friend.[34] In trying to account for Greene's "prejudice" against Parker, she explained to Brownson, she noted that Greene's "deep reverence" had been shocked by Parker's "latitudinarian opinion whose final bearings he saw." She attributed this to Greene's lack of experience with such "secluded students" as Parker, suggesting that Greene could not appreciate "that the religious sentiments do actually survive in individual character," no matter to what heights someone took philosophical speculation. Greene's problem with Parker, she concluded, simply lay in the younger man's inability to acknowledge that, rather than being as rigorous a logician as he, most speculative men (Parker included) in fact were occasionally "inconsistent" in their thought and saw no reason to be embarrassed by this.

Now, in cases where Greene's "taste, and sentiments were first propitiated," Peabody continued, "as in Waldo Emerson's and some other person's instances,—the young man had formed [a] correct judgment" of their character. But when "false opinions" were "the first things that [struck] his mind—the prejudice is liable to be so strong—that he hardly afterwards can see the truth." Peabody considered herself fortunate in this regard, for her own relationship to Greene, she explained, remained one of a "fascination" that still had "not passed away." But in an apparent attempt to excuse his impolitic behavior by assuming some of the blame, she admitted that early in their relationship she had allowed Greene to treat and speak to her too frankly, so that it appeared to others that he had little respect for her. As she put it, she regretted that she "did not require of him *that deference* due to sixteen years advance of him," for when she found that "E[liza]. F[arrar]. and others took up the notion that he did *not know how to respect*—founded on his bearing to me,—[she] felt conscience stricken."[35]

Clearly, Peabody was deeply pained by Greene's indiscretions and strove mightily to explain their causes. As Parker's "intimate friend," she vehemently denied Greene's suggestion that Parker had "made a mistake ... in his wife" and that he now allowed himself to be "pitied by female friends" for his poor choice of a helpmeet. Further, Peabody observed that "the time when the curse against transcendentalism broke out" in Greene's conversation, "and *the time* when this 'evil thing' of a specific character about Parker took shape," was when Greene's own plans "about going to Europe" had changed, "and when something personally painful had taken place."

Parker's own journals for this period provide an important clue to this mystery, for in the unhappiness of his marriage he had become very taken with the same Anna Shaw whom Greene soon enough would marry! Peabody either never discovered or chose to conceal what that something was, but she observed "that this painful matter . . . pressed on him personally" and even assumed some blame herself. Greene "talked a good deal of being injured," she noted, and as well said of her that she was "*a character* that he would not vote for . . . to belong to his church."[36]

This tempest in a Transcendental teacup also involved none other than Brownson, who during Greene's escalating difficulties with Parker had made known his "feeling" that in a recent sermon (probably *Of the Transient and Permanent in Christianity* [1841]) Parker had plagiarized Benjamin Constant, the French apostle of Eclecticism, and him. Trying to explain Greene's attack on Parker, Peabody admitted that at first she had "conjectured" that Brownson had instigated it by making "*some specific charge* against Parker" and thus "*intensified*" Greene's previous "prejudices & present state of feeling" so much that he was driven to his outburst about Parker's personal life. She knew that Brownson and Greene "had shared for a time the same opinion" of Parker but was pleased that Brownson had "afterwards reason to distrust the whole," that is, to discount what Greene had suggested about Parker's marital affairs.[37]

Peabody evidently had communicated with Greene about the whole affair, trying in vain not to "disturb his feelings"; he had in fact become very angry. Among other things, he was upset that his close friend Brownson now seemed to "take up against him" by dissociating himself from his young friend's impolitic comments. The situation had only gotten worse, for "evil reports" about Parker's domestic arrangements continued to circulate in the Transcendentalists' parlors. Miss Shaw herself probably had become part of the scandal, for some people openly suggested that Parker's intolerable home life had made him look outside marriage for female company. In Peabody's euphemistic account, "it was said [that] P neglected his wife—sought the society of other ladies—was pitied by some of his female friends for not being free to marry her sisters!"[38]

I cite this missive at such length, first, because of its window onto the complex rivalries among the Transcendentalists themselves during this period, but more importantly to indicate Greene's growing estrangement from some key members of the movement—including his mentor Brownson—as he was about to join the ministry. Whatever had occurred in his personal life to so disenchant him with Transcendentalism now made him attack even more strongly the hyperindividualism that he had come to associate with Transcendental philosophy, and to speak more and more to

the social millennium envisioned by the French socialists to whom Brownson had introduced him.

This is the roiled background to Greene's two essays in the *American Review*, which with very few changes he republished in 1849 as his pamphlet
on *Transcendentalism*. Suffice it to say, in these efforts, as in other polemical writings, Greene subjected the movement to the rigors of his logic. On
his very first page, for example, he declared Transcendentalism "that form
of Philosophy which sinks God and Nature in man." Those who take their
point of departure as God alone, he explained, are most often brought to
Pantheism, and those who start in nature become Materialists. But "others
start with man alone, and end as Transcendentalists."[39]
    After a redaction of Kant in which Greene emphasized how Kantian
idealism implied that an individual's sensory perceptions are ultimately erroneous because subjective, he spoke to the Transcendentalists' perceived
solution to this dilemma, to *transcend* space and time because man cannot
know them absolutely. But he found this reasoning "confused" because it
led to the conflation (in his word, "sinking") of God and nature in man that
Greene deplored. "When a man has cut himself off from every thing which
is not himself, (which he must do if he attempts to transcend space and
time)," Greene noted, "he must find the reason of all things in himself."
But, Greene declared, "the reason of God and the universe are not to be
found in man." If one believed that they were, as did the Transcendentalists, this was "a sort of human Pantheism" (12–14).
    Despite Greene's pointed criticism of the egocentric basis of Transcen-
dentalism, he dedicated his book to Emerson, whom he considered "the
profoundest metaphysician, after Jonathan Edwards, which this country
has ever produced" (6). Obviously worried about how Emerson would take
his criticism, in a letter to the Concord sage he explained that in *Transcendentalism* he had sought "not to refute" but to "popularize" Emerson's doctrine, along with the "doctrine of the East and of John's Gospel."[40] In the
pamphlet, however, there was less foot-shuffling, for despite his respect for
Emerson's undeniable spirituality, Greene strongly objected to the Transcendentalists' claim that finally each individual "soul creates all things."
"This amounts to an identification of man with God," and thus to what he
termed a "*Human Pantheism*," an "*absorption of God in the human soul.*"
In his pamphlet, Greene quoted one of his friends, himself a pantheist,
who had memorably explained the result of his absorption: "'I hold myself
to be a leaf, blown about by the winds of change and circumstance, and
holding to the extreme end of the branches of the tree of universal exis-

tence.'" But the Transcendentalists, he continued, "*think themselves to be some of the sap*" (18).

As elsewhere in his religious writings, Greene here sought to preserve the notion of a majestic divinity totally other than man. "The fact is," he argued, that "the body builds the soul, and the soul builds the body, but it is God who builds both." Just as it requires a man to create a poem, "so it requires a living and transcendent God, to create this transcendent poem which we call nature and man, or the visible universe" (21–22). And further, again echoing Edwards, in his posthumously published *End for Which God Created the World* (1765), "So the world is the thought of God, but that thought rendered firm and stable in its manifold relations, by the simple volition of the Divine mind" (32). Because both the Vedas and the Gospel of John preserved this sense of divine omnipotence, Greene wanted people to focus the ideas of thinkers like Emerson through the lenses ground by the authors of these mystical texts. "Man is dependent, for the continuance of his life," Greene concluded, "upon that which is not himself" (41). To think otherwise deified the ego in an illusory manner.

In Greene's assessment of Transcendentalism, we thus find a continued engagement with conservative Christian theology, even as he attempted to corroborate such doctrine by recourse to other scriptures like the Vedas. It should come as no surprise that as he assumed his pulpit in West Brookfield, he continued such explorations, particularly given the conservative position of most of the neighboring clergy. Thus, in another pamphlet of the same period he issued *Remarks in Refutation of the Treatise of Jonathan Edwards on Freedom of the Will* (1848); and in another that same year addressed the doctrine of *The Incarnation*.

His discussion of Edwards continued a long dialogue with this theologian, for as he had made evident in his *First Principles*, Greene found Edwards's notion of the will a main stumbling block to a Unitarian understanding of Scripture. Now he tackled head-on Edwards's central assumption that although the will makes choices and thus appears free, it cannot choose its choices—that is, that an individual has no final power over his general disposition as saint or sinner. Greene simply dismissed this idea. He granted Edwards, for example, that it is wrong to maintain that "the will determines its determinations, chooses its choices." But, like Nathaniel William Taylor and other clergymen who were transforming the "New Divinity" into yet more novel forms, Greene sought to preserve the notion of man's moral liberty and thus observed that while he did not conceive "that freedom consists in a man's willing as he wills to will," he held that "man *wills*, and that the very word *will* includes the idea of freedom."[41] Refusing Edwards's gambit, Greene could not "even discern any

meaning in the expression that liberty consists in the power of choosing between different choices." "If I choose between two objects," he declared,
"is it not *I* that choose?"

Having satisfied himself as to man's liberty—and thus of his moral ac-
countability—Greene turned his attention, in his other important effort
from his first years in the ministry, to the continuing significance (even to
liberal Christians) of maintaining an enlarged understanding of Christ's
role. Rather than supporting the egotheism of the Transcendentalists,
Greene encouraged contemplation of solidarity with all humanity, the low
as well as the high. Under the pretense of humbly asking the venerable
John Fiske, who had ministered to the neighboring town of New Braintree
literally for half a century, for advice about how to understand the incarnation, Greene presented his own sophisticated Unitarian view of Christ as
"the middle term through whom the perfections of God may descend upon
the children of Adam."[42] Because "none of us can attain God directly,"
Greene noted, we must "attain, if we attain at all," through Christ, "for he
is, as it were, the ladder reaching from heaven to earth" (12).

Thus far Greene's theology was unexceptional, but in detailing its implications he moved to the more radical ground that had been surveyed by
Brownson in his *The Mediatorial Life of Jesus* (1842) and owed a more
complete canvass to the French thinkers in whom, probably at Brownson's
counsel, Greene had read.[43] In light of such influences, his study of the
New Testament convinced him that therein "is taught the great doctrine of
the mutual *solidarity* of the members of the Christian Church; and by
implication, the *solidarity* of the whole human race." And by "solidarity,"
he explained, glossing the fourth section of Leroux's *De l'Humanité*, he
understood "that connection of things with each other which makes it impossible that one should be influenced without the influence being transmitted, through that *one*, to *all*" (27).

Greene's understanding of the Fall was directly related to his notion of
each person's linkage, and thus responsibility, to all others. When man was
first created, he explained, "all his passions, feelings, sentiments, and aspirations, were in harmony with the course of universal nature." But as soon
as "each made his own private enjoyment the main end of his life, the harmony of the universe was broken, the unity of the human race was shattered
into as many fragments as there were individual men, and these fragments
repelled each other, for each was intensely selfish, and each cared for his
own, and not for the common good." The only remedy to this wholesale
capitulation to sin was through the Incarnation. The work of "the second
Adam" was "to make men *to be one in the bond of charity*—it was to make
men *be one in the unity of a common Life*" (41–43).

Needless to say, such Christian charity was not rampant in a society in which the enthronement of an individual's inalienable rights to life, liberty, and the pursuit of happiness (and profit) was protected by legislative fiat. Thus Greene discerned and spelled out what thenceforth became the main theme of his life and work, a championing of that very "solidarity" with all people typified by Christ and, concomitantly, an attack on what Leroux called "the property caste." Borrowing an analogy from one of the pseudo-sciences of the day, Greene memorably stated his doctrine and tipped his hand regarding what he saw as his own privileged role in the coming reorganization of society. While he knew "but little of the truth or falsehood of mesmerism," he wrote, it seemed an apt metaphor for what he sought to express of man's relation to God. "As one man by a prolonged and earnest gaze," he continued, "can obtain control over another, transmitting his thoughts and feelings into the mind of the other, bringing the will of the other into complete subjection to his own, so the Father, by the might of the overpowering effulgence of his glory, magnetized our Lord, bringing him into conformity with the perfect image of his own infinite holiness." In turn, Christ "magnetized" his disciples, "and these others still others," so that "the succession has come down to the present day, and the disciples of Christ, at this present hour, are able to transform the unconverted into the form and image of Christ, through the magnetism of a holy life" (25–27). Seemingly unaware of the implicit elitism this analogy sanctioned, Greene no doubt saw himself in this apostolic succession.

From his pastorate in West Brookfield Greene demonstrated his commitment to this ethic of Christian mutualism by involving himself in practical activities for the realization of social harmony. Always the proselytizer, in 1849 he publicized his humanitarian message through a seventy-four-page pamphlet, *Equality*, issued by a local printer, which (like his contemporaneous effort on *Mutual Banking*) illustrates Pierre-Joseph Proudhon's influence on him. Instigated by the number of state banks chartered to support the region's burgeoning industrialization, Greene's *Equality* was a weighty broadside against such usurious financial institutions which, as monopolies of capital, prevented competition, raised interest rates, and contributed to increased acrimony between capital and labor. "Every blow aimed at competition," he declared, "is a blow aimed at liberty and equality, for competition is but another name for that liberty and equality which ought to exist in every manufacturing and commercial community."[44] Banks allow lenders to "escape their fair share of the general competition," he observed, and thus "confer exclusive privileges upon a certain class" (3).

Much of his pamphlet consists of examples of unfair advantages that bank incorporation made possible, but its main interest lies in the ways that Greene linked his opposition to banking to universal questions of "Equality, Justice, and Charity" (29). Not surprisingly, given his contemporaneous writing, in so doing he argued for a radical respect for each individual based in a Christian's obligation to his fellow man. Greene deplored the distance between worker and capitalist and, citing an example from Henri de Saint-Simon, noted that those who loaned money were but unprofitable drones in an economy to which they felt no organic relation. The "sudden disappearance" of a thousand capitalists, he noted, "would cause a sentimental evil only, without occasioning any serious inconvenience to society," unlike, say, the death of fifty of the state's best surgeons (32).

Thus, in the second part of his treatise, addressed "To the Philosophers and Politicians," Greene turned his attention specifically to the plight of labor. First, he dissected what he saw as the three main economic systems by which man related to God and nature: communism, capitalism, and socialism. Recycling some of his recently published thoughts on Transcendentalism, Greene noted that *"The man who denies the rights of capital, is a transcendentalist in political economy."* For what is capital, he asked?

> It is that outward object with which man is related, which man labors upon, which man transforms. Transcendentalism is the denial in the most unqualified terms of the very existence of capital, that is of things which are not man, and with which man is related: and communism is an application of transcendentalism in a more limited sphere of science. (61)

The materialist was no better, Greene observed, for if the transcendentalist "denies the existence of capital, and therefore denies its rights," the materialist affirms its existence "and denies the existence of the laborer, and therefore denies the rights of the laborer." Thus, while the transcendentalist is "a fanatical radical," the materialist is "a bigoted conservative" (62). And what of the socialist, who advocated state intervention in men's private affairs to replicate what they supposed a "Divine Order"? Socialism "is the philosophy of a Theocracy" that wants the state to intervene in men's private lives and as such "is destructive to both liberty and equality" (64).

Because none of these explanations alone seemed correct, Greene's solution was to champion a combination of the three systems, to allow them to "limit, modify, and correct each other." It is only "in their union and harmony," he declared, "that the truth is to be found," a truth formed in equal parts of the liberty of the transcendentalist, the equality of the materialist, and the fraternity of the socialist (64–65). To his dismay, because the "division of labor, and the increase of artificial wants" have "revolutionized our social condition," and because *"the principle of the* DISTRIBUTION *of the values produced, is divorced from the principals of the* PRODUCTION *of those values"* (65), men were being led, *"with gigantic strides, towards—* SOCIALISM!!!!" (67–68). Effectively reshaping society as it allowed banks to monopolize capital, the Commonwealth of Massachusetts thus intervened in society *"for the distribution of wealth in some order other than that which would follow from the prevalence of* FREE COMPETITION" (69).

Greene's reaction to the evil tendencies of socialism was strident. Socialism, he declared, "gives us *but one class, a class of slaves,"* with but one master, "the state." Further, the worst evil of this system lay in its proclivity to pantheism, for "Pantheism is beginning already to prevail extensively in the community; and, as for the fullness of pantheism which is requisite for the completeness of a system of socialism, it would be furnished by the first Phalansterian who might happen to present himself" (70). So much for the communitarian promise of Brook Farm!

To Greene's mind, "Love" was the only answer to the inevitable social strife engendered by the industrial revolution. "We all gravitate toward the same God," he wrote, "and this upward gravitation is to us the revelation of our destiny." Further, because "All men are brothers," they "all gravitate toward the same spiritual Sun, toward the same common Father" (71). If people were centered fully in "INDIVIDUALISM," which Greene believed to be "a holy doctrine," they would respect their fellow beings because they too had to be recognized as holy individuals. "He that contends against the rights of an individual man," he concluded, "contends against God," for "it is the indwelling of God in every individual soul, that is the origin and foundation of all human rights" (72–73). "The mystical triangle which ought to be inscribed on the colors of every republic" had at its points liberty, equality, and fraternity, "a sacramental formula" that guaranteed not an "absolute democracy" in which individuals cared primarily for themselves, but rather the "Constitutional Democratic Republic" based firmly in Christ's principles, which Greene sought for his fellow men (74).

One yearns to know how Greene's townspeople received this unusual pamphlet, parts of which he earlier had published in the *Worcester Palladium*, a Democratic weekly, and to know whether discontent with his radicalism contributed to his request for dismissal. In any event, we have finally arrived at the mature expression of the radical individualism alluded to in my title. Greene called for an appreciation of his fellow man based profoundly in *Christianity*, not in Emerson's egoism or the misguided socialism of a George Ripley. Although Greene conceded that Emerson's thoughts "radiate always in right lines," he also found the Transcendental-

ists "incapable of grasping some things [including people] in their relations"
(60). Greene's primary contribution to American social thought thus
resided in his sponsorship of a radically egalitarian Christian individualism
for the salvation of a nation profoundly lost to market capitalism. As others
have observed, in *Equality* (as in Greene's pamphlet on *Mutual Banking*,
in which he argued for the establishment of "mutual" banks much like
modern credit unions in their nonprofit nature and their use of real estate
to secure loans), Greene derives many of his ideas from Proudhon.[45] But
more important is the novelty of their sponsorship at a time when virtually
all other Transcendentalists, including Brownson himself, offered very different solutions to the growing problems between labor and capital.
Greene's recurrence to a Christian mysticism based as much in his reading
of Edwards as in the French mutualists is a truly novel contribution to
American liberalism.

We can gauge the degree of this novelty by citing Brownson's own reaction
to his erstwhile disciple. In a review of Greene's last major work from his
West Brookfield pastorate, his *Remarks on the Science of History; Followed
by an A Priori Autobiography* (1849) published after Brownson had meta-
phorically left Concord for Rome, Brownson assessed Greene's contributions to contemporary philosophical discourse.[46] The piece is particularly
poignant because of Brownson's introduction of Greene to the French
thought by which he became so influenced and which Brownson now renounced.[47]

In this work, Brownson observed, Greene ambitiously sought to demonstrate, using as a basis "the great Logical Series by Nines" (elaborated by
Buchez in his *Introduction to the Science of History*), how one could write
"universal history under the form of a biography" and "biography under
the forms of universal history." But Greene's outline of the universal
progress of history in fact occupies but a few pages, with the majority of the
work given over to "a sort of imaginary spiritual Autobiography" through
which Greene sought to demonstrate how each individual recapitulates
the progress of the entire human race, through the "grand epochs" of "Desire," "Reasoning," and "Realization." Approvingly citing Emerson's essay
on "History," that "there is a relation between the hours of life, and the
centuries of time," Greene detailed what obviously was the story of his own
hard-won spiritual progress.[48]

Brownson, however, found many problems in the work. He immediately
lit into Greene's acknowledgment of Jacob Boehme (whose mysticism also
lent itself to organization by such a series of progressions) and Buchez, for

he thought them "the last from whose works we should expect materials suitable for a work to be composed and published by a professedly Christian minister."[49] Of Leroux, to whom Greene dedicated the book, Brownson had little more good to say, though he admitted that he himself held "the very questionable honor of being the first to introduce [Leroux] to the American public" during the "brief period when [that French thinker] exerted a very great influence over his own philosophical speculations." Indeed, in this review Brownson painfully confronted the ghosts of his own philosophical past, confessing that the study of Leroux's writings once had formed "an epoch in [his] mental history," particularly during 1842 and 1843 when Brownson was constructing and publishing his *Synthetic Philosophy* (215).[50] Although his refutation of Leroux was lengthy, we might characterize Brownson's greatest disappointment in him as having led readers to "disregard all distinction between intuition and reflection, and therefore to contend that reflection, as well as intuition, reproduces the order of being." After more mature consideration Brownson had come to see that this implied "the absurdity of supposing that, in the order of being, the abstract precedes the concrete, the possible the real, and that the creator is filled or completed in the creature" (215–216).

Even as he praised the ambition and intelligence of his onetime disciple, Brownson regretted Greene's uncritical acceptance of Leroux's ideas. Displaying his usual erudition, Brownson became most exercised over what he called Greene's "autotheism," the same sort he found in Fichte, Emerson, and Alcott. For these people, Brownson noted, all that is or exists is "I or Ego" (222–223), a philosophical position that presented the same difficulties as the pantheism which he (and, supposedly, Greene) had rejected. Criticizing Greene's attempt, "consciously or unconsciously," to "combine Cartesianism and Platonism in a single doctrine"—an example of what Brownson considered a general fault of "modern philosophy"—Brownson noted that "ideas, the forms, essences, or possibilities of things, are before the science and will of God only in the order of reflection, not in the order of being" (234). "Neither ontologically nor psychologically," he reminded his pupil, "neither in the order of being nor in the order of knowledge, . . . is the abstract prior to the concrete, the possible to the real, the essence to the subsisting being, or the being to the attributes to God" (236).

Brownson's review consists of forty pages of similarly dense philosophical commentary (talk of being taken seriously in a review!), but contains virtually nothing about the rich detail in the autobiographical portion of the work. Characterizing the work as "ambitious," Brownson yet lamented its "marks of haste." The book is not, as Brownson put it, "equally elaborated throughout, and it wants artistic conception and finish." Further, "its several parts do not seem . . . to cohere, or to have originated in the same design," for it "lacks unity and regular scientific development" (216). Brownson could not see the connection between the brief "Remarks on the Science of History" and the "Autobiography." There was nothing to lead the reader, he observed, "to regard it as any thing else than an autobiographical sketch of the religious experience of a serious young man, of a speculative turn, exhibiting with spirit and fidelity the various doubts he encountered, and the methods and reasonings by which he solved or attempted to solve them." But because Brownson recognized in the author a "philosophical genius," he was willing to consider that in Greene's own mind the several parts of the work in fact were connected. That, said Brownson, is what "we must seize in the best way we can, and appreciate, as the condition of understanding and appreciating what he has written" (217).

Greene had had a sense of what he would be in for if his mentor reviewed the book, for upon sending him a copy on January 24, 1849, he expressed his chagrin at the "wide gulph" between them. There was no one, he added, with whom he "desire[d] more to labor side by side with than you." And though he knew well, as he put it, that upon reading his book Brownson would think him "not a mere heretic, but heretical all over," Greene still sought intellectual and personal rapprochement. He never ceased to hope, he wrote, "that we may come together again."[51] Brownson, too, acknowledged their erstwhile closeness. He knew the anonymously published book's author, he admitted at the outset of his review, "a Unitarian minister, in whom, while he was pursuing his preparatory studies," Brownson had taken "a deep personal interest," and who was one of his "most intimate and highly esteemed young friends" (214).

But the review indicated that these two thinkers had drifted far apart. Despite Brownson's gruff attempts at politeness, the overall tone of the review was severe, if not totally dismissive. Does this help to explain why shortly thereafter Greene left for Europe? Surely, if anyone could understand what he sought to articulate about the mutualism necessary to save America from industrial feudalism, it should have been Brownson—he who even earlier than Greene had drunk at the wells of French social thought, he to whom Greene had confessed that he owed more, "philosophically and theologically, than I do to any other five men living."[52]

But by 1850 Greene had passed beyond Brownson and Transcendentalism. To whom could he speak and be understood? In another great individualist of the age, Henry Thoreau, Greene would find little comfort: the Concord saunterer's criticism more often than not bore marks of sarcasm and pity rather than of the true Christian compassion Greene counseled. Greene championed an equally demanding and heroic but different respect for the individual, one marked by an understanding of how as Christians all men were indissolubly linked. For him the operative word remained "mutualism," and his ethic, compassion. How ironic, then, that Greene now finds his small place in history books among those whom we have labeled "anarchists" and "libertarians" but who often lacked his deeply religious vision, one based as much in Edwards's understanding of the nature of true virtue as in Emerson's essays.

Throughout the 1860s and 1870s Greene's thought only widened and deepened. By 1872, still a religious seeker, he published *The Blazing Star; with An Appendix Treating of the Jewish Kabbala*. Continuing to insist that mutual association was the foundation of social progress and that true freedom was guaranteed only if one recognized each being as significant as one's self, Greene now drew sustenance from the Jewish mystical tradition, which reinforced his sense of the centrality of man in divine creation. The world, Greene observed in his "Appendix," is "in one aspect, a poem; in another, it is a logical argument." But "in every aspect, the universe is a work of art."[53] Such mysticism moved him beyond Transcendental egotism to a more inclusive faith. Too long sidetracked by trailing him in the paths of philosophical anarchists, we should return him to his rightful place among the heralds of American liberal religion and recognize that he was indeed a memorable example of Emerson's "Man Thinking."

NOTES

1. Ralph Waldo Emerson, "Historic Notes of Life and Letters in New England," *Lectures and Biographical Sketches* (1883), in *Complete Works of Ralph Waldo Emerson*, ed. Edward Waldo Emerson (Boston and New York, 1903–1904), 10:329; Margaret Fuller to Ralph Waldo Emerson, Nov. 9, 1841, cited in *The Letters of Ralph Waldo Emerson*, ed. Ralph L. Rusk (New York, 1939), 2:462n.

2. For a succinct overview of the Transcendentalists' influence on liberal Christianity, see William R. Hutchison, *The Transcendentalist Ministers: Church Reform in the New England Renaissance* (New Haven, 1959).

3. On Brownson, see Arthur M. Schlesinger, Jr., *Orestes A. Brownson: A Pilgrim's Progress* (Boston, 1939); and Thomas R. Ryan, *Orestes A. Brownson: A Definitive Biography* (Huntington, Ind., 1979). The standard account of French influence on American Transcendentalism is Walter Leatherbee Leighton, *French Philosophers and New-England Transcendentalism* (Charlottesville, 1908). Also see William Girard, "Du Transcendentalism consideré essentiellement dans sa définition et ses origine françaises," *Univ. of California Publications in Modern Philology* 4(Oct. 18, 1916):351–498; and "Du Transcendentalism consideré dans son aspect social," *Univ. of California Publications in Modern Philology* 8(Aug. 6, 1918):153–226.

4. On Brook Farm and Fourierism, see Carl Guarneri, *The Utopian Alternative: Fourierism in Nineteenth-Century America* (Ithaca, 1991); and Richard Francis, "The Ideology of Brook Farm," *Studies in the American Renaissance 1977*, ed. Joel Myerson (Boston, 1977), 1–48. The market economy during this period is explored in Charles Sellers, *The Market Revolution: Jacksonian America, 1815–1846* (New York, 1991).

5. Obituary in the *Boston Evening Transcript*, June 1878, reprinted in Kenneth Walter Cameron, "Emerson and William Batchelder Greene's Creativity and Questioning," *American Renaissance Literary Report X* (Hartford, 1996), 82; quoted in Elizabeth Palmer Peabody, *Reminiscences of Rev. William Ellery Channing, D. D.* (Boston, 1880), 435.

6. The main biographical sources for Greene are George Willis Cooke, *An Historical and Biographical Introduction to Accompany the Dial* (Cleveland, 1902), 2:117–128; Joel Myerson, *New England Transcendentalists and The Dial: A History of the Magazine and the Contributors* (Rutherford, 1980), 155–156; and Cameron, "Greene's Creativity," *passim*.

7. Peabody, *Channing*, 435ff.

8. Peabody, *Channing*, 435ff; Cameron, "Greene's Creativity," 22.

9. William B. Greene, *The Incarnation: A Letter to Rev. John Fiske, D. D.* (West Brookfield, Mass., 1848), 20; Thomas Wentworth Higginson, *Cheerful Yesterdays* (Boston, 1898), 106.

10. Ralph Waldo Emerson to Frederic Henry Hedge, Nov. 25, 1842, in *Letters of Ralph Waldo Emerson*, 3:99; William B. Greene to Orestes Brownson, Aug. 24, 1842, Orestes Brownson Papers, University of Notre Dame, South Bend, Indiana (cited hereafter as UND).

11. Kenneth Walter Cameron, "Emerson, Thoreau, and the Town and Country Club," *Emerson Society Quarterly* 8(1957):46, 11.

12. William B. Greene, *Socialistic, Communistic, Mutualistic, and Financial Fragments* (Boston, 1875).

13. See Cameron, "Greene's Creativity," 82–83.

14. Indeed, Greene's intellectual development might profitably be compared not only to that of Marsh, whose "Preliminary Essay" appended to his edition of Coleridge's *Aids to Reflection* (1829) marked an epoch in New England's intellectual life, but also to that of other conservative clergy who similarly were touched by philosophical Idealism without ever becoming bona fide Transcendentalists (Caleb Sprague Henry, for example). See Ronald V. Wells, *Three Christian Transcendentalists: James, Marsh, Caleb Sprague Henry, and Frederic Henry Hedge* (New York, 1943); John J. Duffy, ed. *Coleridge's American Disciples: The Selected Correspondence of James Marsh* (Amherst, Mass., 1973); and Peter C. Carafiol, *Transcendent Reason: James Marsh and the Forms of Romantic Thought* (Gainesville, Fla., 1982).

15. Henry F. Brownson, *Orestes A. Brownson's Middle Life: From 1844–1855* (Detroit, 1899), 209.

16. On Buchez, see especially D. G. Charlton, *Secular Religion in France, 1815–1870* (London, 1963), 182–184; Robert Flint, *The Philosophy of History in Europe* (Edinburgh and London, 1884), 1:242–252; Edward Berenson, *Populist Religion and Left-Wing Politics in France, 1830–1852* (Princeton, 1984), 42–44; Shirley M. Gruner, *Economic Materialism and Social Moralism: A Study of the History of*

Ideas in France from the Latter Part of the 18th Century to the Middle of the 19th (The Hague, 1977), chap. 20; and François-André Isambert, *Politique, religion et science de l'homme chez Philippe Buchez* (Paris, 1967).

17. On Leroux see especially Flint, *Philosophy of History in Europe*, 1: 252–258; David Owen Evans, *Social Romanticism in France, 1830–1848* (Oxford, 1951); Charlton, *Secular Religion in France*, 82–87; and Jack Bakunin, *Pierre Leroux and the Birth of Democratic Socialism* (New York, 1976).

18. [William B. Greene], *Remarks on the Science of History; Followed by an A Priori Autobiography* (Boston, 1849), 25–26.

19. Peabody, *Channing*, 439–440; [Greene], *Autobiography*, 37; Greene, *The Incarnation*, 28–29.

20. [William B. Greene], "First Principles," *The Dial* 2(Jan. 1842):275–276.

21. See Allen C. Guelzo, *Edwards on the Will: A Century of American Theological Debate* (Middletown, Conn., 1989), for a penetrating treatment of the topic. Oddly, Guelzo does not mention Greene's refutation.

22. [Greene], "First Principles," 278; William B. Greene, *The Doctrine of Life with Some of Its Theological Applications* (Boston, 1843), 42.

23. Jonathan Edwards, *Freedom of the Will* (1754; New Haven, 1957), 142; [Greene], "First Principles," 281.

24. Martin K. Doudna, introduction to William B. Greene, *"Transcendentalism" (1849) and "Equality" (1849)* (Delmar, N.Y., 1981), ix.

25. Greene, *Doctrine of Life*, 30–31.

26. Greene, *Doctrine of Life*, 57–58, 74; Peabody, *Channing*, 364.

27. Higginson, *Cheerful Yesterdays*, 106–107; Peabody, *Channing*, 435.

28. Ednah Dow Cheney, "Reminiscences of Mr. Alcott's Conversations. Part I," *Open Court* 2(Aug. 9, 1888):1131–1133; reprinted in Kenneth Walter Cameron, *American Renaissance Literary Report VI* (Hartford, 1992), 95.

29. Peabody, *Channing*, 435–436.

30. Peabody, *Channing*, 435.

31. See Bruce P. Ronda, ed., *Letters of Elizabeth Palmer Peabody, American Renaissance Woman* (Middletown, Conn., 1984), 29–34; and Orestes Brownson, *The Laboring Classes* (Boston, 1840).

32. Peabody, *Channing*, 436; Ronda, *Letters of Peabody*, 235.

33. Ronda, *Letters of Peabody*, 235.

34. Elizabeth Palmer Peabody to Orestes Brownson [1842], Orestes Brownson Papers, UND.

35. In his own letter to Brownson during this period, Greene said almost the same thing *of her*! Peabody, he wrote, "is a strange character—entirely too hard for me." "Every general remark that I make," he continued, "she applies to herself, and wants me to ease her mind upon difficult points of which I cannot even conceive. If I had known that this would have been the consequence, I should have been very careful of letting [her] become so well acquainted with me." Greene to Brownson, Aug. 24, 1842, Orestes Brownson Papers, UND.

36. Dean Grodzins makes clear this very personal reason for Greene's anger at Parker and quotes extensively on the matter from Parker's manuscript journal. Grodzins, "Theodore Parker and Transcendentalism" (Ph.D. diss., Harvard University, 1993), esp. 173–195. Peabody to Brownson [1842], Orestes Brownson Papers, UND.

37. Peabody to Brownson [1842], Orestes Brownson Papers, UND.
38. Greene to Brownson, Aug. 24, 1842; Peabody to Brownson [1842], Orestes Brownson Papers, UND.
39. William B. Greene, *Transcendentalism* (West Brookfield, 1849), 1. Subsequent references cited parenthetically in text.
40. Ralph Waldo Emerson to William B. Greene, [May 2, 1843?], paraphrased in *Letters of Ralph Waldo Emerson*, 3:171.
41. On Taylor, see Sidney Earl Mead, *Nathaniel William Taylor, 1768–1858: A Connecticut Liberal* (Chicago, 1942); Bruce Kuklick, *Churchmen and Philosophers: From Jonathan Edwards to John Dewey* (New Haven, 1985), 43–65; and Guelzo, *Edwards on the Will*, 112–139.
42. Greene, *The Incarnation*, 6. Subsequent references cited parenthetically in text.
43. Orestes Brownson, *The Mediatorial Life of Jesus*, vol. 4, *Works of Orestes A. Brownson*, ed. Henry F. Brownson (Detroit, 1882–1887), 4:140–172.
44. [William B. Greene], *Equality* (West Brookfield, 1849), 2. Subsequent references cited parenthetically in text.
45. See, for example, James J. Martin, *Men Against the State: The Exposition of Individualist Anarchism in America, 1827–1908* (Colorado Springs, Colo., 1970), 34–35; William O. Reichert, *Partisans of Freedom: A Study in American Anarchism* (Bowling Green, 1976), chap. 3; and Rudolph Rocker, *Pioneers of American Freedom: Origin of Liberal and Radical Thought in America* (Los Angeles, 1949), 97–112.
46. The essay review first appeared in the Jan. 1850 number of *Brownson's Quarterly Review* and is reprinted in Brownson, *Works*, 1:214–252.
47. See, for example, Brownson's "Leroux on Humanity," from the *Boston Quarterly Review* for July 1842, reprinted in *Works*, 4:100–139.
48. [Greene], *Autobiography*, viii–ix.
49. Brownson, "An A Priori Autobiography," *Works*, 1:214. Subsequent references cited parenthetically in text.
50. First published in the *Democratic Review* for Dec. 1842 and Mar. 1843, and reprinted in *Works*, 1:58–129.
51. William B. Greene quoted in H. F. Brownson, *Brownson's Middle Life*, 209–211.
52. H. F. Brownson, *Brownson's Middle Life*, 211.
53. William B. Greene, *The Blazing Star; with An Appendix Treating of the Jewish Kabbala* (Boston, 1872), 80.

Transcendentalism's
Cultural Legacy

"Our National Glory"

Emerson in American Culture, 1865–1882

RICHARD F. TEICHGRAEBER III

ANY EFFORT TO UNDERSTAND RALPH WALDO EMERSON'S central place in American culture must pay special attention to the development of his reputation during the era of Reconstruction and the first years of the Gilded Age. It would be a mistake to say it was during this period that he secured his identity as the "founder" of his nation's culture. No one figure ever has earned that title, and Emerson never claimed it for himself, though at the time of his death he was as inescapable a presence in America's intellectual and cultural life as Lincoln was in its politics. Emerson's post-Civil War career is best understood as a time when most of his contemporaries came to see him not only as America's leading man of letters, but also as one of its preeminent public moralists, a figure the example of whose life and writings urged them on to more strenuous efforts to realize shared national ideals. "He is an accepted fact," one contemporary reviewer of *Letters and Social Aims* (1875) commented more bluntly, "just as we accept Shakespeare." There is still a tendency among biographers, cultural historians, and literary critics to treat Emerson's entire postbellum career as a prolonged mental twilight, a tendency encouraged by the gradual but relentless decline of his eyesight and memory and by the uncertainty surrounding his precise role in the arrangement of his final publications. Despite an element of truth in that familiar picture, it needs to be complemented by study of the reasons why Emerson was such a highly visible figure during the last seventeen years of his life and of how his activities and ideas figured in public debate about the shape of postbellum culture.[1]

This is especially true of the years 1865–1872, the period which will be the main focus of this essay. The years immediately following the Civil War, one contemporary witness later observed, were a time when "none but

Emerson himself noted the approach of old age." More significantly, they were also a time when Emerson became "an accepted fact" in American life. He entered into a sort of Indian summer as a public speaker early in 1865, and over the course of the next five years he enjoyed his most active and lucrative years on the national lecture circuit. The first collected edition of his writings—the pirated two-volume *Complete Works of Ralph Waldo Emerson*—appeared in London in 1866, and by the late 1870s three other multivolume collected editions had been published in Boston. Honors, such as election to the Harvard Board of Overseers and to a vice-presidency of the New England Woman Suffrage Association, also pressed upon him—as did a new set of admirers ("Emersonidae," James Russell Lowell called them) who made Emerson himself into something of a cultural cause and who included Franklin Sanborn, Moncure Conway, James Elliot Cabot, and Charles William Eliot. Further evidence of his fame can be found in the steady stream of invitations to lecture, publish, sit for photographs, and travel which continued to find their way to his Concord home over the course of the 1870s. There can be little question that when Emerson reached the end of his creative life in 1872, he was among the most famous figures of his time.[2]

No one reading this book will need to be reminded that most phases of Emerson's career, and almost all aspects of his writings, have been subject to intensive study and are comparatively familiar. (The early stages of his intellectual development now rank among the most thoroughly explored identity crises in history.) But neither the last two collections of essays published during his lifetime nor the final, and in many ways quite distinct, phase of his public career have received anything like such close attention.[3] A step-by-step recounting of every facet of the development of the later Emerson's reputation, however, would extend well beyond the boundaries of a single paper. So here I touch only in passing on his poetry and literary essays. What I offer primarily is a picture of Emerson as an aging but still active public moralist who presented his views to a growing variety of audiences that became available to him as one of postbellum America's best-known figures. My two main concerns are (i) to recover an Emerson who wanted to help his contemporaries grapple with the problems of their lives (and in the process to characterize both Emerson's ideas and a particular style of presentation that defined his stance as a public moralist) and (ii) to reconstruct some of the more important ways in which his activities and ideas gained national attention during the last years of his life. My commitment to restore Emerson to his historical context has made for a paper that is comparatively short on theory and long on efforts, first, to allow the later Emerson to speak for himself, something he is rarely allowed to do in modern scholarship; and, second, to attend to the various ways in which his contemporaries viewed his career and his postbellum lectures and writings. One consequence of this approach is a fairly generous supply of quotations. Another is a sensitivity to the importance of questions surrounding the history of Emerson's reception that nonetheless resists their promotion to an infallible method of identifying the immediate significance of Emerson's body of work without careful reference to the work itself. Doubtless it makes sense to think of Emerson's lectures and essays in terms of the economic and social interests of those willing to pay for or write about them. Whatever truth this familiar approach may contain, however, it is not very near the whole truth. We must therefore begin with a broader view.

This was part of the editorial eulogy of Emerson that appeared in the *Boston Daily Advertiser* the day after he died:

> he is not the property of any class, but our common possession and our national glory whose works read like the great ledger entries of our merchants, whose acts betray the shrewdness and prudence of the typical New Englander and whose words are the outcome of our national development, our joy, our honor, and withal a part of every fine American, so that his axioms and surprises of 1840 have become our proverbs of 1882. If one wishes to have the summary and quintessence of this new continent, and its people, their thought and the very spirit of modern New England, it is all in Emerson, of whom only the mortal frame can be destroyed by the angel of death.

Writing the obituary of a "national glory" is no easy task, and in skirting the question of how axioms of a typical New England in the 1840s became national proverbs in the early 1880s, this passage perhaps betrays the strain. Yet the *Daily Advertiser*'s characterization of Emerson as a "national glory" was amplified and echoed in countless other obituary tributes across the country during the spring and summer of 1882. The *New York Herald's* editorial eulogy proclaimed that "nobody who has watched the growth of the intellectual life in America can have a doubt about the permanence of his influence upon its development. No American writer of any time is acknowledged by a wider intellectual audience to have been the stimulus to it most liberal thinking." The *Chicago Daily Tribune* said that at the time of his death Emerson had come to be "recognized as the representative mind of his country." The *San Francisco Chronicle* offered perhaps the most lavish praise of all, observing that Emerson "belongs like DANTE, GALILEO, MONTAIGNE, NEWTON, and DARWIN, not so much to his own as to future times, and his works will be classics in all languages centuries after his contemporaries of higher-flown pretensions and reputations are forgotten." Dissenting notes, predictably, were sounded in Southern newspapers, but usually qualified with grudging recognition of his achievements. At the time of his death, began the obituary in the *Charleston News and Courier*, Emerson was widely recognized as "the most distinguished of American essayists"; he "had no prototype and will have no successful imitator."[4]

It is right to see this nationwide tribute as perhaps both a symptom of Emerson's extraordinarily high public standing and a cause of its further growth. In tracing the historical origins of this final remarkable apotheosis, however, we should be careful not to let it obscure the very different character of Emerson's reputation during earlier stages of his career. In the 1830s, he had first gained national attention as a figure who had inspired a radical break with existing Protestant literary and philosophical traditions in New England. In the 1840s and into the 1850s, his lectures, essays, poems, and other publications won him a transatlantic reputation as the most original man of letters American culture had yet produced. In 1859 and 1860, he joined Henry David Thoreau in defending John Brown at a time when news of his Harpers Ferry's raid met almost universal condemnation in Northern states, and when the Civil War began, one of his most widely known contributions to public debate was his controversial description of Brown as "the Saint . . . whose martyrdom, if it shall be perfected, will make the gallows as glorious as the cross." Against this background, it is interesting to speculate how different Emerson's obituaries would have been had he died, say, early in the summer of 1863, after major Union military defeats at Fredericksburg and Chancellorsville. Not only would it have been more to difficult place him in the history of American culture— "twenty years before his death," William Dean Howells once reminded students of Emerson's popular reputation, "he was the most misunderstood man in America"—it seems likely he would have been remembered by many, North and South, as something of a sectional ideologist whose antislavery speeches had given abolitionism an important measure of cultural legitimacy.[5] Nor, of course, would Emerson have established a close attachment to Harvard, the full story of which forms an important episode in the development his postbellum reputation. Only when Harvard's "own darling sons [started] dying on the field of battle," Sanborn observed in the year of the Emerson centenary, did its official appreciation of him begin to rise to "something like justice."[6] He could have added that, during the last decades of the nineteenth century, the increasingly close association of Emerson's name with Harvard would provide new ground for the building of his reputation.

It is difficult to measure what Emerson himself made of his postbellum fame. While he hardly thought of himself as a sectional ideologist, he did prize his regional identity. And yet he never longed for followers. Emerson said he found satisfaction less in his possible direct influence on others than in successfully encouraging kindred spirits to pursue their own paths. "This is my boast," he had written in his journal in 1859, "that I have no school & no follower. I should account it a measure of the impurity of insight if it did not create independence" (*JMN*, 14:258).[7] Nor did he view his own publications as sacred texts. In some moods, he dismissed the commercial success of his later publications as the predictable by-product of his longevity. Referring to *Society and Solitude*, he remarked in an 1870 journal entry that "My new book sells faster, it appears, than either of its foregoers. This is not from its merit, but only shows that old age is a good advertiser. Your name has been seen so often that your book must be worth buying" (*L*, 6:55). As he grew older, he also became increasingly uncomfortable with his status as cultural celebrity. "We should all be public men if we could afford it. I am wholly private," he wrote in a journal entry of July 12, 1872, "such is the poverty of my constitution" (*JMN*, 16:275-276). His discomfort with popular acclaim was fed by his sense that he often came across as a "hack lecturer" (*L*, 6:123). As much as he believed in the transforming power of good lecturing, Emerson never escaped doubts about his effectiveness as a speaker, doubts that were intermittently triggered in the late 1860s by indifferent audiences and satirical newspaper accounts of his talks. Finally, several entries in his letters and journals betray a growing frustration at his inability to keep up with his many commitments; and by 1868 his sense of dwindling intellectual energy crossed with an anxiety that expressed itself in various ways, including efforts to block newspaper coverage of his lectures in Boston and New York.[8]

All that said, there is little question that Emerson recognized that his services as a lecturer and a writer were more in demand between 1865 and 1872 than at any previous time in his career. "I have never had so many tasks as in the last twelve months" (*L*, 6:123), he commented in a letter of July 7, 1869, looking back on a year during which he had given forty-five lectures in Massachusetts, Rhode Island, Connecticut, and New York; corrected six earlier volumes of his essays for publication in a new two-volume collection of *Prose Works* that Fields, Osgood & Co. would publish in October; participated in deliberations that led Harvard's Board of Overseers to appoint Charles Eliot as president; served as curator of the Concord Lyceum; and begun work on the first chapters of *Society and Solitude*. And yet the two previous years in fact had been even busier; 1866 and 1867 were arguably the most ambitious years of Emerson's entire career as a lecturer. He gave forty-three lectures in 1866 in fourteen different New England and mid-western states; the next season he accelerated his pace, delivering eighty lectures altogether, and for the first time went as far west as Minnesota and Kansas. During the late 1860s, his fame as a lecturer also came to be matched by his economic prosperity. In the mid 1850s, Emerson had begun to command a comparatively large income from lecturing: his fees for individual public lectures typically ranged between $25 and $50, and the largest sum he received for private lectures was $1,166 for a series on "Topics of Modern Times" in Philadelphia in January 1854. The Civil War, however, brought a sudden and drastic reduction in Emerson's income. Dividends from his stocks and bonds were discontinued, and demand for his lectures and books largely dried up. As a result, Emerson was forced to borrow to meet his financial needs, and he was in considerable debt when the war ended. But his financial pinch was short-lived. By the winter of 1865, the western lecture circuit had been re-established, and that year the Unitarian Church in Milwaukee paid Emerson $300 for a series of six lectures on "American Life." By December 1867, his fee for individual public lectures in Ohio, Illinois, Missouri, and Iowa had risen to $100. Eight months later, he netted $1,655.75 for a miscellany of six private lectures in Boston, managed by his publisher Ticknor & Fields—"which is by much the largest sum I ever received for work of this kind" (*L*, 6:54-55), he wrote in gratitude to James T. Fields. Because of his declining eyesight and memory, Emerson rarely lectured outside New England after 1870, but his fees remained high: $250 for "Nature and Art" in Chicago on November 27, 1871; $1,457 for six private "conversations" on literature in Mechanics Hall, Boston, in April 1871; and $300 for "Eloquence" at the Academy of Music in Philadelphia, where three thousand people gathered to hear him speak on March 18, 1875. The question of what contemporaries made of his last public performances will be addressed later in this essay. Here the point that deserves emphasis is simply that the satisfaction they took from direct encounters with a celebrity were the currency of Emerson's old age.

Emerson also knew that the power and prestige of his publishers had as much to do with his late success as his longevity. While publishing was never a labor of love for him, Emerson was no tyro when it came to the American book trade.[9] Phillips and Sampson, his publisher during the 1850s, was known for its relatively aggressive marketing of American writers. A more crucial chapter in the story of the cultural production of the later Emerson, however, began in 1860, when he was taken on by

Fields, who by then had established his reputation as the first great publisher-patron of American authors. (By 1860, Ticknor and Fields's publishing list included Whittier, Longfellow, Holmes, Lowell, and Thoreau.) Fields was one of the great cultural entrepreneurs of the middle decades of the nineteenth century, and one way to summarize his role in enhancing Emerson's reputation during the 1860s might be to say simply that he used his extensive network of friendly ties with editors of newspapers and magazines in which he advertised his books to secure a prominent place for Emerson within America's emerging national literary culture. Fields's power is most evident in the initial reception of *Conduct of Life*, not only Emerson's most immediate commercial success, but also his most widely reviewed book. Yet in another sense Fields's chief service in Emerson's behalf may have been less that he helped market his writings to a national audience, than that he used his power to limit the full play of market forces in determining the standing of Emerson's writings after 1860. The advertising campaigns Ticknor and Fields launched on behalf of its writers typically were not designed to sell its costly and elegantly produced books— the first two volumes of Emerson's *Prose Works* (1869) were priced at $5—so much as to make national the fame of the writers it chose to sponsor. The niche within the mid-nineteenth-century literary marketplace Ticknor & Fields controlled was one in which success was defined more in terms of status than sales. And so the mere appearance of Fields's name on title pages of Emerson's publications sufficed to locate his books immediately within that niche.[10]

Can these disparate bits and pieces of Emerson's career between 1865 and 1872 be put into a single coherent narrative? Or, more precisely, what bearing do they have for an understanding of Emerson's place in postbellum culture? The received account encourages us to think of the late Emerson as an uncomplicated, almost predictable presence in national life. Rather than a person active in responding to and shaping historical events, he works mostly as a symbol—Apostle of Culture or the Transcendentalist *par excellence*. To appreciate the symbol, we need to know little about the person.[11] But various threads of the story of Emerson in his mid sixties, when pulled, require us to construct a more complicated narrative that focuses on his sense of himself as a public moralist. To begin with, there is the fact that Emerson in his mid sixties still thought of himself as the holder of unpopular views, despite his rapidly growing national reputation. In broad terms, it is correct to think of the later Emerson as a progressive liberal. He was democratic, egalitarian, and secular, openly

sympathetic with the radicals in Reconstruction and the new movement
for woman's suffrage, and even more openly suspicious of his countrymen's
preoccupation with money and status—and such views hardly commanded
immediate assent·in the lecture halls and parlors of postbellum America.
The reporter who recorded Emerson's January 12, 1866, reading of "Social
Aims" before the Oberlin College Societies Library Association, for example, clearly thought he spoke for many when he underlined the unortho-
doxy of the speaker's views: "Mr. Emerson has little sympathy, we suppose,
with the faith that is dearest to us of Oberlin.... [H]is philosophy fails beside the faith of thousands of illiterate believing souls." Five months before
Emerson's visit to Oberlin, James Fields had refused to publish Emerson's
new essay on "Character" in the *Atlantic*, saying it was "not suited to the
magazine. Ordinary readers would not understand him and would consider it blasphemous."[12]

Such episodes help to explain why, in some moods, the later Emerson
viewed himself as a figure who stood alone, a counselor without followers,
sustained primarily by his desire to awaken his countrymen to their latent
capacities for independent thought and action. And certainly the identity
of an idealistic outsider is one that any champion of self-reliance and self-
trust might have found comforting, since it simultaneously celebrates the
inner resolve of a solitary individual, defines a sense of public purpose, and
explains away perceived failure. Occasionally, then, the later Emerson still
sounds like an American Jeremiah, and although he encountered other
reminders of his unpopularity in the late 1860s, it is fair to say that exag-
gerating the strength of popular opposition to his views remained one
of his polemical strategies.[13] The most important instances of this—not
surprisingly—usually involved discussions of popular attitudes towards
religion and education. In "Character," for example, Emerson depicted
mankind at large as resembling "frivolous children" who were "impatient
of thought and wish to be amused. Truth is too simple for us; we do not like
those who unmask our illusions" (W, 10:109). In "Education," he described
advocates of educational reform as confronting a society in which "the
word Education has so cold, so hopeless a sound" and asserted that "a treatise on education, a convention for education, a lecture, a system, affects us
with slight paralysis and a certain yawning of the jaws" (W, 10:133). "Character," it is worth noting, first appeared in the April 1866 *North American
Review*—three months before Emerson received an honorary degree of
Doctor of Laws from Harvard; "Education" was the lead lecture in a successful series on "American Life" he initially presented in Boston, Worcester, and Milwaukee, in the winter of 1864, a year that had begun with his
election to the American Academy of Arts and Sciences.[14]

As the invocations of "us" and "we" in "Character" may suggest, however, even in his most polemical moods Emerson intended to project his differences with his contemporaries in ways he thought would be reassuring. He in fact did not see himself speaking from a position located entirely outside the circle of mankind. "The religions we call false," he acknowledged, "were once true. They also were affirmations of the conscience correcting the evil customs of their times" (*W*, 10:104-105). Emerson, while pointedly questioning popular belief in the need for any particular institutional manifestation of religion—especially, of course, Protestant Christianity—remained confident of the enduring moral energy of his contemporaries. His task as public moralist, then, was to persuade them to continue to move in the right direction, and central to that task was persuading them to recognize that the route he recommended was simply an extension of a path that others before had already followed successfully. The following passage in "Character" is particularly revealing here:

> The Church, in its ardor for beloved persons, clings to the miraculous, in the vulgar sense, which has even an immoral tendency, as one sees in Greek, Indian, and Catholic legends, which are used to gloze every crime. The soul, penetrated with the beatitude which pours into it on all sides, asks no interpositions, no new laws—the old are good enough for it,—finds in every cart-path of labor ways to heaven, and the humblest lot exalted. Men will learn to put back the emphasis peremptorily on pure morals, always the same, not subject to doubtful interpretation, with no sale of indulgences, no massacre of heretics, no female slaves, no disfranchisement of women, no stigma on race; to make morals the absolute test, and so uncover and drive out the false religions. There is no vice that has not skulked behind them. It is only yesterday that our American churches, so long silent on Slavery, and notoriously hostile to the Abolitionist, wheeled into line for Emancipation. (*W*, 10:114)

This may have been one of the passages that made "Character" "blasphemous" in Fields's view. But Emerson's purpose was complex in ways this label does not manage to suggest. The passage is notable, as David Robinson has observed, in its equation of nineteenth-century movements for feminism and racial equality with the struggle against the most egregious historical examples of religious bigotry. But the passage at the same time served to voice Emerson's overriding concern with the new American culture he saw emerging from the success of the cooperative effort represented by the antislavery movement and the Civil War. Here Emerson wanted to drive home at least two related points: first, the specific "immoral tendency" of the American churches had been their commitment to defend an arbitrary resting place along the route of moral progress; and second, the moral impetus of American culture as a result had passed from its churches to its various reform movements.[15] Taken together, the two claims, in the end, reflected not so much Emerson's "heretical" views as they did his renewed confidence in his countrymen. "We see the dawn of a new era," he wrote in an 1865 journal entry, "worth to mankind all the treasure & all the lives it has cost, yes, worth to the world the lives of all this generation of American men, if they be demanded." Emerson knew what the Civil War had cost in lives, but he also wanted to believe it had "made many lives valuable that were not so before" and so had effectively "*moralized* cities & states" (*JMN*, 15:64).

As careful reading of "Character" suggests, Emerson did not stand in a purely adversarial relation to postbellum American culture, precisely because he was appealing to certain shared national values and experiences at the same time that he was criticizing his contemporaries for not living up to their agreed shared standards. His essays, Oliver Wendell Holmes remarked in a letter of October 30, 1869, were "peaceful battle songs"; they did not make men "set their teeth and knit their foreheads, but sent them forward smiling to think their thoughts and say them."[16] Emerson was not attempting to reverse or subvert his country's cultural and moral sensibilities, but instead to refine them and to call them more effectively into play on public issues. In these circumstances, however, he was also running at least two risks as he contrasted the farsightedness and consistency of his own positions with the generally self-interested confusions and inconsistencies he had to impute to those who, while sharing the same premises, had failed to draw the same conclusions. The first, ironically enough, was the risk of not being understood at all; the second, that of standing too close to those he criticized—of sounding too "peaceful" in his criticism—and thereby not being understood correctly. Both of these considerations also bring us to the final aspect of Emerson's general performance as public moralist that I want to discuss here: his characteristic style and manner of argument.

Nothing seemed more apparent about Emerson to his postwar audiences than the difficulty of his language. Some admirers (such as Bret Harte) praised him for doing more than any other American thinker "to voice the best philosophical conclusions of American life and experience." But others remarked that he did so in ways that made it difficult to sum up neatly the conclusions he was endorsing, as one might sum up this or that more conventional contribution to contemporary American social criticism or literature. There is no need for extensive citation here except to illustrate briefly how the difficulty of Emerson's prose sometimes served to obscure his performance in the role of public moralist. A particularly instructive example in this regard is the laudatory review of *Letters and Social Aims* that appeared in the February 26, 1876, *Saturday Review*. At first glance, the review appears to be a straightforward rebuttal of the complaint that Emerson's writing was "fanciful and rambling, and does not teach one anything in particular." As the rebuttal unfolds, however, it becomes clear that the complaint contains an important element of truth. For Emerson's achievement, according to the *Saturday Review*, lay precisely in the fact that his writings were not accessible to those who approached them looking for "rules and propositions." In his work, "matter" and "form" were as inseparable as they were in "the best talk"; yet also as with the best talk, this meant there was something in Emerson's writing that "would not be fixed." The *Saturday Review* was by no means divided in its praise of Emerson's achievement. What makes its defense of the difficulty of his prose instructive, however, is that it loses sight of the fact that Emerson thought of himself as a social critic who was describing what was wrong with his culture in ways that suggested practical remedies. The more difficult his language, then, the greater the distance between him and his audience, and the more obscure his criticism was likely to be.[17]

It would be misleading to suggest, however, that most encounters with Emerson's language during the 1860s and 1870s produced the impression of a writer whose views resisted straightforward translation. (The young Henry James, for example, had little trouble in offering a reliable précis of his ideas in an otherwise historically threadbare and somewhat condescending account of Emerson in his 1879 biography of Hawthorne.[18]) What is perhaps more striking about the language of *Society and Solitude* and *Letters and Social Aims*, especially when read in conjunction with contemporary newspaper accounts of Emerson's lectures and public addresses in the mid to late 1860s, is the extent to which his prose in fact took various forms. Throughout his career, no one ever doubted that Emerson's language presented a formidable challenge to ordinary intelligence. But his essays, lectures, and speeches also displayed mastery of prose styles that ranged from moral indictment and political censure at one extreme to satiric comment and utopian speculation at the other. This list may sound strange to some modern literary critics and theorists, but I expect it captures the experience of many of Emerson's contemporaries who knew him mostly by way of listening to him talk or reading excerpts from his books in literary reviews and summary accounts of his lectures in newspapers. Any one interested in understanding the growth of Emerson's reputation in the

1860s and early 1870s would be wise not to lose track of a lecturer and writer who could employ this sort of rhetoric:

> I think the genius of this country has marked out her true policy. Opportunity—doors wide open—every port open; if I could have it, free trade with the world, without toll or custom-house; invitation as we now make to every nation, every race and skin—white man, red man, yellow man, and black man; hospitality, a fair field, and equal laws to all. (*UL*, 6)

> The young men in America at this moment take little thought of what men in England are thinking or doing. That is the point which decides the welfare of the people; *which way does it look?* ... We have come to feel that "by ourselves our safety must be bought;" to know the vast resources of the continent, the good-will that is in the people, their conviction of the great moral advantages of freedom, social equality, education, and religious culture, and their determination to hold these fast, and, by them, to hold fast to the country and penetrate every square mile of it with this American civilization. (*W*, 8:101–102)

> Therefore I praise New England because it is the country in the world where is the freest expenditure for education. We have already taken, at the planting of the Colonies ... the initial step, which for its importance might have been resisted as the most radical of revolutions, thus deciding at the start the destiny of this country,—this, namely, that the poor man, whom the law does not allow to take an ear of corn when starving, nor a pair of shoes for his freezing feet, is allowed to put his hand into the pocket of the rich, and say, You shall educate me, not as you will, but as I will: not alone in the elements, but, by further provision, in the languages, in sciences, in the useful and elegant arts. The child shall be taken up by the State, and taught, at the public cost, the rudiments of knowledge, and, at last, the ripest results of art and science. (*W*, 10:125–126)

Here clearly was a public moralist ready to offer "rules and propositions," and confident enough of his standing that he did not need to use specialized or esoteric language to convey his message. Here too was a figure who openly identified himself as a member of his community, and the ideals he promoted come across as strong versions of the ideals his countrymen themselves claimed to live by.[19]

All that said, perhaps Emerson's most common rhetorical strategy was (as Richard Poirier has labeled it) troping, taking hold of the everyday language of his contemporaries and raising it to a higher pitch of moral intensity and interpretive power.[20] This fact also underlines my earlier point about Emerson's reliance on a certain community of values between himself and his audience: for without a shared understanding of the current use of language, efforts to turn that language in new and unexpected directions seem destined to fall on deaf ears. Similarly, if Emerson's troping aimed to free the thinking of his contemporaries from predetermined meanings of what he took to be the key words in their culture, at least one understanding of each term being transformed had to be widely shared; otherwise, the attempted transformation would have little persuasive force. The whole of Emerson's essay on "Wealth" in *Conduct of Life*—still widely circulated in various forms during the late 1860s and 1870s—can be regarded as an extended exercise in troping, or, more specifically, an exhibit of Emerson's determination to uncover nobler purposes he felt certain were contained with the characteristically American "demand to be rich." While the essay sometimes has been read as providing a rationale for Gilded Age entrepreneurs, ultimately it was a selective rationale that welcomed only those ready to join Emerson in the still undone work of giving all Americans "access to the masterpieces of art and nature" and of creating a society whose economic abundance would be used primarily to provide every one of its members "the means and apparatus of science and the arts." That in essence was Emerson's vision of the unique double meaning of "wealth": an egalitarian culture where the benefits of civilization, reserved for the opulent few in Europe, would now be enjoyed by all in America.[21]

The rhetorical strategy of troping so characteristic of Emerson's essays and lectures in the 1840s and 1850s also figured prominently in those he composed in the second half of the 1860s. It was evident, to begin with, in his choice of titles: "Character," "Success," "Courage," "Hospitality," "Greatness," and "Eloquence." All these pieces pursued are "Emersonian" as Poirier has defined the term, in wanting both to "prevent words from coming to rest" and "to dissuade us from hoping that they ever might." The "constant interest" in "manners" Emerson appeared to affirm at the outset of "Social Aims," for example, turned out to be grounded in an understanding of "manners" that expanded and redefined the term to include Emersonian ideals of self-command and independence. He accepted the popular definition of "manners," in other words, only to turn that definition on its head. The man of true "manners and talent" does not need a fine coat, for "it is only when mind and character slumber that the dress can be seen. If the intellect were always awake, and every noble sentiment, the man might go in huckaback, or mats, and his dress would be admired and imitated" (W, 8:87). The later Emerson offered no explicit praise for a life of voluntary poverty; otherwise he sometimes sounded much like Thoreau.[22]

As a rhetorical strategy for a public moralist, troping was not without its drawbacks. There is little evidence showing that Emerson's contemporaries understood the full complexity of his challenge exactly as he offered it. As we have seen, some despaired of understanding it at all; others heard Emerson's acknowledgement of their concerns and then overlooked or ignored his criticism.[23] Robinson's description of the prose in "Success" as "walking a thin line" could also be applied to several of his postbellum essays. Emerson was a figure who thought he could speak to his culture, Robinson reminds us, because he so deeply shared its values, and this familiar characterization draws attention to the fact that his effort to reclaim the notion of success by divorcing it from the search for quick and superficial achievement was of a piece with his effort to preserve the ideal of success on individualistic grounds. In recognizing that these two views of success were of a piece, however, we can also see why contemporaries who put Emerson back into close company with American prophets of the gospel of material success did not entirely misconstrue his original intentions. The potential for such a half-reading was latent in the strategy of troping itself. In speaking the language of his countrymen, Emerson never managed to sustain an oppositional tone strong enough to prevent many of them from mistaking his language for a roundabout endorsement of existing social and economic practices. Emerson's protest against the culture of his day, Holmes remarked in looking back on the course of his career, was one that "outflanked the extreme left of liberalism," yet it was at the same time "so calm and serene that its radicalism has the accents of the gospel of peace." He was, in short, "an iconoclast without a hammer, who took down our idols from their pedestals so tenderly that it seemed like an act of worship."[24] Not entirely true, and curious coming from Holmes since he doubtless knew that slavery and the Civil War had prompted Emerson to deliver openly partisan, and at times violently polemical, lectures and addresses. But Holmes also knew that Emerson was never comfortable with the role of political spokesman.

In considering Emerson's performance as a public moralist during the final years of his life, as well as the whole complicated question of his status as one of the Gilded Age's leading cultural celebrities, special attention has to be paid, finally, to his role in the transformation of American higher education, and here the chronological framework I've employed so far needs to be broadened somewhat. His influence in this realm—especially in the case of Charles Eliot's implementation of the elective system at Harvard—has provoked conflicting interpretations in modern scholarly commentary, interpretations which, interestingly enough, mirror divisions of opinion first displayed by late nineteenth-century observers of Emerson's career. A general conviction that Emerson was a spokesman for fundamental educational reform was first voiced during the 1840s and 1850s when he emerged as a favorite lecturer on college campuses and before various young men's associations. After the Civil War, Emerson also found admirers who argued that his condemnations of the "deadness" of American education had prompted his most concrete recommendations for reform:

> it would be well for those who affect to regard him as a harmless mystic, to know that no other man, for years, has left such an impress upon the young collegiate mind of America; that his style and thought go far to form the philosophic pothooks of many a Freshman's thesis; that from a secular pulpit he preaches better practical sermons on the conduct of life than is heard from two-thirds of the Christian pulpits of America.[25]

In a similar though much less defensive vein, Eliot would announce in the Emerson centenary year that he had "laid down in plain terms the fundamental doctrines" on which Harvard's new elective system rested. Supporting his position with quotations drawn from essays ranging from "The American Scholar" to "Education," he identified Emerson as "a prophet and inspirer of reform" who had left the hard work of "giving practical effect to his thought" for others to do. Yet Eliot, the most influential academic reformer of his generation, also left no doubt that it was Emerson, above all others, who had inspired the work of curricular reform that had begun when he took office as Harvard's president in 1869, with Emerson himself—then in the second year of his first term on the Board of Overseers—sitting among the front-row guests at his inaugural address.[26]

Several years before Eliot underlined Emerson's credentials as an American "prophet," another set of admirers had put forward a different and apparently contrasting image. James Elliot Cabot's *Memoir of Ralph Waldo Emerson* (1887) provided an influential early statement of this view with his observation that Emerson's doctrines in fact had never gained many converts, because he "had never identified himself with his precepts, but was always ready to reverse them, however categorical they might be, with equal emphasis and as coolly as if he had never heard of them. He was not compiling a code." The alternative suggestion here was that Emerson was important not because he had helped to reshape nineteenth-century Amer-

ican culture but because he had contemplated that culture from the vantage point of an original mind. This was an Emerson who George Santayana
would say, admiringly, "had no doctrine at all." Those who knew Emerson
personally, he remarked, never judged him as a poet or philosopher, nor
identified his "efficacy" with that of his writings. Yet his cultural efficacy, on
Santayana's account, seemed beside the point, since the picture of Emerson he presented was that of a detached, Olympian figure who generally
held himself above the fray of controversy, and so was "in no sense a
prophet for his age or country."[27]

On closer inspection, it may not be hard to see that these two interpretations are not quite the opposites they may appear at first. They implicitly
agree in discounting the modest effectiveness Emerson claimed for himself in reflecting on his career. Both "American prophet" and "American
mystic" are descriptions of a figure who wielded a peculiarly powerful influence on the educated elite of his time. (By the end of the century, Emerson's more well-informed admirers collectively had begun to sense that he
could be enlisted in many causes or none at all.) But what if we consider
Emerson's complex and disputed contribution to the transformation of
American higher education in the broader context of this discussion of his
role as public moralist? That contribution falls into place if we approach it,
in the first place, as an integral part of his distinctive effort to interpret and
defend the newness of American culture. Santayana was right in saying
that Emerson had no gospel to proclaim, at least not in the usual sense. But
that hardly meant he was prepared to defend American "education" as he
found it. For what he found manifested only mistrust and timidity—that is
to say, failure to honor the distinctively American belief that all the nation's
institutions "existed for the individual, for the guardianship and education
of everyman."[28] The entire system was "a system of despair," Emerson
complained. It omitted "the vast and the spiritual," as well as "the practical
and the moral" (W, 10:133). The true object of education was both more
idealistic and more worldly than its current generation of providers chose
to recognize.

So the content of a distinctively American "education" had yet to be determined, and Emerson hoped to have—and for a time clearly did have—
a voice in that determination. Several lectures he delivered frequently during the second half the 1860s—especially "Resources," "Social Aims,"
"Education," and variously titled lectures on the topic of "culture"—should
be read in terms of his long-standing commitment to a cultural transformation in which his central strategy was to awaken his listeners to their
own deepest values and in which the chief objects of his criticism were
skepticism and complacency. "There is much criticism, not on deep

grounds, but an affirmative philosophy is wanting." Emerson called on a new generation of American scholars to join him in assuming the responsibilities of "counselor" and "upholder," "imparting pulses of light and shocks of electricity, guidance and courage" (W, 10:325). "Guidance" here was, in part, synonymous with a renewal of faith in "the good will that is in the people," a renewal that—in Emerson's case—had been wrought by the Civil War: "The whole history of the Civil War is rich in a thousand anecdotes affecting the fertility of resource, the presence of mind, the skilled labor of our people" (W, 8:139). (During the war itself, Emerson had said: "We will not again disparage America now that we have seen what men it will bear" [W, 11:322].) Another part of his guidance was focused on long-standing cultural questions: "Amidst the calamities which war has brought on our county this one benefit has accrued—that our eyes are withdrawn from England, withdrawn from France, and look homeward." Emerson himself was "looking homeward" in his postbellum lectures and essays, and what he saw was a profound cultural transformation in the making—a transformation whose accomplishment he held up as the primary measure of America's worth as a reunified nation.

Despite his free-trade convictions, the later Emerson was neither a nationalist on behalf of a rising professional middle class nor an idealistic mouthpiece for a new entrepreneurial ethos. Unlike other Northern celebrants of the Civil War and its heroes, he also never waved the bloody shirt. His vision of the "progress of culture" in America took other forms. One—largely overlooked by students of the last phase of his career—was a remarkably pointed defense of immigration. Emerson's message at the outset of his second Phi Beta Kappa address at Harvard in 1867, for example, was that there had been an unprecedented "fusion of races and religion" in America, a fusion which had made it "the answering facility of immigration, permitting every wanderer to choose his climate and government" (W, 8:197). The generational categories in which Emerson often expressed himself arguably fit immigrants better than the middle class or corporate entrepreneurs. The new postbellum American nation was one where "men come hither by nations" (W, 8:197) and promised—as he had put it in an 1864 lecture before the Parker Fraternity in Boston—by "perpetual intermixture to yield the most vigorous qualities and accomplishments of all."[29] Emerson was also sympathetic to new efforts to speed the political and economic assimilation of freed African Americans. He had identified himself publicly with the great revolution of the middle of the Civil War: the acceptance of black men into the Union Army.[30] After the war, he endorsed the Reconstruction as an end to the "false relations" of slavery and the beginning of an effort to create a just order in which "every man shall have what he honestly earns" and an "equal vote in the state, and a fair chance in society" (*JMN*, 15:301–302).

What would "education" in this America become? Emerson professed not to know. "We confess that in America everything looks new and recent" (*W*, 8:202). He knew only that the very purpose of America entailed embracing the "new and recent"—thereby promising an escape from "the ruts of the last generation"—and that here education would not imitate the European model, with churches and "hereditary aristocracy" imposing their values on ordinary people. With the Civil War over, Emerson also knew that his own exemplary New Englanders no longer formed a separate country, but were now caught up in America's "fusion of races and people," and they would betray their own democratic values if they resisted the assimilation of those coming "from crowded, antiquated kingdoms to the easy sharing of our simple forms" (*W*, 8:203). "The democratic opening of all avenues to all," Emerson proclaimed, "is the fixed advantage which our institutions give, the solver of all conceits" (*UL*, 7). The progress of democracy, then, would generate radically new concepts of "culture" and "education" whose richness could only be intimated. Repress American "hospitality," constrain the choices of ordinary men and women, and the result will be to extinguish the egalitarian spirit that is "our power." America's alternative to European education—its "one point of plain duty"—was "to educate every soul. Every native and every foreign child that is cast on our coast shall be taught, at the public cost, all the rudiments of knowledge, and at last the ripest results of art and science" (*UL*, 7).

A multinational America, "the answering facility of immigration" where individual identity is not static but progressive and ever-changing, and where the object of education was to teach every person "self-trust": that was Emerson's vision of a postwar America with its "doors wide open." How much of this version of Emerson reappeared in Eliot's famous centenary address? Important parts of it, to be sure. Eliot recognized (and shared) Emerson's confidence in the uniqueness of what was transpiring in America, and the same was true for Emerson's belief that there was no pre-established model for American education available in Europe. But this is perhaps the wrong question to explore at length here if we want to understand the main historical significance of the Emerson-Eliot connection. It does not require close reading of Eliot's centenary tribute to see that it was largely a picture of Emerson in his thirties. His career as a lecturer received only brief mention, and its remarkable revival in the late 1860s—including Emerson's second Phi Beta Kappa Address at Harvard—went unmentioned. The part of Emerson's life that interested Eliot ended in 1843, because in that year he saw the development of the central maxims

of his thought as coming to an end. Emerson's contributions to the abolitionist movement in the 1840s and 1850s were more important than Eliot
may have known at the time, though there were other voices celebrating
Emerson in 1903—above all, Franklin Sanborn, who was then the chief
eulogist and self-appointed historian of American Transcendentalism—
who had already made much of this side of his career. Moreover, it was
almost entirely in antebellum New England that Eliot put Emerson—the
world of Concord, Harvard, and Boston, not the postbellum America of
immigrants and entrepreneurs. Finally, and perhaps most obviously, he
saw Emerson through the spectacles of his own understanding of what
counted as progressive reform at the outset of the twentieth century, with
the result that Emerson was viewed as a prophet of various other developments ranging from "the cultivation of manners" and the ascendancy of
"athletic sports" in American higher education to "the absurdity of paying
all sorts of service at one rate, now a favorite notion with some labor
unions." Even Eliot's claim that Emerson had been the main source of
his commitment to the elective system turned out to be somewhat self-
serving. We know that elective reforms endorsed by both of Harvard's governing boards were already underway at the time of Eliot's inauguration,
and the new president was expected to continue the advance. And while it
was hardly surprising that Eliot traced his intellectual pedigree back to
Emerson, he in fact had displayed little concern with the elective principle
before his election.[31]

Whatever its limitations, large or small, Eliot's centenary lecture on
Emerson forms an important part of the larger story of how Emerson's
name and ideas gained national attention and authority during the Gilded
Age. Eliot of course was in no position to dictate a national consensus
regarding Emerson, even if he had managed a more faithful rendering of
his career and ideas. But he did hold institutional power that he used
to provide what was arguably a more important service: the publicity
needed to keep Emerson visible in American culture at large. The entire
course of their relationship might be described as a feedback loop. At first,
Eliot borrowed strength from the reputation of a living, embodied Emerson. Here we should remind ourselves how young Eliot was when, after he
was elected president, he began to have frequent contact with Emerson—
he was thirty-five, younger than any previous president, and Emerson was
sixty-six—just as we should remind ourselves that he had not been the
overwhelmingly popular choice of the Harvard Overseers. The Emerson
that Eliot sought out in the 1870s was not simply one of the sixteen overseers who had voted for his appointment—eight had voted against it—but
a figure recently accepted as part of Harvard's great past and an eager

ally in the cause of institutional reform.[32] Near the end of his term, however, it was Eliot, now widely recognized as America's most influential educational reformer, who helped to build Emerson's posthumous reputation. In fact, by the turn of the century, Eliot's public identity within American culture began to resemble the later Emerson's in some respects. The labels "oracle," "prophet," and "sage" were now used to describe his relationship with the public at large. Harvard's President Eliot had become America's President Eliot, and it was in that role that he helped to confer new luster on Emerson. Two years after the centenary address, he found what turned out to be a more permanent way of identifying Emerson as a vital agent of Harvard's past and future, dedicating the University's new Emerson Hall—the first building in America dedicated to the study of philosophy—on the dual occasion of the one-hundredth anniversary of his birth and Harvard's hosting the annual convention of the American Philosophical Association. Four years later, Eliot made Emerson the chief American beneficiary of his labors as editor of the new "Harvard Classics" in yet another project that served to tie Emerson's name even more closely to an institution that once had wanted nothing to do with him. In Eliot's fifty volumes, Emerson was among a remarkably small handful of American writers who earned inclusion in an otherwise all-British and European pantheon; and while he was one of two Americans whose writings earned publication as a separate volume, Eliot singled him out as "the greatest of American thinkers."[33]

The story of the later Emerson's career traced in this essay differs in several important respects from that usually told by modern interpreters. First of all, we have seen that the public image of Emerson in American culture during the 1860s and 1870s was more manifold than is typically suggested. The familiar image of the later Emerson as a revered literary figure of the recent past, a New Englander who survived in the Gilded Age as a symbolic remnant of a better age, is too foreshortened (if not altogether misleading) to take in all the details displayed in a full history of his postwar activities and reputation. Against the familiar image of "exquisite" Emerson (the adjective comes from the young Henry James), I have set another that in fact bears resemblance to one first sketched shortly after his second Phi Beta Kappa Address. As it appeared in the September 21, 1867, issue of *Every Saturday*, the assessment ran as follows:

> The enthusiasm with which Ralph Waldo Emerson is greeted in
> every part of the United States is a phenomenon which cannot es-

cape the attention of those who study the affairs and tendencies of that country. During the last few years we find him at one time called to Washington to address the national representatives on the condition of the country, and afterwards engaged in a consultation with President Lincoln; last year Harvard University bestowed on him the honorary degree of Doctor of Laws; during the past winter he visited the West, and addressed the populations of its most important cities which turned out crowds to welcome and listen to him; at St. Louis he held conversations with a Hegelian club, which certain educated Germans have formed there; and more recently he has been unanimously chosen to deliver the chief oration at the Cambridge Commencement, having the day before been elected by the legislature of Massachusetts an overseer of that institution, the oldest and most important in the country. Thus, in his sixty-fourth year, and after a literary career of more than forty years, in which he has advocated the most sweeping heresies of the age, and been regarded as an incomprehensible visionary, the seer opens the "garden-gate," once sternly slammed in the face of the world, and steps into the arena; the prophet's mantle is thrown aside for the captain's armor.[34]

The verdict here is not precisely the one I have tried to support—and it was Harvard alumni, not the Massachusetts Legislature, who elected Emerson Overseer—but it comes close. It was in the second half of the 1860s that Emerson achieved the stature of a national presence, although the story told here recognizes that in the process his "heresies" were not simply forgotten, nor did his countrymen suddenly stop viewing him as an "incomprehensible visionary" as they sought greater familiarity with the man and his writings and ideas. The broad opening claim of this assessment, however, seems accurate enough, if in proclaiming Emerson a national presence *Every Saturday* meant to draw attention to two relatively straightforward points. First, despite the fact that actual sales of American editions of Emerson's writings remained relatively modest over the course of the 1860s and 1870s, some sort of confrontation with Emerson—the man, the image, his lectures and his writings—became virtually obligatory for literate Americans of diverse backgrounds and interests. Second, the same could not yet be said for any other nineteenth-century American writer and lecturer, either in Emerson's own generation or in its successor. There was in fact no one else who had lived a life like Emerson's or represented what he had come to represent—a poet-philosopher central to the emerging high culture of the Gilded Age and at the same time a peripatetic public moralist who, for more than three decades, had attempted to address the cultural and political concerns of everyday Americans.

These conclusions are also significant in pointing to new questions concerning developments that served to enhance and maintain Emerson's reputation after his death. We still know surprisingly little about the story of what became of Emerson's reputation during the last two decades of the nineteenth century. During his lifetime, it seems clear that the centrality of Emerson was not imposed on his countrymen, but accepted, sometimes with amusement, confusion, and reluctance. As important as his ties to postbellum Harvard may have proved to be, no one set of cultural institutions ever "constructed" Emerson's reputation while he was alive. It is of course true that he needed to be familiar to be respected—to become "an accepted fact" before he became our "our national glory"—but over the entire course of his lifetime the repeated performances most important to public acceptance included his lectures and newspaper accounts of those lectures, as well as publications and institutional attachments under his direct control. To carry the story I have told in this essay beyond 1882, then, we would need to know more about the cultural identities of those who guaranteed the familiarity of an Emerson who lived on largely as the author of books. Eliot was only one of a large number of players in this story, and a latecomer at that.

At the time of Emerson's death, the *New York Herald* commented that "there is a difference of opinion [regarding] how long Mr. Emerson's books will continue to be read."[35] Over the course of the next twenty-five years, however, dozens of publishers moved to assure that reading Emerson would became a national practice by packaging his writings for every level of the American literary marketplace. Some examples: beginning in 1883, his books and essays became a staple for middle-class home libraries in a new format Houghton Mifflin Company perfected to identify and bring to market America's "classic" authors: the Riverside Edition of the Complete Works. Three years later, his work began to reappear in numerous cheap cloth and paperback editions, thereby spreading Emerson even more widely throughout American culture. Between 1882 and 1909, some forty-six different miscellaneous collections of Emerson's writings were printed by various American and British publishers. Also, prior to the appearance of the "Harvard Classics," *English Traits* and *Representative Men* had been republished in the "World's Classics" of Oxford University Press in 1903, as well as in the new "Everyman's Library" series—a joint undertaking of J. M. Dent in London and E. P. Dutton in New York.[36]

The complex pattern of the reprintings of Emerson's writings between 1882 and 1909 suggests plainly that during this period popular demand for those writings was much greater than at any time during the course of his life. This is not the same, however, as saying that an abundant supply of his writings signaled that Emerson had become the dominant or representative cultural figure of the time. Perhaps more interestingly, it also is not the same as saying that his high cultural standing was dependent on any one text or set of texts. Most late nineteenth- and early twentieth-century Americans probably either avoided or remained indifferent to the question of which of his writings gave Emerson authority within American culture. There were, to be sure, some voices who proclaimed that his early essays formed the ideal center of a new field of professional study called "American literature," but these were as yet few in number and their immediate influence is difficult to measure.[37] A preference for the writings of the younger Emerson seems to be a general cultural taste Americans acquired after the end of the World War I, and the notion of a falling off in the later Emerson had not yet attracted many adherents either.

How and why, then, did Americans come to believe that there is little in the career or thinking of the later Emerson to compare with the Emerson of the 1830s and 1840s? The story told in this essay suggests that that question is worth another close look, both because it involves the interesting spectacle of the full complexity of the historical Emerson fading from sight as his cultural authority increased and because it draws our attention to a more general cultural change in our purposes in reading Emerson or contemplating his career. Or put another way, while scholarly interest in Emerson's texts has undergone a remarkable revival during the past two decades, with a new mood of interpretive charity guiding many sophisticated reinterpretations, contemporary studies of the intellectual and rhetorical demands Emerson's writings continue to make on readers have been exploring questions that appear only indirectly relevant to the effort to understand the various identities Emerson has had over time. We will begin to find our way here, perhaps, as we more carefully establish and come to terms with the changing institutional settings within which the status of his work has been debated and defined.

Notes

1. J. A. Bellows, "Mr. Emerson's New Book," *Liberal Christian*, Jan. 22, 1876. The *Liberal Christian* (1845–1877) was a Unitarian weekly published in New York. As with Shakespeare in nineteenth-century America, the later Emerson was so familiar he sometimes became an object of parody, perhaps most famously in a speech Mark Twain delivered at a Dec. 17, 1877, dinner in Boston given by the publishers of the *Atlantic Monthly* to commemorate John Greenleaf Whittier's seventieth birthday.

Twain's speech—a literary burlesque in which Emerson, Holmes, and Longfellow were portrayed as seedy confidence men preying on a naive California miner—attracted national attention. That most Boston newspapers that reported the speech presented it sympathetically as an amusing satire suggests the aging Emerson was not held in unthinking reverence in his home state. More importantly, the newspaper controversy surrounding the speech shows that talk about Emerson at times was popular entertainment during the Gilded Age. See Henry Nash Smith, *Mark Twain: The Development of a Writer* (Cambridge, 1962), chap. 5.

2. Franklin Sanborn, "The Portraits of Emerson" in *Transcendental and Literary New England*, ed. Kenneth Walter Cameron (Hartford, 1975), 184; Lowell, as quoted in *Uncollected Lectures by Ralph Waldo Emerson*, ed. Clarence Gohdes (New York, 1932), vi. Emerson also had a substantial transatlantic reputation that reinforced his standing at home. See William J. Sowder, *Emerson's Impact on the British Isles and Canada* (Charlottesville, 1966).

3. A more definitive assessment of Emerson's postbellum career (which should include a careful reexamination of late nineteenth-century critics and scholars who presented Emerson as the epitome of Transcendentalism) awaits not only the completion of the new edition of Emerson's *Collected Works*, but also a comprehensive secondary bibliography that includes all newspaper and magazine accounts of Emerson's lectures. Although missing important items, Robert E. Burkholder and Joel Myerson, *Emerson: An Annotated Secondary Bibliography* (Pittsburgh, 1985), provides the most up-to-date general inventory. My account of Emerson's career between 1865 and 1882 draws from the still invaluable Ralph Rusk, *The Life of Ralph Waldo Emerson* (New York, 1949), and John McAleer, *Ralph Waldo Emerson: Days of Encounter* (Boston, 1984).

4. Anon., "Ralph Waldo Emerson," *Boston Daily Advertiser*, Apr. 22, 1882; anon., "Ralph Waldo Emerson," *Chicago Daily Tribune* Apr. 30, 1882; anon., "Death of Emerson," *San Francisco Daily Chronicle* Apr. 28, 1882; anon., "Ralph Waldo Emerson," *Charleston Daily News and Courier*, Apr. 29, 1882. For an extended review of Emerson's obituaries, see H. L. Kleinfield, "The Structure of Emerson's Death," *Bulletin of the New York Public Library* 65(1961):47–64.

5. William Dean Howells, *Literary Friends and Acquaintances*, ed. D. F. Hiatt and E. H. Candy (1900; Bloomington, 1968), 57. More recent studies of Emerson's antebellum reputation include my *Sublime Thoughts/Penny Wisdom: Situating Emerson and Thoreau in the American Market* (Baltimore, 1995), chaps. 7 and 8; Mary Kupiec Cayton, "The Making of an American Prophet: Emerson, His Audiences, and the Rise of the Culture Industry in Nineteenth-Century America," *American Historical Review* 92(1987):597–620; and Len Gougeon, *Virtue's Hero: Emerson, Antislavery, and Reform* (Athens, Ga., 1990).

6. Franklin Sanborn, "Harvard's Treatment of Emerson," in *Transcendental and Literary New England*, 351–352.

7. The following abbreviations are cited parenthetically in the text to refer to various editions of Emerson's writings: *CW: The Collected Works of Ralph Waldo Emerson*, ed. Alfred R. Ferguson et al. (Cambridge, Mass., 1971–); *JMN: The Journals and Miscellaneous Notebooks of Ralph Waldo Emerson*, ed. William H. Gilman et al. (Cambridge, Mass., 1960–1982); *L: The Letters of Ralph Waldo Emerson*, ed. Ralph L. Rusk and Eleanor Tilton (New York, 1939–); *UL: Uncollected Lectures*

of Ralph Waldo Emerson, ed. Clarence Gohdes (New York, 1932); *W: The Complete Works of Ralph Waldo Emerson*, ed. Edward Waldo Emerson (Boston, 1903–1904).

8. In a letter of Nov. 25, 1868, for example, Emerson remarked that he had asked the leading Boston newspapers in advance of a new round of lectures not to report him and that, for the most part, they obliged (*L*, 6:45). Emerson's efforts to keep himself "safe from reporters" also reflected his desire to provide fresh material for his lecture audiences. In November 1865, looking forward to a new lecture tour in several Midwestern states, Emerson told a correspondent that he was reluctant to lecture in Brooklyn and New York for fear that future audiences in the Midwest might see accounts of early versions of his lectures in the national edition of the *New York Tribune* (*L*, 5:436).

9. It is worth noting that, while a growing number of his contemporaries were attempting to become self-supporting writers, Emerson was well protected by money and social position from the full force of the nineteenth-century literary marketplace to shape his life and determine how he would represent himself in his writings. By the late 1860s, he was a wealthy man by contemporary standards. His income from investments and lectures not only provided him with financial freedom, it also allowed him to pay printing and composition costs and retain copyright of all his authorized publications.

10. It is of course no less true that Emerson's growing national reputation as America's leading poet-philosopher helped confer new luster on Fields's publishing house and magazines, especially the *Atlantic Monthly*. On Fields, see W. S. Tyron, *Parnassus Corner: A Life of James T. Fields* (Boston, 1963); Richard H. Brodhead, *The School of Hawthorne* (New York, 1986); and Ellery Sedgwick, *The Atlantic Monthly, 1857–1909: Yankee Humanism at High Tide and Ebb* (Amherst, Mass., 1994), chap. 3. Fields's efforts on Emerson's behalf would be continued by the several firms that succeeded Ticknor & Fields as Emerson's publisher during the last three decades of the nineteenth century: Fields, Osgood, & Company; James R. Osgood; and—after Henry Houghton bought out the failing Osgood—Houghton Mifflin Company.

11. The last 17 years of Emerson's life occupy little more than 21 pages in the most recent, 573-page biography by Robert D. Richardson, *Emerson: The Mind on Fire* (Berkeley, 1995); the Library of America edition of Emerson's *Essays and Lectures* (New York, 1983) does not include a single essay Emerson published after 1860.

12. *Lorain County News* (Oberlin, Ohio), Jan. 17, 1866, as quoted in *L*, 5:449n; Fields, as quoted in Carlos Baker, *Emerson among the Eccentrics: A Group Portrait* (New York, 1996), 457.

13. Emerson continued to be stigmatized with the label "infidel" in the postwar years. A few weeks after he read "Social Aims" on the evening before commencement exercises at Ripley Female College (later Green Mountain Junior College), an anonymous letter in the July 27, 1865, *Christian Advocate and Journal* (New York) protested Emerson's presence by asking rhetorically, "Will not our children learn infidelity fast enough without being taught it at school by the high priest of infidelity?"

14. "Character" appeared anonymously in the *North American Review*, then under the editorship of Charles Eliot Norton and James Russell Lowell, and owned by James Fields.

15. David M. Robinson, *Emerson and the Conduct of Life: Pragmatism and Ethical*

Purpose in the Later Work (New York, 1993). My understanding of the later Emerson is much indebted to Robinson's important study, but I also think (for reasons discussed later in this paper) he tends to overdraw the "oppositional" attitudes of the later Emerson.

16. Holmes, as quoted in *L*, 6:78n, wrote to Emerson after receiving gift copies of the first two volumes of his *Prose Works*, published by Fields, Osgood & Co. in Boston, on Oct. 27, 1869.

17. Bret Harte, review of *Society and Solitude*, in *Overland Monthly* (Oct. 1870): 386–387; anon., "Emerson's Letters and Social Aims," *Saturday Review* 41(Feb. 26, 1876):275–276. The *Overland Monthly* (1868–1923), published in San Francisco, was California's leading literary magazine during the last decades of the nineteenth century; its circulation was 10,000 at the time of Harte's review.

18. Henry James, *Hawthorne* (New York, 1879), 80–84. Of Emerson's central ideas, James wrote: "Emerson expressed, before all things . . . the value and importance of the individual, the duty of making the most of one's self, and living by one's personal light, and carrying out one's own disposition."

19. For a more extended discussion of Emerson's antebellum essays and his response to the Civil War along these lines, see my *Sublime Thoughts/Penny Wisdom*, chaps. 1, 4, and 6. The traditional view of the Civil War simply as a facilitator of Emerson's accommodationism and Northern cultural imperialism turns on a selective reading of his lectures and writings. More often a critic of the North's compromising stance than of the South's injustice during the 1850s, Emerson was a disunionist when the war began in April 1861. It is true that he welcomed the outbreak of war as an unanticipated opportunity to accomplish quickly the political redemption of the South. But he also insisted that only if Union forces fought for emancipation, as well as for union, would their cause be just.

20. Richard Poirier, *The Renewal of Literature: Emersonian Reflections* (New York, 1987), 13–19, 131–132.

21. "Wealth," in *Conduct of Life* (1860), reprinted in *Selected Writings of Ralph Waldo Emerson*, ed. Brooks Atkinson (New York, 1940), 705, 700–701, 699. In 1875, James R. Osgood arranged for separate re-publication of "Wealth" in its new and relatively less expensive *Vest Pocket Series*. In 1876, *Conduct of Life* was reprinted as vol. 6 of the "Little Classics Edition" of Emerson's extant works.

22. Poirier, *Renewal of Literature*, 16.

23. Focusing mostly on Midwestern newspaper accounts of early lecture versions of "Success," Cayton, "The Making of an American Prophet," has argued persuasively that during the 1850s Emerson's stature grew because he was misread as a proponent rather than as a critic of the American success myth. It would be interesting to know if the same process repeated itself during Emerson's last great lecture tours of the Midwest in the late 1860s.

24. Robinson, *Emerson and the Conduct of Life*, 162; Holmes, as quoted in Baker, *Emerson among the Eccentrics*, 472. Howells would later remark that Emerson simply was not taken seriously before the Civil War. "It would be hard to persuade people now," he wrote in 1900, "that Emerson once represented to the popular mind all that was most hopelessly impossible, and that in a certain sort, he was a national joke, the type of the incomprehensible, the byword of a poor paragraph." Howells, *Literary Friends*, 56.

25. Harte, review of *Society and Solitude*, in *Overland Monthly* 5(Oct. 1870):387.

26. Charles W. Eliot, "Emerson," in *Charles W. Eliot, the Man and His Beliefs*, ed. William Allan Neilson (New York, 1926). This essay was first presented as a lecture in Symphony Hall, Boston; it first appeared in print as "Emerson as Seer" in the *Atlantic Monthly* (June 1903):844–855, and later also reprinted in Eliot, *American Leaders* (1906).

27. James Elliot Cabot, *A Memoir of Ralph Waldo Emerson* (Boston, 1887), 625–626; George Santayana, "Emerson," in *Interpretations of Poetry and Religion* (1900), reprinted in *Selected Critical Writings of George Santayana*, ed. Norman Henfry (Cambridge, 1968), 117–127. In standard modern accounts of the emergence of the American university during the last decades of the nineteenth century, Emerson has been assigned the role of active and influential reformer. See, for example, Burton Bledstein, *The Culture of Professionalism: The Middle Class and the Development of Higher Education in America* (New York, 1976), 259–268; yet he also has received only passing mention in Laurence Veysey's *The Emergence of the American University* (Chicago, 1965).

28. Ralph Waldo Emerson, "Historic Notes of Life and Letters in New England," in *The American Transcendentalists: Their Prose and Poetry*, ed. Perry Miller (Garden City, N.Y., 1957), 5.

29. Emerson, as quoted in Cabot, *Memoir*, 2:789. Also see the somewhat more well-known 1845 journal entry where Emerson hailed the American continent as an "asylum of all nations," which drew "the energy of Irish, Germans, Swedes, Poles, and Cossacks, and all the European tribes—of the Africans and the Polynesians," creating in the process a "new race" as "vigorous as the new Europe which came out of the smelting pot of the Dark Ages" (*JMN*, 9:299–300). In commenting on this passage, David Hollinger recently has grouped Emerson with Crevecoeur and Melville as American thinkers whose national ideal is not quite pluralist, because they did not explicitly envision a series of enduring groups, nor unambiguously cosmopolitan, because they emphasized "the diversity not of the final product, but only of the materials going into it." After the Civil War, the Emerson we encounter at the outset of the "Progress of Culture" might be seen as anticipating the more full-blown cosmopolitanism of figures such as Randolph Bourne. See David Hollinger, *Postethnic America: Beyond Multiculturalism* (New York, 1995), 86–87; and Lawrence W. Levine, *The Opening of the American Mind: Canons, Culture, and History* (Boston, 1996), 105, 107, 110.

30. Emerson was also one of the *Atlantic's* principal spokesmen for the cause of rapid emancipation, after abandoning his disunionist position when the war began. On Emerson's career during the Civil War, see Gougeon, *Virtue's Hero*, chap. 8. Abolitionists saw the formation of Negro regiments and the regular use of Negro soldiers as important elements of the struggle to establish the equality of free blacks. On Mar. 20, 1862, Emerson spoke to a Boston fundraising gathering for the soon to be famous Massachusetts Fifty-fourth, a Negro regiment commanded by Robert Gould Shaw. After its ill-fated assault on Fort Wagner in South Carolina, Emerson published the poem "Voluntaries" in the October 1863 *Atlantic* as a memorial to the regiment.

31. Eliot, "Emerson," 521–522, 526. My account of Eliot borrows primarily from Hugh Hawkins, *Between Harvard and America: The Educational Leadership of Charles*

W. Eliot (New York, 1972), and Kim Townsend, *Manhood at Harvard: William James and Others* (New York, 1996), chap. 2.

32. Hugh Hawkins has told us that during the first dozen years of his presidency Eliot attended chiefly to Harvard's internal organization and finances, and it was precisely in these areas that he enlisted Emerson's support. As a member of the Overseers Visiting Committee, for example, Emerson inspected classes in various departments. He also reviewed and voted on faculty appointments, and solicited funds from his classmates.

   It might also be said that what makes the first phase of the Emerson-Eliot connection an important episode in postbellum cultural history—rather than simply another instance of the slippery ways in which an intellectual relationship based on "influence" usually works—is the fact that Eliot briefly seized on Emerson (along with Charles Eliot Norton and Henry Adams) as a figure of new cultural possibility: the academic intellectual. In the summer of 1870, Eliot appointed Emerson to the Harvard faculty as Lecturer in Philosophy and during the winter of 1870–1871 as Lecturer on Natural History. Emerson's performance in Eliot's short-lived experiment in "University Lectures" was, in the view of both men, something of a failure. But it also signaled the beginning of Eliot's successful effort to transform Harvard into a graduate research university.

33. Eliot's selections from Emerson's work for vol. 5 of the Harvard Classics included 18 essays—all but one of which were published before 1844—and the entirety of *English Traits*. Selections from Benjamin Franklin, John Woolman, and William Penn appeared in vol. 1; the entirety of Richard Henry Dana's *Two Years Before the Mast* in vol. 23; and single essays from Channing, Poe, Thoreau, and Lowell in vol. 28: *Essays English and American*.

34. James, *Hawthorne*, 82; "Mr. Emerson at Harvard," *Every Saturday*, Sept. 21, 1867. *Every Saturday* (1867–1874) was an eclectic weekly published in Boston by Ticknor & Fields, Emerson's publisher at the time.

35. Anon., "RWE," *New York Herald*, Apr. 28, 1882.

36. For a detailed description of the many miscellaneous collections of Emerson's writings published in this period, see Joel Myerson, *Ralph Waldo Emerson: A Descriptive Bibliography* (Pittsburgh, 1982), 571–577. James Elliot Cabot (with the assistance of Emerson's daughter Ellen) also worked to make Emerson appear to be an even more productive author of books than he ever was. Between 1884 and 1893, Cabot collected or re-created dozens of previously unpublished lectures, addresses, and essays in *Miscellanies* (1884), *Lectures and Biographical Sketches* (1884), and *Natural History of the Intellect* (1893). Beginning in 1883, other hands were responsible for the publication of Emerson's private letters and, beginning in 1909, his voluminous journal entries.

37. See Nina Baym, "Early Histories of American Literature: A Chapter in the Institution of New England," *American Literary History* (1989):459–488.

Transcendentalism from the Margins

The Experience of Caroline Healey Dall

HELEN R. DEESE

> *For myself, I am a Transcendentalist of the old New England sort.*
>
> —CAROLINE HEALEY DALL,
> *Transcendentalism in New England*

IN THE SUMMER OF 1840 A BRILLIANT, WELL-READ, ARTICULATE, and morally earnest young woman entered the bookshop of Elizabeth Palmer Peabody at 13 West Street in Boston for the first time. In doing so Caroline Healey opened the door into a new world, a gathering place favored by the Transcendentalists for its foreign books and periodicals, where it would not be unusual to encounter perhaps Ralph Waldo Emerson or Margaret Fuller or Theodore Parker. Here the eighteen-year-old Healey must have felt herself in a bibliophile's paradise—and a bibliophile she already was. But she was hardly more struck by the riches of the wares than by what Peabody herself represented to her: a woman of vast learning, myriad intellectual interests, enormous enthusiasm, and, not of least importance, great personal warmth. For Healey, the daughter of a mother who disparaged her every literary endeavor and constantly urged upon her the practical advantages of skill with a needle over proficiency with a pen, Peabody was no trivial discovery. Caroline Healey's entrance into this bookshop may well have been the most important step of her life.

Though by the age of eighteen Healey had already for several years sat in various public halls and Unitarian churches listening to lectures and sermons by male Transcendentalists, it was this woman, Peabody, who was to provide her entrée into their circle. The opening of her acquaintance with Peabody occurred at a crucial, formative point in Healey's development. It was to have ramifications both for the direction that her own life was to take and for her later perspective as an historian of Transcendentalism. For the path to Peabody's bookstore led on to the venue of Margaret Fuller's conversations and eventually to the pulpit, the lecture hall, and innumerable reform conventions, committee rooms, and legislative halls where Caroline Healey Dall would be engaged in acting out her moral imperatives. Fuller's influence on Dall's life and thought was to be so profound that Dall's analysis of the Transcendentalist movement a half-century later elevated Fuller to the role of its chief protagonist. Dall was thus the first interpreter of Transcendentalism to give it a distinctly feminist spin.

In the history of the Transcendentalist movement Caroline Healey Dall (1822–1912) is a marginal figure. She was younger than the major players— five years younger than Henry David Thoreau, the youngest of the group. She did not attend a single meeting of the Transcendental Club. None of the major figures of the movement seem to have counted her as belonging to the inner circle. Neither early histories of Transcendentalism nor biographical studies of its leading participants recognize her role. Yet in addition to Elizabeth Palmer Peabody, those with whom she was on close personal terms at various times included Theodore Parker, James Freeman Clarke, A. Bronson Alcott, Cyrus Bartol, William Henry Channing, and Frederic Henry Hedge. She was an inveterate consumer of the lectures, sermons, conversations, and publications of all the members of the group. Emerson was a father figure whose approval she sought, and Margaret Fuller was her most important role model. Peripheral as she was, Dall was close enough to the movement's center that she was profoundly affected by its participants, their thought, and their actions. Caroline Healey Dall was in many ways the result of the Transcendentalist movement.

Dall was not the only one of that younger generation whose lives were touched by the Transcendentalists to have been so affected by the association, of course; one thinks of Franklin Benjamin Sanborn, one of John Brown's "secret six" and a leader in the social science movement; of Thomas Wentworth Higginson and Robert Gould Shaw, acting out their idealism at the head of black regiments in the Civil War; of George William Curtis, a son of Brook Farm, who spoke out his social conscience. The roster of women so influenced by the Transcendentalists to become leading social activists might include, besides Dall, Ednah Dow Cheney and Julia Ward Howe. Of this latter group Dall was, it seems to me, the most thoroughly imbued with the Transcendentalist imperative of what she called "lofty living." Much of her long life was devoted to such causes as abolitionism, the woman's movement—in which she enacted a leading role early on through her lectures and publications—and the social science movement. Dall was a bridge between the sort of idealistic reform movements typical of the antebellum period and the later progressive, "scientific" approaches.

In addition to her social activism she engaged in journalistic and literary endeavors and even what we might today call "women's studies," then in her later years became an active apologist, historian, and interpreter of the Transcendentalist movement. This essay attempts to see Transcendentalism through her eyes. It will focus both on Dall's contemporary journal accounts of her participation in the movement and on her retrospective rendering of it from the distance of half a century. The versions of Transcendentalism that emerge, filtered through Dall's perspective, say much about the movement and its participants—and perhaps more about Dall herself.

The daughter of wealthy Boston merchant and banker Mark Healey and Caroline Foster Healey, the young Caroline Wells Healey was the oldest of eight children. She enjoyed the special favor of her father and a fine education that ended, nevertheless, its formal phase when she was fifteen. She had begun attending lectures in Boston by Emerson, among others, at the age of twelve. She later reflected that it was considered a great extravagance in 1835 for a person so young to have a separate ticket to a lecture series, but she recalled that her father was willing to indulge her in this luxury on one condition: that she write a summary or "abstract" of each lecture. Her first efforts at such reporting were rough and incomplete, but her skills of careful listening and meticulous reporting increased markedly to the point that years later, when James Walker, future president of Harvard, gave a course of Lowell Lectures, he said (she claimed) that he could hardly distinguish her notes from his own manuscript and "would quite as lief print from one as the other!"[1] Dall also recorded the daily events of her own life in a journal kept for some seventy-five years. Her ingrained habit of remembering and recording has had fortunate consequences for posterity: not only do her works serve as a substantial source of information on Transcendentalism, abolitionism, the women's movement, and sundry other nineteenth-century reform and intellectual movements, they also preserve the poignant story of her own fascinating life in both its private and its public aspects.

When Dall entered Elizabeth Peabody's bookshop in 1840 she took a step that brought her into a much closer proximity to the Transcendentalist circle than had her attendance at lectures. In Peabody, Dall found a willing mentor. "I love to hear her talk—," she wrote in her journal,

> to see her smile—although I return from both—amazingly humbled in my own conception— So deep learning—so youthful joyousness so great experience & perfect simplicity I never saw

united in one character. She told me much of her early life—of her opportunities—of her progress—& the unfolding of truth—& religion to her view. It repaid me for a great deal to know—that she was willing to teach me.[2]

In the course of long talks at the bookshop Peabody, who was twice Healey's age, advised her to practice self-culture, introduced her to Samuel Taylor Coleridge's works, and explained to her the faculties of Reason and Understanding. Before long Dall wrote in her journal (no doubt accurately) that Peabody was trying to make a Transcendentalist of her. At the time, Healey resisted, insisting to her journal, "I think she cannot succeed—common sense—I have—and that is apt to—look upon the speculations of so styled wiser heads as *uncommon nonsense*" (MS Journals, August 7, 17, 22, 28, 29, 1840; October 2, 1840).

But this vaunted common sense did not prevent Healey's association with the Transcendentalists from being raised to yet another level when, in the spring of the following year, Peabody recruited her for Margaret Fuller's conversation series. There she found herself in the company of George and Sophia Dana Ripley (at whose home all but one of the gatherings took place), Clarke, Emerson, Alcott, Hedge, Jones Very, Charles Stearns Wheeler, and other votaries of the movement. "It was," she understated later, "a great opportunity."[3] But the experience proved to be anything but comfortable for the youngest member of the group (Healey was still only eighteen). Headstrong, she seems to have blundered into these gatherings of the elite as if she were among equals, questioning, commenting, disputing. Fuller not only did not give her instant sympathy as had Peabody, but instead found her positively irritating, viewing her as an "upstart child." Fuller required of newcomers "a sort of personal submission," and Healey "would not bow" because she felt herself "as much the child of my Heavenly Father as she."[4] Even the heretofore sympathetic Peabody took Healey severely to task for her temerity in joining fearlessly in the discussion at the conversations. She made it clear to Healey that "the circle is composed of intimate friends—among whom I [Healey] am the only stranger—and—that it is not intended for conversation" (MS Journals, March 23, 1841). Emerson too was apparently aghast at Healey's audacity, for Peabody told her, "It is because you are nearsighted that you make so many mistakes. . . . [I]f you had only seen Emerson look at you, last night, I am sure you would never have said some things you did" ("Conversations," 419).[5] When Healey attempted to make peace with Fuller by presenting her, at great cost and effort, a bouquet of her favorite flower, the heliotrope, Fuller received it coldly. Elizabeth

Peabody intimated to Healey that her gesture had been a *faux pas* ("Conversations," 419).

In the face of such antagonism, one might expect this young interloper, duly chastened, to have retreated into silence for the duration of the series. But to do so was not in Caroline Healey's nature. To Peabody's rebuke concerning Emerson, she responded in a private reminiscence,

> I could not help smiling inwardly. I had felt through eyes that never made mistakes, the full measure of Emerson's contempt, the night before, but I had not felt humiliated by it. I had asked a question which ought to have been inoffensive. He had a right to think it silly, but he had *no* right to feel as he did towards me, in consequence. ("Conversations," 419)

She told Peabody that she would try to control herself in the gatherings, "but if she could not remember it long enough—she must be forgiven" (MS Journals, March 23, 1841; "Conversations," 416). This resolution to remain silent was futile; she continued to speak up, even to disagree with Fuller, though she felt she was on the brink of being asked by Peabody or Fuller to drop out of the group. Her own view was that she "had paid a certain number of hard dollars for my place in it, & valued it too much as a means of culture, to give it up" ("Conversations," 416). She might well have added that one had a reasonable expectation of being allowed to speak in a forum labeled "conversation." But whatever Healey may have learned from the Transcendentalists, it is clear that she did not have to learn self-assertiveness from them. Her confidence in her own opinions, her willingness to engage in debate with her elders and betters, had already been fostered by her father, who from her childhood had demanded her participation in sophisticated argument.

What Caroline Healey found in her first sustained contact with the larger Transcendentalist circle was not welcoming sympathy or validation of her worth or her opinions. Instead she found a new way of thinking. In the conversation series that Healey attended, Fuller used ancient mythology to explore archetypes; as Dall remembered it, from there Fuller "proceeded to open all the great questions of life."[6] Most of all, Healey imbibed a devotion to the truth and a revulsion against hypocrisy. "If I were to characterize [Fuller] in two words," Dall declared in a lecture nearly two decades later, "it would be as 'Truth-teller and Truth-compeller.' She not only spoke what she thought . . . but she compelled us to do the same. There was something in her presence which tore away all disguises: even unconscious pretension could not bear it."[7] In reflecting on her personal experience with Fuller, Dall confirmed the judgment of many of Fuller's contemporaries by asserting that "Margaret's conversational powers were [never] approached on this continent" (MS Journals, March 20, 1852). Perhaps most significant, she found in Fuller's erudition and brilliance an even more attractive role model than Peabody's less ordered enthusiasm. For even at the time, Healey recognized the value of her exposure to the personalities and the ideas of the circle. When the series ended she wrote in her journal, "I could have wept—easily when we parted—never have I enjoyed any society so much as that of these 'reunions'—" (MS Journals, May 6, 1841).

For the rest of her life Dall regarded this experience as a positive and pivotal, if somewhat uncomfortable, point in her intellectual develop- ment. But in retrospect she also felt that it was to her "self-assertion" in these conversations that she owed "much of the misunderstanding & su- perficial condemnation which has made my public life, unnecessarily painful & severe"; she was perceived, she felt, as "self-conceited" when she was actually obeying "an instinct of self *possession*" ("Conversations," 417). A lifelong pattern was established in which Dall's assertiveness served her both well and ill: it would allow her to enter such daring new realms for a woman as lecturing, preaching, and addressing legislators, but it also served to alienate her from many friends, acquaintances, and potential allies.

At the same time that she was enrolled in Fuller's conversation series Caroline Healey was bombarded on yet another front by the "newness": for the first time on April 4, 1841, she heard Theodore Parker preach, another momentous point in her development. The effect on her was profound: "His sermon startled me waked me up—into admiration and dread. I felt that talents like his might do what they pleased with me—and yet that upon a common mind, his views would have the worst effect" (MS Journals, April 4, 1841). Despite the reservations here expressed, a few weeks later, when Parker's delivery of his South Boston sermon put him at the center of a storm of controversy, Dall defended him to her more conservative West Church friends and found that she was consid- ered "an infidel for my pains" (MS Journals, June 11, 1841). In the fall of 1841 she was in the audience for Parker's course of public lectures on religion and before the series was over felt herself largely in sympathy with his radical views, though she wondered if she had the courage and independence to declare publicly her allegiance to him (MS Journals, Oc- tober 27, 1841).

With Theodore Parker, Healey was to develop one of the most personal of her relationships with any Transcendentalist. Whereas she had felt an aloofness in both Fuller and Emerson, and Peabody had dealt with her as a pupil in need of correction and advice, Theodore Parker treated Healey from the beginning as an equal. In December 1841 she wrote to him a letter that was generally admiring, yet was critical of what she believed to be his shock tactics. Parker endeared himself to her by taking her criticisms seriously and responding without condescension. A few months later Healey made a public and irrevocable commitment to the doctrines of Parker, declaring herself before a West Church Bible class "a humanitarian—a disciple of Theodore Parker's in part—a more venturesome—thinker in part" (MS Journals, April 17, 1842). And it is to Parker's example more than any other person's that she owed what became one of the driving forces of her own life—the impulse to social reform. As Parker became engaged in the cause of abolitionism, Dall, seeking his guidance, did so as well. From there it was only a step to her early leadership role in the women's movement and, later, in the social science movement.

The life that Dall lived in her most active and productive years was the natural outgrowth of her Transcendentalist legacy, as she early developed a reputation as a radical. She delivered public lectures. She organized and participated in woman's rights conventions. She addressed a committee of the Massachusetts state legislature, urging the franchise for women. She occasionally preached in Unitarian pulpits, claiming to have been the first woman to have done so. Her landmark publication *The College, the Market, and the Court; or, Woman's Relation to Education, Labor and Law* (Boston, 1867) was widely regarded as the most significant statement of the day on the woman question. In 1868 her reform impulse found a broader arena as she became a founder and longtime officer of the American Social Science Association. In recognition of her pioneering role Dall was in 1878 awarded an honorary doctorate from Alfred University. Her less controversial activities included her prolific writing for Unitarian publications, as well as for the *Index*, a publication of the Free Religious Association; her reporting for newspapers on scientific conferences; and her publication of literary criticism, reviews, historical research, children's books, and reminiscence. She was in effect a freelance writer who took all fields as her province. After 1878, largely retired from active reform work, Dall lived in Washington, D.C., where she became the friend of political and scientific luminaries, the intimate of First Lady Frances Cleveland, the leader of a reading group for young women, and a well-known hostess.

. . .

In Dall's late years she recognized that the period of her young woman-hood in the Boston area had been no ordinary time. She saw it as a kind of New England Golden Age that she had been in a position to observe, and she felt an obligation to preserve her own record of it. In the 1890s she made arrangements to leave her journals (which already covered more than sixty years) and other papers to the Massachusetts Historical Society after her death. For at least the last quarter of the century she had been self-consciously recording in her journals her encounters with the aging and dying Transcendentalists. As the density of details that she recorded about these figures increased markedly, one gets the sense that Dall was realizing that she was on the brink of the end of an era, and that as a second-generation Transcendentalist she was responsible for preserving its vestiges for posterity. In addition to this private contemporary record in her journals that Dall realized would not be tapped until after her death, she also turned—perhaps motivated by the hope of fame and monetary reward as well as by a sense of duty or the muse of history—to publishing recollections and interpretations of the movement and its participants.

Dall was not, however, the earliest historian of the Transcendentalist movement. Octavius Brooks Frothingham published his *Transcendental-ism in New England: A History* in 1876, and the correspondence, "life and letters" compilations, and biographies of individual Transcendentalists had regularly been making their appearances following the deaths of their re-spective subjects. The first of these was the *Memoirs of Margaret Fuller Ossoli*, edited in 1852 by Emerson, Clarke, and William H. Channing.[8] From the mid 1870s into the twentieth century (perhaps stimulated in part by Frothingham's work) Transcendentalism assumed a respectability that was reflected in a steady stream of retrospective, sometimes romanticized treatments of the movement and its participants, most of them from the pens of members (like Dall) of the younger generation who had been asso-ciated with the Transcendentalists.[9] Thus by the mid 1890s, in addition to several brief general examinations of the movement, two more biographies of Fuller had appeared, as well as two of Parker, four of Thoreau, a half-dozen of Emerson, and one of Alcott. Dall read and commented in her journals on most of these publications; often she published reviews of them, most frequently in the *Springfield Republican*. And by the 1890s she began formulating her own reminiscences. In 1895 she published her transcription of the Margaret Fuller conversation series that she had at-tended in 1841, *Margaret and Her Friends*. (Dall thus appropriated the title originally intended for Emerson, Clarke, and Channing's *Memoirs of*

Margaret Fuller Ossoli.) In the same year she delivered in Washington, D.C., a lecture that she published two years later as *Transcendentalism in New England: A Lecture*. (The lecture had first taken the form of an article in the *Journal of Speculative Philosophy*, then was reprinted as a pamphlet). In 1900 she produced *"Alongside": Being Notes Suggested by "A New England Boyhood" of Doctor Edward Everett Hale*, a more general reminiscence of the Boston of her youth.

Of her retrospective publications on Transcendentalism the most original and provocative is *Transcendentalism in New England*. Though Lawrence Buell has recognized this work as "especially interesting as a feminist appraisal of the movement,"[10] it has otherwise generally received little attention. Dall's full title, *Transcendentalism in New England: A Lecture*, deliberately plays off Frothingham's publication of two decades earlier, *Transcendentalism in New England: A History*. At the time that Dall prepared her lecture, Frothingham's work was the nearest thing in existence to a standard comprehensive history of the movement—and, in fact, the same might be said today. Even though critics have from the beginning pointed out various shortcomings, Frothingham's history remains the starting point of almost all serious considerations of Transcendentalism and an inevitable touchstone for treatments of individual Transcendentalists. Dall and Frothingham were contemporaries, born into the same Unitarian Boston milieu in the same year (1822), and both came under the influence of the Transcendentalists. The son of prominent Unitarian minister Nathaniel Langdon Frothingham and the grandson of wealthy merchant Peter Chardon Brooks, Frothingham had enjoyed the privileges accorded to male Boston Brahmins: Boston Latin School, Harvard, the Harvard Divinity School, and prestigious pulpits in New England and the New York City area. Emerson was a friend of the family as the young Frothingham grew up, often present, he recalled, "at my father's table diffusing the radiance of serene ideas, and heralding the diviner age that was to come."[11] His father was invited by Emerson, but declined, to participate in the organizational meeting of what became the Transcendental Club. Both his family connections and his gender provided Frothingham with more of an insider's view than Dall had. He certainly at one time considered himself a Transcendentalist and history has so depicted him, though by the time he wrote his history of the movement Frothingham was himself somewhat ambivalent toward it.[12]

Dall's history of the movement was created as an hour-long lecture, only a fraction of the length of Frothingham's book, and thus lacks the scope and depth of the latter. When she delivered this lecture Dall was nearly seventy-three years old. She could easily have used the stores of her memory and her journals to produce an entertaining talk filled with personal anecdotes of the now-celebrated Transcendentalists. But she was speaking before the Society for Philosophical Enquiry in Washington, D.C., and she aimed to be more than entertaining: instead of telling after-dinner tales she undertook to construct a revisionist interpretation of the movement. Dall was in a situation that might have been daunting to a lesser person. A woman in male territory (and a woman, it will be remembered, whose education had ended at age fifteen), she had agreed to address an audience primarily of scholars and professionals, among whom were William T. Harris, the U. S. commissioner of education and the leading light of the Hegelian school of philosophy in the country; James Macbride Sterrett, professor of philosophy at Columbian (now George Washington) University in Washington; and Edward Farquhar, professor of history at Columbian. But Dall appears to have been no more intimidated by this situation than she had been at age eighteen when she refused to be silenced at Fuller's conversations. She deliberately chose to challenge the standard history of Transcendentalism.

When Dall first read Frothingham's history shortly after its publication, certain aspects of it had disturbed her, and now she had an opportunity to respond publicly. Not that she attacked Frothingham by name or disagreed with all that he said; in fact, to some extent Dall relied upon his history, even in a few instances borrowing its phraseology, covering herself with only an acknowledgment in her preface. But despite a certain indebtedness, when Dall's lecture is read side by side with Frothingham's history the inescapable conclusion is that much of the lecture is a deliberate rejoinder to the history. Dall's revisionist reading is based upon the different perspective that her more marginal relationship to the movement provided. Even with Dall's history of activism it is still a little amazing that she came up with an interpretation of Transcendentalism so original and so radical. For Dall's reconstruction of New England Transcendentalism is, among other things, unabashedly feminist.

The Transcendentalist movement began and ended, Dall asserted, with a woman. Its history "stretched along two hundred years, beginning with a woman's life and work in 1637, and ending with a woman's work and death in 1850. The arc, which we call transcendental, was subtended by a chord, held at first by Anne Hutchinson, and lost in the Atlantic waves with Margaret Fuller."[13] Dall saw in the Antinomian controversy and in Hutchinson, the very earliest notable New England woman, the germ of the essential element of the movement, the belief in "the immanence of the Divine in the Human" (*TrNE*, 25). With the observation that "little is known of Anne Hutchinson," Dall attempted to rectify history's neglect by devoting several paragraphs to what she presented as a heroic and tragic story. Hutchinson, gathering scores of women into her home from far and near, became, according to Dall, the spokesperson and exemplar of exaltation, enthusiasm, and free speech in Puritan New England. At her meetings there was "perfect freedom of remark and question." Further, and very importantly for Dall's purposes, Hutchinson acted out her faith in a life of "generous help and efficient sympathy in household dilemmas, childbirth, and mortal sicknesses" (*TrNE*, 6–7, 9).

Portraying Hutchinson as a martyr to a tradition-bound patriarchal system, Dall depicted the struggle between Hutchinson and the church authorities as gender-based. She was "attractive to women," and it was her growing power through her influence over women that jeopardized the male power structure. The synod of ministers, threatened by "this woman who sets herself up as an authority among us," boldly "engag[ing] with the abstrusities of metaphysical divinity," decided that "the women of New England must be rescued from her clutches," Dall declared. Hutchinson was accused of Antinomianism, her opinions "caricatured, misrepresented, and perverted." Dall speculated that "It is probable that there were no men in the synod capable of understanding her simple declarations: they were not mystical enough for the theologians of the period." To demonstrate Hutchinson's incipient Transcendentalism Dall highlighted a single quotation from her: "The Spirit is most powerful in the saint when it endeavors least." The statement "might have been cut from the pages of 'The Dial' two hundred years later," Dall maintained, and then pressed home: "I think I hear Emerson saying it" (*TrNE*, 7–9).

Dall was not arguing that the nineteenth-century Transcendentalists were conscious of a direct line of influence from Hutchinson to them. But she found support for her subversive genealogy in a remark in Emerson's essay "The Transcendentalist." "The Transcendentalist," she quoted Emerson, "might be counted an *Antinomian*, because he asserts that he who has the Lawgiver may not only neglect but contravene every written command!" (*TrNE*, 11). Though Dall conceded that Emerson did not make the connection to Hutchinson herself, she was confident that he would not have overlooked this link ten years later when, she assumed, his consciousness in such matters had been raised.[14] Even so, he was with this statement recognizing "the ripple left by [Hutchinson's] movement" (*TrNE*, 11).

Bound up with Dall's claim for Hutchinson as the forerunner of Transcendentalism is her assertion that the movement was indigenous. Whereas Frothingham had devoted more than a quarter of his history to tracing the European roots of Transcendentalism in Germany, France, and England, Dall argued that it was a growth native to New England soil. The Transcendentalist impulse had been felt in New England (through Hutchinson) more than a hundred years before Kant's *Critique of Pure Reason* had been printed, and it existed "independently of the causes which brought that philosophical classic into existence." Reasserted in the sermons of William Ellery Channing, it was a natural development out of the "One originating cause" that underlay the system of Puritanism and was unique to New England. Though Dall acknowledged that in the nineteenth century the flowering of the movement had been stimulated by the influence of Kant and other Germans and by the English Romantics, she asserted that "out of New England, Transcendentalism had no practical existence." Her emphasis is on the word *practical*, and her perspective throughout is on the practical working out of the philosophy. In Germany, she argued, Transcendentalism was an idea that "belonged to the scholars, and never affected popular life" (*TrNE*, 5). The New England Transcendentalist made "an extravagant demand on human nature—that of lofty living," and thus in New England the philosophy led to social and political action—to Brook Farm, to abolitionism, to heroism and sacrifice in the Civil War. Dall's emphasis on this aspect of the movement anticipates such approaches as Anne C. Rose's *Transcendentalism as a Social Movement* and the renewed recent interest in the antislavery and other social and political involvement of the Transcendentalists. Dall even made bold to fine tune Emerson's definition of Transcendentalism in "The Transcendentalist" ("Idealism as it appears in 1842") to the key of her own bent and experience, offering the variation "idealism made practical as it appeared in 1842" (*TrNE*, 23).

Frothingham himself had observed that Transcendentalists were in the vanguard of the struggle for woman's rights, and not unpredictably Dall too emphasized this particular manifestion of the reform spirit within the movement. "Like Dryden," she wrote, "every Transcendentalist was ready, and indeed had good reason, to assert that there was 'no sex in souls'" (*TrNE*, 24). But later in the lecture she recalled a seemingly contradictory episode in the history of the movement. When in 1849 a group of Transcendentalists and others in the Boston area formed the Town and Country Club, Emerson had opposed the admission of women. Her own husband, Unitarian minister Charles Henry Appleton Dall, had gone to join the club, she recounted, with ten dollars in his pocket, intending to pay dues for them both, but finding women excluded he had returned home without joining. The club was, she claimed, "wrecked" on the rock of the exclusion of women (*TrNE*, 29–30).

In point of fact, Dall proves to be an unreliable witness in this matter. Her contemporary journals of the Town and Country Club period reflect no such incident, and indeed make reference to Charles Dall's having attended several meetings of the club with his wife's blessings (MS Journals, April 15, 22, May 2, October 16, 1849). Has Dall deliberately distorted the truth here? It is impossible to know for sure. I find it unlikely that she would have consciously manufactured an incident to serve her own purposes. But at best some bending of the truth, consciously or unconsciously, is taking place. What does Dall gain from distorting the facts of this incident? She makes herself and her husband look more progressive than they actually were at the time, and she draws attention to the bias of Emerson, who did in fact strike through the names of the women proposed for membership. While this incident seems to negate or at least modify Dall's claim of gender equality within the movement, perhaps it represents a little evening of old scores that Dall could not resist, even at the expense of undercutting her own point.

Dall's feminist stance more obviously leads to her attempts to revise Frothingham's reading of Margaret Fuller. Although he devoted an entire chapter to Fuller—only Emerson, Alcott, Parker, and Ripley fared as well—Frothingham depicted her simply as "the critic." Early in his discussion of Fuller he declared that, "Strictly speaking, she was not a Transcendentalist."[15] As one who had experienced and observed Fuller's real effect on people's lives, Dall found this view inadequate. She admitted the futility of conveying "any idea of Margaret Fuller" or "any impression of her being and influence" to those who never knew her, but she nevertheless felt compelled to give her personal testimony to the far-reaching influence of Fuller's life. Like Anne Hutchinson, Fuller attracted women to her circle and, Dall declared, her own influence so pervaded the group that there were "no low, ignoble motives, no vanity, no poor ambitions, no coquetries, no looking to marriage as an end, no proneness to idle gossip." The difference in Margaret Fuller's time and Anne Hutchinson's was that as both of them attracted "larger and larger crowds of women," in Hutchinson's case the patriarchy became threatened and effected a power play to annihilate the threat, whereas Fuller's male acquaintances "begged admittance to her audience." The result however was disappointing, at least in terms of the formal conversations that Fuller conducted: "It was only with women that [Fuller] became both priestess and oracle," Dall observed (*TrNE*, 35–36).

Dall countered Frothingham's depiction of Fuller as simply an intellectualized, detached "critic" by emphasizing her practical Transcendentalism, best seen in her attempts to improve the lives of other women. At Brook Farm, Fuller had "interested herself in the single women longing for something better than they knew, and without resources" (*TrNE*, 37). She followed the lives of such women and "helped them to independence."[16] Likewise, in New York she offered aid to women at Sing Sing

prison through both public addresses and private counseling. In Italy she
not only became involved in the Italian Revolution and wrote its history
but also superintended a hospital. Dall's point is to rectify an error made by
Frothingham and other interpreters of Fuller: the "common feeling that
she valued intellect above character, and felt neither sympathy nor affection for commonplace persons." According to Dall, "The very reverse of
this was true" (*TrNE*, 37–38). Besides Frothingham, Dall must have had in
mind her own experience with Charles Robinson, a Unitarian minister
personally acquainted with Fuller, who in 1858 "baffle[d] any memory" of
Dall's about Fuller by saying that "she had no republicanism about her, that
she despised common people" (MS Journals, December 30, 1858). Dall's
defense of Fuller stressed the fact that like Anne Hutchinson Fuller was
distinguished not only by her intellectual achievement but by her practical
service to other women.

When Fuller left America for Europe in 1846, according to Dall, the
"impulse" of her life continued to be felt. Even after her death four years
later, Dall contended, "the glory of Margaret's life did not perish." Her
death "left a vacancy greater than any space she had filled." It coincided
with the real end of the Transcendentalist movement. Dall argued in a final
footnote that despite the fact that Emerson and others survived Fuller by
decades, Emerson "belonged to the whole world," and the other survivors
similarly were not contained by their identification with this movement;
but Fuller's status was different, her own life and influence inextricably
bound up with the movement. Dall concluded, "I do not think I am mistaken in saying that what is meant by New England Transcendentalism
perished with Margaret Fuller" (*TrNE*, 35, 38).

Dall attempted another corrective to Frothingham by taking issue with
his version of the *dramatis personae* of the movement. Emerson, Alcott,
Fuller, Parker, and Ripley had figured as Frothingham's major luminaries;
among the "minor prophets" with whom he dealt briefly were William H.
Channing, Ellery Channing, Cyrus Bartol, Clarke, Samuel Johnson,
Samuel Longfellow, T. W. Higginson, and even David Wasson and John
Weiss. Dall's first revision in this cast of characters was to resurrect two key
figures whom Frothingham had ignored: Frederic Henry Hedge and
Henry David Thoreau. Dall was especially at pains to establish the central
role played by Hedge early in the movement. She and Hedge had discussed
Frothingham's work soon after it first appeared, and she found Hedge
"more out of patience" with it than she herself. "He claims," she wrote in
her journal, "to have organized Transcendentalism in the United States—
the Club always being called Hedge's Club" (MS Journals, January 28,
1877). Following up on this lead, Dall asked Hedge to write out a statement

of his "connection with the Transcendental movement." Hedge obliged by detailing in a letter his early publication on Coleridge in the *Christian Examiner* vindicating German metaphysics and his introductory notices of the German philosophers in his *Prose Writers of Germany*. Dall apparently asked for more detailed information about the Transcendental Club, for another letter shortly followed listing the names of those who participated in the club. Taking considerable editorial latitude, Dall conflated portions of these two letters and published them in *Transcendentalism in New England* as proof that Hedge was the "commander of this fleet" that brought "Leibnitz, Spinoza, Kant, Goethe, Herder, Schleiermacher, and Jean Paul . . . sailing all at once into Boston harbor." Hedge thus represented the crucial connection through whom "the latent idealism of his own people"—the idealism that had briefly come to the surface in Anne Hutchinson—"sprang gladly to meet that which had already taken shape abroad." Restraining herself from being "betrayed into a biography of Dr. Hedge," Dall concluded that a history of Transcendentalism that omitted Hedge was like "the play of 'Hamlet' with the part of Hamlet left out!" (*TrNE*, 12–17).

Dall also undertook to suggest that Henry Thoreau played more of a role in the movement than would be apparent from reading Frothingham's history. Frothingham mentioned Thoreau's name only twice, once in a list of contributors to the *Dial* and once as the subject of Ellery Channing's biography. Dall's own view of Thoreau was limited by the fact that she had had less personal involvement with him than with any of the other major Transcendentalists. Thoreau had not attended the Margaret Fuller conversations that had facilitated her early acquaintance with many members of the circle. Dall heard Thoreau lecture on a few occasions and regularly read his publications, both before and after his death. But her estimate of him was colored by the fact that at least initially she considered him a reclusive thinker who was above the fray of practical reform. Nevertheless, she was impressed upon hearing him lecture in defense of John Brown, remarking appreciatively, "I was surprised—for I had thought Mr Thoreau, only a philosopher" (MS Journals, November 1, 1859). On his side, Thoreau had heard and apparently approved a lecture given by Dall at the Concord Lyceum (MS Journals, December 15, 1859). Though Thoreau was, Dall observed in her history of the movement, "little known outside [his] special walk," she nevertheless recognized that his was a significant role, if only to mark the boundaries of the movement's tendency at one pole to extreme individualism. Though she admitted that through figures like Thoreau Transcendentalism was in "danger that the eccentricities of the individual should be attributed to the philosophy," she showed herself a fair appreciation of Thoreau's individualism, characterizing him as being "in his own person a practical refutation of the theories of the Socialists" (*TrNE*, 20–21). Though her treatment of Thoreau is ambivalent, Dall clearly implied the folly of Frothingham's complete omission of his role in the movement.

If she wished to add Hedge and Thoreau to Frothingham's list of Transcendental worthies, Dall was determined to remove Bronson Alcott. Her attack on him is one of the apparent mysteries of her *Transcendentalism in New England*. Frothingham had devoted a chapter to Alcott as "The Mystic," according him a place of preeminence in the movement second only to Emerson. In fact, Frothingham went so far as to claim that in 1837 it was Alcott and not Emerson who was "the reputed leader of the Transcendentalists."[17] Dall countered this by admitting that Alcott was "prominent in the public eye" and that Emerson was "enamored" of him, but she explained Emerson's misconception as the result of his being "himself so sweet and unselfish that he never felt, and therefore never could recognize, his opposite." She asserted that Alcott "did more than any one to bring ridicule upon the movement" and stated flatly that "he had no significant influence." Dall attributed to Alcott the "mountainous self-conceit" more often associated with Margaret Fuller and, more damning, suggested that his life did not accord with his philosophy (*TrNE*, 22–23). And she proceeded to heap ridicule on the Orphic Sayings published by Alcott in the *Dial*, quoting a college friend's parody of them as "Gastric Sayings": "The frying-pan globes, the griddle orbs all things" is a fair sample (*TrNE*, 30). Thus Dall mercilessly disparaged Alcott's place in the movement.

The mystery lies in the fact that this stance marks a turn-around in Dall's assessment of Bronson Alcott. Some of the richest passages in her journal detail her observations of and her relationship with him. In 1851 and again in 1856, Dall became a regular participant in Alcott's Boston conversations and reported on them, sometimes in detail, in her journal.[18] She declared a feeling of affinity for him and once waxed so enthusiastic as to express her belief that the city of Boston should pay Alcott simply to live there (MS Journals, January 13, 1851). In 1856 she opened her home to him as a site for his conversations (MS Journals, April 21, 1856). In 1864 Dall spent several days in the home of the Alcotts in Concord, and shortly thereafter, acutely aware of their financial pressures, she helped Alcott's daughter Louisa to find a publisher for the novel *Moods* (her first novel to be published) and assisted another daughter, May, to sell her art work in Boston. Dall once also proposed to arrange for Abigail May Alcott, Bronson Alcott's wife, a position as matron of a woman's prison. In short, Dall had been on intimate terms with the Alcott family and clearly admired Bronson Alcott. What, then, made her turn on him in this history?

The reason is not obvious, but a reading of Dall's journals and of her published and unpublished comments on Alcott after his death suggests a possible explanation for her about-face. Dall's faith in Bronson Alcott may have been profoundly shaken by the revelations of his own daughter. A lengthy conversation with Louisa in March 1888 (less than two years before the deaths of both Bronson and Louisa) seems to have been the basis for later remarks by Dall on the relationship between this daughter and father. Though Dall's journals are niggardly in details of the conversation, a subtext running through the discussion seems to have been Louisa's resentment, long pent up, at having to serve as the breadwinner for her entire family. Following the deaths of both father and daughter, Dall mentioned in her journal that the newspapers were comparing Louisa's devoted attachment to her father with that of Ellen Emerson to her father. Dall called the comparison "absurd." "Ellen *loved* her father," Dall protested, while "Louisa served hers from a sense of *duty* & strong family feeling. She was deeply conscious of his weaknesses and could not thoroughly respect him" (MS Journals, March 8, 1888). When she read Sanborn and Harris's biography of Alcott[19] Dall declared that the biographers had given his life a dignity it did not deserve, charging that the book skillfully covered up "every disagreable trait of the man, and every evil fact in his life" (MS Journals, June 25, 27, 1893). In a review of T. W. Higginson's *Contemporaries*, Dall wrote that Alcott "had a dark side which only those who lived in the house with him could see, but of which Louisa to her very latest hour was very free to speak."[20] In short, the evidence seems to point to the fact that Louisa in an unguarded moment had expressed to Dall frustration and resentment toward her father. One is tempted to speculate that this resentment stemmed from the fact that providing for his family's material wants was a low priority for Bronson Alcott, resulting in the family's impoverishment (indeed they had almost literally starved in the wake of the collapse of the Fruitlands experiment) and eventual dependency on Louisa's earning power. At any rate, after this conversation, Dall never again spoke of Bronson Alcott in any but a disparaging manner, and her animosity, engendered, it seems likely, by what she believed was his indifference to the physical needs of his family, boils over in this history. She was no longer able to credit his positive achievements and contributions to the Transcendentalist movement in light of what she now saw as the disparity between his idealism and his life, a disparity that she most likely saw demonstrated in his taking advantage of his wife and daughters.

Dall's revisions of what passed for the authorized history of the movement amount to more than mere quibbles; she attacked Frothingham's work on several fronts. Most striking is her evaluation of the feminine component of the movement as essential, even preeminent. This was a

wide departure from Frothingham's depiction of a dominantly male con-
federation whose precursors were wholly male. Her related point that
one did not have to go to Germany or Italy in search of the movement's
roots was a reaction to Frothingham's Eurocentric analysis of its sources.
Though Frothingham himself noted the reforming tendencies of the
movement, the effect of his devoting only one of fifteen chapter to "Practical Tendencies"—while opening with five chapters on the movement's
European roots—was to give the work the character of a history of ideas.
Dall reordered the emphasis, urging the centrality of social action to the
identity of the movement. It is clear also that Dall viewed the movement
more as a social organism than did Frothingham. When Dall looked back
at the movement it was not primarily a philosophical system that she saw,
but people, individuals who interacted with her and with each other and
whom she judged by how well they lived out their ideals. Margaret Fuller's
centrality was manifested, Dall felt, not just through her ideas or her function as critic, but through the force of her character, her personal influence, especially for other women. In Dall's reconstruction of this social
organism her friend Henry Hedge must be reinstated to his rightful place
and her former friend Bronson Alcott removed from the central position
allotted him by Frothingham. Her restoration of Henry Thoreau to the circle was done on more objective grounds; Dall was never close to him, but
was near enough to the group as a whole to understand the injustice of
omitting him. Thus as a marginal figure herself Dall was rehabilitating certain figures whom Frothingham had, for various reasons, marginalized:
Fuller perhaps because of her sex, Hedge perhaps because of his Bangor
residence, and Thoreau because of his personality.

Because of her early involvement with the movement, her longevity, and
her commitment to recording and interpreting the events in which she
participated, Caroline Healey Dall provides a unique vantage point on
New England Transcendentalism. What does she tell us about the movement? The inconsistent and amorphous nature of Transcendentalism has
always made it difficult to define precisely. Dall gives us one way of viewing it, a view from the margins. Not one of the inner circle, she nevertheless was herself a living legacy of the movement and was astute enough
to make sense of it. She defined and judged Transcendentalism not only by
the principles of its philosophy but also by its practical effects on society. As
she read it, the key elements of the movement were the imperatives to
truth-speaking and to social action. As far as she was concerned, in her
experience, Transcendentalism *was* a social movement. Moreover, she
emphasized the significance of its feminine faces. She revealed also that, in
her case at least, the group was less open to outsiders than one might have

imagined. But Dall's response even in light of a certain exclusiveness in the circle testifies to the attraction that these thinkers and their thought held for a seeker such as herself: as the major figures presented themselves at timely points in her life as mentors and role models, she found their thought and lives to be so compelling that to a large extent she fashioned her own life after theirs.

What do Dall's accounts and analyses reveal about her own character and perspective and about her objectivity as an historian? Clearly, the Transcendentalism that she recovers, with its feminist perspective and its emphasis on social activism, echoes her own interests and serves to position herself within the context of the movement, thus conferring on her life a kind of thematic unity. Her designation of Anne Hutchinson as a fore-mother of Transcendentalism is a bold stroke of revisionist interpretation. (Two-thirds of a century later the peculiar Americanness of the movement would be underscored by Perry Miller.[21]) Her contention for the centrality of Margaret Fuller's role is a corrective to most nineteenth-century and, indeed until recently, twentieth-century depictions of the movement. It is also something of a tribute to Dall's disinterestedness: despite Fuller's apparent disdain for her, Dall became one of her primary apologists. But Dall did not always rise above her own prejudices. Her account of the Town and Country Club and her dismissal of Bronson Alcott suggest the unmistakable sound of the grinding of axes. If we want from Dall factual details of the movement, we should go to her contemporary journals. When the facts go through the prism of her biases and her memory, especially after the passage of decades, they sometimes suffer distortion. The accuracy of her memory seems particularly vulnerable to the temptation (conscious or unconscious) to justify old resentments. What she was writing in *Transcendentalism in New England* is after all (as is true of the works of Frothingham, Sanborn, and others of the same generation) subjectively based history. Such history has its pluses as well as its minuses. A look at the movement through the eyes of this woman, whose independence of thought and devotion to reform were in part fixed by her early encounter with Transcendentalism, can give us a new sense of the power that the movement wielded for her generation and beyond.

NOTES

1. Caroline H. Dall, *"Alongside": Being Notes Suggested by "A New England Boy-hood" of Doctor Edward Everett Hale* (Boston, 1900), 49–50.
2. Manuscript Journals, Aug. 17, 1840, Caroline Dall Papers, Massachusetts Historical Society. Cited hereafter parenthetically within text as "MS Journals."

3. Caroline H. Dall, *Margaret and Her Friends: Or Ten Conversations with Margaret Fuller upon The Mythology of the Greeks and Its Expression in Art* (Boston, 1895), 9.

4. From an account written by Dall on Aug. 7, 1859, and copied into a manuscript journal at the Schlesinger Library entitled "Conversations upon the Mythology of the Greeks." Cited hereafter parenthetically within text as "Conversations"). It is printed in Joel Myerson, "Caroline Dall's Reminiscences of Margaret Fuller," *Harvard Library Bulletin* 22(1974):414–428. A slightly different version of this account appears in Caroline H. Dall, "Margaret Fuller Ossoli," *North American Review* 91(1860):122.

5. As a matter of fact, Healey's self-reported contributions to the conversations (admittedly not the most objective rendering) generally seem to this reader no more out of order or pedantic than those of numerous other participants. And by Healey's account, Peabody herself "acknowledge[d] that what I said at the last meeting was as good in itself, and as well delivered—as anything—said, there—save by Ralph Emerson" (MS Journals, Mar. 23, 1841).

6. Dall, *Margaret and Her Friends*, 6.

7. Dall's lecture, advertised under the heading "Individuals whose lives modify Public Opinion, and Exhibit the Spirit of the Age. Mary Wollstonecraft, Sidney Morgan, Anna Jamieson [*sic*], Charlotte Bronte, and Margaret Fuller," was first delivered in Boston on Nov. 15, 1858 (Boston *Daily Evening Transcript*, Nov. 1, 1858). It is printed in Dall's book *The College, the Market, and the Court; or, Woman's Relation to Education, Labor and Law* (Boston, 1867), 83–130.

8. Dall herself had come near writing a biography of Fuller. The Fuller family, having been pleased by Dall's treatment of Fuller in her lectures in the late 1850s, proposed the biography to her and lent her many of the family papers. Dall expressed some reluctance at undertaking such a task, uncharacteristically feeling herself unworthy, and protesting to the Fullers that "Margaret . . . never loved me." Fuller's mother, however, responded that "She would have loved you dearly had she lived." But the project never came to fruition; Arthur Fuller, who was attempting to arrange for the publication, was killed in the Civil War and his mother had died in 1859, a year after having met Dall. See Joel Myerson, "Mrs. Dall Edits Miss Fuller: The Story of *Margaret and Her Friends*," *Papers of the Bibliographical Society of America* 72(1978):187–200; MS Journals, Nov. 3, 6, 1858.

9. For a useful survey of these early reminiscences, see Lawrence Buell, "The Transcendentalist Movement," in *The Transcendentalists: A Review of Research and Criticism*, ed. Joel Myerson (New York, 1984), 9–13.

10. Buell, "Transcendentalist Movement," 10.

11. O. B. Frothingham, *Recollections and Impressions, 1822–1890* (New York, 1891), 21.

12. It is worth observing that Frothingham, but not Dall, is granted a chapter in the standard bibliographical work on the Transcendentalists, Myerson's *The Transcendentalists: A Review of Research and Criticism*. For Frothingham's shifting views on Transcendentalism, see J. Wade Caruthers, *Octavius Brooks Frothingham: Gentle Radical* (University, Ala., 1977), *passim*.

13. Caroline Healey Dall, *Transcendentalism in New England: A Lecture* (Boston, 1897), 6. Cited hereafter parenthetically within text as *TrNE*.

14. For Dall's view of Emerson's position on the women's movement see Helen R. Deese, "'A Liberal Education': Caroline Healey Dall and Emerson," *Emersonian Circles: Essays in Honor of Joel Myerson*, ed. Wesley T. Mott and Robert E. Burkholder (Rochester, N.Y., 1996), 237–260.

15. Octavius Brooks Frothingham, *Transcendentalism in New England: A History* (New York, 1876), 285.

16. Elsewhere, Dall stated that after Fuller had supported the education of her brothers, she had made "large gifts or loans of money" to women in distress. Dall, "The Hawthorne Book Censured," *Springfield Daily Republican*, Dec. 15, 1884.

17. Frothingham, *Transcendentalism in New England*, 249, 257.

18. See Helen R. Deese, "Alcott's Conversations on the Transcendentalists: The Record of Caroline Dall," *American Literature* 60(1988):17–25.

19. Franklin Benjamin Sanborn and William Torrey Harris, *A. Bronson Alcott: His Life and Philosophy* (Boston, 1893).

20. T. W. Higginson, *Contemporaries* (Boston, 1899); Caroline Healey Dall, *Springfield Republican*, Nov. 11, 1899.

21. Perry Miller, "New England's Transcendentalism: Native or Imported?" in *Literary Views*, ed. Carroll Camden (Chicago, 1964), 115–129.

Christopher Pearse Cranch

Painter of Transcendentalism

NANCY STULA

I N SEPTEMBER 1841 — JUST SIX YEARS AFTER COMPLETING HIS studies at Harvard Divinity School—the young Unitarian minister Christopher Pearse Cranch (1813–1892) confessed to Ralph Waldo Emerson: "I become more and more inclined to sink the minister in the man, and abandon my present calling *in toto* as a profession."[1] Cranch's inspiration to abandon the ministry stemmed from his having "very vigorously" taken up landscape painting. Today, however, Cranch is best known as a poet linked with the New England Transcendentalists; that his involvement with the new philosophy led him from a fledgling career as a Unitarian minister to a career as a landscape painter is seldom considered.[2]

Despite the recent interest among literary historians in Cranch as a disciple of Emerson, his career as an artist has not been recognized and his paintings have received almost no attention. Perhaps this lack is partially due to the fact that the majority of Cranch's surviving paintings remain hidden away in private collections. Also responsible, however, are suggestions by scholars that Cranch was a dilettante. The scholarship of American Transcendentalism, greatly influenced by Perry Miller's *The Transcendentalists: An Anthology* (1950), has unfortunately accepted Miller's pronouncement that Cranch was one of "the most futile and wasted talents. . . . [H]e gave up the pulpit, not . . . to take on serious work, but to become, by deliberate intention, a dilettante."[3]

Clearly this was not the case. Christopher Cranch considered painting his "chosen life profession,"[4] and during his forty-five year career as a landscape painter, he met with success. He was elected "Academician"—the highest rank an artist could attain—at the prestigious National Academy of Design in New York. Along with fellow Hudson River School artists, he contributed to major American exhibitions, very often to critical acclaim.[5] Cranch was also among an elite group of Americans in Paris in the 1850s

548

to gain entrance to the highly competitive Salon; notwithstanding the formidable competition and absence of any connection to the French atelier system, he succeeded in having his *American Sunset* hung "on the line."[6] He exhibited at three Paris Salons as well as at the 1855 Exposition Universalle. In addition, Cranch wrote extensively on the role of art and the artist within the context of Transcendentalism; these writings comprise a coherent theory of art.

Despite his successes, Cranch's name is quite unknown among art historians today. Perhaps we may blame Cranch himself for not assuring his fame: in Henry James's words, it was not in his nature "to emphasise or insist."[7] Cranch's diffidence, more than any aesthetic qualities or deficiencies in his paintings, worked to insure his obscurity. Cranch was in fact a gifted painter. Possessed of a receptive mind, he was able to give voice to a wide range of ideas current in the philosophical climate of nineteenth-century America, of which Emersonian Transcendentalism was a significant part.

We are thus faced with the need not merely for revision, but for an initial consideration of Cranch as an artist who was a Transcendentalist. Cranch was the only New England Transcendentalist who painted and his landscapes readily lend themselves to a reading of Emersonian philosophy made visual. His most intense association with Transcendentalism extended into the late 1840s, a period which coincides with a fruitful time in his career as a painter. These paintings must be viewed in the context of his Transcendental interests.[8] While Cranch's well-known caricatures of the late 1830s and early 1840s provide us with the most explicit link between Emersonian philosophy and his landscape paintings (for in drawing these caricatures, Cranch explored the visual potential of Transcendental ideas), only his paintings will be treated here.[9]

This essay will grapple with the question of what constitutes a Transcendental painting, if indeed such a thing exists. Many scholars have accepted luminist paintings (such as those produced by the American artists Fitz Hugh Lane, John Frederick Kensett, Sanford Robinson Gifford, and Martin Johnson Heade) as visual corollaries to the writings of Emerson and, by extension, to Transcendental philosophy.[10] The relationship of luminism to Transcendentalism, however, is tenuous.[11] Instead, I will propose that Christopher Cranch, rather than any of the luminists, is the more appropriate link between American landscape painting and Transcendental thought.

Cranch's first career was in the Unitarian ministry. Upon graduating from Columbian College in 1832 he was confronted with having to choose between the three "learned professions." Settling on the ministry, he enrolled in Harvard Divinity School along with John Sullivan Dwight and Theodore Parker and graduated in the summer of 1835. Although Cranch was never ordained, he set out as a supply preacher on the eastern seaboard, an undertaking that involved substituting for the permanent preacher at various parishes. Despite an inborn diffidence, Cranch became acclimated to preaching. During his first year he was exhilarated with his new career: "I have had some most glorious moments in the pulpit, moments which have carried with them an excitement I do not remember ever to have experienced elsewhere, or ever so deeply."[12]

Cranch's exhilaration was short-lived. Experiencing doubts as to his suitability for the Unitarian pulpit, he complained: "I cannot forget myself.... Nothing goes from me that has not passed under the eyes of self.... I am not free enough." His journals from these years are consumed with pledges to improve himself, to be bolder: he realized that his inborn reserve and diffidence "keeps me again and again silent."[13] Increasingly, the Unitarian ministry proved inhibiting. While his thoughts still flowed on paper, he had difficulty speaking publicly. He found himself virtually unable to preach.

The problem lay in what he termed his lack of "spontaneousness," and the cure, he decided, was to be found in the West. Encouraged to travel to St. Louis by his cousin William G. Eliot, he commenced his ministry at large in 1836, substituting first for Eliot and then for James Freeman Clarke in Louisville. Cranch was especially content with his situation in Louisville, for he was able to combine preaching with his love of writing, which he did as contributor to, and substitute editor of, *The Western Messenger*. In fact, he was so satisfied that he considered permanent settlement in the West and even suggested that Clarke ordain him. Three months later, however, Cranch was once again on the road and in February of 1839 he returned permanently to the East.

Before heading west, Cranch had some insight into the "new views" of Unitarianism, but it was during his years in the Ohio Valley that he blossomed as a Transcendentalist. Cranch and Clarke had known each other briefly as students as Harvard Divinity School, but in the West Cranch discovered in Clarke a soul sympathetic to those liberating views that had been labeled "Transcendentalism." Self-doubt and dissatisfaction with his career had been exacerbated by the restrictions that the Unitarian ministry placed on him. It is not surprising that by 1838 Transcendental precepts consumed Cranch's language; by 1840, recognizing that his theological views had undergone a complete metamorphosis, he burned twenty-four sermons and believed "others will follow before long. They are old clothes. I feel myself too large to get into them again. I do not stand where I stood a year ago."[14]

Transcendentalism was a Romantic impulse. By the 1830s Unitarianism had lost its "emotional appeal" for many of the younger generation. Young Christopher Cranch wanted to trade dry, rational Unitarianism for something "more satisfying to the soul," something that would allow him to express his religious views freely.[15] Initially he sought emotion and intensity. To appreciate the wonder of God's creation entailed breaking away from convention and routine—what Thomas Carlyle called "Custom."

Cranch credited his rapid conversion to Transcendentalism to two primary influences: Thomas Carlyle and Ralph Waldo Emerson.[16] He read Carlyle's *Sartor Resartus* (1836) and was most inspired by the religious pantheism he encountered in the chapter "Natural Supernaturalism." There Carlyle encouraged a transcendence of mundane appearances in order to recognize the miraculous in nature, even when "Custom" persuades us that "the Miraculous, by simple repetition, ceases to be Miraculous." Cranch first read Emerson's *Nature* (1836) shortly after it was published, and for him it was an eye-opening experience which he likened to a sunrise. He would re-read *Nature* several times over the course of his life. But it was Emerson's "Divinity School Address" (1838) that "drew the dividing line between the old and the new school of Unitarianism" and defined Transcendentalism for Cranch. He wrote of Emerson's address: "To some of my contemporaries it was dangerous heresy, to me it was a gospel of truth." Even though some considered Emerson's doctrines heretical, as "downright atheism, mysticism, or perhaps nonsense," Emerson remained for Cranch the "master mind of New England."[17]

While Cranch was not as radical in his views or as outspoken as Emerson, he did encounter opposition as a result of his ties to Transcendentalism.[18] In the spring of 1840, when Cranch delivered the commemorative poem he had written for the Quincy, Massachusetts, bicentennial, he publicly pleaded the case of Transcendentalism.[19] In so doing he attracted the attention of several prominent Quincy citizens, including his father's cousin John Quincy Adams. By June, news of Cranch's Transcendental tendencies reached his father, William Cranch (1769–1855), the chief justice of the Circuit Court in Alexandria, Virginia, and Christopher had to defend his radical new views.

In his letter to his father Cranch played with semantics, avoiding any commitment to that dangerous term "Transcendentalism," which he craftily assigned to the German school:

> I know very little about this system of philosophy. . . . of Kant, Fichte, Hegel, Schelling, etc., which is what I suppose to be the Transcendental philosophy, has always, from the very slight idea I have of it, struck me as a cold, barren system of Idealism. . . .

> But somehow the name "Transcendentalist" has become a nick-
> name here for all who have broken away from the material philos-
> ophy of Locke, and the old theology of many of the early Unitari-
> ans. . . . It has almost become a synonym for one who . . . preaches
> the spirit rather than the letter.
>
> The name has been more particularly applied to Mr. Emerson.

Nevertheless, Cranch reassured his father that Emerson "seems to be very
far from Kant or Fichte. His writings breathe the very spirit of religion and
faith. . . . [T]here is nothing in anything he says, which is inconsistent with
Christianity." He added: "Since we cannot avoid names, I prefer the term
'New School' to the other long name."[20]

Cranch finally met Ralph Waldo Emerson in Boston in the winter of
1839–1840 when he attended the first three of Emerson's ten lectures on
"The Present Age." That March, Cranch initiated a correspondence with
Emerson, sending him two poems for inclusion in the premier issue of
The Dial. In his letter he expressed his gratitude: "I have owed to you more
quickening influences and more elevating views in shaping my faith, than I
can ever possibly express to you."[21] Emerson likewise was impressed with
the young poet; he praised Cranch's verse and invited him to Concord to
"compare notes a little farther, to see how well our experiences tally."[22]
Cranch was one of the "many promising youths" about whom Emerson was
enthusiastic.[23] For the next year at least they remained in contact, but by
October 1841, Emerson's estimation of Cranch's work appears to have
fallen and he distanced himself from the young poet. Despite the ensuing
one-sided relationship, Emerson's writings remained an unceasing influence on Cranch.

From his first reading of *Nature*, Cranch became interested in exploring
Emersonian concepts and phraseology through visual means, initially
through caricature. Conservative Unitarians criticized the heretical ideas
of Transcendentalism, but the popular audience objected more to the
language of Transcendentalism, describing it as odd to the point of being
incomprehensible. In his essay "Transcendentalism," published in the
Western Messenger, Cranch defended the language of the Transcendentalists, but his defense is in essence recognition that inarticulate passages
did exist.[24] He too found humor in the wording, and these phrases provided material for the caricatures he and James Freeman Clarke began
drawing in the 1830s. Emerson's phrase "Almost I fear to think how glad I
am!", for example, provided Cranch with the image of Emerson dashing

FIGURE 1. "Transparent Eyeball," ink drawing on paper
"Journal, 1839," Cranch Papers, Massachusetts Historical Society,
Boston, Massachusetts.

across a lawn, stepping in puddles, and waving his arms—simultaneously
running scared and exhilarated.[25] But perhaps Cranch's most famous
image is his caricature of Emerson's line in *Nature* "I become a transparent eye-ball" (figure 1), which earned him the reputation of being the
most playful of the Transcendentalists. Emerson is depicted as an enormous eyeball, optic nerve tied in a ponytail, perched atop a minuscule
body in top hat and tails.[26] Cranch's sarcastic prophesy to Clarke—"We
are linked in celebrity, and thus will descend to posterity as the immortal
illustrators of the great Transcendentalist!"—ironically had come to pass:
this image has been reproduced more often than Cranch's other caricatures or any of his paintings.[27]

The details of their history notwithstanding, the significance of these
caricatures is that, in choosing to create images from Emerson's key
phrases, Cranch located his conception of Transcendentalism in the realm
of the visual. It was probably a combination of the very material quality
of the words Emerson used as well as Thomas Carlyle's graphic method of
presentation in *Sartor Resartus* that convinced Cranch of the suitability of

visual images to the expression of Transcendental ideas.[28] Cranch realized
that the graphic actuality of language is precisely where the fusion between
text and image occurs and similarly allows images to grow from the text.
The expression of Transcendental philosophy through visual means, initiated in his caricatures, ultimately found the ideal vehicle in landscape
painting. Before committing himself to a career in painting, however,
Cranch first had to reach a crisis point.

The controversy surrounding Transcendentalism, combined with the
demands of the Unitarian ministry, seriously affected Cranch; he suffered
a mental and physical breakdown of sorts. Because of his affiliation with the
Transcendentalists, he was unable to find pulpits to supply. By the summer
of 1840, shortly after his poems appeared in the *Dial*, Cranch complained
that "Most of the religious societies were afraid of the 'New Views.' The
pulpits were barred against me."[29] Continuing to encounter opposition
from his ties to the new philosophy, and oppressed by the limitations of the
Unitarian ministry, he lamented "a clergyman's life is the life of a slave. . . .
He cannot own a soul, and a mouth of his own." Cranch vowed never to
be ordained. Confiding in John Sullivan Dwight that his career goals were
changing, Cranch searched for alternatives to preaching and even expressed interest in joining Ripley's Brook Farm. The continual worry that
the Unitarian churches were "ridding themselves of all their best ministers"
hastened Cranch's abandonment of the Unitarian ministry.[30]

The search for new vocations and rejection of the ministry was characteristic of the Transcendental movement. Emerson had left the ministry in
1832 to write and lecture. George Ripley and John Sullivan Dwight also
gave up preaching for other pursuits. Cranch ultimately abandoned the
ministry, but the break with his first career was neither easy nor well defined, occuring sometime between 1841, when he declared that he had
"given up everything but the . . . glorious brush and palette," and 1844,
when he claimed that he was "completely free from the clerical yoke."[31]

Nevertheless, trading a career in the ministry for one in the fine arts has
been viewed as an unusual, if not extreme, conversion. Julie M. Norko, in
her 1992 article, proposes that Cranch viewed art and religion as "conflicting interests" that ultimately resulted in his "movement from religion to
aestheticism." But the conflict, I would argue, is not between religious
duty and aestheticism, or "vocation" and "inclination," as Norko suggests,
but rather between the new views Cranch had adopted and steadfast Unitarianism; Transcendentalism, in fact, could be aligned with the fine arts in
its opposition to mainstream Unitarianism.[32] For Cranch, preaching and
painting were not separate activities but simply two sides of the same coin:
celebrations of God in Nature. Painting, like prayer, became an act of

devotion, and thus, Cranch's goals remained constant.[33] Released from the Unitarian ministry, Cranch allowed nature to take on the role of the pulpit and continued to express his new religious views through prayer, poetry, and painting. As a result, theology and painting intertwine.

The alignment of religion with art was commonplace in the nineteenth century. Landscape, according to the American art critic James Jackson Jarves in his *Art-Idea* (1864), was "the creation of the one God—his sensuous image and revelation, through the investigation of which by science or its representation by art men's hearts are lifted toward him." Art led men to God, so artists could in some measure replace preachers. Barbara Novak, referring to the artists of the nineteenth century as "priests of the natural church," observes that "since artists were created by God and generously endowed by him with special gifts, the powers of revelation and creation extended to them too." In fact Cranch would exclaim: "I feel, while painting, the joy of a Creator, as if I were the Spring, making the trees put out leaves and . . . calling up clouds and lighting them with sunset glories."[34]

Perry Miller implicitly supported the link between painting and religion in his alignment of Transcendental literature with religion. According to Miller in *The Transcendentalists*, after Unitarianism rendered theological disputation obsolete, the Transcendental "revival of religion had to find new forms of expression instead of new formulations of doctrine, and it found them in literature"—or in Cranch's case, in painting. "The self-consciously literary character of the movement should not deceive us into regarding it as no more than a school of aestheticians," Miller cautioned; "worship remained the controlling motive." Like Thoreau writing of the daily trials of life on Walden Pond and Emerson on nature, Cranch too was attempting in his landscapes, in Miller's words, to "create a living religion without recourse to . . . the obsolete jargon of theology."[35]

Cranch recognized that the role of the artist—like the poet or preacher—was to give his audience insight into "the light of that truth," which was God manifested in Nature. In an essay published in the *Western Messenger* in 1838, Cranch addressed the need for a creative outlet which would align itself with religious aims. Emphasizing the close relationship between religion and art, he grappled with art theory, maintaining that the artist not only strengthens his own religious feelings through the act of expression but also makes spirituality available to his audience. Given the fusion of God and nature in nineteenth-century American culture, George William Curtis's comment that "some beautiful landscapes that I saw of [Cranch's] . . . made my heart 'babble of green fields' to itself for some days afterwards" demonstrates Cranch's success in his mission.[36]

That Curtis was a Transcendentalist confirms Cranch's ability to speak to a Transcendental audience. In fact, several members of this community, including Margaret Fuller, John Sullivan Dwight, and Theodore Parker, admired Cranch's work. Both Curtis and Fuller would praise Cranch in their published reviews of his paintings, and Parker owned Cranch's *Cascades of Tivoli*, which he lent to the Boston Athenaeum for exhibition in 1850.

One of Cranch's first attempts at landscape painting is *A River View of Uptate New York* (1843), painted at the height of his immersion in Emersonian Transcendentalism.[37] He presents us with a pristine landscape broken only by the inclusion of a few tiny figures: a hunter stands on the shore with his dog while Native Americans pass below in a canoe. It is in every way a scene of man in harmony with nature, embracing Emerson's view of nature as commodity, in which the physical needs of man are supplied (the hunter and fishermen), and as beauty and spirit. The foreground consists of a rocky promontory and a storm-blasted tree; the latter, having fallen across the chasm, provides a natural bridge, facilitating the viewer's access into the scene. The fortuitously placed log and large rocks not only offer the viewer access into the landscape but a secure place to stand as well, encouraging direct contact with nature.

Cranch maintained that we "must enter the great temple of the invisible and spiritual through the door of the visible." Here Cranch attempted to transcend sensual "understanding," as defined by Samuel Taylor Coleridge in *Aids to Reflection* (1825), in order to access "Reason,"—an extension of Emerson's moral sentiment which was the direct and immediate knowledge of the spiritual. Once we enter into Cranch's image of the beauty and power of God in nature, we transcend sensuality. Like George William Curtis, whose admiration of Cranch's landscape led him to remember actual landscapes, and finally to relive his own past experiences in nature, we too transcend the visual before Cranch's painting. Internalizing such scenes of nature, the Transcendental viewer becomes mesmerized, so to speak: "We fall into trances and almost abnormal spheres of life when we yield ourselves to her [Nature's] power." Then, "locked to the heart of Nature,"

> [we] feel the same spirit thrilling through her and us. We breathe the same breath, we are filled with the same joy with which the Infinite Fountain of Love inspires her . . . as these revelations of God are incessant, a flowing river of delight and instruction; so the soul of man shall be a corresponding receiver thereof, and his interior nature be a true reflection of the Kosmos—the immense world of beauty that forever shines around us.

John Sullivan Dwight, like G. W. Curtis, a viewer well versed in Emersonian concepts, noted of Cranch's work, "Were there not these still mirrors to reflect the beauty of the heavens to us, it might be lost to eyes so seldom lifted upwards."[38]

Cranch's *River View* offers us the tranquility necessary for such reflection. Sailboats glide across the calm river under a blue sky accented with fair-weather cirrus and cumulus clouds. But Cranch's image is not the "still mirror" which so aptly describes luminist painting: here the light appears cool and palpable as it settles over the distant mountains, but one is aware of Cranch's short, curling brushstrokes, which cause the light to circulate and shimmer over the landscape. The image as a whole is not still or quiet.

As mentioned above, several scholars have linked American luminism with Transcendental philosophy as the luminist vision finds a corollary in Emersonian precepts, specifically to certain phrases found in Emerson's *Nature*.[39] The absence of brushstroke, for example, is a particularly fitting parallel to the absence of ego suggested by Emerson's description of becoming a "transparent eyeball" and allowing the currents of the Universal Being to circulate through him. When the artist's labor trail of brushstrokes is invisible—as it is in luminist painting—then, as Emerson wrote, "all mean egotism disappears." The stillness and expansiveness inherent in Emerson's imagery, "my head bathed in blithe air and uplifted into infinite space," find a visual equivalent in the hard, cool light of the luminists' landscapes and in the dominant horizontality of their compositions.

It is significant, then, in light of the alignment of luminism with Transcendentalism, that Cranch, who was immersed in Emersonian philosophy, did not produce luminist paintings. Only on rare occasions did he employ the extended format featuring the strong unbroken horizon line favored by the luminists. His delicate, rounded brushstrokes create a pattern offering quite the opposite effect from that achieved by the magically invisible stroke of luminist painters. Their crystalline clarity is traded for a soft shimmering or vibrating effect in Cranch's work. His landscapes are not composed of the spare outlines favored by Lane and Kensett, but rather are diverse to the point of appearing crowded. His paintings are filled with activity and sound.

The fact remains that Cranch, who did not participate in luminism, was both a painter and a Transcendentalist who endeavored to render visible Transcendental ideas. Cranch's brand of Transcendentalism bypasses the "transparent" aspect to celebrate a nature that is sound-filled and motion-filled—the nature Emerson called "ecstatic." The luminist emphasis on the "transparent," with its compositional structure privileging the horizontal and its absence of brushstroke, causes these landscapes to become quiet and still. In effect, time stops. This militates against the flux, the continual shifting and metamorphosing that Emerson celebrated as one of nature's

FIGURE 2. *Landscape* (1849), oil on canvas,
signed and dated lower center, 32" x 48"
©New-York Historical Society, New York.

methods. The stoppage of time plays no role in this aspect of Emersonian
Transcendentalism where perpetual motion and change are evident everywhere in the natural world. As Emerson noted, there was "every hour, a
picture which was never seen before, and which shall never be seen
again."[40] It is this facet of Transcendentalism—in which the galvanizing
flow of energy as the Universal Spirit moves through nature, or moves nature through us—that we see characterized in Cranch's landscapes. It is
not surprising that Cranch found his voice in the Emersonian celebration
of the energy in nature, for motion—wandering and searching—was a
defining element in his personality and his career. Cranch's search for a
vocation and inspiration were in essence his search for a voice.

The New-York Historical Society's *Landscape* (1849) (figure 2) provides
a visual counterpart to the flux in nature that Emerson celebrated. The
scene is energized with activity, sound, and endless variety. A bald mountain looms large over the right side of the composition and is balanced by a
smaller peak at the left; both are echoed in several rounded mountain
peaks in the far distance. Deciduous and evergreen trees encircle a calm
lake which erupts into a waterfall; it, in turn, dashes down either side of the
large rock that obstructs the stream in its center. In the foreground is a
storm-blasted tree trunk that lends an element of the sublime to the richly

varied scene; its presence recalls the past violence of some storm and all of its attendant motion and thunder. The sublimity is balanced—in the Emersonian sense of the inherent balance of polarized forces in nature—by the calm sky above.[41]

But the scene as a whole is fictitious. It is not a transcription of an actual American view but rather a composite of several landscapes, and in this sense it is conceptual. Emerson had experimented with the possibility that nature may exist only in our minds, a projection instilled in us by God, and Cranch too had remarked upon the power of the mind independent of matter.[42] In a parallel manner, a conceptual approach informs his image. Conceptual attitudes often bore two-dimensional results and Cranch's *Landscape* does in fact contain passages that militate against the compositional devices that attempt to locate the objects in deep space. Here Cranch attempted a Claudian composition[43] featuring a central pool of water framed by trees, all infused with a golden light; however, the conceptual underpinnings of this scene become apparent: the calm lake in the middleground tilts towards the picture plane and the distant mountains flatten in the hazy light and push forward. This wavering back and forth between two- and three-dimensionality warps the Claudian construct and militates against any sense of tranquility in the scene, or in the mind of the viewer.

The sound- and motion-filled nature that Cranch celebrates corresponds to Emerson's belief that "when God speaketh he should communicate, not one thing, but all things; should fill the world with his voice; should scatter forth light, nature, time, souls, from the centre of the present thought; and new date and new create the whole." In keeping with the rush of sound as God's voice and varied presence fills the world, Cranch's paintings and poems are rarely silent. "Field Notes," written in 1842, celebrates the wealth of sounds and species in nature. Cranch's choice of words for their phonetic qualities reinforces his portrayal of a sonorous Nature:

> Heareth wisdom musical in a low-toned waterfall,
> Or the pine grove's breezy rush,
> Or the thrilling of a thrush, . . .

Or, of the endless variety of nature:

> Vines that creep and spikes that nod,
> Golden-helmet, golden-rod,
> Orchis, milk-weed, elder-bloom,
> Brake, sweet-fern and meadow broom. . . .[44]

In his paintings, including *Landscape* (figure 2) and *Landscape with Waterfall* (1851) (figure 3), sound is transmuted into visual activity as a sign

FIGURE 3. *Landscape with Waterfall* (1851) oil on canvas, 36" x 54"
Courtesy, Biggs Museum of American Art, Dover, Delaware.

of the continual flux in the natural world. In the painting from 1851, the dominant motif—a waterfall, which is the epitome of sound and motion—sets the tone for the scene. Placed against the picture plane, the cataract begins to invade the viewer's space, in essence moving sound into the foreground. The waterfall supplants the calm Claudian coulisse entirely.

At first glance the composition of *Landscape with Waterfall* appears Claudian, but on close observation one senses again a deviation. The river, viewed on an acute angle, twists the composition so that the river banks appear parallel to each other, retreating into the distance in a semicircular motion. The vanishing point appears to be located at the extreme left of the composition, at a point on the horizon hidden from view by the birch trees. Thus the resulting landscape appears to be in motion, oddly and slowly revolving.

During the late 1840s and 1850s Cranch was repeatedly drawn to certain motifs that include this "split waterfall." That motif is featured in the New-York Historical Society *Landscape* and *Landscape with Waterfall*, discussed above, as well as in *Autumn Landscape with Boy Fishing* (1845, not illustrated). Given Cranch's immersion in Transcendental philosophy during these years, these landscapes can be read as visual expressions of Emersonian concepts of flux, polarity, and unity in variety. Because such images were intended to be "read" by the viewer, iconography is privileged over technique and other formal issues.

During these years, Cranch was fascinated by the writings of Emanuel Swedenborg. In his journal entries from 1839 through the 1870s he grappled with Swedenborgian concepts.[45] In *Heaven and Its Wonders and Hell* (1758) Swedenborg took care to label natural symbols; he supplied links between individual species of trees, for example, and very specific moral attitudes.[46] Echoing Swedenborg's belief that every object in nature was attached to a moral law, Cranch, in his poem "Correspondences," likened Nature to "a scroll,—God's handwriting thereon," thus forging a relationship between word and image.[47] Like Swedenborg, Cranch endeavored to pierce through the externalities of nature to locate underlying spiritual messages. Certainly the correspondence theory was predominant in his mind when he began painting in the 1840s; it was not long before he was able to translate Swedenborgian concepts into visual form. While Cranch demonstrated little of Swedenborg's interest in assigning such specific attributes to natural forms, the emphasis on allowing external, sensual form to stand in for spiritual truths had ramifications on Cranch's iconography.

A "transcendental landscape," then, might be replete with natural symbols, such as the waterfall. The split waterfall motif—best described as a stream that invariably splits around a central rock causing the water to rush around both sides before ultimately rejoining—appears to have held special significance for Cranch. A clue to the symbolism and emotional significance of this favored motif may be found in the last stanza of Cranch's "Enosis" (1840). In these lines he celebrates the inherent, though sometimes obscured unity between two kindred souls, perhaps between himself and Ralph Waldo Emerson:

> We like parted drops of rain
> Swelling till they meet and run,
> Shall be all absorbed again,
> Melting, flowing into one.[48]

The stream of water in the landscape, in an identical manner, when separated, will flow around an obstacle and ultimately be reunified.

For Cranch, the split/reunified waterfall, like the drops of rain flowing into one, can be read as a symbol of Transcendental friendship. While the waterfall is encountered almost exclusively in the landscapes of the 1840s and early 1850s—the period of Cranch's immersion in Transcendental philosophy—it appears in only one later painting: the *Landscape* Cranch painted as a gift for Emerson in 1874 as a testament to his lasting influence.[49] This image, above all else, must be read as a statement of the philosophical debts he owed Emerson and as a visual manifestation of his words.[50]

It is significant that Cranch, after abandoning the waterfall motif for almost two decades, reinstalled it as the dominant motif in this landscape. The painting, which today still hangs on a wall in Emerson's house in Concord, Massachusetts, is a sunset landscape. The central body of water, colored by the setting sun, flows toward the viewer before cascading over a wall of large rocks in the foreground. The effect is that of the split waterfall. Painted several years after Cranch and Emerson lost contact, this landscape can be read as Cranch's attempt at renewing their friendship. This intention is apparent in the motifs Cranch chose: one strong, well-branched tree stands above the rest and towers over the landscape. The stream below, which breaks over the rock passage forcing the water into small streamlets, each separate from the other but composed of the same stuff, are ultimately reunited. The composition is balanced and Claudian: trees on the rocky banks frame the lake and waterfall. A golden light—warm, palpable, and in motion—envelops and unifies the scene. Cranch's palette and technique developed sophistication over the years; here his stroke is quite painterly, a result of his contact with Barbizon painting in the late 1850s, and he experiments with the interaction of reflected colors imbuing the foreground objects with a red hue as the sun sets behind them.[51]

Cranch's feeling for light, evidenced throughout his career in his landscapes, emerged in his poetry as well. "The Artist," published in the *Dial*, is one who "breathed the air of realms enchanted" and "bathed in seas of dreamy light."

> A sky more soft than Italy's
> A halcyon light around him spread;
> And tones were his and only his,
> So sweetly floating o'er his head.[52]

Other poems, including "The Ocean" (1844), in which Cranch likens mankind to "Spirits bathing in the sea of Deity," contain passages in which the senses are transcended. "The Music of Nature" (1836), begins with such a passage:

> I wandered with a calm surprise
> Half on the earth, half on the air,
> And sometimes I went gliding where
> The ocean meets the skies.
> O, it was sweet to roam away!
> No cumbrous limbs to clog the motion.[53]

These lines approach the light-filled clarity of the "transparent eyeball" aspect of Transcendentalism, yet even Cranch's closest approaches to luminism are not quiet or still. When gliding "half on the air," or transcending the body and senses, as he does below, there remains a concern with motion and sound that breaks the characteristic silent stillness of luminism:

> Whilst slept the limbs and senses all,
> Made everything seem musical;
> How could I cease to hear?[54]

As with Cranch's paintings, in which brushwork militates against any sense of tranquility, the concern with sound and motion in his poetry dilutes the power of the quiet mood evoked.

When Emerson first encouraged Cranch to break away from the Unitarian ministry to pursue landscape painting in 1841, he championed self-reliance.[55] Asserting his Romantic belief in the sacredness of the individual, Cranch broke away from institutional religion and pursued his inner calling to celebrate God's work as a painter of nature. Yielding to Emerson's precept to "insist on yourself," Cranch asserts his presence in painting through the application of paint and through his arrangement of landscape elements. Applying paint in curving motions with his characteristic light stroke, Cranch achieves a roundness of form and a constant, albeit subtle, surface activity. He is present in all of his images. (Conversely, the luminists, through the suppression of brushstroke and rejection of conventional composition, became, in essence, "invisible.")

For Cranch, as for Emerson, traces of the artist's life experiences, such as were carried in brushwork and compositional structures, were an essential part of true art. Nevertheless, in America at mid century, it was commonly understood that an artist must not assert himself in landscape painting to a degree that would cause the image to deviate from truth to God's creation. Cranch never privileged technique over content, which for him was the poetry or religious spirit in nature. Instead his presence was meditative, his "spirituality" was "of the still, contemplative sort; breathings, aspirations," detectable in his "constant tendency to converse with the essence and souls of things through the outward form."[56]

In his essay "On the Ideal in Art," published in 1845, Cranch refuted the popular Lockean notion that art is merely the skillful "imitation" of nature. He argued instead that visible nature must pass through "the refining fire of human genius, before she takes her highest degree," developing Emerson's idea that "thus is Art a nature passed through the alembic of man." Cranch acknowledged that "No one denies that Nature is the material basis of Art, that Nature must be accurately imitated"; however, it is "the

Mind, the Soul, after all, which perceives nature; the eye is but an optical instrument." No artist can be completely objective and imitative in the Lockean sense, but neither can he tamper with God's Nature: "Let us strive to imitate Nature; but there will be unconsciously imparted to the imitation a treatment which is strictly our own. Nor is this departing from Nature. For there is an ideal as there is an actual Nature." He accepts that while attempting accurately and truthfully to transcribe the landscape onto his canvas, his conception, as well as the mark of his brush, will remain visible. His characteristic brushstrokes and complex compositional structure should then be read as an assertion of self and of the image of nature in the artist's Mind and Soul.[57]

Ultimately, Cranch's art is a function of the compromise that "Art is neither wholly material nor wholly spiritual," but rather "the beautiful child of the wedlock between Nature and the Soul; and she is the more beautiful, the more she bears a resemblance to both parents."[58] Straddling the line between the real and the ideal in his theory of landscape painting, Cranch spoke as a New England Transcendentalist whose philosophy was located a distance from the materialism of John Locke—which stressed reliance on the senses, and correspondingly on the imitation of nature—and somewhat closer to the idealism of Kant—which emphasized the processes of the mind, of which imagination was a large part. These were issues that concerned Cranch as an artist over the course of his life.

Cranch's method had always required an intense communion with nature which was itself an act of devotion. Allowing nature to sink into his soul, he extracted its essence in "rare landscapes of soft mellow tone."[59] His early landscapes of the 1840s and 1850s, the period when he was most closely associated with Transcendentalism, are encyclopedic and necessarily fictitious views that included every natural phenomenon imaginable in an effort to reveal the flux and endless variety in nature. In his later paintings, Cranch sought out quiet, arcadian landscapes—scenes of Venice bathed in light and tranquil views of the Hudson River (see figure 4)—that cultivate a mood of contemplation and a spirituality stemming from Transcendentalism. Yet all of his landscapes support an intimate dialogue between man and nature.

Rather late in his career, Cranch published an essay, "The Unconscious Life," in which he continued to promote a form of painting that would rely on the imagination to filter sensory information received from its models (nature) but that was also the result of various unconscious, intuitive processes. This essay was published in 1890—just two years before his death—but it found its genesis in his "Commonplace Book" circa 1876, reflecting the direction Cranch's Transcendentalism took in the 1870s and

FIGURE 4. *Sunset Landscape*, oil on canvas, 15" x 30"
1960.7, gift of Mrs. Henry R. Scott
©Addison Gallery of American Art, Phillips Academy,
Andover, Massachusetts. All Rights Reserved.

1880s.[60] Cranch explored the implications of the unconscious in directing the painting process. As paintings are often "injured, if not spoiled, by being overlabored," he sought to locate the truest image in the "first fresh impression" without regard for technique or composition. In this context, even the roughest oil sketch would be valuable as a record of direct contact with God in nature. The unconscious allows the artist to intuit truth in nature, thus taking on the role of Emerson's moral sentiment, through these first impressions. An unfinished sketch would enable us to feel "how small things may suggest the greater—the drop of water image the firmament."[61]

Over the years Cranch's painting style and technique gained sophistication, and his brand of Transcendentalism developed into a system in which painting and theology function as one. Nevertheless, one aspect of his life as an artist remained unchanged. Cranch, the Transcendentalist, was in communion with God when he painted his landscapes and sketched outdoors. Breathing the fresh air, opening his heart and mind to the beauties of the landscape, he received the moral sentiment. Transcribing nature onto canvas became an act of devotion, an integral part of the intimate relationship he found with the Universal Spirit in Nature. Christopher Cranch was unique in that he painted as a Transcendentalist. Whether he was painting the Grand Canal in Venice or a cedar tree in Fishkill, his goals were inherently religious. While Transcendentalism can be found, to a limited degree, in his paintings—that is, in his approach and in his iconography—it remains that for Cranch the very act of painting the landscape was Transcendentalism.

Notes

1. Christopher Pearse Cranch to Ralph Waldo Emerson, Sept. 12, 1841, in Leonora Cranch Scott, *The Life and Letters of Christopher Pearse Cranch* (Boston and New York, 1917), 60.

2. Recent scholarship has focused on Cranch as a Transcendentalist within the context of his relationships with Ralph Waldo Emerson, Theodore Parker, and the Transcendental circle in general. J. C. Levenson was among the first to write about Cranch in "Christopher Pearse Cranch: The Case History of a Minor Artist in America," *American Literature* 21(1950):415–426. Hazen C. Carpenter, in his article "Emerson and Christopher Pearse Cranch," *New England Quarterly* 37(1964): 18–42, traced the often one-sided relationship between the two Transcendentalists; Elizabeth R. McKinsey's study *The Western Experiment: New England Transcendentalists in the Ohio Valley* (Cambridge, Mass., 1973) offered insight into his psyche. These essays were followed by a series of articles published in the 1970s and 1980s by: David Robinson, "The Career and Reputation of Christopher Pearse Cranch: An Essay in Biography and Bibliography," *Studies in the American Renaissance 1978*, ed. Joel Myerson (Boston, 1978), 453–472; David Robinson, "Christopher Pearse Cranch, Robert Browning, and the Problem of 'Transcendental' Friendship," *Studies in the American Renaissance 1977*, ed. Joel Myerson (Boston, 1977), 145–153; Joel Myerson, "Transcendentalism and Unitarianism in 1840: A New Letter by C. P. Cranch," *CLA Journal* 16(1973):366–367; Francis B. Dedmond, "'A Pencil in the Grasp of Your Graphic Wit': An Illustrated Letter from C. P. Cranch to Theodore Parker," *Studies in the American Renaissance 1981*, ed. Joel Myerson (Charlottesville, 1981), 345–357; Francis B. Dedmond, "Christopher Pearse Cranch: Emerson's Self-Appointed Defender," *Concord Saunterer* 15(1980): 6–19; Francis B. Dedmond, "Christopher Pearse Cranch's Journal. 1839," *Studies in the American Renaissance 1983*, ed. Joel Myerson (Charlottesville, 1983), 129–150; and Shelly Armitage, "Christopher Pearse Cranch: The Wit as Poet," *American Transcendental Quarterly* 1(1987):33–47. Most recent is Julie M. Norko's 1992 article, "Christopher Pearse Cranch's Struggle with the Muses," *Studies in the American Renaissance 1992*, ed. Joel Myerson (Charlottesville, 1992), 209–228. Recent monographs of Transcendental periodicals—*The Western Messenger*, *The Dial*, and *The Harbinger*—also contain substantial discussions of Cranch's role.

3. Perry Miller, *The Transcendentalists: An Anthology* (Cambridge, Mass., 1950), 179. It is unclear why Miller did not view Cranch's painting as "serious work," but his pronouncements have had ramifications on Cranch's reputation. Lawrence Buell, for example, quoting Miller, refers to Cranch as a "would-be artist." *Literary Transcendentalism* (Ithaca, 1973), 42, n. 42.

4. Christopher Pearse Cranch, "Autobiography," unpaginated, unpublished MS, private collection.

5. Cranch exhibited widely during his career. For a listing of exhibitions in which he participated see James Yarnall and William H. Gerdts, *The National Museum of American Art's Index to American Art Exhibition Catalogues* (Boston, 1986). Cranch belonged to the group of New York-based artists who later came to be

known as the "Hudson River School." These landscape painters exhibited at the National Academy of Design, spent summers sketching along the Hudson River, and congregated at the Century Club in New York City. As a group, their paintings typically combined precisely observed detail with the ideal elements of the Claudian composition. Cranch was one of the least well known participants in the Hudson River School, but his work deals with the same issues and functions within the same parameters as that of the other Hudson River artists.

6. "On the line" refers to the exhibition practice of honoring certain paintings with a prime location on the wall, that is on the "line" that is eye-level. On the other hand, those paintings considered inferior by the hanging committee were "skied," meaning that those painting were hung close the ceiling, far above the visitor's eye level and easily overlooked.

   The Paris Salon was held every other year during Cranch's stay in France (1853–1863), and his paintings were accepted for the Salon every year that it was held: 1855, when he exhibited two landscapes; 1857, when he exhibited four paintings; and 1861, when he exhibited one landscape. Cranch returned to New York in 1863.

7. Henry James, *William Wetmore Story and His Friends* (Boston, 1903), 1:110.

8. In a letter to John Sullivan Dwight, dated July 22, 1841, Cranch wrote: "A friend of mine here, who paints very sweet landscapes, offers to give me some instruction in the practical parts of painting, and then I can go on of myself. I am all impatience to begin." In the same breath, he continues: "Do you ever see Emerson? His last book has been a living fountain to me," thus confirming the concurrence of Emersonian inspiration with the urge to paint. Cranch to Dwight, July 22, 1841, Cranch Papers, Massachusetts Historical Society.

9. These caricatures can be found in the collections of the Houghton Library at Harvard University, the Massachusetts Historical Society in Boston, and the Albany Institute of History and Art in Albany, New York. For an in-depth treatment of Cranch's caricatures, see F. DeWolfe Miller's excellent study *Christopher Pearse Cranch and His Caricatures of New England Transcendentalism* (Cambridge, Mass., 1951).

10. Through the suppression of brushstroke and rejection of conventional composition, the luminists become, in essence, invisible. This elimination or suppression of self causes the artist to become transparent and allows the "currents of the Universal Being" to circulate through him as well as through the viewer without mediation. A visual corollary is provided to Emerson's "a light shines through us upon things and makes us aware that we are nothing, but the light is all. Emerson, "The Over-Soul," in *Selected Essays*, ed. Larzer Ziff (New York, 1982), 208.

11. In fact, so tenuous is the link between the luminists and Transcendentalism that Elizabeth Garrity Ellis observed that, while it is unlikely that luminist Fitz Hugh Lane (1804–1865) knew Cranch's caricature of Emerson's "transparent eyeball," "Cranch's top-hatted creature towering over field and hills . . . has nonetheless dominated discussions of the luminist paintings [Lane] produced from the mid 1850s until his death in 1865," thus suggesting a link between Lane's paintings and Emerson. Ellis, "Cape Ann Views," in *Paintings of Fitz Hugh Lane* (Washington, D.C., 1988), 19.

   Most recently, however, an article published by Mary Foley in *The American Art Journal* puts forth a stronger case for Lane having some familiarity with Emerson's ideas. Until the publication of her article, only the fact that Lane's name had been found on a list of members of the American Union of Associationists tied him with a group of former Brook Farmers. Elizabeth Garrity Ellis, "Fitz Hugh Lane and the American Union of Associationists," *The American Art Journal* 17(1985):89. Foley discovered Lane was also active in the Gloucester Lyceum after 1848, where he was appointed to the board of directors in September 1849. The fact that Emerson lectured at the Lyceum encourages the possibility that Lane may have heard him lecture or may even have spoken with him. Mary Foley, "Fitz Hugh Lane, Ralph Waldo Emerson, and the Gloucester Lyceum," *The American Art Journal* 27(1995–1996):99–101. While Lane may have heard Emerson speak in Gloucester, there is still no evidence that connects Lane with Transcendentalism on a deeper level.

12. Cranch to John Sullivan Dwight, June 15, 1836, in Scott, *Life and Letters*, 26.

13. Cranch to Margaret Cranch (sister), Oct. 15, 1837, in Scott, *Life and Letters*, 40; Cranch to Julia Myers, Aug. 10, 1837, in Scott, *Life and Letters*, 35. Cranch's 1839 "Journal" begins with a New Year's resolution on Jan. 8, 1839: "I must begin to *Live* more in earnest, than I have done. . . . At present I only *dream*. Half of my existence seems to be *dreaming*. A deadly *indifference* hangs over me—like a lethargy." "Journal," Cranch Papers, Massachusetts Historical Society.

14. Journal entry of 1840, transcribed in Cranch, "Autobiography."

15. Cranch to William Cranch, July 11, 1840, in Scott, *Life and Letters*, 50.

16. "Carlyle was an early love with me . . . [as was] Emerson. To these two great minds, among others, I was mostly indebted for the change that gradually took place in my theological belief. . . . These two leaders marshalled me the way my natural tendencies were impelling me." Cranch, "Autobiography."

17. Thomas Carlyle, *Sartor Resartus* (Boston and New York, 1897), 235; Cranch, "Autobiography"; Cranch to Julia Myers, Feb. 4, 1840, in Scott, *Life and Letters*, 47.

18. In Maine, during the winter of 1840, Cranch wrote: "I came across some people who called Emerson crazy and sneered at . . . 'transcendentalism.' . . . I spoke in defense. I long to utter my mind to these Philistines, but I anticipate some squalls here. If it comes to this I shall clear out of Portland pretty quick" ("Autobiography"). Once labeled a Transcendentalist, Cranch encountered difficulty in finding pulpits to fill. He voiced his frustration to John Sullivan Dwight through sarcasm: "Let me advise you . . . to repent of your heresies, to renounce R. W. E. and all his evil works and return to good old fashioned Unitarianism." Cranch to Dwight, Apr. 20, 1840, Cranch Papers, Massachusetts Historical Society.

19. Cranch's poem was published as *Poem Delivered in the First Congregational Church in the Town of Quincy, May 25, 1840, the Two Hundredth Anniversary of the Incorporation of the Town* (Boston, 1840).

20. Cranch to William Cranch, July 11, 1840, in Scott, *Life and Letters*, 49–51.

21. William Cranch to Ralph Waldo Emerson, Mar. 2, 1840, in Scott, *Life and Letters*, 58.

22. Emerson to Cranch, Mar. 4, 1840, in Scott, *Life and Letters*, 60. Emerson praised "Enosis" and "Aurora Borealis" as "true" and "brilliant" and "one more authentic sign . . . of a decided poetic taste, and tendency to original observation in our Cambridge circle" (5n). Cranch was unable to go immediately to see Emerson so the visit did not take place until August. A letter from Cranch to Emerson dated

Sept. 12, 1841, refers to additional visits "enjoyed with you under your roof and occasionally in Boston." In Scott, *Life and Letters*, 60–61.

23. Emerson exclaimed to Margaret Fuller that Cranch, along with Henry David Thoreau and William Ellery Channing comprised "the best club that ever made a journal." Quoted in William H. Moss, "'So Many Promising Youths': Emerson's Disappointing Discoveries of New England Poet-Seers," *New England Quarterly* 49(1976):55. Moss also notes that "Emerson had followed this same pattern several times before in his relationships with young poets" at first enthusiastic and later disenchanted with their productions (47).

24. "Truth dawns like light upon nations," Cranch explained. "All who are true . . . feel its coming, though they only *feel*, in dim, vague glimmerings of imagination and hope, but cannot *think* their dream into shape—much less speak it. . . . They are like infants who have but a confused inarticulate language of their own." "Transcendentalism," *Western Messenger* 8(Jan. 1841):405–409.

25. The original of this caricature in the archives of the Houghton Library, Harvard University, has been torn; the remaining portion, from Emerson's feet to his neck, is on the reverse of Cranch's "disagreeable things" cartoon (many thanks to Jennie Rathbun at the Houghton Library for locating this item). A "reconstruction" appears in F. DeWolfe Miller, *Christopher Pearse Cranch and His Caricatures of New England Transcendentalism* (Cambridge, Mass., 1951).

26. Several versions of this caricature exist: one, in the Houghton Library at Harvard University; a second version in the Albany Institute of History and Art in Albany, New York; a third in Cranch's 1839 "Journal," Cranch Papers, Massachusetts Historical Society, in which the name Ralph Waldo Emerson inscribed over the walking eyeball has been crossed out.

27. Cranch to James Freeman Clarke, May 20, 1839, Cranch Papers, Massachusetts Historical Society. While Cranch's caricatures have a wide audience today, it remains unclear just who their intended audience was in the 1830s and 1840s. Cranch confessed to Clarke that he lent to his cousin William Henry Furness "my Emersonian scraps . . . and it seems by sundry external signs upon them . . . that they have been considerably thumbed and pocketed. Great men have looked upon them." But it is not clear whether Emerson ever saw the caricatures.

28. In 1839, according to his "Journal," Cranch wrote a "Sartorish letter" illustrated with images that have what Cranch called "a sense—a Carlylean graphic-ness and truth. There can be a touch of comicality in them too—to give them a relish." Cranch, Jan. 9, 1839, "Journal," Cranch Papers, Massachusetts Historical Society.

29. Cranch, "Autobiography." Cranch complained of not having had a preaching engagement in the previous two months because "My name is expunged from the list of *safe* men. . . . I have the misfortune to have associated with Emerson, Ripley, & those corrupters of youth, and have written to the Dial, and these are unpardonable offenses." Cranch to John Sullivan Dwight, Nov. 17, 1840, in Myerson, "Transcendentalism and Unitarianism," 366–367.

30. Cranch to John Sullivan Dwight, July 22, 1841, Cranch Papers, Massachusetts Historical Society. Cranch made several visits to Brook Farm in West Roxbury, Massachusetts, and although supportive of the venture, he never became a member: "I have . . . no plans; or prospects, save of the vaguest sort. I want to see something of Ripley's establishment, and know if there is any work held out there to me in which

I can earnestly engage." Cranch to Dwight, July 22, 1841, Cranch Papers, Massachusetts Historical Society.

In the 1830s and until the early 1840s, before Cranch began to paint, he contributed poetry and essays to the various Transcendental periodicals: the *Western
Messenger*, the *Dial*, and the *Harbinger*. This involvement not only demonstrated
his commitment to Transcendentalism but also points to his increasing need for an
outlet for his "new views" outside of the Unitarian pulpit. For a complete discussion
of Cranch's involvement with Transcendental periodicals, see Robert D. Habich,
*Transcendentalism and the "Western Messenger": A History of the Magazine and Its
Contributors, 1835–1841* (London and Toronto, 1985); Joel Myerson, *The New
England Transcendentalists and the Dial: A History of the Magazine and Its Contributors* (London and Toronto, 1980); and Sterling F. Delano, *"The Harbinger"
and New England Transcendentalism: A Portrait of Associationism in America*
(London and Toronto, 1983).

31. Cranch to Julia Myers, Aug. 2, 1841, in Scott, *Life and Letters*, 67; Cranch, "Autobiography."

32. Norko, "Christopher Pearse Cranch's Struggle with the Muses," 210. Norko proposes as her thesis:

> Cranch spent a large portion of his early years attempting to ignore or unsuc-
> cessfully reconcile his concept of duty with his natural inclinations. . . . His
> prose of the period after he accepted the call to preach Unitarianism in the
> Ohio Valley demonstrates the development of the tension between vocation
> and inclination. In the prose, missionary zeal confronts his eventual movement
> from religion to aestheticism. (210)

Furthermore, Norko provides support for her view of painting as not only "inclination" but "amusement" for Cranch with the observation that Cranch's father would
only tune his piano on "days of leisure": "Perhaps [father] William Cranch's classification of the arts as leisure activities explains not only why Cranch could not be
formally trained in them, but also why he could not seriously consider a career in
them" (210). That few opportunities for "formal training" in painting existed in
America in the 1830s notwithstanding, Norko never mentions a detail of critical
importance: Christopher Cranch's older brother John was an artist who toured Italy
with Thomas Cole and whose drawings can today be found in the collection of the
Metropolitan Museum of Art, New York.

33. Further support for this alignment of nature and God can be found in the writings
of the Hudson River School artists, of which the best known is Asher B. Durand's
"Letters on Landscape Painting" (published in *The Crayon* in 1855), as well as in
contemporary art criticism.

34. James Jackson Jarves, *The Art-Idea*, ed. Benjamin Rowland, Jr., (1864; Cambridge
Mass., 1960), 86; Barbara Novak, *Nature and Culture: American Landscape and
Painting, 1825–1875* (New York, 1980), 9; Christopher Pearse Cranch, "The
Painter in the Woods," *Sartain's Union Magazine* 10(Jan. 1852):44–45.

35. Miller, *The Transcendentalists*, 9. Miller cautioned that "unless this literature be
read as fundamentally an expression of a religious radicalism in revolt against a rational conservatism, it will not be understood" (8). He also observed that "This inherently religious character of New England Transcendentalism has not been
widely appreciated, mainly because most students are not acquainted with all the

writings . . . [and] because all the insurgents strove . . . to put their cause into the language of philosophy and literature rather than of theology" (8–9).

36. Christopher Pearse Cranch, "Expression, the Mother of Sentiment," *Western Messenger* 5(Sept. 1838):375; George William Curtis to John Sullivan Dwight, Dec. 22, 1845, in *Early Letters of George Wm. Curtis to John S. Dwight: Brook Farm and Concord*, ed. George Willis Cooke (New York, 1898), 237.

37. This image can be found in Nancy Stula, *Lured by the Muses: Christopher Pearse Cranch, 1813–1892* (New York, 1997).

38. Christopher Pearse Cranch, "Ralph Waldo Emerson," undated, unpaginated MS, Cranch Papers, Massachusetts Historical Society; Cranch, "Painter in the Woods," 44–45; John Sullivan Dwight, review of Cranch's *Poems* [1844], *The Harbinger* 1(July 26, 1845):105–107.

39. John I. H. Baur identified luminism in his 1954 article "American Luminism: A Neglected Aspect of the Realist Movement in Nineteenth-Century American Painting," *Perspectives U. S. A.* 9(1954):90–98; but Barbara Novak, in *American Painting of the Nineteenth Century: Realism, Idealism, and the American Experience* (New York, 1969), first stressed the links between luminism and the transparent and tranquil aspect of Transcendentalism. More recently, Novak has stated: "There is perhaps little direct influence. But we can claim affinity. Luminism is the purest visual formulation of mid-century transcendental philosophy." *Nineteenth Century American Painting: The Thyssen-Bornemisza Collection* (New York, 1986), 30.

40. Emerson, *Selected Essays*, 44. Barbara Novak, in a footnote to her discussion of luminism in *American Painting of the Nineteenth Century*, acknowledges that several scholars (including John McCoubrey and John Kouwenhoven) have "put forth the idea of flux as the essentially American quality."

> If a dominant American quality is, as I maintain, not flux but an absolute in time and space that fortifies the constant existence of both thing and thought, it is perhaps because we have indeed had an awareness of flux that has engaged us even more intensely in a search for the underlying absolutes. . . . For Emerson, the task seems to have been to find that unity beneath the flux. (300n)

41. This painting was completed just after Cranch's return from Italy in 1849. While the Italian landscape and ruins had been a source of associations, the pristine wildness of the Catskills and Adirondacks put Cranch in touch with the power of God. The sublime, with its attendant rawness and power, spoke of Creation itself.

42. In his "Commonplace Book," circa 1872, Cranch wrote: "If Mind has this tendency and this power of making a magic lantern of itself, with eyes . . . to see its own hidden pictures thus made real—does it not argue a power independent of matter . . . ?" Cranch, "Commonplace Book," 26, Cranch Papers, Massachusetts Historical Society.

43. "Claudian" composition refers to the compositional structure employed by the French artist Claude Lorraine (1600–1682). This landscape structure consists of framing trees, a middle ground punctuated by water—usually a central coulisse— and a distance bathed in a golden light. Nineteenth-century American artists found Claude's compositions especially well suited to conveying the aesthetic of the beautiful. Cranch, as a young art student, studied Claude's *Liber Veritatis* in the Library of Congress, admiring his landscapes for their "truth" and "ideality." Cranch to John Sullivan Dwight, June 9, 1841, in Scott, *Life and Letters*, 71.

44. Emerson, *Selected Essays*, 188; Christopher Pearse Cranch, "Field Notes," in *Poems* (Philadelphia, 1844), 82–86. This poem is dated July 1842.

45. Cranch delved into Swedenborg's *Arcana Coelestia: or Heavenly Mysteries Contained in the Sacred Scriptures* (Boston, 1794) very early, in 1839, and while he denied that he had become a "Swedenborgian," the theologian's influence is nonetheless apparent in several of his poems of this period as well as in his paintings. In his "Commonplace Book," circa 1872, Cranch continued to grapple with Swedenborg: "All depends on which side we approach him. If on the philosophical, common sense side he is a help to us. . . . [T]hrow out his contradictions of statement and then strain his philosophical creed through the seive of Reason . . . and Swedenborg become a great light in our hands." Cranch, "Commonplace Book," 11, Cranch Papers, Massachusetts Historical Society.

46. Swedenborg set forth that "Vines and laurels correspond to affection for truth . . . while olives and fruits [trees] correspond to affection for good." *Heaven and Its Wonders and Hell* (New York, 1900), 79.

47. Christopher Pearse Cranch, "Correspondences," *Dial* 1(Jan. 1841), 381.

48. Cranch, "Enosis," in *Poems*, 51–52.

49. This oil on canvas, c. 9" x 12", is owned by and can be seen at the Ralph Waldo Emerson House in Concord, Mass.

50. Cranch's letter to Emerson, dated Apr. 27, 1874, which accompanied the painting, is transcribed in Scott, *Life and Letters*, 280–281.

51. Cranch spent ten years in France, from 1853–1854, and during this decade he was inspired by the painters who worked in the area around Barbizon and in the Forest of Fontainebleau. This group of painters often took unassuming landscapes for their subjects and developed an approach characterized by broad brushstrokes that obliterated fine detail.

52. Christopher Pearse Cranch, "The Artist," *Dial* 3(Oct. 1842):225. When published in 1844 with his collection of *Poems*, "halcyon" was replaced so that line 12 reads: "Their wealth of light around him spread."

    In an 1872 entry in his "Commonplace Book," Cranch sings a "Prayer to the Sun-God . . . I worship thee—Joy of the Universe! Today, by thy light, let me paint as I never painted before. And the joy of thy light, And the joy of my work, shall be my best reward! N.Y. Feb. 7 1869." "Commonplace Book," 6–7, Cranch Papers, Massachusetts Historical Society.

53. Cranch, "The Music of Nature," in *Poems*, 14–20. The poem is dated June 1836. In an undated manuscript entitled "Dreams," Cranch described a similar sensation, but one in which he cannot transcend the senses as walking on air required extreme physical exertion: "I have a strange vivid dream, now and then, of walking in the air. I don't mean that flying sensation some have, but a plain rising and stepping, only accomplished by strong effort of will and usually just a few feet above the heads of my companions. . . . I sink only when I relax my will and muscular effort." "Dreams," undated, unpaginated MS, Cranch Papers, Massachusetts Historical Society.

54. Cranch, "The Music of Nature," 20.

55. Emerson wrote to Cranch in Oct. 1841: "that the beauty of natural forms will not let you rest, but you must serve and celebrate them with your pencil, and that at all hazards you must quit the pulpit as a profession, I learn without surprise. . . . The

Idea that rises with more or less lustre on all our minds, that unites us all, will have its way and must be obeyed." Emerson to Cranch, Oct. 10, 1841, in Scott, *Life and Letters*, 62.

56. John Sullivan Dwight, review of Cranch's *Poems*, 105–107. Of Cranch's nature, Dwight wrote: "There is nothing in him which could by any possibility tyrannize over others. You feel that here is a gentle nature . . . who would rather sit silent hours and days than *impose* the influence of his speech, and who would suffer all the consequences of inaction, rather than *take* the lead" (106).

57. Christopher Pearse Cranch, "On the Ideal of Art," *The Harbinger* 1(Aug. 23, 1845):170–171; Emerson, *Selected Essays*, 47; Cranch, "On the Ideal of Art," 170–171. For Cranch, genius was the artist's "God-given privilege of infusing . . . Imagination into the dead materials it has collected together, breathing upon dry bones and clothing them in the garb of life and beauty."

58. Cranch, "On the Ideal of Art," 170–171.

59. Cranch, "The Artist," 225.

60. Christopher Pearse Cranch, "The Unconcious Life," *Unitarian Review* 33(Feb. 1890):97–122. Excerpts from the first draft of this essay are found in Cranch's "Commonplace Book" entry for Nov. 11, 1876, Cranch Papers, Massachusetts Historical Society. An essay also titled "The Unconscious Life" was read before the Sunday Club of Boston on Oct. 12, 1880 (Minutes of the Sunday Club, Cranch Papers), before the essay was published in the *Unitarian Review*.

61. Cranch, "The Unconscious Life"; Cranch, "Painter in the Woods," 44–45.

Later Manifestations of Concord

Charles Ives and the Transcendentalist Tradition

Michael Broyles and
Denise Von Glahn

C HARLES IVES'S INTEREST IN TRANSCENDENTALISM, AND IN Ralph Waldo Emerson and Henry David Thoreau in particular was of long duration, his reading in the field of some depth. This essay approaches that interest through his Piano Sonata No. 2 (*Concord, Mass., 1840–1860*). It considers not only the score but also a book-length program, *Essays Before a Sonata*, that Ives wrote to accompany the piece.[1] While Ives often provided interpretive insights and programmatic associations for his compositions, either in the scores or in his autobiography, *Memos*,[2] *Essays Before a Sonata* is unique in its length and scope. Why he felt compelled to write such an extensive explication is open to conjecture. Music and prose together provide greater insight into Ives's thinking on the subject than either would have done singularly.

It has been said that "in the entire range of American literature there is no stronger tie between a writer and a place than the tie between Henry Thoreau and Concord, Massachusetts."[3] It can also be said that in the entire history of American music, no composer has understood the power of place as thoroughly and profoundly as Charles Ives. Born in 1874 into an established Connecticut family that could trace its lineage back to the earliest settlers, Ives thrived upon social privilege, financial security, a generations-long commitment to active citizenship, an Ivy League education, and a deeply felt identification with the New England of his ancestors. Though he later lived and worked in Manhattan, regular extended visits to his fourteen acres in West Redding, Connecticut, renewed him physically and spiritually. His home in its bucolic setting offered a place away from the too busy and volatile world of the city.

Place, however, meant more than mere retreat. Judging from his autobiography, Ives customarily recalled when a piece was composed by citing where it was composed; times and places were indivisible aspects of a thought. Like his recollections, Ives's scores also brim with references to specific places. Many of them actually bear the name of the place in their titles. In these cases, naming a location went beyond being a convenient mnemonic device. Places organized ideas, and for Ives ideas were paramount; ideas animated his music. It should come as no surprise then to find that the idea of time and place inspired some of Ives's most moving works: *The "St. Gaudens" in Boston Common, Putnam's Camp, Redding, Connecticut, The Housatonic at Stockbridge,* and *From Hanover Square North,* to name just a few. Each of these "place pieces" proclaims the intimate and unique relationship that Ives understood existed between a time and a place. But capturing time and place in music required an unconventional approach to composition, one that emphasized atmosphere over action. Using techniques that Robert Morgan has termed "spatial," Ives succeeded in weaving the place into the musical fabric.

Although spatial techniques are commonplace in *late*-twentieth-century Western composition, non-linear approaches to musical construction and form were rare in the early decades of the century. The nineteenth-century tradition that Ives inherited was premised upon predictable harmonic motions, trackable temporal sequences, and a dominant, single trajectory that determined the hierarchy of all elemental relationships and behaviors. By contrast, Ives's spatially conceived pieces manifested harmonic stasis, circular melodic gestures, a weakened sense of lapsed time, multilinear activity, and large-scale reflective structures that defied conventional objectives.[4] If unyielding progress towards an irresistible, audible goal drove the music of the common-practice era, equipoise among musical elements characterized spatially conceived pieces.[5]

For many composers, spatial techniques were their own *raison d'être,* but for Ives they were means to an end. Ives wanted what the techniques could create: room to render place in sound. Absent the irresistible push and pull of rhythmic drive and harmonic determinism, spatially conceived pieces allowed listeners the opportunity to fasten their aural gaze on where they were, rather than on where they were headed; spatial techniques secured "time" to contemplate the atmosphere of a location. Thus, in Ives's "place pieces," time operates in two ways: first, as part of a place-time duality, time is a basic motivating idea for a piece; second, as an essential component of music, time is manipulated in such a way as to suggest the minimization of its passage.

Ives's Piano Sonata No. 2 (*Concord, Mass., 1840–1860*), often referred to as the *Concord* Sonata, is one of his most famous contemplations of place. The nineteenth-century village memorialized in the piece resonates with meaning for students of American history, literature, and philosophy, but it was also personally significant for Ives. At least two earlier generations of Ives family members claimed associations with the bard of Concord, Ralph Waldo Emerson. Though it is difficult to determine at what point Ives developed a mature understanding of Emerson, or of any of the other Concord Transcendentalists for that matter, it is accurate to say that he was aware of these men and their work relatively early in his life.

Charles's paternal grandmother, Sarah Hotchkiss Wilcox Ives, was an admirer of Emerson, as was her son, Ives's "Uncle Joe." Family myth tells of Joseph Ives meeting Emerson and James Russell Lowell in Boston in the mid 1850s and of Emerson later staying with the Iveses when he lectured in Danbury. Though difficult to corroborate, stories that appeared in the *Danbury Times* between 1856 and 1859 announcing Emerson's lecture schedule might actually support the family legend. Lyman Brewster, a young attorney who would later marry Ives's paternal aunt Amelia, was corresponding secretary of the Danbury Lyceum, a "venerable institution . . . inspired with the determination . . . to make its mark upon the literary history of the town."[6] As secretary of the Lyceum, Brewster shared responsibility with its president, J. Marshall Guion, for arranging speakers for the yearly lecture series. A number of well-known orators were secured, including Horace Greeley, Wendell Phillips, and Henry Ward Beecher. Though Emerson was scheduled and rescheduled for the 1856–1857 season, it was not until three years later, on December 7, 1859, that he spoke to the Lyceum on "Success." If the Iveses hosted Emerson at all, it was most likely during his stay in Danbury in December of 1859. Given the prominence of the Ives home in antebellum Danbury, such would not be surprising. Certainly Lymen Brewster's role in securing Emerson for the Lyceum would have endeared him to the Iveses, and once he married into the family all his efforts in this realm would have been absorbed into their own history.

But Charles Ives had his own, if less direct, connection with the famous philosopher. In his senior year in college Ives wrote a paper on Emerson's influence and submitted it to a Yale literary magazine.[7] That the paper was never published and there are no extant copies make it difficult to assess Ives's youthful grasp of Emerson or Transcendentalism. It is possible, however, that parts of this paper formed the nucleus for the essay entitled "Emerson" in *Essays Before a Sonata*. Regardless of the sophistication of Ives's thinking in 1898, it is clear that he eventually went beyond a vague inherited family predisposition towards Emersonian Transcendentalism. Ives's habitual paraphrasing of lines from Emerson essays indicates that at some point he read widely in Emerson's writings.[8]

Recently, psychiatrist-music historian Stuart Feder has explored Ives's ties to another favorite son of Concord, Henry David Thoreau. Although Ives's understanding of Thoreau seems to have been confined to *Walden*, which he read for the first time before entering college in 1894 and again, most likely, in 1919 when he was writing the essay to accompany the fourth movement of the *Concord* Sonata, Feder traces Ives's "sentimental and intellectual attachment to Thoreau" to "his father, George Edward Ives. In Thoreau . . . Ives perceived a worthy and loveable maverick through whom he could idealize his father." When George Ives died unexpectedly during Charles's first semester at Yale, the composer remembered it was to Thoreau that he turned for comfort. Beyond the fourth movement of the *Concord* Sonata, Ives's interest in Thoreau is attested to in a number of songs he wrote, including "Remembrance," "Walking," and most especially "Thoreau." Although the *Concord* Sonata reveals an acquaintance with the works of Hawthorne, especially the short stories "The Celestial Railroad" and "Feathertop: A Moralized Legend," and with the character of Bronson Alcott and his family, Ives's sense of Transcendentalism was shaped, more or less, by his reading of Emerson and Thoreau.[9]

Determining the depth of Ives's knowledge of Transcendentalism is problematic, especially if one attempts to go beyond his oft-stated beliefs in the innate goodness of man, the unity of diversities found in nature, and the idea of the presence of the universal in the local. Even *Essays Before a Sonata*, by far his most extended discussion of Transcendentalism, fails to present a coherent statement on the philosophy. Scholars must slog through Ives's verbal quagmire hoping to discover just what about Concord and Transcendentalism impressed him. But Ives was first and foremost a composer, and his most articulate remarks are found in the music itself and in the preface to that work. With this piece as with others, Ives sets out to explore the ideas associated with a particular place in a particular time.

In composing a piece on Concord, Massachusetts, Ives chose a town rich with historic and symbolic meaning, "a town both real and mythical."[10] The Transcendental Concord was clearly central to Ives's conception of his sonata. But Concord had great historical significance prior to Transcendentalism. Its role in the Revolutionary War is secured in our national memory, immortalized in part by a Cambridge rather than a Concord bard, Henry Wadsworth Longfellow. Its historical importance far predated even the Revolutionary War, however. Concord was among the first inland communities in New England, and its founding was achieved with great difficulty and hardship. Those who settled it interpreted their mission within the framework of seventeenth-century Puritan orthodoxy. They saw themselves making—barely —a garden out of a desert. In 1654 Edward Johnson characterized these efforts: "Thus this poore people populate this howling Desert, marching manfully on (the Lord assisting) through the greatest difficulties, and forest labours that ever any with such weak means have done."[11] Concord, in Puritan terms, was thus perhaps the first inland garden, the first wresting of a piece of interior America out of the desert. It was the beginning of the march westward, the Puritan view of the wilderness providing the first rationale for why the American continent should submit to the European conquest.

Ives did not see the Puritan side of Concord directly. Instead he saw the literary Concord, and he was quite specific about that in the title of the sonata. He did, however, embrace a view of nature, manifest in Emerson and Thoreau, which is traceable to Puritan New England.[12] Emerson and Thoreau were indirect heirs of the beliefs about nature of at least one important New England theologian, Jonathan Edwards. Unlike most Puritans, Jonathan Edwards found in nature a solace, a place of inner peace and contemplation. The Edwardsian vision of nature was mystical. Paula M. Cooey characterized Edwards's view of nature as anagogic, that point in which nature "becomes the body of infinite, eternal spirit."[13] Edwards, however, was not a pantheist; he distinguished that which was created from the creator, although his detachment was not absolute.[14] Nature was a coded message, God's way of revealing the divine to man.

Emerson, like Edwards, saw God in nature. The shape of God varied but the spirituality was the same. Nature was a refuge, a place of contemplation. In the stillness and contemplation of the moment the Divine resided. In Emerson the tangible, judgmental, omniscient, hellfire-brimstone God of Edwards became the Universal Being, but nature remained a source of meditation in which man achieved a mystical unity with his world. Thoreau's vision of nature was similar, owing much to his mentor, Emerson; if anything Thoreau took the idea of nature as a vehicle for meditation and hence surrender of self even further than Emerson.

Charles Ives embraced the Emersonian view of nature. Living in a post-industrial-revolution world from which he desperately wanted to escape, Ives could not accept his own generation's view of nature as a resource to be exploited for capitalism's profit. But he was not comfortable with an exclusively grandiose Romantic view of nature, with the "operatically sublime" conception of the American landscape favored by some nineteenth-century painters. For Ives neither the Romantic, secularized view of "nature sublime" nor the modern view of "nature subdued" was sufficient. Like the Transcendental philosophers and the luminist painters, Ives also sought in nature the "still small voice," an approach that enveloped nature and spirit in a shroud of stillness.[15] Both the grandiose and the contemplative approaches are found in the *Concord* Sonata, the first in "Emerson," the second in "Thoreau."

Although Ives himself did not talk about Edwards, he did not miss the Puritanism in Emerson, and Ives's friends and early supporters were quick to notice a similarity between Edwards and Ives.[16] In fact much of the "Emerson" movement of the sonata is about the philosopher's struggle with Puritanism. In a marked first edition referred to in *Memos* Ives wrote, "This movement . . . attempts to suggest the struggle that seemed to go on in Emerson, in reconciling . . . the influence of the old Puritan canon, dogma, etc., with his individual growth—that is, theology vs religion. In fact the whole movement has more to do (and more than I intended) with the struggles of his soul than that peace of mind which he commands even in his struggles—though the music tries to end with that feeling."[17]

So how does Ives map out Concord? What of its history and symbolism does he capture? Does Ives's belief in "innate goodness" or "the presence of the universal in the local" actually manifest itself in his music? How does he capture the stillness of place that permeates Thoreau's Walden? Accepting programmatic associations for any piece of music is difficult, and it is especially so when a work is a pastiche of movements originally conceived in relation to other projects, as were the movements of the *Concord*.[18] How important was Transcendentalism to the work? What was the significance of naming a piano sonata after a village? There are a number of possible explanations. Given the geneses of each of the movements, scholar J. Peter Burkholder concludes, "Not even the 'Concord Sonata' itself is a wholly Transcendentalist work. *It is Concord*, not Transcendentalism, that is the connecting thread between the four movements" [italics added].[19] Others might decide that the movements' titles—"Emerson," Hawthorne," "The Alcotts," and "Thoreau"—suggest that the composer was primarily interested in four individuals more or less associated with Transcendentalism rather than the locus of their activities. Indeed copious interpretive comments that Ives wrote in the margins and between the staves of a 1920 score owned by pianist John Kirkpatrick appear to support the contention that the *Concord* Sonata is a piece more about people than anything else. But the title of the larger work, *Concord 1840-1860*, tells us otherwise, as does the preface to *Essays Before a Sonata*, in which Ives writes about "the spirit of Transcendentalism that is associated in the minds of many with Concord, Mass., of over a half century ago."[20] And in the *Essays* spatial and geographical metaphors abound. Although their character varies from movement to movement, that variance itself hints at an interpretive pattern of the overall sonata. That Ives included almost all geographical references from the *Essays* in the excerpts that precede each movement suggests their importance to the composer. His remarks introducing "The Alcotts" and "Thoreau" in particular focus on specific places in Concord village and the ways in which they "bear a consciousness that its past *is living*."[21] For Ives, regardless of the genesis of the sonata, in the final form of the work the town and the philosophy are equally important and the village of Concord is as much a part of the Transcendental tradition as Emerson or Thoreau.

The variety of geographical and spatial references found in Ives remarks can best be understood by mapping Ives's Concord as an artistic space. One view would be as in Diagram 1. In some cases the geography is real: Ives describes the third movement, "The Alcotts," as a walk "down the broad-arched street, passing the white house of Emerson," eventually to arrive "beneath the old elms overspreading the Alcott house."[22] Ives also depicts Thoreau's Walden in detail, referring to the "Indian summer" in which "mists rise," revealing Thoreau standing "on the side of the pleasant hill of pines and hickories in front of his cabin," then going "down the white-pebbled and sandy eastern shore," eventually to climb "the path along the 'bolder northern' and 'western shore, with deep bays indented,' arriving at the railroad track."[23] (We will return to these movements later in the essay.) In "Emerson" and "Hawthorne" places are either symbolic or imaginary: Ives situates Emerson on a mountain: "We see him standing on a summit . . . peering into the mysteries of life, contemplating the eternities, hurling back whatever he discovers there,—now thunderbolts for us to grasp."[24] Ives freely admits that "Hawthorne" is about fantasy; nevertheless there is a railroad, the Celestial Railroad, "that frosty Berkshire morning," a church and churchyard, Main Street, and the "Stamford camp meeting."[25]

This blending of real places and symbolic or fantastical spaces is one of the keys to understanding the *Concord* Sonata. Nature is at the heart of *Concord*, and some writers have considered it a "nature piece."[26] But like

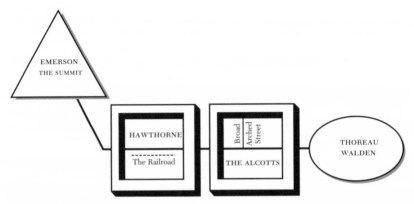

DIAGRAM 1. Ives's Concord Village: A Spatial-Spiritual Landscape

Emerson, Ives found in nature a vehicle for deep spiritual contemplation. What Ives considered real and what he considered spiritual must be sorted out before the sonata can be understood. Approached from that point of view, *Concord* consists of two spiritual, transcendent outer movements, enclosing two human, down-to-earth inner movements. Emerson is the giant peering down from the summit, trying to take it all in, to comprehend it in one concentrated vision. His weapon is thunderbolts. Thoreau is the philosopher, the meditator considering nature and existence; the "Thoreau" movement is a quiet contemplation interrupted by intrusions from the outside world. The world of abstract transcendence may have captivated Ives, but it was not his only passion. In between are two inner movements in which the cosmos is put aside while the parallel struggle of life goes on. These middle movements are about Ives's world of boyhood dreams and adult responsibility. We should not forget both how deeply Ives felt about these topics and how they intertwined in his life and thought.

"Hawthorne" depicts the youthful, playful, fantastical life of the boy, a life that Ives remembered vividly, as many of his pieces demonstrate. The images in "Hawthorne" are down-to-earth, chaotic, noisy, rambunctious. They ultimately rest on Hawthorne's stories themselves, many of which are anything but childish; nevertheless Ives's own interpretation, as seen in the preface and the music itself, is one of childhood fantasy. "The Celestial Railroad" probably had a double meaning to Ives. As Ives conceived "Emerson," the philosopher had already conquered the Puritans, and now Hawthorne, that is Ives, can laugh at them. They are no longer threatening. Ives admitted that he did not want to deal with the "influence of sin upon conscience," which he considered central to any conception of Hawthorne.[27] "The Celestial Railroad" may also have attracted Ives because of his own childhood fascination with trains. In a diary Ives kept in 1914 when commuting by train between New York City and his new home in West Redding, Connecticut, he described just how strong that fascination was:

> Traveling down and back to Redding now every day.
> —A sleepless night when I was 10 years old or so always preceded a trip to New York in the cars from Danbury. The excitement and anticipation was greater than a trip to England would be now—I went to a new world—the only hard part of commuting now is that each time I fear I may get further and further away from my boy time dreams. Cannon/?/ station—So. wilton winnipauk, Darien; when names that had a mystical meaning in our imagination—

> trains were run on the Ives Bros RR under the clothes line to these
> places and back a hundred times . . .

Ives then describes in considerable detail how they set up the imaginary
train, how they used the dinner bell and other items, how they made the
sounds, the whistle, the sissle, and the accents of the brakemen—note the
emphasis on sounds—how their "passengers" would get up and answer
the door bell when they were not in a station, etc., and how his father
would play with them, discovering that he could imitate certain train
sounds on the violin. Ives then observes:

> How thankful we feel now, that father dreamed with us, how cir-
> cumspect our lives would be now if he hadn't. It is always the
> "minute after" life that everyone lives. Immortality is but a hope a
> component substance we now must be full of hope—riding up and
> down from Redding as I do now, might stifle it if we hadn't had our
> RR under the clothes line.[28]

"The Alcotts" depicts the grown man and his milieu. Ives's vision of manhood has posed a problem for some scholars, who have found his rhetoric
macho and even misogynist. Yet to Ives manhood was not Rooseveltian
bluster—he absolutely detested Theodore Roosevelt and what he symbolized, including war and hunting—but something very different. Ives's primary vision of a real man was a caring husband and devoted father, which
he interpreted in Victorian terms: a man's primary duty was to take care of
his family. This belief determined his business practices, his personal life,
and his zealous but inept ventures into politics. Ives's insurance career was
no mere convenience providing him the financial freedom to pursue his
art. He considered his work a mission, which he approached as idealisti-
cally as any aspect of his intellectual or creative worlds. Both his work in
life insurance and his ventures into politics were driven by issues of man's
responsibility to his fellow man, for Ives saw in his insurance prospects the
"average man," which he equated explicitly with "humanity."[29]

As we saw, Ives placed Emerson on the summit in the first movement.
The physical landscape was a perennial and powerful metaphor in Ives's
music. But in spite of the considerable time that he spent in the Adirondacks and the Berkshires, and even though he made many references to
nature, he seemed indifferent to mountains as part of the natural landscape.[30] From 1910 ascending a mountain or being on a summit invariably
had spiritual or metaphorical meaning to Ives. In that year he wrote *Evidence*, one of a group of songs collected in *114 Songs*, whose text, in Ives's
own words, was "either by Harmony Twitchell Ives or her husband":

There comes o'er the valley a shadow, the hilltops still are bright;
There comes o'er the hilltop a shadow, the mountains bathed
in light;
There comes o'er the mountain a shadow but the sun ever shines
thro' the night.

Frank Rossiter, in the first scholarly biography of Ives, noted that "Ives himself had long used the symbol of the mountain to suggest spiritual transcendence and the hard and lonely way of truth."[31] In his Second String Quartet, the symbolic nature of the mountain is clear: "S[tring] Q[uartet] for four men—who converse, discuss, argue (in re 'politick'), fight, shake hands, shut up—then walk up the mountain to view the firmament.'" In 1935, in a memorandum associated with a letter to Franklin D. Roosevelt, arguing for more direct participation of the people in the political process, Ives waxed poetically: "But some morning—GLORIOUS—(not tomorrow)—these answers will be 'right about facing' and the Tread up the mountain, resounding around the world, will bring a new Horizon to all."[32]

In his musical world, the only figures that Ives allowed on the mountain were Emerson, Robert Browning, and Thoreau. Emerson alone stood on the summit, "at the door of the infinite." Ives had great respect for Browning; he described him as "too big a man to rest in one nice little key, his inward tough[ness] & strength he walked on the mountains not down a nice proper little aisle. . . . His mind had many roads, not always easy to follow—the ever flowing changing, growing ways of mind & imagination—over the great unchanging truths of life & not death."[33] Musically Ives viewed Browning and Emerson similarly; Ives's *Browning Overture* has the same weighty, dense, chromatic sound that "Emerson" does.[34] Finally Ives used the mountain as pure metaphor to describe both Emerson and Thoreau: "to me their thoughts (Emerson, Thoreau especially), substance, and inspiration change and grow, rise to this mountain, then to that, as the years go on through time to the Eternities."[35]

The Sounds of Concord

i "EMERSON"

"A subtle chain of countless rings
The next unto the farthest brings"

While one can easily sympathize with Ives as he struggled to articulate the philosophical implications of what Concord and Transcendentalism meant to him, no matter how much prose he wrote, he was primarily a composer. As a philosopher and an essayist alone he would surely be forgotten. Thus we turn to the central question: What can the music tell us? A brief examination of each movement serves to introduce Ives's thinking. A more detailed exploration of the final movement, "Thoreau," sharpens our appreciation of Ives's understanding of Concord and Transcendentalism.

Earlier we presented a map of Ives's Concord. To help translate the sounds themselves into a visual image, the equivalent of an aerial tour of the sonic terrain might be useful. If one were to conduct such an overview, the four-movement sonata might appear as a chain of wedge-shaped constructions alternately expanding to encompass the entire region and contracting to focus in on a particular locale. As often with Ives, however, even the terrain can appear contradictory; thus expansion and contraction can appear simultaneously, depending on the vantage point of the observer.

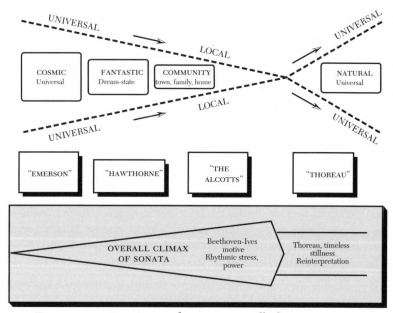

DIAGRAM 2. Ives *Concord* Sonata: Overall Plan, Two Views

Indeed, if judged by musical characteristics alone, such a perception would not be wide of the mark. The first movement, "Emerson," unfolds precipitously with an expanding wedge of sound that claims the entire keyboard cosmos as its own. Beginning at the center of the instrument and steadily moving out in both directions, a pianist unleashes an attack that covers the extremes of the instrument in a matter of seconds. The first line of the score is its own best graphic representation, itself depicting a mountain or summit.

Ives, *Concord* Sonata, "Emerson," beginning

The music starts loud and becomes louder. Unencumbered by traditional time and key signatures, sounds hurl themselves into musical space. The air is filled; it pulsates with energy. With no single melodic line to focus the ear, no prescribed pulse to lock in a rhythmic course, there is only an agitated torrent of sound whose steady state is flux. This is music about vastness and possibilities, and Ives's composition clutches at the whole world of sound. This is Ives's vision of Emerson "standing on a summit at the door of the infinite," Emerson, "an invader of the unknown—America's deepest explorer of the spiritual immensities—a seer painting his discoveries in masses and with any color that may lie at hand." Just as Ives experienced "the futility of attempting to fasten on Emerson any particular doctrine, philosophic, or religious theory," listeners also grapple with the realization that there is no obvious elemental or structural goal to guide them. Although musical logic does indeed control individual movements and the larger work, it is not immediately apparent: initially, surface gestures appear disconnected and autonomous. Perhaps this is Ives's musical manifestation of Emerson's writing style: "His underlying plan of work seems based on the large unity of a series of particular aspects of a subject, rather than on the continuity of its expression. As thoughts surge to his mind, he fills the heavens with them, crowds them in, if necessary, but seldom arranges them along the ground first." At the very least Ives seems to follow Emerson's admonition: "For it is not metres, but a metre-making argument that makes a poem—a thought so passionate and alive that like the spirit of a plant or an animal it has an architecture of its own, and adorns nature with a new thing."[6]

But Ives does not wish to present Emerson or Emersonian Transcendentalism as inchoate; vastness does not have to suggest defuseness or disorganization. Quite the opposite, vastness includes the range of expression from the most freely formed to the most tightly controlled; vastness leaves room for the unity of dissimilar things. And so it is with the "Emerson" movement. If Ives's opening gambit cuts loose, he "grounds" Emerson and Transcendentalism using at least two musical devices: first, a melodic gesture; second, a compositional technique. Into the seemingly chaotic sonic universe of the *Concord* Sonata Ives interjects a musical touchstone, perhaps the most famous motive in all of Western art music: the four-note tattoo from Beethoven's Fifth Symphony. The universally recognized motive becomes a familiar moment in an ofttimes confusing mélange of sound. Though we hear it differently in this exotic context, it offers a comforting focal point in an otherwise dizzying musical landscape.

Why choose to incorporate this particular musical tagline? What are the ramifications of the interpolation? Though having *structural* precursors in earlier four-movement piano sonatas, the sounds of the *Concord* were dramatically different from any prior work bearing the appellation "sonata." Historically, sonatas were thematic showcases relying upon the presentation and development of contrasting melodic and harmonic groups for formal coherence and unity. Although Ives does borrow "freely from the ubiquitous nineteenth-century techniques of cyclic form, thematic transformation, and the development of motive families,"[37] there is no mistaking Ives's sonata for any creation by an earlier master. As the highly non-tonal opening of "Emerson" denies listeners conventional sonata expectations and hence the most obvious connections to that genre, the piece relies upon the famous four-note quotation from a classical symphony to tie itself to earlier models and validate the Ives sonata as a legitimate entry in the Western tradition. By extension the quotation validates Emerson and Concord as legitimate topics for such a work.

But what is the connection between Emerson and Beethoven? Why import a European high-art relic into a work celebrating American philosophers and an American place? Hadn't Emerson himself chided Americans for listening too long to the courtly muses of Europe? By the fourth decade of the nineteenth century, Beethoven's Fifth Symphony was invested with a profundity and celebrity exceeding that of any similar piece. It had become universal in its appeal, and this universe included Concord and the Transcendentalists, who held the work and its creator in particularly high esteem. The Fifth grew from a work of musical interest and value in 1808 to a piece of musical art with unrivaled symbolic importance in a matter of a very few years. And in America it achieved that status precisely in Boston, where it was repeatedly programmed in the 1840s, its fame aided in no small measure by lengthy discussions by several Transcendental writers including John S. Dwight, J. F. Tuckerman, and Margaret Fuller.

Whether the four-note motive connoted "fate knocking at the door" or some other equally abstract sentiment was beside the fact; its cachet was undeniable. In this way the motive was the perfect articulation for the "Emerson" movement, a movement that Ives claimed sought to convey universal truths, a movement determined to reconcile differences. By incorporating Beethoven into a movement entitled "Emerson," Ives elevated the movement and the larger work to a level equal to the greatest European artistic creations and invested it with unassailable significance. With Beethoven present in "Emerson" the work could shift from aggressive assertions to gentle meditations and remain universal and unified.[38] While the Beethoven quotation permeates the "Emerson" movement, it is not the only material Ives borrowed. In the fourth movement listeners hear the only other borrowing acknowledged by Ives—Stephen Foster's song "Massa's in De Cold Ground."[39]

In addition to claiming parity with Beethoven by commandeering the four-note motive and all it connoted, Ives champions the range of Emerson in a second, more purely musical way. Having begun the movement with the freest expression of musical thought—a meterless, keyless cavalcade of sound—and having explored the widest range of musical styles, from Impressionistic meanderings[40] to jazzy uppercuts,[41] at a point approximately two-thirds of the way through the piece, Ives works his way toward a fugato passage reminiscent of the contrapuntal writing of the greatest Baroque master, Bach.[42] Although the music refuses to develop along strict guidelines of fugal technique, the implication of tight control is palpable. Ives's music informs us that Emerson's universe is all-inclusive; it contains free-forms as well as fugues, watery arpeggios and chordal jabs, the known and the unknown.

As the movement draws to a close Ives offers numerous directions to the pianist to slow down, to become softer, to play notes in such a way that they are "heard as a kind of an overtone." In the last line of music sounds fade to a "scarcely audible" *pppp*. If, as the beginning of the piece demonstrates, Emerson is capable of the grand gesture, Ives tells us he is also capable of the most introspective utterance, a reverent humility. A note written by Ives following the final measure of "Emerson" in a first-edition score says, "[I] Have played an Amen A E *ppppp*." And as we noted earlier Ives wrote of this movement that it "attempts to suggest the struggle that seemed to go on in Emerson, in reconciling . . . the influence of the old Puritan canon, dogma, etc., with his individual growth—that is, theology vs religion. In fact the whole movement has more to do (and more than I intended) with the struggles of his soul than [with] that peace of mind which he commands even in his struggles—though the music tries to end with that feeling."[43] With "Emerson" Ives opens his sonata to the most abstract and accommodating universe. This is the cosmic

Concord, a place of unbridled passions and possibilities, a place of thunderbolts and caresses.

II "HAWTHORNE"
III "THE ALCOTTS"

If "Emerson" invites listeners to contemplate an infinite cosmos, "Hawthorne" and "The Alcotts" attempt to focus attention on more and more specific places: one imaginary, one real. Like Hawthorne's tale "The Celestial Railroad," the second movement takes listeners on a wild ride from one fictional scene to another; the music careens as if with Hawthorne's train from the dream-state station house to "the ancient city of Vanity." In "Hawthorne" Ives has taken seriously Thoreau's observation that "transcendental philosophy needs the leaven of humor to render it light and digestible." The composer's chatty remarks found in a first edition suggest the mood he was after. Ives advises pianists: "For the most part this movement is supposed to be played as fast as possible, lightly and not literally. Marks of tempo, expression, etc. are used as little as possible. If the score itself, the preface or an interest in Hawthorne suggest nothing, marks will only make things worse. Besides it all depends on the time of day or year it is played or not played—the marks for me may not do for another." In "Hawthorne" Ives declares that he wants to "suggest some of [Hawthorne's] wilder, fantastical adventures into the half-childlike, half-fairylike phantasmal realms." The music is breathless and wide-eyed. As in "Emerson," the music is alternately frantic and halcyon, rag-like and impressionistic, but it is also more rooted in place. According to Ives, the writings of Hawthorne had "more to say about the life around him—about the inherited mystery of the town"—than did the works of Emerson: "A novel, of necessity, nails an art-effort down to some definite part or parts of the earth's surface; the novelist's wagon can't always be hitched to a star."[44] So while Hawthorne's fantastic tales may animate scarecrows and take their characters on trips to imaginary Celestial Cities, a key aspect of the works is a sense of place.

Ives's marginal notes in a first edition pair particular musical moments with specific narrative scenes. But his comments are not necessary to recognize a certain scenic quality in his music. Listening to the movement unaided by a score or Ives's markings, one might liken the experience to visiting a number of musical *locations*. The piece lurches forward and then rests, temporarily grounded in key or rhythm. At these resting places listeners take in the sonic setting. Those with a score read that an oscillating rhythmic pattern (on page 23/line 2) is a manifestation of Feathertop's pipe with its dancing demons, and a repeating whole-tone scale run is the "Scarecrow look[ing] in on the vagabond's band" (page 24/lines 1-2).[45]

When Ives wants to evoke "distant bells over the grave yard . . . heard by the ghosts" he relies upon a narrow felted board 14 3/4 inches long to depress specific clusters of black keys too widespread for a single hand to reach. These triple *piano* chords float over a gentle rolling piano part. Immediately the music manifests a sense of perspective and depth; we hear distinct musical foregrounds and backgrounds. Additional scribbled comments identify music "sounding as singing in the distance." Clearly spatial differentiation is an important concern for Ives in this movement and increasingly in "The Alcotts" and "Thoreau." When in "Hawthorne" Ives pre-echoes tonal (harmonically rooted) passages from "The Alcotts" movement (see page 33/line 1; page 34/line 2 and perhaps most conspicuously the final seconds of the piece), we witness the composer subtly working his way toward the final particularization of place that will be achieved in the "Thoreau" movement.

With Ives's note to "The Alcotts," all doubts of the central importance of place to the *Concord* Sonata are removed. Ives narrows his focus and moves from cosmic landscape in "Emerson" and the fantastical grand tour in "Hawthorne" to Concord itself and the Alcotts' family home, "Orchard House." Ives sees the village as "remind[ing] one of that common virtue lying at the height and root of all the Concord divinities. As one walks down the broad-arched street, passing the white house of Emerson—ascetic guard of a former prophetic beauty—he comes presently beneath the old elms, overspreading the Alcott house. It seems to stand as a kind of homely but beautiful witness of Concord's common virtue—it seems to bear a consciousness that its past *is living*, that the 'mosses of the Old Manse' and the hickories of Walden are not far away."

Ives paints a serene tableau for "The Alcotts" by opening the movement with a four-part, hymn-like improvisation on the Beethoven motif. His musical language is no accident. In *Essays* Ives refers to the "commonplace beauty" and "spiritual sturdiness" of Orchard House and thinks of it as "a kind of common triad of the New England homestead, whose overtones tell us that there must have been something aesthetic fibered in the Puritan severity."[46] "The Alcotts" gently overflows with common triads as listeners experience passages in A-flat, E-flat, B-flat, F, and C majors, yet the music is anything but traditionally unilinear in its trajectory. "Here is the home of the 'Marches'—all pervaded with the trials and happiness of the family and telling, in a simple way, the story of 'the richness of not having.'"

"The Alcotts" is infused with the four-note Beethoven motive as the essay preceding the movement is filled with references to the composer. Ives ties Beethoven to the Alcott family: "And there sits the little old spinet-piano Sophia Thoreau gave to the Alcott children, on which Beth played the old Scotch airs, and played at the Fifth Symphony." He also relates the composer to the Concord philosophers: "All around you, under the Concord sky, there still floats the influence of that human faith melody, transcendent and sentimental enough for the enthusiast or the cynic respectively, reflecting on innate hope—a common interest in common things and common men—a tune the Concord bards are ever playing, while they pound away at the immensities with a Beethovenlike sublimity, and with, may we say, a vehemence and perseverance—for that part of greatness is not so difficult to emulate." Although the movement is never content to stay within one key area for very long, except for two passages that are almost aggressive in their rootlessness (see page 54/lines 2-3; page 56/line 4-page 57/line 1) the movement is remarkable within the sonata for showcasing functional harmonic relationships and for its overall stability. With music that hides its complexity under a veil of tonal simplicity, Ives has domesticated Transcendentalism; he has brought it down from the Emersonian summit and invited it into our community and homes.

"The Alcotts" is the only movement that ends big, with the biggest climax of the entire sonata, although the music suddenly tapers off to a pianissimo in the final few beats. The climax is reached on an unusual passage, an expanded statement of the Beethoven motive that commands the entire keyboard just as it had in much of the "Emerson" movement. Here it encompasses five and one-half octaves beginning with the third lowest note on the piano. Unusual about this passage, however, is its harmony; it consists entirely of principal triads in the key of C major. Nothing like that happened in "Emerson," although it is presaged in the appearance of the hymn in "Hawthorne" and the beginning of "The Alcotts." Here for several seconds the entire piano reverberates with pure, consonant, diatonic triads. And the rhythm, although still lacking metric notation, is nevertheless rooted in a clear, straightforward, pounding duple meter. This trails off at the end, as both a foreign note, a B-flat, and an irregular rhythmic pattern are introduced, but C is maintained, the movement closing with the pure triad.

Scholars have debated at length the source of the expanded motive, the continuation of the Beethoven tattoo heard here so clearly, and their conclusions bear directly on how the sonata is conceived. In reference to the *Concord* Sonata David Hertz states, "But most of Ives' quotations are not from the pantheon of European high culture. The quotations are not usually taken from works like Beethoven's Fifth Symphony, and even that conspicuous reference is reshaped through the sounds of the American hymnal."[47] Hertz and others suggest that the Ives motive, with its continuation, is a pastiche of several sources, including Beethoven's *Hammer-*

Ives, *Concord* Sonata, "Alcotts," ending.

klavier Sonata, Op. 106, and two hymns, Simeon Marsh's "Martyn" and Charles Zuener's "Missionary Chant." The hymn associations are ironically circular, themselves Beethoven derivatives, for Zeuner almost certainly took his own tune from Beethoven's Fifth Symphony. Such was standard practice for the early nineteenth-century hymnists, who baldly, consistently, and thoroughly plundered European art music for tunes. They were driven by religious more than aesthetic considerations, foremost in their minds the desire to find good melodies free of secular (textual) associations. What better source than European high art? Here was a wealth of material that, until the 1840s at least, few Americans knew. Ives may have been influenced by the Zeuner tune in the second phrase, after it comes to rest on the second scale degree, but the continuation is probably Ives's own, and the expanded motive is best described as the Beethoven-Ives motive.

The power and prominence of the Beethoven motive points to the relation among the first three movements. This motive appeared frequently in "Emerson," although often its presence is obscured by the dense complexities in which it is set. The initial appearance of the motive at the end of the first line of music is a good illustration of this point. The vigorous opening of the piece distracts one from the mid-range statement of Beethoven's Fifth hiding within a right-hand filigree pattern. A second statement of the motive, while more audible and identifiable than the first, is relegated to the lowest octaves of the keyboard, where it sounds more like a vaguely familiar rumble than the undeniable touchstone it will become. It takes until page 6, line 2, for the motive to command the full attention of the music and listeners. Set within seventh and ninth chords, Beethoven goes head-to-head with sounds we have come to associate with jazz. This is undeniably Beethoven, but Beethoven in a new land. Thereafter the four-note tattoo weaves in and out of the musical fabric. The movement ends with a gentle, pianissimo iteration of the motive.

The four-note motive is not omnipresent in the second movement. The music of "Hawthorne" appears alternately too busy and too distracted to be concerned with Beethoven. Instead of an outright confrontation with the motive proper, Ives introduces an expanded version of the idea (referred to above), known among Ives scholars as the "human faith melody," a phrase taken from Ives's remarks preceding "The Alcotts." Listeners must wait until twelve pages into the score to catch a sonic glimpse of the four-note motive. It appears briefly, riding on the crest of left-hand arpeggios, but the arpeggios exhaust themselves and the Beethoven motive fades. Subsequent appearances of the motive in this movement are infrequent and inconspicuous and always part of the expanded theme.

As if to make up for its prolonged absence, the Beethoven motive and its derivatives permeate every aspect of the third movement. One might even think of "The Alcotts" as a prolonged rumination on the subject. The climax at the end of "The Alcotts" brings together the first three movements of the sonata and suggests, in retrospect, a second way of hearing the overall work: three powerful but individual movements followed by a final, summarizing movement that nevertheless shifts to a different emotional realm. Emerson may have been quite abstract and spiritual, but to Ives his was the spirituality of thunderbolts whose final target was the powerful tonal assertion at the end of "The Alcotts." The resonating declaration of the Beethoven-Ives motive at the end of "The Alcotts" functions as a cumulative statement toward which Ives had been building for three movements. In one sense the climax of "The Alcotts" also functions to effect a transition, achieved by a technique similar to Beethoven's segue into the choral finale of the Ninth Symphony. When Beethoven wanted to interrupt the serene, ethereal mood of the slow movement of the Ninth Symphony, he began the finale with what Wagner called a *Schrekenfanfare*, a piercing fortissimo dissonance that wiped out the effects of the previous variations. Ives may have intended the same effect in reverse here. With "Thoreau" we enter a world of stillness and meditation, and Ives's use of musical spatial techniques comes to the fore. The sheer tonal and rhythmic rootedness of the closing of "The Alcotts" sets us up for the immense temporal and harmonic freedom to be enjoyed in the illimitable inner world of "Thoreau."

IV "THOREAU"

"I think I could write a poem to be called Concord."[48]

"Thoreau" emerges softly, slowly in a chromatic wash of sound. In the first minute and a half of music there is no suggestion of key or meter, only the reiteration of subtly transforming figures that circle in upon themselves.[49] Listeners have a sense of being somewhere, even if they do not know where. In what initially appears paradoxical, this interior place is most powerfully present in music that refuses to be bounded, in music that thwarts traditional expectations for harmonic and rhythmic behavior. Absent conventional linear implications that accompany functional harmony and barred rhythms, which force a concern with progress and the passage of time, "Thoreau" allows listeners to bask in an atemporal contemplation of the sonic landscape. By incorporating such spatial techniques, Ives suspends our interest in the narrative aspects of "Thoreau" and concentrates our focus on the place.

Having explored cosmic, fantastical, and domestic realms in the first three movements, Ives goes one additional step. In "Thoreau" Ives probes a specific site of resounding significance to Transcendentalism; he goes to Walden Pond and looks and listens. In the note preceding the movement, Ives describes his musical landscape in luxurious detail. It is autumn, "Indian summer at Walden"; we are told of "the mist and haze over the pond"; we learn the flora of the woods as Thoreau "stands on the side of the pleasant hill of pines and hickories in front of his cabin." Later in the note we track the Concord woodsman "down the white-pebbled and sandy eastern shore" and "along the 'bolder northern' and 'western shore, with deep bays indented,' then along the railroad track, 'where the Aeolian harp plays.'" Ives appeals to all of our senses.

In "Thoreau" Ives offers his most personal and intimate response to Concord and Transcendentalism. His note at the bottom of page one of a first-edition score sheds light on the scale of this more "interior" piece: "This Thoreau movement is supposed to be played in a lower dynamic ratio than usual; i.e. the 'forte' [loud] here is about the 'mezzo piano' [medium soft] of the preceding movements."[50] As the fourth movement opens, Ives invites us into a peaceful and contemplative setting with soft, gentle, inward-turning gestures. For each arpeggiated figure that expands, there is a circular motion that contracts.

But Walden is not always benign. Nature and Thoreau change moods. Ives shows a more aggressive side in louder and faster-paced passages. (See page 59/line 4; page 60/line 3; page 61/lines 1, 3, 4.) Marginal scrib-

Ives, *Concord* Sonata, "Thoreau," beginning

blings in a first-edition score explain Ives's thinking. At the first sustained rhythmic passage Ives inserts: "He [Thoreau] gets after somebody or something." When the music relaxes he writes: "He quiets down again." Back and forth Ives hears the music and Walden through Thoreau's imagined actions. When Ives repeats an earlier contemplative section he inserts: "He sits down again and listens to nature"; as the music flips to a rag-like passage Ives writes "something begins to stir him again."[51]

Energetic as the rhythmic moments are, they do not jar or overwhelm the predominantly peaceful musical world Ives has created. The movement is anchored by a series of pedal points that ground the work and by the reappearance of tonal areas that rein in the most flighty harmonic excursions. Like Thoreau, Ives captures both the spiritual and the savage aspects of nature; they coexist with no contradiction.[52] Without benefit of grids or charts, and making no attempt to convey precise topographical features, Ives maps out Walden in music that is at times dreamily impressionistic and unfettered—music that floats freely in time and space—and is at other times tonally confined and driven. Listeners hear the bounded, physical specificity of the Walden woods in recurring pitch and rhythm patterns and in extended key-centric areas. They also hear the limitlessness of Thoreau's vision of nature in fully saturated chromatic passages, in numerous echo effects, and in the veiled flute solo that wafts in at the movement's end as if from another world.[53]

Ives's use of echoes is one of the most resonant gestures of "Thoreau." Thoreau wrote extensively on echoes in his chapter "Sounds":

> Sometimes, on Sundays, I heard the Lincoln, Acton, Bedford, or Concord bell, when the wind was favorable, a faint, sweet, and as it were, natural melody, worth importing into the wilderness. At a sufficient distance over the woods this sound acquires a certain vibratory hum, as if the pine needles in the horizon were the strings

of a harp which it swept. All sound heard at the greatest possible
distance produces one and the same effect, a vibration of the universal lyre, just as the intervening atmosphere makes a distant
ridge of earth interesting to our eyes by the azure tint it imparts to
it. There came to me in this case a melody which the air had
strained, and which had conversed with every leaf and needle of
the wood, that portion of the sound which the elements had taken
up and modulated and echoes from vale to vale. The echo is, to
some extent, an original sound, and therein is the magic and
charm of it. It is not merely a repetition of what was worth repeating in the bell, but partly the voice of the wood; the same trivial
words and notes sung by a wood-nymph.[54]

Ives was especially sensitive to "Sounds" and the phenomenon of echoes.
A paraphrase of this paragraph appears at the top of his song "Thoreau"
and in the excerpts from his essay "Thoreau" that precede the movement.
Echoes force one to consider the effects of distance on sound, a phenomenon that interested Ives throughout his compositional career, and one that
he associated with his father, who was an indefatigable experimenter with
musical phenomena. Although an annotated first edition of "The Alcotts"
contains three passages marked "echo," these comments do not appear in
the later edition.[55] Echoes were not of primary importance to the scene
Ives was creating in the third movement. The "Thoreau" movement, however, derives much of its essential character from echoes, the interplay of
foreground and background, the meeting of the present and the past, basic
issues of place and time. In all, "Thoreau" includes seven instances where
the performer is instructed to play in an echo-like manner.[56]

As pianists realize Ives's instructions and listeners take in the seemingly
distant sounds, one wonders what exactly the echoes represent. Are they
no more than the voiced reverberations of tones normally at the outer limits of human perception, or are they more like recollections of long-gone
sounds, memories of people, events, places, times, perhaps even earlier
movements? Or are they expressions not yet quite fully formed, fragments
of a nascent composition? Is the echo real or symbolic or both? To what
degree is the echo a musical manifestation of Thoreau's foremost symbol,
Walden Pond?

Richard J. Schneider, in his essay "Walden," discusses the rich ambiguity of the pond "representing nature as both knowable and unknowable."
The glass-like surface "symbolically mediates between the material and
spiritual worlds represented by the earth and sky." At the same time "the
pond reveals new views to the alert observer and provides an art gallery of

nature's masterpieces. . . . The reflections . . . are never mere duplicates of the scene reflected. . . . The air and water always add something new. Thus the pond represents as well the eye of the artist/writer, whose task is to connect the material and the spiritual and thereby reveal new and beautiful truths to others."[57]

Ives's song "Remembrance," known as "The Pond" in its chamber music version, connects the image of a lake with distant sounds and memories both in that text, which reads "A sound of a distant horn, / O'er shadowed lake is borne, my father's song," and in the closing notes that quietly whisper the first three notes of "Taps."[58] It too mediates between "the material and spiritual worlds." In the fourth movement of the *Concord* Sonata Ives similarly fuses now with then, here with there, the local and particular with the universal and cosmic. Ives deftly maneuvers through the landscape surrounding Walden Pond using a combination of compositional techniques that alternately fix and free our senses of musical time and place.

In a second seeming paradox, Ives minimizes the sense of time passing as he clears space to meditate on the thematic importance of time in *Walden*. He writes extensively on Thoreau's concept of time in the essay preceding the last movement:

> Throughout *Walden,* a text that he is always pounding out is "Time." Time for inside work out-of-doors; preferably out-of-doors, though "you may perhaps have some pleasant, thrilling, glorious hours, even in a poor house." Wherever the place—time there must be. Time to show the unnecessariness of necessities which clog up time. Time to contemplate the value of man to the universe—and of the universe to man—man's excuse for being. Time *from* the demands of social conventions. Time *from* too much labor (for some) which means too much to eat, too much to wear, too much material, too much materialism (for others). Time *from* the "hurry and waste of life." Time *from* the "St. Vitus Dance." *But,* on the other side of the ledger, time *for* learning that "there is no safety in stupidity alone." Time *for* introspection. Time *for* reality. Time *for* expansion. Time *for* practicing the art, of living the art of living.[59]

In "Thoreau" Ives creates time "to" and "for" by subduing our concern with the inevitable march of musical time. As we are fixed *in* time, we are able to study it and our place in the expanded moment. This innermost place is without boundaries. Ives, like Thoreau, allows us to consider our relationship to the many worlds we inhabit—the supremely personal and interior world found through the contemplation of the sylvan setting of Walden, the familiar and comfortable world of our villages and homes, the dream-like fantasy world of imaginary places, and the limitless cosmos that embraces our planet.

Though an unconventional final movement, it is no surprise that Charles Ives ends the *Concord* Sonata with the soft-spoken meditations of "Thoreau." For Ives, creator of monumentally large symphonic works and treacherously difficult virtuosic displays, the personal was always the orientation point. With "Thoreau" Ives once again claims the personal as most important, as the goal of all strivings. The third movement of the sonata closed with a statement of the Beethoven-Ives motive, strong, powerful, rooted. It reappears in the last two pages of "Thoreau," transformed. It sounds quietly, from afar on the flute, interwoven with the "human faith melody" and Stephen Foster. It has lost both its accent and metrical certainty; rhythmically it hesitates, suspended. The universal Beethoven motive, exemplar of the noblest achievements of mankind, so omnipresent and controlling in the first and third movements, is tucked into the final two pages of "Thoreau" and mediated, as it were, by a much humbler theme.[60] As Beethoven's motive wafts across the pond on the sounds of a flute, it must compete for air-time with Stephen Foster's Civil War song "Massa's in De Cold Ground." The flute is associated with Thoreau and, more importantly, is George Ives's first instrument. Its unexpected appearance in the final minutes of the forty-five-minute work is Charles Ives's ultimate personal statement.[61] Into the infinitely boundless world of Transcendentalism Ives interjects a simple solo flute. With this gesture, the universal has come home; it can be found in Concord.

As with many of Ives's most thoughtful works, "Thoreau" closes with an open ending. There is no tonal resolution, no rhythmic declaration of finality, no structural denouement. The music fades from our hearing and literally drifts off into the cosmos. The last line of the piece combines a recollection of the first sounds of the movement with a subdued statement of the Beethoven motive, thereby connecting the first and fourth movements. Ives gives musical meaning to the opening sentence of his "Thoreau" essay: "Thoreau was a great musician, not because he played the flute but because he did not have to go to Boston to hear 'the Symphony.'"[62] Coming full circle, Ives has joined the particular, local world of Thoreau and Walden with the all-embracing, universal world of Emerson. Concord is the universe, and the universe is Concord.

NOTES

1. Charles E. Ives, *Essays Before a Sonata, The Majority, and Other Writings*, ed. Howard Boatwright (New York, 1970), 11–36.
2. Charles E. Ives, *Memos*, ed. John Kirkpatrick (New York, 1972).
3. Robert D. Richardson, Jr., "Thoreau and Concord," in *The Cambridge Companion to Henry David Thoreau*, ed. Joel Myerson (Cambridge, 1995), 12.
4. In an essay entitled "Spatial Form in Ives," Robert Morgan offers a concise statement distinguishing between Ives's reflective structures and traditional ABA form: "It is important to note that these repetitions have a fundamentally different meaning from the restatement of previous material—recapitulation—in classical forms. The latter brings about a resolution of tonal tension and, equally important, generates a new wave of motion—one destined to stay within the principal key area and thus balance the preceding one. In Ives these restatements are nothing more than brief allusions which link the closing with the opening through explicit association. Whereas in the classical recapitulation there is a confirmation and regeneration of motion, in Ives the repetition is its negation. The piece, at this stage, is not going anywhere; it is over, yet its ending is also its beginning. The musical significance of this seems considerable to me: if the material which initiates a motion can also terminate it, then relative to traditional musical concepts, the meaning of motion has been fundamentally altered. Indeed, so have the meanings of beginning and ending, for there is a strong suggestion at the close of these movements that the whole process could begin over again—that is, that they could become truly circular and unending." Robert P. Morgan, "Spatial Form in Ives," in *An Ives Celebration*, ed. H. Wiley Hitchcock and Vivian Perlis (Urbana, 1977), 148–149.
5. It is a given that music requires the passage of time simply to occur, to say nothing of achieving form, substance, and meaning. In most Western art music composed prior to the twentieth century, rhythm, harmony, and melody work together with single-minded purposefulness to propel the music (and listeners) towards a logical conclusion. Marking progress towards the final goal was part of the initial conception of a piece. While listeners might not be aware of the exact length of their musical experience, they were conscious of moving forward on a dominant, linear trajectory towards some kind of resolution. But such linearity, an essential aspect of an art that takes place through time, does not have to dominate musical behavior or listener perception. Ives, along with other early twentieth-century composers, understood that individual musical elements could be separated and made to behave in ways that weakened, undermined, or obscured the power of a single linear trajectory. Composers no longer concerned themselves exclusively with the passage *through* time, but admitted the possibility of contemplating the synchronous moment *in* time. The degree to which musical elements combine to maximize or minimize the peception of lapsed time plays a large role in determining whether a piece is considered linear or spatial.

   It might be useful to think of spatially conceived pieces as similar to landscape paintings that contain numerous points of interest, but in which no single focal point catches the eye immediately. Viewers take time to roam the canvas and take in the scenery.

6. *Danbury Times*, Nov. 20, 1856.

7. See Ives, *Memos*, 83.

8. A cursory survey of Ives's chapter on Emerson in his *Essays Before a Sonata* reveals references to over a dozen different works by Emerson, including essays from both the first and second series, the series entitled "The Conduct of Life," and "Nature." In the postface to *114 Songs* (Redding, Conn., 1922) Ives refers to Emerson's essay "Over-Soul." In *Memos* the composer paraphrases from "Circles" (201 n. 14), "Self-Reliance" (225 n. 23), and "Politics" (214 n. 10), among other Emerson essays.

9. Ives, *Memos*, 2–3. In an unpublished paper Feder states that "his father, George Edward Ives, . . . introduced Charles to Thoreau in family readings of the Transcendentalists," thus suggesting a lifelong acquaintance with Thoreau. See Stuart Feder, "Charles Ives and H.D. Thoreau: 'A Transcendental Tune of Concord,'" (paper presented at the annual meeting of the Sonneck Society, Worcester, Mass., Apr. 9, 1994), 2. The authors have been unable to corroborate this family activity with materials that are currently available. The only reference Ives appears to make to a long history with Thoreau is in *Memos*, where he waxes on "my years of friendship with Emerson, Alcott, Thoreau [and] Hawthorne" (192).

10. Jan Swafford, *Charles Ives: A Life with Music* (New York, 1996), 266.

11. Edward Johnson, "Planting this Wilderness," in *Puritanism and the American Experience*, ed. Michael McGiffert (Reading, Mass., 1969), 158.

12. Sacvan Bercovitch, in "Emerson, Individualism, and the Ambiguities of Dissent" *South Atlantic Quarterly* 89(1990), refers to a "line from Mather to Edwards to Emerson" regarding views of nature. Here we are only arguing a similarity in the contemplative approaches to nature that Edwards, Emerson, and Thoreau took.

13. Paula M. Cooey, *Jonathan Edwards on Nature and Destiny: A Systematic Analysis* (Lewiston, N.Y., 1985), 118.

14. Cooey, *Jonathan Edwards on Nature and Destiny*, 2–3.

15. The terms "operatically sublime" and the "still small voice" are from Barbara Novak, *Nature and Culture: American Landscape and Painting, 1825–1875* (New York, 1980), 28, 18. The terms "nature sublime" and "nature subdued" are from the title of a lecture given by Donald Worster on "Nature Sublime; Nature Subdued: John Wesley Powell's Exploration of the Colorado River," University Park, Penn., November 1996.

16. Lawrence Gillman observed a similarity between Ives's music and Edwards's prose. "Music," *New York Herald Tribune*, Jan. 31, 1927. Henry Bellaman made a similar connection in "Charles Ives: The Man and His Music," *Musical Quarterly* 19(1933):45–58.

17. Ives, *Memos*, 199 n. 3.

18. J. Peter Burkholder explains: "Each movement was first conceived for a different medium from any of the others: the Emerson movement as an overture for large orchestra or a concerto for piano and orchestra (Ives referred to this earlier version as the *Emerson Overture* or the *Emerson Concerto*): the Hawthorne movement as a piece for piano, two pianos, two pianos with four players, or even 'a dozen pianos': the Alcotts movement for organ or for piano with voice or violin, as well as in the form of the *Orchard House Overture*; and the Thoreau movement 'in terms of strings, colored possibly with a flute or horn.' The orchestral version of the Emerson movement was once grouped with a set based on abolitionist themes, and the

Thoreau movement was projected as the last movement of a set entitled *Sounds*, suggesting that Ives did not always see the Transcendentalist aspect of these movements as the most important." J. Peter Burkholder, *Charles Ives: The Ideas Behind the Music* (New Haven, 1985), 30.

19. Burkholder, *Charles Ives*, 30.

20. Ives, *Essays*, xxv.

21. Charles Ives, *Second Pianoforte Sonata: "Concord, Mass., 1840–1860,"* 2d ed. (New York, 1947), 52.

22. Ives, *Second Pianoforte Sonata*, 52.

23. Ives, *Second Pianoforte Sonata*, 58.

24. Ives, *Second Pianoforte Sonata*, unnumbered page preceding page 1.

25. Ives, *Second Pianoforte Sonata*, 20.

26. Mark Tucker, "Of Men and Mountains: Ives in the Adirondacks," in *Charles Ives and His World*, ed. J. Peter Burkholder (Princeton, 1996), 188.

27. Ives, *Second Pianoforte Sonata*, 20.

28. Ives loose diary pages, Charles Ives Papers, MSS 14, box 45, folder 12, Yale University Music Library.

29. Ives's thoughts on this topic are captured most eloquently in an article written by Henry Bellamann in 1933. In response to an inquiry by the author regarding the dual life of a businessman and composer, Ives responded: "My business experience revealed life to me in many aspects that I might otherwise have missed. In it one sees tragedy, nobility, meanness, high aims, low aims, brave hopes, faint hopes, great ideals, no ideals, and one is able to watch these work inevitable destiny. . . . It is not even uncommon in business intercourse to sense a reflection of a philosophy—a depth of something fine—akin to a strong beauty in art. To assume that business is a material process, and only that, is to undervalue the average mind and heart. To an insurance man there *is* an 'average man' and he is humanity. I have experienced a great fullness of life in business. The fabric of existence weaves itself whole. You can not set an art off in the corner and hope for it to have vitality, reality and substance. There can be nothing *'exclusive'* about a substantial art. It comes directly out of the heart of experience of life and thinking about life and living life. My work in music helped my business and my work in business helped my music." Bellamann, "Charles Ives: The Man and His Music," 49–50.

30. Two of Ives's early instrumental works use the word *mountain* in the title: *From the Steeples and the Mountains*, written in 1901/1902, and *An Autumn Landscape from Pine Mountain*, written in 1904. In the former the mountain is incidental, even trivial to the conception of the piece, which was titled in the sketch "From the Steeples—a New Sexton—telephone Smith's." The score for the latter piece is lost, but Ives's own description suggests that it is about hearing his father's cornet coming from afar, specifically from Ridgebury, a town near Pine Mountain.

31. Frank R. Rossiter, *Charles Ives and His America* (New York, 1975), 269.

32. Ives, *Essays*, 224.

33. John Kirkpatrick, *A Temporary Mimeographed Catalogue of the Music Manuscripts and Related Materials of Charles Edward Ives, 1874–1954,* (New Haven, 1960), 32.

34. Relentlessly so—in fact so much so that Ives himself faulted the composition for being "too carefully made." Ives, *Memos*, 76.

35. Metaphorical landscapes have been invoked recently in many fields. In one area in particular, the science of complex adaptive systems, or complexity, the concept of a fitness landscape closely resembles Ives's spiritual landscape. Stuart Kauffman, who pioneered the term, mapped a biological landscape in which the peaks represent high fitness; lower levels, foothills; and valleys, lower fitness. In Kauffman's conceptualization fitness means how capable an organism, or a molecule, is to maintain itself, reproduce, and continue. Kauffman states: "We will find in this book that whether we are talking about organisms or economies, surprisingly general laws govern adaptive processes on multipeaked fitness landscapes. . . . In scaling the top of the fitness peaks, adapting populations that are too methodical and timid in their explorations are likely to get stuck in the foothills, thinking they have reached as high as they can go; but a search that is too wide ranging is also likely to fail." Although Ives had in mind spiritual fitness, about which he had very specific ideas, he could easily have written the latter sentence. See Stuart A. Kauffman, *At Home in the Universe: The Search for Laws of Self-Organization and Complexity* (New York, 1995), 27.

36. Ives, *Essays*, 12, 11, 14, 22; Ralph Waldo Emerson, "The Poet," in *Essays and Lectures*, ed. Joel Porte (New York, 1983), 450.

37. Geoffrey Block, *Ives, Concord Sonata: Piano Sonata No. 2 ("Concord, Mass., 1840–1860")* (New York, 1996), 31.

38. Creative theorizing has led certain Ives scholars to suggest a range of possible borrowed materials. These include Debussy's "Golliwogg's Cake-Walk," Stravinsky's "Petrushka," Schubert's Ninth Symphony, Brahms's F-sharp Minor Piano Sonata, and assorted pieces by Bach, Chopin, and Wagner, as well as American hymnists. It is not the intention of this essay to support or refute these "sightings."

39. Charles Ives acknowledges the Beethoven Fifth borrowing in his "Emerson" essay in *Essays*, 36, and makes a reference to Stephen Foster's "Massa" in his remarks in unnumbered pages at the end of the second edition of the *Concord* Sonata: "Sometimes, as on pages 62–65–68, an old Elm Tree may feel like humming a phrase from 'Down in the Corn Field,' but usually very slowly." See Ives, *Second Pianoforte Sonata*.

40. See Ives, *Second Pianoforte Sonata*, 8.

41. Ives, *Second Pianoforte Sonata*, 6. See second measures on second line.

42. Ives, *Second Pianoforte Sonata*, 13. See bottom two staves.

43. Ives, *Second Pianoforte Sonata*, 19; John Kirkpatrick Papers, John Herrick Jackson Music Library, Yale University; Charles Ives, *Second Pianoforte Sonata "Concord, Mass., 1840–60"* (Redding, Conn., 1920), 18, Ives Collection, John Herrick Jackson Library, Yale University; Ives, *Memos*, 199 n. 3.

44. Nathaniel Hawthorne, *The Complete Novels and Selected Tales of Nathaniel Hawthorne* (New York, 1937), 1071; Henry David Thoreau, *Early Essays and Miscellanies*, ed. Edwin Moser and Joseph J. Moldenhauer (Princeton, 1975), 235; Ives, *Second Pianoforte Sonata* (1920), 21; Ives, *Essays*, 40, 41.

45. See Hawthorne, "Feathertop: A Moralized Legend," *The Complete Novels*, 1092–1106.

46. Ives, *Essays*, 47.

47. David Michael Hertz, *Angels of Reality: Emersonian Unfoldings in Wright, Stevens, and Ives* (Carbondale, 1993), 130.

48. Henry David Thoreau, Sept. 4, 1841, *Journal*, ed. John C. Broderick et al (Princeton, 1981–), 1:330.

49. Is this musical circularity the sonification of Thoreau's remark: "Our voyaging is only great-circle sailing"? *Walden*, ed. J. Lyndon Shanley (Princeton, 1971), 320.

50. Ives, *Second Pianoforte Sonata* (1920), 61.

51. Ives, *Second Pianoforte Sonata* (1920), 62, 63, 66, Ives Collection, John Herrick Jackson Library, Yale University.

52. See Joyce Carol Oates, introduction to *Walden*, ed. J. Lyndon Shanley (Princeton, 1989), xvi.

53. The ambiguous, unresolved ending of "Thoreau," a type of echo of the opening passage of the movement, suggests a return to the infinite and universal from the local.

54. Thoreau, *Walden* (Princeton, 1989), 123.

55. See Charles Ives, "Concord Sonata," Box 74/Folder 716, p. 55, ll. 1, 2, John Kirkpatrick Papers, John Herrick Jackson Library, Yale University.

56. Indications for echo effects are found in "Thoreau": p. 60, ll. 3 and 4; p. 61, l. 3; p. 62, l. 2; p. 66, l. 1; p. 68, ll. 2 and 4.

57. Richard J. Schneider, "Walden," in *Cambridge Companion to Henry David Thoreau*, 101.

58. See Charles Ives, *114 Songs*, song 12, p. 27.

59. Ives, *Essays*, 55–56.

60. Stuart Feder offers an insightful interpretation for the downplaying of the Beethoven motive in the "Thoreau" movement. Referring to Thoreau, whom Ives identified as "a great musician . . . because he did not have to go to Boston to hear 'the Symphony,'" Feder observes: "The great natural musician . . . Ives rationalized, was too sensitive to cast his passionate emotions in Beethovenian form." *Charles Ives*, 270.

61. For a discussion of Ives's associations of the flute with Thoreau and his father, see Feder, "Charles Ives and H.D. Thoreau."

62. Ives, *Essays*, 51. Given Ives's propensity for puns, one can only wonder whether he was enjoying a play on words by using the phrase "the Symphony." Given the significance of the Beethoven Fifth motive to the *Concord* Sonata, and the careful placement of the four-note motive at the end of the "Thoreau" movement, Ives makes it clear that "the Symphony" could, indeed, be heard at Walden.

Transcendentalism
and the Critics

Transcendentalist
Literary Legacies

Lawrence Buell

TRANSCENDENTALISM WAS THE FIRST LITERARY MOVEMENT in U. S. history whose repercussions continue to be felt even now.[1] That fact alone will ensure that it remains of permanent interest to scholars in the field of American literature, however the field may henceforth be re-defined, and whether or not the first chapter of the comprehensive annual conspectus of Americanist scholarship—*American Literary Scholarship*—continues as it has for the first thirty-odd years of its existence to be devoted to "Emerson, Thoreau, and Transcendentalism." But before we who have devoted substantial fractions of our careers to investigating the movement become complacent about its sure-fire durability as an area of speciali-zation, it behooves us to recognize that Transcendentalism is no longer so central a preoccupation within American literary studies as it once was. In pressing this point throughout the first half of this essay, in no sense do I in-tend to depreciate the other contributions to this forum, by whose overall quality I have been much impressed; nor to retract anything I myself have previously written about literary Transcendentalism; nor to disown my deep, ongoing interest in the movement. Much less would I wish to be un-derstood as prophesying the exhaustion of Transcendentalism as a subject of inquiry; in fact, the second half of this paper will reverse the momentum of the first and make some very strong claims for its importance as a lens through which even Americanists who would not by any stretch of the imagination consider themselves to be Transcendentalism specialists not only should but in fact do view what they see, whether or not they realize the fact. By the same token, however, those of us for whom Transcenden-talism remains a central subject of direct inquiry will, I suspect, do our work best if we begin from the awareness that not only has "Transcendentalism" ceased to be an unproblematically crucial point of explicit reference in U. S. literary scholarship generally, but that this fact of the history of literary scholarship should be thought of as an opportunity, not a disaster.

My own scholarly generation started from the conception of an ante-bellum literary cosmos in which Transcendentalism (through Emerson's agency especially) played a more crucial role than any other contempora-neous cisatlantic influence in furthering national literary emergence. This had been the version of history handed down within both American liter-ary scholarship and the American studies movement from the seminal fig-ures in the professionalization of those two enterprises, F. O. Matthiessen and Perry Miller. My teachers were their students, literally or by osmosis. Starting in the late 1960s, however, this myth came under pressure from several fronts.

First, canonical revisionism—not to mention the more radical ques-tioning of the validity of canonicity as a way of thinking—made it clear that many previously neglected writers who now seem deserving of seri-ous study had scant interest in Transcendentalism. Did the sentimental-ists? the slave narrators? the writers of popular sensationalist exposés like George Lippard or T. S. Arthur? Nina Baym, William Andrews, and David Reynolds—to name only those who have done the most extensive reclamation work in these three respective areas—have shown that the answer is in each case no.[2] As Frederick Douglass and Harriet Beecher Stowe, then Catharine Maria Sedgwick, Lydia Maria Child, Susan War-ner, Maria Cummins, Harriet Jacobs, and Harriet Wilson have come to be studied with increasing respect and systematic intensity, the notion of Transcendentalism's centrality within the antebellum literary scene has become less self-evident. A telling indication of this is the fact that most contemporary scholarship on the authors just listed except for Child feels no particular obligation to refer to literary Transcendentalism except peripherally.

Second, in keeping and sometimes self-consciously allied with the level-ing effect of canonical revisionism, but operating from its own distinct set of commitments, the so-called history of the book movement has challenged Transcendentalism's centrality—effectively if not explicitly—by holding up as the central fact of antebellum literary culture the emer-gence of a full-fledged literary marketplace. By redirecting attention from "major" intellectual movements and literary figures to the institutions of authorship, reading, and publishing, the implication if not the overt argu-ment of history of these is that Longfellow and Stowe are at least as impor-tant foci for the period as Emerson, Louisa May Alcott more so than Thoreau and incomparably more so than her father, Bronson.[3] Weighed by the criteria of cultural diffusion and cultural representativeness, *Godey's Lady's Book* seems a more significant publishing event than the *Dial*. Only on the lyceum circuit did Transcendentalism (meaning Emerson, particularly) come close to achieving a degree of entrepreneurialism and a breadth of dissemination to rival the best-selling authors.[4]

Third, the understanding of what counts as Transcendentalism has significantly changed, resulting in a shrinkage of its seeming importance as an autonomous force. The perceived importance of Margaret Fuller, Mary Moody Emerson, and other women associated with the movement has risen sharply; with this new interest has come a new sense of the importance of Transcendentalism as gendered discourse, whether that be conceived in terms of androcentric constraint of female voices or, oppositely, as a feminist challenge to patriarchy.[5] The thrust of this new work, broadly speaking, has been less to reconstitute Transcendentalism from a more gynocentric perspective than to reimagine its gender dynamics as part of a more extensive web of emerging middle-class culture within which Transcendentalism was one nodal point. Roughly the same can be said of the critical shift of attention away from the movement's religiocentrism relative to its social and political dimensions, which are now taken much more seriously. No longer are Brook Farm or even Fruitlands dismissed so easily with a satirical chuckle, nor Fuller's partisanship in the Italian Revolution reduced to romance with Ossoli, nor Emerson's antislavery convictions written off as half-hearted and atypical.[6] These are clearly net gains. Yet the shift of attention from "religion" toward "politics," and from moral ideas to ethics *vis-à-vis* social reform movements, has lessened interest in the epistemological-theological discussions and debates that constituted the most pervasive unifying concern of Transcendentalism *qua* movement.

Fourth, the putative extent of Transcendentalism's literary influence has been challenged by reconception of the terms of the intellectual genealogies of certain figures once commonly aligned with it. In particular, Emily Dickinson has come to be envisioned much less routinely as a legatee of a post-Calvinist sensibility in an Edwards-Emerson lineage and more often in relation to a transatlantic sorority of nineteenth-century women poets, both American and British.[7]

Altogether, then, Transcendentalism's "market niche" has contracted as the interests of literary scholarship have evolved and diversified. The antebellum literary scene now seems much more full of actors than formerly. Not only is slave narrative part of every properly balanced antebellum literature syllabus, but it is no longer respectable to pretend to represent the genre by a single figure. The internal variety of domestic fiction and the subtler quarrels of its practitioners with the generic conventions that Baym defined as recently as 1978 (at that time practically a lone voice crying in a wilderness created by decades of deprecation) have now become a topic of specialization in itself.[8] The familiar narrative of cisatlantic literary emergence (Puritanism begat Unitarianism, which begat Transcendentalism, which begat everything else), which the vigorous persistence of Puritan legacy studies from Miller to Sacvan Bercovitch seemed to have established through the 1980s as the preferred myth of premodern American cultural continuity, today looks less sufficient than it did only yesterday, as it were, as an explanation for the antebellum literary landscape. The advancement of the study of premodern Southern culture and renewed interest in the literature of westwarding as genderized discourse and as arena of cultural collision in which Native American and Mexican voices disputed with those of Yankees and Euroamerican immigrants have further underscored the provincialism of a Transcendentalist-centered map of antebellum U. S. literary culture.[9] This notwithstanding the fact that from the 1970s through the 1990s our access to the Transcendentalist writings and commentary thereon has dramatically improved, with better and fuller scholarly editions of the works of Emerson, Thoreau, Fuller, Very, and the Alcotts, and a wealth of textual and bibliographical work published in *Studies in the American Renaissance* (1978–1995) and by such houses as G. K. Hall, Garland, and the University of Pittsburgh Press.

On the other hand, and by the same token, the attention paid a certain number of individual writers associated with the movement has not only held firm but increased. Emerson and Thoreau now elicit a smaller percentage of the totality of antebellum literary scholarship than they did at mid century, but the quantity is at least greater than ever. Interest in the women literati associated with the movement, Fuller particularly, has never been keener. To be sure, graduate students in literature departments today may not be asked to master the movement's intellectual history, nor to study the lives and works of the secondary figures, as they were a generation ago, when Miller's two anthologies were required reading. Even those male writers other than Emerson and Thoreau who were considered indisputably "major" Transcendentalists are less widely studied than formerly: Bronson Alcott, Orestes Brownson, Theodore Parker, George Ripley.

Indeed, owing to the continuing pattern of centrifugalism that marks literary studies of the 1990s across the board—a smörgasbord of competing paradigms, many of them loosely arrayed under the sign of "Cultural Studies"—today's hypothetical student is less likely to encounter under the sign of Transcendentalism those movement literati who *are* widely studied than in the company of other figures who had nothing to do with the movement. To find Emerson, for example, in juxtaposition with Frederick Douglass and W. E. B. Du Bois, Thoreau in relation to John Muir and Aldo Leopold, Fuller in relation to Mary Wollstonecraft and Sarah Josepha Hale. Yet when any of these three Transcendentalist figures are taught, discussed,

and written about by literary scholars, the claims made—or presumed—
for their significance as cultural markers are likely to be more exalted than,
for example, almost anybody's claims for Fuller before 1970; or the briefs
(such as they were) set forth for Emerson by Matthiessen (to whom he
seemed a precursor rather than a giant) and by Miller (to whom Emerson
seemed an ironic declension from Edwards and less interesting as a
barometer of antebellum thought than Charles Grandison Finney); and it
has long since ceased to seem necessary, as it so clearly did to Matthiessen,
to argue the case for Thoreau's gifts as a writer—or to put Emerson's in
their place.

Emerson's durability is an especially striking phenomenon. During the
first third of the twentieth century his standing began to look vulnerable,
rather like that of the schoolroom poets. Miller's and Matthiessen's luke-
warmness reflect this tendency, short-lived as it turned out, to cut Emerson
down to size either as intellectually effete (Miller) or artistically deficient
(Matthiessen). Within a decade, however, Emerson's reputation began to
be revived with the help of the Stephen Whicher's powerful if reductive
hypostasis of an essential Emerson (still reflecting an equivocal estimate of
his achievement), based on a highly selective fraction of his writings from
Nature through "Experience" and "Fate" that seemed to yield a narrative of
antinomian assertion followed by conservative lapse.[10] Conceivably, Emerson might have suffered another serious reversal with the new historicist
turn to unmasking supposedly oppositional eminences as actually centrist
and indeed hegemonic in their underlying ideological allegiances. Yet despite some incisive reappraisals of this kind,[11] not to mention astringent
revaluations of Emerson's limits from a gender studies standpoint, this did
not happen. Why? The recent revival of sympathetic interest in the "political" Emerson has doubtless been one factor. But a prior and more fundamental influence than this late development was surely the turn toward
"theory" that began in the late 1960s. Almost overnight, post-Matthiessen-
ish formalist critiques of Emerson's artistry came to seem irrelevant
quibbling; and the genre of the self-reflexive literary essay-meditation on
great ethical, moral, and cultural issues became newly interesting. In the
1970s and 1980s, Emerson became seized upon as a central figure in at least
four ambitious and influential projects of Americanist reconception:
Harold Bloom's mythic narrative of American poetic (and ultimately also
religious) succession, which posits Emerson as primal ancestor; Sacvan
Bercovitch's identification of Emerson as a key point in the transmission of
post-Puritan rituals of ideological consensus; Stanley Cavell's repossession
of Emerson as the key American figure in the transmission of Kantian
thinking to Nietzsche and thence to Heidegger; and the reinterpretation

of American literary and intellectual pragmatism that Cornel West, Richard Poirier, and others have advanced.[12]

These bodies of work have been influential not only in sustaining interest in Emerson as a central subject of literary Americanist inquiry,[13] but also in reinforcing the pre-existent, new-critical-begotten penchant for a major-figures, major-texts approach as against extensive study of the full Transcendentalist canon in an empirical-historical context. What has engaged all four Emersonians above has not for the most part been his Transcendentalist nexus but Emerson as defined by scrutiny of his texts in the light of a conceptual configuration whose coordinates fall largely outside the movement *per se*. To the extent that their projects confirm the significance of Transcendentalism *qua* movement, they do so for the most part obliquely and by implication via a broader thematic envisioned as instantiated and energized by Emerson rather than *via* reconstruction of the history of Transcendentalism or its antecedent origins in Boston Unitarian or Anglo-Saxon culture.

Thus the current image of Transcendentalism's place in antebellum literary history rests for contemporary literary scholarship more (perhaps I should say "even more") on the evidential base of select texts by select figures—Emerson, Thoreau, and Fuller particularly—than it did a quarter century ago. Scholars who specialize in critical interpretation have tended to bypass the movement's other figures and to consider most aspects of the social history of the movement as comparative detritus, for the sake of pursuing intensive examination of their writers of choice in the interest of whatever superintending vision, while, on the other hand, those literary scholars most committed to empirical research in the areas of cultural history, publishing institutions, reading practices, and textual editing devote a smaller percentage of their effort to the Transcendentalists.

When we extend our inquiry, therefore, to the broader question of literary Transcendentalism's import for U. S. literary history generally, it comes as no surprise to find that it seldom gets addressed these days. The conspicuous exception is the treatment of the movement in our new full-dress literary histories. Within the first two volumes of *The Cambridge History of American Literature*, Barbara Packer's account stands out not only for its intrinsic merits as the best monograph-length history of the Transcendentalist movement ever written but also as by far the most extensive treatment accorded by *The Cambridge History* to any single American literary coterie before 1860.[14] The *Columbia History of American Literature* not only has one chapter explicitly devoted to a summary of the movement but another that virtually is.[15] In *The Columbia History* as well as the Cambridge, Transcendentalism is the only pre-1860 movement to get chapter-length treatment. The same holds for *The Columbia History of American Poetry*.[16] Except for these and briefer handbook-type surveys, however, it is relatively uncommon nowadays to find articles or books that situate Transcendentalism, or some strand thereof, as a chapter in a broader narrative of U. S. literary history, or that attempt to trace "the Transcendentalist influence" on American literature. Contemplation of Transcendentalism's import, holistically considered, as an American literary phenomenon seems, in short, largely reserved for occasions when one cannot escape being magisterial.

Yet that scarcely means Transcendentalism lacks such broader import. On the contrary, at the level of prevailing critical assumptions about the shape and distinctiveness of U. S. literary history, Transcendentalism has maintained all along something like its old centrality, if only as a kind of unacknowledged Shelleyan legislator. How can this be? In the remainder of this essay, I shall try to make sense of the paradox by reviewing four ways in which literary Transcendentalism has effectively continued to shape prevailing assumptions about what distinctively constitutes U. S. literary discourse beyond what most Americanists today consciously realize.

First and perhaps most fundamentally, the Transcendentalists' standing as the first coterie in U. S. literary history to produce (via its major writers) a substantial body of work thought to have enduring literary importance has helped ensure that the boundary between fictive and so-called nonfictional genres in our conception of what counts as American literature would remain forever blurred. Whether one accepts or rejects the claim, the very fact that the sententious Emerson has so often been held to be the most seminal figure in U. S. literary history bespeaks a more elastic notion of the scope of the literary canon than prevails in British literary studies. Despite their obvious salience from the early eighteenth century to the late nineteenth, the genres of essay and autobiography, not to mention homiletic and political discourse, within the British literary canon overall look rather modest compared with the American. The same holds not only for the traditional U. S. canon (Euroamerican and predominantly male) but also for the extended canon ushered in by feminist and ethnic revisionisms, which includes not just the autobiographies of Benjamin Franklin, Henry David Thoreau, and Henry Adams, but of Douglass, Jacobs, Richard Wright, and N. Scott Momaday; the homilies of Martin Luther King, Jr., as well as those of Jonathan Edwards and Emerson; the intellectual prose of Fuller and Charlotte Perkins Gilman and W. E. B. Du Bois and James Baldwin as well as that of Thomas Jefferson, James Madison, Emerson, Abraham Lincoln, and William and Henry James.[17] Even if female and minority figures have more often been held up for their "difference" from or "opposition" to the patriarchal canon than for their interconnections with it, their retrieval has been facilitated by the prior legitimacy accorded nonfictional prose by the unusually capacious genre parameters of the pre-existing canon.

The Transcendentalist reinforcement of the prior tendency for American literary expression to transgress the boundaries of the fictive, at the very point when authorship was just becoming established as a profession in the U. S., both reflected and reinforced the interdependence of aesthetic play with didactic and utilitarian motives in the writing of the colonial and early national periods, especially in the north. One sees the longer-range impress not simply in the historic legitimacy accorded nonfictional genres, but also within the fictive genres themselves, poetry especially. Two quite different poetic legacies figure here: the resistance to defining poetry in terms of formalism, which Emerson picked up from Coleridge and transmitted to Whitman and so on down;[18] and the recrystallization of poesis as gnomic wisdom literature in writers like Dickinson and Frost—the laconic face of bardism, as against the shamanistic.[19]

The James brothers, William and Henry, disclosed more than they realized when they wrote Emerson's epitaph in two opposite ways. William characterized him as "an artist whose medium was verbal and who wrought in spiritual material." Henry gave substantially the same point the opposite spin when he characterized Emerson as "a striking exception to the rule that writings live in the last resort by their form."[20] As these dicta suggest, to the extent that Emerson remains a literary founding father, the attempt to define a national aesthetic accomplishment in terms of fictive craftsmanship will always seem restrictive, even as the case for defining it in terms of "the strength of [its] message alone" (Henry James's equivocal characterization of Emerson's potency) may seem uncomfortably lax.

Hardly less typical of American literary discourse than blurred genres has been the principal rhetorical scene of both Transcendentalist poems and literary prose: a presiding consciousness in the act of beholding, recording, formulating the flow of environmental phenomena in the context of an interactive relation between the observing consciousness and that environment. This denominator links Emerson's "Experience," Thoreau's *Walden*, Fuller's *Summer on the Lakes*, with their longer meditative poems as well as Sylvester Judd's novel *Margaret* and Louisa May Alcott's favorite and most "Transcendentalist" novel, *Moods*. Such work thrusts in either or both of two directions, both of which are strongly marked in U. S. literary history generally: on the one hand, toward autobiographical discourse or protagonist-centered narrative; on the other hand, extrospectively toward a descriptive or ethnographic engagement with the physical environment.

Neither move was invented by the Transcendentalists, of course: vide the rich antecedent traditions, reaching back to the early colonial period, of spiritual autobiography and travel narrative. But literary Transcendentalism (instanced especially by Emerson's "Self-Reliance" and Thoreau's "Resistance to Civil Government" and "Economy") remains the locus classicus in discussions of the centrality of the idea of the single individual as central to U. S. literary structures as well as cultural values, whether for better or for worse. The same can be said of the role of Emerson's *Nature* and especially Thoreau's *Walden* as points of reference in the service of all accounts of "nature" discourse in U. S. literary history.

Third, the Transcendentalist literati helped canonize in U. S. literary thought the Romantic idealization of childlike vision. Initially the most influential embodiments were supplied by the domestic fiction (Warner, Cummins, and Stowe) and poetry (Sigourney and Elizabeth Oakes Smith) of popular women writers whose relation to the Transcendentalist movement was at best tangential and generally hostile. But the ethico-spiritual case for the superiority of intuition to formal learning and the necessity of reinventing culture theory anew in light of that insight, was pressed to a greater and more self-conscious extreme by Emerson and Thoreau, with Bronson Alcott, Jones Very, and Ellery Channing playing supporting roles and Louisa May Alcott supplying retrospective confirmation of the still insufficiently studied symbiosis between Transcendentalism and sentimentalism as post-Romantic formations. Although domestic fiction was doubtless more directly influential than Transcendentalism in prompting the next generation of American writers to invent figures like Milly Theale and Huck Finn, literary Transcendentalism has played a more significant role in underpropping arguments that "innocence" was a core ingredient of American cultural self-definition, and in identifying the experience of wonder as a promising ground-condition for the literary sensibility.[21]

Animating the Transcendentalists' neo-Romantic idealization of intuition was the quest for a core or essence of spirituality underlying the forms, rituals, and theology of historical religions. Emerson's "Divinity School Address" and Theodore Parker's *Discourse on the Transient and Permanent in Christianity* show that this project to purify Protestantism to the utmost by retrieving from it something like a religion of pure spirituality had both an affirmative and a demolitional aspect. Considered as a movement standing primarily for the transition from piety to secularism, Transcendentalism was instrumental in promoting within the U. S. the role of literary figure as sage or social arbiter/prophet that Coleridge and Carlyle,

and Alexander Pope and Samuel Johnson before them, had introduced to
Britain. Considered as a movement standing primarily for the deparochial-
ization of historical Christianity, Transcendentalism was influential in the
formation of the earliest form of "multicultural" theory in the United
States: comparative religious thought. An early instance was Thoreau's
"Ethnical Scriptures" for the *Dial*—wise epigrammatic sayings from various sources—including what seem to have been the first Buddhist texts
published in the U. S.[22] Thoreau wrote both with anti-provincial animus
against a moribund-seeming post-Puritan theology (hence his naughty
praise, in *A Week on the Concord and Merrimack Rivers*, of Greek and
Hindu religion at the expense of Protestant Christianity) and from a more
post-Enlightenment commitment to all religious traditions—all "great" religions, anyhow—as analogous expressions, all legitimate as far as each
went, of divine spirit.

It was not until the end of the century and the "World's Parliament of
Religions" at the 1893 Chicago Exposition[23] that America at large came
round to institutionalizing anything like the comparatist effort that Thoreau, Emerson, and Fuller in her own way (with her classical mythography)
initiated. Their vision was pursued more systematically by Transcendentalists who continued active into the late nineteenth century: Lydia Child,
Thomas Wentworth Higginson, Moncure Conway, and especially James
Freeman Clarke and Samuel Johnson.[24] When one of Buddhism's (very
few) premodern American converts, Bostonian William Sturgis Bigelow,
undertook during an early stage of his initiation to describe its essence to
Boston clergyman Phillips Brooks, the best he could do by way of summary
was: "As far as I have got it, Buddhist philosophy is a sort of Spiritual Pantheism—Emerson almost exactly.'"[25]

It is understandable that no one, at least to my knowledge, has thought
to link the Transcendentalists' predilection for educing thematic affinities
between the "great" religious traditions to contemporary multiculturalist
thinking. After all, the Transcendentalists' quest was chiefly for the supposed spiritual unity underlying cultural variety, and cultural difference
per se therefore often seemed to them epiphenomenal, even impedimen-
tary. But to the extent that they committed themselves to a dethronement
of Protestantism and indeed western thought generally from its position of
preeminent spiritual authority they made it possible, as Walt Whitman for
example realized, to imagine Jehovah, Brahma, Buddha, Allah, and Osiris
in the same breath as precursors of a mature contemporary identity.[26] This
quasi-openness to a myth of multiple cultural antecedence, in turn, has
unquestionably had something to do with the fact that more non-Anglo
writers throughout the Americas have claimed Whitman as a primal ances-

tor than any other premodern American precursor.[27] When Maxine Hong Kingston named the protagonist of her even more hybridized *Tripmaster Monkey* Whitman Ah Sing, she was partly signifying on Whitman for overstepping his perceptual limits (e.g. by associating him with one of the most notorious early stereotypical "Chinamen," Bret Harte's "Ah Sin"),[28] but partly paying Whitman a sort of homage, as James Joyce and Derek Walcott paid Homer in their rewritings of the Odyssey in their own postcolonial venues.

These reflections lead one to a conclusion both hopeful and sobering. Yes, literary Transcendentalism is likely to endure as a significant formative influence in American theory whether self-consciously acknowledged as such or not—likely to endure as such well into the twenty-first century, beyond all our professional lifetimes if not forever. But the way in which it is likely to endure is in synechdoche form via selected works by a few figures, such as Emerson, Thoreau, and Fuller. Transcendentalism's dead white males are likely to remain neglected for the indefinite future. In particular, the movement's generally overlooked later literary phases after the deaths of Fuller and Thoreau and after Emerson's senescence—ironically, the very point in literary history when the process of literary Transcendentalism's broad dissemination is most apparent even as the movement *qua* movement winds down—will probably continue to be short-shrifted. But perhaps after all it is not to be expected, or even to be desired, that Transcendental literary discourse should regain the *felt* centrality it enjoyed at mid century until the pendulum of scholarly fashion has swung so far to a contrary extreme that the intimation of the extent of Transcendentalism's continuing pertinence to our evolving myths of national literary history will hit its rediscoverers with the force of a really fresh revelation. Such an experience as this, of something like a genuinely original relation to the universe of Transcendentalist discourse, may well produce a more momentous result than any we can now anticipate.

NOTES

1. The two previous movements worthy of the name were the Connecticut Wits of the late eighteenth century and the Knickerbockers of the early nineteenth, neither of which had the impact Transcendentalism did. Some would argue that Puritanism's literary legacy was more important to the antebellum "renaissance" than Transcendentalism's (indeed, that Transcendentalism was part of that legacy), but although this position is respectable—if not altogether convincing—Puritanism was of course not itself a literary movement to the same degree that Transcendentalism was.

2. Nina Baym, *Woman's Fiction: A Guide to Novels by and about Women in America, 1820–1870* (Ithaca, 1978); William Andrews, *To Tell a Free Story: The First Century of Afro-American Autobiography, 1760–1865* (Urbana, 1986); David Reynolds, *Beneath the American Renaissance: The Subversive Imagination in the Age of Emerson and Melville* (New York, 1988).

3. The patriarch of history of the book studies, William Charvat, studied Longfellow's professional career with great care but, at least in his published scholarship, paid little attention to Emerson. Transcendentalism has been of marginal interest in such recent significant contemporary studies of antebellum print institutions as Michael Winship, *American Literary Publishing in the Mid-Nineteenth Century: The Business of Ticknor and Fields* (Cambridge, 1995); Ronald J. Zboray, *A Fictive People: Antebellum Economic Development and the American Reading Public* (New York, 1993); Susan Coultrap-McQuin, *Doing Literary Business: American Women Writers in the Nineteenth Century* (Chapel Hill, 1990); and Patricia Okker, *Our Sister Editors: Sarah J. Hale and the Tradition of Nineteenth-Century American Women Editors* (Athens, Ga., 1995). The latter two monographs exemplify the potential synergy between canonical revisionism and book history, which has been especially strong in literary historiography of women writers, as the previous work of Cathy Davidson (*Revolution and the Word: The Rise of the Novel in America* [Oxford, 1986]) and the ongoing work of Nina Baym (e.g. *American Women Writers and the Work of History, 1790–1860* [New Brunswick, 1995]) attests.

4. This is by no means to say that the Transcendentalists were disengaged from the antebellum marketplace, or that their work is not relevant to marketplace-valenced analysis. See, for example, Steven Fink, *Prophet in the Marketplace: Thoreau's Development as a Professional Writer* (Princeton, 1992), which shows that Thoreau was more greatly interested in accommodating himself to marketplace trends than has been realized; and Richard F. Teichgraeber III, *Sublime Thoughts / Penny Wisdom: Situating Emerson and Thoreau in the American Market* (Baltimore, 1995), which appraises both writers' stances of accommodation *and* dissent in terms of negotiation of marketplace attitudes and realities.

5. A significant indicator of the Fuller revival under feminist-revisionary auspices was the appearance and the influence of Bell Gale Chevigny's biographical-critical anthology, *The Woman and the Myth: Margaret Fuller's Life and Writings* (Old Westbury, N.Y., 1976). Since then, Fuller has become handsomely monumentalized, e.g. by Robert Hudspeth's six-volume scholarly edition of *The Letters of Margaret Fuller* (Ithaca, 1983–1994), and Charles Capper's *Margaret Fuller: An American Romantic Life* (New York, 1992–). Phyllis Cole initiated the rediscovery of Mary Moody Emerson in "The Advantage of Loneliness: Mary Moody Emerson's Almanacs, 1820–1855," *Emerson, Prospect and Retrospect*, ed. Joel Porte (Cambridge, Mass., 1982), 1–32, and other essays that have formed part of the basis of her *Mary Moody Emerson and the Origins of Transcendentalism* (New York, 1998), while Nancy Craig Simmons has edited *The Selected Letters of Mary Moody Emerson* (Athens, Ga., 1993). Bruce A. Ronda's edition of Elizabeth Peabody's letters, *Letters of Elizabeth Palmer Peabody, American Renaissance Woman* (Middletown, Conn., 1984), and Delores Bird Carpenter's edition of Ellen Tucker Emerson's *The Life of Lidian Jackson Emerson* (Boston, 1980) have helped attract new attention to all three figures. The Louisa May Alcott revival has been less a result of her Transcendentalist connections than of the rise of con-

temporary interest in nineteenth-century women writers and domestic fiction, but Transcendentalist scholars have contributed significantly, e.g. Joel Myerson, Madeleine B. Stern, and Daniel Shealy in their edition of *The Journals of Louisa May Alcott* (Boston, 1989).

6. On Brook Farm, see for example Carl J. Guarneri, *The Utopian Alternative: Fourierism in Nineteenth-Century America* (Ithaca, 1991), and Richard Francis, *Transcendental Utopias: Individual and Community at Brook Farm, Fruitlands, and Walden* (Ithaca, 1997). On Fuller, see Larry J. Reynolds and Susan Belasco Smith, eds., *"These Sad but Glorious Days": Dispatches from Europe, 1846–1850* (New Haven, 1991). The map of Emerson's involvement in political and specifically antislavery activity has been recharted by Len Gougeon, *Virtue's Hero: Emerson, Antislavery, and Reform* (Athens, Ga., 1990), and Len Gougeon and Joel Myerson, eds., *Emerson's Antislavery Writings* (New Haven, 1995). Albert von Frank's *The Trials of Anthony Burns: Freedom and Slavery in Emerson's Boston* (Cambridge, Mass., 1998) presents a "cultural history" of the controversy surrounding the Burns case, which claims for Emersonian Transcendentalism a catalytic role in abolitionist discourse not claimed for him since Stanley Elkins's *Slavery: A Problem in American Institutional and Intellectual Life* (Chicago, 1959).

7. Albert V. Gelpi's *Emily Dickinson: The Mind of the Poet* (Cambridge, Mass., 1966) is a good presentation of the traditional New England genealogy. Sandra Gilbert and Susan Gubar, *The Madwoman in the Attic: The Woman Writer and the Nineteenth-Century Literary Imagination* (New Haven, 1979), 539–560, began the revisionary process extended by Cheryl Walker, *The Nightingale's Burden: Women Poets and American Culture before 1900* (Bloomington, 1982), and many others. I do not mean to imply that the two genealogies are irreconcilable; see for example, Barton Levi St. Armand, *Emily Dickinson and Her Culture: The Soul's Society* (Cambridge, 1984), which brings them together.

8. See, for example, Susan K. Harris, *19th-Century American Women's Novels: Interpretive Strategies* (Cambridge, 1990); Shirley Samuels, ed., *The Culture of Sentiment: Race, Gender, and Sentimentality in Nineteenth-Century America* (New York, 1992); and Lora Romero, *Home Fronts: Domesticity and Its Critics in the Antebellum United States* (Durham, 1997).

9. Studies of the genderization of westwarding literature start with Annette Kolodny, *The Lay of the Land: Metaphor as Experience and History in American Life and Letters* (Chapel Hill, 1975), and *The Land Before Her: Fantasy and Experience of the American Frontiers, 1630–1860* (Chapel Hill, 1984). Myra Jehlen directly links Emersonian Transcendentalism with hegemonic expansionism in *American Incarnation: The Individual, the Nation, and the Continent* (Cambridge, Mass., 1986), 76–122; Eric J. Sundquist further explores the ideological implications of expansionist discourse and takes account of the Hispanic and Indian voices that expansionism overrode in "The Literature of Expansion and Race," in *The Cambridge History of American Literature*, ed. Sacvan Bercovitch (Cambridge, 1995), 2:127–238.

10. For further detail, see my editorial "Introduction" to *Ralph Waldo Emerson: A Collection of Critical Essays* (Englewood Cliffs, N.J., 1993), 1–12; and "Emerson's Fate," *Emersonian Circles*, ed. Wesley T. Mott and Robert E. Burkholder (Rochester, N.Y., 1997), 11–28.

11. E.g. Jehlen, *American Incarnation*, and David Simpson's pejorative contrast of what he takes to be the Transcendentalist will to monoglossic hegemony as against James Fenimore Cooper's greater acknowledgment of vernacular linguistic diversity in *The Pioneers. The Politics of American English, 1776–1850* (New York, 1986), 230–259. Simpson is acknowledged but this aspect of his argument effectively bypassed in Michael P. Kramer, *Imagining Language in America: From the Revolution to the Civil War* (Princeton, 1992), as Kramer goes on to recall Emerson in his traditionally accepted role as stimulus to Whitman's more self-conscious advocacy of vernacularization.

12. Bloom's argument for an Emerson-generated American poetic mainstream from Whitman to Stevens and beyond began with "Bacchus and Merlin: The Dialectic of Romantic Poetry in America" (1970), in his *The Ringers in the Tower: Studies in Romantic Tradition* (Chicago, 1971), 291–322; Bercovitch's Puritan legacy/American consensus reading of Emerson starts with *The Puritan Origins of the American Self* (New Haven, 1975), 157ff; Cavell's engagement with Emerson as a philosopher starts with "Thinking of Emerson" (originally a 1978 address), in his *The Senses of Walden*, rev. ed. (San Francisco, 1981), 123–138. For the pragmatist repossession, see especially Cornel West, *The American Evasion of Philosophy: A Genealogy of Pragmatism* (Madison, 1989), 9–41; and Richard Poirier, *Poetry and Pragmatism* (Cambridge, Mass., 1992), 37–75.

13. I do not mean to imply that the four traditions of retrieval I have just listed are either entirely original in their arguments or entirely laudatory toward Emerson in their analysis of him—only that they have been influential in ensuring that his work and thought continue as a central reference point in American literary studies.

14. Barbara Packer, "The Transcendentalists," in *Cambridge History of American Literature*, 329–604.

15. Lawrence Buell, "The Transcendentalists," in *The Columbia Literary History of the United States*, ed. Emory Elliott (New York, 1988), 364–378; Michael Colacurcio, "Idealism and Independence," in *Columbia Literary History of the United States*, 207–226.

16. Lawrence Buell, "The Transcendentalist Poets," in *The Columbia History of American Poetry*, ed. Jay Parini (New York, 1993), 97–120. Indeed, there are only three other "historical movement" chapters in the entire volume: "The Poetry of the Harlem Renaissance," "Beat Poetry and the San Francisco Renaissance," and "The Black Arts Poets."

17. I prefer to waive discussion of whether canonical revisionism has or at least ought to have made the notion of "canon" itself obsolete, suspect, or unusable. I incline to think not, but this is not the place to examine the issue with the thoroughness it deserves.

18. Emerson's famous dictum that "meter-making argument," not "meters" per se, makes a poem is anticipated by if not directly pillaged from Coleridge's Shakespearean criticism. The Emersonian roots of this dimension of American poetic practice have been insisted on most famously by Harold Bloom (with a degree of resistance to the Miltonic and Romantic influence on Emerson that I have never been able to fathom). But there is a much older tradition of identifying form-breaking as a distinctively American swerve that begins at least as early as the American modernists themselves: e.g. Ezra Pound, "What I Feel about Walt Whitman" (1909), in *Selected Prose: 1909–1965*, ed. William Cookson (New York, 1973),

145–146; and T. S. Eliot, "American Literature and Language" (1953), in his *To Criticize the Critic* (London, 1965), 59.

19. Robert Frost, "On Emerson," *Daedalus* 4(1959):712–718; reprinted in *Emerson: A Collection of Critical Essays* (Englewood Cliffs, 1962), ed. Milton Konvitz and Stephen Whicher, 12–17.

20. William James, "Address at the Centenary of Ralph Waldo Emerson, May 25, 1903," in his *Writings, 1902–1910* (New York, 1987), 1120; Henry James, "Ralph Waldo Emerson" (1887), in his *Literary Criticisms—Essays on Literature, American Writers, English Writers* (New York, 1984), 270.

21. Cf. R. W. B. Lewis, *The American Adam: Innocence, Tragedy, and Tradition in the Nineteenth Century* (Chicago, 1955), and Tony Tanner, *The Reign of Wonder: Naivety and Reality in American Literature* (Cambridge, 1965). It should be noted in this regard how sentimentalism generally refrains from radical Transcendentalist endorsement of the intuitive. Notwithstanding cases like Stowe's Eva St. Clare and Smith's sinless child, domestic fiction tends to remain more pragmatically committed to a narrative of the maturation of (female) youth into self-disciplined, socially functioning adult.

22. Thomas A. Tweed, *The American Encounter with Buddhism, 1844–1912* (Bloomington, 1992), xix. Tweed also points out that a concurrent (1844) lecture by Edward Elbridge Salisbury to the American Oriental Society was more influential.

23. Richard Hughes Seager, *The World's Parliament of Religions: The East/West Encounter* (Bloomington, 1995), is the best scholarly analysis, though a little too driven by the thesis that the parliament was controlled by the liberal Protestant agenda that called it into being.

24. The best surveys to date are Carl T. Jackson, *The Oriental Religions and American Thought: Nineteenth-Century Explorations* (Westport, Conn., 1981), chaps. 6–7; and Arthur Versluis, *American Transcendentalism and Asian Religions* (New York, 1993), chap. 8. The most important works by this group were Clarke's *Ten Great Religions: An Essay in Comparative Theology* (Boston, 1871, subsequently much revised and reprinted) and Johnson's three-volume *Oriental Religions and Their Relation to Universal Religion* (Boston, 1872–1885), neither of them models of scholarship (neither man knew any non-European languages except Hebrew), but exemplary—Johnson's work in particular—for the attempt to treat "exotic" faiths on a plane of respect equal to the author's own traditions. Higginson's "The Sympathy of Religions," *The Radical* 8(Feb. 1871):1–23, and other papers were widely read in their day, and Conway has a special importance as the first and only Transcendentalist to undertake a pilgrimage to Asia.

25. Quoted in Tweed, *American Encounter with Buddhism*, 73.

26. As in Whitman's "Song of Myself," in his *Leaves of Grass: Comprehensive Reader's Edition*, ed. Harold Blodgett and Sculley Bradley (New York, 1965), 75.

27. Jim Perlman, Ed Folsom, and Dan Campion, eds., *Walt Whitman: The Measure of His Song* (Minneapolis, 1981), includes many such tributes.

28. Harte's intent, in his poem about Ah Sin if not in the play he wrote jointly with Mark Twain, was to satirize anti-Chinese racism rather than to perpetuate racist stereotypes: *v.* Gary Scharnhorst, "'Ways That Are Dark': Appropriations of Bret Harte's 'Plain Language from Truthful James," *Nineteenth-Century Literature* 51(1996):377–399.

Contributors

NINA BAYM, Professor of English and Jubilee Professor of Liberal Arts and Sciences, University of Illinois at Urbana-Champaign

MICHAEL BROYLES, Distinguished Professor of Music and Professor of American History, The Pennsylvania State University

LAWRENCE BUELL, John P. Marquand Professor of English, Harvard University

CHARLES CAPPER, Associate Professor of History and American Studies, University of North Carolina at Chapel Hill

PHYLLIS COLE, Associate Professor of English and Women's Studies, Pennsylvania State University—Delaware County

HELEN R. DEESE, Professor of English Emerita, Tennessee Technological University

JOHN PATRICK DIGGINS, Distinguished Professor of History, Graduate Center, City University of New York

DEAN GRODZINS, Lecturer in History and Literature, Harvard University

ROBERT A. GROSS, Murden Professor of History and American Studies, College of William and Mary

CARL J. GUARNERI, Professor of History, St. Mary's College of California

PHILIP F. GURA, Professor of English and American Studies, and Adjunct Professor of Religious Studies, University of North Carolina at Chapel Hill

ALAN D. HODDER, Associate Professor of Religion, Hampshire College

BARBARA PACKER, Professor of English, University of California, Los Angeles

DAVID S. REYNOLDS, Distinguished Professor of English, Graduate Center, City University of New York

ROBERT D. RICHARDSON, JR., former Professor of English, University of Denver, currently an Independent Scholar

DAVID M. ROBINSON, Professor of English and Distinguished Professor of American Literature, Oregon State University

NANCY STULA, 1997 Ph.D. in art history, Columbia University

RICHARD F. TEICHGRAEBER III, Professor of History and Director, Murphy Institute of Political Economy, Tulane University

ALBERT VON FRANK, Professor of English, Washington State University

DENISE VON GLAHN, Assistant Professor of Music, Florida State University

CONRAD EDICK WRIGHT, Ford Editor of Publications and Director, Center for the Study of New England History, Massachusetts Historical Society

MARY SARACINO ZBORAY, Independent Scholar, Atlanta, Georgia

RONALD J. ZBORAY, Associate Professor of History, Georgia State University

Index

Ballou's Pictorial Drawing Room Companion, 351
Bancroft, George, 126, 240
  economic views of, 242, 243
  reader comments on, 338
  Schleiermacher and, 130
Bancroft, Lucretia, 341
Barber, John, 273
Barker, Anna, 418
Barnum, P.T., 301
Barrett, Martha Osborne, 330
Barrett, Capt. Nathan, 257
Barth, Karl, 143
Bartlett, S.R., 274–275
Batchelder, Susan, 472
Baym, Nina, 168–189, 330
Beard, Charles, 13
Beecher, Catharine, 421
Beecher, Henry Ward, 295
Beethoven, Ludwig van, 586–587, 589, 590–592, 597
Bellamann, Henry, 600
Bellamy, Edward, 464–465
Bercovitch, Sacvan, 394, 450–452, 609
Berlant, Lauren, 466
Bhagavad Gita, 191–192, 193, 203, 212–214, 221–222, 489
"The Bhagvat Geeta, and The Doctrine of Immortality" (Greene), 480
Biblical Repository, 131, 133, 140
Bigelow, William Sturgis, 614
Blake, Harrison, 212, 216, 301
Blood, Thaddeus, 254
Bloom, Harold, 609
Boehme, Jacob, 490–491
Bonaparte, Napoleon, 284
Book of the Seasons (Howitt), 173–174
Boorstin, Daniel, 448
Boott, Francis, 343
Boston Daily Advertiser, 501
Boston Female Anti-Slavery Society (BFASS), 420–421, 424
Boston Public Latin School, 163
Boston Recorder, 133
Boston Statesman, 472
Boston Vigilance Committee, 85
Boston Woman's Rights Convention, 434
Bowditch, Nathaniel, 152
Bowen, Francis, 339–340
Brackett, Mrs. Samuel E., 385
Brahmins, 98–99, 218–219
Brewster, Lyman, 576

Brisbane, Albert, 154–155, 447, 462
  The Social Destiny of Man, 150
  on social equality, 460, 461
Brook Farm, 256–257, 428–429, 607
  Brooks on, 10
  collapse of, 157–158, 463–464
  Cranch and, 569–570
  Emerson and, 431
  Fourierist era of, 156–157, 447–470
  Fuller and, 431, 539–540
  Schleiermacher and, 141
  utopianism and, 65, 235
Brooks, Philips, 614
Brooks, Van Wyck, 10, 235
  America's Coming-of-Age, 10
  The Flowering of New England, 16–17, 22, 245, 255
Brown, John, 91, 92, 305, 502
Browne, Sarah Smith, 321, 352
Browning Overture (Ives), 583
Brownson, Orestes. *See also* Brook Farm
  compared with Emerson, 60–61
  Greene and, 471, 490–492
  "The Laboring Classes," 64–65
  The Mediatorial Life of Jesus, 486
  Miller on, 23
  New Views of Christianity, 53, 55–56, 59–60, 64–65, 134
  on popular culture, 285
  reformism of, 64–65, 94
  Schlesinger on, 17, 389
  slavery and, 396
  on society, 231, 235
  on source of religious impulse, 58–60
  on Unitarianism, 57
Broyles, Michael, 574–602
Buchez, Philippe, 471
Buell, Lawrence, 27, 605–619
Bultmann, Rudolf, 128
Bunker Hill Memorial Association, 262, 269, 273
Burnouf, Eugène, 197
Burns, Anthony, 31, 319, 358, 396
Bushnell, Horace, 140
Buttrick, Maj. John, 259

Cabot, Elizabeth Dwight, 319, 327, 334, 335, 336, 337, 343, 361
Cabot, James Elliot, 319, 513
Calendar of the Natural Year (Aikin), 173
Calhoun, John C., 389
Calvinism, 229–250